THE
LAST DAYS
AND THE
VILE MAN OF DANIEL

ROBERT PELLETIER

ISBN 978-1-953223-12-8 (paperback)
ISBN 978-1-953223-14-2 (digital)

Copyright © 2020 by Robert Pelletier

All rights reserved. No part of this publication may be reproduced, distributed, or transmitted in any form or by any means, including photocopying, recording, or other electronic or mechanical methods without the prior written permission of the publisher. For permission requests, solicit the publisher via the address below.

Rushmore Press LLC
1 800 460 9188
www.rushmorepress.com

Printed in the United States of America

CONTENTS

Preface..5
Chapter 1: The Right Division of the Word of God...................11
Chapter 2: The Last Days 23
Chapter 3: The Mystery of the One Body of Christ and
             the Seventy Weeks of Daniel 43
Chapter 4: God Reveals the Man of Sin.................................102

    Section 1: Isaiah Chapter 14:1–27; References 1, 2, and 3....112
    Section 2: Daniel Chapters 7–12: References 4, 5, 6, 7,
        and 8...121
        Reference 4: Daniel 7:1–27: "The Little Horn" 126
        Reference 5: Daniel 8:1–27: "The King of
          Fierce Countenance" 160
        Reference 6: Daniel 9:23–10:6: "The Prince
          that Shall Come" 199
        References 7 and 8: Daniel 11:1–12.13: "The
          Vile Man" and "The Willful King"......................236
    Section 3: 2 Thessalonians Chapter 2:1–13: References 9,
        10, and 11 340
    Section 3: Revelation Chapter 12:13–13:18: Reference 12...362
    Section 3: Revelation Chapter 17: 1–18: Reference 13 401
    Section 3: Revelation 19:20–21: Reference 14.....................492

Appendix A: God's Covenant People...501
Appendix B: The Holy Place and the Abomination of
              Desolation of Matthew 24.....................................523
Appendix C: The Twenty-Three Hundred Days of Daniel 8:14...542
Appendix D: The Final Timelines 570

Appendix E:	The Seven Heads and Ten Horns of Revelation and Daniel 582
Appendix F:	The Four Latter-Day Beasts 625
Appendix G:	The Millennial Kingdom of Our Lord Jesus Christ 652
Appendix H:	The Composite Description and Identification of the Beast 673

PREFACE

IT IS WITH A SENSE of awe and love of God and father of our Lord and Savior, Jesus Christ, that I present this book in his service. I have endeavored to take a fresh look at the words of God related to the last days—the time of the end. The end-times include the end of the rule of natural man on the earth replaced by the rule of our Lord Jesus Christ. The book is committed to revealing the truths of God regarding the time of the end through biblical research and an outward as well as inward recognition of the perfection of the Word of God. This work is based on the foundational works of Mr. E. W. Bullinger but takes his foundation up to the present-day understanding. Two of his monumental works: *The Companion Bible* and *Commentary on Revelation* are referenced in this work. These two works exemplify Mr. Bullinger's love for God's Word and his pursuit of objective accuracy in interpretation. His approach and reverence for the Word of God, to me, is unparalleled. I firmly believe that if Mr. Bullinger were alive during these last times, he would have reached a great deal of the conclusions that are written in this work. I could try to document the methodology and biblical research principles used in this book, but I think that they are described in the following excerpts from Mr. Bullinger's own preface provided in *Commentary on Revelation*. Consider the following:

> It is with a sense of devout praise to God that this exposition of the Apocalypse is now completed. It will be found to differ in its conclusions from any other work that has been

issued with the same design. It may be permitted here to specify briefly the reason of such departure: for the reader will find that traditional teaching is set aside, and history is never appealed to substantiate any of the events of this prophetic portion of the Holy Word.

There are numberless expositions based on historical lines; and it must be admitted, when the different writers come to be examined, no two of them agree as to the historical events that are said to fulfil, or are put forward as fulfilling, the judgments either of seals, trumpets, or vials. Good reason, therefore, exists for attempting a more self-consistent principle of interpretation. It may be said by some that there is no authority, in any previous writer, for the views presented in the following pages; and it is true. Very few care to be thought what is termed singular or peculiar, and therefore they like to have some names to appeal to. But this is the very reason why the mists of tradition have been allowed to take the place of independent research.

Tradition is like the tether which prevents an animal from getting a blade of grass beyond the length of that tether. We thankfully acknowledge that there are a few who have been delivered from that bondage, and have given us the results of their labours in a more or less fragmentary form.

Our own work is the result of years of study devoted to the book. During these years, notes have been gathered, and are now brought together and used as forming so many links in

> the chain which brings to completion the work we now send forth.[1]
>
> Let us say at once that we believe, and must believe (1), that God means what He says; and (2), that He has a meaning for every word that He says. All His works and all His words are perfect, in their choice, order and place: so perfect, that, if one word or expression is used, there is a reason why no other would have done.[2]

Needless to say, this work lines up with the same reverence of the Word of God that Mr. Bullinger describes in the section above. The same type of independent research has been employed, and the handcuffs of traditional teaching only play second fiddle to the accuracy and integrity of the Word of God. This work is also the result of many years of research as well as the observance of current world conditions compared to the written Word of God to test the times that we live in. I believe that the methodology is sound and the strict observance to the period of time known as the mystery of the one body of Christ will be strictly adhered to. It is this correct division of the Word of God concerning the time of the mystery of the one body of Christ, and how God uses it in his Word, that is critical to what God would have us know concerning the last days.

The book is founded on a directive given by the Lord Jesus Christ in his response to his disciples concerning their question regarding the time of the end and the last days. Consider Matthew 24:3–21 KJV; my emphasis:

> And as he sat upon the mount of Olives, the disciples came unto him privately, saying, Tell us, when shall these things be? and what shall be

---

[1] E. W. Bullinger, *The Apocalypse or "The Day of The Lord"*, Kindle Edition, Kindle locations 112–133. Second Edition (Revised and Corrected) 1909. Michael Fortner Publisher, Great Plains Press.

[2] Ibid., Kindle Locations 282–284.

the sign of thy coming, and of the end of the world? And Jesus answered and said unto them, Take heed that no man deceive you. For many shall come in my name, saying, I am Christ; and shall deceive many. And ye shall hear of wars and rumours of wars: see that ye be not troubled: for all these things must come to pass, but the end is not yet. For nation shall rise against nation, and kingdom against kingdom: and there shall be famines, and pestilences, and earthquakes, in divers places. All these are the beginning of sorrows. Then shall they deliver you up to be afflicted, and shall kill you: and ye shall be hated of all nations for my name's sake. And then shall many be offended, and shall betray one another, and shall hate one another. And many false prophets shall rise, and shall deceive many. And because iniquity shall abound, the love of many shall wax cold. But he that shall endure unto the end, the same shall be saved.

And this gospel of the kingdom shall be preached in all the world for a witness unto all nations; and then shall the end come. **When ye therefore shall see the abomination of desolation, spoken of by Daniel the prophet, stand in the holy place, (whoso readeth, let him understand:)** Then let them which be in Judaea flee into the mountains: Let him which is on the housetop not come down to take any thing out of his house:

Neither let him which is in the field return back to take his clothes. And woe unto them that are with child, and to them that give suck in those days! But pray ye that your flight be not in the winter, neither on the sabbath day: For then shall be great tribulation, such as was not since the beginning of the world to this time, no, nor ever shall be.

The Lord is asked concerning the last days and the end of the current age. He responds by explaining what will transpire before the terrible Day of the Lord. Part of his explanation instructs the disciples to look in the book of Daniel to understand future events. Many have read these same words, and there are many various interpretations with respect to which section of the book of Daniel this represents. This work takes the directive of the Lord Jesus Christ and examines the book of Daniel to understand what would take place in the last days. The book also develops the reader's understanding through the revealed Word of God regarding the identity of the vile man, who is first mentioned in the book of Daniel, and traces his steps as he rises on the world stage at the time of the end. The vile man is also one of the many names God assigns to the final Antichrist. Many interpreters have found the scripture that the Lord is referring to in Matthew 24 is located in Daniel 11.31, but few have gone back far enough into the book of Daniel to understand the characteristics and acts of the final man of sin.

Daniel records a significant amount of prophecy concerning the last days, all of which is interrelated and must be ingested to understand the picture God is portraying regarding the Antichrist. Each of these scriptures is evaluated, without contradiction, and assembled together, painting an accurate picture of the final man of sin. The other critical clue that must be adhered to, with respect to future events, is the time period skipped over by God—the time of the mystery of the body of Christ. Once this time period is adhered to in the Old Testament, large sections of the prophecy given to Daniel come to life and clearly reveal the perfection of the Word of God. These two processes are the two critical methods missing from the various commentaries concerning the prophecies of Daniel and how they relate to the last time. Systematically attending to these biblical principles allows God's Word to speak to us in a very unique way.

In closing, I once again refer to Mr. Bullinger in his hope for his work as documented in his Commentary on Revelation. My hope is that this work is indeed a progression of the foundation that he blazed over a hundred years prior. I can attest that this work is indeed an earnest desire to believe God and to receive what he has said regardless of praise or criticism. Consider the following:

> We pray God to accept and bless our humble effort to interpret this wonderful and important Book. We believe He has ruled it; but where, through any infirmity, we have misused His gifts, we pray Him to over-rule it. None are more cognisant of imperfection and failure than ourselves; and, after all we have done, there is still much left for others to do. We do not exhaust the book; and may, after all, have only laid out a road on which others may follow with far greater success. We claim only one thing - an earnest desire to believe God; and to receive what He has said, regardless alike of the praise of man or the fear of man; and quite apart from all traditional beliefs or interpretations. May the Lord own and use and bless our efforts for His own Glory and the good of His people. E.W. Bullinger 25 Connaught St., London W. July 1st, 1902.[3]

Robert J. Pelletier

---

[3] Ibid., Kindle Locations 226–233.

CHAPTER 1

The Right Division of the Word of God

MUCH HAS BEEN WRITTEN AND discussed concerning the biblical account of the last days of man's rule on the earth as documented throughout the Bible. The Bible is clear that wrath of God will come upon the earth in the last days, and it will be such a wrath as has never been seen on the earth before. The wrath will be swift and complete and will end the rule of man on the earth while initiating the reign of Jesus Christ on the earth. God has divided the people on the earth into three categories: the Jews, the Gentiles, and the church of God.[4] The church of God was last to appear on the earth, and it consists of Jews and Gentiles who now have God as their Father through a new birth in Jesus Christ. The church of God, made up of former Jews and Gentiles, is currently on the earth (2020), and members of the church are the offspring of God through a new birth and a new gift given to them by God and through faith in Jesus Christ. The church of God, or the church of the one body of Jesus Christ, will not be present for the wrath of our holy God as documented in the book of Revelation.[5] The church of God will have been raptured or removed from the earth before the final wrath of our holy God as recorded in the book of Revelation.

---

[4] 1 Corinthians 10:32.
[5] 1 Thessalonians 1:10.

The wrath of a holy God toward a world that has rejected him in every way is the great subject of the book of Revelation. Additionally, the book of Daniel and the Old Testament is the foundation for the book of Revelation. It will be clear in this work that without Old Testament understanding, the book of Revelation is hopelessly left to imagination. The wrath of God, as depicted in the book of Revelation, marks the transition period between the current grace administration and the Day of the Lord. The grace administration, the current administration (as of 2020), is characterized by God's grace, mercy, and forgiveness toward both Jew and Gentile through believing in Jesus Christ and receiving God's gift: eternal life. The last days of mankind's rule on earth, as documented in the book of Revelation, ends with the Lord's Day, or the day when the Lord rules on the earth. In this work, the time between these two administrations (the transition period) will be known as the last days or the time of the end—that is, the end of Man's rule on the earth. The transition will encompass the time known as the last days.

The scriptures are not silent concerning the judgment of God enacted on an evil generation during the last days—a generation that God declares is destroying the earth that God created for *his pleasure.*

> Thou art worthy, O Lord, to receive glory and honour and power: for thou hast created all things, and for thy pleasure they are and were created. (Revelation 4:11 KJV; my emphasis)
>
> And the nations were angry, and thy wrath is come, and the time of the dead, that they should be judged, and that thou shouldest give reward unto thy servants the prophets, and to the saints, and them that fear thy name, small and great; and shouldest destroy them which destroy the earth. (Revelation 11:18 KJV; my emphasis)

God's Word is the most plagiarized book in the world. People have used it, abused it, changed it, deleted it, destroyed it, laughed at it, joked about it, misconstrued it, made a profit with it, obtained votes with it, and ignored it. The people who know their God love it, live by it, and believe it, and the true God empowers them by it.

The numerous theories concerning the end times and the fallacy of false interpretations lead unbelievers to question and joke about any talk of the apocalypse. This is in spite of the considerable number of scriptures dedicated to this very same subject throughout the Bible. Almost every book of the Bible contains some reference to God's final plan for man's deliverance from sin and death. God has taken significant effort to warn mankind of the terrifying consequences of sin and death, their destructive power, and how sin and death are dealt with in the last days. God has provided the remedy: *receive the gift of God through faith in Jesus Christ*. The books of Daniel and Revelation contain substantial descriptions of factual events and timelines that will be frequently referenced and expanded in this work. The books of Daniel and Revelation complement each other regarding the last days—the final days of man's rule on the earth. These two books are critical to understanding the last days, and one cannot be understood without the other.

The Bible states clearly that the time of the end will result in mankind hiding itself from the terror of God.[6] In the current age of grace, before the events of the last days, God offers humanity eternal life through belief in his son, Jesus Christ:

> "For this is good and acceptable in the sight of God our Saviour; Who will have all men to be saved, and to come unto the knowledge of the truth. For there is one God, and one mediator between God and men, the man Christ Jesus; Who gave himself a ransom for all, to be testified in due time" (1 Timothy 2:3–6).

The heart of this document is intended to warn of the coming days of God's holy judgment. The hope is twofold: (1) that those who do not know the truth may know and be saved, and (2) that

---

[6] Revelation 6:15–17.

those who do know become more knowledgeable of the events of the last days and the timelines that God has documented in his Word. Consider the following scripture from 1 Thessalonians, in which God states that his church, the announced body of Christ, will be knowledgeable of the last days as they approach: "For when they shall say, Peace and safety; then sudden destruction cometh upon them, as travail upon a woman with child; and they shall not escape. *But ye, brethren, are not in darkness, that that day should overtake you as a thief. Ye are all the children of light, and the children of the day: we are not of the night, nor of darkness. Therefore, let us not sleep, as do others; but let us watch and be sober"* (1 Thessalonians 5:3–6 KJV).

The fundamental principle and basis of our study is that all scripture concerning the end times will be fulfilled exactly as documented in the Word of God. Those called of God will clearly understand the last days as they approach through the scriptures. Biblical events in the Word of God will be fulfilled with God's precision. The end-time theories and mind pictures must be sanitized through the accuracy and integrity of the Word of God. The initial coming of the Lord Jesus Christ was vividly foretold in the Old Testament through many Old Testament scriptures. God documented clearly in his word information regarding the birth and the first coming of his only begotten Son. The return of Jesus Christ is also documented in the Word of God by the Patriarchs, the prophets, the law, the Gospels, the epistles of Paul, and the book of Revelation. At the time of the end, it will be the lovers of God, the born-again believers as well as the remnant of believing Israel, who will know of the times and of the seasons through the revealed Word of God. The wicked will continue to be deceived and blinded through their unbelief. The blinding of the wicked at the time of the end is foretold in the book of Daniel:

> "And he said, Go thy way, Daniel: for the words are closed up and sealed till the time of the end. **Many shall be purified, and made white, and tried; but the wicked shall do wickedly: and none of the wicked shall understand; but**

> **the wise shall understand"** (Daniel 12:9–10 KJV; my emphasis).

Understanding and right division of the Word of God will keep us out of darkness, and it will assure us that the last days will not overtake us as a thief. The believer must test the traditional teachings of man against the written Word of God. Wrong interpretation or wrong division of God's Word will leave us unaware of the information God has provided concerning the last days. It is always the decision of the believer to reject or accept the written Word of God, regardless of belief; the Word of God will stand and be fulfilled exactly as God recorded it.

It is the will of the Lord for the believer and the searcher of scripture to understand what God has revealed in his word. The believer is required to study the Word of God and believe what God states in his word. God looks on the hearts of his people and approves of those who study, digest, and believe his word with patience, humility, and meekness. Consider the following scriptures:

> No man that warreth entangleth himself with the affairs of this life; that he may please him who hath chosen him to be a soldier. And if a man also strive for masteries, yet is he not crowned, except he strive lawfully. The husbandman that laboureth must be first partaker of the fruits. Consider what I say; and the Lord give thee understanding in all things. Remember that Jesus Christ of the seed of David was raised from the dead according to my gospel: Wherein I suffer trouble, as an evil doer, even unto bonds; but the Word of God is not bound. Therefore I endure all things for the elect's sakes, that they may also obtain the salvation which is in Christ Jesus with eternal glory. It is a faithful saying: For if we be dead with him, we shall also live with him: If we suffer, we shall also reign with him: if we deny

him, he also will deny us: If we believe not, yet he abideth faithful: he cannot deny himself. Of these things put them in remembrance, charging them before the Lord that they strive not about words to no profit, but to the subverting of the hearers. Study to shew thyself approved unto God, a workman that needeth not to be ashamed, rightly dividing the word of truth. But shun profane and vain babblings: for they will increase unto more ungodliness. And their word will eat as doth a canker: of whom is Hymenaeus and Philetus. (2 Timothy 2:4–19 KJV)

… and the brethren immediately sent away Paul and Silas by night unto Berea: who coming thither went into the synagogue of the Jews. **These were more noble than those in Thessalonica, in that they received the word with all readiness of mind, and searched the scriptures daily, whether those things were so.** (Acts 17:10–11 KJV; my emphasis)

The Word of God was given to man as an instruction book pertaining to life and godliness. The scriptures require studious effort, as well as removing oneself from controversy, bickering, and infighting. A patient, forgiving, and contrite heart ensures that the believer, with the mind of Christ, is growing in acknowledgement and understanding of the Word of God.

The prince of the power of the air will always provide temptation—especially to those who live in godly fashion on the earth. The Lord Jesus Christ was always careful to reply to the devil with the Word of God: "*It is written.*" Confrontation with temptation from Satan, in any other way, is flirting with disaster.

Today, many people are ignorant of the rightly divided Word of God as written down by holy men of God. The Word of God, because of wrong division, is looked down upon by many as a home for religious zealots. Our minds must always be disciplined to respond to temptation with the revealed Word of God, either with words or in our thoughts and actions. Faith in the Word of God is considered the sword of the spirit and will quench all of the fiery darts of the devil. Consider the following:

> For we wrestle not against flesh and blood, but against principalities, against powers, against the rulers of the darkness of this world, against spiritual wickedness in high places. Wherefore take unto you the whole armour of God, that ye may be able to withstand in the evil day, and having done all, to stand. **Stand therefore, having your loins girt about with truth, and having on the breastplate of righteousness; And your feet shod with the preparation of the gospel of peace; Above all, taking the shield of faith, wherewith ye shall be able to quench all the fiery darts of the wicked.** And take the helmet of salvation, and the sword of the Spirit, which is the Word of God. (Ephesians 6:12–17; my emphasis)

The faithful servant of Christ is apt to continually search the scriptures daily, allowing God to feed his spirit and grow in the knowledge of the Word of God. Divisions in the Christian church of today are a result of the ignorance one has of the scripture and the power of God. Men tend to honor religious tradition in place of God's Word.

The idea of the last days of natural man's rule on earth is a biblical concept and has roots throughout scripture. The last days of man's rule, or the time in which man judges the affairs of the earth, is one of the many subtopics contained in the book of Revelation. The historical record of the last days is contained throughout scripture, in both the Old and New Testaments. This work will examine a substantial amount of these accounts, which God has accurately documented in his Word. The many and various accounts of the vile man, or the Antichrist, will be listed individually and also collectively compiled at the end of this work. It will be shown how each record complements and expands on the interrelationships between it and the others. The searcher of scripture must first understand that the Word of God, in its original form, was and is perfect and holds no contradictions. Contradictions are introduced via man through mistranslations, false interpretations, words taken out of context, and the failure to recognize fundamental principles of biblical research. God's Word, in and of itself, is complete, powerful, and sharper than any two-edged sword. A particular topic may have many references located on several passages and written down by many prophets, but there can be no contradiction. The point is that each verse or passage can add additional information, but each does not contradict or in any way devalue the other. The records may seem to be different, but careful study must be applied to resolve apparent contradictions. Key to understanding apparent differences is knowing how God, in his own style, gives further details through separate records. The summation of the records together reveals the total revelation and information that God wishes to set forth. The process by which God builds information regarding a particular event, through several records regarding the same subject, is known as *scripture buildup*. The process of scripture buildup is never more employed than it is in the study of the last days and the transition between man's day and the Lord's Day. This transition is fully manifested in the book of Revelation, but God foreshadows and complements the book of Revelation through a significant amount of Old and New Testament scriptures.

The books of Daniel and Revelation stand alone in their importance to our study of the last days. One of the main themes in Daniel's revelation is the abundance of prophecy concerning the last days. The theme is especially evident in God's final dealings with his original chosen people, Israel: their land, the holy place of God, and the Day of the Lord. The events leading up to the Day of the Lord, the day when the Lord reigns on the earth, are initiated by the appearance of the vile man, or the Antichrist. It is the vile man, commonly referred to in this work as the Antichrist, who will propel the world into forty-two months of horrible tribulation on earth. At the end of the final forty-two months, our Lord Jesus Christ will destroy the vile man by the brightness of his coming for Israel. He will then usher in the Day of the Lord, or the day when the Lord rules on earth. Consider the following:

> **And then shall that Wicked be revealed, whom the Lord shall consume with the spirit of his mouth, and shall destroy with the brightness of his coming:** Even him, whose coming is after the working of Satan with all power and signs and lying wonders, And with all deceivableness of unrighteousness in them that perish; because they received not the love of the truth, that they might be saved. And for this cause God shall send them strong delusion, that they should believe a lie: That they all might be damned who believed not the truth, but had pleasure in unrighteousness. (2 Thessalonians 2:8–12; my emphasis)

The Lord's appearing for Israel will signal the beginning of the millennial kingdom and the physical reign of our Lord and Savior, Jesus Christ, on the earth. His appearing, also known as the revelation of Jesus Christ, also marks the end of natural man's rule on the earth. Before his coming for Israel, the Lord will rapture his called out born-again believers from the earth, who will then be with the Lord forever.

Through the permissive will of God, and because of the arrogance of an evil generation, the man of sin—the Antichrist or the vile man—will be allowed to have dominion for a period of forty-two months. Consider the following:

> And I stood upon the sand of the sea, and saw a beast rise up out of the sea, having seven heads and ten horns, and upon his horns ten crowns,

and upon his heads the name of blasphemy. And the beast which I saw was like unto a leopard, and his feet were as the feet of a bear, and his mouth as the mouth of a lion: and the dragon gave him his power, and his seat, and great authority. **And I saw one of his heads as it were wounded to death; and his deadly wound was healed: and all the world wondered after the beast. And they worshipped the dragon which gave power unto the beast: and they worshipped the beast, saying, who is like unto the beast? Who is able to make war with him? And there was given unto him a mouth speaking great things and blasphemies; and power was given unto him to continue forty and two months.** (Revelation 13:1–5; my emphasis)

The final forty-two months will complete the seventy weeks of years documented in Daniel 9:24. The seventy weeks of years will be covered later in this work. It is important to understand that God set a timetable for Israel's deliverance. It will be at the conclusion of Daniel's prophecy of seventy weeks of years (490 years, the final seven years still being in the future in 2019) when God fulfills all covenant promises made to Israel. The end of the forty-two months will also end the time of the Gentiles, or the time when man judges on the earth. The time of the Gentiles is a time when the Gentiles have dominion over the earth and the rule over God's holy place. The end of the seventy weeks of years is when God finishes his dealings with the Jews and the Gentiles and ushers in the Day of the Lord. This work will also identify the significant number of Old Testament scriptures concerning Israel and Israel's future, which still await fulfillment. The end of the final forty-two months will also mark the fulfillment of many of these scriptures.

The basis of this work is the accurate examination of the multitude of scriptures God reveals concerning the end time, or the end of natural man's rule on earth. It is not the intent of this document to convince the reader of the possibility of the last days but to prayerfully examine the scriptures and let God's Word speak concerning the subject. Our duty is to honestly and humbly study the Word of God—not deceitfully but in accordance with God's interpretation principles. The scriptures must be allowed to speak and reveal truth to us. When this truth is revealed and believed, then God is allowed to change our thinking to his ways and laws. Our traditional ideas and understanding cannot influence what God is foretelling through his writings. It is of no consequence whether we change scripture to line up with our theology; God will not change his word for us. Regardless, the outcome has already been documented in the Word of God, and it is God's Word that will be exhaustively fulfilled. *"For the prophecy came not in old time by the will of man: but holy men of God spake as they were moved by the Holy Ghost"* (2 Peter 1:21 KJV).

God's acceptance in our lives is directly related to our faith in Jesus Christ through the Word of God. Righteous standing before God can be accomplished only through the grace of God, expressed through faith in Jesus Christ. God's approval is granted when we believe his word and realign our thinking to God's thinking. The true believer began his association with God by faith and must continue by faith. Consider the following:

> "That if thou shalt confess with thy mouth the Lord Jesus, and shalt believe in thine heart that God hath raised him from the dead, thou shalt be saved. For with the heart man believeth unto righteousness; and with the mouth confession is made unto salvation. For the scripture saith, Whosoever believeth on him shall not be ashamed" (Romans 10:9–11 KJV).

Faith, in Romans 10:9–10, allows us to receive the gift of God—that is, his gift of the Holy Spirit as new seed inside of us. Faith in Jesus Christ also allows us to become a new creature in Jesus Christ. When a man or woman believes in his heart in the resurrection of

Jesus Christ and confesses with his tongue Jesus Christ as Lord, God acts to seat that person in the heavens with Christ; this is his ultimate gift to man—eternal life. The amazing gift of God comes only through faith, and faith comes through the Word of God. The will of God for his saints is to come to a full knowledge of the truth through his word. Knowledge of the truth can be accomplished only through faith in his word and a disciplined study of his word. The disciple of Christ must develop a disciplined lifestyle of faithful study of the Word of God.

The above foundational truths were laid out of necessity to support our study of the Word of God concerning the great subject of the last days. It is imperative that we handle the Word of God with the utmost reverence and respect. I pray that this work blesses you immensely through faith in his word. God is holy and God is spirit. God gives his gift of the Holy Spirit to whomsoever he chooses. God's gift of the Holy Spirit provides teaching, guidance, comfort, and peace with God. Our living Lord and Savior, Jesus Christ, is the captain and head of our salvation and, ultimately, the reason for our existence. I pray that you logically, prayerfully, and sincerely search the scriptures on the great subject of the last days, which is the focus of this book, and find the answers you seek. In this work, may God lead us into an accurate knowledge of his Word as we diligently seek him with regard to the last days. If no one believes God's Word, it is still the Word of God and it will come to pass exactly how God documented it and spoke it into being.

CHAPTER 2

The Last Days

THE SUBJECT OF THE LAST days and the transition between man's rule on earth and the Lord's Day, or the day that the Lord rules on earth, has intrigued Bible enthusiasts and theologians since the fall of man, documented in Genesis. God's Word is far from silent regarding the last days and provides significant direction and instruction. Throughout the Word of God, the scriptures provide extensive information and detail regarding the Day of the Lord. The Day of the Lord can be thought of as the day when God, who created all things for his pleasure, forcibly takes back his created earth and gives it to his son, Jesus Christ, and those who follow him. The transition time between man's rule and the Lord's Day is known as the time of the end or the last days—that is, the last days of man's rule on earth. God's Word regarding the last days is sprinkled throughout the entire Bible, each reference providing unique information. All such scriptures are accurate, unique, and provide further information, building upon what has already been revealed. Right division of scripture requires the reader to specially attend to context and to whom it is addressed. Biblical right division requires faithful biblical research, especially regarding the different administrations in the Word of God. With regard to the last days, the faithful searcher of scripture who adheres to God's interpretation principles will eventually be rewarded with a clear picture of the last days. God did not intend nor does he desire for the many and varied interpretations of his Word with respect to the last days. God's Word interprets itself, builds upon itself, and inspires the searcher to examine the bible further and deeper. The searcher need not leave the Word of God to properly understand God's heart and God's plan regarding the last days. Consider the following:

> Whom shall he teach knowledge? and whom shall he make to understand doctrine? them that are weaned from the milk, and drawn from the breasts. **For precept must be upon precept, precept upon precept; line upon line, line upon line; here a little, and there a little: For with stammering lips and another tongue will he speak to this people. To whom he said, This is the rest wherewith ye may cause the weary to rest; and this is the refreshing: yet they would not hear. But the word of the LORD was unto them precept upon precept, precept upon precept; line upon line, line upon line; here a little, and there a little.** (Isaiah 28:9–13 KJV; my emphasis)

The Word of God interprets itself, each scripture adding additional information to related scriptures such that the message is clear and concise. God has provided signposts, marks, and figures of speech used for emphasis in his Word for guidance. Understanding and utilizing these tools correctly and faithfully helps direct the Bible student into proper interpretation. One of the objectives of this work is to recognize and reveal to the humble searcher these signposts, marks, and guides concerning the last days, each scripture adding information and building upon the previous scripture or scriptures here a little and there a little.

The *Vile Man of Daniel* does not spend a great deal of time convincing the reader of the reality of the last days nor is it argumentative with respect to previous commentaries and their statements concerning the last days. The focus of this work will be focused on a notable figure, a man, who rises during the last days and is mentioned extensively by God in his Word, especially in the book of Daniel. It will be presented that the book of Daniel contains a great deal of the information regarding the last times and the rise of the beast. The associated study around this individual will begin to paint a picture, which will allow the reader to understand the representation that God intends. The result is a methodical analytical process leading to increasing faith and understanding of the Word of God with respect to the great subject of the last days. The last days are inextricably tied to the man of sin, the end of the rule of man, the rapture of the church of God, and the final deliverance for Israel. All of these subjects are related to each other in purpose and time and reach their climax during the last days. The last days also initiate the earthly rule and revelation of our Lord and Savior, Jesus Christ.

The work will begin with a macro view of God's plan—the different administrations and divisions of scripture as they relate to the last days. The work will then focus on the personage of the Antichrist, also known as the *Vile Man*, and the other titles associated with him as documented in the Word of God. It will be shown that these titles all refer to the same man, each divinely inspired and contributing to the identification of the Antichrist. His identification, through this process of scripture buildup, will be open and clear. The process will reveal his identity by considering all references individually and together, line by line, here a little and there a little. It will be demonstrated how the Holy Spirit frequently utilizes this method of accumulated information to reveal individuals and events. This was evident to the few who understood the first coming of the Lord Jesus Christ to the earth.

Scriptural study needs to start with an understanding of the fivefold division of the Bible, which emphasizes the separate divisions of time, or administrations established by God. These administrations can be enumerated or depicted as follows:

1. The Old Testament
   a. The Creation and the Fall
   b. The King and his coming kingdom in promise and prophecy

      c. The calling out of Israel and the period of the law
2. The four Gospels
      a. The King on the earth
      b. The kingdom offered and rejected
      c. The King crucified by Israel in the land
3. The Acts and earlier Pauline Epistles
      a. The King and Kingdom reoffered to Israel and rejected by the dispersion in Rome.[7]
4. The later Pauline Epistles
      a. The kingdom in abeyance
      b. The King made head over all things to the church of the Body
      c. Salvation through faith in Jesus Christ
      d. God through Christ calling out the one body consisting of former Jews and Gentiles
5. The Apocalypse
      a. The kingdom set up on earth with divine judgment, in power and glory
      b. The King enthroned[8]

Each section of the Word of God can be placed into one of the divisions listed above. References and prophecies regarding the future vile man, both political and religious, are contained in each of the divisions. It will be shown that the vile man, or the Antichrist, is mentioned and foretold of in each of the five divisions. The Antichrist is the final embodiment of man's rebellion against God's sovereignty and rule. After the last days, and after man's rebellion is put down, God rules in the heavens and on earth through his son, Jesus Christ. The last days of man's rule on Earth are immediately followed by the setting up of the everlasting kingdom of our Lord and Savior, Jesus Christ.

---

[7] Acts 3:19, 21; 28:25, 26.
[8] Bullinger, *Commentary on Revelation*, Kregal Publications, Grand Rapids Michigan, Pg3.

The starting point for understanding God's plan for the ages is examining God's purpose for the earth. Admittedly, the last days, and the activities of the vile man, are intricately tied to many of the scriptures associated with God's final dealings with Israel. To accurately comprehend the last days, it is paramount to understand God's final dealings with Israel and how God divides the people on the earth. God divides the inhabitants of the earth into three categories: the Jews, the Gentiles, and the body of Christ, or the church of God.[9] Per the Word of God, the whole purpose purposed upon the earth is listed in Isaiah 14:21–27. The purpose is that God called out a people on the earth to be his, most of whom rejected him. Their rejection allowed God to reach the whole earth with the message of salvation. The message is proclaimed throughout the earth and saves those who believe and are called according to his purpose. After the removal or the rapture of the body of Christ, the last days will unravel God's plan to rescue the remnant of Jacob's physical seed during the last time. God, during the last days, will also fulfill his covenant promises to the Patriarchs. Consider the following:

> Prepare slaughter for his children for the iniquity of their fathers; that they do not rise, nor possess the land, nor fill the face of the world with cities. For I will rise up against them, saith the LORD of hosts, and cut off from Babylon the name, and remnant, and son, and nephew, saith the LORD. I will also make it a possession for the bittern, and pools of water: and I will sweep it with the besom of destruction, saith the LORD of hosts. **The LORD of hosts hath sworn, saying, Surely as I have thought, so shall it come to pass; and as I have purposed, so shall it stand: That I will break the Assyrian in my land, and upon my mountains tread him under foot: then shall his yoke depart from off**

---

[9] 1 Corinthians 10:32.

> **them, and his burden depart from off their shoulders. This is the purpose that is purposed upon the whole earth: and this is the hand that is stretched out upon all the nations. For the LORD of hosts hath purposed, and who shall disannul it? and his hand is stretched out, and who shall turn it back?** (Isaiah 14:21–27 KJV; my emphasis)

If this is God's purpose, then it would make sense that God would spend a good deal of his prophetic revelation on this very subject. He does. Careful examination of the scriptures reveals exactly this; significant portions of God's Word reveal how he will bring his purpose to pass. The Lord Jesus Christ, his only begotten son, is highly exalted and works together with God to bring God's purpose to pass. Scriptures relating to the millennial kingdom and latter-day events, as well as those dealing with God's final dealings with Israel, are the main theme of the Word of God. Scriptures relating to the vile man or the Antichrist are closely tied to God's purpose. The end time ("*suntaliea*" in Greek) represents the time of the end and describes the events leading to the final days of natural man's rule on earth. The events of the last days are the central theme of this study and will evolve into expounding God's purpose that he purposed upon the whole earth.

The scripture teaches us that the Lord Jesus Christ always did God's will. The Lord Jesus Christ will once and for all bring God's will to pass in the last days concerning his bride, Israel. The called out of God today are a special called-out people who are known as the one body of Jesus Christ. The body of Christ consists of former Jews and Gentiles who have received eternal life through new birth and through the gift of God—the Holy Spirit. The called-out born-again believers are a group who are holy and who have been separated for God's purposes. Their future is to be received up into glory and to be with God; their head and leader is Jesus Christ. They are the *firstfruits* of the earth of those with the seed of Jesus Christ born within them. The body of Christ will be called up into glory before the horrific events of the last days—especially the final forty-two months.[10]

The understanding of these great principles is critical to the right division of the Word of God. Once these foundational principles are understood, the scriptures will come to a new reality and the reader will be empowered to accurately unravel the events of the last days. The lack of understanding of these fundamental principles has caused a great deal of confusion and wrong division of the Word of God. In fact, the confusion regarding the last days has led many to believe that there is no one accurate interpretation. Consequently, most believers are content to simply throw out what God has revealed and accept the traditional belief that the truth of the last days is hidden from our understanding. God has stated clearly that he would not have his children in darkness; rather, he would have them understanding what the will of the Lord is. God would not have us ignorant of his revealed revelation of future events.

The last days include all Old Testament visions and prophecies as well as what Jesus Christ foretold in the four Gospels concerning these days. It is the vile man of Daniel who will appear on the world stage and fulfill all that is written about him in the scriptures. His appearance will unmistakably mark the beginning of sorrows for the nations and usher in the time of Jacob's trouble. The fact that God lists days, times, midpoints, sequences of events, people, and signs to look for emphatically reveals that God has always planned for his people to know the events and timetable concerning the end time. God reveals in his Word all the important events that will take place during the last days of his wrath and judgment. The scriptures make known that it is the wicked that will not understand in that day, but the wise will understand.[11] Consider the following scripture directed to the church of God:

> But of the times and the seasons, brethren,
> ye have no need that I write unto you.

---

[10] Philippians 3:20, 21.
[11] Daniel 12:10.

> For yourselves know perfectly that the day of the Lord so cometh as a thief in the night. For when they shall say, Peace and safety; then sudden destruction cometh upon them, as travail upon a woman with child; and they shall not escape. **But ye, brethren, are not in darkness, that that day should overtake you as a thief. Ye are all the children of light, and the children of the day: we are not of the night, nor of darkness. Therefore let us not sleep, as do others; but let us watch and be sober**. For they that sleep, sleep in the night; and they that be drunken are drunken in the night. But let us, who are of the day, be sober, putting on the breastplate of faith and love; and for an helmet, the hope of salvation. **For God hath not appointed us to wrath, but to obtain salvation by our Lord Jesus Christ,** Who died for us, that, whether we wake or sleep, we should live together with him. Wherefore comfort yourselves together, and edify one another, even as also ye do. (1 Thessalonians 5:1–11 KJV; my emphasis)

And further, consider the following scriptures:

> Now we beseech you, brethren, by the coming of our Lord Jesus Christ, and by our gathering together unto him, That ye be not soon shaken in mind, or be troubled, neither by spirit, nor by word, nor by letter as from us, as that the day of Christ is at hand. **Let no man deceive you by any means: for that day shall not come, except there come a falling away first, and that man of sin be revealed, the son of perdition; Who opposeth and exalted himself above all that is called God, or that is worshipped; so**

that he as God sitteth in the temple of God, showing himself that he is God. Remember ye not, that, when I was yet with you, I told you these things? And now ye know what withholdeth that he might be revealed in his time. For the mystery of iniquity doth already work: only he who now letteth will let, until he be taken out of the way. And then shall that Wicked be revealed, whom the Lord shall consume with the spirit of his mouth, and shall destroy with the brightness of his coming: Even him, whose coming is after the working of Satan with all power and signs and lying wonders, And with all deceivableness of unrighteousness in them that perish; because they received not the love of the truth, that they might be saved. And for this cause God shall send them strong delusion, that they should believe a lie: That they all might be damned who believed not the truth, but had pleasure in unrighteousness. **But we are bound to give thanks alway to God for you, brethren beloved of the Lord, because God hath from the beginning chosen you to salvation through sanctification of the Spirit and belief of the truth: Whereunto he called you by our gospel, to the obtaining of the glory of our Lord Jesus Christ. Therefore, brethren, stand fast, and hold the traditions which ye have been taught, whether by word, or our epistle.** (2 Thessalonians 2:1–15 KJV; my emphasis)

But this is that which was spoken by the prophet Joel; And it shall come to pass in the last days, saith God, I will pour out of my Spirit upon all flesh: and your sons and your daughters shall prophesy, and your young men shall see visions, and your old men shall dream dreams: And on my servants and on my handmaidens I will pour out in those days of my Spirit; and they shall prophesy: And I will show wonders in heaven above, and signs in the earth beneath; blood, and fire, and vapour of smoke: The sun shall be turned into darkness, and the moon into blood, before that great and notable day of the Lord come: And it shall come to pass, that whosoever shall call on the name of the Lord shall be saved. (Acts 2:16–21 KJV)

And I heard, but I understood not: then said I, O my Lord, what shall be the end of these things? And he said, Go thy way, Daniel: for the words are closed up and sealed till the time of the end. Many shall be purified, and made white, and tried; but the wicked shall do wickedly: and none of the wicked shall understand; but the wise shall understand. And from the time that the daily sacrifice shall be taken away, and the abomination that maketh desolate set up, there shall be a thousand two hundred and ninety days. Blessed is he that waiteth, and cometh to the thousand three hundred and five and thirty days. (Daniel 12:8–12 KJV)

Daniel 12 reveals to us that God seals the words associated with the last days. God also states that it will be the wise ones alive during the last days who will be able to put these words together and understand the scriptures. None of the wicked will understand, as stated above in Daniel. Theologians in previous generations did not understand these records. God sealed them until the last days; therefore, they could not have understood. These verses indicate that the seal will be taken off in the last days, but only the wise in those days will understand and be able to interpret the final days from the Word of God.

The above scriptures, as well as many others, state emphatically that certain events must pass before the great and terrible day of the Lord. These events will be known and understood at the time of the end by the wise alive in those days. The wise—those who study and believe God's Word—will have a thorough knowledge and understanding of the last days. This understanding will be key to performing his will in the last times. The scriptures state emphatically that men's hearts will fail for the things that are coming on the earth. The great trials of the end times will be a vehicle to inspire those who are called of God, both Jew and Gentile, to seek his forgiveness, repent, and do the will of God.

God instructs his people to watch and to be sober and not to continue as others—those who do not believe the scriptures. Further, God states that the day of his wrath should not overtake us as a thief as it will others; that is, we will not be unaware of the last times.[12] The body of Christ will know full well of the approaching Day of the Lord from the Word of God. God intends for his sons and daughters to know of the beginning of the time of sorrows related to the last days. Nevertheless, there will be those that will refuse to believe what God has revealed. The question is not whether it is God's will for us to know but rather what it is that we should look for. When are we to look for it? Where do we find it in God's Word?

It is evident that the end-time events occupy a unique role in God's Word. God has a reason for everything that he says, where he says it, when he says it, whom he says it to, and why he says it. The duty of the believer is to patiently search the scriptures to seek God's explanation through right division of his word. Once God does enlighten us, it is our responsibility to seek his guidance and wisdom and to walk in accordance with his will for our lives.

The fact that God dedicates significant portions of his word to explaining the last days and the glorious end for Israel is additional encouragement for us to study and understand God's Word. All evidence that God provides needs to be examined and digested, thereby allowing God to reveal his word and will through the

---

[12] 1 Thessalonians 5:4.

scriptures. Each word examined must be scrutinized and patiently pieced together through faith and prayer. The process allows God to speak from his heart to our heart. It is God's will to inform his children of the approaching last times. God utilizes his word to reveal the divine sequence of events related to the restitution of all things. The searcher of the Word of God is required to be patient, diligent, and disciplined, adhering to God's biblical research principles. The student must attain a disciplined process of being like-minded with God, thereby rejecting man's nonbiblical traditions and thoughts. Our ability to change our thinking to line up with God's thinking will be the measuring stick for success. The Word of God must speak and we must listen. Our thoughts must be reformulated to properly align with God's Word. The Word of God is deliberate and clear in its depiction of God's controversy with mankind. It is this controversy, taking center stage during the last days, that will be the main focus of this work. God's final controversy and resolution regarding man's rebellion has far-reaching effects beginning in the heavens, resounding on the earth, and affecting the sun, moon, stars, and all of God's creation.

Theologians through the years have pieced together events leading up to the second coming of our Lord Jesus Christ. It is clear and understood with mainstream Christianity that Jesus Christ will return as King of kings and Lord of lords. Questions have resulted from the various attempts to accurately portray last-time events. There are many and varied interpretations, which together result in mass confusion. The confusion has had the effect of forcing one to agree with one of the many interpretations. The result is diverse opinions and discord among the brethren. Will anyone know of God's timetable? What will be the signs of these times? Will Israel once again be the habitation of God and of his anointed one? Will the events of the book of Revelation truly come to pass as they are represented in God's Word? Who can be saved after the gathering together of the saints? The answers to these questions must be in the Word of God. God requires believers to approach his word humbly—with a broken heart and contrite spirit.[13] It is this humility before his throne that will produce good understanding.[14] God reveals his Word to those who fear him and humbly and prayerfully come before his throne through Jesus Christ. There are answers, and God's Word provides them; God states that his word contains all things that pertain to life and godliness.[15]

Many believe that it is not for anyone to know the timetable of the last days. This erroneous belief opposes all the information that God has provided. The scripture lists days, months, years, and events in specific order. Those who do understand and believe that God has provided signposts and a roadmap are typically narrowly looked upon. It is an accurate and rightly divided understanding of the Word of God that gives believers good understanding. An example of how scripture can be misunderstood is a scripture used to convince many that God's dealings with mankind are hidden. It will be shown that the scripture is written to state just the opposite. Examine the following from God's Word with context in mind: *"When they therefore were come together, they asked of him, saying, Lord, wilt thou at this time restore again the kingdom to Israel?* ***And he said unto them, It is not for you to know the times or the seasons, which the Father hath put in his own power. But ye shall receive power, after that the Holy Ghost is come upon you: and ye shall be witnesses unto me both in Jerusalem, and in all Judaea, and in Samaria, and unto the uttermost part of the earth"*** (Acts 1:6–8 KJV; my emphasis).

The disciples asked Jesus a logical question: what will happen next for Israel? From their perspective, in the first century, this was a legitimate question. The disciples were all Jewish and well-schooled in Old Testament scriptures, which emphatically foretell of the glorious end for Israel. Their question was related to God's purpose for Israel—the restoration of national Israel and the removal of Satan's

---

[13] Psalm 51:17.
[14] James 1:21.
[15] 2 Peter 1:3.

yoke from God's people and land. They were biblically literate, strong in their Old Testament knowledge, and what God promised to their fathers. They knew many of the scriptures concerning Israel were still unfulfilled at this point in the first century. With this background, they asked the Lord a logical question concerning Jewish prophecy fulfillment. The disciples closely examined Old Testament scripture after Christ's resurrection to determine what would happen next. The result was an honest question—a question that was burning in their hearts and minds. They now had firsthand understanding from the scriptures and recent events as to his suffering, crucifixion, and resurrection just witnessed. The resulting question was, what would happen next? Their frustration with the answer to this question led them to address the Lord before his taking up into heaven. The chatter among them must have been about how and when the Lord was going to restore the glory to Israel—the promises that God made to their fathers. Finally, they went and asked the Lord himself, as written in Acts 1:6. The question was both legitimate and logical for the situation they were in. The Lord was present, and they were all together. They now had the ability to clear up this burning question in their minds. The reply to their question by the Lord Jesus Christ is found in Acts 1:7–8: *"It is not for you to know the times or the seasons, which the Father hath put in his own power. But ye shall receive power, after that the Holy Ghost is come upon you: and ye shall be witnesses unto me both in Jerusalem, and in all Judaea, and in Samaria, and unto the uttermost part of the earth"* (Acts 1:7–8; my emphasis).

    The Lord effectively refocused their attention from their burning question to a new command: *"Go to Jerusalem and wait for the promise of the father."* Indeed, it is true that the times and seasons are truly in the Father's hands, including the time and season for the restoration of Israel. God controls the times and the seasons as he sees fit. The instruction to the apostles in Acts 1 is still an accurate instruction today to the body of Christ. The restoration is documented in every part of the Word of God. Now, at the time he spoke with the disciples, as recorded in Acts 1, that day was still a long way off. Of more importance was the day that was upon them at that time in the first century—that is, the day of God's grace to mankind through Jesus Christ. The day of God's grace begins in the book of Acts and represents a new period when God puts the Holy Spirit in each believer through a new birth in Jesus Christ. The new time that was now upon them required a new focus: winning souls for Christ. The period of the mystery of the body of Christ was now thrust upon them. The mystery period is found nowhere in the Old Testament scriptures, which contributed to their confusion regarding the times and seasons. Their question was honest and logical, and the Lord's answer was practical. The mystery period, the time when God's grace is abundant on the earth, was at that time present; and the glorious end for Israel was still far in the future.

The reality is that all times and seasons are controlled by God. But God also gives accurate details about times and seasons when they begin and progress on the earth. Stated another way, the times and seasons are initiated by God, but once initiated they travel along a prescribed path in accordance with God's Word. The prescribed path is also laid out by God in his Word. If this were not so, hundreds of scriptures relating to future events, personages, and timetables would have to be ignored. God's Word, as written in these very same scriptures, will one day come to life and meticulously and accurately be fulfilled when the season of the last time is initiated by God. The prophetic scriptures and timetables are part of God's Word; they are purposed by God and are as important as any other subject in the Bible. They are simply waiting for their season of fulfillment. Acts 1:7–8 provokes the question, If God does not want us to know the times or seasons of the last days, why does he provide so much information regarding this same time? God provides a sequence of events, personages, days, months, events, durations, judgments, and instructions regarding the last days. Why provide all this data if we are not to understand? Why would God state a definite time of 1,260 days, 42 months, and 3.5 years if it meant nothing? There must be a logical answer that incorporates the perfection of God's Word. There is an answer, and it has to do with right division of the Word of God and the understanding of the mystery of the body of Christ. Additionally, the Greek and Hebrew words used in Acts 1:7–8 must be understood in their context.

Examination of the Bible reveals several instances in which God uses prophetic words to warn his people of coming events, seasons, and times. The final of these warnings is indeed that of the events of the last days and the glorious end for Israel. Study of other biblical events reveals God's utilization of prophecy to protect and warn his people. For example, God continued to warn Israel of their impending Babylonian captivity if they would not turn from their idols. The season of Babylonian captivity came upon them after they refused to heed God's warnings. God warned Nineveh of its impending judgment through Jonah. This warning was adhered to and a great slaughter was averted. God warned the Israelites in Egypt of each plague before it happened. Israel's knowledge of the coming events allowed them to have courage and strength during the fearful Egyptian plagues. God warned Lot and Abraham of the destruction of Sodom and Gomorrah before it came to pass. Through this warning, Lot could save himself and his family from destruction. The list goes on and on and the purpose is clear: God comforts, cares, and warns those that fear and reverence him during times of great trouble. If God warned his people of these troubled times, why would God not warn his own people before the time of the greatest tribulation that would ever come to Earth? Each future-event prophecy has the protracted purpose of warning those who fear and reverence him during turbulent times and seasons. Now, examining the true meaning of Acts 1:7–8, the key to the interpretation is contained in the meanings of the Greek words used for *times and seasons*. The Greek words used and their meanings are as follows:

> χρόνους; translated KJV (Acts 1:7) as "times"; This word perceives time quantitatively as a period measured by the succession of objects and events and denotes the passing of moments.[16]
> καιροὺς; translated KJV (acts 1:7) as "seasons"; Season, opportune time. It is not

---

[16] Zodhiates, S. *(2000). The Complete Word Study Dictionary: New Testament (electronic ed.). Chattanooga, TN: AMG Publishers; 1992*

merely as a succession of minutes, but a period of opportunity (though not necessity)[17]

These words, "times" and "seasons," taken in their context and in accordance with their Greek meanings, are used by the Lord in Acts 1:7–8 and refer to God's retaining knowledge of the initiation of certain periods of time and keeping it a secret. God would leave these times to his own power to initiate. It is also clear that once these times and seasons are initiated by God, they will follow a prescribed path documented in the Word of God. The point of Acts 1:7–8 is that the disciples' discussions and questions concerning end times and Israel's glorious end were not the focus of God's plan at that time. The restoration of Israel, closely associated with the end-times period, was still thousands of years away at the time when this question was asked. Jesus Christ instructed them of a new time—the period of the mystery of the one body of Christ. The mystery period was the time that was at hand and the time they were to focus on in the present. The times and the seasons of the last days—those days related to Israel's restoration—were still far off in the future. The time and season for God to provide his gift of the Holy Spirit through faith in Jesus Christ was now upon them and would last for almost two thousand years. The disciples were not aware of this new grace administration time period that was now thrust upon them. It was unclear to them because their Old Testament study did not reveal anything about the time of the mystery of the one body of Christ. The grace administration, or the administration of the one body of Christ, was hidden from all generations and secure in the heart of God. This mystery period was first revealed to the apostle Paul only in the first century.[18] The Lord stated in Acts 1 that a new time or administration was coming on the earth—that is, the time of the mystery of the one body of Jesus Christ. The new church of the body would be made up of both the Jews and Gentiles and given God's

---

[17] Zodhiates, S. *(2000). The Complete Word Study Dictionary: New Testament (electronic ed.). Chattanooga, TN: AMG Publishers; 1992*

[18] Colossians 1:26–27.

unmerited divine favor through faith in Jesus Christ. The mystery period will be studied in detail in the next chapter, but for now, Acts 1:7–8 can be summarized as follows:

- The question concerning Israel's restoration in Acts was asked thousands of years before the actual restoration would occur. This restoration will take place at some time in the future, after the final seven years of Daniel's prophecy of seventy sevens of years.[19]
- The vast amount of scripture concerning Israel will be fulfilled in the future exactly as God set it forth in his word, as recorded in both Old and New Testament scriptures.
- What the disciples thought to be fulfilled two thousand years ago, the restoration of Israel, is still awaiting fulfillment. The fulfillment, when it is initiated by God, will come to pass exactly as written in God's Word, with not one word failing.
- God will initiate the final times and seasons of the last days when he sees fit. Once initiated by God, the time and season of the last days will follow the prescribed path set by God in both the Old and New Testaments.
- Understanding the events of the last times, as documented in the Word of God, will enlighten the believer as to the events surrounding the last times, and the lover of God will not be caught unaware.

Israel, also known as the bride of Christ, will be purified through the final forty-two months of the final seven years also known as Jacob's trouble. This is detailed in many Old Testament scriptures and will be examined in this work. The scriptures extensively speak of the last days and God's glorious end for Israel. The prophecies regarding the last days will be the focus of this work. The period known as the mystery of the one body of Christ, initiated by God two thousand years ago, continues today (2020) and was kept secret

---

[19] Daniel 9:24–27.

in the Old Testament. The disciples were ignorant of this gap in time, since it was not revealed in the Old Testament but was kept hidden in the heart of God.[20] Since the disciples were unaware of the secret mystery period, they rightly believed in Acts 1:7–8, which stated that the restoration of Israel, the final seven years, would immediately begin. We know now that the restoration of Israel has been held in abeyance until God initiates the end times, the final seven years, as he sees fit.

It is true that Acts 1:7–8 begins to hint at a new period initiated by God—the mystery administration of the one body of Jesus Christ. The initiation of the last seven years, or the window of time when God restores Israel, is in God's hands. God will initiate this time in accordance with his own hidden plans. The last seven years, or end times, is the period of the final seven years, or "*last week*," of Daniel's prophecy of the seventy sevens of weeks.[21] Once God sets this last "*week*" (week of years, or seven years) into motion, God, through his Word, has provided enormous amounts of information relating to these last seven years. All the scripture written about these last days can be understood and expected to come to pass with precision and accuracy. Those alive and who fear and reverence God during this time will have perfect knowledge as to the sequence of events set forth by God in his Word. The understanding of the sequence of events will allow the believer to "*not be overtaken as a thief*"[22] and will provide the events to "*watch for*,"[32] as instructed by the Lord. Only God knows when he will initiate and put into motion the last times and seasons. God's people today are instructed to "*watch and not to sleep*"—to be cognizant of the events of the world and compare them to God's Word. Through this process, the believer can determine whether God has set this time and season into motion. What to watch for is one of the central themes of this work. Through study and right division of the Word of God, the initiation of the last seven years can be accurately understood: "*for that day will not overtake you*

---

[20] 1 Corinthians 2:7.
[21] Daniel 9:24.
[22] 1 Thessalonians 5:1–6.

through thievery." This is consistent with God's will. Consider the following: "For yourselves know perfectly that the day of the Lord so cometh as a thief in the night. For when they shall say, Peace and safety; then sudden destruction cometh upon them, as travail upon a woman with child; and they shall not escape. **But ye, brethren, are not in darkness, that that day should overtake you as a thief**" (1 Thessalonians 5:2–4 KJV; my emphasis).

Our study now examines the time of the mystery of the one body of Jesus Christ. The scripture states that the body of Christ consists of former Jews and Gentiles made one and given eternal life through faith in Jesus Christ.[23] The mystery administration was kept hidden in God throughout Old Testament times, and even the times of the Lord's presence on earth. The one body of Jesus Christ and its members were kept secret in the heart of God until revealed to the apostle Paul in the first century.[24] The proper understanding of the scriptures regarding this time is paramount to the understanding of the last times. This fact cannot be overstated and is critical to right division of the Word of God. Our study will reveal that the administration of the one body of Jesus Christ is missing, nowhere mentioned in the Old Testament and therefore not understood from the vantage point of the Old Testament. An accurate understanding of this missing period of time from the Word of God is required to rightly divide God's Word. Ignorance of this mystery period leads to extensive misunderstanding and wrong interpretation of the Word of God, especially concerning the last days. Daniel's prophecy of the seventy sevens of years cannot be accurately understood without a right understanding of this period of time.

---

[23] 1 Corinthians 12:13.
[24] Ephesians 3:1–5.

CHAPTER 3

The Mystery of the One Body of Christ and the Seventy Weeks of Daniel

THE RIGHT DIVISION OF THE Word of God is essential to understanding the last days, or the time of the end of man's rule on the earth. Fundamentally, the right division concerning the administration of the one body of Jesus Christ is paramount to right division and accurate understanding of the last days of man's rule on Earth. If the mystery administration is accurately understood, all last-day references recorded in the Word of God, especially Old Testament references, will perfectly fit together. Before we delve into the last days, it is critical for proper interpretation to examine the meaning of the one body of Jesus Christ and how it fits into the administrations listed in God's Word.

The one body of Jesus Christ is referred to in the Word of God as the church of God. The church of God, and the power that it brings into the life of a believer, is one of the least understood subjects of scripture. The majority of revelation in God's Word concerning the administration of the body of Christ was revealed by God to Jesus Christ. Jesus Christ then revealed it in the first century to the apostle Paul, who subsequently wrote it down and documented it in his epistles as instructed by the Lord Jesus Christ. The mystery of the one body was a secret administration kept secret in the heart of God; it was not revealed in Old Testament scriptures but was revealed to Paul in the first century. The plan for salvation for both Jew and Gentile, through faith in Jesus Christ, was a new concept hidden in the heart of God. Paul's letters were inspired by God and given through the Lord Jesus Christ through special revelation from Jesus Christ. The apostle Paul received revelation not from men but from the Lord Jesus Christ, and ultimately from God. Consider the following verses in Galatians: *"For do I now persuade men, or God? or do I seek to please men? for if I yet pleased men, I should not be the servant of Christ.* ***But I certify you, brethren, that the gospel which was preached of me is not after man. For I neither received it of man, neither was I taught it, but by the revelation of Jesus Christ"*** (Galatians 1:10–12 KJV; my emphasis).

Paul received revelation from our Lord and Savior, Jesus Christ. The revelation that Paul received was a new revelation and was the information, the final piece of the puzzle, that made the Word of God complete. The information regarding the mystery of the one body of Jesus Christ was from God handed down to Jesus Christ and ultimately revealed and written down by the apostle Paul. It will be shown that one of the greatest revelations Paul received was this doctrine of the mystery of the one body of Jesus Christ. In Colossians, Paul states that the revelation of the mystery was given to him in order to fulfill or make complete the Word of God: *"Whereof I am made a minister, according to the dispensation of God which is given to me for you, to fulfill the Word of God; Even the mystery which hath been hid from ages and from generations, but now is made manifest to his saints: To whom God would make known what is the riches of the glory of this mystery among the Gentiles; which is Christ in you, the hope of glory"* (Colossians 1:25–27; my emphasis).

Colossians 1:25–27 indicates a missing piece of information regarding the Word of God. The missing piece is inserted before the book of Revelation but after the Gospel period. Something cannot be completed (fulfilled) unless there is a missing part. The Greek word translated here as "fulfill" is "*pleroo*," and it is used as an infinitive of "purpose"—that is, as a verbal noun showing completion of an action. The missing part of the Word of God was intentionally left out by

God until revealed to Paul in the first century. God did not reveal, or even hint at, the one body of Jesus Christ in any other part of God's Word. This missing part, the mystery of the one body of Jesus Christ, was a secret up until the first century. Right division of the one body of Christ is critical and forms a central basis for accurate interpretation of the last days. The revelation that the Lord gave to the apostle Paul will simply not make much sense without getting the mystery period clear in our minds. Accurate knowledge of the mystery of the one body of Jesus Christ reveals hundreds of otherwise little-known verses of scripture. These scriptures will be fundamental to understanding the last days, or the time of the end. Accurate knowledge of this timely subject is simply of critical necessity. Paul's letters contain the whole truth concerning the mystery period that was to fulfill the Word of God. Paul's letters were inspired by God and are of equal weight as all other scripture. They have the same profit as other scriptures and are mainly written to those who have accepted Jesus Christ as Lord and Savior. *"All scripture is given by inspiration of God, and is profitable for doctrine, for reproof, for correction, for instruction in righteousness: That the man of God may be perfect, thoroughly furnished unto all good works"* (2 Timothy 3:16–17 KJV; my emphasis).

The Word of God continually supplies doctrine, reproof, and correction to the lover of God. It is our duty to patiently and methodically study the scriptures and digest the doctrine, reproof, and correction that God provides daily. God, through his Word, is molding us into the image of his dear son, Jesus Christ, as we grow in his gift of the Holy Spirit. The scriptures must be believed in order for them to be energized in our lives. This believing faith comes from a daily diet of the Word of God. Faith in Jesus Christ saves us and justifies us with God. Justification by faith, not of the law, is a new concept brought into being as part of the administration of the one body of Jesus Christ. It is critical that God's Word be read and studied. The most important issue concerning faith in God is faith in the Word of God and the right division of his Word. God approves of our lives as we study and rightly divide his Word of Truth. During the mystery age—that is, the time of the one body of Christ on Earth, salvation can come only through faith in Jesus Christ. All who come to him during this period must accept him as their personal Lord and Savior. Salvation through faith will continue until the gathering together or the rapture of the body of Christ. The time of the last trumpet[25] is the time when the body of Christ will meet the Lord in the air. Salvation after the rapture of the body of Christ will come about only through works and through the trials enumerated in the book of Revelation and certain Old Testament scriptures. In short, deliverance will once again be based on works. In contrast, those who have been saved by the gift of God through faith in Jesus Christ are also approved by God through right division of his Word. Consider the following:

> Of these things put them in remembrance, charging them before the Lord that they strive not about words to no profit, but to the subverting of the hearers. **Study to show thyself approved unto God, a workman that needeth not to be ashamed, rightly dividing the Word of Truth.** But shun profane and vain babblings: for they will increase unto more ungodliness. And their word will eat as doth a canker: of whom is Hymenaeus and Philetus; Who concerning the truth have erred, saying that the resurrection is past already; and overthrow the faith of some. Nevertheless the foundation of God standeth sure, having this seal, The Lord knoweth them that are his. And, Let every one that nameth the name of Christ depart from iniquity. **But in a great house there are not only vessels of gold and of silver, but also of wood and of earth; and some to honour, and some to dishonour. If a man therefore purge himself from these, he shall be a vessel unto honour, sanctified, and meet for the master's use, and prepared unto every good work.** (2 Timothy 2:14–21 KJV; my emphasis)

---

[25] 1 Corinthians 15:52.

God reveals his approval process for those in his family resulting in vessels of honor. God also reveals vessels of dishonor in the same house—members of the same family. The two important requirements for a vessel of honor are the right division of the Word of God and a holy life before God. This is the high calling and the standard that he calls all of his sons and daughters to. The right division of the Word of God is important to God, and therefore it should be important to us. His instruction is that we rightly divide—make the right cut—when studying his Word.

The mystery of the one body of the Lord Jesus Christ must be understood in light of right division of God's Word. Methodically, each scripture must be addressed and digested and sanctified in our heads in accordance with God's biblical interpretation principles. Failure to understand the mystery of the one body of Christ and its relation to the bride of Christ, Israel, will result in confusion and misinterpretation. The body of Christ is the body of Christ, and the bride of Christ is the bride of Christ; these are two separate and distinct bodies. The difference between the two groups must be clearly understood to completely understand the Word of God in our minds. The study of the last days, or time of the end is built upon our understanding of the complete Word of God.

The Word of God is multifaceted and reveals the manifold wisdom of God. The Word naturally contains instruction for all peoples, times, ages, and administrations. God expects his approved ones to rightly divide and utilize his Word in their daily lives. Conformance and discipline according to God's Word leads to being conformed into the image of Christ and attaining a personal relationship with the risen Christ. God supernaturally reveals his Word to those who humbly come to it through faith. Without faith, it is impossible to please him; and failure to rightly divide will lead to guesswork and confusion. The error concerning the mystery of the one body of Jesus Christ has led to great confusion. The body of Christ is not the same as the bride of Christ and must be rightly divided to avoid confusion. God does not use words interchangeably; he has a reason and purpose for every word that he documents in his Word. The body of Christ is indeed Christ's body and consists of all those, both Jew and Gentile, who have believed in their heart that God raised Christ from the dead and confessed with their mouth that Jesus Christ is Lord.[26] The bride of Christ, as will be shown in this work, always refers to Israel—the physical descendants of Abraham, Isaac, and Jacob. It will be the remnant of these descendants that God will supernaturally save in the last days, fulfilling his promises to their fathers. These two groups, the bride and the body, are separate and distinct and have different standings before God. Interpreting these groups in any other way causes innumerable contradictions and confusion. When God says, "body of Christ," he means "body of Christ," and when he says, "bride of Christ," he means "bride of Christ"; these are two distinct groups of people. The final marriage feast, as documented by God in the Gospels and the book of Revelation, is the marriage of the body of Christ and the bride of Christ. This marriage feast is not fulfilled until Revelation 19:7.

    The first-century Christians were unified in their belief and understanding of the Word of God and secure in their standing as the one body of Jesus Christ. Through this knowledge, they had great witness and power in their daily lives and in their witness for Christ. Consider the following:

> And when they had prayed, the place was shaken where they were assembled together; and they were all filled with the Holy Ghost, and they spake the Word of God with boldness. And the multitude of them that believed were of one heart and of one soul: neither said any of them that ought of the things which he possessed was his own; but they had all things common. And with great power gave the apostles witness of the resurrection of the Lord Jesus: and great grace was upon them all. Neither was there any among them that lacked: for as many as were possessors of lands or houses sold them, and

---

[26] Romans 10:9.

brought the prices of the things that were sold. (Acts 4:31–34 KJV)

An essential ingredient for the remarkable power and witness of the first-century Christians was their thorough knowledge of the mystery of the one body of Jesus Christ. Unification is not possible without accurate and right division of the Word of God. Numerous problems result when the Word of God is not rightly divided. The resulting confusion gives way to division, strife, anger, and hatred. God means what he says in every scripture—where he says it and why he says it. A synchronized life is one in which the Word of God lives and dominates the behavior of a believer, resulting in God's power being self-evident.

The history of the Christian church reveals that the devil first stole the central concept of the mystery of the one body of Jesus Christ and replaced it with religious tradition. Discord and division quickly followed, and it expanded with time as the church heeded and submitted to the traditions and doctrines of men. The one body of Christ and the reality of *Christ in you* by a new birth through faith in Christ was replaced by tradition, robbing the church of power. The great miracle of the new birth in Jesus Christ was soon replaced by religion, in which all religion not based on faith in Christ can be summed up as outward justification through works of the flesh. The church was left powerless, resulting in religious tradition and being hopelessly stuck in mediocrity. In spite of this, God still provides his power when his people rise up and rightly divide his Word through faith.

The one body of Jesus Christ was kept hidden in God for ages and generations and was never revealed until first revealed to the apostle Paul in the first century. Why did God keep the body of Christ hidden and never reveal it to any of his created beings? To answer this question, we must first understand the two major subjects of the entire Bible: *"And I will put enmity between thee (the serpent) and the woman, and between thy seed and her seed (Christ); it shall bruise thy head, and thou shalt bruise his heel"* (Genesis 3:15 KJV).

Genesis 3:15 lays the foundation for the events and actions documented in the Word of God after the fall in Genesis. The events in this passage are not chronologically listed but are listed in accordance to importance to God. The bruising or destruction of Satan is listed first but will happen last. The reality of Satan's bruising consists of his total destruction along with his plans, aspirations, power, and authority. This is signified by the bruising of the head of the Satan—the brain, or the source of all Satan's thinking and strategy. The second part of the scripture deals with the bruising of the heel of the seed of the woman. This is the horrific crucifixion of our Lord and Savior, Jesus Christ. The sufferings and the glory of our Lord Jesus Christ are the main theme of the Bible. His glorious resurrection accomplishes man's redemption and further will fulfill all of God's will for the heavens and the earth. Through Jesus Christ, all are saved who are called by God and believe in accordance with his will. Through Jesus Christ, the curse is removed, death is defeated, sin is no more, the earth is restored, and God's great purpose is accomplished.

Satan's attempt to destroy the seed of the woman, Jesus Christ, is clear throughout scripture. The Old Testament contains historical information regarding God's actions in repelling Satan's attempts to destroy the woman's seed—that is, the Lord Jesus Christ. God continuously protected and watched over his plan to provide a promised seed for man's redemption in spite of the best efforts of Satan. Time and time again, the devil attacked the people of God in an attempt to ruin God's redemptive plan laid out in Genesis 3:15. The following are some of the actions taken by Satan in his attempt to thwart the redemptive plan of God by destroying the seed of the woman:

1. The giants in the land before Abraham arrived to occupy God's holy place
2. The attempted killing of Joseph after his dream was revealed to Jacob
3. The occupation of the land in the time of Moses
4. The destruction of the Jewish male infants at Moses's birth to remove the promised seed

5. The elimination of the Jews through Haman to eradicate the Jews from the earth
6. The giants at the time of the flood and during the time of Noah contaminating the bloodline of man
7. The killing of the infants and toddlers in Bethlehem in a futile attempt to destroy God's promised seed at the time of the birth of Jesus Christ
8. The crucifixion of Jesus Christ, in which Satan believed that he finally rid himself of the promised seed

These attempts were nothing other than Satan attempting to nullify God's redemptive plan and the promise of Genesis 3:15. In all of these attacks, God protected his plan and divinely intervened to nullify Satan's attacks. Satan's attacks reached a climax when he orchestrated the crucifixion of our Lord Jesus Christ. The death of Jesus Christ at Calvary seemed to Satan to be the elusive victory that he pursued throughout the Old Testament. Satan thought that he had finally destroyed the promised seed. Satan believed that he finally drove a stake into God's plan as stated in Genesis 3:15. His strategy to kill the promised seed and eliminate man's redeemer appeared to be accomplished and final. Satan believed that the crucifixion at Calvary was the final nail in the coffin of God's plan to redeem mankind from sin and death. In contrast, and through this very action, Satan himself ushered in the administration of the one body of Christ, or the period of the mystery. The mystery period would be a new period in which everyone who would believe and confess Jesus Christ would become sons and daughters of God through a new miraculous spiritual birth.

The mystery administration would be a time of God's grace allowing all that would accept Jesus Christ to gain access to the Holy Spirit seed through a new inner birth. The new birth would give power to all who would receive the gift to overcome the prince of the power of the air. Satan's own action at Calvary opened the door for the gift of the Holy Spirit to be given to those Jews and Gentiles who would believe and accept. The devil effectively provided the means for the new birth to be given to any man or woman to be a son or daughter of God through faith in Jesus Christ. The new birth gave rise to the Holy Spirit's spiritual power, born anew, in men and women who would believe in the risen Christ. The new birth, Holy Spirit, would be greater spirit than that which was in the world—a spiritual birth greater than any of the evil spirits of Satan's realm. In effect, Satan orchestrated his own doom in the like manner of the story of Haman of the Old Testament, who foreshadowed this very event. If Satan knew that the killing of Christ would open the door and allow millions of people to escape certain death, he would not have crucified Jesus Christ.[27] It is evident that Satan did not know the end result of his actions *because God kept it hidden from ages and from generations.* God effectively gave Satan the rope that would seal his own doom. God, through his infinite wisdom, allowed Satan to be the initiator of the gift of the Holy Spirit to be given to millions. His error of killing Jesus Christ resulted in the most miraculous plan God had ever devised for man. The fitting end is exactly how God chose to seal Satan's doom.

A similar event in the Old Testament, as previously mentioned, is documented in the book of Ester. Haman, a proud high-ranking official to the king, planned to kill off all Israel. His reason for killing off Israel was because of one certain subject of the king—Mordecai. It was Mordecai who would not bow before Haman as he walked through the king's terrace. God allowed Haman to go so far as building gallows to destroy Mordecai. Haman believed that he would be finally be able to rid himself of the Jews and Mordecai. After this, Haman was invited to the king's dinner to celebrate and be honored, only to discover that he was the one that would be hanged on his own gallows. Thus, God foreshadowed how another proud being, Satan, would bring doom to himself hundreds of years later.

The reason that God kept the period of the mystery of the one body of Jesus Christ secret was to seal the fate of Satan and give the earth to the Lord Jesus Christ and his called-out ones. The scripture states that Satan would not have killed the Lord Jesus Christ if he had known what God was going to do next. Consider the following:

---

[27] 1 Corinthians 2:7–8.

> Your faith should not stand in the wisdom of men, but in the power of God. Howbeit we speak wisdom among them that are perfect: yet not the wisdom of this world, nor of the princes of this world, that come to nought: **But we speak the wisdom of God in a mystery, even the hidden wisdom, which God ordained before the world unto our glory: Which none of the princes of this world knew: for had they known it, they would not have crucified the Lord of glory.** But as it is written, Eye hath not seen, nor ear heard, neither have entered into the heart of man, the things which God hath prepared for them that love him. (1 Corinthians 2:5–9 KJV; my emphasis)

Satan's crucifixion of our Lord allowed millions of people, for almost two thousand years, to be saved from sin and death through faith in Jesus Christ. Consider the following:

> For this cause I Paul, the prisoner of Jesus Christ for you Gentiles, If ye have heard of the dispensation of the grace of God which is given me to you-ward: How that by revelation he made known unto me the mystery; (as I wrote afore in few words, Whereby, when ye read, ye may understand my knowledge in the mystery of Christ) **Which in other ages was not made known unto the sons of men, as it is now revealed unto his holy apostles and prophets by the Spirit; That the Gentiles should be fellowheirs, and of the same body, and partakers of his promise in Christ by the gospel**: Whereof I was made a minister, according to the gift of the grace of God given unto me by the effectual working of his power. Unto me, who

am less than the least of all saints, is this grace given, that I should preach among the Gentiles the unsearchable (untraceable) riches of Christ; And to make all men see what is the fellowship (administration) of the mystery, which from the beginning of the world hath been hid in God, who created all things by Jesus Christ: To the intent that now unto the principalities and powers in heavenly places might be known by the church the manifold wisdom of God, According to the eternal purpose which he purposed in Christ Jesus our Lord. (Ephesians 3:1–11 KJV; my emphasis)

These scriptures fortify the truth that God kept his plan of salvation hidden and secret regarding the Mystery of the one body of Jesus Christ until revealed to Apostle Paul. None of the information regarding the mystery period was contained in the Word of God before the first century; this includes both the Gospels and the Old Testament. The devil knew of the sufferings and the future glory of Jesus Christ as King of kings and Lord of lords through God's revealed word. Satan did not know what God was planning between the sufferings and the glory of Christ—the grace and forgiveness that would be given to man through Jesus Christ. This interim period of time, which Satan had no knowledge of, is the time of the mystery of the one body of Christ. The hidden time would be a time when Jew and Gentile would be made one (body) through faith in Jesus Christ. This information was kept secret in the heart of God.

The devil believed that by killing our Lord he had thwarted God's plan of salvation. The devil knew what the Old Testament stated about the sufferings and the glory concerning Jesus Christ. The devil did not know anything of the new birth and eternal life for Jew and Gentile, or God's plan to create, through a new spiritual birth, the manifold, multifaceted body of Christ. God kept this great truth hidden in his heart in order to redeem mankind. This is why no reference to this plan can be found in the Bible before it was revealed to Apostle Paul in the first century. The reality of the new birth—being born again not of corruptible seed but of incorruptible, or sinless, seed was a new thing on the earth.[28] The Jew and Gentile would both be partakers of the same body of Jesus Christ, effectively being joined together as one body with no difference. The disciples knew of the glory that would one day come to Israel, but they had no knowledge of the mystery period of time. Their lack of understanding of this mystery period logically led them to their question in Acts 1:4–10 concerning Israel. Their Old Testament studies led them to believe that the restoration of Israel followed immediately after the crucifixion. With this in mind, they asked the question to the Lord in Acts. Consider the following:

> And, being assembled together with them, commanded them that they should not depart from Jerusalem, but wait for the promise of the Father, which, saith he, ye have heard of me. For John truly baptized with water; but ye shall be baptized with the Holy Ghost not many days hence. **When they therefore were come together, they asked of him, saying, Lord, wilt thou at this time restore again the kingdom to Israel?** And he said unto them, It is not for you to know the times or the seasons, which the Father hath put in his own power. But ye shall receive power, after that the Holy Ghost is come upon you: and ye shall be witnesses unto me both in Jerusalem, and in all Judaea, and in Samaria, and unto the uttermost part of the earth. And when he had spoken these things, while they beheld, he was taken up; and a cloud received him out of their sight. And while they looked stedfastly toward heaven as he went up, behold, two men stood by them in white apparel. (Acts 1:4–10 KJV; my emphasis)

---

[28] 1 Peter 1:23.

Their question concerning Israel from their understanding of the Word of God was reasonable. Would the glorious end for Israel now be accomplished? All of their teaching and understanding of the Word of God pointed toward Israel being restored as the next event in the sequence after the suffering of Christ. Their understanding from the Old Testament directed them to believe that the coming of Israel's Messiah and his rule on earth as King of kings and Lord of lords would follow directly after the sufferings of Christ. No scripture hinted at any delay between the two events; therefore, naturally, they believed that the glory for Israel would immediately follow.

The sufferings and glory of the Messiah were nothing new and were frequently prophesied in the Old Testament. Conversely, there was not even the slightest hint in the Old Testament of Jew and Gentile being grafted into a unified body of Christ through a new spiritual birth. The Old Testament referred to both groups as completely separate and distinct. God kept this mystery hidden in his heart. This truth would be one of many testaments that would reveal his manifold wisdom to the world. Truly, when one finally understands this mystery of the one body of Jesus Christ, the majesty and sovereignty of our Holy God is understood by his created beings.

> **And to make all men see what is the fellowship (administration or time period) of the mystery, which from the beginning of the world hath been hid in God, who created all things by Jesus Christ: To the intent that now unto the principalities and powers in heavenly places might be known by the church the manifold wisdom of God,** According to the eternal purpose which he purposed in Christ Jesus our Lord: (Ephesians 3:9–11 KJV; my emphasis)

The foundational reality of the one who is joined to Christ is that he is free from the domination of sin and the deception of Satan, with Satan no longer having rule of a believer through death. The way of life is through the liberty that comes through faith in Jesus Christ. In the end, it will be Jesus Christ who will crush the head of Satan and all his plans as documented in Genesis 3:15. The firstfruits, the beginning of that freedom, are given to those whom God calls out to be members of the one body of Jesus Christ. Consider the following:

> Knowing this, that our old man is crucified with him, that the body of sin might be destroyed, that henceforth we should not serve sin. For he that is dead is freed from sin. Now if we be dead with Christ, we believe that we shall also live with him: Knowing that Christ being raised from the dead dieth no more; death hath no more dominion over him. For in that he died, he died unto sin once: but in that he liveth, he liveth unto God. Likewise reckon ye also yourselves to be dead indeed unto sin, but alive unto God through Jesus Christ our Lord. Let not sin therefore reign in your mortal body, that ye should obey it in the lusts thereof. Neither yield ye your members as instruments of unrighteousness unto sin: but yield yourselves unto God, as those that are alive from the dead, and your members as instruments of righteousness unto God. For sin shall not have dominion over you: for ye are not under the law, but under grace. (Romans 6:6–14 KJV)

In this section, God, through the Apostle Paul, reveals a new standing for those who will live together with God eternally. Christ, having been raised from the dead, cannot die again. His resurrection was unlike that of Lazarus who did again meet with death. Christ's resurrection broke forever the tyranny of death and the author of death—that is, Satan. Death can no longer exercise any power over those sanctified through faith in Jesus Christ. Satan believed that the crucifixion of Jesus Christ put an end to the promise of God in Genesis 3:15. Instead it marked the beginning of the end of Satan and his hold on man through death and sin. The cross was Satan's final move, and the resurrection was God's checkmate, rendering all of Satan's strategies powerless. The game is over. God is now calling out his saints and is patient to wait for all those who will believe. The end of Satan is separated only by time. Christ died to sin once and for all, and all of mankind are invited. The freedom and reality of the new birth are now being realized to all those who will believe and who are called according to his purpose. The one body of the Lord Jesus Christ grows stronger with each new member.

The Old Testament writings contain future events for Israel and for Israel's Messiah, Jesus Christ. The scriptures concerning the Antichrist in the Old Testament are also future and accurate in accordance with God's Word and will. Jacob's time of trouble, as described in the Old Testament, concerns the last days of man's rule on Earth and is still future. The church of the one body of Jesus Christ is a special group called to God for a special purpose on Earth: to represent the absent Christ (that is, absent in his glorified body only). The standing of the body of Christ is a gift and is through faith. The instructions to the body of Christ are contained in the writings of Paul through the revelation of Jesus Christ. The body of Christ was hidden in the Old Testament and was revealed only to Paul through the revelation of Jesus Christ in the first century. Because it was hidden in the Old Testament, the instructions to the body of Christ, and even the existence of the body of Christ, cannot and did not come into concretion in the scriptures until Paul received it in the first century. Consider the following:

> "Let every one of us please his neighbor for his good to edification. For even Christ pleased not himself; but, as it is written, The reproaches of them that reproached thee fell on me. **For whatsoever things were written aforetime were written for our learning, that we through patience and comfort of the scriptures might have hope**" (Romans 15:2–4; my emphasis).

Scriptures written before the time of the Mystery period on Earth were written for our learning and *not* directly written to the body of Christ. A good deal of information gleaned from Old Testament scriptures concerns events of the last days, but there is nothing concerning the one body of Jesus Christ. It will be the Old Testament scriptures that will identify the future vile man of Daniel, the Antichrist, and Satan's final actions through him. The Old Testament scriptures also provide information regarding the final time periods and timelines that will come to pass and have a future fulfillment. They provide information regarding when the final days begin as well as the final glory for Israel, including the final sequence of last-day events. The Old Testament reveals the continual struggle of Israel, their turning away from God, and their returning to God. When Israel walked with God, they were a powerful, successful nation; and when they were stiff-necked toward God and disobeyed, captivity ensued.

Satan knew through Genesis 3:15 that the seed of the woman would one day come and crush his head. God prophesized that David's house would produce the seed. The scriptures revealed information about the first coming of the Lord Jesus Christ. In fact, the Lord states that the entire Bible contained scriptures that spoke of him.

> "Search the scriptures; for in them ye think ye have eternal life: and they are they which testify of me. And ye will not come to me, that ye might have life. I receive not honour from men. But I know you, that ye have not the love of God in you. I am come in my Father's name, and ye receive me not: if another shall come in his own name, him ye will receive. How can ye believe, which receive honour one of another, and seek not the honour that cometh from God only?" (John 5:39–44 KJV)

It is evident from the Old Testament that the devil sought to defeat God's plan of salvation for mankind. The believing Jews knew from the Old Testament that glory would one day come to Israel through their Messiah. The Jews also understood that the Messiah would suffer but would also have a glorious end. This glory was not a mystery in the Old Testament but was a continual theme that was revealed through many Old Testament scriptures. The sufferings of Christ, which were revealed in the Old Testament were not as well known; they were understood only through an accurate study of the Word of God. The sufferings of Christ were vividly portrayed in many areas of the Old Testament, yet they were little understood by Old Testament-believing Jews. Psalm 22 and Isaiah 53 as well as other similar scriptures reveal the reality of the sufferings of Messiah. The coexistence of both glory and suffering for the Messiah led to questions and theories of how one could relate to the other. How could the Messiah suffer and have such a glorious end? Stated another way, how could the Messiah receive so much glory and be burdened with so much pain and agony? To resolve the contradiction, they decided to ignore sufferings and believe only the glorious end for Israel, stumbling at the revelation concerning his suffering. The Jews still look for their glorious Messiah without the sufferings. This lack of understanding was apparent when our Lord confronted Jewish believers in the book of Luke:

> And when they found not his body, they came, saying, that they had also seen a vision of angels, which said that he was alive. And certain of them which were with us went to the sepulchre, and found it even so as the women had said: but him they saw not. **Then he said unto them, O fools, and slow of heart to believe all that the prophets have spoken: Ought not Christ to have suffered these things, and to enter into his glory? And beginning at Moses and all the prophets, he expounded unto them in all the scriptures the things concerning himself.** And

> they drew nigh unto the village, whither they went: and he made as though he would have gone further. But they constrained him, saying, Abide with us: for it is toward evening, and the day is far spent. And he went in to tarry with them. And it came to pass, as he sat at meat with them, he took bread, and blessed it, and brake, and gave to them. And their eyes were opened, and they knew him; and he vanished out of their sight. And they said one to another, Did not our heart burn within us, while he talked with us by the way, and while he opened to us the scriptures? (Luke 24:23–32; my emphasis)

The Lord's followers were instructed to believe all that was written concerning Christ. The consensus belief of Israel was that Christ would not suffer. The Lord himself confronted and corrected their wrong division of scripture in the above passage. The wrong division of the Word of God will always cause stumbling and confusion. The scriptures vividly depicted a suffering Messiah who would one day enter glorious standing with God and man. Another attempt to convince Israel of the sufferings of Messiah was his final words on the cross. The Lord recited the first and last words from Psalm 22 (please read) as his final words on earth: "*My God My God, why has thou forsaken me*" and "*It is finished.*" These words were spoken by the Lord to bring Israel into remembrance of Psalm 22, which accurately and definitively describes the crucifixion in minute detail. Psalm 22 was recorded hundreds of years earlier. The lesson is that believing all scripture is paramount to spiritual maturity. Believing all scripture related to the last days is critical to the understanding of the last times; if we do not heed this, we too will stumble. Our prayer to God is to lead us into his truth concerning the last days by examining and believing all that God has revealed in his Word.

The whole of the Old Testament reveals God's plan and will for Israel and the Gentiles. God is the God and creator of all people, Jews and Gentiles. A great deal of the Old Testament scripture was addressed to Israel, God's chosen people. After the promise to Abraham and to his seed, the sections directed to the Gentiles are few and far between, but they are there for those with focused eyes. The blessing of the Gentiles would come through Israel, specifically in the form of the promised seed, Jesus Christ. The Gentiles were to be blessed through Abraham's seed, but the method that God was going to use to bless the Gentiles was unknown, or a mystery. The clear plan that is documented in the Old Testament was, *and still is*, how God chose to redeem Israel, the bride of Christ. The sufferings and glory of the Messiah coming to Israel are clearly stated through an abundance of Old Testament scripture. The Messiah coming to the world was originally revealed in Genesis 3, but all scriptural fulfillment was to occur through Israel. Concerning the mystery of the one body of Jesus Christ, the Old Testament scriptures were silent. Failure to adhere to this simple principle will distort the understanding of the Word of God. Lack of understanding will lead to wrong division and confusion. Consider the following excerpt from E. W. Bullinger:

> Many readers of the Bible treat it as though it were a "puzzle picture," where we have to "find a face," or "a man," or some other object. No matter what part of the Bible is read, the one object seems to be to "find the Church." For, the "Word of truth," not being rightly divided or divided at all, the whole Bible is supposed to be about everyone in every part, and in every age; and the church is supposed to be it's one pervading subject. This arises from our own natural selfishness. "We" and therefore all "we" read "we" take to ourselves, not hesitating to rob others of what belongs to them. Here is a case in point. In Isaiah chapter 30, the headings at the Bible for these chapters read, "Judgment upon Jerusalem," and "God's mercies to his church." This is a dividing of the word indeed! but whether it is "rightly dividing" is another matter. The book is declared to be "the

vision of Isaiah which he saw concerning Judah and Jerusalem." And in spite of this, the blessings which he saw concerning Judah and Jerusalem are taken away and given to the church while the curses which are spoken are kindly left for "Judah and Jerusalem"![29]

In this system of interpretation, the Bible is useless for the purposes of divine revelation. It is made derisive to its enemies, a ground for the attacks of infidels, while it becomes a stumbling block to its friends. And yet it is on this same principle that the Apocalypse is usually treated. Everywhere the church is thrust in: John (in chapter 4:1) represents the church; the living creatures, the cherubim (chapter 4), represent the church; the four and twenty elders are the church; the one hundred forty-four thousand are the church; the great multitude is the church; the woman clothed with the sun is the church; the man child is the church; the bride is the church; the New Jerusalem is the church; the seven churches are the church; and so they go, on and on, until the humble reader of the book is bewildered and disheartened. No wonder the book is neglected. The wonder would be if it were not.[30]

---

[29] *Commentary on Revelation*; creator(s): Bullinger, E.W.: Print Basis: F.H. Revell, 1909
Rights: Public Domain; CCEL Subjects: All; Kregal Publications, PO Box 2607, Grand Rapids, Mi 49501; 1993; pp 1.

[30] *Commentary on Revelation;* creator(s): Bullinger, E.W.: Print Basis: F.H. Revell, 1909
Rights: Public Domain; CCEL Subjects: All; Kregal Publications, PO Box 2607, Grand Rapids, Mi 49501; 1993; pp 1, 2.

Failure to rightly divide scripture has precipitated many erroneous doctrines in the body of Christ. The church seems determined to exclude both Jew and Gentile from the holy scriptures. To totally exclude Israel from God's plan of redemption for faithful Israel or those who trust in the almighty God results in error, leading to more error. There are whole sections of Old and New Testament writings that one must ignore to believe this error. When God says that former Jews and Gentiles who believe on Jesus Christ as their Lord and Savior are one body and constitute the body of Christ on Earth until his return, God means exactly that. He does not mean that in one place we are the body of Christ and in another place we are the bride of Christ. This method of interpretation leaves words without meaning and language without understanding; it allows a cat to be a dog and a lion to be a bear. The erroneous method encourages well-meaning believers to interpret anything in scripture any way they would like to. The church of the one body of Christ is not the bride of Christ. God means "body" when he says "body" and "bride" when he states "bride." If Israel is not to be dealt with by God in the last days as the bride of Christ, then whole sections of scripture fall apart and are replaced by confusion and random interpretation. Paul, through revelation from Jesus Christ, addresses this confusion in Romans 11:

> I say then, Hath God cast away his people? God forbid. For I also am an Israelite, of the seed of Abraham, of the tribe of Benjamin. God hath not cast away his people which he foreknew. Wot ye not what the scripture saith of Elias? how he maketh intercession to God against Israel, saying, Lord, they have killed thy prophets, and digged down thine altars; and I am left alone, and they seek my life. But what saith the answer of God unto him? I have reserved to myself seven thousand men, who have not bowed the knee to the image of Baal. **Even so then at this present time also there is a remnant according to the**

election of grace. And if by grace, then is it no more of works: otherwise grace is no more grace. But if it be of works, then is it no more grace: otherwise work is no more work. What then? Israel hath not obtained that which he seeketh for; but the election hath obtained it, and the rest were blinded (According as it is written, God hath given them the spirit of slumber, eyes that they should not see, and ears that they should not hear;) unto this day. And David saith, Let their table be made a snare, and a trap, and a stumblingblock, and a recompence unto them: Let their eyes be darkened, that they may not see, and bow down their back alway. I say then, Have they stumbled that they should fall? God forbid: but rather through their fall salvation is come unto the Gentiles, for to provoke them to jealousy. Now if the fall of them be the riches of the world, and the diminishing of them the riches of the Gentiles; how much more their fulness? For I speak to you Gentiles, inasmuch as I am the apostle of the Gentiles, I magnify mine office: If by any means I may provoke to emulation them which are my flesh, and might save some of them**. For if the casting away of them be the reconciling of the world, what shall the receiving of them be, but life from the dead? For if the firstfruit be holy, the lump is also holy: and if the root be holy, so are the branches. And if some of the branches be broken off, and thou, being a wild olive tree, wert graffed in among them, and with them partakest of the root and fatness of the olive tree;** Boast not against the branches. But if thou boast, thou bearest not the root, but the root thee. Thou wilt say then, The branches were broken off, that I might be graffed in. Well; because of unbelief they were broken off, and thou standest by faith. Be not highminded, but fear: For if God spared not the natural branches, take heed lest he also spare not thee. Behold therefore the goodness and severity of God: on them which fell, severity; but toward thee, goodness, if thou continue in his goodness: otherwise thou also shalt be cut off. And they also, if they abide not still in unbelief, shall be graffed in: for God is able to graff them in again. For if thou wert cut out of the olive tree which is wild by nature, and wert graffed contrary to nature into a good olive tree: how much more shall these, which be the natural branches, be graffed into their own olive tree? **For I would not, brethren, that ye should be ignorant of this mystery, lest ye should be wise in your own conceits; that blindness in part is happened to Israel, until the fulness of the Gentiles be come in. And so all Israel shall be saved: as it is written, There shall come out of Sion the Deliverer, and shall turn away ungodliness from Jacob: For this is my covenant unto them, when I shall take away their sins. As concerning the gospel, they are enemies for your sakes: but as touching the election, they are beloved for the fathers' sakes.** For the gifts and calling of God are without repentance. For as ye in times past have not believed God, yet have now obtained mercy through their unbelief: Even so have these also now not believed, that through your mercy they also may obtain mercy. For God hath concluded them all in unbelief, that he might have mercy upon all. O the depth of the riches both of the wisdom and knowledge of God! how unsearchable are his judgments, and

> his ways past finding out! For who hath known the mind of the Lord? or who hath been his counsellor? Or who hath first given to him, and it shall be recompensed unto him again? For of him, and through him, and to him, are all things: to whom be glory forever. Amen. (Romans 11:1–36 KJV; my emphasis)

The gifts and calling of God are without repentance; they do not change. God will fulfill all his promises to Israel; this is one of the central themes of the end times. The verses concerning Israel are extraordinary and must be studied and rightly divided to be accurately understood. Israel has become a people surrounded by controversy, anger, hate, and tragedy to this day. Few can accurately give an account from the Word of God concerning their glorious future. In fact, it is impossible to rightly divide the sequence of events concerning the last days without understanding the way God once and for all deals with Israel. Our responsibility before God is to believe all that is written regarding a subject—in this case, the time of the end. Romans 11 states that God has made an everlasting covenant with national Israel and will fulfill his commitments. Only a remnant of Israel will be saved through the tribulation, and it is only God who knows who of Israel will be saved. God does not save Israel because they deserve it but because he promised their fathers, the patriarchs. The subject of Israel and its documentation in the Old Testament is handled more extensively in appendix A. The study of God's Word cannot be based on private interpretation but must be understood in light of God's rightly divided Word.

Scripture reveals the sufferings and glory of the Messiah, Jesus Christ, from the Old Testament. The Old Testament did not distinguish between the times of the sufferings of Christ, represented by his crucifixion, and his glory on Earth following his death and after the great tribulation. We know now that the two time periods are separated by the administration of the one body of Jesus Christ. The time—that is, the time of the one body of Jesus Christ on Earth—was purposely not documented by God in the Old Testament but was kept hidden by God. The prophets searched diligently for this period of time but could not find it. Consider the following:

> Peter, an apostle of Jesus Christ, to the strangers scattered throughout Pontus, Galatia, Cappadocia, Asia, and Bithynia, Elect according to the foreknowledge of God the Father, through sanctification of the Spirit, unto obedience and sprinkling of the blood of Jesus Christ: Grace unto you, and peace, be multiplied. Blessed be the God and Father of our Lord Jesus Christ, which according to his abundant mercy hath begotten us again unto a lively hope by the resurrection of Jesus Christ from the dead,
>
> To an inheritance incorruptible, and undefiled, and that fadeth not away, reserved in heaven for you,
>
> Who are kept by the power of God through faith unto salvation ready to be revealed in the last time.
>
> Wherein ye greatly rejoice, though now for a season, if need be, ye are in heaviness through manifold temptations: That the trial of your faith, being much more precious than of gold that perisheth, though it be tried with fire, might be found unto praise and honour and glory at the appearing of Jesus Christ:
>
> Whom having not seen, ye love; in whom, though now ye see him not, yet believing, ye rejoice with joy unspeakable and full of glory: **Receiving the end of your faith, even the salvation of your souls.**
>
> **Of which salvation the prophets have enquired and searched diligently, who prophesied of the grace that should come unto you: Searching what, or what manner of time the**

> **Spirit of Christ which was in them did signify, when it testified beforehand the sufferings of Christ, and the glory that should follow.**
>
> **Unto whom it was revealed, that not unto themselves, but unto us they did minister the things, which are now reported unto you by them that have preached the gospel unto you with the Holy Ghost sent down from heaven; which things the angels desire to look into …**
>
> (1 Peter 1:1–12 KJV; my emphasis)

The Old Testament prophets saw a time period but could not find any information from God concerning it. According to verse 11, the Holy Spirit, which was in them, spoke only concerning the future sufferings and glory of Christ. They knew, or thought, it was not logical for the glory of Christ as King of kings on the earth to follow directly in time with his sufferings; that is, there had to be a period of time in between. Naturally, they searched the Word of God diligently for the answer. The answer was hidden in the heart of God, not revealed until Paul received it through the revelation of Jesus Christ and documented it in his writings. The special time period, which is known as the period of the mystery of the one body of Jesus Christ, was first revealed to the apostle Paul after Pentecost. The Old Testament prophets could not have found it, because it was not documented anywhere in the Old Testament; they searched diligently but could not find it.

It was this mystery or secret of God, hidden in the heart of God, that would ultimately seal Satan's doom. When the mystery period is understood, including the reason that God kept it secret, then the final puzzle piece of scripture is completed. God's master plan for the redemption of mankind is complete. It is the revelation of the mystery period that reveals the manifold wisdom of God. Paul states in Colossians 1:25 that he was given the revelation that completed, or fulfilled, the Word of God—the mystery of the one body of Jesus Christ. The completion of this picture allows understanding of the Word of God to be taken to a new level. Consider the following:

> And you, that were sometime alienated and enemies in your mind by wicked works, yet now hath he reconciled In the body of his flesh through death, to present you holy and unblameable and unreproveable in his sight: If ye continue in the faith grounded and settled, and be not moved away from the hope of the gospel, which ye have heard, and which was preached to every creature which is under heaven; whereof I Paul am made a minister; Who now rejoice in my sufferings for you, and fill up that which is behind of the afflictions of Christ in my flesh for his body's sake, which is the church:
> **Whereof I am made a minister, according to the dispensation of God which is given to me for you, to fulfil (to fill up, to finish) the Word of God; Even the mystery which hath been hid from ages and from generations, but now is made manifest to his saints: To whom God would make known what is the riches of the glory of this mystery among the Gentiles; which is Christ in you, the hope of glory:** Whom we preach, warning every man, and teaching every man in all wisdom; that we may present every man perfect in Christ Jesus: Whereunto I also labour, striving according to his working, which worketh in me mightily. (Colossians 1:21–29 KJV; my emphasis)

The administration of the mystery of the one body of Jesus Christ began on the day of Pentecost and will continue until the gathering together of the body of Christ in the clouds:

> But I would not have you to be ignorant, brethren, concerning them which are asleep, that ye sorrow not, even as others which have no hope. For

if we believe that Jesus died and rose again, even so them also which sleep in Jesus will God bring with him. For this we say unto you by the word of the Lord, that we which are alive and remain unto the coming of the Lord shall not prevent them which are asleep. **For the Lord himself shall descend from heaven with a shout, with the voice of the archangel, and with the trump of God: and the dead in Christ shall rise first: Then we which are alive and remain shall be caught up together with them in the clouds, to meet the Lord in the air: and so shall we ever be with the Lord. Wherefore comfort one another with these words.** (1Thessalonians 4:13–18 KJV; my emphasis)

The body of Christ, consisting of both Jew and Gentile—those who have made Jesus Christ their personal Lord and Savior—will be raptured, or removed from the earth, before the wrath of Almighty God as documented in the book of Revelation. Jews and Gentiles who accept Jesus Christ as their Lord and Savior are no longer Jews or Gentiles but members of the body of Christ—the church of God. Each becomes an individual member of the same body of Jesus Christ with no difference in his or her standing before God. Consider the following:

But the scripture hath concluded all under sin, that the promise by faith of Jesus Christ might be given to them that believe. But before faith came, we were kept under the law, shut up unto the faith which should afterward be revealed. **Wherefore the law was our schoolmaster to bring us unto Christ, that we might be justified by faith. But after that faith is come, we are no longer under a schoolmaster. For ye are all the children of God by faith in Christ Jesus. For as many of you as have been baptized into**

> **Christ have put on Christ. There is neither Jew nor Greek, there is neither bond nor free, there is neither male nor female: for ye are all one in Christ Jesus. And if ye be Christ's, then are ye Abraham's seed, and heirs according to the promise.** (Galatians 3:22–29 KJV; my emphasis)

The body of Christ, or church of God, is a special group set apart for God and saved in accordance with God's promise of salvation through faith in Jesus Christ. They are neither Jews nor Gentiles but part of the body of Christ. Conversely, the Jews—the physical lineage of Abraham, Isaac, and Jacob as discussed in this work—are keenly associated with the events of the last days. These Jews, after the removal of the church from the earth, are the actual physical descendants of Abraham, Isaac, and Jacob, and they will be the central focus of God's dealings on the earth. So, God, during the last days, hears the prayers of the Jews in Jerusalem and answers their prayers in accordance with his promise to their fathers. His answer is to reveal to them the Lord Jesus Christ, taking away the veil from their eyes. As for the one body of Jesus Christ, the church that began on the day of Pentecost, it will continue until it is miraculously removed from the earth. Consider the following:

> For this cause I Paul, the prisoner of Jesus Christ for you Gentiles, If ye have heard of the **dispensation of the grace of God** (administration of God's grace) which is given me to you-ward: How that by revelation he made known unto me the mystery; (as I wrote afore in few words, Whereby, when ye read, ye may understand my knowledge in the mystery of Christ) **Which in other ages was not made known unto the sons of men, as it is now revealed unto his holy apostles and prophets by the Spirit; That the Gentiles should be fellowheirs, and of the same body, and partakers of his promise in**

Christ by the gospel: Whereof I was made a minister, according to the gift of the grace of God given unto me by the effectual working of his power. Unto me, who am less than the least of all saints, is this grace given, that I should preach among the Gentiles the unsearchable (untraceable) riches of Christ; And to make all men see what is the fellowship (administration) of the mystery, which from the beginning of the world hath been hid in God, who created all things by Jesus Christ: To the intent that now unto the principalities and powers in heavenly places might be known by the church the manifold wisdom of God, According to the eternal purpose which he purposed in Christ Jesus our Lord: In whom we have boldness and access with confidence by the faith of him. Wherefore I desire that ye faint not at my tribulations for you, which is your glory. For this cause I bow my knees unto the Father of our Lord Jesus Christ, Of whom the whole family in heaven and earth is named, That he would grant you, according to the riches of his glory, to be strengthened with might by his Spirit in the inner man; That Christ may dwell in your hearts by faith; that ye, being rooted and grounded in love, May be able to comprehend with all saints what is the breadth, and length, and depth, and height; And to know the love of Christ, which passeth knowledge, that ye might be filled with all the fulness of God. Now unto him that is able to do exceeding abundantly above all that we ask or think, according to the power that worketh in us, Unto him be glory in the church by Christ Jesus throughout all ages, world without end. Amen. (Ephesians 3:1–21 KJV; my emphasis)

The revelation of the mystery was kept secret by God from before the foundation of the world. Why did God keep this revelation secret? The answer to this question is foundational to our understanding and proper division of the Word of God. Consider the following from 1 Corinthians 2:

> And I, brethren, when I came to you, came not with excellency of speech or of wisdom, declaring unto you the testimony of God. For I determined not to know anything among you, save Jesus Christ, and him crucified. And I was with you in weakness, and in fear, and in much trembling. And my speech and my preaching was not with enticing words of man's wisdom, but in demonstration of the Spirit and of power: That your faith should not stand in the wisdom of men, but in the power of God. Howbeit we speak wisdom among them that are perfect: yet not the wisdom of this world, nor of the princes of this world, that come to nought: **But we speak the wisdom of God in a mystery, even the hidden wisdom, which God ordained before the world unto our glory: Which none of the princes of this world knew: for had they known it, they would not have crucified the Lord of glory.** But as it is written, Eye hath not seen, nor ear heard, neither have entered into the heart of man, the things which God hath prepared for them that love him. But God hath revealed them unto us by his Spirit: for the Spirit searcheth all things, yea, the deep things of God. For what man knoweth the things of a man, save the spirit of man which is in him? even so the things of God knoweth no man, but the Spirit of God. Now we have received, not the spirit of the world, but the spirit which is of God; that we might know the things that

are freely given to us of God. Which things also we speak, not in the words which man's wisdom teacheth, but which the Holy Ghost teacheth; comparing spiritual things with spiritual. But the natural man receiveth not the things of the Spirit of God: for they are foolishness unto him: neither can he know them, because they are spiritually discerned. (1Corinthians 2:1–14 KJV; my emphasis)

The above section of scripture reveals the fundamental reason why God kept the mystery of the one body of Jesus Christ secret. According to verses 7 and 8, if the devil knew that God would save millions from destruction through faith, he, the devil, would not have crucified Jesus Christ. It was Satan working in the hearts of men who killed Jesus Christ, and it was Satan who was defeated when Jesus Christ rose from the dead. Men and women can now be saved and given new inner life through a new perfect gift of God by way of faith in the risen Lord Jesus Christ. Consider the following:

That if thou shalt confess with thy mouth the Lord Jesus, and shalt believe in thine heart that God hath raised him from the dead, thou shalt be saved. For with the heart man believeth unto righteousness; and with the mouth confession is made unto salvation. For the scripture saith, Whosoever believeth on him shall not be ashamed. For there is no difference between the Jew and the Greek: for the same Lord over all is rich unto all that call upon him. For whosoever shall call upon the name of the Lord shall be saved. (Romans 10:9–13 KJV)

Satan and the spiritual princes of this world would not have crucified the Lord Jesus Christ if they had known that God was going to resurrect his son and save millions of people from destruction.

Satan thought that by destroying the promised seed, Jesus Christ, he would destroy God's plan to redeem man. Without the resurrected Christ, sin and death would have had no cure for the penalty of sin is death. Someone had to pay for our sins. God, in his manifold wisdom, did not reveal his intentions to raise Christ and save millions until after Christ's death. His secret was secure and unknown to all of his creation, including Satan and his spirit agents. Satan habitually pays close attention to what God documents and reveals in his word. The devil would rather have had Jesus Christ in one place at one time than to have millions of new eternal beings with Christ in them. These new creations of God, born-again believers, would also be given the powerful gift of Holy Spirit and would have Christ in them through a new birth. The new creations would also, through faith, have a greater spirit in them than that which is in the world.[31] The reality is that these new creations of God meant certain destruction for Satan.

    The heart of God contains his true redemptive plan for mankind. His plan regarding the new birth was hidden—never mentioned in the Old Testament or the Gospels—until revealed to the apostle Paul. The previous scriptures, those before the revelation given to Paul, did not mention one word about the mystical body of Jesus Christ consisting of both Jews and Gentiles given eternal life through a new birth. There is nothing about a gift of Holy Spirit coming down from God and giving new birth to those Jews and Gentiles called by God. There is no mention of being born again or, more accurately, what exactly the new birth would mean. The scriptures are silent about God putting Christ in every believer who believes in his son. Nowhere is there any mention of men and women becoming sons and daughters of God through a new birth. These miraculous truths simply were nowhere to be found in scripture until revealed to and documented by the apostle Paul in the first century. Understanding these truths from God's Word fuels the fire in a believer that never extinguishes. It's no wonder why Satan would not have crucified Jesus Christ if he had understood what God planned to do. Understanding

---

[31] 1 John 4:4.

this foundational truth also allows us to go to the Old Testament scriptures, which document the vile man who rises in the last days of man's rule on earth and rightly divide God's Word. The church of God, made up of called-out born-again believers, is nowhere mentioned in the Old Testament. I will not try, as so many do, to insert—or, more accurately, to force—the church of God, the born-again believers, into the Old Testament, where it should not be. We also will not insert the mystical one body of Jesus Christ made up of former Jews and Gentile on Earth into the book of Revelation. The insertion of the church of God, the born-again believers, into the Old Testament or the book of Revelation only causes confusion and wrong division of the Word of God. Not inserting the church of God into the Old Testament or the book of Revelation will allow the Word of God to interpret itself—especially with respect to the last days, which are the focus of this work.

The Old Testament must always be read with the realization that the mystery of the one body of Jesus Christ is nowhere to be found in the Old Testament. The Old Testament contains the history of mankind and his fall from his beginnings, when he was created by God. It also contains the story of God calling out Israel, as well as God's plan for man's redemption through the promised seed of Christ; this is also a main theme in the Old Testament. The children of Israel became God's special vehicle to bring about the Messiah. The Old Testament also contains truths that are specifically for Israel's past, present, and future. Understanding that the mystery of the one body of Jesus Christ is nowhere contained in the Old Testament is key to understanding the end times. Right division of the Word of God concerning the mystery is fundamental to understanding the significant portion of scripture that relates to the last times.

When we rightly divide the Word of God regarding the mystery administration, time divisions will become clear and the perfection of the Word of God will be understood. Through understanding these time divisions, whole sections of Old Testament scripture become remarkably evident. Suddenly, the prophecies of Daniel concerning the end for Israel (still future in 2020) will give new light, being understood in view of the mystery administration, which is not mentioned in Old Testament scripture. The searcher of scripture will understand that God skips the time period of the mystery of the one body in the Old Testament, fast-forwarding to the end times. Through the knowledge of the mystery period, Old Testament scriptures can be rightly divided as per God's divisions. All Old Testament prophecies concerning Israel focus on God's will for Israel only. Stated another way, the church of God, made up of Jews and Gentiles, is never mentioned or referred to in any Old Testament scripture. Failure to adhere to this simple truth leads to confusion and error, which will obscure right interpretation. The error will especially be evident in any study regarding the last times. The sufferings and the glory of the Lord were both well documented and understood throughout the Old Testament Scriptures; in contrast, the mystery period was hidden in God.

The book of Daniel reveals angels as carriers of revelation to Daniel from God. The angels revealed information regarding the millennial kingdom of Jesus Christ, the final heaven and earth, the final doom of Satan, Jacob's trouble, and the future glory for Israel. The final glory of the Jews includes their final deliverance by God through the specific events of the last times. The glory restored to Israel occurs after the removal of the church of the one body of Jesus Christ. It is evident that the angels were completely knowledgeable of all these events except for the administration of the mystery of the one body of Jesus Christ. Consider the following verse in 1 Peter 1:12:

> "Unto whom it was revealed (the angels), that not unto themselves, but unto us they did minister the things, which are now reported unto you by them that have preached the gospel unto you with the Holy Ghost sent down from heaven; **which things the angels desire to look into.**" (1 Peter 1:12 KJV; my emphasis)

What new thing on earth did the angels *"desire to look into"* as recorded in this verse? The angels were astonished to see new spiritual creations in Jesus Christ for everyone who believed in Jesus

Christ. The new creation was undocumented in the Old Testament and therefore surprised even the angels. The new body of Christ, created through a new spiritual birth in each believer, was simply unprecedented. The new mystical body of Christ, which was made of former Jews and Gentiles, was now in operation and was simply amazing to the angels. The mystery period is the centerpiece of God's truth, completing God's plan for the complete redemption of mankind. The mystical body of Jesus Christ is the cornerstone to understanding God's ultimate plan for mankind. Christ is the acting head of the church, making all strategic decisions and providing direction for all members of his body. This mystical body effectually operates through each believer as each one allows the head to provide direction and nourishment to all the body parts in accordance with the will of God.[32]

The Word of God speaks loud and clear in the Old Testament concerning the last days and specific sequential events leading up to God's final dealings with the heavens and the earth. Although there are numerous scriptures referring to the last times, it is Daniel that provides core information concerning the last days, especially regarding the deliverance of Israel. The prophecy given to Daniel mainly concerned Daniel's people, Israel. All prophecies in Daniel are specific to Israel and Jerusalem and cannot be directed to the hidden church of God. The present mystery administration is a time when God, through his unmerited divine favor, opens salvation to all who believe. This truth is not so in the Old Testament, in which Israel is the center of God's focus. The promised seed was promised to national Israel and was opened to the Gentiles only because of their rejection. Their deliverance is still future when the time of the Gentiles are fulfilled. The promises of God do not change; God will fulfill all that he promised to Israel. Their deliverance is held in abeyance until the last times. Daniel was a prophet beloved of God, and God revealed to him revelation regarding the last days. Consider the following:

---

[32] Colossians 2:19.

> Wherefore king Darius signed the writing and the decree. Now when Daniel knew that the writing was signed, he went into his house; and his windows being open in his chamber toward Jerusalem, **he kneeled upon his knees three times a day, and prayed, and gave thanks before his God, as he did aforetime. Then these men assembled, and found Daniel praying and making supplication before his God.** (Daniel 6:9–11 KJV; my emphasis)

Daniel was indeed a man beloved of the Lord. His continual prayer and supplication to his God separated him as a man of prayer. He prayed continuously for his people and for knowledge concerning Israel and their end. Consequently, God sent his angel to make Daniel understand the end for Israel in response to his prayer. The revelation given to Daniel is first and foremost prophecy having to do with Israel and their end. Daniel prayed to understand what would be the end for his people, Israel. Consider the following:

> And now, O Lord our God, that hast brought thy people forth out of the land of Egypt with a mighty hand, and hast gotten thee renown, as at this day; we have sinned, we have done wickedly. O Lord, according to all thy righteousness, I beseech thee, let thine anger and thy fury be turned away from thy city Jerusalem, thy holy mountain: because for our sins, and for the iniquities of our fathers, Jerusalem and thy people are become a reproach to all that are about us. **Now therefore, O our God, hear the prayer of thy servant, and his supplications, and cause thy face to shine upon thy sanctuary that is desolate, for the Lord's sake. O my God, incline thine ear, and hear; open thine eyes, and behold our desolations, and the city

> **which is called by thy name: for we do not present our supplications before thee for our righteousnesses, but for thy great mercies. O Lord, hear; O Lord, forgive; O Lord, hearken and do; defer not, for thine own sake, O my God: for thy city and thy people are called by thy name.** And whiles I was speaking, and praying, and confessing my sin and the sin of my people Israel, and presenting my supplication before the LORD my God for the holy mountain of my God; Yea, whiles I was speaking in prayer, even the man Gabriel, whom I had seen in the vision at the beginning, being caused to fly swiftly, touched me about the time of the evening oblation. And he informed me, and talked with me, and said, O Daniel, I am now come forth to give thee skill and understanding. At the beginning of thy supplications the commandment came forth, and I am come to shew thee; for thou art greatly beloved: therefore understand the matter, and consider the vision. (Daniel 9:15–23 KJV; my emphasis)

Daniel was asking God what the end of his people would be and when they would be delivered. The answer came from an angelic messenger of God. The messenger proceeded to give Daniel an overview of Israel from the time the temple was to be rebuilt until the time of Israel's final deliverance. The summation given by the angel must be understood in light of the hidden time of the mystery of the one body of Jesus Christ. ***The Word of God must be rightly divided and the time of the mystery must be skipped over to understand the prophecy.*** The time of the mystery (to date almost two thousand years) is not contained in any prophecy given to Daniel. When we make this right division of the Word of God, the Old Testament prophecies, especially Daniel, begin to make perfect sense. Consider the following:

> Yea, whiles I was speaking in prayer, even the man Gabriel, whom I had seen in the vision at the beginning, being caused to fly swiftly, touched me about the time of the evening oblation. And he informed me, and talked with me, and said, O Daniel, I am now come forth to give thee skill and understanding. At the beginning of thy supplications the commandment came forth, **and I am come to show thee; for thou art greatly beloved: therefore understand the matter, and consider the vision. Seventy weeks are determined upon thy people and upon thy holy city, to finish the transgression, and to make an end of sins, and to make reconciliation for iniquity, and to bring in everlasting righteousness, and to seal up the vision and prophecy, and to anoint the most Holy.** (Daniel 9:21–24 KJV; my emphasis)

These scriptures reveal how God is going to wrap up and fulfill all of his promises to Israel. Verse 24 sets forth God's timetable—the seventy sevens of years, a 490-year timetable. God reveals that after the 490 years, the following will have been accomplished for Israel:

1. The transgression will be finished.
2. The sins will have ended.
3. Reconciliation will have been made for iniquity.
4. Everlasting righteousness will have been brought in.
5. Vision and prophecy will have been sealed.
6. The Most Holy will have been anointed.

At this present time, 2020 and counting, none of these events have taken place for Israel. The fulfillment of these promises of God still await fulfillment for Israel in the future. God's Word and God's promises are true and will come to pass exactly as documented in his Word. Their fulfillment will be in accordance with God's timetable.

God is not a man; he does not lie. The 490-year prophecy is God's timetable for fulfilling these promises to Israel. The 490 years require right division of the Word of God***, including the realization that the mystery period is hidden and skipped over.*** It will be shown that the period of the mystery is between the sixty-ninth and seventieth week of years of Daniel's prophecy. The mystery period is skipped over, and God fast-forwards to the final seven years of the prophecy of seventy sevens of years. The 490-year period excludes the period of the great mystery period hidden in the heart of God. For this reason, it is not part of any Old Testament scripture. The visions and prophecies given to Daniel concerned only Israel and the Jews, their land, Jerusalem, and the holy place. Understanding this will be fundamental to our study of the end times.

Before continuing further in our study, it is important to understand God's heart concerning proper interpretation of his Word. There is a pervading opinion that many interpretations can be gathered from any particular scripture. This is fallacy and is untrue. There may be more than one fulfillment, but there is always one interpretation. Consider the following:

> The secret things belong unto the LORD our God: but those things which are revealed belong unto us and to our children forever, that we may do all the words of this law. (Deuteronomy 29:29 KJV)
>
> Knowing this first, that **no prophecy of the scripture is of any private (Greek: one's own) interpretation.** For the prophecy came not in old time by the will of man: but holy men of God spake as they were moved by the Holy Ghost. (2 Peter 1:20–21 KJV; my emphasis)

According to Deuteronomy 29:29, God has secrets that he does not reveal about himself or about his creation. In contrast to what God has not revealed, he has given us the ability to divide and understand the scriptures he has revealed. Consider the following scripture sections:

> But thou hast fully known my doctrine, manner of life, purpose, faith, longsuffering, charity, patience, Persecutions, afflictions, which came unto me at Antioch, at Iconium, at Lystra; what persecutions I endured: but out of them all the Lord delivered me. Yea, and all that will live godly in Christ Jesus shall suffer persecution. But evil men and seducers shall wax worse and worse, deceiving, and being deceived. **But continue thou in the things which thou hast learned and hast been assured of, knowing of whom thou hast learned them; And that from a child thou hast known the holy scriptures, which are able to make thee wise unto salvation through faith which is in Christ Jesus. All scripture is given by inspiration of God, and is profitable for doctrine, for reproof, for correction, for instruction in righteousness: That the man of God may be perfect, thoroughly furnished unto all good works.** (2 Timothy 3:10–17 KJV; my emphasis)
>
> Simon Peter, a servant and an apostle of Jesus Christ, to them that have obtained like precious faith with us through the righteousness of God and our Saviour Jesus Christ: Grace and peace be multiplied unto you through the knowledge of God, and of Jesus our Lord, According as his divine power hath given unto us all things that pertain unto life and godliness, through the knowledge of him that hath called us to glory and virtue: **Whereby are given unto us exceeding great and precious promises: that by these ye might be partakers of the divine**

> **nature, having escaped the corruption that is in the world through lust. And beside this, giving all diligence, add to your faith virtue; and to virtue knowledge; And to knowledge temperance; and to temperance patience; and to patience godliness;** And to godliness brotherly kindness; and to brotherly kindness charity. For if these things be in you, and abound, they make you that ye shall neither be barren nor unfruitful in the knowledge of our Lord Jesus Christ. (2 Peter 1:1–8 KJV; my emphasis)

The believer and lover of God must rely on what God has delivered to mankind through his Word. Understanding the doctrine, reproof, and correction of the Word of God is essential to understanding life and the times we live in. The result of adhering to God's Word is proper godly living and knowledge of all things that pertain to life and godliness.

Proper understanding of God's Word concerning the end times is required for right division of the Word of God. False teachings and failure to adhere to God's requirements for right doctrine has led to chaos and confusion. Consider the following:

> "But there were false prophets also among the people, even as there shall be false teachers among you, who privily shall bring in damnable heresies, even denying the Lord that bought them, and bring upon themselves swift destruction" (2 Peter 2:1 KJV)

The prophecies of Daniel have definite purpose in the Word of God, especially regarding the end times. Daniel's prophecies, when rightly divided, will give great revelation regarding the events that lead to the last times. Our mission is to search the scriptures with patience, with prayer, and with a humble broken heart before God.

Through this process, we will be enlightened to God's truth, receiving with meekness his engrafted Word. Consider the following:

> Every good gift and every perfect gift is from above, and cometh down from the Father of lights, with whom is no variableness, neither shadow of turning. Of his own will begat he us with the Word of Truth, that we should be a kind of firstfruits of his creatures. Wherefore, my beloved brethren, let every man be swift to hear, slow to speak, slow to wrath: For the wrath of man worketh not the righteousness of God. **Wherefore lay apart all filthiness and superfluity (abundance) of naughtiness (wickedness), and receive with meekness the engrafted word, which is able to save your souls. But be ye doers of the word, and not hearers only, deceiving your own selves. For if any be a hearer of the word, and not a doer, he is like unto a man beholding his natural face in a glass:** For he beholdeth himself, and goeth his way, and straightway forgetteth what manner of man he was. But whoso looketh into the perfect law of liberty, and continueth therein, he being not a forgetful hearer, but a doer of the work, this man shall be blessed in his deed. (James 1:17–25 KJV; my emphasis)

A method of interpretation that we will employ in this work is called scripture buildup. Scripture buildup requires examination of all scripture relating to a subject or event, and it "builds up" information from each reference. Through this process, the total picture that God wishes to convey can be assembled together. The process is like an artist's masterpiece being crafted and formed through time. Each scripture requires examination, along with the realization that there can be no contradictions in any one reference as compared to an associated reference. Each reference can supply additional information but there can be no contradictions. Once completed, all information is gathered together from each of the scriptures, and the final story or picture is accurately understood. Consider the following:

> Know therefore and understand, that from the going forth of the commandment to restore and to build Jerusalem unto the Messiah the Prince shall be **seven weeks**, and **threescore and two weeks**: (69 of the seventy weeks mentioned n Daniel 9:24) the street shall be built again, and the wall, even in troublous times. And after **threescore and two weeks shall Messiah be cut off,** but not for himself: and the people of the prince that shall come shall destroy the city and the sanctuary; and the end thereof shall be with a flood, and unto the end of the war desolations are determined. And he shall confirm the covenant with many for **one week**: and in the midst of the week he shall cause **(begin to cause)** the sacrifice and the oblation to cease, and for the overspreading of abominations he shall make it desolate, even until the consummation, and that determined shall be poured upon the desolate. (Daniel 9:25–27 KJV; my emphasis)

Daniel 9:25–27 is God's final timetable concerning Israel. At the end of these seventy sevens of years, God will once and for all deliver Israel and fulfill his promises to the patriarchs and complete the promises he listed in Daniel 9:24. The prophecy of seventy sevens of weeks (490 years) in ***Daniel 9:24 cannot be understood without rightly dividing the scripture concerning the mystery period***. The mystery period is skipped over by God and is not contained in the prophecy of seventy sevens of years. The period known as the mystery of the one body of Jesus Christ, which is up to now almost two thousand years old, can be placed between the sixty-ninth and seventieth weeks of years as listed in Daniel 9:24. Stated another way, there is already almost two thousand years between the sixty-ninth and seventieth weeks of years as presented in Daniel 9:24–27. When these scriptures are rightly divided concerning the mystery period, the scriptures will fit perfectly and be in harmony with each other and the rest of God's Word. If this is not understood, constant confusion and innumerable interpretations will persist, resulting in no real trusted interpretation. Daniel 9, and several other sections of Daniel as well as the Old Testament, will be critical to our understanding of the vile man of Daniel. The understanding of the secret time of the mystery not revealed in the Old Testament is essential to any understanding of the last days of natural man's rule on Earth.

Daniel 9:25 states, "From the going forth of the commandment to restore and build Jerusalem unto the Messiah the Prince shall be seven weeks and three score and two weeks." These sixty-nine weeks of years of verse 25 represent 483 years. The time period begins with the command to restore and build Jerusalem. This time began in the twentieth year of Asteiages, the time of Darius the Median, or approximately 454 BC. The completion of the first sixty-nine weeks of years, or 483 years, is marked by the cutting off of the Messiah in AD 29, as stated in verse 26. Historically, we know that our Lord Jesus Christ was indeed cut off (killed) after the sixty-nine weeks of years in AD 29, exactly as documented. The cutting off of the Messiah represented the completion of the first sixty-nine weeks of years, leaving one seven-year period to be fulfilled. Further investigation reveals that the commandment to build the temple was given by Asteiages in 454 BC, 454 years before the birth of Christ. According to Daniel's prophecy given by God through the angel, the completion of the 483 years was to be the year of the "cutting off of the Messiah." What the Messiah's cutoff actually meant to the Jews at the time of Daniel and before it actually happened was not entirely clear from the passage. The cutting off was indeed the crucifixion, which occurred in AD 29. (Note: from history, we know that the Julian calendar was off by approximately three or four years). It is clear that some Old Testament scriptures were not understood entirely until the time of their fulfillment; the cutting off of the Messiah certainly is in that category.

The crucifixion of our Lord, the cutting off of the Messiah, completes the first sixty-nine weeks of years of Daniel's prophecy of seventy sevens of years. [33] The completion of the sixty-nine weeks leaves one week, or one seven-year period, of unfulfilled prophecy intended for Israel. As noted, the completion of the seventy weeks will be marked by the fulfilling of all the promises listed in Daniel 9:24. The Old Testament vantage point at the time of Daniel suggests that the seventy sevens of years are consecutive in time. The key to understanding the seventy weeks is the fact that between the sixty-ninth and the seventieth week of years is the period of the mystery. God did not make known the mystery period to anyone in heaven or Earth until he made it known to the apostle Paul in the first century. The fact that God broke out the seventieth week of years from the other sixty-nine weeks of years in Daniel 9:24–27 is the first clue. The separation should have raised a flag and spurred additional study. The reality of the mystery of the one body of Christ, kept hidden by God, crystallizes the prophecy of the seventy weeks of years for Israel. The last seven-year period is still yet to be fulfilled, but it will be fulfilled in its entirety.

The beginning of the last week, or seven-year period, is in the Father's hands as stated in Acts 1:7. But God has provided in his word, especially the book of Daniel, significant and specific information about the events that will occur during the final seven years, including the event that will initiate it. God, through his word, identifies the man of sin early in the seven-year period through Daniel's prophecies. The last seven years will be a cataclysmic culmination of God's plans for all on the earth: Jews, Gentiles, and the church of God. A change in the heavens will also be included, as Satan will be cast out of the heavens.[34] The called-out Jews—that is, the remnant of Israel to be saved, will go through their tribulation and will be delivered by God through forty-two months of tribulation on earth. They will be

---

[33] Daniel 9:24.
[34] Revelation 12:7–9.

delivered at the end of the forty-two months and will live in the land with Jesus Christ as their Lord and David as their king. The Gentiles will see their rule on earth, the time of the Gentiles, end abruptly at the hands of the Antichrist. The church of God will be raptured from the earth, but this will not occur until the identity of the vile man and Antichrist is revealed through the Word of God. His identity can occur only after the initiation of the last seven years, as indicated in Thessalonians. Consider the following:

> Now we beseech you, brethren, by the coming of our Lord Jesus Christ, and by our gathering together unto him, That ye be not soon shaken in mind, or be troubled, neither by spirit, nor by word, nor by letter as from us, as that the day of Christ is at hand. **Let no man deceive you by any means: for that day shall not come, except there come a falling away first, and that man of sin be revealed, the son of perdition; Who opposeth and exalteth himself above all that is called God, or that is worshipped; so that he as God sitteth in the temple of God, shewing himself that he is God.** Remember ye not, that, when I was yet with you, I told you these things? And now ye know what withholdeth that he might be revealed in his time. For the mystery of iniquity doth already work: only he who now letteth will let, until he be taken out of the way. And then shall that Wicked be revealed, whom the Lord shall consume with the spirit of his mouth, and shall destroy with the brightness of his coming. (2 Thessalonians 2:1–8 KJV; my emphasis)

A great many of the events contained in the last seven years are documented in Daniel's prophecies. The important elements at the core of these prophecies are listed as follows:

- the event that initiates the beginning of the last seven years
- the identity of the Vile man or Antichrist before his seemingly miraculous resurrection.
- the events leading up to the middle of the last seven years
- the events of the middle of the last seven years
- the commotions and wars occurring during the last half of the last seven years (the final forty-two months)
- the events surrounding and defining the 2,300 days, "*the times, time and half of time*": the 1,260 days, the 1,290 days, and the 1,335 days
- the first and second resurrections—that is, the resurrections of the just and of the unjust after the last seven years

It is no wonder that the Lord, as he spoke to his disciples concerning the last days, pointed them back to Daniel to be enlightened. Consider the following:

> And many false prophets shall rise, and shall deceive many. And because iniquity shall abound, the love of many shall wax cold. But he that shall endure unto the end, the same shall be saved. And this gospel of the kingdom shall be preached in all the world for a witness unto all nations; and then shall the end come. **When ye therefore shall see the abomination of desolation, spoken of by Daniel the prophet, stand in the holy place, (whoso readeth, let him understand:)** Then let them which be in Judaea flee into the mountains: Let him which is on the housetop not come down to take anything out of his house: Neither let him which is in the field return back to take his clothes. And woe unto them that are with child, and to them that give suck in those days! But pray ye that your flight be not in the winter, neither on the sabbath day: For then shall be great tribulation, such as was not

> since the beginning of the world to this time, no, nor ever shall be. And except those days should be shortened, there should no flesh be saved: but for the elect's sake those days shall be shortened. (Matthew 24:11–22 KJV; my emphasis)

Curiously, the Lord states in verse 15, "Whoso readeth, let him understand," indicating that it will take a right division, or right cut, of the Word of God to truly understand. In all the prophecy of Daniel—or the Old Testament, for that matter—there is not one hint of the existence of the mystery period or the church of the one body of Christ. The period of the mystery of the church of Jesus Christ was kept hidden in the heart of Almighty God. Oh, the greatness and manifold wisdom of our holy God and Father.

God's heart in giving this information to those who love him is to make his people aware of the last times. The information God gives makes the believer aware of the last times, meaning that he or she will not be in darkness regarding the last days. There is still one additional week of years (seven years) left for the fulfillment of all God prophesized for Israel. The final week fulfills a great deal of God's plan for mankind on the earth, including the crushing of Satan's head as prophesized in Genesis 3:15. Israel, the last days, the end of man's rule on earth, and the establishment of the eternal kingdom of Jesus Christ on Earth are all included. The events of the seventieth week, studied extensively in this work, will be clear to the wise in those days and at the time of their fulfillment. Consider the following:

> "And I heard, but I understood not: then said I, O my Lord, what shall be the end of these things? And he said, Go thy way, Daniel: **for the words are closed up and sealed till the time of the end. Many shall be purified, and made white, and tried; but the wicked shall do wickedly: and none of the wicked shall understand; but the wise shall understand**" (Daniel 12:8–10; my emphasis)

The understanding is sealed until the time of the end. The administration of the mystery of the one body of Christ, the time that was hidden in God, sequentially follows the first sixty-nine weeks, or 483 years. In this work, all time periods—days and years—listed as part of the last seven years will be rightly divided with due recognition to the mystery period.

Ignoring the times, days, years, and events in the Old Testament is denying the accuracy and the integrity of the Word of God. The final events and times of the last seven years, as documented by God, will be the lifeline for the people alive during the terrible time of the end. These scriptures will give them the hope and strength required to make it through the last days. Additionally, the body of Christ will not be left in darkness:

> But of the times and the seasons, brethren, ye have no need that I write unto you. For yourselves know perfectly that the day of the Lord so cometh as a thief in the night. For when they shall say, Peace and safety; then sudden destruction cometh upon them, as travail upon a woman with child; and they shall not escape. **But ye, brethren, are not in darkness, that that day should overtake you as a thief. Ye are all the children of light, and the children of the day: we are not of the night, nor of darkness.** Therefore let us not sleep, as do others; but let us watch and be sober. For they that sleep sleep in the night; and they that be drunken are drunken in the night. But let us, who are of the day, be sober, putting on the breastplate of faith and love; and for an helmet, the hope of salvation. For God hath not appointed us to wrath, but to obtain salvation by our Lord Jesus Christ, Who died for us, that, whether we wake or sleep, we should live together with him. Wherefore comfort yourselves

together, and edify one another, even as also ye do. (1 Thessalonians 5:1–11 KJV; my emphasis)

That day shall not overtake us (the church of the body of Christ) as a thief, for we are all the children of light. The season of the end time, the last seven years, is in the Father's hands. God will put the last seven years into motion at the time that God chooses; it is at God's own discretion. The goal of the searcher of the scripture is to understand from scripture the sequence of events that follow the beginning of the final seven years or the seventieth week. The sequence of events during the last seven years will not be a mystery or be hidden from the understanding of those who God will enlighten during the last times. This is stated emphatically at the directive of the Lord: "*watch and not to sleep as do others.*" In order to watch, we must first have something to watch for. The information must, by necessity, be from the Word of God; otherwise, there could be no basis for it. God has given many scriptures that unravel the final seven years; many of them are contained in the Old Testament, especially the book of Daniel. The final seven-year sequence of events that led up to the end is indeed well documented in God's Word. It will be these scriptures that will give light to the final days and reveal the truth and identity of the characters and time frames. "*God would not have us in darkness … that day shall not overtake us (The Body of Christ) as a thief*" (1 Thessalonians 5:4; my emphasis).

As searchers of truth, we will now move forward to the sequential events contained in the final week of Daniel's prophecy of seventy sevens of weeks. From the foundation laid in the previous chapters, we understand that God has given us signposts, directions, and instructions concerning the last days. Once God initiates the last seven years, the Word of God instructs us by giving accurate accounts of days, months, years, activities, events, and character behavior. By rightly dividing the Word of God, we become instructed from the Word of God with this information; therefore, our path and understanding are on solid ground. Throughout these last-time events, the wicked will be blind to what is occurring on the earth. The scriptural events and characters who rise during the last seven years, as depicted especially in Daniel and Revelation, will take center stage during the last seven years. These events and characters are what we are to look for, or "*watch.*"

There is full assurance from scripture that it is the will of the Father for us to be aware of the last days regardless of what men may tell us. The vile man of Daniel focuses on the scriptures relating to the final seven years. The focus will come about through the examination and the right division of the Word of God. The result is that the man of God will be thoroughly furnished with and knowledgeable of the things that are shortly coming to pass. Those who understand will also be in awe of the accuracy and exactness of the Word of God. We must examine all scripture concerning the last days, especially Daniel and Revelation, to understand what God would have us watch for. The scriptures depicting the final week are filled with an enormous amount of detail concerning the last times. The Old Testament contains most of the information regarding the final seven years; consequently, we will spend a great deal of time in Old Testament scripture to unravel the final seven years. The book of Revelation gives specific details concerning the final forty-two months of the last seven years and focuses on the actions of the Antichrist. It is this Antichrist and his followers that will bring the wrath of God upon the earth.

Chapter 11 of Romans provides a clue as to when the last time or season will begin. Consider the following:

> For I would not, brethren, that ye should be ignorant of this mystery, lest ye should be wise in your own conceits; **that blindness in part is happened to Israel, until the fulness of the Gentiles be come in.** And so all Israel shall be saved: as it is written, There shall come out of Sion the Deliverer, and shall turn away ungodliness from Jacob: For this is my covenant unto them (Israel), when I shall take away their sins. As concerning the gospel, they are enemies for your sakes: but as touching the election,

they are beloved for the fathers' sakes. (Romans 11:25–28 KJV)

The fullness of the sins of the Gentiles is associated with the times growing worse and worse. Consider the following: "*Yea, and all that will live godly in Christ Jesus shall suffer persecution.*
But evil men and seducers shall wax worse and worse, deceiving, and being deceived" (2 Timothy 3:12–13)
As stated earlier, there must not be contradictions in the Word of God and all must be fulfilled. God will initiate the last days not when man has finally attained peace but when sin is so bad that God will not stand by any longer and allow man to destroy the earth. Consider the following:

"And the nations were angry, and thy wrath is come, and the time of the dead, that they should be judged, and that thou shouldest give reward unto thy servants the prophets, and to the saints, and them that fear thy name, small and great; **and shouldest destroy them which destroy the earth**" (Revelation 11:18 KJV; my emphasis).

The above verse indicates an interesting fact: humanity will be destroying the earth. God will not allow this to happen, for we know that God created the earth for his pleasure:

And the first beast was like a lion, and the second beast like a calf, and the third beast had a face as a man, and the fourth beast was like a flying eagle. And the four beasts had each of them six wings about him; and they were full of eyes within: and they rest not day and night, saying, Holy, holy, holy, Lord God Almighty, which was, and is, and is to come. And when those beasts give glory and honour and thanks to him that sat on the throne, who liveth for ever and ever, The four and twenty elders fall down before him that sat on the throne, and worship him that liveth for ever and ever, and cast their crowns before the throne, saying, **Thou art worthy, O Lord, to receive glory and honour and power: for thou hast created all things, and for thy pleasure they are and were created.** (Revelation 4:7–11 KJV; my emphasis)

God, at the time of the end, steps into the doings of man not when peace and calm are attained but when the sins of man are so putrid that he cannot stand by and allow it to continue any longer. As stated earlier, God's prophecy to Daniel contains a good deal of the blueprint concerning the final days of man's rule on Earth. To understand the blueprint, it is imperative that the searcher of scripture understand the mystery, or hidden time, of the one body of Jesus Christ. The key to understanding is making the right division of Daniel's prophecy of seventy sevens of weeks. Some final points regarding the final seventy sevens, or 490 years, documented in Daniel 9:24–27, are as follows:

- The Messiah will be cut off in AD 29, 483 years after the command to build the second Judean temple (Daniel 9:25).
- After the cutting off of the Messiah from the earth, a period of time will come that was never foretold in the Old Testament. The period was hidden by God and is known as the mystery of the one body of Christ. To date, it has lasted almost two thousand years (Ephesians 3).
- The period of the mystery will last until God sets in motion the last times. (The times and the seasons are in the Father's hands.)
- The time of the end will begin with Antichrist strengthening himself with a covenant with many people.
- The final week, or seven years, will begin after the fullness of the times (sin) of the Gentiles has come in or been

completed. The last seven years will be initiated by the Antichrist rising up after he makes a strong league with a powerful Gentile nation, as noted in Daniel 11.23.

- God, and God only, will initiate the last seven-year period, or the time of the season of the end. When the last days, or the last seven years, begin, the sequential events (days, times, seasons, years, people, and events) will be fulfilled exactly as God has documented in the Old and New Testaments. Not one Word of God will fall to the ground.

A great deal of sequential data referencing the final seven years are contained in the Old Testament and are not hidden by God. The rapture of the church will conclude the time of the mystery and will mark the end of acquiring salvation through a new birth in Jesus Christ. The new birth is a new beginning as an offspring of God; hence, it is known as being born again of the spirit of God. After the rapture, the wrath of God, including Jacob's trouble, will come upon the earth. Time will again revert to Jew and Gentile being separated, as in the Old Testament, and man will achieve status with God by works. (See Revelation 2; 3). Additionally, the veil of the temple will once again be established between Jew and Gentile.

God tells us to watch and be sober, indicating that he has provided information and events to watch for in his Word. The quest for the information that God has provided is the basis of this study. God states that there will be a special blessing to those who rightly divide the scriptures concerning the last days. Consider the following: *"The Revelation of Jesus Christ, which God gave unto him, to shew unto his servants things which must shortly come to pass; and he sent and signified it by his angel unto his servant John: Who bare record of the Word of God, and of the testimony of Jesus Christ, and of all things that he saw.* ***Blessed is he that readeth, and they that hear the words of this prophecy, and keep those things which are written therein: for the time is at hand***" (Revelation 1:1–3 KJV; my emphasis).

Our heart to our Holy God is to diligently seek his word regarding the last-day events with humility, meekness, and a contrite or broken heart. It is God who will enlighten and teach us through his gracious gift of Holy Spirit. Our attitude before our Holy God must be that of a broken heart together with a contrite Spirit. True humility with a contrite or broken heart is the only safe ground before our Holy God and our Lord Jesus Christ. Consider the following:

> Let that therefore abide in you, which ye have heard from the beginning. If that which ye have heard from the beginning shall remain in you, ye also shall continue in the Son, and in the Father. And this is the promise that he hath promised us, even eternal life. These things have I written unto you concerning them that seduce you. **But the anointing which ye have received of him abideth in you, and ye need not that any man teach you: but as the same anointing teacheth you of all things, and is truth, and is no lie, and even as it hath taught you, ye shall abide in him.** (1 John 2:24–27 KJV; my emphasis)

God has revealed an abundance of information concerning the last seven-year period. The information is for our learning and because he loves his people. God is a God of love, not the author of confusion. God always wants his people in full understanding of his dealings with the world. I believe that the following sections will provide all the necessary information from the Word of God for the man of God to be informed. The study is not watered down with traditions of men, whether they be religious or secular. I pray that this work, before God, is undiluted and accurately documents the last days once they are set into motion by God. The writings that follow are not exhaustive regarding the subject but rather provide enough information to "*Watch*," as commanded by the Lord.

> But of the times and the seasons, brethren, ye have no need that I write unto you. For yourselves know perfectly that the day of the Lord so cometh as a thief in the night.

> For when they shall say, Peace and safety; then sudden destruction cometh upon them, as travail upon a woman with child; and they shall not escape. **But ye, brethren, are not in darkness, that that day should overtake you as a thief. Ye are all the children of light, and the children of the day: we are not of the night, nor of darkness. Therefore let us not sleep, as do others; but let us watch and be sober.**
>
> For they that sleep sleep in the night; and they that be drunken are drunken in the night.
>
> But let us, who are of the day, be sober, putting on the breastplate of faith and love; and for an helmet, the hope of salvation. For God hath not appointed us to wrath, but to obtain salvation by our Lord Jesus Christ. (1 Thessalonians 5:1–9 KJV; my emphasis)

In summary, God refers to the body of Christ as children of light that are appointed not to wrath but to salvation by our Lord Jesus Christ. This work describes the sequence of how the last days unfold as stated in the Word of God. The time of the last days is a culmination of God dealing with all three groups of people: Jews, Gentiles, and the church of God—the one body of Jesus Christ. The latter of these will be raptured from the earth before the great and terrible Day of the Lord. The work contains the momentous events that will unfold on the earth during the last seven years of man's rule on the earth. At the time of these events, God will deliver the body of Christ from wrath by removing the church from the earth before the wrath of Almighty God has truly come upon the earth.[35] God will initiate the last days and then the final seven years through two lightly considered events on the earth that only the wise to the Word of God will understand. It is the covenant and league with a strong powerful nation by the Antichrist which will initiate the events of

---

[35] 1 Thessalonians 5:8–10.

the last days that will lead up to his rising and reign of terror.[36] These events will also usher in the final 2,300 days.[37] The time and season when God initiates these events are hidden in God but the events that follow after the initiation will be understood by the wise at the time of their occurrence on the earth. God, and only God, will put these last time events into motion.

The last week, or seven years, is still awaiting fulfillment and will be fulfilled exactly as God documented it in his Word. A great deal of scripture describing the last seven years in both the Old and New Testaments still awaits fulfillment but will be fulfilled accurately as described. At the end of the final seven years, all promises made to Daniel concerning Israel and listed in Daniel 9:24 will be accurately fulfilled. The period of the mystery of the one body of Jesus Christ was hidden in the heart of God and is nowhere to be found in Old Testament scripture. Accurate understanding of the mystery period is foundational to right division of the Word of God concerning the last days. Once the mystery period is understood and rightly divided, God's manifold wisdom and greatness, as well as the accuracy of his Word, move to a new level. How perfectly it will fit together for the searcher and lover of God's holy scriptures! To our great and mighty God, who knows the end from the beginning and who loved the world so much that he gave us his only begotten son. He is blessed forever and ever. Amen.

---

[36] Daniel 9:27.
[37] Daniel 11.23.

CHAPTER 4

God Reveals the Man of Sin

OUR ATTENTION NOW SHIFTS TO the vile man of Daniel and what God's Word states about him. Most of chapter 3 was dedicated to proving how the time of the mystery of the one body of Christ was hidden in the Old Testament. Understanding the secret mystery period is fundamental to rightly dividing the Word of God regarding the last days. All references to the last times, especially concerning the Old Testament scriptures, must be rigty divided and understood in lieu of the absence of the mystery period. When this is adhered to, God's Word will then be allowed to speak and identify the vile man as he rises to prominence in the last days. In addition to the term "vile man" in Daniel chapter 11:21, many other titles exist in the Bible that describe the same individual. Some of these titles include *"the king of Babylon," "the son of perdition," "the Assyrian," "the willful king," "the man of sin,"* and *"the Antichrist."* The concept of scripture buildup must be employed in our study to accurately attain the focused picture that God is revealing. Each of these titles will be studied individually in their context and will add additional information to the makeup of the vile man. Each description is referring to the same individual but adds additional information regarding his rise and fall during the last times. The study of the vile man will focus on most of the references in the Bible concerning this man of sin. Proper understanding will require all tradition and private interpretation to be cast aside; the scriptures must be allowed to speak to our hearts and minds. It is the Word of God that will be our sole source of knowledge for inspiration, understanding, and prophecy.

The books of Daniel and Revelation reveal to us that the vile man is present on the earth during the seventieth week of Daniel's prophecy of seventy sevens of years. The gospels, the epistles of Paul, the book of the revelation of Jesus Christ, and other Old Testament scriptures will bear this out as well. The man of sin is called by twelve different names in scripture, but the same individual is referenced each time. God uses the method of scripture buildup to build the image of the vile man through many unique scriptures referring to the same individual. Scripture buildup is an ingenious tool used by God to reveal, through several separate interrelated accounts, descriptions of the same individual. The result will be a complete, unmistakable picture of the vile man. Each scripture builds up or adds information without contradiction to that which has already been revealed from other scriptures. The entire revelation revealed by God can then be considered together to paint an unmistakable portrait. The Word of God is perfect; consequently, all scripture within the Word of God must be perfect, with no contradictions. Apparent contradictions, when they arise, typically are caused by mistranslation, lack of understanding, context-related issues, or failure to adhere to the scripture's addressee. Scripture study requires disciplined right division of the Word of God through due diligence of all God has revealed. The reward for right division is the truth of the Word of God, which cannot be stolen by tradition. God's Word is written only to people who desire to know and love God. The Old Testament is written to believing Israel and those of the Gentiles who hold the true God in high esteem. Both groups will be alive during the last days: the believing Jews, who are the lineage of Abraham, Isaac, and Jacob; and those who seek to love God. These will once again be the focus during the final seven years of Daniel's prophecy of the seventy sevens of years.[38] The end days culminate in God's

---

[38] Daniel 9:24.

final dealings with the Jews and Gentiles. Before the wrath of God on the earth, and during the last seven years, the church of God, will already have been removed. The culmination of these events also marks the time of the blindness being taken away from Israel as stated in Romans 11. The removal of the blindness from Israel, as stated in Romans 11, is a central theme of the last days. The book of Revelation is the account of the final forty-two months leading up to the purifying of the bride of Christ, Israel. This is clearly stated in Revelation 20. Consider the following:

> And after these things I heard a great voice of much people in heaven, saying, Alleluia; Salvation, and glory, and honour, and power, unto the Lord our God: For true and righteous are his judgments: for he hath judged the great whore, which did corrupt the earth with her fornication, and hath avenged the blood of his servants at her hand. And again they said, Alleluia. And her smoke rose up for ever and ever. And the four and twenty elders and the four beasts fell down and worshipped God that sat on the throne, saying, Amen; Alleluia. And a voice came out of the throne, saying, Praise our God, all ye his servants, and ye that fear him, both small and great. And I heard as it were the voice of a great multitude, and as the voice of many waters, and as the voice of mighty thunderings, saying, Alleluia: for the Lord God omnipotent reigneth. **Let us be glad and rejoice, and give honour to him: for the marriage of the Lamb is come, and his wife hath made herself ready. And to her was granted that she should be arrayed in fine linen, clean and white: for the fine linen is the righteousness of saints. And he saith unto me, Write, Blessed are they which are called unto the marriage supper of the Lamb. And**

he saith unto me, These are the true sayings of God. (Revelation 19:1–9 KJV; my emphasis)

The fulfillment of Romans 11:26 and Revelation 19:1-9 will be accomplished at the completion of Daniel's seventy sevens of years. The completion of this time also coincides with the marriage of the lamb (the body of Christ) with Israel (the bride of Christ). Proper interpretation of these great truths allows God to give his people—those present at the time of fulfillment—extensive information and instruction concerning the final seven years. The remnant of Jews alive during Jacob's trouble and the called of God will utilize this information in a masterful way. The instruction will be critical for God's people to come safely through the darkest time in human history.

The man of sin, one of the alternative titles of the Antichrist, including all his descriptions and behaviors, will initially be studied from the Word of God. It is the Word of God that gives the accurate details regarding his rising and his behaviors in the last days. The book of Revelation and the book of Daniel provide the core of information regarding the man of sin. The books are woven together through a perfect balance of coordinated information that only God could have conceived. In-depth understanding of either book requires cross-referenced information from the other. God wove these two books together to associate the revelation of Jesus Christ on the earth to be understood in light of Old Testament prophecy to the Jews. Information from these two books will be invaluable for those alive during the horrific events described in the book of Revelation. The frightful times of Revelation will require an accurate knowledge of the Word of God for survival. It will be the persecution associated with the last days that will require those who love God to seek Jesus Christ as their Messiah. The two books, Daniel and Revelation, and the man of sin are intrinsically woven together in the contextual fabric of each end-times prophecy. The Word of God reveals the man of sin, who further reveals the sequence of events initiated by him. Through this method, his actions and behaviors will be understood and will be instrumental in revealing the events of the last days as they unfold. The references to the Antichrist are not intended to elevate him but to convey that his presence on Earth reveals the last days and the cataclysmic events that follow. Both books also inform the reader of the plight of the Gentiles and of the heavens and the earth. In short, the end-time scriptures reveal the future for all of God's creation.

The study of the vile man, or man of sin, necessarily needs to examine each of the names given in the Word of God. In this study, each name given to the vile man *will be marked in italics for emphasis.* The behavior of the vile man will also be in bold to bring attention to his actions. The study will begin in the Old Testament and progressively work through each reference. The final references will culminate with the extraordinary references regarding the beast in Revelation. After each section, or each reference to the vile man, commentary will be added for further explanation. Each verse will be listed and commented on as appropriate. At the end of each commentary and interpretation, the attributes associated with the vile man related to that section will be listed. Through this process, God's intended picture and meaning will be rebuilt accurately through careful examination of the Word of God. It will be God's Word, through this process of scripture buildup, that will methodically build an accurate picture of the man of sin. The process will also reveal a sequence of events in the last days that cannot be misinterpreted.

Scripture buildup is a process that builds up a focused picture relating to an important biblical event or individual through the conglomeration of several verses concerning the same matter or individual. The focus of this work will be references to the vile man and his behaviors during the last days. The finished portrait will comprehensively assemble an accurate portrayal of the picture that God intended to convey. Six fundamental rules for scriptural interpretation and scripture buildup are as follows:

1. Common referenced scriptures associated with the same event or individual cannot have contradictions.

2. Scriptures, as originally written down, are perfect and must be studied in their inherent perfection in accordance with the language and culture at the time. The Hebrew, Aramaic, or Greek must be examined in accordance with the grammatical rules of each language.
3. The searcher must be careful not to be influenced by previous bias or, put another way, accepted traditional beliefs.
4. Each scripture must be interpreted in the context of the section it is written in, with recognition of the addressee.
5. Lack of understanding or apparent contradictions must be mitigated through accepted biblical research techniques (e.g., context, remote context, word or words used before in scripture, original texts, related verses, biblical exegesis, and right division in accordance with whom a given scripture is written to).
6. The addressees are summarized as follows:

    a. The Old Testament is primarily written to Israel.
    b. The Gospels are written to Jew and Gentile.
    c. The Pauline Epistles are predominantly written to the church of God, the body of Christ.
    d. The book of Revelation is written to Jew and Gentile. To the Jews it contains detailed information for Israel, the bride of Christ.

These six principles will guide the analysis and interpretation regarding the vile man of Daniel.

Consider the following:

> Therefore seeing we have this ministry, as we have received mercy, we faint not; But have renounced the hidden things of dishonesty, not walking in craftiness, **nor handling the Word of God deceitfully; but by manifestation of the truth commending ourselves to every man's**

conscience in the sight of God. But if our gospel be hid, it is hid to them that are lost: In whom the god of this world (Satan) hath blinded the minds of them which believe not, lest the light of the glorious gospel of Christ, who is the image of God, should shine unto them. (2 Corinthians 4:1–4 KJV; my emphasis)

Adherence to the above six fundamental rules will reveal the deep things of God placed in his Word for those who diligently seek him. God requires that the searcher of scripture, who wishes to understand the deep and diverse things of God, be established and full-grown in relationship to God and his son, Jesus Christ. God states emphatically in 1 Corinthians chapter 3 that if envy and strife exist in your life you will not move past the beginning principles of salvation—Christ and him crucified. Paul could not go beyond the original oracles of the Word of God in his teachings to the Corinthians because of envy and strife in their assemblies. God is not mocked. God requires obedience from those who wish to understand the deep and spiritual things revealed in his Word. His requirements to those who study his Word are to love God with all your heart through Jesus Christ and love your neighbor as yourself. If these two ingredients are not present, then understanding the deep things of God's Word, in this case the last days, will be unfruitful. The reader will not be able to go beyond the first oracles of faith. If there is envy and strife, there will also be divisions that will abound, along with gossip and backbiting. If these are present, then understanding the deep things of God's Word will be elusive at best. Be sure to adhere to God's two great commandments: love God with all your heart, mind, soul, and strength, and love your neighbor as yourself. If you discipline yourself to abide in these two great commandments, then you will have good success in your study and receive the blessings of God. The scriptures that follow are set forth for enlightenment. May our Heavenly Father and our Lord Jesus Christ bring life to these truths in his perfect Word. We can do nothing without him!

The scripture verses listed from the Word of God taken together as a whole describe the man of sin in detail. The fundamental ingredient will be scripture buildup. Each reference must be studied and understood word by word and line by line in context. The Word of God must be rightly divided to receive the full blessing that God intended. Through this process, the accuracy of the Word of God concerning the last days will be clearly evident. Each verse and precept build upon the preceding. Consider the following:

> But they also have erred through wine, and through strong drink are out of the way; the priest and the prophet have erred through strong drink, they are swallowed up of wine, they are out of the way through strong drink; they err in vision, they stumble in judgment. For all tables are full of vomit and filthiness, so that there is no place clean. **Whom shall he teach knowledge? and whom shall he make to understand doctrine? them that are weaned from the milk, and drawn from the breasts. For precept must be upon precept, precept upon precept; line upon line, line upon line; here a little, and there a little:** For with stammering lips and another tongue will he speak to this people. To whom he said, this is the rest wherewith ye may cause the weary to rest; and this is the refreshing: yet they would not hear. (Isaiah 28:7–12 KJV; my emphasis)

A sizable portion of the scriptures examined concerning the vile man are contained in the Old Testament. A significant amount of the information and detail concerning the last seven years is also contained in Old Testament. The apocalypse, or the book of Revelation, expounds, expands, and complements the information given in the Old Testament scriptures regarding the last days. The apocalypse can be thought of as focusing on the final forty-two months of the last seven years for Israel and the Gentiles. The scriptures in this study are listed as they appear in scripture sequence, with references to other scriptures as appropriate. The sections examined are directly or indirectly related to the vile man or the Antichrist. The vile man is a man, an individual, who increases with strength and power as he learns to walk with Satan and experiences the depths of satanic power during the last days. The overall process is to assemble each piece of information from each verse of scripture and then combine the various references together as one focused portrait. In this manner, the related scriptures will lead us to the representation God intended. The final product will be an astonishingly accurate picture with both clarity and detail.

The methodology will be to list the names and various references of the vile man throughout the Bible. Each reference will then be examined and documented as per the details provided. The book of Daniel will be handled separately owing to the volume of information listed. Daniel, since it contains significant information, will be developed and expounded through sectional divisions within the book of Daniel. Both the references in Daniel and references in other scriptures will then be integrated into one portrayal.

Following is the list of direct or alternate names used in the Word of God for the vile man. The list is not exhaustive but includes the core names that refer to one and the selfsame man. The references will be the focus of this study and will provide the core knowledge concerning the timing of the actions of the vile man. The names and titles are the starting point that God has used as pointers in his word. The names and titles provide a critical mass required for proper understanding of the last days. Indirect references to the vile man and his aliases are added as appropriate, but the references below compose the core of the information God has provided in his word with respect to the vile man. The references are broken down into sections or groupings, each one revealing additional attributes of the vile man. The result will be an accurate representation of the vile man and will once again display the perfection of the Word of God, each section or grouping adding information without contradiction.

THE LAST DAYS AND THE VILE MAN OF DANIEL

The Twelve Titles and References of the Antichrist:[39]

Section 1; Isaiah 14: References 1, 2, and 3
1. "King Of Babylon"; Isaiah 14.4
2. "The Assyrian"; Isaiah 14.25
3. "Lucifer, Son of the morning"; Isaiah 14.12

Section II; Daniel 7–12: *References 4, 5,6,7,8*
4. "The Little Horn", Daniel 7.8; Daniel 8.9
5. "The King of Fierce Countenance"; Daniel 8.23
6. "The Prince that shall come"; Daniel 9.26
7. "The Vile Person"; Daniel 11:21
8. "The Willful King"; Daniel 11: 36

Section III: New Testament References: *References 9,10,11,12*
9. "The Man of Sin"; 2 Thessalonians 2:3
10. "The Son of Perdition"; 2 Thessalonians 2:3
11. "That Wicked (or Lawless) One"; 2 Thessalonians 2:8
12. "The Beast with Seven Heads and Ten horns"; Revelation 13:1
13. "The Beast that was and is not and is again"; The Beast and the Great Whore; Revelation 17:8

The study will examine each of the titles listed above in the order in which they appear in the Word of God. Each will be scrutinized and studied in its original context and in accordance with the interpretation principles listed above. The result will be a composite picture or portrait listed in appendix A. May the Lord God enlighten and bless us in this study of his Word.

---

[39] Bullinger, *Companion Bible, King James Version, Kregal Publications, Grand Rapids Michigan; published 1990;* P1192.

Section 1: Isaiah Chapter 14:1–27; References 1, 2, and 3
"King of Babylon," "The Assyrian," "Lucifer, Son of the Morning"
These three titles will be handled together since all three are contained in the same chapter of Isaiah.

- Reference 1: king of Babylon, cast to the ground (Isaiah 14:4 KJV)
- Reference 2: Lucifer, son of the morning (Isaiah 14:12 KJV)
- Reference 3: the Assyrian (Isaiah 14:25 KJV)

> Isaiah 14; 1–27:
> For the LORD will have mercy on Jacob, and will yet choose Israel, and set them in their own land: and the strangers shall be joined with them, and they shall cleave to the house of Jacob. And the people shall take them, and bring them to their place: and the house of Israel shall possess them in the land of the LORD for servants and handmaids: and they shall take them captives, whose captives they were; and they shall rule over their oppressors. And it shall come to pass in the day that the LORD shall give thee rest from thy sorrow, and from thy fear, and from the hard bondage wherein thou wast made to serve. That thou shalt take up this proverb against the **king of Babylon, and say, How hath the oppressor ceased! the golden city ceased! The LORD hath broken the staff of the wicked, and the sceptre of the rulers. He who smote the people in wrath with a continual stroke, he that ruled the nations in anger, is persecuted, and none hindereth**. The whole earth is at rest, and is quiet: they break forth into singing. Yea, the fir trees rejoice at thee, and the cedars of Lebanon, saying, Since thou art laid down, no feller is come

up against us. **Hell from beneath is moved for thee to meet thee at thy coming: it stirreth up the dead for thee, even all the chief ones of the earth; it hath raised up from their thrones all the kings of the nations. All they shall speak and say unto thee, Art thou also become weak as we? art thou become like unto us? Thy pomp is brought down to the grave, and the noise of thy viols: the worm is spread under thee, and the worms cover thee. How art thou fallen from heaven, O Lucifer, son of the morning! how art thou cut down to the ground, which didst weaken the nations! For thou hast said in thine heart, I will ascend into heaven, I will exalt my throne above the stars of God: I will sit also upon the mount of the congregation, in the sides of the north: I will ascend above the heights of the clouds; I will be like the most High. Yet thou shalt be brought down to hell, to the sides of the pit. They that see thee shall narrowly look upon thee, and consider thee, saying, Is this the man that made the earth to tremble, that did shake kingdoms; That made the world as a wilderness, and destroyed the cities thereof; that opened not the house of his prisoners? All the kings of the nations, even all of them, lie in glory, every one in his own house. But thou art cast out of thy grave like an abominable branch, and as the raiment of those that are slain, thrust through with a sword, that go down to the stones of the pit; as a carcase trodden under feet. Thou shalt not be joined with them in burial, because thou hast destroyed thy land, and slain thy people: the seed of evildoers shall never be renowned. Prepare slaughter for his children for the** iniquity of their fathers; that they do not rise, nor possess the land, nor fill the face of the world with cities. For I will rise up against them, saith the LORD of hosts, and cut off from Babylon the name, and remnant, and son, and nephew, saith the LORD. I will also make it a possession for the bittern, and pools of water: and I will sweep it with the besom of destruction, saith the LORD of hosts. The LORD of hosts hath sworn, saying, Surely as I have thought, so shall it come to pass; and as I have purposed, so shall it stand: That I will break the Assyrian in my land, and upon my mountains tread him under foot: then shall his yoke depart from off them, and his burden depart from off their shoulders. This is the purpose that is purposed upon the whole earth: and this is the hand that is stretched out upon all the nations. For the LORD of hosts hath purposed, and who shall disannul it? and his hand is stretched out, and who shall turn it back?** (Isaiah 14:1–27 KJV; my emphasis)

Reference 1,2,3; Commentary: Section 1: "King of Babylon," "The Assyrian," "Lucifer, Son of the Morning"

Isaiah chapter 14 contains the first direct reference to the vile man in the Bible. The first reference in the Bible typically contains crucially important characteristics concerning a subject. In this first occurrence, God takes us back to Genesis and to the root of the problem—that is, Satan and his attempt to usurp the sovereignty of Almighty God. The final attempt of Satan's rebellion will be the Antichrist and his attempt to rule the earth and declare himself God. The first characteristic associates the last days with the *king of Babylon* and *Jacob's time of trouble.* This first occurrence does not provide a great deal of specifics related to the vile man but rather sets the foundation or cause for God's judgment. God initially states in verse 1 that he will have mercy on Israel and will fulfill all the promises to the patriarchs and fathers of Israel. This opening statement assures us of God's faithfulness to Israel and to their fathers; the Patriarchs, to whom he made everlasting promises. The declaration and promise to Israel is first mentioned before all the horrific trouble that ensues in Isaiah 14. The second item of importance is the association of the *King of Babylon* whose physical presence will affect all the nations of the earth. It will be all nations, peoples, and tongues of the world that will be involved in the God's final-days controversy with mankind. The importance of Babylon is first related to the revolt of unified nations in Genesis under the sway of Nimrod as documented in Genesis chapter 11. The first rebellion foreshadows the final rebellion of the Antichrist. The revolt of the Antichrist at the time of the end will also be linked to the unified nations under the sway of Satan. The last days will see the *Assyrian*, or *king of Babylon*, rise in the stead of Nimrod. Appropriately, the *king of Babylon* is associated and mentioned in this chapter with Satan. The final rebellion is the final revolt against God and his Christ during the last days. In the final reference to the Antichrist, the beast of Revelation, the Babylonian reference once again associates him with "*Mystery Babylon.*"[40] The final days will once again feature the revolt of nations, tongues, and peoples of the world against the true God and under the sway of the Antichrist. The third significant characterization is the unification of the *king of Babylon* with Lucifer and Satan. As will be seen in the references and scriptures that follow, Satan, through his instrument the *king of Babylon*, will act in unison to attempt to usurp God; that is, his people and his sovereignty. In the end, their futile attempt will amount to nothing but will bring on eternal damnation to both the Antichrist and Satan. The final revolt will, however, bring an end to the dominion of the Gentile nations of the world signified as Babylon and result in the Lord Jesus Christ taking up his rightful position as King of kings and Lord of lords. The final significant fact in this section finds the King of Babylon and the destruction

---

[40] Revelation 17:5.

instigated by Satan as amounting to nothing. It will be God that will protect those who fear and reverence him, even during the horrific time of the end. Jacob is finally delivered, and God's purpose that is purposed upon the whole earth will be fulfilled, as noted in verse 26.

Jacob's final deliverance, the saving of the remnant of Jacob during the last days, is a foundational principle throughout the Bible. The foundational truth of Jacob's deliverance runs as a red thread throughout the entire Bible. God will remember and keep all promises made to Israel and to their fathers. Consider the following:

> For I would not, brethren, that ye should be ignorant of this mystery, lest ye should be wise in your own conceits; that blindness in part is happened to Israel, until the fulness of the Gentiles be come in. **And so all Israel shall be saved: as it is written, There shall come out of Sion the Deliverer, and shall turn away ungodliness from Jacob: For this is my covenant unto them, when I shall take away their sins.** As concerning the gospel, they are enemies for your sakes: but as touching the election, they are beloved for the fathers' sakes. For the gifts and calling of God are without repentance. (Romans 11:25–29 KJV; my emphasis)

Isaiah 14 complements Isaiah 13 and describes God's judgment of the whole earth, represented by Babylon. Babylon originally symbolized the first gathering together of nations for rebellion led by Nimrod, the great rebel of Genesis.[41] In the final rebellion by the Antichrist, God states that he will save a remnant of his people, Israel, after judging the nations represented by Babylon. The leader of *mystery* or *secret* Babylon, the one who rises in the last days, is represented by the king of Babylon—that is, the Antichrist or vile man (verse 4). The last attempt by the king of Babylon to rebel against

---

[41] Genesis 10; 11.

God will be similar to the first attempt by Nimrod, the mighty rebel of Genesis 11. Nimrod was the initial rebel who gathered the nations together in rebellion against God. His rebellion is listed in Genesis 10 and 11 and resulted in the tower of Babel, a symbol of a man's futile attempt to elevate himself to the level of God.

Isaiah 14: 4–6 documents the events that transpire after God's deliverance of the remnant of Israel and the destruction of the *king of Babylon* in the last days, God documents the prior activities of the King of Babylon. The oppressor and the golden city have ceased, the Lord has broken the staff of the wicked, and the man who continuously and unchangeably smote the earth with hate and ruled the nations in anger is now persecuted. The Lord himself will be the one that destroys him.[42] The Antichrist is depicted here and described by his arrogance and pride, which result in the destruction of the cities and peoples of the earth.

Isaiah 14: 7–21 describe the peace of the millennial kingdom and look back at the destruction of the *man of sin*. He called himself God, and now he is brought to nothing. The scripture in verse 12 goes on to equate the Antichrist with Lucifer, the son of the morning. In comparison, Revelation 13 describes the final beast energized by Satan and taking on the characteristics of Satan. Lucifer is described as the son of the morning and the one who weakened the nations. Verse 13 reveals the heart of Satan and, subsequently, the heart of the Antichrist. These two will act in unison in their attempt to thwart the sovereignty of God, for they know their time is short. It will be Satan's instrument, the Antichrist, together with unsaved natural man, who will unify together with delusional desires to be God. They will contrive a futile attempt to remove any remembrance of the true God and his son, Jesus Christ, from heaven. These final actions and alliances will bring onto the earth the final wrath of God as documented in the book of Revelation. Satan sums up the eternal purpose in his heart in verse 13: *"I will ascend into heaven, I will exalt my throne above the stars of God, I will sit also upon the mount of the congregation in the sides of the north: I will ascent upon the heights*

---

[42] 2 Thessalonians 2;8.

of the clouds; I will be like the most high." The true natural desire of Satan and his instrument, the Antichrist, is to ascend to the throne of God and usurp his authority. You will see further on in this study how the *man of sin* does indeed declare himself God as he sits in the temple of God.[43] Man also has this innate desire to be his own God. The only remedy that is approved by God is the cleansing that God provides through faith in Jesus Christ. The Antichrist acting in unison with Satan and wanting to be God agrees with all related scriptures describing the man of sin. The Word of God reveals the true intentions of all those who follow and worship the beast. God knows the heart of man and the heart of the beast. God's Word reveals the true intentions of the beast and Lucifer. The strategies of Satan, operating through the Antichrist, are thrown down and judged by God in verses 15–24. Some attributes of the Antichrist that can be collected from this section are as follows:

1. He will be brought down to hell, to the sides of the pit. (v.15)
2. He will narrowly be considered and the power he once had will be scoffed at. (v.16)
3. He is described as the man that made the world a wilderness; indicating how he destroyed the nations and cities therein; Mystery Babylon. (v.17)
4. He will not be permitted to rest in death like all others but will be roused from death and cast into the everlasting torment of hell. The fact that he is the first to be cast into hell is documented in several other scriptures. (v.18–20)

Isaiah 14: 21–24 describe God's judgment of the nations represented by Babylon. The nations will no longer possess the earth or fill the world with their cities. The destruction of the nations will be accomplished via Satan and his instrument, the Antichrist. Later, and toward the end of the final seven years, God's vengeance toward the kingdom of the beast and the nations will be poured out on the

---

[43] 2 Thessalonians 2:4.

earth. The kingdoms of the earth will become Christ's as King of kings and Lord of lords.

Isaiah 14:25–27 describes the Assyrian, another name for the Antichrist. The Assyrian is not another character, but the same character representing distinctive characteristics or a different viewpoint of the Antichrist. What is the significance of the name "the Assyrian"? The name represents the origin of the Antichrist on the earth, while "King of Babylon" represents his short-lived dominion over the earth. God states that he will break the yoke of the *Assyrian* from the people of God in the last days. God further states that he will break or destroy him in the land of Israel. The word "*Assyrian*" is derived from "Assur"—the name of one of the sons of Shem, whose image was worshipped by the Assyrians as a god. The people who populated Assyria derived from Babylon and were an extension of, yet more developed than, the Babylonians. The Assyrians also were often at odds and at war with Israel in the Old Testament. The story of Hezekiah and his deliverance from the Assyrians exemplifies the defiance of the Assyrians against God and his people.[44] The Hezekiah story concerns the king of Assyria coming up against Israel and taking it. He then comes up against a small remnant of Jews (Judah) led by Hezekiah in Jerusalem. As part of these exploits, the king of Assyria requires submission to his god and rejection of the true God. Hezekiah, against all odds, resists and puts his complete trust in the Lord. Hezekiah is taunted for his belief in the true God, but he stands his ground. God responds by destroying the army of the Assyrians and delivering Hezekiah and Israel. The story foreshadows the last days, the final seven years (Jacobs's trouble), and the events that occur during the Day of the Lord. The story also foreshadows the origin of the *man of sin*; he will ascend from the remnants of the Assyrian empire that will be present in the last days. Scripture reveals how God will once again destroy the Assyrian in his land, which agrees with various other scriptures related to the same topic.[45] God reveals in verse 26 his purpose, which is purposed upon the whole

---

[44] 2 Kings 18.
[45] Daniel 11:45.

earth. God rules in the heavens and the earth and will give the earth to the Lord Jesus Christ and those who fear God through him. The land promised to Abraham, Isaac, and Jacob will be given to their offspring, those written in the book of life, at the end of the final seven-year period. God has purposed this in his heart, and it will happen just as it is written.

Section 1, Reference 1,2,3: *Attributes Associated with the Antichrist (Isaiah 14:1–27)*

In summary, the following key informational points can be gathered from Section 1, references 1, 2, and 3:

1. The Antichrist, or king of Babylon, will eventually direct his anger against Israel, but the remnant of Israel will be saved from destruction. This is the purpose that God has purposed upon the whole earth (vv. 1–4, 25–27).
2. He will represent Satan on Earth with arrogance, pride, destruction, and a claim to be God (vv. 9–14).
3. He will be brought down to hell and be the first to be cast into hell and not buried in the earth (vv. 15–20).
4. He will narrowly be considered, and the power he once had will be scoffed at (v. 16).
5. He is described as the man that made the world (mystery Babylon) a wilderness, indicating how he destroyed the nations and cities therein (v. 17).
6. After his rule of the nations of the world and their subsequent destruction, the nations will be no more. The rule over the earth will be given to God and his Christ (v. 21–23).
7. He will rise from the Assyrian territory and grow in strength and power, finally ruling over all the earth.
8. He will be destroyed in the land of Israel (v. 25).

Section 2: Daniel Chapters 7–12: References 4, 5, 6, 7, and 8

"The Little Horn", "The King of Fierce Countenance, "The Prince that Shall Come", "The Vile Person", The Willful King"

These references contain the core of the information regarding the Antichrist or vile man. Daniel chapters 7–12 contain the next five records of the vile man. The book of Daniel was written in both Hebrew and Aramaic. God divides the book according to Jew and Gentile. The initial part of Daniel (Daniel 2–7), written in Aramaic, pertains to the times of the Gentiles up until Gentile rule was put down by God and given to the Lord Jesus Christ as recorded at the end of chapter 7. The second half of the book of Daniel, written in Hebrew, is focused on the Jews and brings us up to the same point, the dominion of Jesus Christ, but from the Jews' perspective (Daniel 8–12). God uses this format to call attention to the fact that, in the eyes of God, Jews and Gentiles are two separate and distinct groups in the Old Testament. Both groups will answer to almighty God, and both will account for their lives on the earth. The things concerning the Jews and their future, including the end times, are documented in chapters 8 through 12 and are written in Hebrew. The book of Daniel documents a significant amount of future prophecy for both the Jews and Gentiles, but the time of the one body of Jesus Christ is not found since it was hidden in the Old Testament. Truly God is the God of both the Jews and the Gentiles; he is the true God who created the heavens and the earth and the universe and all therein. The language division of the book is God's way of drawing unique attention and providing emphasis as he sees fit. The part written to the Jews is distinct from the times of the Gentiles and their end (chapters 2–7). The focus of this study will be on the Hebrew section, Daniel 8–12. Daniel chapters 2 and 7 will be included as needed, since they contain essential information regarding the final Gentile dominions during the end times. It will be these sections in Daniel that will reveal specific details regarding the actions of the vile man and his end. The story is one of God utilizing the Antichrist and the horrific chaos that he will represent to test the entire world, beginning with Israel. Although the Gentiles are adversely affected by the Antichrist, it is Israel that goes through the greatest transition. Daniel 7 also acts as the documented transitional period between the time of the Gentiles, the last days, and the everlasting rule of Jesus Christ. The following is the general structure of the book of Daniel:

1. Daniel 1–7:28—Gentiles: The Captivity of Judah
    a. Beginning of Gentile dominion
    b. The time of the Gentiles
    c. The end of Gentile dominion
    d. The beginning of the kingdom of Jesus Christ, God's son
2. Daniel 8:1–12:13—The Jews
    a. Desolations of Jerusalem
    b. Jacob's trouble
    c. End of Judah's captivity
    d. Beginning of the kingdom of Jesus Crist, God's son
    e. The actions and timelines of the Antichrist

As noted, the second section of Daniel will be our focus. Section 2, chapters 8–12, is focused on the last days and defines the actions, behaviors, and events, along with an accurate description of the Antichrist or vile man. Daniel 8–12 is structurally broken down as follows:

1. Daniel 8–12: The kingdoms/dominions both past and future, interpretations, the Beast amplified, who they are and what their actions will be, the twenty-three-hundred-day vision in general, and Daniel's lack of understanding
2. Daniel 9–10:1: Timeline of 1 above, seventy sevens, the final seven, and Daniel's understanding
3. Daniel 11:2–11:45: The individual kings, interpretations, the Beast amplified, their individual actions, and the interpretation of the twenty-three-hundred-day vision

The book of Daniel is purposely divided by God through language—that is, Aramaic and Hebrew. The language format divides the book into two separate sections; each section is addressed to the Gentiles and the Jews, respectively. Daniel 7 is the transitional section between the two groups and integrates the last times of the Gentiles with the last days of man's rule on the earth. Daniel 7 lists the last three superpower Gentile dominions that arise on the earth during the last days. These Gentile dominions are followed immediately by the dominion of the beast, which will incorporate all three in his kingdom. The last three Gentile dominions on the earth are coexistent and will be present on the earth when the dominion of the Antichrist begins. The chapter ends with the setting up of the everlasting kingdom of the Lord Jesus Christ on earth as King of kings and Lord of lords. Section 2 (Daniel 8–12) focuses specifically on the time of the end—especially how it relates to the Jews and God's final fulfillment of the promises to their fathers. Any discussion concerning man's final rule on earth as well as the Jews' deliverance through Christ necessarily must include the Antichrist or the vile man. The man of sin is woven into the fabric of all events of the last days. It is as if God uses this man to bring about the prescribed outcome for all three groups: Jews, Gentiles, and the church of God. The association of the vile man and the last days is documented in all related sections of scripture.

As we examine each reference in Daniel, the methodology will break down and list the section structures as appropriate. Recall that structure is used by God to add clarity and aid in the general interpretation of his Word. Theologians, and those who study the Word of God, have always noticed the symmetry and parallelism associated with scripture. The exactness of this structure is undeniable and emphasizes the perfection and care that God used in the creation of his Word. Truly, the verse in psalms comes alive when this is understood:

> The words of the LORD are pure words, Like silver tried in a furnace of earth, Purified seven times.
> You shall keep them, O LORD, You shall preserve them from this generation forever. (Psalm 12:6–7 NKJV)

Realization of the flawless structure and breakdown of the words of God reveals the inherent faultlessness and perfection of the Word of God. Through the realization of the exactness of structure in God's Word, the student cannot help but be in awe of the precision and perfectness of our great God and father of our Lord Jesus Christ. The parallelism in structure is divided into several categories. The categories are listed below for clarity. The structures themselves, as depicted in the book of Daniel, will aid precision and understanding, shedding light on individual parts through structure division. The linguistic structure categories of parallelism are related to figures of speech used by God to emphasize portions of his Word. The classification of structural divisions is given as follows, with scriptural references as examples. These structures will become clear as we move through the book of Daniel. A general description of the main structures is listed below. To get a more detailed explanation of the structures in the Word of God, refer to the works of E. W. Bullinger.[46] (Note: these structures will become clear when the actual example in Daniel is listed.)

The types of structures and parallelism used are as follows (Note: Scripture examples are also provided):

1. Simple, synonymous, or gradational: This structure occurs when the lines are parallel in thought and in the use of synonymous words (e.g., Genesis 4:23–24).
2. Simple, antithetic, or opposite: This structure occurs when the two or more lines are contrasted, being opposed in sense to one another (e.g., Proverbs 10:1).
3. Simple, synthetic, or constructive: This structure occurs when the parallelism consists only in the similar form or construction. (e.g., Psalm 19:7–9).
4. Complex, alternate: This structure occurs when the lines are placed alternately (e.g., Genesis 19:25).

---

[46] E. W. Bullinger, "Figures of Speech used in the Bible," *Companion Bible; Kregal Publications, Grand Rapids Michigan; Published 1990; appendix 6; p.8.*

5. Complex, repeated alternation: This refers to the repetition of two parallel subjects in two or more lines (e.g., Isaiah 65:21–22).
6. Complex, extended alternation: This refers to alternation extended so as to consist of three or more lines (e.g., Judges 10:17).
7. Complex, introversion: This structure occurs when parallel lines are placed so that the first corresponds with the last, the second with the second to last, and so on. (e.g., Genesis 3:19; 2 Chronicles 32:7–8).

The understanding of parallelism supports proper division of the Word of God and proper interpretation. As you read and study the words of God and the perfection of parallel verses, the structures will become apparent. The perfection ultimately makes known God's power and glory. The structure defines the scope, which in turn captures the context, thus giving additional true meaning to each of the words in the Word of God.

The prophecy given to Daniel was revealed through various visions and revelations received while Daniel was in captivity in Babylon. The records are related to each other and build on each other. The deliberate process is line by line, precept by precept. Each reference will be evaluated individually, listing characteristics after each assessment. Individual sections will be evaluated with regard to structure and proper rules of interpretation. Each section reveals distinctive characteristics of the Antichrist/vile man, blending into a comprehensive depiction of the subject matter. Daniel 11 contains the core of information regarding the vile man's actual behavior in the last days. The chapter personifies the attributes of the Antichrist/vile man, which are the one central focus of this work. The references of section 2 span several chapters in Daniel and document the visions he received through revelation as he documented them in the Word of God. The visions and revelations Daniel received from God came primarily through angelic messengers during the Babylonian captivity period of Israel's history (496 to 426 BC). The continuation of reference names is listed in accordance with the twelve titles of the Antichrist and as follows. Each reference will be expanded and evaluated in the pages that follow.

- Reference 4: "The Little Horn" (Daniel 7:8; 8:9)
- Reference 5: "The King of Fierce Countenance" (Daniel 8:23)
- Reference 6: "The Prince that Shall Come" (Daniel 9:26)
- Reference 7: "The Vile Person" (Daniel 11:21)
- Reference 8: "The Willful King" (Daniel 11:36)

Reference 4: Daniel 7:1–27: "The Little Horn", The Vision and Interpretation of the Four Great Latter-Day Beasts

The structure of Daniel 7 (repeated alteration) is as follows:

A. 7:1–8: The four beasts (vision)
  B. 7:9–14: The judgment of the Son of Man (vision)
    C. 7:15–16: Daniel's perturbation and inquiry
A. 7:17: The four beasts (interpretation)
  B. 7:18: The judgment of the Son of Man (interpretation)
    C. 7:19–22: Daniel's inquiry
A. 7:23–25: The four beasts (interpretation)
  B. 7:26–27: The judgment of the Son of Man (interpretation)
    C. 7:19–22: Daniel's perturbation[47]

> Daniel 7; 1–27:
> In the first year of Belshazzar king of Babylon Daniel had a dream and visions of his head upon his bed: then he wrote the dream and told the sum of the matters. Daniel spake and said, I saw in my vision by night, and, behold, the four winds of the heaven strove upon the great sea. And four great beasts came up from the sea, diverse one from another. The first was

---

[47] Bullinger, *Companion Bible, King James Version*, Kregal Publications, Grand Rapids Michigan; published 1990; P1192.

like a lion, and had eagle's wings: I beheld till the wings thereof were plucked, and it was lifted up from the earth, and made stand upon the feet as a man, and a man's heart was given to it. And behold another beast, a second, like to a bear, and it raised up itself on one side, and it had three ribs in the mouth of it between the teeth of it: and they said thus unto it, Arise, devour much flesh. After this I beheld, and lo another, like a leopard, which had upon the back of it four wings of a fowl; the beast had also four heads; and dominion was given to it. **After this I saw in the night visions, and behold a fourth beast, dreadful and terrible, and strong exceedingly; and it had great iron teeth: it devoured and brake in pieces, and stamped the residue with the feet of it: and it was diverse from all the beasts that were before it; and it had ten horns. I considered the horns, and, behold, there came up among them another little horn, before whom there were three of the first horns plucked up by the roots: and, behold, in this horn were eyes like the eyes of man, and a mouth speaking great things. I beheld till the thrones were cast down, and the Ancient of days did sit, whose garment was white as snow, and the hair of his head like the pure wool: his throne was like the fiery flame, and his wheels as burning fire. A fiery stream issued and came forth from before him: thousand thousands ministered unto him, and ten thousand times ten thousand stood before him: the judgment was set, and the books were opened. I beheld then because of the voice of the great words which the horn spake: I beheld even till the beast was slain, and his body destroyed, and**

given to the burning flame. As concerning the rest of the beasts, they had their dominion taken away: yet their lives were prolonged for a season and time. I saw in the night visions, and, behold, one like the Son of man came with the clouds of heaven, and came to the Ancient of days, and they brought him near before him. And there was given him dominion, and glory, and a kingdom, that all people, nations, and languages, should serve him: his dominion is an everlasting dominion, which shall not pass away, and his kingdom that which shall not be destroyed. I Daniel was grieved in my spirit in the midst of my body, and the visions of my head troubled me. I came near unto one of them that stood by, and asked him the truth of all this. So he told me, and made me know the interpretation of the things. These great beasts, which are four, are four kings, which shall arise out of the earth. But the saints of the most High shall take the kingdom, and possess the kingdom for ever, even for ever and ever. **Then I would know the truth of the fourth beast, which was diverse from all the others, exceeding dreadful, whose teeth were of iron, and his nails of brass; which devoured, brake in pieces, and stamped the residue with his feet; And of the ten horns that were in his head, and of the other which came up, and before whom three fell; even of that horn that had eyes, and a mouth that spake very great things, whose look was more stout than his fellows. I beheld, and the same horn made war with the saints, and prevailed against them; Until the Ancient of days came, and judgment was given to the saints of the most High; and the time came that the saints possessed the**

kingdom. Thus he said, The fourth beast shall be the fourth kingdom upon earth, which shall be diverse from all kingdoms, and shall devour the whole earth, and shall tread it down, and break it in pieces. And the ten horns out of this kingdom are ten kings that shall arise: and another shall rise after them; and he shall be diverse from the first, and he shall subdue three kings. And he shall speak great words against the most High, and shall wear out the saints of the most High, and think to change times and laws: and they shall be given into his hand until a time and times and the dividing of time. But the judgment shall sit, and they shall take away his dominion, to consume and to destroy it unto the end. And the kingdom and dominion, and the greatness of the kingdom under the whole heaven, shall be given to the people of the saints of the most High, whose kingdom is an everlasting kingdom, and all dominions shall serve and obey him. (Daniel 7:1–27; my emphasis)

Reference 4: Daniel 7:1–27; Commentary: "The Little Horn", The Vision and Interpretation of the Four Great Latter-Day Beasts.

Daniel 7 documents the four beasts which arise prior to and during the last days which will represent the final four Gentile kingdoms on the earth. The beasts—the lion, the bear, and the leopard—are not part of any previous prophecies in Daniel or related to the time of Daniel. Neither are they related in any way to any previous kingdom or dominion mentioned in the Old Testament. Instead, they are related to the time of the end. The first three animal-like Gentile nations will arise immediately before the kingdom of the fourth beast, just prior to the last days. The fourth terrible kingdom or dominion which results in the production of the Antichrist, will arise and take control from the previous three. Both the animal-like Gentile dominions and the fourth terrible beast and kingdom will be contemporary and part of the last times. Daniel 7 associates the final four beasts, dominions, and nations with the last days and the final Gentile dominion on the earth. The chapter covers the transition of time from the last days of Gentile rule, or man's day, to the time of the Lord's dominion, or the Day of the Lord. It is important to realize that the final four beasts are associated with the last days and are not part of any kingdom mentioned in the Old Testament or that existed before. I stress this because many commentaries try to associate these last-day dominions with the Old Testament, resulting in critical error. They arise in the last days and will be understood by the words that characterize them in Daniel. In contrast, the Lord's Day, which will be established after the destruction or the disarmament of these final four, will be characterized by the rule of Jesus Christ as King of kings and Lord and lords.

Recall that God uses beasts when referring to Gentile rulerships or dominions.[48] The kingdom of our Lord Jesus Christ follows the fourth and final terrible beast, which is associated with the final Gentile dominion as described in Daniel 7. The fulfillment and destruction of the final or fourth beast will complete and bring an end to the time of the Gentiles. Daniel 7 chronicles the transition from the time of the Gentiles to the time of God's everlasting kingdom established on the earth—the Day of the Lord. The Day of the Lord, or the everlasting age of the kingdom of God, will reveal Jesus Christ as King of kings and Lord of lords on the earth.[49] The final kingdom is an everlasting kingdom in which God rules over the earth and becomes all in all. Consider the following:

> For as in Adam all die, even so in Christ shall all be made alive. But every man in his own order: **Christ the firstfruits; afterward they that are Christ's at his coming. Then cometh the end, when he shall have delivered up the kingdom to God, even the Father; when he**

---

[48] Daniel 8:20–27.
[49] Daniel 7:27.

THE LAST DAYS AND THE VILE MAN OF DANIEL

shall have put down all rule and all authority and power. For he must reign, till he hath put all enemies under his feet. The last enemy that shall be destroyed is death. For he hath put all things under his feet. But when he saith all things are put under him, it is manifest that he is excepted, which did put all things under him. And when all things shall be subdued unto him, then shall the Son also himself be subject unto him that put all things under him, that God may be all in all. (1 Corinthians 15:22–28 KJV; my emphasis)

The Vision of Daniel Chapter 7

> In the first year of Belshazzar, king of Babylon, Daniel had a dream and visions of his head upon his bed: then he wrote the dream and told the sum of the matters. Daniel spake and said, I saw in my vision by night, and, behold, the four winds of the heaven strove upon the great sea. And four great beasts came up from the sea, diverse one from another. The first was like a lion, and had eagle's wings: I beheld till the wings thereof were plucked, and it was lifted up from the earth, and made stand upon the feet as a man, and a man's heart was given to it. And behold another beast, a second, like to a bear, and it raised up itself on one side, and it had three ribs in the mouth of it between the teeth of it: and they said thus unto it, Arise, devour much flesh. After this I beheld, and lo another, like a leopard, which had upon the back of it four wings of a fowl; the beast had also four heads; and dominion was given to it. (Daniel 7:1–6)

The first three beasts or Gentile nations that arise in Daniel 7 are listed in sequential order in verses 3–6; this is the order in which they arise in the last days. God uses symbolic beasts or wild animals in his word to describe Gentile nations or dominions. For example, in Daniel 8, God uses a ram and he-goat to represent Media-Persia and the king of Greece, Alexander the Great, respectively. The final three Gentile dominions that arise in the last days—the lion, the bear, and the leopard—characterized by wild animals, eventually become part of the fourth dominion, the terrible beast described in Daniel 7:7. The nations represented by the lion, bear, and leopard will also be shown to represent six heads of the final seven-headed beast, as documented in Revelation 13.[50] There is one head for the lion, one head for the bear, and four heads associated with the leopard as documented in Daniel chapter 7, bringing the total number of heads together for the three beasts to six heads in all. It will be shown that the seventh head, the wild beast or Antichrist himself, will rise last and will initially hold ten horns. The fourth and last dominion mentioned in Daniel chapter 7 will be the final Gentile power on the earth and will initially be made up of the lion, bear, and leopard together with the wild best or Antichrist, amounting to seven heads; the same seven heads and ten horns are documented in Revelation chapters 13 and 17 showing how both books are interwoven together. In time, the seventh head will arise as the Antichrist/vile man, who will then replace three of the first ten horns (leaders) and go on to rule the earth with his ten horns. This gets ahead of the story a little bit, but it will be expanded on as we study the book of Revelation. For now, it is important to understand that the beasts in total represent the seven-headed-ten-horned beast of Revelation 13 and 17 in unified form. Thus, there is no contradiction concerning the beasts of Daniel and Revelation; each scripture reference complements the other while also providing important information regarding the same final Gentile dominion. Additionally, we see how God purposely skips over the time of the one body of Jesus Christ and fast forwards to the time of the end as we detailed in chapter 2 of this work. The unified beast represented

---

[50] Revelation 13; 1–3; 17.

by the lion, bear, leopard, and Antichrist in Daniel chapter 7 will eventually make up the fourth terrible beast of Revelation 13:1–3 and Revelation 17.

Revelation 13:1–3 represents the condition on the earth at the time of the middle of the final seven years. The lion, bear and leopard are also seen by John in Revelation 13 as being in a unified state as opposed to separate in Daniel chapter 7. This will be further explained when we examine the book of Revelation. At the time of the end, the fourth beast will be coming into power and will initially consist of the three previous final-day beasts or Gentile dominions. Once again, the connection between Daniel and Revelation is clear—the two books complement and expound on the information that each record provides. One book cannot be interpreted without the other. The four beasts mentioned in Daniel 7 will be studied further in appendixes F and G. The fourth beast, and most important, will be the final Gentile kingdom on the earth and will have the Antichrist as its head. The fourth beast will be the focus of this segment and will be studied in detail. The three prior beasts mentioned in Daniel 7 give a history as to the makeup of the fourth and final beast, the focus of the chapter. The characteristics of the fourth terrible beast represent the dominion of the Antichrist/vile man. It is important to keep in mind that the lion, bear, and leopard rise to prominence and power in the last days. They are dominions, or great superpower Gentile nations, that have never been on the earth before at the time of Daniel's prophecy, and therefore they are not part of any Old Testament prophecy as many commentaries claim. God uses separate and distinct unclean animals to represent these Gentile nations in the last days.

Daniel 7 traces time from the rising of the first three beasts to the consolidation of all earthly dominion in the fourth terrible beast. The fourth beast, said to be different from all others and having great iron teeth, will devour the whole earth and waste it. The time of the fourth beast rising is not defined in these scriptures but will be understood by those alive during the last days, who will understand through various other scriptures in both Daniel and Revelation studied in this work. In any event, the millennial kingdom of Jesus Christ will follow the destruction of the fourth terrible beast. The matter is then concluded;

God will set up an everlasting dominion on the earth with his son, Jesus Christ, as King of kings and Lord of lords. Those with him will be those who fear God and accept Jesus Christ as Lord and believe in their heart that God raised him from the dead. The fourth beast's time of dominion will be short; his rule will be a short but terrible forty-two months (the final one-half of the last seven years). During these forty-two months, he will be given the ability, and in many cases supernatural ability, to destroy the earth as a direct result of man's complete rebellion against God. Consider the following:

> And then shall that Wicked be revealed, whom the Lord shall consume with the spirit of his mouth, and shall destroy with the brightness of his coming: **Even him, whose coming is after the working of Satan with all power and signs and lying wonders, And with all deceivableness of unrighteousness in them that perish; because they received not the love of the truth, that they might be saved.** And for this cause God shall send them strong delusion, that they should believe a lie: That they all might be damned who believed not the truth, but had pleasure in unrighteousness. (2 Thessalonians 2:8–12 KJV; my emphasis)

Each wild animal documented in Daniel 7 reveals specific characteristics of these latter-day dominions. These latter-day Gentile nations will be easily identified by those alive at the time of their rising. Their identification will be apparent through the animal-like characteristics God gives them in Daniel 7. They will be future beasts, powerful Gentile nations, and will fit with God's description of them as documented in Daniel 7. God uses wild animals, as opposed to domesticated animals or animals that can be trained, to indicate that these Gentile countries or governments cannot be trained or tamed. These wild Gentile dominions cannot and will not pay heed to the oracles and laws of God; thus, God considers them wild and untrainable.

The animals listed in Daniel 7 represent nations and power bases that arise in the last times. These kingdoms will be wild by nature and stand in opposition to God's laws and God's ways. In fact, there has never been a Gentile nation or government, either present or past, that has completely followed God's law and God's ways, even to this day. Individuals within all nations may get born again or follow the laws of God, but Gentile nations and their governmental leaders do not. Additionally, God mentions only Gentile nations in the Old Testament in relation to their contact with Israel—his land and people that he called. This explains why, although there have been hundreds of Gentile nations, only a handful are mentioned in the Word of God.

The three end-times Gentile beasts mentioned in Daniel 7 will eventually be unified with the fourth—the kingdom of the Antichrist. The fourth beast, which is partially made up of the first three, will eventually have dominion over God's land and people; therefore, all four beasts are mentioned here. The fourth of these latter-day beasts will be the most terrifying and will eventually be headed by the Antichrist. The time for the dominion of the fourth beast will be forty-two months as will be seen in other references related to the Antichrist. The association of these nations with God's land and people explains why God mentions only them and disregards hundreds of other Gentile nations throughout history. The only Gentile nations important to God are the nations that come into contact with his covenant land and people. The church of God—or the body of Christ, made up of Jews and Gentiles—is not part of any country but of individuals called out by God to eternal life through Jesus Christ. The church of God is a secret group called out by God and destined for eternal life with Jesus Christ. The church exists through individual members called out from every nation on the earth. The church of God will never rule or dictate a Gentile government—or, for that matter, any government. Their destiny is to rule with Christ as his body when he comes to rule the heavens and the earth as King of kings and Lord of lords. The existing Gentile nations are compared to wild animals; they are wild by nature and will remain wild until the kingdoms of the earth are forcibly given to the Lord Jesus Christ by God. Additionally, God uses horns to represent individual kings or leaders within these Gentile dominions or nations. The horns appear throughout this study of the beast and will be further explained as the study progresses.

The key portion and focus of Daniel 7 is the fourth beast, which comes into power during the last times, the final Gentile dominion on the earth. Daniel 7:7 states that the fourth beast is to be "diverse" (different) from the previous three. The word "diverse" used in this section of scripture has a Hebrew origin: "יְשַׁנֵּא." This word means "To be different from previous," and it indicates, in this context, that this fourth kingdom will be of a different kind or genus from the previous three. This indicates that the fourth kingdom, or worldly dominion, will be different from all other sovereign kingdoms that came before it throughout the history of man on the earth.

The different nature of the fourth beast will be traced to supernatural characteristics that will be associated with the kingdom of the Antichrist. The Antichrist will be a man, initially of small beginnings, who evolves into a supernatural being energized by Satan himself. The leadership of the world by a supernatural being on the earth has never occurred on the earth since the beginning of time. The supernatural nature, or differentness of the fourth beast, will be further developed as we move further into our study—especially our study of the book of Revelation. In short, the final Gentile dominion over God's land and people will be a supernatural beast from the earth energized by Satan himself and having dominion over Jerusalem and the entire earth.

The dominion of the final kingdom of the Antichrist at the time of the end will rise and consolidate the first three superpower Gentile dominions mentioned in Daniel 7—that is, the lion, bear, and leopard. This is further made clear in Revelation 13 in which all three animals are shown as one beast. In addition, the first three Gentile dominions will be coexistent and will not, at least initially, war with each other. They will also be present at the time of the rising of the fourth terrible beast. The first three dominions mentioned in Daniel 7 become a powerful foundation for the fourth terrible dominion of the Antichrist. The association and agreements developed among all four together will occur sometime in the first half of the last seven years.[51] The fourth beast will consolidate power to advance the secret plan of Satan for world dominion. Development of this topic will be further refined with scriptural references of notable events, treaties, covenants, and leagues made with the vile man. The result will be the short forty-two-month dominion of the Antichrist, who will claim to be god but will be energized by Satan. His iron and terrifying rule, allowed by God, will extend over the entire earth as a result of man's pride and arrogance.

The kingdom of the Antichrist will be different from anything that the earth has ever seen before; it will have supernatural powers. The fourth beast will gain dominion over the previous three Gentile superpowers after they submit to his *supernatural* power in the latter days. The fourth beast will supernaturally charm the first three beasts into cooperation, resulting in the relinquishing of their power during the final forty-two months. The fourth beast will then consolidate into one colossal supernatural power, which will rule the earth and break it to pieces. The fourth beast will eventually seize all power from the previous three Gentile powers and sustain world dominion for forty-two months, as documented in Revelation.[52] During the last days, the first three Gentile dominions, or wild animals, will be present in some form when the fourth beast rises. Daniel 7:7 states that "He will stamp the residue (of the first three) with his feet." Additionally, Revelation 13:2 corroborates this and reveals the fourth beast as consisting of the previous three. The one colossal beast will then assume control over the earth. Consider the following:

> "And the beast which I saw was like unto a leopard, and his feet were as the feet of a bear, and his mouth as the mouth of a lion: and the dragon gave him his power, and his seat, and great authority" (Revelation 13:2 KJV).

---

[51] Daniel 9:27.
[52] Revelation 13:5.

Revelation 13:2 reveals the fourth beast coming together as one colossal worldly power at the time of the end. The history of the lion, bear, and leopard requires an understanding of Daniel 7. Daniel 7 documents separate beasts with separate characteristics each rising during the last times. Daniel 7:7 depicts the fourth beast as stamping the residue of the previous three beasts with his feet, which indicates his conquest of the previous three. The fourth beast will then utilize the power of the previous three beasts to attain world conquest. Daniel 7 summarizes the beginnings of the lion, bear, and leopard: where they came from, their characteristics, their behavior, and their association with the last days. Revelation 13 indicates how they will come together as part of the fourth terrible beast and the result of their coming together. The three chapters: Revelation 13 and 17, and Daniel 7, complement each other and each cannot be understood without the others. God fuses these two sections of his word together and thereby provides additional information through scripture buildup, each section providing unique information without contradiction. The information gathered through scripture buildup is individually important, but the whole cannot be understood without the information from each individual part. Through this process the final picture can be assembled together as documented later in this work.

> "After this I saw in the night visions, and behold a fourth beast, dreadful and terrible, and strong exceedingly; and it had great iron teeth: it devoured and brake in pieces, and stamped the residue with the feet of it: and it was diverse from all the beasts that were before it; and it had ten horns" (Daniel 7:7).

The fourth beast arises and is described as dreadful, terrible, and exceedingly strong. This section should also be compared to Revelation chapter 13 in which God expands on the dread and strength of the fourth beast through specific events that will occur on the earth. It has great iron teeth, as compared to the others before it. The fourth beast is also the fourth kingdom that rises as depicted in

Daniel 2:40. Daniel 2 represents the whole of the Gentile dominion on the earth. The time of the Gentiles is defined as the time when the Gentiles will have rule over God's land and people on the earth. We once again apply the principle of not considering the time of the one body of Jesus Christ on the earth which are hidden in these verses. The reign of the final Gentile dominion will end with the coming of the Lord Jesus Christ to deliver Israel. The time when Israel, as a nation, learns to say "Blessed is he who comes in the name of the Lord" will mark the end of the time of the Gentiles. The nations represented as animals in Daniel 7 do not represent any one of the dominions listed in Daniel 2 but rather represent the feet and the toes of the great image of Daniel 2. The beasts of Daniel 7 are an amplification of the last days of Gentile rule on the earth. In this section, God uses the noun "horn" to indicate powerful individuals associated with kingdoms or dominions. The ten horns of verse 7 are the same ten horns of Revelation 13:1 and Revelation 17:3. They are also represented by the ten toes of the great image in Daniel 2. Consider the following:

> "And the beast that was, and is not, even he is the eighth, and is of the seven, and goeth into perdition. And the ten horns which thou sawest are ten kings, which have received no kingdom as yet; but receive power as kings one hour with the beast. These have one mind, and shall give their power and strength unto the beast. These shall make war with the Lamb, and the Lamb shall overcome them: for he is Lord of lords, and King of kings: and they that are with him are called, and chosen, and faithful" (Revelation 17:11–14 KJV)

The ten kings mentioned in both Daniel 7 and Revelation 17 are in subjection to the beast after one hour with the beast, in accordance with Revelation 17:12–13. The above scripture indicates that the ten kings, or horns, are individuals and kings or leaders. The ten kings do not appear on the scene as powerful leaders until the beast ascends to supernatural power as one raised from the dead. The phrase "*the beast had ten horns*" in Daniel 7:7 indicates that the beast already possessed the ten horns that are now part of his kingdom.

The fourth beast exhibits ten horns arising out of the earth, which take control of all the nations of the world. The strength of the beast is represented by dread and terror, exceedingly strong, and great iron teeth. God's description of awesome power needs no further explanation. In time, the fourth beast will require the previous three to surrender and become subject to the fourth. The fourth beast, a supernatural force, then crushes the residue of the first three beasts (see Daniel 7:7) and gives power to ten kings, whom he himself appoints. The supernatural beast, the ten kings (horns), and the remnant of the first three beasts will make up the fourth different wild beast. The fourth beast will then go on to ruthlessly rule the earth for the final forty-two months. God allows this through his permissive will in response to the monumental sins of the people of the earth—their rebellion against his law and their rejection of his son, Jesus Christ.

> "I considered the horns, and, behold, there came up among them another little horn, before whom there were three of the first horns plucked up by the roots: and, behold, in this horn were eyes like the eyes of man, and a mouth speaking great things" (Daniel 7:8).

Daniel considered the horns. The word "considered" in verse 8 has a Hebrew stem that means "to diligently seek after the origin of." Daniel was interested in the origin of the ten horns. Where did they come from? How did they receive their power? God answers Daniel's question in the verses that follow. The Hebrew origin of "horn" translates to "kings" or "leaders."[53] The word must be understood in accordance with its Hebrew origin. *Horn* is used frequently in references to the last days throughout scripture and is understood

---

[53] Revelation 13:12.

through previous usage in the Word of God. From the previous usage of "horn," we can get an accurate understanding of its meaning from similar usages. Consider the following:

> And as I was considering, behold, an he goat came from the west on the face of the whole earth, and touched not the ground: **and the goat had a notable horn between his eyes. And he came to the ram that had two horns,** which I had seen standing before the river, and ran unto him in the fury of his power. (Daniel 8:5–6 KJV; my emphasis)
>
> Now as he was speaking with me, I was in a deep sleep on my face toward the ground: but he touched me, and set me upright. And he said, Behold, I will make thee know what shall be in the last end of the indignation: for at the time appointed the end shall be. **The ram which thou sawest having two horns are the kings of Media and Persia. And the rough goat is the king of Grecia: and the great horn that is between his eyes is the first king.** (Daniel 8:18–21 KJV; my emphasis)

The clear meaning of the word "horn" in Daniel 7 can be gathered from the usages in Daniel 8 above. This meaning also agrees with the same word used in Revelation 17:12. The word, as it is used in this context of Gentile leaders, can be said to refer to proud, powerful leaders representing nations, kings, powers, or principalities, typically apt to shed blood and godless in their behavior and pursuit of power. The vile man is also described, initially, as *"a little horn"* in Daniel 7:8. He is designated as a little horn or a horn (man) of small beginnings. It is also stated in verse 8 that another *horn* comes up (rises up) among the first ten horns. This latter horn subdues three of the first ten horns and, in time, increases in strength. The interpretation of this *horn* is also noted in verse 24. The *"little horn"*, the Antichrist, or the horn of small beginnings, is also documented in Daniel 11:21–24. Consider the following:

> And in his estate shall stand up a **vile person**,(the little horn) to whom they shall not give the honour of the kingdom: but he shall come in peaceably (a time of careless security), and obtain the kingdom by flatteries. And with the arms of a flood shall they be overflown from before him, and shall be broken; yea, also the prince of the covenant. And after the league made with him he shall work deceitfully: **for he shall come up, and shall become strong with a small people.** He shall enter peaceably even upon the fattest places of the province; and he shall do that which his fathers have not done, nor his fathers' fathers; he shall scatter among them the prey, and spoil, and riches: yea, and he shall forecast his devices against the strong holds, even for a time. (Daniel 11:21–24 KJV; my emphasis)

Daniel 7:8 further states the little horn will replace or pluck up three of the first horns by the roots. The little horn begins as a man of small beginnings and then grows in strength. The little horn conquers or replaces three of the first ten horns by the roots, revealing discord among the ten horns. In any event, the beast or little horn will be given power over the earth for forty-two months, as stated in Daniel 7:25. It appears that the three horns that are replaced by the little horn are kings or leaders in and around Israel. The three appear to be associated with three areas conquered by the vile man as documented in in Daniel 8: the south, the east, and the pleasant land. Daniel 7:8 goes on to say that the little horn becomes a man speaking great things. The great things that he speaks are documented in several other scriptures; most notably, he declares himself god after his supernatural resurrection.[54] Daniel 7:8 also states, "*He has eyes like the eyes of a man,*" indicating that he, initially at least, is a mortal man. The mention of eyes in this verse also indicates that he has plans and keen understanding as he schemes for world dominion.

> I beheld till the thrones were cast down, and the Ancient of days did sit, whose garment was white as snow, and the hair of his head like the pure wool: his throne was like the fiery flame, and his wheels as burning fire. A fiery stream issued and came forth from before him: thousand thousands ministered unto him, and ten thousand times ten thousand stood before him: the judgment was set, and the books were opened. I beheld then because of the voice of the great words which the horn spake: I beheld even till the beast was slain, and his body destroyed, and given to the burning flame. (Daniel 7:9–11)

Daniel, by revelation, is given the description of the great judgment of our great God, which comes after the destruction of the beast and after the last seven years. These verses reinforce the fact that these scriptures in Daniel are descriptive of the last days of man's rule on earth. The description of God's judgment in this section is consistent with other descriptions of God as the glorious judge and creator of the earth. His judgment is set, and the books were opened. The first one to be judged is the vile man or the Antichrist. The Antichrist is thrown bodily into the lake of fire to be burned and be in torment forever and ever. From the book of Revelation, we know that the false prophet, not mentioned in this verse, is also thrown into the lake of fire with the vile man.[55] The judgment scene depicted here is the first of two great judgment scenes in God's Word:

---

[54] See verses 11, 20, 25; 8:11; 11:36–37; 2 Thessalonians 2:3–4; Revelation 13:5–6.
[55] Revelation 19:20.

the resurrection of the just and the resurrection of the unjust. The resurrection of the unjust, also known as the great white throne judgment, occurs some one thousand years after the resurrection of the just.

Daniel continues to describe and document his long-duration vision concerning the beast that he received from the angel. The judgment scenes are explained through these verses once again, associating Daniel's vision with the last days. The vision corroborates several other scriptures related to this event. Consider associated verses in Revelation 19:

> And I saw heaven opened, and behold a white horse; and he that sat upon him was called Faithful and True, and in righteousness he doth judge and make war. His eyes were as a flame of fire, and on his head were many crowns; and he had a name written, that no man knew, but he himself.
> And he was clothed with a vesture dipped in blood: and his name is called The Word of God. And the armies which were in heaven followed him upon white horses, clothed in fine linen, white and clean. And out of his mouth goeth a sharp sword, that with it he should smite the nations: and he shall rule them with a rod of iron: and he treadeth the winepress of the fierceness and wrath of Almighty God. And he hath on his vesture and on his thigh a name written, KING OF KINGS, AND LORD OF LORDS. And I saw an angel standing in the sun; and he cried with a loud voice, saying to all the fowls that fly in the midst of heaven, Come and gather yourselves together unto the supper of the great God; That ye may eat the flesh of kings, and the flesh of captains, and the flesh of mighty men, and the flesh of horses, and of them that sit on them, and

the flesh of all men, both free and bond, both small and great. **And I saw the beast, and the kings of the earth, and their armies, gathered together to make war against him that sat on the horse, and against his army. And the beast was taken, and with him the false prophet that wrought miracles before him, with which he deceived them that had received the mark of the beast, and them that worshipped his image. These both were cast alive into a lake of fire burning with brimstone.** And the remnant were slain with the sword of him that sat upon the horse, which sword proceeded out of his mouth: and all the fowls were filled with their flesh. (Revelation 19:11–21 KJV; my emphasis)

Revelation 19 describes the same event documented in Daniel 7, but in more detail. John's vision in Revelation does not contradict but adds additional information to Daniel's vision. The beast exists until the very end—that is, the end of the last seven years. He is then judged and destroyed at the coming of (the Revelation of) the Lord Jesus Christ with the saints and heavenly forces. Jesus Christ destroys the beast with the brightness of his coming to the earth to take his rightful place. Consider the following:

For the mystery of iniquity doth already work: only he who now letteth will let, until he be taken out of the way. **And then shall that Wicked be revealed, whom the Lord shall consume with the spirit of his mouth, and shall destroy with the brightness of his coming: Even him, whose coming is after the working of Satan with all power and signs and lying wonders, And with all deceivableness of unrighteousness in them that perish; because they received not the love of the truth, that they might be saved.** And for this cause God shall send them strong delusion, that they should believe a lie: That they all might be damned who believed not the truth, but had pleasure in unrighteousness. (2 Thessalonians 2:7–12 KJV; my emphasis)

The descriptions in these verses and the judgment scenes are self-descriptive and need no interpretation by man. These descriptions are given for the reader to read and be in awe of the glory and power of God and of his son, Jesus Christ. Daniel 7:11 states that the horn speaks great words. The great words are words of blasphemy against God and the Holy Spirit. Through these words, the vile man commits the unforgiveable sin and is thrown bodily into the lake of fire prepared for Satan and his angels. Consider the following:

"As concerning the rest of the beasts, they had their dominion taken away: yet their lives were prolonged for a season and time. I saw in the night visions, and, behold, one like the Son of man came with the clouds of heaven, and came to the Ancient of days, and they brought him near before him. And there was given him dominion, and glory, and a kingdom, that all people, nations, and languages, should serve him: his dominion is an everlasting dominion, which shall not pass away, and his kingdom that which shall not be destroyed" (Daniel 7:12–14).

Daniel 7.12 informs us that the rest of the beasts—the bear, the lion, and the leopard—had their dominion or power taken away but could exist for a season and a time. Stated another way, the prior Gentile superpowers, before the rising of the beast, will have all their power taken away but could exist as sovereign countries for a season and a time. The word "time" in verse 12 is the same word, in its inflected form, used for the time period of one year in Daniel 7:25. It is reasonable to assume that the other Gentile dominions—the lion, bear, and leopard—will be allowed to exist after the destruction of the beast but will be without power for what seems to be a one-year period. It is reasonable to assume that the temple plans given to Ezekiel by God and documented in Ezekiel 40–48 will now, at the end of the final seven-year period, be implemented. The year following the destruction of the beast may then be the acceptable year of the Lord—the year that the Lord provides recompense or the judgment of the nations. The acceptable year of the Lord will only be fully understood at the time of the end. Consider the following verses in which the acceptable year is always mentioned along with the Lord's vengeance:

> For it is the day of the **LORD'S vengeance, and the year of recompences** for the controversy of Zion. And the streams thereof shall be turned into pitch, and the dust thereof into brimstone, and the land thereof shall become burning pitch. The Spirit of the Lord GOD is upon me; because the LORD hath anointed me to preach good tidings unto the meek; he hath sent me to bind up the brokenhearted, to proclaim liberty to the captives, and the opening of the prison to them that are bound. (Isaiah 34:8–9 KJV; my emphasis)
>
> To proclaim the acceptable year of the LORD, and the day of vengeance of our God; to comfort all that mourn … (Isaiah 61:1–2 KJV)
>
> **To me belongeth vengeance, and recompence**; their foot shall slide in due time: for the day of their calamity is at hand, and the things that shall come upon them make haste.
>
> For the LORD shall judge his people, and repent himself for his servants, when he seeth that their power is gone, and there is none shut up, or left. (Deuteronomy 32:35–36 KJV; my emphasis)

> I have trodden the winepress alone; and of the people there was none with me: for I will tread them in mine anger, and trample them in my fury; and their blood shall be sprinkled upon my garments, and I will stain all my raiment. **For the day of vengeance is in mine heart, and the year of my redeemed is come.** And I looked, and there was none to help; and I wondered that there was none to uphold: therefore mine own arm brought salvation unto me; and my fury, it upheld me. (Isaiah 63:3–5 KJV; my emphasis)

The scripture does not go into detail about how the three Gentile kingdoms have their power taken away, but they will be powerless during this time. It is also reasonable to assume that all other nations still intact after the final forty-two months also will have their power taken away as the Lord Jesus Christ will now rule as King of kings and Lord of lords. All their weapons of war will be powerless. Daniel 7:13 goes on to describe the setting up of the kingdom of our Lord and Savior, Jesus Christ, as King of kings and Lord of lords.[56] The setting up of the Lord's everlasting kingdom will follow immediately after the destruction of Antichrist. The Lord comes in the same way he was taken up, but this time he comes to the earth in glory and power. The rulership and everlasting dominion of the earth has now been transferred to Christ, which has been given to him by God. The glorious scenes in these verses fulfill several prophecies in both the Old and New Testaments. Consider the following:

> When they therefore were come together, they asked of him, saying, Lord, wilt thou at this time restore again the kingdom to Israel? And he said unto them, It is not for you to know the

---

[56] See Daniel 7:18, 27; 2:35, 44; 4:3; 6;26; Psalms 45:6; 145:13; 146:10; Isaiah 9:7; Obadiah 21; Micah 4:7; Luke 1:33; John 12:34; and Hebrews 1:8; also read Psalm 2 and Revelation 20.

times or the seasons, which the Father hath put in his own power. But ye shall receive power, after that the Holy Ghost is come upon you: and ye shall be witnesses unto me both in Jerusalem, and in all Judaea, and in Samaria, and unto the uttermost part of the earth. **And when he had spoken these things, while they beheld, he was taken up; and a cloud received him out of their sight. And while they looked stedfastly toward heaven as he went up, behold, two men stood by them in white apparel; Which also said, Ye men of Galilee, why stand ye gazing up into heaven? this same Jesus, which is taken up from you into heaven, shall so come in like manner as ye have seen him go into heaven**. (Acts 1:6–11 KJV; my emphasis)

Why do the heathen rage, and the people imagine a vain thing? The kings of the earth set themselves, and the rulers take counsel together, against the LORD, and against his anointed, saying, Let us break their bands asunder, and cast away their cords from us. He that sitteth in the heavens shall laugh: the Lord shall have them in derision. **Then shall he speak unto them in his wrath, and vex them in his sore displeasure. Yet have I set my king upon my holy hill of Zion. I will declare the decree: the LORD hath said unto me, Thou art my Son; this day have I begotten thee. Ask of me, and I shall give thee the heathen for thine inheritance, and the uttermost parts of the earth for thy possession. Thou shalt break them with a rod of iron; thou shalt dash them in pieces like a potter's vessel.** Be wise now therefore, O ye kings: be instructed, ye judges of the earth. Serve the LORD with fear, and rejoice with trembling. Kiss the Son, lest he be angry, and ye perish from the way, when his wrath is kindled but a little. Blessed are all they that put their trust in him. (Psalm 2:1–12 KJV; my emphasis)

The Angel's Interpretation of the Chapter 7 Vision

"I Daniel was grieved in my spirit in the midst of my body, and the visions of my head troubled me. I came near unto one of them that stood by, and asked him the truth of all this. **So he told me, and made me know the interpretation of the things. These great beasts, which are four, are four kings, which shall arise out of the earth. But the saints of the most High shall take the kingdom, and possess the kingdom for ever, even for ever and ever**" (Daniel 7:15–18; my emphasis).

Daniel asks the angel for the interpretation of the vision that he witnessed in the first part of chapter 7. Many times, God-fearing men attempt to interpret the Word of God based on their own imaginations and compelled by their own convictions. Daniel does not rely on his own understanding but goes to the source for the interpretation. The angel first interprets the three beasts—the lion, bear, and leopard—and then goes on to a more detailed description of the fourth terrible beast. The angel explains that the kings represent Gentile nations that possess extraordinary warlike powers. These are not the only Gentile nations, but they will be the strongest of Gentile nations at the time of the end. These four beasts will rise on the earth during the last days. As stated earlier, these beasts cannot be any previous kingdoms mentioned in Daniel or any other Old Testament scripture, since they are separate and distinct animals and are associated with the last days. Previous scripture reveals that these nations will be contemporary with the beast and will eventually form the foundation for the Antichrist's world domination. Daniel 7:18, goes on to direct our attention to the most important fact in the chapter—that the everlasting kingdom of the Lord Jesus Christ will be on earth following the destruction of the fourth terrible beast. Consider the following:

> Then I would know the truth of the fourth beast, which was diverse from all the others, exceeding dreadful, whose teeth were of iron, and his nails of brass; which devoured, brake in pieces, and stamped the residue with his feet; And of the ten horns that were in his head, and of the other which came up, and before whom three fell; even of that horn that had eyes, and a mouth that spake very great things, whose look was more stout than his fellows. I beheld, and the same horn made war with the saints, and prevailed against them; Until the Ancient of days came, and judgment was given to the saints of the most High; and the time came that the saints possessed the kingdom. Thus he said, The fourth beast shall be the fourth kingdom upon earth, which shall be diverse from all kingdoms, and shall devour the whole earth, and shall tread it down, and break it in pieces. And the ten horns out of this kingdom are ten kings that shall arise: and another shall rise after them; and he shall be diverse from the first, and he shall subdue three kings. And he shall speak great words against the most High, and shall wear out the saints of the most High, and think to change times and laws: and they shall be given into his hand until a time and times and the dividing of time. But the judgment shall sit, and they shall take away his dominion, to consume and to destroy it unto the end. And the kingdom and dominion, and the greatness of the kingdom under the whole

> heaven, shall be given to the people of the saints of the most High, whose kingdom is an everlasting kingdom, and all dominions shall serve and obey him. (Daniel 7:19–27; my emphasis)

Daniel 7:19–27 is the interpretation and amplification of the fourth terrible beast on the earth, as mentioned earlier in the chapter. God uses seven verses in this section to describe the terrible beast, compared to only one verse describing the previous three. In this way, God indicates the importance of the fourth terrible beast, the most important of the beasts mentioned in the chapter. The previous three beasts are mentioned regarding their relation to the fourth beast; they add information concerning the origin of the fourth beast. The information details how the fourth beast came to be and where the fourth got its power—that is, initially from the previous three. Verse 19 states again that the fourth latter-day beast will be diverse or different from all other previous Gentile kingdoms or dominions on the earth. Daniel describes the beast as being "exceedingly dreadful" or dreadful beyond belief. The fourth beast stamps the residue (what is left of the previous three beasts) with his feet, indicating how all the earth will be put under the feet of the fourth beast, who will have total dominion for a time, and times, and half a time—or one year, plus two years, plus half a year—that is, forty-two months. Note also how the fourth beast stamps the residue of the previous beasts with his feet. Form Revelation 13.2 we know that the feet of the final terrible beast were the feet of a bear. It is reasonable to assume that whatever Gentile nation is represented by the bear—the feet of Revelation 13.2—will be utilized by the beast to destroy the earth. These scriptures agree with Revelation 13:5. The uniqueness of the fourth beast stems from the beast being supernatural in nature.

The differentness of the fourth beast is related to the fourth beast's ability to operate in the supernatural realm in the sight of men. An earthly beast or kingdom such as this has never been on the earth before, and therefore God labels this Gentile kingdom "*diverse*" or different from all previous kingdoms.

Daniel 7:24 goes on to describe and interpret the ten horns, which are part of the final beast, as ten kings that shall arise in the last days. Recall that the ten kings, or horns, are also documented in Revelation 17 as receiving power after one hour with the beast. The ten horns give their power to the beast and are instrumental in war with the lamb and shall destroy the whore of Revelation 17.[57] The destruction of "*Mystery Babylon*" is further described in Revelation 18. In Daniel chapter 7, another horn is then noted to arise in verse 24 and subdue three kings or leaders, presumably through force or intrigue. The last horn or king that arises is noted to be different from the other ten, indicating supernatural abilities. It is this latter horn, which is diverse from the others, that will provide supernatural capabilities and be the focus of power. The latter horn also speaks great words or blasphemies against God, declaring himself as divine. The latter horn is the vile man or the Antichrist and is in supernatural form. He will rise as a corrupt leader in mortal form. Eventually, he will rule over the entire earth for forty-two months. Revelation 13 also documents a second beast, a false prophet, who rises after the first and is once again supernatural in nature but is in unison with the first. Although Daniel 7 is silent concerning the second beast or false prophet, Revelation 13 is clear concerning his existence and behavior.[58] Whereas the first beast is political in nature, the second beast or the false prophet, will be religious in nature. The false prophet will be responsible for creating a universal idolatrous system of worship in the final forty-two months.[59] The false prophet will be studied as part of Revelation 13. The final wild beast and the false prophet, which will both be energized by Satan and will have supernatural characteristics, now become the center of power for the final terrible kingdom on the earth. It is important to note that these two individuals, the wild beast and the false prophet, will be individual men supernaturally energized by Satan. It will be these

---

[57] Revelation 17:12.
[58] Revelation 13:11–18.
[59] Revelation 13:11–15; 2 Thessalonians 7–11; Revelation 19:20.

two men who will be permitted to go and deceive the whole earth for forty-two months.

Consider the following:

> "Even him, whose coming is after the working of Satan with all power and signs and lying wonders, And with all deceivableness of unrighteousness in them that perish; because they received not the love of the truth, that they might be saved. And for this cause God shall send them strong delusion, that they should believe a lie: That they all might be damned who believed not the truth, but had pleasure in unrighteousness" (2 Thessalonians 2:9–12 KJV).

Daniel 7:8 contains the first mention of the title "*little horn*"—the label given to Antichrist or the vile man. The horns represent kings or leaders who arise in the last days. From the scripture, these ten leaders will arise in and around the Middle East and have a strong relationship with the vile man. The little horn or vile man will begin as a man of small beginnings and the leader of a small people.[60] But through political sharpness, he will increase in strength and dominance. His power will not be his own, but he will be assisted by powerful nations.[61] As his power grows, he begins his worldly conquest by defeating three of the first ten horns or leaders. The three kings he replaces are kings of the south, the east, and the pleasant land.[62] The full understanding of the dynamics of the ten kings, who they are, and how they are replaced will be fully understood at the time of the end and the time of fulfillment. For now, it is important to understand that they will be associated with the wild beast or vile man and will serve to further the vile man's ambitions. Daniel 11:23 documents the vile man's small beginnings as the leader of a small

---

[60] Daniel 11:23.
[61] Daniel 8:24.
[62] Daniel 8:9; 11.

people—hence the title *"little horn."* Although his beginnings are small, he quickly increases in power and strength in an astonishing meteoritic rise to power. All this occurs as the world watches with a somewhat helpless gaze. It is the little horn who will rise during the finals seven years, of which, it is the final 3.5 years which constitute Jacob's trouble.

During the final 3.5 years, the beast or little horn will declare himself God. His mouth will be the mouth that speaks "great things" (Daniel 7:8, 20). His transformation into the wild supernatural beast occurs after the middle of the seventieth seven and will be marked by a miraculous satanic resurrection. The little horn will make war with those who sanctify God in their hearts and will prevail against them (v. 21). Verse 25 states that the little horn will also change times and laws; the world and the kingdoms thereof being given into his hand for a time, times, and the dividing of time—3.5 years.

The final forty-two-month period will constitute Satan's last-ditch effort to usurp God's authority. Satan, understanding from scripture that his time is short, will energize the supernatural beast and attempt to usurp God's authority. God allows the deception of Satan to be virtually irresistible, led by legions of deceiving spirits. God allows deception through his permissive will as a result of mankind's complete rejection of God and his son, Jesus Christ.

The last seven-year reality depicted in Daniel is vividly portrayed in this work and will follow exactly as documented in the written Word of God. The two 3.5-year periods or the two separate careers of the beast make up the seventieth week of years of Daniel's prophecy of seventy sevens.[63] After the seven years, the three initial beasts listed in Daniel 7 1–6 will be allowed to continue without power, dominion, or weapons, only for a season and a time.[64]

The key to an accurate understanding of the career of the beast will be to trace the evolution of the beast through Daniel and Revelation, as well as other key scriptures. The rise of the beast as the Antichrist will be undetected by the vast majority and will come

---

[63] See Daniel 9:24–27.
[64] Daniel 7:12.

upon the earth as surprisingly as the days of Noah and the flood. Only a keen understanding of what to look for from the Word of God will allow one to navigate through and identify the future wild beast. The reader will at once observe the cohesiveness and similarities of all scriptures taken together through scripture buildup. The man of small beginnings, the little horn, begins his ascent during the first half of the last seven years. He increases in power; he associates with, and begins his conquest of, foes, propelling a hidden agenda of world conquest. At the middle of the seventieth week, he sets up the abomination that causes desolation—that is, destruction at the holy place in Jerusalem. At or about the time of the middle of the seven years, the beast is assassinated and miraculously comes back from the dead.[65] After his satanic resurrection, he becomes the seventh head of the supernatural beast. The wild beast then goes on to deceive the world. Legions of willing evil spiritual agents will assist him and make his final earthly conquest of the earth different (by way of their supernatural quality) from all others that were previously on the earth.[66]

Section 2, Reference 4: Attributes Associated with the Antichrist (Daniel 7:1–27)

Daniel 7:1–6 tells us that the last days will feature three powerful Gentile dominions represented as beasts—a lion, a bear, and a leopard with four heads—will arise in the last days before the fourth terrible beast. It is stated that these three *shall arise during the last time.* They individually will arise in the last days as superpower Gentile dominions or governments. The three beasts will be powerful nations on the earth, each having characteristics associated with the representative animal of each Gentile nation in Daniel 7. God's people, at the time of the end, will recognize and understand the nations at their rising through scriptural characteristics documented in Daniel 7. These nations will arise and fulfill the scripture related to them, probably beginning some fifty to one hundred years before

---

[65] Revelation 13:3; 17:8–13.
[66] 2 Thessalonians 2:4.

the initiation of the last seven years. The three will not attack one another but will be present at the rising of the fourth terrible beast. The fourth beast will conquer and consolidate these three and use them as his power base for world dominion. The fourth beast will provide the seventh head, the vile man, being then equivalent to the seven-headed beast in Revelation 13 and 17.

Daniel 7:7 states that the fourth terrible beast or the kingdom of the Antichrist will arise after the three beasts of Daniel 7:1–6. The fourth beast is also the final Gentile dominion to rule the earth and relates to the feet and toes of the image portrayed in Daniel 2. The first three beasts in Daniel 7 are associated in time with the fourth terrible beast. The ten toes represent the ten kings or horns of the fourth terrible beast. The fourth beast of Daniel 7 will have great iron teeth, which represent its ability to kill and destroy and conquer the earth. The fourth kingdom will also be as strong as iron but as fragile as clay, indicating strong nations together with weak nations. The various peoples will not mingle or cleave together with one another but will associate only as per world dominion. [67] The wild beast will eventually be the ruler of this fourth kingdom and conquers the world. The fourth latter-day beast will be different or diverse from all previous dominions on the earth. The statement reveals the supernatural abilities of the beast to conquer. The fourth beast will have ten horns, which represent ten contemporaneous kings or rulers that will receive power after one hour with the beast.[68] It is probable that the ten kings will receive their power at the same time the beast is miraculously resurrected.

Daniel originally saw ten horns or kings. In Daniel 7:8, he sees a little horn coming up and replacing three of the first ten. The little horn will arise sometime after the rise to power of first ten kings. Examination of the little horn, from other related passages, identifies him as the Antichrist or the vile man. He is described as a little horn due to his small beginnings or his beginning with a small group of

---

[67] Daniel 2:40–44.
[68] Daniel 11:36; 2 Thessalonians 2:4; Revelation 13:5, 6; 17:12.

people.[69] The little horn will be a man supernaturally energized and speaking very great things. Other scriptures make clear that the great things he speaks are blasphemies against God and his declaration of himself to be God while also changing laws and times.[70]

Daniel 7:9–10 states that the dominion of the Antichrist will be immediately followed by the setting up of the millennial kingdom of Christ as King of kings and Lord of lords. For this reason, the fourth latter-day beast is associated with the last days of man's rule on earth—the end of the times of the Gentiles.[71] The fourth latter-day beast is present in time just before the judgment of God and the first resurrection: the resurrection of the just.[72]

Daniel 7:11 states that the beast will be slain and thrown into a burning fire. The same fate of the beast is listed in the book of Thessalonians, as well as the book of Revelation. It will be the Lord Jesus Christ that will destroy the beast with the brightness of his coming for Israel. [73] The beast will be thrown bodily into the lake of fire since he will have already suffered the first death.

In Daniel 7:12, the millennial kingdom of Jesus Christ begins with the destruction of the beast, the false prophet, and the confederate nations.[74] God will give the dominion and rulership over the nations and Israel to the Lord Jesus Christ. The rulership of Jesus Christ over Israel and the nations fulfills the promises made to Abraham, Isaac, and Jacob, specifically listed in Daniel 9:24. The previous three beasts or Gentile nations—the lion, bear, and leopard—will be allowed to exist for a season and a time but without power.

Daniel 7:23–25 tells us that the fourth latter-day beast will be different (because of supernatural abilities) from all previous beasts and dominions that have been on the earth. The fourth terrible beast will be the fourth prevailing kingdom to have rule over the entire earth. The fourth latter-day beast also represents the feet and toes of

---

[69] See Daniel 11:23; 8:9.
[70] Daniel 7:25; Revelation 13; 2 Thessalonians 2:3–4.
[71] Daniel 2:34, 44.
[72] John 5:25–29.
[73] 2 Thessalonians 2:8; Revelation 19:20.
[74] Revelation 20:1–4; Psalm 2.

the great image in Daniel 2.[75] The ten horns are ten kings that shall arise during the time of the fourth latter-day beast. Out of the ten horns, a "*little horn*" shall arise and shall be different from the previous ten. The last little horn represents the Antichrist—a being who will have supernatural ability and will be miraculously resurrected from the dead, deceiving the entire world. God uses horns to represent strong, powerful leaders. The "*little horn*" or vile man shall arise and subdue three of the first ten kings or representatives of their respective nations. The "*little horn*" shall speak great words and declare himself to be God. He shall also persecute the saints of God and will have dominion for three and one-half years or forty-two months.

Daniel 7:26–27 states that it will be the Lord Jesus Christ who will destroy the beast with the brightness of his coming for Israel. The church of the body of Christ will have previously been raptured. [76]

In summary, the following key informational points can be gathered from section II, reference 4:

1. The fourth latter-day beast or kingdom headed by the Antichrist listed as part of the latter day beasts of Daniel chapter 7 will be dreadful, terrible, and extremely strong; with great iron teeth and nails of brass; and it will devour, stamp, and break into pieces the residue of the three contemporary beasts, or nations—the lion, bear, and leopard (v. 7).
2. The fourth latter-day beast will be different from all previous Gentile nations (dominions, kingdoms) that preceded it on the earth. The fourth beast, headed by the Antichrist, will have supernatural characteristics after its miraculous resurrection not ever seen on the earth before; hence it shall be different (v. 7).
3. The beast will have ten horns—representative kings or rulers appointed by the beast. The Antichrist will arise as a "little horn" and will replace or subdue three of the first ten

---

[75] Daniel 2:40–44.
[76] 2 Thessalonians 2:8–10; Revelation 19:20.

horns. The horns he replaces are identified as those of the south, the east, and the pleasant land. (vv. 7, 8).
4. The "little horn" will declare himself God and speak blasphemies against God and his people and be allowed to rule, deceive, and destroy for forty-two months (vv. 8, 25).[77]
5. The beast, Antichrist, or vile man will be destroyed by the Lord Jesus Christ at the end of the final forty-two months of the seventieth seven-year period. The beast will be destroyed by the brightness of the coming of the Lord Jesus Christ, who will set up his millennial kingdom immediately after the destruction of the beast. The beast will then be judged by God and thrown into the lake of fire forever and ever (vv. 11–14, 27).[78]
6. The Antichrist or *"little horn"* will make war with the saints of the Most High and will prevail against them. The destruction of the nations and the beast's hatred of the true God and God's people will begin in earnest during the midst (middle) of the seventieth week and continue for the final forty-two months (vv. 19, 21, 23, 25).[79]
7. The Antichrist will wear out the saints of the Most High and will change times and laws, including the covenant law of God given through Moses and the prophets. He will do this according to his will for time, times, and half of time—three and one-half years (v. 25).[80]

Reference 5: Daniel 8:1–27: "The King of Fierce Countenance", The Gentile Kingdoms in General and the Twenty-Three Hundred Day Vision

The structure of Daniel 8 (introversion and extended alternation) is as follows:

---

[77] Daniel 7:7, 19–20, 24; Daniel 8:9.
[78] Daniel 7:11; 2 Thessalonians 2:8; Revelation 19:20.
[79] Daniel 7:21; 9:27; 11:31–35.
[80] Daniel 7:25; 11:31–36.

THE LAST DAYS AND THE VILE MAN OF DANIEL

A. v. 1: the king; time
B. vv. 1–2: the vision; prophecy
  a) vv. 3–4: ram
    b) v. 5: he-goat
      c) vv. 5–7: great horn
        d) v. 8: great horn broken
          e) v. 8: four horns
            f) v. 9: little horn arises (future prophecy)
              g) vv. 10–12: little horn practices and prospers (future prophecy)
                h) vv. 13–15: supernatural appearance; mighty warrior: time (future prophecy)
                  i) vv. 16–17: vision understood; appearance not understood (future prophecy)

B. vv. 18–19: the vision; interpretation
  a) v. 20: ram
    b) v. 21: he-goat
      c) v. 21: great horn
        d) v. 22: great horn broken
          e) v. 22: four horns
            f) vv. 23–24; little horn arises (future prophecy)
              g) vv. 24–25; little horn practices and prospers (future prophecy)
                h) v. 26; supernatural appearance; mighty warrior: time (future prophecy)
                  i) vv. 26–27; vision understood; appearance not understood (future prophecy)

A. v. 27: the king; his business

    Daniel 8; 1–27:
    1 In the third year of the reign of king Belshazzar a vision appeared unto me, even unto

me Daniel, after that which appeared unto me at the first. And I saw in a vision; and it came to pass, when I saw, that I was at Shushan in the palace, which is in the province of Elam; and I saw in a vision, and I was by the river of Ulai. Then I lifted up mine eyes, and saw, and, behold, there stood before the river a ram which had two horns: and the two horns were high; but one was higher than the other, and the higher came up last. I saw the ram pushing westward, and northward, and southward; so that no beasts might stand before him, neither was there any that could deliver out of his hand; but he did according to his will, and became great. And as I was considering, behold, an he goat came from the west on the face of the whole earth, and touched not the ground: and the goat had a notable horn between his eyes. And he came to the ram that had two horns, which I had seen standing before the river, and ran unto him in the fury of his power. And I saw him come close unto the ram, and he was moved with choler against him, and smote the ram, and brake his two horns: and there was no power in the ram to stand before him, but he cast him down to the ground, and stamped upon him: and there was none that could deliver the ram out of his hand. Therefore, the he goat waxed very great: and when he was strong, the great horn was broken; and for it came up four notable ones toward the four winds of heaven. **And out of one of them came forth a little horn, which waxed exceeding great, toward the south, and toward the east, and toward the pleasant land. And it waxed great, even to the host of heaven; and it cast down some of the host and of the stars to the ground, and stamped upon them.**

THE LAST DAYS AND THE VILE MAN OF DANIEL

Yea, he magnified himself even to the prince of the host, and by him the daily sacrifice was taken away, and the place of his sanctuary was cast down. And an host was given him against the daily sacrifice by reason of transgression, and it cast down the truth to the ground; and it practiced, and prospered. Then I heard one saint speaking, and another saint said unto that certain saint which spake, how long shall be the vision concerning the daily sacrifice, and the transgression of desolation, to give both the sanctuary and the host to be trodden under foot? And he said unto me, Unto two thousand and three hundred days; then shall the sanctuary be cleansed. And it came to pass, when I, even I Daniel, had seen the vision, and sought for the meaning, then, behold, there stood before me as the appearance of a man. And I heard a man's voice between the banks of Ulai, which called, and said, Gabriel, make this man to understand the vision. So he came near where I stood: and when he came, I was afraid, and fell upon my face: but he said unto me, Understand, O son of man: for at the time of the end shall be the vision. And he said, Behold, I will make thee know what shall be in the last end of the indignation: for at the time appointed the end shall be. The ram which thou sawest having two horns are the kings of Media and Persia. And the rough goat is the king of Grecia: and the great horn that is between his eyes is the first king. Now that being broken, whereas four stood up for it, four kingdoms shall stand up out of the nation, but not in his power. **And in the latter time of their kingdom, when the transgressors are come to the full, a king of fierce countenance, and understanding dark**

sentences, shall stand up. And his power shall be mighty, but not by his own power: and he shall destroy wonderfully, and shall prosper, and practice, and shall destroy the mighty and the holy people. And through his policy also he shall cause craft to prosper in his hand; and he shall magnify himself in his heart, and by peace shall destroy many: he shall also stand up against the Prince of princes; but he shall be broken without hand. And the vision of the evening and the morning which was told is true: wherefore shut thou up the vision; for it shall be for many days. And I Daniel fainted, and was sick certain days; afterward I rose up, and did the king's business; and I was astonished at the vision, but none understood it. (Daniel 8:1–27; my emphasis)

Reference 5: Daniel 8:1–27; Commentary: "The King of Fierce Countenance", The Twenty-Three-Hundred-Day Appearance.

Daniel begins the Hebrew section of the prophecy given to him by signifying the interrelationship between historical Gentile dominions and the final Gentile dominion that rises during the last time. It will be this final Gentile dominion which rises in the last time that will mark the end of Gentile rulership of the world. The final Gentile dominion will also mark the time of the deliverance of the set-apart Jews—the nation that will be called by God. The focus of chapter is the final Gentile dominion, the kingdom of the Antichrist, and the events leading up to the final days. The perspective of time relates the Jews' future from Daniel's time up to and including the last days but skipping over the time of the mystery of the one body of Christ. In contrast to chapter seven, which focused on the last kingdoms or dominions of the Gentiles in the last days, chapter eight focuses on God's land and people in the last days—Israel. The previous chapters of Daniel (Daniel 1–7) were written in Aramaic, indicating their focus on the Gentiles. Daniel 8–12 focuses on God's final dealings with Israel—God's land and God's people. Although the focus is Israel, the entire world is affected, and the day in which natural man is the judge on the earth ends abruptly.

Daniel is informed that the Antichrist will be a king of fierce countenance and goes on to describe the same individual from a different vantage point while also providing additional information about the same man (beast) from chapter 7. In Daniel chapter 8 the origin of Antichrist is traced back to the four dominions remaining after the fall of Alexander the Great. Alexander's residual four dominions are ancient history, but out of one of them, in the latter days, the Antichrist emerges. Once again, God skips over thousands of years to focus on the point of the chapter—the Antichrist and Israel's time of deliverance. Daniel pinpoints the origin, or rising, of the Antichrist to one of Alexander's four dominions that remained after the death of Alexander. The connection hints that the Antichrist will be the next to rule over the earth as one man much the same as Alexander the Great. In this manner, God pieces together an accurate picture of the same individual building up information from another viewpoint and from another area of scripture.

In Daniel chapter 8 Daniel sees another vision that is like the vision of chapter 7. Daniel goes on to describe the vision of two animals—a ram and a he-goat—that aggressively attack one another. The animals represent Gentile kingdoms or dominions. God also symbolizes leaders of countries by the term "horns." The two animals of Daniel 8 are separate and distinct from the animals' representative of kingdoms and dominions in Daniel 7: the lion, the bear, and the leopard. The Gentile nations of chapter 7 are necessarily linked to the last days. The ram and the he-goat of chapter 8 are historical dominions and were the next Gentile dominions to rise after the fall of Nebuchadnezzar around 500 BC. The chapter 8 Gentile dominions are historical and are identified in chapter 8 to be Media-Persia, and the dominion of Alexander the Great. This also allows God to associate wild animals with Gentile kingdoms which can now shed light on the lion, bear, and leopard of Daniel chapter 7 as great Gentile nations who have yet to arise. The final kingdom mentioned (Daniel 8:9) is that of the Antichrist, who is identified in this chapter as the little horn or a horn of small beginnings. The little horn emerges from one of the four residual dominions of Alexander's kingdom, but it does so in the last days thousands of years after the fall of Alexander, once again skipping over the time of the Mystery of the one body of Christ on earth. Both chapters 7 and 8 focus on the little horn, who will now, along with the fate of Daniel's people; Israel, become the focus of the rest of the prophecy given to Daniel. Chapter 7 and chapter 8 reveal characteristics of the little horn, providing critical information with respect to the fourth and final terrible, wild Gentile beast, but from different perspectives. The final beast is understood to be the kingdom of the Antichrist—the final ruler during the time of the Gentiles. The ram and he-goat of chapter 8 are depicted as conquering or warring with each other. The he-goat is documented as conquering the two-horned ram and then becoming the next Gentile dominion on earth. The Gentile beasts listed in Daniel 7 do not war with each other but come together as part of the one unifying wild beast during the last days. The Gentile nations listed in chapter 8 do attack each other: therefore, the animals of chapter seven and chapter eight are not the same but are different Gentile dominions completely, both in time and in behavior characteristics.

The identities of the nations or animals of chapter 8—that is, the ram and the he-goat—are clear from the Word of God, history, and every reputable commentary written about this chapter. God has also interpreted these animals for Daniel and gives the identities in his word to ensure that there can be no mistake (see interpretation section below). In contrast, God does not interpret the animals or nations listed in chapter 7, implying that the animals in chapter 7 are still future.

God, in Daniel 8, goes on to discuss the four notable dominions or nations that are the remnant of the he-goat (Alexander the Great) depicted in verse 5 after the fall of Alexander in 323 BC. The four notable dominions that replaced Alexander's dominion are also understood from antiquity, or from any good history book. The four Gentile dominions remaining after the death of Alexander came into being after Alexander's death (approximately 323 BC). The four kingdoms that remained after the fall of Alexander were scattered to the north, south, east, and west, as stated in Daniel 8:8. The kingdoms included Seleucids (Syria, Babylonia, and Persia), Ptolemy (Egypt), Cassandra (Macedon), and Lysimachus (Thrace and Asia Minor). God states that these four horns, or leaders, became new nations after the death of Alexander and were divided toward the four winds of heaven—that is, the north, south, east, and west.

> **And out of one of them came forth a little horn, which waxed exceeding great, toward the south, and toward the east, and toward the pleasant land. And it waxed great, even to the host of heaven; and it cast down some of the host and of the stars to the ground, and stamped upon them. Yea, he magnified himself even to the prince of the host, and by him the daily sacrifice was taken away, and the place of his sanctuary was cast down. And an host was given him against the daily sacrifice by reason of transgression, and it cast down the truth to the ground; and it practiced, and prospered.** (Daniel 8:9–12; my emphasis).

In this section, God reveals additional information about the vile man as the "*little horn*" who "*waxes*" or becomes exceedingly "*great*." The "*little horn*" then becomes the focus, or the most important subject for the balance of the chapter. At this point God also skips over the thousands of years associated with the time of the one body of Jesus Christ. The other nations mentioned earlier in chapter 8—that is, the ram and he-goat—only provide information as to the origin of the "*little horn*"; therefore, God uses only a couple of verses to describe them. A good deal, if not all, of the remainder of chapter 8 of Daniel is relevant and explanatory regarding the "*little horn*"—his behavior, actions, wars, and the time of the end. The "*little horn*" of chapters 7 and chapter 8 is the same individual arrived at from two different routes or viewpoints. Both viewports are orchestrated by God but arrive at the same destination. Each path adds information and builds upon the other. Chapter 8 answers the questions, Where did the "*little horn*" originate from? and What nations did the "*little horn*" replace of the ten horns in chapter 7? Daniel 8:9 states that the "*little horn*" will arise from one of the four nations or dominions formed after the fall of Alexander, but not until the last days. This marks a critical fact revealed by the Word of God; that is, the Antichrist will rise from one of the four dominions in and around the Middle East in the last days. Daniel 8:9 also states that the "*little horn*" will replace three horns or kings as per Daniel 7:8—namely, a leader of the south, and one from the east, and whoever will be ruling the pleasant land—the land of Israel—at the time of the end. Daniel 8:9 goes on to say that the "*little horn*" or vile man will "*wax great*," indicating how he initially conquers toward the south, the east, and "*the pleasant land*," Israel. After this initial assault, he goes on to world dominion through supernatural means. At the time of the end, the vile man will evolve from one of the remnant nations that came into being after Alexander's breakup. That nation will be intact and will produce the little horn or vile man. We will see that God is even more specific as to which nation this is in Daniel 11.

From the standpoint of location, the compass center is always centered at the Holy of Holies in Jerusalem—the geographical center point that God uses to deal with his people, Israel, in the Old Testament. When these tragic last time events begin, Israel, Jerusalem, and the Holy of Holies will again become center stage for God's dealings with both the Jews and the Gentiles. The church of the one body of Jesus Christ *will* have been raptured before these final last-day events are fully realized. After the rapture of the *one* body of Christ, the focus will once again be on Israel, with Jerusalem at its center. God will fulfill, once and for all, the promises made to their fathers. From God's perspective, the Holy of Holies is the center of God's dealing with Israel. The Holy Mount, or rock in Jerusalem, is the place where God made his original promises to Abraham after he offered to sacrifice his son Isaac. It is this place where God will deal mercifully with latter-day Israel. Consider the following:

> "And it came to pass, when Solomon had finished the building of the house of the LORD, and the king's house, and all Solomon's desire which he was pleased to do, That the LORD appeared to Solomon the second time, as he had appeared unto him at Gibeon. **And the LORD said unto him, I have heard thy prayer and thy supplication that thou hast made before me: I have hallowed this house, which thou hast built, to put my name there forever; and mine eyes and mine heart shall be there perpetually**"
> (1 Kings 9:1–3 KJV; my emphasis)

Daniel 8:10 states that the beast waxed great even to the host of heaven and that it cast down some of the host and of the stars to the ground. The dragon (Satan) and his angels (stars) will be cast out of heaven in accordance with Revelation 12:7. His final casting out of heaven will occur during the final seven years or during the last days. Additionally, it is stated that the beast will overcome the saints—some of the set-apart ones of the remnant of the seed of Israel.[81] The trial of the sanctified ones during the last days is consistent with other records regarding the falling of the sanctified ones.[82] The world will be under the sway of the Antichrist, who will successfully persecute those who attempt to put their faith in God. Verse 11 goes on to state that the beast will magnify himself above the prince of the host, God himself, the creator and ruler of the starry host or the Lord God of Hosts. The beast will laud himself to be some great one on the earth, leading to his proclamation to the world that he is God. Once again, this is consistent with other related scriptures concerning the Antichrist. Consider the following:

> And the king shall do according to his will; and he shall exalt himself, and magnify himself

---

[81] Daniel 11:33–35.
[82] See Daniel 11:28–35; Revelation 13:5–9; Matthew 24:3–20.

above every god, and shall speak marvellous things against the God of gods, and shall prosper till the indignation be accomplished: for that that is determined shall be done.

Neither shall he regard the God of his fathers, nor the desire of women, nor regard any god: for he shall magnify himself above all. (Dan11:36–38 KJV)

… Who opposeth and exalteth himself above all that is called God, or that is worshipped; so that he as God sitteth in the temple of God, shewing himself that he is God. (2 Thessalonians 2:4 KJV)

Daniel 8:11 states that the vile man or the Antichrist will take away the Jewish daily sacrifice, which correlates to other related verses.[83] The Jewish daily sacrifice will most likely be a prayer sacrifice that the remnant of Israel will offer to God in Jerusalem at the temple mount site. The scripture regarding this will become clear to the wise at the time of the end. The daily sacrifice may even be the daily prayer offerings that are offered at the Western Wall in Jerusalem. The Western Wall theory is also supported in Daniel 9:25 by the peculiar word translated as "wall," which is from a Hebrew word meaning "dug out or cut off." The wall that is prayed to today in Jerusalem is the lone remnant of the original wall from Old Jerusalem or the city of David. The wall was "dug-out" or "cut off" from the original city that was destroyed around AD 70. The meaning and placement of this word in Daniel 9:25 seems to baffle translators. Could this have been the Jerusalem Western Wall of today (2020) in Israel? The Western Wall, which appeared thousands of years after this prophecy, could have been foretold by God in Daniel 9:25, only to be fulfilled thousands of years later. This is also consistent with how God skips over the mystery period, knowing the end from the beginning. The

---

[83] See Daniel 9:27; 11:31; 12:11.

THE LAST DAYS AND THE VILE MAN OF DANIEL

daily sacrifice, even thousands of years later, was known by God, who knows the end from the beginning and foretells future events in these Old Testament scriptures. In any event, the ending of the daily sacrifice becomes the focus of many end-times scriptures and marks the middle of the last seven years. The scripture states that a key signpost signaling the end times is the vile man, for reasons unspecified, begins the process of prohibiting the daily sacrifice from occurring as stated in Daniel 9.27. Another key signpost signaling the beginning of the end times will be the vile man strengthening himself with a league or covenant with a great superpower nation. The final seven years and the beginning of the 2,300 days both begin sometime after the league Antichrist makes with a powerful Gentile nation.[84] Each of the time periods begin at different points within the last days. The covenant of (Daniel 9.27) and the league (Daniel 11.23) appear to be the same; each adding additional information to the event. They both involve the Antichrist/vile man joining himself with a powerful Gentile nation.

The midst of the seventieth week marks the central critical crisis point of the last seven-year period. At the mid-point of the last seven years, the final forty-two months of the final seven years begin. The other events associated with the midst of the week are the dispersion of Israel from the holy city, the casting down of the holy place or sanctuary, and the setting up of the abomination that causes desolation.[85] This will also be the time that Satan is cast out of the heavens with his angels, as documented in Revelation 12 (examined later in this work). Daniel 8:11 states that the Holy of Holies or the sanctuary is cast down.

Daniel 8:12 states that the beast is given a host (a strong, powerful force or army) because of transgression—that is, because of the excessive sins of mankind at the time of the end. The sins of mankind at the time of the end will result in deceit and lawlessness prospering on the earth and the truth being cast to the ground and

---

[84] See Daniel 11.23
[85] See Matthew 24:15–24.

forgotten about. These details, once again, associate this section with Antichrist and the last days.[86] The beast and his host will go on to practice and prosper for the next forty-two months. God allows the desolation of the last forty-two months in response to the rebellion of national Israel and the general rejection of God and his word by mankind. The beast and his short-duration kingdom will be allowed to practice and prosper for forty-two months, as mentioned in several other scriptures, including Thessalonians and Revelation. Consider the following:

> Let no man deceive you by any means: for that day shall not come, except there come a falling away first, and that man of sin be revealed, the son of perdition; **Who opposeth and exalteth himself above all that is called God, or that is worshipped; so that he as God sitteth in the temple of God, shewing himself that he is God.** Remember ye not, that, when I was yet with you, I told you these things?
>
> And now ye know what withholdeth that he might be revealed in his time. (2 Thessalonians 2:3–6 KJV; my emphasis)
>
> And I saw one of his heads as it were wounded to death; and his deadly wound was healed: and all the world wondered after the beast. **And they worshipped the dragon which gave power unto the beast: and they worshipped the beast, saying, Who is like unto the beast? who is able to make war with him? And there was given unto him a mouth speaking great things and blasphemies; and power was given unto him to continue forty and two months. And he opened his mouth in blasphemy against God, to blaspheme his name, and his tabernacle,**

---

[86] See 2 Thessalonians 2:9–11.

THE LAST DAYS AND THE VILE MAN OF DANIEL

and them that dwell in heaven. And it was given unto him to make war with the saints, and to overcome them: and power was given him over all kindreds, and tongues, and nations. And all that dwell upon the earth shall worship him, whose names are not written in the book of life of the Lamb slain from the foundation of the world. If any man have an ear, let him hear. (Revelation 13:3–9 KJV; my emphasis).

At the time of the middle of the final seven-year period the beast prospers and prevails for the next forty-two months—the next three and one-half years—on the earth. The next section of Daniel reveals an additional time of twenty-three hundred days, which must be understood to begin after the beginning of the final seven years, or Daniels final week of years and as documented in Daniel 9.24. This time period will be studied later in this work.

Then I heard one saint speaking, and another saint said unto that certain saint which spake, **How long shall be the vision concerning the daily sacrifice, and the transgression of desolation, to give both the sanctuary and the host to be trodden under foot? And he said unto me, Unto two thousand and three hundred days; then shall the sanctuary be cleansed.** And it came to pass, when I, even I Daniel, had seen the vision, and sought for the meaning, then, behold, there stood before me as the appearance of a man. And I heard a man's voice between the banks of Ulai, which called, and said, Gabriel, make this man to understand the vision (appearance). So he came near where I stood: and when he came, I was afraid, and fell upon my face: but he said unto me, Understand, O son of man: for at the time of the end shall be the vision. Now as he was speaking with me, I was in a deep sleep on my face toward the ground: but he touched me, and set me upright. And he said, Behold, I will make thee know what shall be in the last end of the indignation: for at the time appointed the end shall be. (Daniel 8:13–19; my emphasis)

The twenty-three-hundred-day vision or appearance mentioned above is critical to understanding the sequence of events associated with the last days. Daniel 8:13–19 depicts two saints or angels discussing a future vision that occurs twenty-three hundred days before the cleansing of the sanctuary. The vision is related to God's final dealings with Israel and the final seven years. The prophecy concerning the vision will require twenty-three hundred days to be fulfilled as spoken by the angel. The end of the prophecy is the cleansing of the sanctuary sometime close to the end of the final seven years and during the last days of man's rule on earth. The cleansing of the sanctuary at the end of the twenty-three hundred days will also be a key transitional point related to the transition of the rule of the earth from the Gentile nations to the rulership of the Lord Jesus Christ. The meaning of the twenty-three-hundred-day time-period has baffled researchers for hundreds of years. The verse has generated several diverse and different meanings over the centuries. It is beyond the scope of this document to discuss all the various interpretations, but the same interpretation tools that were identified at the beginning of this work will be used to understand the twenty-three-hundred days. As more information becomes available, and especially as the last days approach, the interpretation may be refined and better understood. The interpretation will center on the mistranslation of the English word "vision" in several verses in chapters 8, 9, and 10.

The English word "vision" is translated from the Hebrew via two main Hebrew words—*"hazon"* and *"mare."* We will focus only on their use in the book of Daniel. The two Hebrew words are always translated into the English as either "vision" or "appearance" in the book of Daniel. For proper interpretation, the reader needs to understand which word is being used in each instance. The context can be understood only through proper understanding of the Hebrew word used in each verse. The two interpretations of "vision" and their derivative Hebrew words are listed to clarify the meaning in each context. The first usage in chapter 8, regarding the vision of the ram, the he-goat, and the final "little horn," encompasses the entire prophecy or vision *"hazon"* of chapter 8. This word is clear, and we will not spend a great deal of time on its translation and meaning, since it is related to general prophecy given to Daniel. The second Hebrew word used, *"mare,"* is of more interest and will be studied in detail. The true meaning has been lost in translation into English, since this word is translated into English as the word "vision." The second Hebrew word used for "vision" in this section, *"mare,"* has to do with a physical supernatural appearance. The first time *"mare"* is used is in Daniel is in Daniel 8:15, and it is related to a supernatural appearance that Daniel saw. The Hebrew word *"mare"* is properly translated as "appearance" in its first usage in Daniel 8:15 but is mistranslated thereafter. The other instances of *"mare"* in this section and in the sections that follow are always mistranslated as "vision." Curiously, the *Young's Literal Interpretation* version does indeed correctly carry the translation "appearance" throughout these sections. The point is that the Hebrew word *"mare"* must be associated with a physical appearance or physical reality that is seen in prophetic revelation. The appearance can be a still shot or a type of progressive video revealing revelation from God. In the instance of the book of Daniel, both are used depending on the context of the scripture verse.

Daniel 8:15; Daniel sees a vision of a great warfare and the wrath of God on the earth. There is also revelation of the man of sin, Antichrist, as he progresses through his actions on the earth. At face value, it seems that the appearance is that of the angel who was speaking with him, which satisfies conventional wisdom. As the chapter develops and subsequent chapters begin, it becomes evident that the "appearance" that Daniel saw was not that of the angel at all but of something much more radiant and astonishing and hard for Daniel to understand. This is supported by the usages of the same Hebrew word, *"mare,"* translated "vision or appearance" in verses 16, 26, and 27 of Daniel 8, as well as the usage of the word in Daniel 9:23 and 10:1. In all these verses, the same word is used for the supernatural appearance but is translated as "vision." Reading the above verses will at once call into question what exactly Daniel saw in the supernatural appearance of Daniel 8:15. To say that the appearance was that of the angel simply does not make sense from the context. There are several reasons why it could not be the angel. First, if it was the angel, why is Gabriel at once commanded to instruct Daniel as to the meaning of the appearance in verse 16? Secondly, the vision is next used in verse 26 about an appearance associated with twenty-three hundred mornings and evenings, which will occur only in the future. Thirdly, Daniel is instructed in verse 29 to seal up and not reveal the prophecy concerning the appearance. And the fourth reason is connected to verse 27, in which it states that Daniel simply did not understand the appearance. The other usages of "vision" and "mare" in chapters 9 and 10 continue to reinforce that the appearance that Daniel saw was something of a more astonishing nature and was related to the final twenty-three hundred days, not the angel. In fact, it is not until Daniel 10:1 that Daniel finally states that he had received understanding of the appearance he saw in chapter 8, but he still does not reveal the meaning. The angel provides explanations and revelations listed in both Daniel 8 and Daniel 9 to get Daniel to the point where he understands the original appearance. One last proof that the vision was not that of the angel is that the angel is instructed to explain the appearance to Daniel in 8:16. Additionally, Daniel is also instructed in verse 26 to shut up or keep the appearance secret—that is, to not document the appearance.

From the above, we know that the vision or appearance was not that of the angel at all. What exactly was the appearance that Daniel saw in Daniel 8:15? One key is the word used for "man" in 8:15. It is stated in verse 15 that Daniel saw something like the *"appearance of a man."* The word "appearance" is translated from *"mare,"* which is translated into English as "vision" in the book of Daniel. The other word of interest is the Hebrew word used for "man," which is not the typical Hebrew word, "adam," used for "man" in the Old Testament. The Hebrew root word used is "*gbr*," which has the basic root meaning "to rise, raise, restore, or rise in arrogance against God." Additionally, derived stems include the idea of being strong or prevailing over something.[87] Once again, to get greater insight into the word, we will examine the first usage of this word "gbr" in the Bible—both that of the manuscript and the root word. The first usage supplies additional insight into the meaning of the word. The Hebrew word "*gaber*" is used in this verse and translated into English as "man." The first usage is in Genesis 10:8 and has to do with Nimrod, the first mighty warrior who rebelled against God. As so often occurs with the Word of God, God uses the first usage of a word to reveal a great deal of information about the word being considered. Consider the first usage in Genesis 10:8–10: *"And Cush begat Nimrod: he began to be a **mighty** one in the earth. He was a **mighty** hunter before the LORD: wherefore it is said, Even as Nimrod the mighty hunter before the LORD. And the beginning of his kingdom was Babel"* (Genesis 10:8–10).

The word "hunter," used twice in verse 9 of Genesis 10 for emphasis, has the meaning of a mighty rebel against God. Nimrod was the author of the tower of Babel in Babylon—the first symbol of mankind coming together as one in arrogance and rebellion against God. Recall that God intervened at the tower of Babel by dividing the languages to confuse the people, thus thwarting their attempt to come together as one, which had resulted in gross idolatry. God intervened in Genesis 10 for the good of mankind. The Hebrew word "*gaber*" is the specific word used and inserted by the Holy Spirit in description of the appearance that Daniel saw in chapter 8. Therefore, Daniel was startled and alarmed. After all, Daniel saw many visions, but this one, Daniel distinctly states, startled him. What Daniel saw must have been associated with the last days and the rising of the Antichrist against God and against man. He saw the increasing dominion of the Antichrist as he propelled the world into chaos,

---

[87] J. N. Oswalt, "גָּבַר," in *Theological Wordbook of the Old Testament*, electronic edition, ed. R. L. Harris, G. L. Archer Jr., and B. K. Waltke (Chicago: Moody Press, 1999), 148.

destruction, and a terrible war. He saw what appeared to be a mighty rebel rising in the earth in the last days. Nimrod was the first mighty rebel who arose to gather the people of the earth as one man against God. What Daniel saw was the last mighty rebel to rise during the last days. Daniel was also instructed to shut up and not to reveal the prophecy and vison that he had just witnessed. Daniel was instructed not to reveal the appearance, but in accordance with Daniel 8:16, he could understand the appearance. The angel explains to Daniel what the appearance meant in the verses that follow. Daniel documents some information as to what he understood of the appearance, but it is not until Daniel 10:1 that Daniel states that he finally understood the vision. The vision of the rising and eventual fall of the Antichrist encompassed twenty-three hundred days, as noted in Daniel 8:14. In Daniel 10:1, Daniel reveals some information about the twenty-three-hundred-day vision—namely that it describes a long period of warfare. Other than Daniel 10:1, Daniel, as instructed, does not document a great deal of information regarding the appearance that he saw. We will see that it will be John in the book of Revelation who will document the events of the last days. Why God waits until the first century to reveal to John the events of the book of the Revelation of Jesus Christ is hidden in God, but is probably related to keeping the information secret and hidden from Satan. Consider the various translations listed below regarding Daniel 10:1 and the great twenty-three-hundred-day period of warfare:

> In the third year of Cyrus king of Persia a thing was revealed unto Daniel, whose name was called Belteshazzar; and the thing was true, **even a great warfare**: and he understood the thing, and had understanding of the vision. (Daniel 10:1 ASV; my emphasis)
>
> In the third year of Cyrus the king of the Persians, a word was revealed to Daniel, who was called by his name Belteshazzar, and the word was reliable and it concerned a **great tribulation**,

> and he understood the word and he received understanding. (Daniel 10:1 LEB; my emphasis)
>
> In the third year of Cyrus king of Persia, a thing is revealed to Daniel, whose name is called Belteshazzar, and **the thing is true, and the warfare is great:** and he hath understood the thing, and hath understanding about the appearance. (Daniel 10:1 YLT; my emphasis)

Daniel 10.1 states that Daniel understood the vision and that *"the matter was revealed to him."* The matter he was documenting was the matter of the rise and fall of the Antichrist in the last days—specifically the final twenty-three hundred days until the cleansing of the sanctuary. The matter was a continuation of the vision ("*mareh*") shown to him in Daniel 8:15. It took Daniel a full chapter of information and his pleading and praying to God in chapter 9 for Daniel to understand the appearance, which he first saw in Daniel 8:15. The only clue that he gives, in accordance with the angel's instruction not to reveal the specifics, is in Daniel 10:1 in which Daniel states that the appearance and the twenty-three hundred days concerned a great conflict, a great warfare, or a great tribulation, as noted in the above translations.

The end of the vision concerning the twenty-three-hundred days is clear and is marked by the cleansing of the sanctuary. In contrast, the beginning of the twenty-three hundred days, as well as the final seven years, is not as clear, but must be pieced together through other sections of scriptures. The twenty-three-hundred-day time period is initiated with the rising of the vile man as he begins his conquests to the South, to the East and to the pleasant land. It appears that his rising to conquer is related to a verse in Daniel 11.23. Consider the following:

> [23] And after the league made with him he shall work deceitfully: for he shall come up, and shall become strong with a small people. [24] He shall enter peaceably even upon the fattest places

of the province; and he shall do that which his fathers have not done, nor his fathers' fathers; he shall scatter among them the prey, and spoil, and riches: yea, and he shall forecast his devices against the strong holds, even for a time.

²⁵ And he shall stir up his power and his courage against the king of the south with a great army; and the king of the south shall be stirred up to battle with a very great and mighty army; but he shall not stand: for they shall forecast devices against him. (Daniel 11:23–25 KJV; my emphasis)

According to the above, he rises sometime after the league or covenant is made with the strong powerful Gentile nation and after the beginning of the final seven years of Daniel's seventy-sevens of years prophecy. From inspection of other sections of scriptures, the twenty-three hundred days begin sometime after the beginning of the last seven years and, in fact, are included within the final seven years. Also included within the twenty-three hundred days will be the bold rising of Antichrist which is alluded to in several scriptures. From all indications the twenty-three hundred days will mark the beginning of sorrows as stated by the Lord in Matthew 24:8. The beginning of sorrows on the earth is associated with plagues, wars, and famines as stated in Matthew chapter 24. These initial judgements will also mark the beginning of the perilous times mentioned in 2 Timothy 3:1. This same time with more specific details is documented by the first four seals of Revelation chapter 6 which indicates a type of acute tribulation period before the middle of the final seven years. As stated earlier, the books of Daniel and Revelation are woven together such that one interprets the other. In this case the twenty-three hundred days are mentioned in Daniel chapter 8 relating to the period of the vision documented in the book of Revelation. There is no such time period mentioned anywhere else in the Word of God or in the book of Revelation. The book of Revelation does mention forty and two months, and 1,260 days, but in reading the book of Revelation it is clear that there are judgement events which occur before the middle of the final seven years. It is the final forty and two months which result in the worst time in human history, but it should be clear that the beginning of sorrows on the earth begin before the final forty and two months. This is further studied in Appendix C.

In Daniel chapter 8, The angel goes on to explain to Daniel what the appearance meant through the information given to Daniel in chapter 9. In Daniel 10:1, Daniel documents that he finally understood the vision or appearance that he saw in Daniel 8:15. He reveals only that it concerned a great conflict, which we know now as the book of Revelation.

The beginning of sorrows begins the twenty-three-hundred days listed in Daniel 8.13. The appearance Daniel sees in Daniel chapter 8, which encompasses twenty-three-hundred days, is that of the warfare contained in the book of Revelation. The time period initiates the beginning of sorrows and the eventual rising of the Antichrist to his end. His rising occurs sometime after he makes his covenant/league with a strong powerful nation and with the many as documented in Daniel 9:27 and after the beginning of the final seven years. The twenty-three-hundred-day appearance includes the entire prophecy given to Daniel beginning in Daniel 8:9 and continuing through Daniel 12, ending with the cleansing of the sanctuary. Consider the following:

> And out of one of them **came forth** a little horn, which waxed exceeding great, toward the south, and toward the east, and toward the pleasant land. And it waxed great, even to the host of heaven; and it cast down some of the host and of the stars to the ground, and stamped upon them. Yea, he magnified himself even to the prince of the host, and by him the daily sacrifice was taken away, and the place of his sanctuary was cast down. And an host was given him against the daily sacrifice by reason of transgression, and it cast down the truth to the

ground; and it practised, and prospered. (Daniel 8:9–12 KJG; my emphasis)

We now understand the appearance of Daniel 8.15 and his understanding of Daniel 10.2. Many of the questions have been answered regarding the appearance that Daniel saw in chapter 8. We know that the appearance, or vision, that Daniel saw was that of sorrows increasing on the earth and the eventual rising and falling of a mighty warrior and an associated warfare that occurs in the last days, namely the events of the book of Revelation. We know that what he saw required twenty-three hundred days to fulfill. We also know that the twenty-three hundred days ends with the cleansing of the sanctuary. Using scriptural buildup, we can now search other scriptures regarding the same subject and compile the additional data that God has provided in his word. Once again, any reference to the same event must not contradict any other. This method also allows us to prove the accuracy of the interpretation. The following scriptures can be used to amass additional information regarding the appearance that Daniel saw. Each one will be listed and the additional information will be discussed. The common thread among these scriptures is the beast coming forth at the beginning of the twenty-three hundred days after the start of the final seven years.

The appearance that Daniel saw in chapter 8 occurred during the time of the "*little horn*" as he rose to power in the last days. The appearance is one of a mighty warrior and a great warfare on the earth (the tribulation) that associates a time and a prophecy to be fulfilled to the time of the end. To put it another way, the vision will require twenty-three hundred days to be fulfilled and is related to the vision John saw in the book of Revelation.

It is now clear that in Daniel chapter 8, Daniel saw some type of a supernatural vision that would take twenty-three hundred days to be fulfilled. The twenty-three-hundred-day vision is related to the last seven years and the time of the end. The vision that he saw was revealed to him during his deep sleep or the trance that he was in, and it was recorded in Daniel 8:18. Additionally, Daniel was instructed not to reveal or write down what he saw in the trance. Since the appearance and the prophecy concerning the vision is part of the last days, by process of elimination we can determine what the twenty-three-hundred-day vision is not.

1. It is not the entire vision or prophecy of Daniel 8, which spans thousands of years and includes the ram and the he-goat. From previous scriptures in Daniel, one can see that these dominions already came and went and are not part of the last seven years.
2. The twenty-three hundred days are not prophecy of the next twenty-three hundred years, as some have believed. Rather, each day is represented by a twenty-four-hour day.
3. It is not a prophecy that has already passed. The twenty-three-hundred-day vision still awaits fulfillment during the last seven years and is related to the book of Revelation and the vision that John saw in the first century.
4. The vision is not an appearance and prophecy that Daniel understood as compared to the ram and he goat, which he did understand.

We can also determine what the vision is:

1. It is a heavenly future vision of an appearance of the rising and falling of a mighty warrior: the Antichrist and the sorrows and warfare that follows. The vision depicts the events associated with the final twenty-three hundred days and as part of the last seven years. Those last seven years are the final seven years of Daniel's seventy sevens prophecy concerning Israel. (See Daniel 9:24.)
2. It is a vision that Daniel is instructed by the angel in Daniel 8:26–27 not to write down but to be kept shut up or sealed.
3. It is a twenty-three-hundred-day vision contained within the final seven years, or 2,520 days. The vision begins approximately 220 days after the beginning of the final

seven years and ends with the cleansing of the sanctuary in Jerusalem.
4. It is a vision of the last twenty-three-hundred days of plagues, sorrows, famines, warfare and tribulation leading to the deliverance of the remnant called out of Israel given to Daniel during the time of his deep sleep. The end of the twenty-three-hundred days will be marked by the cleansing of the sanctuary; the fulfillment of what he saw will take twenty-three hundred days to be accomplished.
5. It is a prophecy of twenty-three hundred days beginning in Daniel 8:9 and ending in verse 12. The prophecy is associated with the last times and the still future. The prophecy itself is represented by an appearance shown to Daniel while he was in a trance.

Daniel 8:13 states that the vision is "*concerning the daily sacrifice, the transgression of desolation, and the sanctuary and host to be trodden under foot.*" The words "concerning" and "sacrifice" in verse 13 were added by translators and are not in the original text; that is, there is no corresponding Hebrew word. Without the added words, the verse should read, "*How long does the vision continue, the transgression of desolation, to give both the sanctuary and the host to be trodden under foot.*" The continuation of time that the vision represents is the focus of the angel's message to Daniel. The prophecy of the ram and the he-goat was clear and was interpreted to us; therefore, the first part of chapter 8 is historical. In contrast, this astonishing vision, which will last twenty-three hundred days, was not understood by Daniel and is still future.

The twenty-three-hundred-day prophecy demands special consideration, since it is critical to understanding important signposts that God provides for warning in the last days. Proper interpretation of the twenty-three-hundred-day vision provides the man or woman of God with understanding and knowledge of the final events as they unfold in the last days. The key concept is that the twenty-three-hundred-day vision is still future (2020) and unique from any other vision in Daniel's prophecy or in chapter 8. Daniel 8 contains two separate and distinct prophecies. The first is the prophecy given to Daniel concerning the he-goat and the two-horned ram. The second prophecy, that of the little horn and his doings, concerns the last days and events that occur at the time of the last seven years. The period of the Mystery of the one Body of Christ is once again skipped over. The second prophecy, as stated earlier, contains the appearance of a mighty warrior who dominates the world stage and the chaos and commotion he causes on the earth for the final forty and two months. There are several pieces of information given by God in his word to support this conclusion. The evidences, along with those listed above, are as follows:

In Daniel chapter 8, the dominions of the ram and he-goat—Media, Persia, and Alexander—spanned several decades in history and were interpreted by the angel in chapter 8. The *little horn* and his actions are also well documented and described in Daniel and other sections of scripture, but these events are still future. The question of what Daniel saw in verse 15 and its meaning is now partly understood; the entire meaning is reserved by God for those alive and of understanding in the last days. The vision that Daniel saw and documented in chapter 8 is also related to what was given to John in the book of Revelation. Additionally, supporting material has been reserved and presented in appendix D, where additional information will be introduced regarding this topic. In this section, it should be abundantly clear that the twenty-three-hundred-day vision is associated with the time of the end—specifically the book of Revelation.

The interpretation of the vision in Daniel 8 by the Angel:

> The ram which thou sawest having two horns are the kings of Media and Persia. And the rough goat is the king of Grecia: and the great horn that is between his eyes is the first king. Now that being broken, whereas four stood up for it, four kingdoms shall stand up out of the nation, but not in his power. **And in the latter time of their kingdom, when the**

transgressors are come to the full, a king of fierce countenance, and understanding dark sentences, shall stand up. And his power shall be mighty, but not by his own power: and he shall destroy wonderfully, and shall prosper, and practise, and shall destroy the mighty and the holy people. And through his policy also he shall cause craft to prosper in his hand; and he shall magnify himself in his heart, and by peace shall destroy many: he shall also stand up against the Prince of princes; but he shall be broken without hand. (Daniel 8:19–25; my emphasis).

Daniel 8:19–25: the narrative and revelation from the angel goes on to give the identities of the ram with two horns and the rough he-goat as being the kings of Media/Persia and the first king of Grecia or Greece—that is, Alexander the Great. These two kingdoms are also represented as part of the great image revealed to Nebuchadnezzar in Daniel 2. The kings of Media/Persia and Alexander are represented in Daniel 2 by the breast of silver and the belly and thighs of brass, respectively. The angel then goes on to focus on the emphasis of the chapter: *the king of fierce countenance—the little horn.* The little horn is stated to evolve from one of the four dominions left after the fall of Alexander, but thousands of years later, when the sin of mankind reaches a peak or is full. The fullness, or fullness to overflowing, of the sins of man is a second characteristic associated with the rising of the Antichrist and is noted in other scriptures describing the man of sin. It will occur when the sins and the atrocities of men on the earth have reached their boiling point in the eyes of God. It will be at this point that God, through his permissive will, will allow the great destruction of the nations of the world brought on by the Antichrist.

History documents that the fall of Alexander resulted in four dominions lying toward the north, south, east, and west, being formed as stated in verse 22. These four dominions, according to Jamieson, Fausset, Brown, and Brown, were the Seleucus empire in the East, including Syria, Babylonia, Media, and Cassander. The western empire included Macedon, Thessaly, Greece, and Ptolemy. The South included Egypt, Cyprus, and Lysimachus. The North was made up of Cappadocia and the northern parts of Asia Minor.[88]

Daniel 8:23 informs us that the vile man or king of fierce countenance will be ejected from one of these four dominions in the latter time of their dominion—that is, in the last days. The time will also be when the sins of rebellious mankind will reach their full end, such that God will intervene. Critical to understanding this section is the realization of a separation of time spanning, as of today (2020) at least 2,350 years between the fall of Alexander's empire and the rising of the "*little horn*" from one of the dominions resulting from the breakup of Alexander's kingdom. Daniel 8:23 states that the Antichrist will be ejected from one of these remaining four dominions, but in the last time. In other words, at least 2,350 years separate verse 22 and verse 23. The words *"the latter time of their kingdom"* account for the time gap between verses 22 and 23. In effect, God fast-forwards to the last days and the time of the end, thereby, associating the Antichrist's kingdom with Alexander's dominion. God associates the two because both men are related to ruling the earth as one man. Additionally, both men—Alexander in antiquity and the Antichrist in the future—require men to pay homage or worship them as divine. Verses 22 and 23 are a foreshadowing of the final Antichrist. Verse 23 also states that the vile man or Antichrist will be ejected at a time when "*the transgressors are come to the full.*" Transgressors or transgressions coming to a full indicates the extent of the sin of man at the time of the end. Man grows worse and worse in his arrogance, pride, and rejection of God. God's wrath and judgment come not because man finds peace but because the heart of man becomes so bad that God finally steps in and intercedes in the affairs of the earth. The world will grow worse and worse until man's transgressions bring on God's wrath. Consider the following:

---

[88] R. Jamieson, A. R. Fausset, D. Brown, and D. Brown, *A Commentary, Critical and Explanatory, on the Old and New Testaments* (Oak Harbor, Washington: Logos Research Systems, Inc., 1997).

> But thou hast fully known my doctrine, manner of life, purpose, faith, longsuffering, charity, patience, Persecutions, afflictions, which came unto me at Antioch, at Iconium, at Lystra; what persecutions I endured: but out of them all the Lord delivered me. Yea, and all that will live godly in Christ Jesus shall suffer persecution. **But evil men and seducers shall wax worse and worse, deceiving, and being deceived.** But continue thou in the things which thou hast learned and hast been assured of, knowing of whom thou hast learned them; And that from a child thou hast known the holy scriptures, which are able to make thee wise unto salvation through faith which is in Christ Jesus. All scripture is given by inspiration of God, and is profitable for doctrine, for reproof, for correction, for instruction in righteousness: That the man of God may be perfect, thoroughly furnished unto all good works. (2 Timothy 3:10–17 KJV; my emphasis)

God finally puts an end to the age of man's rule on the earth as a result of man's transgressions reaching up to the heavens, his sins filled to overflowing.[89] The result will be God allowing a deceiver to prosper and prevail for forty-two months—the worst time in human history.[90] God allows the Antichrist, also known as the vile man or "King of fierce countenance," to deceive the world.[91] His fierce countenance is characteristic of his behavior—impudent, unashamed in trampling down, without fear of God or man. It is also stated that he understands dark sentences, alluding to his understanding of mysteries and his concealing his purpose behind ambiguous words. He is stated to use dissimulation and to be skillful through artifice or trickery.

---

[89] 2 Timothy 3:13; Revelation 18:3–6.
[90] See Matthew 24; Revelation 13; Daniel 12:1–2.
[91] 2 Thessalonians 2:9–12.

Verse 23 describes attributes, activities, and characteristics of the Antichrist at the time he carries out his fateful assignment to an unsuspecting world at the time of the end. The beast will understand dark sentences, be skilled in double-dealing, and be proficient in his understanding of perplexing political situations. This refers to his treatment and analysis of the political spectrum of his time. No doubt this attribute will lead to his coming into power. He will be fierce and unrelenting in his behavior and vile in his acts toward men, women, and children. He will come into power and raise himself up when "*the transgressions of the transgressors are come to a full or filled to overflowing.*" The word "transgressor" is translated as "transgressions" in the Septuagint Vulgate. The Hebrew word is "*Pasha*" and means "rebellions"—the rebellions of man against God. Man declares that peace is advancing and progressing, but God distinctly states that sin and rebellion will get worse and worse. The sins and rebellion against God will eventually bring on God's wrath and judgment.

Verse 24 states that his power shall be mighty, but he will not gain it by his own power. We are not told where his power comes from in this verse, but other references reveal the source: Satan and his spirit agents.[92] Additionally, his power will be enhanced through the league he makes with a strong powerful Gentile nation which will assist him in his conquests; thereby not by his own power. He will also make leagues with other strong nations to ally with them, rewarding them with land and spoil.[93] He will destroy wonderfully or cause fearful supernatural destruction. The Hebrew word that is translated as "*wonderfully*" is used sixteen times in sixteen verses in the scripture and always relates to God's supernatural works. The Antichrist or vile man will use Satan's power to do supernatural works of destruction; these are represented by the word "wonderfully." [94] The first usage of "wonderfully" is related to God's miraculous wonders that he performed at the time that the Israelites went into the Promised Land

---

[92] Revelation 13:2; 2 Thessalonians 2:9–10.
[93] Daniel 11:39.
[94] Revelation 13.

at the time of Joshua.[95] The Hebrew verb is "*Pala*" and is in the *nifal* mood, which indicates the verb's subject; it conveys reflexive action. This verb form is first used in Exodus: *"And I will stretch out my hand, and smite Egypt with all my* **wonders (Pala)** *which I will do in the midst thereof: and after that he will let you go. And I will give this people favour in the sight of the Egyptians: and it shall come to pass, that, when ye go, ye shall not go empty"* (Exodus 3:20–21 KJV).

The vile man is stated to practice and prosper in all that he attempts to do. He will be supernaturally propped up by Satan himself. He will destroy the mighty and the holy people. The supernatural nature of his exploits is clear from the prior usage of this word. The word "wonderfully," used in Daniel 8:24, as stated above, has to do with supernatural power—a supernatural destruction of man on the earth energized by Satan himself. The book of Thessalonians further supports this idea. Consider the following:

> "And then shall that Wicked be revealed, whom the Lord shall consume with the spirit of his mouth, and shall destroy with the brightness of his coming: **Even him, whose coming is after the working of Satan with all power and signs and lying wonders**, And with all deceivableness of unrighteousness in them that perish; because they received not the love of the truth, that they might be saved" (2 Thessalonians 2:8–10 KJV; my emphasis)

Daniel 8:25 states that by cunning and crafty scheming the Antichrist will make deceit prosper. Typically, leaders who are deceitful are successful for only a brief time. The Antichrist will prosper and succeed continually, even after the world understands his deceitful behavior. His cunning has to do with his wisdom through understanding and prudence in decision making as well as the evil spiritual agents and strong Gentile nations which will cause him to

---

[95] Joshua 3:5.

succeed. He will also magnify himself in his heart and think himself to be God.[96] In his own mind, he will magnify himself, or literally *"in his heart he will grow big."* The continual success of his policies and his ability to operate in the supernatural realm gives growth to his feeling of the divine. Through this process, he finally will openly declare himself God. Verse 25 also states that *"by peace he shall destroy many."* This reference is clearly alluding to the suddenness of his rise to power as he increases in power and stature in the world. Consider what is written about this verse by Lange in his work *A Commentary on the Holy Scriptures*: "**And by peace shall destroy many**; rather, 'and unawares shall destroy many.' וּבְשַׁלְוָה does not exactly signify 'in the midst of profound peace' (Job 15:21), but more indefinitely, 'with suddenness, by a malignant surprise.' an illustration of the malice and dissimulation practiced by this tyrant, which were already mentioned in v. 23."[97]

His early career, a man of small beginnings and who people consider vile or of little worth to civilized society, will be built on deceitful promises of peace regarding wars that he is involved in. He agrees to covenants and leagues that he signs deceitfully and through artifice.[98] The agreements will allow his gaining of strength and power, which will be used to destroy many people. Finally, he will stand up against the Prince of princes and will be broken or destroyed "without hand." "Without hand" alludes to the fact that he, a spiritual being energized by Satan, will be destroyed not by man but by the brightness of the coming of our Lord Jesus Christ at the end of the final seven years.[99]

> And the vision of the evening and the morning which was told is true: wherefore shut thou up the vision; for it shall be for many days.

---

[96] 2 Thessalonians 2:4.
[97] J. P. Lange, P. Schaff, O. Zöckler, and J. Strong, *A Commentary on the Holy Scriptures: Daniel* (Bellingham, Washington: Logos Bible Software, 2008), 183.
[98] Daniel 9:27; 11:21–23.
[99] 2 Thessalonians 2:8.

> And I Daniel fainted, and was sick certain days; afterward I rose up, and did the king's business; and I was astonished at the vision, but none understood it. (Daniel 8:26–27)

Daniel 8:26 informs us that the angel assures Daniel that the vision or appearance that he saw concerning the final twenty-three hundred days and explained to Daniel in verses 13–15 was not fictional but true. Daniel is further instructed to shut up or not reveal or write down the revelation concerning the vision. He is to keep it to himself, for it concerns or belongs to the last days. Daniel 8.26 should read as follows considering the original Hebrew:

> "And the appearance that you saw in the revelation given by the angel which represented evenings and mornings is true: wherefore shut thou up the visual revelation given by the angel; for it shall not come to pass until many days have progressed. And I Daniel fainted, and was sick certain days; afterward I rose, and did the king's business; and I was astonished at the revelation given by the angel of the mighty warrior, but none understood it" (Daniel 8: 26–27).

Based on the instructions given by the angel, the only information Daniel could reveal was that the appearance "*mareh*" was to span twenty-three hundred days. Explained differently, the appearance gives revelation regarding twenty-three hundred days condensed into a vision seen by Daniel and associated with the last seven years.

The key point here is that Daniel wrote down only the time that the appearance represented. Other specific information regarding the vision was not written down by Daniel and must be revealed in other sections of scripture. The only information provided was that the twenty-three hundred days represented the beginning of sorrows, the rising of the little horn, the suspension of the daily or continual sacrifice, an abomination that causes desolation, and the sanctuary to be trodden under foot. We are also told that it ends with the cleansing of the sanctuary. In essence, a supernatural vision of a mighty warrior and the wars and desolations on the earth that he represented was shown to Daniel, who was amazed by the spectacle but was instructed not to write it down. The appearance told the story of what would occur for the following twenty-three hundred days on Earth and during the last days. After seeing the vision, Daniel sought for the understanding of the vision and was told only that it would last twenty-three hundred days and that it concerned a long warfare.[100] The angel continued to instruct Daniel concerning the vision in chapters 9, 10, and 11, but Daniel was not to write down the meaning. It will be seen that it is the book of Revelation documented by John in the first century that will provide the details of Daniels vision. The point is that both books will be required to understand the last days.

After careful review and study of the vision of Daniel 8, it becomes clear that Daniel's vision of an appearance fits well and completes the vision seen by John in the book of Revelation. Daniel saw the vision but was not to write down the details of the actual vision; he was to write down only the time it represented, twenty-three hundred days, and some generic events of that time. John explained the vision and wrote down the details, but he did not write down the time it represented. Recording of the details of the vision was completed by the apostle John as part of Revelation 17, but it also included many of the other events and visions documented in the book of Revelation. Both John and Daniel saw a similar vision. John recorded the details and wrote about its meaning; one of those visions is documented in Revelation 17. The key is that both sections of scripture need to be understood in order to understand the entire revelation; one cannot be interpreted without the other. Daniel 8 reveals that the events of the vision are to last twenty-three hundred days and are to end with the cleansing of the sanctuary. The book of Revelation reveals the sequence of events as they transpire during

---

[100] Daniel 10:1.

the final twenty-three hundred days. God, for his own reasons, did not want the secret, or vision, to be recorded or written down until after the death and resurrection of the Lord Jesus Christ. Whatever God's reasons, they are not recorded in his written word. We do know that all of what God does is perfect and fits perfectly with his word. The vision could mark several critical events on earth related to the growing and strengthening of the Antichrist. The initiating event will include the beast coming up and becoming strong with a small people, in accordance with Daniel 8:9 and a strong covenant with a strong powerful Gentile nation occurring before the start of the final seven years. His coming up will initially be in mortal form in the first half of the final seven years, but his strength will continue to increase through his deceit and leagues he makes with allies until he becomes supernatural and declares himself God in the last days.

Daniel 8:27 goes on to state Daniel's astonishment (amazement or wonder) at the appearance and the reality that none, not even Daniel, understood the vision. Daniel was not astonished or amazed at the angel but at the appearance he saw, which, according to verse 26, encompassed twenty-three hundred days. Daniel's lack of understanding confirms that the twenty-three-hundred-day vision was separate and distinct from the revelation of the ram and he-goat. The vision concerning the last days was to be shut up and kept secret until written down and documented by John in the book of Revelation.

In summary, the twenty-three-hundred-day vision includes the beginning of sorrows on the earth and the rising of a a mighty supernatural force and the resulting destruction which ensues during the time of the end. What Daniel saw was not to be revealed or written down. John did write down the vision and he explained it in the book of Revelation While Daniel chapter 8 revealed how long it would last.

Section 2, Reference 5: Attributes Associated with the Antichrist (Daniel 8:1–27)

In Daniel 8:1–8, two Gentile dominions are depicted as rising to power immediately after Nebuchadnezzar. The Gentile dominions are represented by a ram and a he-goat. God utilizes animals— the ram and the he-goat of Daniel 8— fighting with each other to represent Gentile dominions at war with each other. The animal analogy is important, as it represents how God sees Gentile dominions and provides proper interpretation when wild animals are used in the Word of God. In like manner, God uses the bear, the lion, and the leopard of Daniel 7 to depict Gentile dominions associated with the last days. The two Gentile dominions from antiquity and represented in Daniel 8 are listed as a ram and he-goat. The ram represented Media-Persia; and the he-goat, Alexander the Great. Alexander was the last ruler to rule the civilized world as one man and thought himself divine. Alexander is depicted in this section as a he-goat. Alexander's rule ended with his death at an early age. Alexander's rule was succeeded by four notable or conspicuous dominions toward the north, south, east, and west (Daniel 8:8). God, through the interpretation of the angel, gives a summary of the Medo-Persian and Greek empires. God states that out of the original empire of Alexander, but thousands of years later, the Antichrist will emerge from one of the residual nations left after the fall of Alexander in the latter days, or thousands of years later. The empires give historical information pertaining to the next, more important, dominion—that is, the latter-day dominion of the Antichrist, or that of the vile man.

Daniel 8:9–27 includes the focus of the chapter—the dominion or the kingdom of the Antichrist and the last days and the glorious return of Jesus Christ. The Word of God will be fulfilled, every jot and tittle, and all that is in this section will occur exactly as it was documented by God.

In summary, the following key informational points can be gathered from section 2, reference 5:

1. The Antichrist will arise from one of the four dominions that remain after Alexander's death, the northern kingdom of the Seleucids, but this will not occur until thousands of years after Alexander's death.[101] The four dominions are

---

[101] Daniel 8:9.

- the Seleucid empire (modern-day Syria) represented as the king of the North;
- Ptolemy (modern-day Egypt), kings of the South;
- Asia Minor in the East; and
- Greece in the West.

2. The Antichrist will be the next man to rule the earth as one man and declare himself to be a god. He will follow in the steps of Alexander the Great, the last man to rule as one man. This is what is foreshadowed in Daniel 8:9.
3. The Antichrist is depicted as a little horn, a man of small beginnings, who rises in the last days from one of the four residual dominions of Alexander's reign—the northern kingdom.[102] His rising is marked by the league he makes with a Gentile superpower marking the first of two seven year periods listed in Daniel (this will be addressed later in this work). The second seven-year period begins during the middle of the first seven-year period and shortly after this, 220 days later, the twenty-three-hundred days begin with the beginning of sorrows on the earth. (v. 9).
4. The Antichrist will grow and become exceedingly great toward the south, the east, and the glorious land—the land of Israel itself. (Note: God's center of the compass on the earth is always the Holy of Holies in Jerusalem) (v. 9).[103]
5. The Antichrist will become great and will affect even the stars, or the angels of heaven (v. 10). The Antichrist will cast down a third of the stars, or angels, from heaven, revealing how he is cast out of heaven with his evil angels and cast to the earth (v. 10).[104]
6. The Antichrist will magnify himself even to God himself—the God of the starry host.[105] He will believe in his heart

---

[102] Daniel 11: 23.
[103] Daniel 8:9.
[104] Revelation 12:4; Daniel 8:10.
[105] Daniel 8:10; 11:36 Revelation 13; 2 Thessalonians 2:4.

that he is a god through powerful miracles. He will magnify himself in his heart (vv. 11, 25).

7. He will make covenants, or promises of peace, acting deceitfully, which will have the opposite effect; that is, they will cause the destruction of many people and nations (v. 25).
8. The Antichrist will take away the daily sacrifice in Jerusalem. This could be a prayer sacrifice in Jerusalem. The sanctuary, the Holy of Holies in Jerusalem, is also cast down. These events are associated with the midst of the seventieth week and are included in the twenty-three hundred days[106] (v. 11).
9. The Antichrist will be given a military host from those he allies with. Initially, he will use this host to accomplish military victories and then to stop the daily sacrifice in Jerusalem. He will then use the military host and his supernatural powers to accomplish his will (v. 12).
10. The Antichrist will cast God's truth—the laws and practices given through Moses and the prophets—down to the ground. These events will begin at the initiation of the twenty-three hundred days and grow stronger as the time of the middle of the final seven years of Daniel's seventy sevens of years prophecy approach (v. 12).[107]
11. He shall rise to power in the last days, when the sins of the people and of the world have reached their limit—that is, when the world overflows with sin, as in the time of Noah before the flood (v. 23).[108]
12. The wild beast shall be the final Gentile ruler of the earth. He will be a ruler or leader of fierce countenance, or of hard countenance (i.e., impudent, unashamed in trampling down, without fear of God or man, and having no compassion for any human being) (v. 23).

---

[106] Daniel 8:11; 9:27; 11:31.
[107] Daniel 8:12; 11:31–32.
[108] Matthew 24:38.

13. His power shall be great, but he will not gain it by his own power; he will be assisted by a strong superpower, other allies, and by Satanic evil spirits. All of this will be orchestrated by Satan and evil spirits to destroy the nations and people of the earth "wonderfully"—that is, through supernatural means.[109] Satan's power will be unbridled through him (v. 24).[110]
14. He will understand dark sentences or conceal his purpose behind ambiguous words, using dissimulation, forming an artifice (see Daniel 8:25). The unfolding of these qualities is presented in Daniel 8:24–25 (v. 23).
15. The power he uses is power from Satan and from Satan's ability to affect situations supernaturally, beyond human effort. The result of this special power will be fearful destruction, and he will succeed in what he does. He will cause mighty men, mighty nations, and the saints to be conquered (v. 24).
16. By his shrewd understanding, discerning, and feeling of superiority, he shall make deceitful or treacherous speech to prosper under his hand, completely in his control. He will consider himself to be superior and divine. Through utilization of this proud arrogance, he will—without warning, and while there is an air of careless security—unexpectedly cause the destruction of many. Finally, he will raise himself up against God and his son, Jesus Christ, bringing on his own destruction without the help of man, by the brightness of the coming of the Lord Jesus Christ (vv. 23–25).[111]

---

[109] Revelation 13:2; 2 Thessalonians 2:9–10.
[110] 2 Thessalonians 2:9.
[111] 2 Thessalonians 2:8.

Reference 6: Daniel 9:23–10:6: "The Prince that Shall Come", The Prophecy of the Seventy Weeks; the Final Seven Years, and the Vision of the Lord in the Book of Revelation

Chapter 9 continues with Daniel's investigation of the twenty-three-hundred-day appearance and vision he experienced in chapter 8. Daniel 9 introduces the next title for the Antichrist—"The prince that shall come." This is another descriptive title for the same individual we have been studying. Chapter 9 sets the foundational time benchmark in Daniel 9:24–27, summarizing the period for Israel's deliverance: seventy weeks of years–490 years. After these 490 divided years, all of God's promises to the Patriarchs, as documented in Daniel 9.24, will be fulfilled. The actual time continues for a much longer time when it is realized that God skips over the time of the mystery of the one body of Christ, the length of that span being almost two thousand years to date (2020). Recall that the mystery period began with the day of Pentecost and will end with the rapture of the body of Christ. The mystery period of the one body of Jesus Christ is skipped over or hidden by God in the Old Testament. The seventy weeks also forms foundational understanding regarding a considerable number of scriptures in the New Testament and the book of Revelation. Wrong division of this section gives rise to great error and varied interpretations, along with endless questions and imaginations. It is these final seven years of the prophecy of the seventy sevens of years—490 years—that remains in the future. We will see that it is during these final seven years that Daniel, in his writings, receives a significant amount of revelation from God.

Recall that in Daniel 8 the angel instructs Daniel in verse 26 not to reveal the twenty-three-hundred-day appearance he witnessed in Daniel 8:15. The appearance was to be "sealed" (i.e., not documented or written down). The angel instructs Daniel in Daniel 9:23 to *"understand the matter and consider the vision,"* referring to the vision that he saw in chapter 8. The information that the angel gave to Daniel in chapter 9 will allow him to understand the vision as he ponders in his mind what he saw while listening to the angel's explanation. The first part of chapter 9 documents Daniel's prayer for additional understanding of the appearance. God responds to Daniel's request and prayer in Daniel 9 by sending Gabriel to give Daniel additional understanding regarding the appearance. The information provided in Daniel 9 continues to build on the information already provided in chapters 7 and 8, without any contradictions. Consider 9:23 to 10:6:

> Daniel 9:23–10:6:
>
> And whiles I was speaking, and praying, and confessing my sin and the sin of my people Israel, and presenting my supplication before the LORD my God for the holy mountain of my God;
>
> Yea, whiles I was speaking in prayer, even the man Gabriel, whom I had seen in the vision at the beginning, being caused to fly swiftly, touched me about the time of the evening oblation. And he informed me, and talked with me, and said, O Daniel, I am now come forth to give thee skill and understanding. At the beginning of thy supplications the commandment came forth, and I am come to shew thee; for thou art greatly beloved: therefore understand the matter, and consider the vision (mareh). **Seventy weeks are determined upon thy people and upon thy holy city, to finish the transgression, and to make an end of sins, and to make reconciliation for iniquity, and to bring in everlasting righteousness, and to seal up the vision and prophecy, and to anoint the most Holy. Know therefore and understand, that from the going forth of the commandment to restore and to build Jerusalem unto the Messiah the Prince shall be seven weeks, and threescore and two weeks: the street shall be built again, and the wall, even in troublous times. And after threescore and two weeks shall Messiah be cut off, but not for himself: and the people**

of the prince that shall come shall destroy the city and the sanctuary; and the end thereof shall be with a flood, and unto the end of the war desolations are determined. And he shall confirm the covenant with many for one week: and in the midst of the week he shall cause the sacrifice and the oblation to cease, and for the overspreading of abominations he shall make it desolate, even until the consummation, and that determined shall be poured upon the desolate. In the third year of Cyrus king of Persia a thing was revealed unto Daniel, whose name was called Belteshazzar; and the thing was true, but the time appointed was long: and he understood the thing, and had understanding of the vision (mareh). In those days I Daniel was mourning three full weeks. I ate no pleasant bread, neither came flesh nor wine in my mouth, neither did I anoint myself at all, till three whole weeks were fulfilled. And in the four and twentieth day of the first month, as I was by the side of the great river, which is Hiddekel; Then I lifted up mine eyes, and looked, and behold a certain man clothed in linen, whose loins were girded with fine gold of Uphaz: His body also was like the beryl, and his face as the appearance of lightning, and his eyes as lamps of fire, and his arms and his feet like in colour to polished brass, and the voice of his words like the voice of a multitude. (Daniel 9:20–10:6 KJV; my emphasis)

Reference 6: Daniel 9:23–10:6: Commentary: "The Prince that Shall Come," The Prophecy of the Seventy Weeks.

The Hebrew section of Daniel continues to build upon reference 5 with the common thread of a vision or appearance that was revealed to but not understood by Daniel, as stated in Daniel 8:27.

We also understand that the twenty-three-hundred-day vision is also related to the time of Jacob's trouble—a well-known future period of troubled time for Israel documented throughout the Old Testament. Jacob's trouble is described in detail in Jeremiah 30 and is understood throughout Israel as a time of God's visitation and final remediation regarding Israel. God will initiate a final timeline to, once and for all, visit, deliver, rebuke, and save the called of Israel. Through this final timeline, God will fulfill all his promises to Abraham, Isaac, and Jacob. Consider the following verses in Jeremiah 30:1–24:

> The word that came to Jeremiah from the LORD, saying, Thus speaketh the LORD God of Israel, saying, Write thee all the words that I have spoken unto thee in a book. For, lo, the days come, saith the LORD, that I will bring again the captivity of my people Israel and Judah, saith the LORD: and I will cause them to return to the land that I gave to their fathers, and they shall possess it. And these are the words that the LORD spake concerning Israel and concerning Judah. **For thus saith the LORD; We have heard a voice of trembling, of fear, and not of peace. Ask ye now, and see whether a man doth travail with child? wherefore do I see every man with his hands on his loins, as a woman in travail, and all faces are turned into paleness? Alas! for that day is great, so that none is like it: it is even the time of Jacob's trouble; but he shall be saved out of it. For it shall come to pass in that day, saith the LORD of hosts, that I will break his yoke from off thy neck, and will burst thy bonds, and strangers shall no more serve themselves of him: But they shall serve the LORD their God, and David their king, whom I will raise up unto them.** Therefore fear thou not, O my servant Jacob, saith the

LORD; neither be dismayed, O Israel: for, lo, I will save thee from afar, and thy seed from the land of their captivity; and Jacob shall return, and shall be in rest, and be quiet, and none shall make him afraid. **For I am with thee, saith the LORD, to save thee: though I make a full end of all nations whither I have scattered thee, yet will I not make a full end of thee: but I will correct thee in measure, and will not leave thee altogether unpunished.** For thus saith the LORD, Thy bruise is incurable, and thy wound is grievous. There is none to plead thy cause, that thou mayest be bound up: thou hast no healing medicines. All thy lovers have forgotten thee; they seek thee not; for I have wounded thee with the wound of an enemy, with the chastisement of a cruel one, for the multitude of thine iniquity; because thy sins were increased. Why criest thou for thine affliction? thy sorrow is incurable for the multitude of thine iniquity: because thy sins were increased, I have done these things unto thee. Therefore all they that devour thee shall be devoured; and all thine adversaries, every one of them, shall go into captivity; and they that spoil thee shall be a spoil, and all that prey upon thee will I give for a prey. For I will restore health unto thee, and I will heal thee of thy wounds, saith the LORD; because they called thee an Outcast, saying, This is Zion, whom no man seeketh after. Thus saith the LORD; Behold, I will bring again the captivity of Jacob's tents, and have mercy on his dwellingplaces; and the city shall be builded upon her own heap, and the palace shall remain after the manner thereof. And out of them shall proceed thanksgiving and the voice of them that make merry: and I will multiply them, and they shall not be few; I will also glorify them, and they shall not be small. Their children also shall be as aforetime, and their congregation shall be established before me, and I will punish all that oppress them. And their nobles shall be of themselves, and their governor shall proceed from the midst of them; and I will cause him to draw near, and he shall approach unto me: for who is this that engaged his heart to approach unto me? saith the LORD. And ye shall be my people, and I will be your God. Behold, the whirlwind of the LORD goeth forth with fury, a continuing whirlwind: it shall fall with pain upon the head of the wicked. **The fierce anger of the LORD shall not return, until he have done it, and until he have performed the intents of his heart: in the latter days ye shall consider it.** (Jeremiah 30:1–24 KJV; my emphasis)

In chapter 9, immediately after the appearance and vision of chapter 8, Daniel continues his quest to understand the appearance and vision that was shown and told to him. Daniel begins reviewing God's Word to receive further clarification. His review brings him to Jeremiah's prophecies, which document the prophecy of the seventy years of Israel's Babylonian captivity as written in Jeremiah 29.[112] Daniel then reads and understands Jeremiah 30, the prophecy of the time of Jacob's trouble. Daniel understands Jacob's trouble to be a time of future trouble for Israel due to Israel's transgressions throughout their existence. Daniel, realizing Jacob's trouble and the relation to the last times, then understands that the appearance of chapter 8 was somehow related. Because of his partial understanding, he begins to seek God for further revelation and understanding regarding the vision of chapter 8. His prayer and supplications are listed in Daniel 9:1–20.

---

[112] Jeremiah 29:1–12; Daniel 9:1, 2.

THE LAST DAYS AND THE VILE MAN OF DANIEL

Daniel now seeks God in prayer and supplication for understanding of how all of this is related (Daniel 9:1–20). He specifically and deliberately prays to God for understanding, while also confessing the sins of his people, Israel. God responds to Daniel by sending his archangel Gabriel to inform Daniel of what is to come in the latter days. The answer from God begins in Daniel 9:20 and is related to the future of Israel and the land in response to Daniel's prayer. Consider the following:

> …..And whiles I was speaking, and praying, and confessing my sin and the sin of my people Israel, and presenting my supplication before the LORD my God for the holy mountain of my God; Yea, whiles I was speaking in prayer, even the man Gabriel, whom I had seen in the vision at the beginning, being caused to fly swiftly, touched me about the time of the evening oblation. And he informed me, and talked with me, and said, **O Daniel, I am now come forth to give thee skill and understanding. At the beginning of thy supplications the commandment came forth, and I am come to shew thee; for thou art greatly beloved: therefore understand the matter, and consider the vision** (mareh; the vision from chapter 8). (Daniel 9:20–23 KJV; my emphasis)

While Daniel was offering sacrifice (prayer) for his people, the land and the holy mount, God sent his angel to give Daniel insight and understanding regarding the vision ("mareh") of chapter 8. Recall that the vision of chapter 8 encompassed twenty-three hundred days. Interestingly, the same word and root construct that was used three times in chapter 8, in verses 15, 16, and 27 ("mare[h]"), is again used in Daniel 9:23 and 10:1. The evidence builds that all four of these occurrences of "vision" ("mareh") refer to the same twenty-three-hundred-day vision originally documented in Daniel 8:15.[113] The same Hebrew word is once again used in all of these verses further proving that the same "vision" ("mareh") of chapter 8 is meant throughout. The meaning of the expression *"understand the matter, and consider the vision"* in Daniel 9:23 is *"pay attention and listen carefully to the response that God is giving."* Daniel was instructed to pay attention to the vision of the appearance, while also considering the revelation that the angel was about to give. The instructions and revelation from the angel are listed in Daniel in 9:23 and onward. The vision, as we know, is associated with the twenty-three hundred days of chapter 8.[114] Daniel is told to *"consider the matter"* of the discourse about to be revealed to him. Another translation would be *"Consider the words that will follow and understand the appearance which you saw."* Daniel was not allowed to reveal the appearance or write down the vision that he saw in chapter 8.[115] Daniel could receive revelation from God through the angel to understand the appearance or vision, but Daniel was instructed not to write down the specifics of the vision. Gabriel was given the order to have Daniel understand.[116] In summary, Daniel will be given information to understand the vision, but he is instructed to keep the specific details of the vision to himself. Daniel does document in great detail the events of the first half of the final seven years, and a generic description of the final forty and two months, but he is instructed not to document the judgment scenes listed in the book of Revelation.

The vision revealed to Daniel in Daniel 8:15, and Daniel's consideration of the revelation provided in Daniel 9:24–27, will accomplish God's purpose to give Daniel skill in understanding concerning the appearance or vision. His acknowledgment that he understands the vision is documented in Daniel 10:1. Daniel understands how the vision relates to latter days regarding Israel and the great warfare that will then be present on the earth. Daniel

---

[113] Four similar syntactic occurrences, see Daniel 8:16, 27; 9:23; 10:1.
[114] Daniel 8:15, 16, 17, 26, 27.
[115] Daniel 8:26.
[116] Daniel 8:16.

receives the answer from God to his original prayer and supplication in chapter 9. Although Daniel now understands the appearance, he does not write down the specifics of the actual vision of chapter 8, since he is instructed to keep it secret, or *"shut up the vision."*

The verses God gives to Daniel to assist in his understanding of the vision of chapter 8:15 are listed below in 9:24–27. He is given the information that he is to contemplate in verses 24–27 while also considering the twenty-three-hundred-day vision of chapter 8. Finally, in Daniel 10:1, he states that he understands the vision of 8:15, being able to assimilate the words and prophecy given him in Daniel 9:24–27. All these verses are tied together through God's use of the same word for "vision," *"mareh,"* which is used in each verse beginning in Daniel 8:15. The verses below summarize the angel's revelation that allows Daniel to consider and understand the vision of chapter 8:15. Consider the following:

> Seventy weeks are determined upon thy people and upon thy holy city, to finish the transgression, and to make an end of sins, and to make reconciliation for iniquity, and to bring in everlasting righteousness, and to seal up the vision and prophecy, and to anoint the most Holy. Know therefore and understand, that from the going forth of the commandment to restore and to build Jerusalem unto the Messiah the Prince shall be seven weeks, and threescore and two weeks: the street shall be built again, and the wall, even in troublous times. And after threescore and two weeks shall Messiah be cut off, but not for himself: and the people of **the prince that shall come** shall destroy the city and the sanctuary; and the end thereof shall be with a flood, and unto the end of the war desolations are determined. And he shall confirm the covenant with many for one week: and in the midst of the week he shall cause the sacrifice and the oblation to cease, and

for the overspreading of abominations he shall make it desolate, even until the consummation, and that determined shall be poured upon the desolate. (Daniel 9:24–27 KJV)

Daniel 9: 24–26 document God's answer to Daniel's prayer. God's explanation of the seventy weeks allows Daniel to further understand the twenty-three-hundred-day vision of Daniel 8:15 as well as the final seventy sevens of years, or 490 divided years, for Israel. The angel first instructs Daniel concerning the events of the final 490 years, which will be divided (not continuous), or cut off, for Israel. At the completion of the final 490 years (seventy sevens of years, or 490 years), the prophecies listed in 9:24 will be accomplished for Israel and the Jews. The end of the 490 years will result in God fulfilling all the promises made to their fathers. One key to understanding the 490 years is the word used for "weeks" in 9:24. The Hebrew word used for "weeks" is "*sabuim*," which simply means "seven units of time." The time could be in any form; that is, the term could be used of days, years, or other units of time. The closest time context in chapter 9 is years, as recorded in Daniel 9:2. Additionally, several other scriptures are in sequential harmony when years are used as the time reference in this verse. Another key to correctly interpret this verse is the word used for "determined" in verse 24—the Hebrew word "*nehtak*," meaning "to cut off" or "to divide." Putting these facts together in the context of this section, the angel states in verse 24 that after the divided 490 years, six events will have been fulfilled for Daniel's people, the land, and the holy place. The list is as follows:

1. Their transgression will be finished.
2. An end to their sins will be reached.
3. Reconciliation for their iniquity will be complete.
4. Everlasting righteousness will be brought in.
5. Vison and prophecy will be sealed up.
6. The Most Holy will be anointed.

The six prophetic events listed above, at the time of this writing (2020), have never been realized for Israel; all of these events still await their fulfillment. This assures us that this prophecy is related to the future. The key to understanding the apparent time confusion is understanding the word "determined" used in verse 24. The meaning is "to divide" or "to break off": that is, the seventy weeks of years are divided, broken off, or not continuous. God reinforces this idea by dividing the revelation regarding the seventy weeks of years into seven, sixty-two, and one final week of years, as documented in verses 24–27. The final week is the future prophecy and, as will be shown, is the focus of the section. The first sixty-nine weeks are historical and end with the cutting off of the Messiah in or about AD 29, as documented in verse 26. The prophecy began on or around 454 BC and ended with the cutting off of the Messiah on or around AD 29, for a total of 483 years. The section states that after sixty-nine weeks of years, or 483 years (near AD 29), the Messiah will be rejected and "cut off." The Messiah will be "cut off" and not come into the kingdom God prepared for him. His kingdom will be held in abeyance. Of course, from history and the scripture, we know that the Lord was crucified, died, was buried, and on the third day rose again. Although he rose from the dead, the Jews rejected him, and his lordship over Israel and the earth has been held in abeyance for a later time. There will be a future time on earth when the Messiah will rule the earth, which will also coincide with when Israel learns to say, *"Blessed is he who comes in the name of the Lord."*[117] The time is associated with the Revelation of the Lord Jesus Christ—the last book of the Bible. After the sixty-nine weeks of years and the cutting off of the Messiah, one week of years remains for the fulfillment of the Daniel 9:24. The prophecy of what occurs during this last seven years begins in the second part of Daniel 9:26 with *"the prince that shall come."* This prince that shall come is, indeed, the Antichrist. He is the one that will destroy Jerusalem, pose as God, and deceive the world for the final forty-two months of the last seven years. At the end of this last week, or last seven years, and the additional days

---

[117] Matthew 23:37–39.

mentioned in Daniel 12: 11–13 all six events related to Israel as stated in verse 24 will be fulfilled.

As stated, the last seven years is still future and is associated with the book of Revelation, or the Revelation of Jesus Christ as King of kings and Lord of lords on the earth. In other words, there is a significant gap of time between the sixty-ninth week and the seventieth week of Daniel's 9.24 prophecy, which is still future. The key to understanding the seventy sevens is understanding the time gap between the sixty-ninth and seventieth sevens. The gap in time is the time skipped over by God between the cutting off of the Messiah and the future prince or leader that shall come (the Antichrist) as mentioned in verse 26. The gap is almost two thousand years old to date (2020) and includes the time of the period of the mystery of the one body of Christ. Recall that the mystery period was hidden in God and never revealed to anyone until revealed to Paul in the first century. Why did God keep this time hidden or secret from Daniel and the angels and all the Old Testament prophets? Consider the following:

> …For this cause I Paul, the prisoner of Jesus Christ for you Gentiles, If ye have heard of the dispensation of the grace of God which is given me to you-ward: How that by revelation he made known unto me the **mystery**; (as I wrote afore in few words, Whereby, when ye read, ye may understand my knowledge in the mystery of Christ) **Which in other ages was not made known unto the sons of men, as it is now revealed unto his holy apostles and prophets by the Spirit; That the Gentiles should be fellowheirs, and of the same body, and partakers of his promise in Christ by the gospel**: Whereof I was made a minister, according to the gift of the grace of God given unto me by the effectual working of his power. Unto me, who am less than the least of all saints, is this grace given, that I should preach among the Gentiles

the unsearchable riches of Christ; And to make all men see what is the fellowship of the mystery, which from the beginning of the world hath been hid in God, who created all things by Jesus Christ. (Ephesians 3:1–9 KJV; my emphasis)

…Howbeit we speak wisdom among them that are perfect: yet not the wisdom of this world, nor of the princes of this world, that come to nought: **But we speak the wisdom of God in a mystery, even the hidden wisdom, which God ordained before the world unto our glory: Which none of the princes of this world knew: for had they known it, they would not have crucified the Lord of glory.** But as it is written, Eye hath not seen, nor ear heard, neither have entered into the heart of man, the things which God hath prepared for them that love him. (1 Corinthians 2:6–9 KJV; my emphasis)

These spectacular verses reveal that God kept all information regarding the mystery of the one body of Christ hidden from man and the scriptures; it is nowhere to be found in the Old Testament. It is the period of the mystery that came into being between the sixty-ninth and seventieth sevens of years of Daniel 9.24 and as documented by the apostle Paul in the above scriptures. The mystery period was also hidden from the devil, the angels, and the Old Testament prophets. The reason for hiding the information was to assure that the redemption of mankind through Jesus Christ would be accomplished; that is, that the devil would unknowingly crucify Jesus Christ, and through his death many would become sons of God and be saved by God through faith in Christ Jesus, as stated above. The mystery period was just that—a mystery unknown to any of God's creation, including the angels, and kept in the heart of God. Therefore, it was unknown and undocumented in scripture until revealed to Paul in the first century. It was also unknown by Daniel and the Old Testament prophets. Understanding the mystery and applying it to these verses in Daniel reveals that God skips over more than two thousand years in this section of Daniel. The gap is between the sixty-ninth seven of years and the seventieth seven of years. As we have seen other sections of Daniel need to be rightly divided in light of this time gap as well. In terms of actual years, the gap is between the 483rd year and the 484th year of the total 490 years of Daniel's revelation of seventy sevens of years. God does this in Daniel 9 by not mentioning any period in between the 483rd and the 484th years. Realizing the gap of time due to the mystery period between the 483rd year and the 484th year, and putting this together in Daniel 9, the 484th year begins the last seven years that still require fulfillment. The first of two seven-year periods begin with the rising of the Antichrist during the time of the end and after he makes a league with a strong ally (see Daniel 9:26b and Daniel 11.23). The prince that shall come, Antichrist, mentioned in Daniel 9.26 is related to the events of the final seven years. He is described as destroying the city (Jerusalem) and the sanctuary (the Holy Place). Verse 27 mentions the covenant that he makes, and parallel events mentioned in verse 26. These two verses (Daniel 9.26, 27) both allude to the time of the end in short measure. The remaining scriptures in Daniel and the book of Revelation will reach their fulfillment during the last seven years. Additionally, the twenty-three hundred days listed in Daniel 8:9–14 also relate to the Antichrist and await fulfillment during these last seven years.

Once the gap in the seventy sevens is understood and divided accordingly, a substantial number of associated scriptures can be harmonized and rightly divided. It also becomes clear why the Lord pointed to the book of Daniel in Matthew 24 when asked about the last times, since Daniel contains, as we also will see, significant information regarding the last seven years still future. Verse 26 of Daniel 9 goes on to reveal the details of the last seven years for Israel, which are still future and part of the latter days. The last days begin with the Antichrist strengthening himself with a strong nation or nations and many people (see Daniel 9:27). The final twenty-three hundred days, however, begin with the beginning of sorrows on the earth and then the Antichrist rising in strength and power as he begins his conquests (Daniel 8.9). Additionally, verse 26 also describing the works of the

THE LAST DAYS AND THE VILE MAN OF DANIEL

Antichrist states that the prince that will come will destroy the city and the sanctuary. The context of these prophetic events is related to Israel, the land, and the city Jerusalem and the holy place. After this, both verse 26 and 27 describe desolation, war, and destruction to follow on the earth for the final forty-two months. Review figure 1 of Appendix D: "The Final Timelines" which graphically depicts Seventy weeks in totality. From figure 1 of Appendix D it is clear that the first seven weeks of years, or forty-nine years, begins with the building of Jerusalem and ends with the dedication of the temple in Jerusalem. The next sixty-two sevens, or 434 years (7×62), follow immediately after the first seven sevens and continue for the next 434 years. The end of these sixty-two sevens is the cutting off of the Messiah in AD 29 (the Julian calendar being in error by about 4 years). From the second part of Daniel 9:26 until the end of the chapter, the last times and the final seven years are referred to.

The final seven years will be initiated by God when God decides to initiate them and at the last time.[118] The final seven years usher in the last days of man's rule on earth and are reserved for the latter time of the mystery period. The time is also marked by a time when the sins of those on the earth reach their full potential, or are filled to overflowing on the earth, like the time before the flood of Noah's day. The mystery period will end generally around the time of the last seven years, marked by the rapture of the church of Jesus Christ to heaven. The time will be at the discretion of God. The exact timing is only alluded to in the Word of God, but it will be a brief time after the Antichrist declares himself as god at the time of the middle of the last seven years. We know from Thessalonians that it will be after the revelation of the beast on the earth.[119] God, in his word, assures us that the body of Christ will be removed from the earth before the true wrath of God comes upon the earth: *"For he shall save us from the wrath to come."*[120] It is also clear that the church will be on the earth for a portion of the final seven years,

---

[118] Acts 1:7.
[119] 2 Thessalonians 2:3, 4.
[120] 1 Thessalonians 5:9.

since 1 Thessalonians 5:3 states clearly that *"that day (the day of our gathering together) shall not come until there be a falling away first and the Man of Sin is revealed."* The man of sin is indeed the Antichrist, and the falling away is a departure from God's universal laws that govern the earth and mankind. A time when lawlessness will abound. Both conditions need to be met before the gathering-together event occurs. Fundamentally, God saves the church of the body of Christ from the wrath that will come upon the earth. The church will be on the earth from the time of the beginning of the final twenty-three hundred days until sometime after the middle of the final seven years. The twenty-three hundred days mark the beginning of sorrows on the earth.[121] These truths are guaranteed by reading and studying what God has revealed in his word regarding the rapture of the church—especially what is written in 1 and 2 Thessalonians.[122] The period of God's ultimate wrath is slated to occur during a portion of the second half of the final seven years of Daniel's seventy sevens—the final forty-two months. The wrath of God and the judgments of God, as well as all the judgments recorded in Revelation, will require twenty-three hundred days to reach fulfillment, but the true wrath of God as documented in the book of revelation will reach its peak during the final forty-two months. The twenty-three hundred days begin, in heaven, with the opening of the first five seals mentioned in Revelation chapter 6. The final twenty-three hundred days will begin at the time of the overspreading of abominations as stated in Daniel 9.27. As the twenty-three hundred days progress, the Antichrist will then begin his rise and his assaults against neighboring countries. The conclusion of the twenty-three hundred days will be marked by the cleansing of the sanctuary.[123]

    The latter part of Daniel 9:26 goes on to state that a prince will come and destroy the city (Jerusalem) and the sanctuary, ending with a flood. The Hebrew word for *"flood"* in 9:26 signifies an overwhelming force of desolation and destruction. Jesus Christ

---

[121] Matthew 24:8.
[122] 1 Thessalonians 5:1–9.
[123] Daniel 8:9; 8:14; Revelation 6:1, 2; Matthew 24:4–28.

never destroyed and will never destroy Jerusalem or the sanctuary at any time, past, present, or future. There are numerous records of the Antichrist doing both while also destroying the nations and a great many people. The prince of Daniel 9:26 is a reference to the Antichrist and is again explained by the gap in time between the first part of verse 26, ending with the cutting off of the Messiah, and the second part, which regards the prince that shall come. Understanding the gap in time and how God skips over the mystery period to the last days, the days of the false messiah, solves the problem of time. The latter part of verse 26 relates to the Antichrist, the prince or leader that will come in the last days. The word for "prince" here is from an Aramaic root word, "*ngyd*," which simply means "a leader or ruler" in the nominative. The "Prince that shall come"—the Antichrist—is the one who rises in the last time and who will destroy the city and the sanctuary with a military host of people dedicated to him. The destruction of the city and the sanctuary will be followed by forty-two months of desolations. The desolations are characterized in verse 26 by the Hebrew words translated as *"desolations are determined,"* indicating the extent of the destruction on the earth. The height of this destruction will also be accompanied by the wrath of Almighty God and will truly begin in earnest after the midst or middle of the week (last seven years), or during the final forty-two months. The same words are used in Isaiah, in which Isaiah describes the same wrath of almighty God at the time of the end. Consider the following:

> And it shall come to pass in that day, that the remnant of Israel, and such as are escaped of the house of Jacob, shall no more again stay upon him that smote them; but shall stay upon the LORD, the Holy One of Israel, in truth. The remnant shall return, even the remnant of Jacob, unto the mighty God. For though thy people Israel be as the sand of the sea, yet a remnant of them shall return: **the consumption decreed** shall overflow with righteousness. **For the Lord**

GOD of hosts shall make a consumption, even determined, in the midst of all the land.

Therefore thus saith the Lord GOD of hosts, O my people that dwellest in Zion, be not afraid of the Assyrian: he shall smite thee with a rod, and shall lift up his staff against thee, after the manner of Egypt.

For yet a very little while, and the indignation shall cease, and mine anger in their destruction.

And the LORD of hosts shall stir up a scourge for him according to the slaughter of Midian at the rock of Oreb: and as his rod was upon the sea, so shall he lift it up after the manner of Egypt.

And it shall come to pass in that day, that his burden shall be taken away from off thy shoulder, and his yoke from off thy neck, and the yoke shall be destroyed because of the anointing. (Isaiah 10:20–27 KJV; my emphasis)

Daniel 9:27, one of the most important verses regarding the Antichrist, goes on to give additional information regarding the rise to power of the Antichrist during the last days and the last seven years. The Antichrist is said to become strong with a covenant, as stated in the first part of verse 27. The important words to be understood in this verse are "strong" and "covenant." The words used represent a covenant that makes one strong. The emphasis is not on the strength of the covenant but rather on his ability to become strong with the covenant. He makes a promise or agreement with a great nation. The same covenant is described as a league in Daniel 11.23. The league of Daniel 11.23 is in the singular in contrast with the covenant that he makes with the many of Daniel 9.27. Both references describe alliance he makes with strong nations. Considering both verses it appears that one of these nations or peoples is stronger than the others and is responsible for his rise to power. This nation also keeps other Gentile nations from interfering in his dealings. The covenant or league does not start the final seven years but begins a seven-year period in which the league strengthens him up to the time of the middle of the final seven years (see timelines in Appendix D; figure 4). The covenant can be considered as the first action in a sequence of events that lead to the final time. Additionally, it does not appear to be a seven-year formal agreement, but rather a length of time in which he is strengthened by it.

The verb used for "strong" in verse 27 is in the Hebrew stem "*hifil*", indicating that the object of the verb, or the covenant, participates in the action of the verb. Stating this another way, the covenant is responsible, either wholly or partially, for the strength or continued strengthening of the prince that shall come—the Antichrist. His strength continues and grows from this time forward until his demise. Interestingly, the Hebrew word for "strong," with the grammatical inflection used in verse 27, is the only such usage in the Bible. The usage of "covenant" in verse 27 is used for alliances, agreements, or promises. In this case, the covenant is made between the prince that shall come and great nation(s). One of these great nations is the same nation associated with the league of Daniel 11.23. The league or covenant marks the beginning of the first of two seven-year periods, in which the second seven-year period, the final seven years, begins at the midpoint of the first. The agreement seems to stand on its own as the initiating point for the events associated with the time of the end. The agreement also seems to have nothing to do with the conglomeration of nations as documented in Revelation 13:1–2 and Revelation 17:15. It is entirely possible that it may be a secondary event on the earth and not draw a great deal of attention from those on the earth. Daniel 9:27b goes on to indicate that at the time of the middle of the first seven years, the Antichrist begins to develop his plans to cause the sacrifice and oblation to cease. This is also the time of the *middle* of the first seven years which initiates the final seven years as depicted in the final timelines. His method of causing desolation (emptiness) of this place in Jerusalem is mentioned in the next part of the verse: *"the overspreading of abominations."* It is this overspreading of abominations which will both mark the beginning of the final twenty-three hundred days and begin to make the sacrifice and oblation to cease in Jerusalem and become empty. Note: the Hebrew word for *"desolate"* in this verse does not mean destruction, but rather an "emptiness." Whatever this *"overspreading of abominations"* is will be understood at the time of the beginning of the final twenty-three hundred days.

The revelation given to Daniel in chapter 9:23–27 allowed him to understand the appearance, or vision, that he saw and previously recorded in Daniel 8:15. The revelation also begins to enlighten us as to God's time period for the deliverance that would come to Israel. Although this time-period is specific to Israel, its affect will be global—especially that of the last seven years which will shortly begin at the time of the midpoint of the first even years. Additionally, all of these time periods can only be understood when the Old Testament scriptures are rightly divided with respect to the missing mystery period—that is, the time of the mystery of the one body of Jesus Christ on earth as discussed previously. This time gap needs to be placed between the sixty-ninth and the seventieth week of years.

To summarize, Daniel was given a vision of an event; the fulfillment of which would require twenty-three hundred days. The twenty-three hundred days would be contained within the last seven years of Daniel's 9:24 prophecy. The beginning of the last sequence of events would be marked by the Antichrist making a league or covenant with many nations and a particularly powerful ally which allows him to rise in power and prominence with time. The vision of Daniel chapter 8 is now becoming clearer with the revelation he receives from the angel in chapter 9. Eventually the circumstances and events associated with the vision of Daniel chapter 8 would be written down by John in the book of the Revelation of Jesus Christ. The twenty-three hundred days begins in heaven with the opening of the first four of the seven seals, as listed in Revelation 6; the Antichrist told to *"go forth conquering and to conquer" and the famines, wars, plagues and peace being taken away from the earth."*[124] The corresponding event on the earth is the beginning of sorrows on the earth and then the rising of the Antichrist sometime after

---

[124] Revelation 6.2 (KJV)

THE LAST DAYS AND THE VILE MAN OF DANIEL

his league or covenant with a strong Gentile nation. The first seal summarizes the rise of the Antichrist and agrees with the beginning of the twenty-three hundred days that Daniel also witnessed.[125] The vision also included a good many of the judgments in the book of Revelation, as were documented and written by the apostle John, who was given the revelation by Jesus Christ. Daniel's prophecies also provide several of the events associated with the vision in revelation, while also providing additional details, but they do so through a different lens. The net effect of both records in Revelation and Daniel is that the last seven years will require both documents to truly understand the final events of the last days—the time period and the actual events. "*This is the mind that has wisdom.*"[126] God requires right division of his word to accurately understand both sections together. Both must be understood together while also considering the gap of time attributed to the mystery time-period. The mind that has applied wisdom and tediously works to understand the Word of God is required to fully understand the vision. Interestingly, Daniel is also instructed to have applied wisdom and skill to understand the visions and the words he was given.[127] Daniel was a man of great wisdom given to him by God. He was able accurately interpret visons of man and visions and revelations from God. He typified *the man who has wisdom.* The understanding of the vision and the timing set down in Daniel 8 can be fully understood only when both books of the Bible, and the related events, are considered together.

Daniel 9:27 goes on to give further information and events related to the rising of the Antichrist. This verse is hard to understand, but once studied in exegesis, it will be shown that it is in harmony with the other verses regarding the Antichrist. Verse 27 is also directly related to verse 26. The key to the understanding is that there are two intersecting seven-year periods documented in the Word of God at the time of the end. The first seven- year period, which is identified in this verse, is the seven-years in which the Antichrist becomes

---

[125] Daniel 8:9.
[126] Revelation 17:9.
[127] Daniel 9:22–23.

strong with the great nation or people as mentioned in this verse. The second seven-year term is the final seven years of Daniels seventy sevens of years prophecy of Daniel 9.24. The second, and final seven years, begins when the Antichrist begins to formulate in his mind his plans to attack the king of the South, the East, Jerusalem and the nation of Israel; effectively eliminating the Jewish daily sacrifice. These nations will exist at the time of the end, but only remnants of their former greatness. The seven-year periods overlap each other but are not the same; that is, they begin and end at separate times, but are both part of the last days sequence of events. The covenant or league of Daniel 9.27 marks the beginning of the rise to power of the Antichrist and is the first in a series of events associated with the last days. It is during the time of the middle of the first seven years, the Antichrist, for reasons not specified, will begin to formulate in his mind the elimination of the sacrifice and the oblation to cease in Jerusalem. The ceasing of the sacrifice and oblation will not happen quickly but will be a process of deterioration and attacks against the Jewish nation. There are two critical verbs that need to be understood as per their Hebrew stems to properly understand verses 26 and 27 of Daniel 9. Additionally, the structure depicting the related verse sections of both verses 26 and 27 need to be examined. Consider the following structure depicting the related verses of Daniel 9.26–27:

> **Daniel 9.26b (KJV)**
> **A. The Coming Prince**..........*and the people of the prince that shall come.*
>   **B. The City and Sanctuary Destroyed**..........*shall destroy the city and the sanctuary*
>   **C. Determined Desolations; final 42 months** ....*and the end thereof shall be with a flood, and unto the end of the war desolations are determined.*
>
> **Daniel 9.27 (KJV)**
> **A. The Coming Prince**..........*he shall confirm a covenant with many for one week (7 years).*
>   **B. The City and Sanctuary Destroyed; Abomination of Desolation shall be set up**..........*shall cause the sacrifice and oblation to cease and for the overspreading of abominations he shall make it desolate.*
>   **C. Determined Desolations; final 42 Months** ....*even until the consummation and that determined shall be poured upon the desolate.*

Examining the structure, it can be seen at once that both verses are relating the same time and the same events; namely the events that led up to the final forty-two months. Many of the same Hebrew words are also used in both verses which support the idea of each section of each verse has a corresponding section in the other verse. Both verses also introduce the prince that shall come (the Antichrist), but from two different stand points. Verse 26 identifies him as a prince that comes and destroys the city and the Sanctuary (Jerusalem and the Holy Place), while verse 27 reveals how he comes into power (a covenant with a great nation) and the events during the middle of the seven-year covenant which begin to cause the destruction of the city and the Sanctuary; that is, the desolator. Both verses also describe the final forty-two months of God's determined desolations. The accuracy and perfection of the Word of God is astonishing.

God utilizes structure to reveal interpretation throughout his word, these verses are no exception. The other Hebrew words critical to the proper understanding of these verses are the words *"determined"* used in both verse 26 and 27 and the word translated *"he shall cause"* used in verse 27. The Hebrew word translated *"determined"* originates from the same Hebrew word transliterated *neherasah* and is a verb in the *Nifal* Hebrew stem. The verb with this inflection is used three other times[128] in the Word of God besides the usages in verse 26 and 27; each time it is describing the final forty-two months of the wrath of God that he has determined on the earth. The other word we need to better understand is the verb translated into English in verse 27 as *"he shall cause."* The verb has its roots from the Hebrew word transliterated *yasbit* and is inflected from the *Hifil* stem and the imperfect tense indicating an incomplete action. The verb is better translated into English as *"he shall begin to cause."* This verb form allows the verses to be in harmony with the structure related to the two seven-year periods. Based on these facts the following extended English interpretation of verse 26b and 27 is offered:

> In the last days a leader of the people shall come on the scene who shall make a seven-year covenant with great nation(s) At the time of the middle of this seven-year covenant, abominations on the earth shall begin to intensify until the desolation spoken of by the prophets begin and continue until the final end. Additionally, he shall begin to cause the cessation of the sacrifice and oblation. This condition will continue until the time that the city and the sanctuary are destroyed. After this the determined wrath of God will be upon the earth until the final end.

These verses are now in harmony with the other scriptures relating to the same events and shed light on both intersecting seven

---

[128] See Isaiah 10.23, 28.22; Daniel 11.36.

years periods as well as the final 2,300 days. It is these final forty and two months that focus on many of the events of the book of Revelation, especially the supernatural rule of the Antichrist. The time of the end will also fulfill the well documented Jacobs's trouble in the Old Testament. The final forty and two months will include the wrath of God on the earth and the culmination of God's dealings with Jew and Gentile. During this time period, the rapture of the body of Christ will also occur sometime after the Antichrist comes into his supernatural state.[129]

The ceasing of the sacrifice, and oblation caused by the Antichrist, has been the cause for vast differences in commentaries. The best explanation, and one that fits well with the context, is that the Antichrist will cause the worship and prayer of the Jews in Jerusalem to cease in the middle point of the final last seven years. One theory worth noting is the theory of the Western Wall of Jerusalem. The theory has to do with the cessation of prayer and supplications to God at the Western Wall in Jerusalem. Supporting this is the strange use of the Hebrew word translated as *"wall"* in Daniel 9:25 (KJV). The Hebrew word for "wall" in verse 25 is the word *"harus,"* having the basic root meaning of *"to cut out, or to cut off."*[130] "Harus" has been confusing translators throughout the years and is the subject of much speculation. Suppose that God, in his infinite wisdom, understood that in the last time there would be in Jerusalem a Western Wall, where the remnant of believing Israel would provide constant or daily prayer to God. The wall was *"cut out"* and its foundation is the only remains from the great city of David in Jerusalem from antiquity. The wall stands as a monument and reminder to the Jews of the remains of the temple that was built on the holy ground nearby. The Antichrist, in the middle of the last seven years, will put an end to this prayer sacrifice. The place of these actions will be the holy place in Jerusalem, as documented in

---

[129] 11 Thessalonians 2:1–4.
[130] *Theological Workbook of Old Testament*, Harris, R. L., Archer, G. L., Jr., & Waltke, B. K. (Eds.). (1999). Theological Wordbook of the Old Testament (electronic ed., p. ii). Chicago: Moody Press. #752.

many other scriptures.[131] In any event, those alive to see these terrible events at the time of the end will clearly understand the meaning. The second part of verse 27 states that after the middle part of the seven years associated with the covenant; the people of the earth will begin to experience increasing hardships until the time of the final forty-two months: "*the overspreading of abominations shall make it desolate until the indignation of God is consummated* [completed]." The description is one of desolation, destruction, and war and matching the time span of Revelation 13:5. The war will not be just any war; it will be a war backed by the hatred and supernatural force of Satan through his supernatural instrument, the Antichrist. The war is one of man against man and the forces of Satan against those on the earth. It will not only be a physical war on the earth but also a spiritual war in heaven—a war of God and his forces against Satan and his angels. This war will include the supernatural forces of Satan on the earth having great wrath upon the inhabitants of the earth.[132] The war will also feature the wrath of almighty God against unbelieving mankind and the forces of Satan. The destruction will begin with nation rising against nation and kingdom rising against kingdom, initiated by the Antichrist as he ascends to power in the latter part of the first 3.5 years. The holy place in Jerusalem will be the initial focus of destruction at the midst of the last seven years and will spread throughout the world as the Antichrist places the abomination, which causes desolation on the earth. The horrible war and turmoil will foster famine and disease, which will eventually be mingled with the spiritual powers of Satan and then the wrath of almighty God. These conditions will then spread very quickly throughout the world, lasting for the final forty-two months.

The final 3.5 years, or forty-two months, are intrinsically tied to the forty-two months of Revelation—the tribulation. The period is also known as the time of Jacobs's trouble, as referenced earlier. The tribulation period, or final forty-two months, is the central focus of the book of Revelation and the latter chapters of the book of

---

[131] Matthew 24:15; Daniel 11:31.
[132] Revelation 12:12.

Daniel. The final tribulation on the earth is also referenced in other sections of Daniel as well as several other Old and New Testament scriptures. For example, from Daniel 11:31 to the end of Daniel 11, information is provided detailing this final time period. This section of Daniel will be addressed in Section 2, References 7 and 8. The second part of Daniel 9:27 states, "… *that determined is poured out on the desolator.*" The first occurrence of this phrase, as previously noted, is in Isaiah 10 as noted in Section 1; References 1, 2, 3.

With respect to the middle of the final seven years, there are several scriptures that corroborate the same sequence of events. It will be these events that will unmistakably mark the middle of the last seven years. Investigation and comparison with other scriptures concerning the middle of the final seventieth week reveals that several events will mark the midpoint of the seventieth seven or final seven years. The events can be listed as follows:

1. The Antichrist will cause the sacrifice and the oblation at the holy place in Jerusalem to cease.[133]
2. The Antichrist will continue strengthening himself, now through spiritual forces supplied by Satan and evil angels.
3. The abomination that causes desolation will be set up at the holy place in Jerusalem, the holy place being the sanctuary of strength, or Holy of Holies.[134]
4. The final forty-two months begin as depicted in Revelation 13.
5. At or about the middle of the seventieth seven, the Antichrist is assassinated and satanically raised from the dead; shortly thereafter, he declares himself God at the Holy of Holies in Jerusalem.[135]

God's prophecy to Daniel regarding the seventy sevens of years stands as one of the greatest prophecies concerning a time roadmap

---

[133] Daniel 11.31.
[134] Daniel 11:31; 12:11.
[135] Matthew 24:15; 2 Thessalonians 2:4; Revelation 13:1; 17:8, 11.

in the Bible. The prophecy represents the divine road map for the ages, up to and including the return of Jesus Christ to the earth as King of kings and Lord of lords. All groups will be affected: the Jews, the Gentiles, and the Church of God. It will mark God's final dealings with the three groups, especially the remnant of Israel. Key to the understanding of the final time period is the gap in time between the sixty-ninth and seventieth seven-year periods—the time of the mystery of the one body of Christ. The gap in time has now continued for more than two thousand years. The time frame includes the coming of the Messiah, Jesus of Nazareth—both his first coming, his cutting off, and his second coming at the end of the seventy sevens of years (490 years). Messiah will die or be cut off and then raised from the dead. Then, after at least two thousand years encompassing the time of the mystery period, the last seven years will begin at God's initiation. The end of the seven years will usher in the acceptable year of the Lord and the millennial kingdom of Jesus Christ anointed as Lord of lords and King of kings. The final seven-year period marks the end of the mystery period, at which time the body of Christ will be taken up in the clouds of the air. Once the body of Christ is removed from the earth, prophecy reverts to the fulfillment of the final seven years for Israel, and especially the final forty and two months. Upon the completion of the seventieth seven, all of God's promises to Israel, especially those of Daniel 9:24, will have been fulfilled. During the final forty-two months, the city of Jerusalem and the temple will be destroyed by the Antichrist, or the prince that shall come. Additionally, the nations of the world will suffer ruin as documented in Revelation and other scriptures.

The beginning of the last days is marked by an evil ruler, the Antichrist, rising and establishing himself with a firm covenant, or resolution, with many nations. At the time of the middle of this seven-year covenant, abominations on the earth begin to intensify until the time of the middle of the final seven years. At the time of the middle of the final seven years the Antichrist supernaturally persecutes God's people and the nations. His wicked activities will last for the final forty-two months. After this final forty-two months of desolations on the earth, the Lord Jesus Christ will come again and destroy the Antichrist with the brightness of his coming. He will judge the Antichrist and all those who follow him and deliver the same to destruction.

The final twenty-three-hundred days contained within the final seven years includes the opening of the seven seals of Revelation 6.2. The beginning of the twenty-three hundred days therefore initiates events in heaven—namely, the opening of the first four of the seven seals by our Lord Jesus Christ. The opening of the first seal results in the rise of the Antichrist. Each seal opening in heaven corresponds to a reactionary event on the earth. The end of the period is marked by the cleansing of the sanctuary in Jerusalem and also the end of the twenty-three-hundred days. The general order of the seals in heaven and the corresponding judgments on the earth follow the path set forth by God, as documented in Revelation 6. These judgements can be thought of to occur simultaneously or at least after the beginning of the final twenty-three hundred days. Consider the following:

1. The Antichrist conquering; the white horse.
2. Peace taken from the earth; the red horse.
3. Famine spreads on the earth; the black horse.
4. Pestilence and disease spread on the earth; the pale horse.

These are the beginnings of sorrows as also stated by our Lord Jesus Christ in Matthew 24:4–8. In Daniel 8:27, Daniel states that he did not understand the vision of the appearance but was astonished by the vision. Daniel is then instructed to "*shut up*," or seal up, the vision, since it is reserved for the last days. The vision given to Daniel, would eventually be written down by John in the book of Revelation. Daniel 9 documents Daniel's prayer and supplication to God to understand both the vision and the end for Israel. Daniel 9:2 reveals Daniel's search in the book of Jeremiah the prophet for answers to his questions regarding the revelation and visions he received. Through his search, Daniel understands the seventy-year servitude of the Jews in Babylon. Daniel also understands from Jeremiah that a time of Jewish trouble will occur during the last days of man's rule on the earth.[136] Daniel continues in chapter 9 to petition God for forgiveness for his people: the Jews, their land, and the holy temple. In response, God reveals to Daniel focused last-time information regarding the Jews, their land, and the holy temple.[137] Gabriel instructs Daniel in 9:23 to *"consider and understand the matter,"* or the prophetic words of chapters 9–12. Daniel needs to consider both the words given and the vision he received in chapter 8. Daniel is instructed to consider the information, including the seventy weeks, the desolations of Jerusalem, the destruction of Jerusalem, the twenty-three-hundred-day vison, and the persecution of God's people, and, finally, the redemption of God's people. After consideration of these events, Daniel begins to unravel the meaning of the great vision of Chapter 8. The final chapters of Daniel reveal to us that Daniel does finally understand the vision and its meaning. Daniel states (NIV): *"In the third year of Cyrus king of Persia, a revelation was given to Daniel (who was called Belteshazzar). Its message was true and it concerned a great war" (Daniel 10:1 NIV)*. The King James version sheds additional light: *"In the third year of Cyrus king of Persia a thing was revealed unto Daniel, whose name was called Belteshazzar; and the thing was true, but the time appointed was long: and he understood the thing, and had understanding of the vision." (Daniel 10:1 KJV)*. Note how Daniel understood the vision, but the specifics of the vision are only indirectly referenced in Daniel 10.1; that is, *"it concerned a great and long warfare."* This is indicative of the fact that Daniel obeyed the command of the angel to not document the specifics of the vision. The specifics and additional details of the vision was given to John to document in the book of Revelation hundreds of years later and after the resurrection of the Lord Jesus Christ. We also know that the vision was a long duration event (2,300 days).

In summary, the great vision revealed to Daniel in chapter 8 was to be shut up and sealed by Daniel.[138] Although Daniel was instructed to seal and shut up the vision, he sought to understand

---

[136] Jeremiah 30:7.
[137] Daniel 9:22–27.
[138] Daniel 8:26.

it through prayer and fasting. Daniel finally understood the vision, as he pondered the vision and considered the words of God listed in chapters 9–12. Chapters 9–12 effectively decipher the vison that Daniel saw in chapter 8. God answered Daniel's prayer by enlightening Daniel about the events of the last days and an accurate understanding of the vision or matter. After Daniel's petition to God to understand the fate of his people in the latter days (see Daniel 9:1–22), God sends his angel to reveal the latter-day details. At the same time, God reveals the meaning of the vision that he received. The angel instructs Daniel to *understand* the information that follows while *considering* the vision of Chapter 8. The first Hebrew verb used in the verse, "*byn*," is translated as "to understand," having the meaning "To observe with care and pay close attention to." The second verb, "*haban*," is translated as "to consider," with the meaning "To have consideration to the end that understanding is achieved." The inflections of the verbs are interesting. The first verb, translated as "to understand," is an absolute infinitive with the effect of actively intensifying the action—in this case, actively understanding God's Words. The second word, translated as "consider," is the same root word with a different inflection. The inflection is a Hebrew "hifil" stem, which is typically causative in nature. The verb is also in the imperative mood, representing a "command to do." Putting these two verbs together, the angel directs Daniel *to actively ponder the words that have been revealed to him. Through this process, he will understand the vision, the revelation, and the appearance ("mareh") of chapter 8.*

Daniel is instructed to consider the vision ("mareh"), which could only refer to the last vision that he saw, the vision of Daniel 8:15.[139] Daniel 9:23 ties the words of God that follow to both latter-day events and also to the vision of chapter 8. Daniel 10:1 states that Daniel finally comes to an accurate understanding of the vision of chapter 8 and the words that were given to him by the angel. The understanding was achieved after a long time spent pondering and considering the words given to him.

---

[139] Daniel 8:26–27.

In the third year of Cyrus king of Persia, Daniel understood the vision and associated prophecies that were documented in Daniel 7–12. Daniel 10:1 is parallel and related to Daniel 9:23. In Daniel 9:23, Daniel is instructed to understand the vision and consider the matter. Daniel finally understands the vision after several revelations from God and careful consideration of the vision of chapter 8 and the prophecies of chapters 9, 10, 11, and 12. The vision concerned the last days and a long warfare on the earth. The discernment did not come without a great deal of struggle and constant prayer to God for wisdom. The following excerpt from the *Good News Bible* (GNB) is a better interpretation of Daniel 10:1. The GNB clearly indicates Daniel's struggle to understand the visions and revelations that he was given: *"In the third year that Cyrus was emperor of Persia, a message was revealed to Daniel, who is also called Belteshazzar. The message was true but extremely hard to understand. It was explained to him in a vision" (Daniel 10:1 GNB)*

Daniel 10:1 is central to the understanding of chapters 7–12. Daniel 10:1 summarizes Daniel's challenge to understand all the visions and revelations given in chapters 7–12. The verse was written after the writings of chapters 8, 9, and most of 10, 11, and 12. The placement of Daniel 10:1 shows how it is central to the understanding of the entire Jewish prophecy contained in chapters 7–12. All the visions are related to the same central subject—the last days and the events leading up to the deliverance of Daniel's people, the Jews. In Daniel 10:1, Daniel states that he finally understands the visions and prophecies concerning the last time and the end for Israel.

Further examination and study of Daniel 10:1 is of value since it states Daniels understanding the entire Revelation given to him concerning his people: the Jews. Daniel 10.1 states *"In the third year of King Cyrus, a word was revealed."* This clearly refers to more than a single word (the KJV uses "a thing"). Some translations state, *"… a revelation was made."* A better translation would be *"… a message was revealed,"* but in those cases where passive forms cause difficulties, it is better to restructure the sentence and say, *"a revelation came to Daniel."* God revealed the matter to Daniel after a long ordeal of contemplating and considering the revelations concerning the vision he received. Daniel finally understood the twenty-three-hundred-day vision of chapter 8, the seventy sevens of weeks and the actions and behaviors of the Antichrist during the last days. The work to understand the revelation was a great mental struggle for him. It is likely that the two key words in this verse, "*thing*" and "*true*," refer to the struggle involved in understanding the message—that is, the revelation given in Daniel 8–12. Understanding the matter required a significant mental struggle; it was extremely difficult to comprehend. Stated another way, only after much struggle, prayer, and supplication to God did understanding come to

Daniel 10:2–6. After Daniel confesses in verse 1 that, although extremely difficult to comprehend, Daniel arrives at understanding with respect to the visions and revelations regarding the last days, Daniel describes a vison of the Lord in verses 2–6. Consider the following verses in Daniel 10:2–6:

> In those days I Daniel was mourning three full weeks. I ate no pleasant bread, neither came flesh nor wine in my mouth, neither did I anoint myself at all, till three whole weeks were fulfilled. And in the four and twentieth day of the first month, as I was by the side of the great river, which is Hiddekel; **Then I lifted up mine eyes, and looked, and behold a certain man clothed in linen, whose loins were girded with fine gold of Uphaz: His body also was like the beryl, and his face as the appearance of lightning, and his eyes as lamps of fire, and his arms and his feet like in colour to polished brass, and the voice of his words like the voice of a multitude.**
> (Daniel 10:2–6 KJV; my emphasis)

Daniel describes a certain vision that he received in the same days when he was receiving the various revelations and visions from God and the angel. The vision was that of a great man; it was strikingly like the vision that John received thousands of years later of the Lord

Jesus Christ, documented in Revelation 1:13–17. The vision is one of a great, astonishing man who was strikingly similar to the man that appeared to John as documented in Revelation 1. The vision critically ties the book of Daniel to the book of Revelation and the revelation of the Lord Jesus Christ. Consider and compare the record in Revelation 1:13–16, of the Lord Jesus Christ, with the similar description in Daniel 10; the similarity to Daniel 10:5–6 is unmistakable:

> I was in the Spirit on the Lord's day, and heard behind me a great voice, as of a trumpet, **Saying, I am Alpha and Omega, the first and the last:** and, What thou seest, write in a book, and send it unto the seven churches which are in Asia; unto Ephesus, and unto Smyrna, and unto Pergamos, and unto Thyatira, and unto Sardis, and unto Philadelphia, and unto Laodicea. And I turned to see the voice that spake with me. And being turned, I saw seven golden candlesticks; **And in the midst of the seven candlesticks one like unto the Son of man, clothed with a garment down to the foot, and girt about the paps with a golden girdle. His head and his hairs were white like wool, as white as snow; and his eyes were as a flame of fire; And his feet like unto fine brass, as if they burned in a furnace; and his voice as the sound of many waters.** And he had in his right hand seven stars: and out of his mouth went a sharp two-edged sword: and his countenance was as the sun shineth in his strength. And when I saw him, I fell at his feet as dead. And he laid his right hand upon me, saying unto me, Fear not; I am the first and the last: I am he that liveth, and was dead; and, behold, I am alive for evermore, Amen; and have the keys of hell and of death. Write the things which thou hast seen, and the things

THE LAST DAYS AND THE VILE MAN OF DANIEL

which are, and the things which shall be hereafter. (Revelation 1:10–19 KJV; my emphasis)

Both records contain identical characteristics not documented in any other part of scripture. God's Word reinforces the critical connection between Daniel and Revelation, linking both to the last days of natural man's rule on the earth.

Section 2, Reference 6: Attributes Associated with the Antichrist (Daniel 9:20—10:6)

1. Daniel 9:20–23 contains Daniel's prayer to understand the vision of chapter 8 and God's final dealings with Israel. The prayer is heard and answered by Gabriel, the same angel who first revealed the vision to Daniel. Gabriel states that he has come to give skill and understanding to Daniel. Daniel is instructed to understand the word while considering the vision of chapter 8. The vision is related to the last days and the rise of the Antichrist, or the vile man, on the earth in the last days.
2. Daniel 9:24–26 is the section in which the prophecy of the seventy weeks of years, or 490 years, is delivered to Daniel. The 490 years are divided into (1) 483 years until the Messiah is cut off, or crucified; (2) the administration of the mystery of the one body of Christ, which is not listed in this section but is implied and understood via the revelation given to the apostle Paul; and (3)The final seven years for Israel, resulting in all prophecies being fulfilled for Israel (see Daniel 9:24). Verses 26 and 27 contain the prophecy concerning the covenant seven years and the final seven years. Verse 26 goes on to state that the prince (the Antichrist or the vile man) will destroy the city of Jerusalem and the Holy of Holies.
3. Daniel 9:27 states that the Antichrist will make a strengthen himself with a strong covenant with a great nation for a seven-year period (not necessarily the Jews

as many commentators state). The covenant will initiate the final days and eventually the final seven years. In the middle of the seven-year covenant with this great nation, the Antichrist will begin to develop his plans to terminate the Jewish sacrifice in Jerusalem. Additionally, the condition of the earth will begin to grow more intense in its abominations, this will continue until the time of the middle of the final seven years when the city and the sanctuary and the sacrifice will cease. This sacrifice may be the prayer at the Western Wall in Jerusalem or something similar. The midst of the final seven years (week) will also feature the abomination that causes desolation to be set up at the holy place in Jerusalem. It must be clear to the reader that the final seven years is not the initial seven years in which the Antichrist is strengthened by a covenant with a strong nation as indicated in Daniel 9:27, but a subsequent seven year period which begins at the midpoint of the first seven year period (see timelines of Appendix D). The Abomination which causes desolations on the earth could very well be the Antichrist being slain and then raised from the dead and declaring himself God in the Holy of Holies in Jerusalem.[140] At the completion of these events, the final forty-two months—the worst time in human history—begins. The awful events of this time can be examined throughout the Bible, especially in the book of Revelation.

4. Daniel 10:1 informs us that Daniel, after a long struggle, understands the visions that he received from chapter seven on. His understanding fulfills the request by Gabriel as documented in Daniel 8:15. The verses that follow in Daniel 10:2–6 go on to describe a vision of a great and unique man who is seen only by Daniel. The vision and the appearance of the man is like the vision of the son of God in Revelation; both visions represent the only two records of the actual son of God in his glorified body in scripture.

---

[140] Revelation 17:8; 2 Thessalonians 2:4; Matthew 24:15.

THE LAST DAYS AND THE VILE MAN OF DANIEL

In summary, the following key informational points can be gathered from Section 2, reference 6:

1. Seventy sevens of years (490 years) are determined, or cut off, for Israel to fulfill all promises made to their fathers. Four hundred eighty-three of those years have been fulfilled and are in the past. The last seven-year period remains to be fulfilled and will be initiated in accordance with God's timetable. The mystery period of the one body of Jesus Christ lies between the sixty-ninth and the seventieth weeks of Daniel's seventy weeks of years prophecy of Daniel 9:24 (see Daniel 9:24).
2. The prince, or the Antichrist, will come and destroy the city (Jerusalem) and the sanctuary (the holy place) at the time of the end. This event will take place at the midpoint of a seven-year period in which the Antichrist strengthens himself with a strong agreement or covenant with strong nations (Daniel 9.27).
3. The Antichrist will strengthen himself with a strong covenant with a great nation for one seven-year period. The covenant will strengthen the Antichrist both politically and militarily with the many people for one seven-year period. The covenant will mark the first of two seven-year periods in which the second, the final, seven-year period will begin at the midpoint of the first seven-year period (see timeline of Appendix D) (v. 27).
4. During the initial seven years that strengthens the Vile Man, the Antichrist will begin the process of causing the sacrifice and oblation to cease in Jerusalem. This will be the sacrifice and oblation of the Jews at the time of the end. What exactly this is will be clear to those alive at the end. The Jewish sacrifice, whatever it is, will be stopped by the Antichrist as part of the events that take place in Jerusalem (v. 27).
5. The events of the middle of the last, or final, seven-year period will be followed by 3.5 years of desolation

and destruction on the earth—the same destruction documented in the Gospels, Revelation, Daniel, and Isaiah (v. 27).

References 7 and 8: Daniel 11:1–12.13: "The Vile Man" and "The Willful King", The Vile Man Revealed

References 7 and 8 of Daniel chapter 11 are far reaching, possibly the most far reaching, with respect to the information concerning the Antichrist and the events of the last days. The section deals with the final revelation given to Daniel from God with respect to the last days. The section focuses on information regarding the latter days, and events leading to the rise of the Antichrist and specific warning signs that will need to be heeded to understand his identity. Recall that Daniel 10 documents the vision of the Son of God (see Daniel 10:6), as he is also described in Revelation. By the end of section 2, references 7 and 8, Daniel is comforted with the words of the angel and a promise from God (see Daniel 12:13). The revelation given to Daniel regarding the last days and the time of the end begins and ends with the angel giving Daniel specific information regarding the last days. Daniel 12:5 reveals that three angelic beings were sent to Daniel to deliver the revelations from God. The visions are similar to the previous angelic revelations but give significant more information regarding the vile man and his individual actions. The beginning of Daniel 11 traces several individual kings up to the time of the final king of the north as he rises to power in the Seleucid kingdom, the kingdom of the north from antiquity. The final historical verse in chapter 11 is verse 20. The verses concerning the last seven years begin in verse 21, with the final king of the north, the Antichrist, as he rises to power in the last days. The time of the mystery of the one body of Jesus Christ can be placed between verses 20 and 21 of chapter 11. Additionally, the church of the one body of Jesus Christ will be on the earth during the first half of the last seven years. Those in the church of the body of Christ that rightly divide the Word of God will understand how the Antichrist fulfills the verses laid out in first 3.5 years of the final seven years (see Daniel 11:21–35). As these verses are fulfilled, the church will understand that it is indeed the time of the end and the verses in Thessalonians will shortly be fulfilled. Consider the following telling verses written in 1Thessalonians 5 to the church of the one body of Christ beginning in verse 1:

> But of the times and the seasons, brethren, ye have no need that I write unto you. For yourselves know perfectly that the day of the Lord so cometh as a thief in the night. For when they shall say, Peace and safety; then sudden destruction cometh upon them, as travail upon a woman with child; and they shall not escape. **But ye, brethren, are not in darkness, that that day should overtake you as a thief. Ye are all the children of light, and the children of the day: we are not of the night, nor of darkness. Therefore let us not sleep, as do others; but let us watch and be sober. For they that sleep sleep in the night; and they that be drunken are drunken in the night. But let us, who are of the day, be sober, putting on the breastplate of faith and love; and for an helmet, the hope of salvation. For God hath not appointed us to wrath, but to obtain salvation by our Lord Jesus Christ,** Who died for us, that, whether we wake or sleep, we should live together with him. Wherefore comfort yourselves together, and edify one another, even as also ye do. (1 Thessalonians 5:1–11 KJV; my emphasis)

Daniel chapter 11, once again, needs to be understood with respect to the gap of time of the mystery period, and once again, God skips over the more than two thousand years of time represented by the mystery of the one body of Christ. Previous focus in Daniel was on nations, or dominions, and rulers in those nations. References 7 and 8 in section 2 focus on individual rulers and the nations they are associated with. This is especially true of the latter sections in

Daniel 11, which reference the movements and actions of the Antichrist in the latter time. References 7 and 8 also introduce "the vile man," which is another term for the "Antichrist." Arguably, these sections provide the most information regarding the actions of the Antichrist. Core information from these sections allows the lover of God to accurately identify the Antichrist when he arises in the last days. These sections build up and provide critical details of final-time events—the events of the last days, including associated individuals and kings. The latter part of chapter 11, and all of chapter 12, focuses on the critical events that become part of the last-days sequence of events. The segment provides accurate details regarding prophecy of latter-day events and actions, especially those of the Antichrist. Since this is the focus of God's attention, it will be the focus of mine as well.

The second part of chapter 11, beginning in Daniel 11:21 and continuing through the book of Daniel, describes the actions and behaviors of the Antichrist in minute detail and is central to this entire work. This section will be critical to our understanding as the vile man rises to power in the last days. Once again, paying attention to the gap of the mystery period cannot be overstated. The gap represents more than two thousand years in time between Daniel 11:20 and Daniel 11:21; these verses cannot be understood unless this gap is properly inserted. The vile man will satisfy all that God's Word states about him, each word being fulfilled in minute detail. The section ends with the deliverance and resurrection of Israel, and Israel's acceptance of the Lord Jesus Christ as their Messiah. The deliverance of Israel marks the end of the seventy sevens of years (the 490 divided years) of Daniel 9:24–27. The one requirement for Israel's redemption has always been national repentance. Those of Israel who will not believe and repent will be rooted out during the events of the last times, but a remnant will be saved out of it.

Chapter 10 begins with individual details as to Daniel's struggles and his interaction with the angels. The details that begin in Daniel 10 continue into chapter 11 and list several individual kings of the north and south of Israel during the Ptolemaic and Seleucid empires (the Ptolemy and Seleucid dynasties, which lasted from approximately 350 to 163 BC). The section climaxes with the actions and behaviors of the Antichrist, ending with his final destruction and the subsequent deliverance for Israel. Between verses 20 and 21 of chapter 11, God fast-forwards from the final king of the North to the final Antichrist, who will be another king of the north, but he rises at the time of the end. We now understand that this period of time encompasses the Mystery of the One Body of Jesus Christ.

The theme that God portrays uniquely in this section are the individual characteristics of the rulers associated with the kings of the north and south of Israel as they rise and fall during their times. The section first records historical events associated with these kings, which have already lived and ruled, and then fast-forwards to the final king of the North—the Antichrist. The kings of the north and the south mentioned in the section can be thought of today, geographically, as modern-day Egypt and Syria. The section climaxes with the individual characteristics of the Antichrist, the final king of the North, or the final king of the Seleucid (Syrian) kingdom, but thousands of years later in time. It is he who will receive the focus of the attention of the section.

The time begins at approximately 426 BC and continues to the time of the end, culminating with the coming of the Lord Jesus Christ. Once again, the time of the mystery of the one body of Jesus Christ is hidden purposely by God. The section is also roughly equivalent to the 490 years of Daniel 9.24; also skipping over the period of the mystery of the one body of Jesus Christ. This section, by far, provides the greatest detail as to the behavior and actions of the Antichrist during the last seven years. Because of the vast information provided in this section, it is the basis and theme for the entire work. References 7 and 8 are also unusual in that they provide tracking information that will accurately identify the Antichrist as he rises in the last days. The actual prophecy is plain and requires no interpretation if rightly divided in time. The actual fulfillment, from antiquity, of the first part of chapter 11 validates the accuracy of the scripture as per past prophecies. Future prophecies, which begin in Daniel 11:21, are associated with the last days and will occur exactly as documented by God in his word. Following is a breakdown of the structure of this section.

The Structure: Daniel 10:2–12:13 (Introversion and Extended Alternation)

A. **Daniel 10:2–10:21:** Daniel's encounter with the angelic messenger and the great vision of the Lord; Daniel's reaction to the vision; the angelic messenger's revelation to Daniel of latter-day information; Daniel instructed to understand concerning his people Israel and the previous vision.
  B. **Daniel 11:1–11:20:** Israel's past and their captivity; the sixty-nine weeks of years in detail; the kings of the North and the South; the historical information and the future information (that is, information future to Daniel but historical now).
A. **Daniel 11:21–45:** The beginning of the last days, the seventieth seven, or last seven-year period, of Daniel 9:24; the vile man—his doings, his actions, his behaviors, and his end; the future to Daniel, specific to the last seven years.
  B. **Daniel 12:1–12:4:** Israel's deliverance, resurrection and redemption; the seventy sevens completed and all of God's promises fulfilled (Daniel 9:24); the future to Daniel and the present; God's fulfillment of promises to Israel.
A. **Daniel 12:5–12:13:** Daniel's encounter with the angelic messenger; Daniel's reaction to the vision; the angelic messenger as courier of latter-day information; Daniel instructed that the words are closed up and sealed until the time of the end; Daniel's understanding; the prophecy and understanding concerning his people Israel and the previous vision.

The following is the verse reference studied in this section with the verse numbering. Consider: *References 7 and 8; Daniel 11:1–12:13; Commentary: "The Vile Man" and the "Willful King" The Vile Man Revealed.*

Daniel 11:21 onward is central and core to this entire work. The latter part of chapter 11 describes the individual actions and events associated with the Antichrist and how they play out during the seventieth seven. The events of this section condense each of the 3.5-year periods, including the events of the middle of the last seven years. To set the stage for understanding Daniel 11.21–45 we must first summarize the happenings of Daniel chapters 8:1–11:20 and cross references associated with this section. The emphasis is Israel, which is the focus of Daniel chapters 8–12, but the events will have consequences for the entire world. Daniel 11 is parallel and complements Daniel 8 without contradiction. Whereas chapter 8 reveals the vision of the twenty-three hundred days, chapter 11 lists the specific events of the twenty-three hundred days. Whereas chapter 8 states that the Antichrist will emerge from one of the four kingdoms after Alexander's reign, chapter 11 documents which one: the northern kingdom.[141] Chapter 11 focuses on the historical lineage of the northern and southern kings, along with their kingdoms up to and including the future Antichrist or vile man. Whereas chapter 8 lists countries and dominions, chapter 11 goes on to list individual kings and their individual activities related to those dominions. Daniel 8 lists countries represented by animals (he-goat, ram) while amplifying the final beast, or the Antichrist. Chapter 11 lists kings associated with the dominions of chapter 8 while identifying the beast, or the Antichrist, as the vile man, as well as his specific activities. Through this process, God reveals the central focus of chapter 11 as being related to the last days and final judgments concerning Israel. Accordingly, and in conjunction with this purpose, it was appropriate for the Lord Jesus Christ to point all interested parties to Daniel when asked about the last days. Consider the following:

> And as he sat upon the mount of Olives, the disciples came unto him privately, saying, Tell us, **when shall these things be? and what shall be**

---

[141] Daniel 8:8–10.

the sign of thy coming, and of the end of the world? And Jesus answered and said unto them, Take heed that no man deceive you. For many shall come in my name, saying, I am Christ; and shall deceive many. And ye shall hear of wars and rumours of wars: see that ye be not troubled: for all these things must come to pass, but the end is not yet. For nation shall rise against nation, and kingdom against kingdom: and there shall be famines, and pestilences, and earthquakes, in divers places. All these are the beginning of sorrows. Then shall they deliver you up to be afflicted, and shall kill you: and ye shall be hated of all nations for my name's sake. And then shall many be offended, and shall betray one another, and shall hate one another. And many false prophets shall rise, and shall deceive many. And because iniquity shall abound, the love of many shall wax cold.

But he that shall endure unto the end, the same shall be saved. And this gospel of the kingdom shall be preached in all the world for a witness unto all nations; and then shall the end come. **When ye therefore shall see the abomination of desolation, spoken of by Daniel the prophet, stand in the Holy Place, (whoso readeth, let him understand:)–Then let them which be in Judaea flee into the mountains: Let him which is on the housetop not come down to take anything out of his house: Neither let him which is in the field return back to take his clothes. And woe unto them that are with child, and to them that give suck in those days! But pray ye that your flight be not in the winter, neither on the sabbath day:**

> For then shall be great tribulation, such as was not since the beginning of the world to this time, no, nor ever shall be. And except those days should be shortened, there should no flesh be saved: but for the elect's sake those days shall be shortened. (Matthew 24:3–22 KJV; my emphasis)

Matthew 24 is in concert with the revelation given to Daniel; the Lord *specifically points to the book of Daniel for those who seek enlightenment with respect to the last days.* The Lord states that when one sees the *abomination of desolation* spoken of by Daniel, then one is to seek higher ground, for those are the days of God's vengeance. The abomination that causes desolation is written about in Daniel, specifically in Daniel 11:31, validating the idea that Daniel is writing of the last days. Daniel 11:31, in time, describes the events of the midpoint of the last seven years.

The parallels between Daniel 8 and 11 cannot be denied, and the relationships are astonishing and revealing. God perfectly uses structure and scripture buildup to accurately reveal the personage of the Antichrist. Understanding both sections allows the Word of God to accurately interpret itself. The following list compares the parallels between Daniel 8 and 11:

Daniel 8:3: The ram with two horns; Media-Persia; the higher-horn Persia (countries).

Daniel 8:5–8: A he-goat from the West that conquers the ram (Media-Persia); Alexander the Great and the country of Greece conquering the Medo-Persian Empire (countries).

Daniel 8:8: Four notable kingdoms emerging from the fall of Alexander and his empire.

(mystery period skipped)

Daniel 8:9: In the latter days, emergence of the little horn out of one of them (one of the four dominions remaining after Alexander).

Daniel 8:9–14; Daniel 8:23–26: The Little Horn and his activities during the last seven years (latter days) when the transgressors are come to a full (expanded); the twenty-three hundred days.

Daniel 11:2: The rising of three additional kings in Persia (individual kings).

Daniel 11:3: A mighty king, Alexander the Great, standing up and doing according to his will and conquering the king of Persia (individual kings).

Daniel 11:4–20: Alexander's kingdom being divided into four, or toward the four winds of heaven (focus on the kings of the North and the South, two of the four).

(mystery period skipped)

Daniel 11:21–23: Information as to which one of the four the Antichrist, or Vile man, arises from—the northern or Seleucid (Syrian) Empire; emergence of the vile man, or the Antichrist, out of the Seleucid (Syrian) Empire; the final king of the North in the latter days; the strengthening of the vile man from the northern kingdom with a small people (the little horn that grows).

Daniel 11:21–45: The Little Horn and his activities (expanded) during the last seven years (latter days); the specifics of the twenty-three hundred days.

Daniel 11 contains the core of the prophecy concerning the Antichrist, or vile man. The section is divided into two parts. The first part is past and represents history to us but is future to Daniel (Daniel 11:1–11:20). The second part is future to Daniel and is associated with the last seven years (Daniel 11:21–45). The timing of the first part begins in or about 426 BC and ends in or about 167 BC. The second part, Daniel 11:21–45, summarizes the last seven years of Daniel's prophecy of seventy sevens of years. The beginning of prophecy concerning the Antichrist is marked by a covenant between the Antichrist and the many and will begin only at the discretion of God. The covenant begins the seven-year covenant period as listed in Daniel 9.27. The final seven years begin at the time of the middle of the first seven-year period (see timelines in Appendix "D").

Recall that in the beginning of Daniel Chapter10, Daniel was mourning three whole weeks. Daniel sees a great vision of the Son of God, the Lord Jesus Christ, like the vision in Revelation 1. Daniel is then stricken with fear, and he faints and falls to the ground. The same vision is seen by John in Revelation and is associated with the last days.[142] Eventually Daniel finds himself beside the great river and begins to converse with the angel who was sent to give him guidance as to what he saw. At the end of chapter 12, the end of the revelation given to Daniel, the revelation ends. Related to this vision in chapter 10, the final close in chapter 12 is marked by three angels: one on either side of the river, and one above in the middle. It is reasonable to believe that all three angels were present throughout the entire vision. The revelation given to Daniel is bounded by both documented appearances. We also know from Daniel chapter 8 that Daniel was instructed to keep the core of the revelation secret regarding certain of the visions that he received. He is again told in chapter 12 that the words are sealed until the time of the end. Consider the following in Daniel 12:4–10:

---

[142] Revelation 1:13–17.

But thou, O Daniel, shut up the words, and seal the book, even to the time of the end: many shall run to and fro, and knowledge shall be increased. Then I Daniel looked, and, behold, there stood other two, the one on this side of the bank of the river, and the other on that side of the bank of the river. And one said to the man clothed in linen, which was upon the waters of the river, How long shall it be to the end of these wonders? And I heard the man clothed in linen, which was upon the waters of the river, when he held up his right hand and his left hand unto heaven, and sware by him that liveth for ever that it shall be for a time, times, and an half; and when he shall have accomplished to scatter the power of the holy people, all these things shall be finished. And I heard, but I understood not: then said I, O my Lord, what shall be the end of these things? And he said, Go thy way, Daniel: for the words are closed up and sealed till the time of the end. Many shall be purified, and made white, and tried; but the wicked shall do wickedly: and none of the wicked shall understand; but the wise shall understand. (Daniel 12:4–10 KJV)

The scene and visions of this section contains three beings: one on either side of the river, and one above the river. The event resembles the same event, and the same beings, who gave the prophecy to Daniel in chapter 8.[143] God does not reveal the reasoning for this arrangement; that is why there must be three angelic attendants, except that a spiritual battle is mentioned. The man above the river is described as clothed in linen, with loins of gold, a body like beryl, a face of lightning, eyes like lamps of fire, arms and feet like polished brass, and a voice like a multitude. The appearance scares the others;

---

[143] See Daniel 8:13.

only Daniel remains to hear what the angelic beings have to say. The revelation had the effect of sapping the strength from Daniel, affecting his physical appearance. He found himself on the ground in a deep sleep. The scene is similar in nature to the event of Daniel 8:18. Daniel, seeing the vision of the archangel, is awestruck, and his strength is taken from him. The word for "vision" in Daniel 10:8 is the Hebrew word *"mara,"* which refers to supernatural communication from God given through visual images. The word is always used in the sense of a supernatural vision or appearance; the common result is amazement or being awestruck. Daniel 10:9 states that Daniel heard the voice and the words of the angels, which caused Daniel to go into a deep sleep.

In verse 11, the angel begins the prophetic message by explaining to Daniel that he has come to answer Daniel's prayers regarding his people, the Jews, and the land of Israel—especially those of chapter 9. The angel goes on to describe the spiritual battle he is fighting, which prevented him from coming earlier. Michael, the angelic leader, is summoned and is also listed as one that appears in the vision. Michael in the Bible is known as an archangel, or chief of the angels.[144] The prophecy itself is sound and is securely written down by Daniel. The three angels are sent by God as a delegation to give Daniel information concerning the end, or final deliverance for Israel. Further, God singles Daniel out to receive the instruction and prophecy of the last days. In these two sections, there are two named angels: Gabriel and Michael, the only two named angelic beings in scripture. Both angels seem to be present in this instance and the prior instances of chapter 8. Michael is the captain, or chief, of the delegation, as seen in the appearance in this section. Michael is also present in Daniel 8 and 12. Michael is described as the *"great prince who stands for Israel."*[145] The other occurrences that contain named angels are in Revelation 12:7, Luke 1:19, Jude 9, and Daniel 12:1.

The record goes on to document additional prophecy given to Daniel concerning the future, and last days, for Israel. The angel

---

[144] Jude 9.
[145] Daniel 12:1.

reveals what God wants Daniel to write down regarding the future—that is, the future focused on the final days and events concerning Israel. The prophecy begins with the kings of the northern and southern kingdoms and ends with the events of the last seven years—God's record of final deliverance for Israel. These scriptures provide the answers to Daniel's original prayers from chapter 9. Initially the angel describes a supernatural battle that hampered his mission to give prophecy and answers to Daniel. The angel reports that Michael is summoned to remove the resistance and allow the prophecy to be delivered to Daniel. The takeaway from this is the reality of spiritual battle lines between evil forces and the forces of God, which are now present on Earth and in the heavens. The section also reveals Michael's position as archangel, or chief of the angels, and as such, the additional special powers he has been given. Verse 14 goes on to explain the reason for the heavenly visit: to give Daniel understanding concerning what shall befall his people (the Jews) in the latter days. The reason is again stated in verse 21, which describes the core reasoning for the prophecy and special revelations from God. The reason for the appearance was to enlighten Daniel with respect to the latter days for Israel in answer to his prayers of chapter 9. The final revelation in this section strengthens and completes all prior revelation given to Daniel in chapters 7, 8, 9, and 10.

> Also I in the first year of Darius the Mede, even I, stood to confirm and to strengthen him. And now will I shew thee the truth. Behold, there shall stand up yet three kings in Persia; and the fourth shall be far richer than they all: and by his strength through his riches he shall stir up all against the realm of Grecia. **And a mighty king shall stand up (Alexander), that shall rule with great dominion, and do according to his will. And when he shall stand up, his kingdom shall be broken, and shall be divided toward the four winds of heaven;** and not to his posterity, nor according to his dominion which he ruled: for

his kingdom shall be plucked up, even for others beside those. And the king of the south shall be strong, and one of his princes; and he shall be strong above him, and have dominion; his dominion shall be a great dominion. And in the end of years they shall join themselves together; for the king's daughter of the south shall come to the king of the north to make an agreement: but she shall not retain the power of the arm; neither shall he stand, nor his arm: but she shall be given up, and they that brought her, and he that begat her, and he that strengthened her in these times. But out of a branch of her roots shall one stand up in his estate, which shall come with an army, and shall enter into the fortress of the king of the north, and shall deal against them, and shall prevail: And shall also carry captives into Egypt their gods, with their princes, and with their precious vessels of silver and of gold; and he shall continue more years than the king of the north. So the king of the south shall come into his kingdom, and shall return into his own land. But his sons shall be stirred up, and shall assemble a multitude of great forces: and one shall certainly come, and overflow, and pass through: then shall he return, and be stirred up, even to his fortress. And the king of the south shall be moved with choler, and shall come forth and fight with him, even with the king of the north: and he shall set forth a great multitude; but the multitude shall be given into his hand. And when he hath taken away the multitude, his heart shall be lifted up; and he shall cast down many ten thousands: but he shall not be strengthened by it. For the king of the north shall return, and shall set forth a multitude greater than the former, and shall certainly come after certain years with a great army and with much riches. And in those times there shall many stand up against the king of the south: also the robbers of thy people shall exalt themselves to establish the vision; but they shall fall. So the king of the north shall come, and cast up a mount, and take the most fenced cities: and the arms of the south shall not withstand, neither his chosen people, neither shall there be any strength to withstand. But he that cometh against him shall do according to his own will, and none shall stand before him: and he shall stand in the glorious land, which by his hand shall be consumed. He shall also set his face to enter with the strength of his whole kingdom, and upright ones with him; thus shall he do: and he shall give him the daughter of women, corrupting her: but she shall not stand on his side, neither be for him. After this shall he turn his face unto the isles, and shall take many: but a prince for his own behalf shall cause the reproach offered by him to cease; without his own reproach he shall cause it to turn upon him. Then he shall turn his face toward the fort of his own land: but he shall stumble and fall, and not be found. Then shall stand up in his estate a raiser of taxes in the glory of the kingdom: but within few days he shall be destroyed, neither in anger, nor in battle. (Daniel 11:1–20 KJV; my emphasis)

The first part of chapter 11 lists individual kings related to the four dominions remaining after the fall of Alexander. The chapter goes on to reduce the four dominions to two dominions of interest: the kingdoms to the north and to the south of Israel. It will be out of one of these two dominions that the Antichrist/vile man will arise, but this will occur in the latter days. The revelation given to

THE LAST DAYS AND THE VILE MAN OF DANIEL

Daniel is in answer to his prayer from chapter 9: "*...that you may know what will befall your people in the latter days.*"[146] The north and south dominions, and their kings, are listed up to, and including, the emergence of the Antichrist in Daniel 11–21 in the last days, once again skipping the mystery period of the one body of Jesus Christ on Earth. The time of the Mystery period, for this section, can be placed between verses 20 and 21. The Antichrist, or vile man, begins his last day's activities in Daniel 11:21 as a latter-day king of the North who rises out from the Seleucid, or Syrian, kingdom in the last days. He will be a successive, but separated in time, king of the North since he is listed successively with the kings of the North. The northern kingdom—the Seleucid, or Syrian, empire—will be the foundation for his rising in the last days. His record, beginning in Daniel 11:21, is synchronized with the other records regarding the "*little horn*," as listed in chapters 7 and 8. Once again, the records and information must not contradict any of the other records regarding the Antichrist throughout scripture. The information presented in chapter 11 is focused on the dominions of the kings of the North and the South, but after the fall of Alexander. The activities of these kings lead up to the emergence of the future *vile man* arising from the final historical king of the North in verse 21, but thousands of years later. The kings of the North and the South have the commonality of having dominion over Israel and Jerusalem; the final Antichrist will share this commonality as well.

The history of the kings of the North and the South, up until verse 21, and the vile man—a latter-day king of the North—is future to Daniel but is historical to us in the twenty-first century. The section up to the record of the future vile man/Antichrist, beginning in verse 21, is historical. The historical section ends at verse 20, switching to future events beginning in Daniel 11:21 and continuing through the end of the book of Daniel. The description of the vile man beginning in verse 21 also exemplifies the life of Antiochus Epiphanies, a type of Antichrist who lived and ruled in Syria as a king of the North from 175 to 164 BC. Antiochus Epiphanies fulfilled many of the

---

[146] Daniel 10:14.

prophecies written concerning the final Antichrist but did not exhaust the prophecy. Daniel 11:21–45 has in certain areas a double meaning summarizing the behavior of two evil men, both kings of the north; and both enter Jerusalem's Holy of Holies, declaring themselves to be God. It will be the final vile man/Antichrist who will exhaust and fulfill all scripture written in this section; this could not be said for Antiochus Epiphanies.

In Daniel 11, another king of the North is deserving of mention; his name is Antiochus III (see Daniel 11:13–19). He had similar characteristics and also foreshadowed the coming *vile man*, or the Antichrist. In referring to Antiochus III, God reveals his actions and how they affected the Jews of that time in history. In keeping with the angel's purpose, God documents the actions of Antiochus III, and some of those of Antiochus IV, in antiquity, showing the parallels with the final Antichrist who arises in the last days. Antiochus III, or "*the Great*," lived from 241 to 187 BC and ruled from 222 to 187 BC. He represented a type of the future Antichrist, or vile man. The similarities are striking and are listed as follows:

Antiochus III (Daniel 11:13–19)	The Antichrist; the Vile man (Daniel 11 21–45)
1. Man associated with battle and war (Daniel 11:13–19)	1. Man associated with battle and war (Daniel 11:21–45)
2. Attacks king of the South (Daniel 11: 15)	2. Attacks king of the South (Daniel 11:25)
3. Does according to his own will (Daniel 11:16)	3. Does according to his own will (Daniel 11:36)
4. Persecutes God's people, Israel (Daniel 11:14, 16)	4. Persecutes God's people, Israel (Daniel 11:33)
5. Destroys and consumes Jerusalem (Daniel 11:16)	5. Destroys and consumes Jerusalem (Daniel 11:41)
6. His body not found at his death (Daniel 11:19)	6. His body not found at his death (Daniel 11:45)

God reveals valuable information regarding the final Antichrist through the foreshadowing of the behaviors of these previous kings. For example, it takes seven verses to describe the actions of Antiochus III (Daniel 11:13–19), including God's mention of his covenant people, Israel. Comparatively, the vile man has twenty-five verses (Daniel 11:21–45) written about him, with several references to God's people, Israel, and the holy place. Thus, God emphasizes the Antichrist and the final seven years, the people and the land being the focus of his attention. The first part of Daniel 11 is related to Israel's captivity under Gentile dominion or *"The time of the Gentiles."* Throughout this period, up to and including the time of the Antichrist, or the vile man, the Gentiles will rule over Jerusalem and God's holy place. The time of the Gentiles will end with the physical coming of the Lord Jesus Christ when he destroys the Antichrist and all Satanic rule on the earth at the time of the end. The Gentiles will rule until their time is complete and their sins are filled up, or overflowing, finally forcing God to intervene with his wrath and judgment. The end times will be challenging times for believers; they will also be the time when God finally puts the last seven years into motion.[147] Daniel 11 answers the question as to which kingdom or dominion the Antichrist will emerge from as mentioned in Daniel 8:9. Putting together Daniel 11:20–21 with Daniel 8:9, it can be seen that the Antichrist will emerge in the last days from the Seleucid Empire, or the modern-day northern republic of Syria.

Beginning in Daniel 11:21, the actions and behaviors of the future vile man/Antichrist are documented; he arises in the last days, and the record of his activities encompasses the remainder of the chapter. Once again, God skips over thousands of years between verses 20 and 21, fast-forwarding to the time of the end. The mystery period is once again missing in the record, keeping with the other records regarding the future vile man, while also giving Daniel information regarding the latter days.

Individual kings are the focus of Daniel 11, in stark contrast to the Gentile dominions mentioned in Daniel 7 and 8. The individual kings of chapter 11 represent the dominions listed in chapter 8. The

---

[147] See Romans 11:25; Daniel 8:23.

focus of the first part of chapter 11 are the kings of the north and south of Jerusalem, which include modern-day Egypt and Syria. The north and south kingdoms are represented by the Kingdoms of the Ptolemies (the South Kingdom, Egypt) and the Seleucids (the northern kingdom, Syria). The focal point of the prophecy is Jerusalem and God's holy place—the reason these kingdoms are mentioned in God's Word at all. Chapter 11 follows up and builds on the vision and prophecy given in Chapter 8. Chapter 11 reveals more detail and critical information regarding the successors of the ram with the two horns (Media-Persia), and the he-goat with the great horn (Alexander the Great). The first five verses of chapter 11 represent a considerable time and only mildly describe the actions of the first kings. Greater attention is given to the individual kings in the latter part of chapter 11—especially the two that will foreshadow the Antichrist as mentioned above. Beginning in Daniel 11:5, the kings of the North (Syria) and the South (Egypt), and how they interact with each other, as well as Israel and Jerusalem, are summarized in the Word of God. These kings are concisely described in several of the verses in chapter 11. The prophecy of these first kings is future to Daniel but is historical to us in the twenty-first century. The kings can be listed as follows:

Kings of the South	Kings of the North
First king of the South: Ptolemy Soter (Daniel 11:5)	First king of the North: Antiochus (Daniel 11:6)
Second King of the South: Ptolemy III (Daniel 11:7–9)	Second king of the North: Antiochus II (Daniel 11:10)
Second king of the South (Daniel 11:11–12)	Second king of the North: Antiochus III (Daniel 11:13–19)

As in chapter 8, the period of the mystery of the one body of Jesus Christ is skipped over, as time moves forward in the chapter to the final king, or the future vile man. The gap in time, the mystery period, can be placed between verse 20 and verse 21 of chapter 11. The vile man, or the Antichrist, will be the leader of the final Gentile revolt on earth. His short-lived world kingdom (3.5 years) is the focus of the majority of the detail given by God in this section. The kingdom of the Antichrist is immediately followed by the everlasting kingdom of our Lord and Savior, Jesus Christ. Whereas chapter 8 reveals a vision and the subsequent interpretation to Daniel, chapter 11 gives prophetic words of actual historical events that occur on the earth during the time of these kings. Beginning in Daniel 11:21, after the listing of the past kings, the actions and rise of the Antichrist and the last days are quickly arrived at; these are the focus of what God wants to reveal to Daniel, and they remain the focus for the rest of the book of Daniel. The expanded documentation of the final Antichrist, the final Gentile world ruler, is in line with God's purpose to give Daniel information regarding the last days for his people, Israel. The historical section of the prophecies ends in Daniel 11:20. As mentioned above, between Daniel 11:20 and Daniel 11:21 lies a significant period of time. Part of the time includes the time of the mystery of the one body of Christ and is skipped over by God. Verses 21 and following begin future prophecies depicting detailed behavior of the future *vile man/Antichrist.* The prophecy of Antiochus IV is also partially mentioned with respect to how he foreshadows the future Antichrist. Verses 21 and beyond relate to the events of the last days and also, more specifically, to the events and behavior relating to the Antichrist. The prophecy documents his behavior during the final seven years of Daniel's prophecy of seventy sevens concerning Israel.

In Daniel 11:1, the final story begins with a recap by the angel, which began in chapter 10. The recap reviews the previous encounter between the angels and Daniel. The time is the first year of Darius the Mede, or 426 BC. Verse 2 shifts time ahead two years, to the time when the angel is speaking with Daniel, or 424 BC. The angel states that there will still be three kings in Persia, with the fourth king being richer than them all. The fourth will be attacked and conquered by Alexander the Great. Alexander will be conquered, and his kingdom will be divided to the four winds of heaven. His dominion is not left to his posterity and will not have the same power as Alexander's did. The term "Scattered to the four winds," used in verse 4, is an interesting phrase and represents the scattering of world rule to four separate dominions after the rule of Alexander. It is interesting to observe that God uses the same phrase in chapter 7, in which he states in verse 2 that the four winds strove upon the great sea. God is indicating that as Alexander's worldwide dominion was scattered to the four winds of heaven. It is these same four winds that will once again produce a worldwide dominion at the time of the end. The common thread is that world rule, once again headed up by one man at the time of the end, will again be present on the earth. The beginning of the last days is initiated in Daniel 7:2: "*The four winds of Heaven strove upon the great sea.*"[148] Chapter 7 of Daniel goes onto list the three beasts that will make up the fourth and final terrible beast. It is this beast, the Antichrist, who will eventually rule the earth as one man. Combining this with Revelation 13:1, the beasts of Daniel 7 are seen rising out of the sea as one great conglomeration of nations. These nations will eventually pay homage to, and give their power and authority to, the wild beast. Chapter 7 gives information as to the origin of the three last-day superpower Gentile nations that rise to power and authority before the final beast. Also, in chapter 7, Daniel gives the history of where these Gentile powers, also mentioned in Revelation 13.1–2, came from. In contrast, Revelation 13 depicts these three Gentile powers as one, succumbing to the wild beast, or the Antichrist. Revelation 13 goes on to give the account of the specific actions of the unified final beast during the final forty-two months. Once again, Revelation 13 and 17, and Daniel 7, must be read together to rightly divide God's Word and provide proper interpretation.

In Daniel 11, after the fall of Alexander and the scattering of his kingdom in Daniel 11:4, the chapter documents the individual kings that rise after the death of Alexander. Of the four dominions scattered to the four winds of heaven, the dominions of the north and south of Israel are the focus of the first part of Daniel 11. It is these kingdoms, the north and south, at various times during this period, that share dominion over God's land and people. Recall that it is the land of Israel that is of primary interest to God. The other two kingdoms remaining after the fall of Alexander, the eastern and

---

[148] Daniel 7:2.

western kingdoms, did not have any association with God's land and people; therefore, they are not mentioned in the chapter. Daniel 11:5–20 continues this theme and provides information beginning with the death of Alexander in verse 4 and continuing until the prototype of the Antichrist arrives in Daniel 11:21. Part of this early section in chapter 11 includes Antiochus III and Antiochus IV, who both share characteristics of the future Antichrist and therefore both have expanded prophecy. Antiochus III and his doings are listed in Daniel 11:15–20. Antiochus IV is the foreshadowing of the future Antichrist and shares several scriptures with the Antichrist, his deeds similar, but not identical, to those of the future Antichrist. Because his life and deeds are so similar, he shares part of the prophecy as a foreshadowing of the future Antichrist. The prophecy regarding both begins in verse 21 and goes on to the end of the chapter. Although both kings have similar behaviors, their lives are separate and distinct; they are separated in time by more than two thousand years. The prophecy beginning in Daniel 11:21 describes both men, but the prophecy does not exhaust the actions of Antiochus IV; therefore another, the Antichrist, must completely fulfill the prophecy. The prophecy regarding the Antichrist gives the additional details, which will be fulfilled only by the Antichrist at the time of the end. The wise mind needs to differentiate between the two for right division of the Word of God. In effect, the Antichrist will fulfill all actions and activities listed in Daniel 11:21–45.

    The kings of the north and the south of Jerusalem listed in the first part of chapter 11 are the kingdoms that are of interest to God in this section of scripture. God's compass center in the Old Testament is always the Holy of Holies in Jerusalem, unless specifically stated otherwise. The kings listed in chapter 11.1–20 are those who have dominion over God's land and people during Old Testament times and after the fall of Alexander. The final king and kingdom is that of the Antichrist and begins in Daniel 11.21 and continues until the deliverance of Israel. Their deliverance will include God's restoration of Jerusalem and the selected Jewish seed who will once again be established in their land, fulfilling all Old Testament prophecies. These prophecies are fulfilled after the Antichrist is destroyed and his body is thrown into the lake of fire after the final seven years. Daniel 11:2–20 lists the kings and kingdoms over God's land and people from the time the prophecy was given to Daniel up to, and including, the prototype of the Antichrist. Verses 21–45 of chapter 11 relate in detail the actions and behaviors of the Antichrist, from the beginning of the last seven years until his demise at the end of the last seven years.

The study of Daniel 11 will be broken into segments. The initial segment, verses 2–20, will cover the part of the prophecy pertaining to the kings of the North and the South, which was future to Daniel but is historical to us in the twenty-first century AD. The next segment, verses 15–19, describes Antiochus III, who is also a historical figure to us but is a prototype of the final Antichrist. Beginning in verse 21 and through to the end of the of the book of Daniel, the doings of the Antichrist and God's final deliverance for the Jewish nation are documented. It is this final concluding section that is the focus of chapter 11; the prior verses simply provide historical information regarding the origin of the vile man. We will closely examine this concluding section since it impacts our understanding of the Antichrist and reveals his specific behavior patterns during the final seven years. It is this concluding section that provides critical information regarding the Antichrist and will be used to identify him during the final seven years. The concluding section gives specific details regarding his rise, his behaviors, his conquests, and his actions of war during the final seven years. This section encapsulates the final seven years and is future to Daniel. Once again, it will be God who will put this timeline into motion as he sees fit.

Daniel 11 begins with the three additional kings that rise after the death of king Darius. After these three kings, a fourth arises who stirs up the kingdom against Grecia, or against Alexander the Great. The fourth king is defeated by Alexander the Great, who begins a worldwide dominion before dying, and his kingdom is scattered at the height of his power.[149] Alexander's kingdom was to be short-lived,

---

[149] Daniel 11:2.

THE LAST DAYS AND THE VILE MAN OF DANIEL

quickly divided unto the four winds of heaven. The kings listed and approximate time periods are as follows:

A. The remaining three kings in Persia and a fourth "*which will be far richer than them all*" (Daniel 11:2) include

1. Artaxerxes II (404–358 BC),
2. Artaxerxes III (358–337 BC),
3. Arses (337–335 BC), and
4. Darius III (335–330 BC).

Verses 3 and 4 of chapter 11 go on to describe the kingdom of Alexander the Great, who followed Darius III as the next leader with dominion over God's land and people. These verses are parallel to the vision of the he-goat in Daniel 8.[150] Chapter 8 reveals that the he-goat, Alexander the Great, comes up and conquers the ram with the two horns, which represents Media-Persia. The time Alexander ruled in Palestine was short, from 333 to 323 BC, but his rule was significant in that he was the last individual king to rule the known kingdoms of the earth as one man. This characteristic is common to the future Antichrist, who will also rule the earth as one man. The Antichrist, or vile man, will be the next leader to rule the earth as one man.[151] The kingdom of Alexander also had rulership over God's land and people. Rulership over God's land and people is the red thread, or common denominator, that differentiates these kings and countries from all others. The red thread also explains why these are the only kingdoms mentioned while all others are completely overlooked. God's focus is always on his people, the land, and the holy place, which he promised to watch over perpetually. The verses that lead up to verse 21 list the kings of the North and the South who rise and fall but have dominion over God's land and people. Verse 21 brings us up to the rise of the final Antichrist, the vile man, who rises at the time of the end. Once again, God skips over the period

---

[150] Daniel 8:6–8.
[151] Daniel 8:8–9.

of the mystery of the one body of Christ, which in this section of Daniel can be placed between verses 20 and 21. Before covering the Antichrist and his activities, We will first list, in more detail, the remainder of the kings who rise before the Antichrist. Listed below are the kingdoms and kings who rise after the rule of Darius III, as documented in Daniel 11:

> B. The mighty king and those that follow him include (see Daniel 11:3–20):

> 1. Alexander the Great (336–323 BC)
> 2. The four kingdoms after Alexander: Ptolemy's (Egypt, Palestine, and some parts of Asia Minor; kings of the South), Cassandreia (Macedonia, Greece, and surrounding areas), Lysimachus's (Bithynia, Thrace, Mysia), and the Seleucid Empire (Syria, Armenia, territories east of the Euphrates; kings of the North)

The scripture goes on to list the kings of the North and the South after the disbanding of Alexander's kingdom into the four dominant dynasties. These kings ruled over God's land and people. Sections C and D below list the kings in sequential order as they appear in scripture (see Daniel 11:5–20):

> C. The kings of the North and of the South who had dominion over Israel (see Daniel 11:5–20)

> 1. (Verse 5) The first king of the South was Ptolemy Soter, son of Lagus, king of Egypt (323–285 BC). His is noted as a great dominion—one that added Syria to Babylon and Media. (Note: Rulers with the name "Ptolemy" ruled Palestine from approximately 323 BC to 200 BC). One of his princes was also strong with him—Seleucus I Nicator, the first king of the North.
> 2. (Verse 6) At the end of a span of years (approximately sixty-three years), King Ptolemy II's daughter Bernice

and Antiochus I Soter came together both in equitable agreement and in marriage (in approximately 260 BC). [152]
3. (Verses 7–8) A branch (Ptolemy III, her brother) of Bernice's roots (her roots being her father, Ptolemy II) is to come forth. Ptolemy III (Eurugetes) comes to the king of the North and steals his precious vessels and great riches and then returns to his own country, Egypt. Ptolemy II ruled from 246 to 221 BC.
4. (Verses 9–12) His son, Seleucid, *"shall certainly come against"* Antiochus III. (Both kings are from the North; the time frame is approximately from 225 to 187 BC.) Ptolemy will come against Antiochus III and be moved with choler (great wrath). The great assembled forces of Antiochus III will be placed in Ptolemy III's hand. Ptolemy will not receive strengthening.
5. (Verses 13–14) Antiochus renews the war with the Ptolemys with a great army. Verse 14 goes on to say that many shall stand up against the king of the south or Ptolemy V. Additionally, many apostate Jews try by force to establish the vision or to establish God's prophecy concerning Israel. Their attempts fail and have the opposite effect of establishing Antiochus III.

D. Verses 15–20 depict the actions of the king of the North (Antiochus III, who ruled from approximately 223 to 187 BC), who is the antitype of the coming Antichrist or vile man listed in verses 21–45. The king of the North shall come and conquer the king of the South, Ptolemy V. These verses foreshadow the king of the north's antitype—the *"little horn,"* or the vile man. The verses that follow, Daniel 11:16–20, go on to list his accomplishments. These verses should be placed parallel with those of the *"little horn"* listed in Daniel 11:21–45, in accordance with the table listed above. He does not exhaust the action of the future

---

[152] Bullinger, *Companion Bible*, 1202.

Antichrist as listed in 11:21–45 but shows how an individual can fulfill the prophecies of the final Antichrist.[153] Common accomplishments of both the Antichrist and Antiochus III are listed in chapter 11 as follows:

1. The king of the north comes twice against the king of the south (verses 15 and 21–29).
2. He shall do according to his own will; none will be able to stop him (verses 16 and 36).
3. God's chosen people shall not stand; they will have no strength to withstand him (verses 15, and 33–34).
4. He will attack, stand in, and destroy the glorious land, creating havoc and destruction (verses 16 and 31).
5. He negotiates agreements for his own power-hungry ambitions (verses 17 and 23).
6. At his end, he returns back to his land and his body is not found (verses 19 and 45, as well as Isaiah 14:19).

The next section of Daniel chapter 11 reveals the specifics of the final man of sin—the Antichrist or vile man. The section begins in Daniel 11.21 with a vile man rising up at the time of the end, jumping in time to the time of the end, at a time when the Mystery of the One Body of Christ is nearing its end. Skipping this time period is crucial to proper interpretation. The time period is between Daniel 11:20 and Daniel 11.21. Daniel 11.21 begins future prophecy. Consider Daniel 11.21–45:

> And in his estate shall stand up a vile person, to whom they shall not give the honour of the kingdom: but he shall come in peaceably, and obtain the kingdom by flatteries. And with the arms of a flood shall they be overflown from before him, and shall be broken; yea, also the prince of the covenant. And after the league made with

---
[153] Bullinger, *Companion Bible*, 1202.

him he shall work deceitfully: for he shall come up, and shall become strong with a small people. He shall enter peaceably even upon the fattest places of the province; and he shall do that which his fathers have not done, nor his fathers' fathers; he shall scatter among them the prey, and spoil, and riches: yea, and he shall forecast his devices against the strong holds, even for a time. And he shall stir up his power and his courage against the king of the south with a great army; and the king of the south shall be stirred up to battle with a very great and mighty army; but he shall not stand: for they shall forecast devices against him. Yea, they that feed of the portion of his meat shall destroy him, and his army shall overflow: and many shall fall down slain. And both these kings' hearts shall be to do mischief, and they shall speak lies at one table; but it shall not prosper: for yet the end shall be at the time appointed. Then shall he return into his land with great riches; and his heart shall be against the holy covenant; and he shall do exploits, and return to his own land. At the time appointed he shall return, and come toward the south; but it shall not be as the former, or as the latter. For the ships of Chittim shall come against him: therefore he shall be grieved, and return, and have indignation against the holy covenant: so shall he do; he shall even return, and have intelligence with them that forsake the holy covenant. And arms shall stand on his part, and they shall pollute the sanctuary of strength, and shall take away the daily sacrifice, and they shall place the abomination that maketh desolate. And such as do wickedly against the covenant shall he corrupt by flatteries: but the people that do know their God shall be strong, and do exploits. And they that understand among the people shall instruct many: yet they shall fall by the sword, and by flame, by captivity, and by spoil, many days. Now when they shall fall, they shall be holpen with a little help: but many shall cleave to them with flatteries. And some of them of understanding shall fall, to try them, and to purge, and to make them white, even to the time of the end: because it is yet for a time appointed. And the king shall do according to his will; and he shall exalt himself, and magnify himself above every god, and shall speak marvellous things against the God of gods, and shall prosper till the indignation be accomplished: for that that is determined shall be done. Neither shall he regard the God of his fathers, nor the desire of women, nor regard any god: for he shall magnify himself above all. But in his estate shall he honour the God of forces: and a god whom his fathers knew not shall he honour with gold, and silver, and with precious stones, and pleasant things. Thus shall he do in the most strong holds with a strange god, whom he shall acknowledge and increase with glory: and he shall cause them to rule over many, and shall divide the land for gain. And at the time of the end shall the king of the south push at him: and the king of the north shall come against him like a whirlwind, with chariots, and with horsemen, and with many ships; and he shall enter into the countries, and shall overflow and pass over. He shall enter also into the glorious land, and many countries shall be overthrown: but these shall escape out of his hand, even Edom, and Moab, and the chief of the children of Ammon. He shall stretch forth his hand also upon the countries: and the land of

> Egypt shall not escape. But he shall have power over the treasures of gold and of silver, and over all the precious things of Egypt: and the Libyans and the Ethiopians shall be at his steps. But tidings out of the east and out of the north shall trouble him: therefore he shall go forth with great fury to destroy, and utterly to make away many. And he shall plant the tabernacles of his palace between the seas in the glorious holy mountain; yet he shall come to his end, and none shall help him. (Daniel 11:21–45 KJV)

These verses of Daniel 11:21–45 are core to this entire work. The scriptures amazingly and specifically describe in detail the vile man of Daniel and God's depiction of him. These verses will accurately identify the Antichrist before he fully comes into power on the earth, and after he comes into power on the earth—the final forty-two months. They will be used to identify him at the time he arises. This section, without doubt, is the most significant information that God gives regarding the Antichrist's rise to power, his world rulership, and his eventual destruction. Without these accurate scriptures in the Word of God, the Antichrist would be next to impossible to identify until his supernatural resurrection and subsequent world rulership. These initial verses describe a man who rises unexpectedly in an era of dictators and evil men. He will initially not be as evil as some that arose in antiquity; however, his utter ruthlessness will be manifested during the second part of the last seven years. Beginning in verse 21, and continuing to the end of the chapter, the scriptures describe a future king who rises in the foundation of the previous king of the north. A good many of the behaviors and actions were partially fulfilled by Antiochus IV, who truly did rise after the king of the north mentioned in verses 19 and 20. He did fulfill some of the prophecy in this section, but he did not exhaust the prophecy in this section. However, the focus of the prophecy is centered on the vile man/Antichrist, who arises during the last days and fulfills all scripture beginning in verse 21, continuing until the end of the chapter. Verse 21 simply fast-forwards thousands of years to the end times, or the last seven years, and picks up as if no time had elapsed. The same literary tool is used by God several times in Daniel and in the other sections of the Old Testament, keeping the time of the Mystery of the body of Christ hidden.

The Antichrist rises in verse 21 *"in his estate (foundation),"* referring to the estate of the previous king of the North (Seleucid, leader of the Syrian Empire), and begins his ascent to power.[154] The first clue of his identity is laid out; he will be another king of the North, meaning he will come from what is left of the Seleucia empire from antiquity, but in the final time, thousands of years later (modern-day Syria). As mentioned earlier, there was another king from antiquity who arose at that time in the Old Testament, Antiochus IV (175–163 BC). He fulfilled some of the scriptures of this section and was another antitype of the final Antichrist. He also arose in the stead of the previous king of the North from the Seleucid empire, but he did not exhaust all the scripture written in this section. In contrast to Antiochus IV, the scriptures beginning in verse 21 will be exhaustively fulfilled only by the final Antichrist. It will be the final Antichrist who will fulfill all of Daniel 11:21–45. These scriptures beginning in Daniel 11:21 and continuing to the end of the chapter will be the core of our study. Additionally, certain parts of these scriptures have double meanings: a meaning relevant to that time in history, and a future meaning revealing the activities of the future Antichrist.

Another example of double meaning in the Word of God is found in 2 Samuel chapter 7. In 2 Samuel 7, David makes a request to God, through the prophet Nathan, to be allowed to build a temple for the ark of the covenant. In response, God announces that he, through David's son, or offspring, will build a house for David that will last forever. The scripture refers to two sons of David. The first is Solomon, who built the physical temple in Jerusalem that was eventually destroyed (did not last forever); the second is Jesus Christ, also an offspring of David, according to the scriptures, who is also

---

[154] Daniel 11:21.

building a house for God. This house is made of fleshly stones and is built upon the foundation of the apostles and prophets. The house he builds will last forever and will be a habitation of almighty God. Jesus Christ is currently building the temple made without hands. This also explains Jesus Christ's words: "*I will destroy this temple made with hands and rebuild it in three days, speaking of the temple of his body.*" The foundation of the Lord's temple is built up with people, spiritual stones, who believe and are saved. The temple built by Jesus Christ will last forever and will exhaustively fulfill the prophecy listed in 2 Samuel 7.[155] 2 Samuel 7 shows how a scripture can have a current and a future meaning. The current meaning is similar, but not exhaustive, while the future meaning fulfills all scripture. This dual meaning is a figure of speech used by God in his word to provide emphasis and call out important parts of scripture. The figure of speech is known as *amphibologia*, meaning "double meaning." This is the same figure of speech used in Daniel 11:21–45 to describe a current meaning and a future meaning, each referring to different individuals.

The importance of Daniel 11:21–45 cannot be overstated and is key to understanding and identifying the vile man as he rises to power in the last days, fulfilling the scriptures written about him. These scriptures written of him will be the only sure way to identify him as he arises. To the world, he will appear to be another power-crazy dictator bent on war as he hides behind peace, but to those with wisdom, he will unmistakably be identified as the Antichrist. He will be identified through these very verses before his final supernatural ascent and his declaration of the divine. Daniel 11:21 and forward is especially important regarding the activities of the Antichrist in the first 3.5 years of the final seven-year period. Although there are many records of the Antichrist's doings during the last forty-two months, Daniel 11:21 through 33 are the only scriptures that acutely describe the Antichrist's actions during the first 3.5 years. The information contained in this section, the first 3.5 years, will allow the skilled discerner of God's Word to identify the Antichrist as he goes through his documented actions. The first 3.5 years contain information, key

---

[155] John 2:15–25; Ephesians 2:19–22.

activities, attributes, behaviors, and time periods of the Antichrist that he will fulfill during the first half of the last seven years. The understanding of the vile man's activities during the first half of the last seven years is critical and key to proper identification of the Antichrist in his time. The scriptures in Daniel 11 reveal what nation he rises out of, how he comes to power, and how he deceives and manipulates world leaders during the first forty-two months of the final seven-year period. Accordingly, this section will be exhaustively studied and scrutinized. I will take on a twofold systematic approach for analysis utilizing the following process:

A. The last seven years will be broken down into the three critical parts: the first 3.5 years, the midst of the week, and the second 3.5 years. The three-tier breakdown is how God divides the last seven years, so we will follow suit and break down the period this way.

B. Commentary for each verse based on item A above will be discussed. Critical words will be studied individually and included in the commentary for each verse.

Refer to Figures 3 and 4 Appendix D *"The Final Timelines"* For a graphical representation of the text of Daniel 11.21–45 (Figure 3) and a timeline of the final seven years (Figure 4). A graphical representation of two seven-year periods is also included in Figure 4 of Appendix D.

Commentary (Daniel 11:21–11:45); The Vile Man Revealed
Daniel 11.21: *"And in his estate shall stand up a vile person, to whom they shall not give the honour of the kingdom: but he shall come in peaceably, and obtain the kingdom by flatteries."* In the estate of the previous king of the North, the Syrian kingdom, a new king shall arise, but he will do so thousands of years later, in the latter days. This is not the next king in succession, but the final Antichrist, who rises thousands of years later. The final Antichrist is the vile man; it is he who will rise during the last days. It is this final vile man who will exhaustively fulfill these scriptures. Also, it is he who is emphasized

THE LAST DAYS AND THE VILE MAN OF DANIEL

and who is the focus of this section of Daniel 11. Between verses 20 and 21, God fast-forwards to the end times and describes this final vile man as he rises. He is not just another king from the North, he is from modern-day Syria, or the modern day remains of the Seleucid empire from Antiquity and is the final Antichrist. That he comes from the North indicates his rising north of Jerusalem out of one of the divisions remaining from Alexander's time. His initial rising as documented in the Word of God begins with a covenant or league with strong nation(s) initiating the first of two seven-year periods (see Appendix D). The time gap is at least twenty-two hundred years between verses 20 and 21 and includes the hidden mystery period. God skips over this period and fast-forwards to the last seven years and the time of the end. The new king who arises is a future king or leader who arises out of the northern kingdom and is described as a vile man, or despicable person. In accordance with Daniel 9:27, the act that initiates his rise is a covenant with the many. The covenant or league with many seems to be an agreement, or resolution, between the king, or leader, and a strong powerful nation. The covenant will be clearly understood by those who will be looking for the fulfillment of this scripture at the time of the end. The covenant or league will allow him to become strong for seven years and is not necessarily a seven-year agreement. It is this league with a strong ally which initiates the last days and is the first of two intersecting seven-year periods. The second seven-year period, the final seven years, is the final seven years of Daniels seventy sevens of years documented in Daniel 9.24. These time periods along with the prophecy concerning them will identify the vile man as he continues to satisfy what is written in Daniel chapter 11.

Verse 21 indicates that the latter-day leader will rise and be identified as a vile, despicable man. He will be a man given little worth and will not be given the honor of the kingdom; that is, he will not be approved of by most of the people in his country. He also will be given little worth, or will be looked down upon, by the world. The description of this man as vile has an implication of his being of little worth, despicable, contemptible, and looked on with disdain. He will be a future king or leader and will emerge from one of the four remnant dominions—Seleucia, the northern kingdom, or in and around modern-day Syria—the remains of the northern kingdom left after Alexander's fall. The scriptures, from Daniel 11:21 up until the end of chapter 11, refer to him and his activities. It will be this future king, this vile man or Antichrist, who will exhaust and fulfill Daniel 11:21–45. The prophecies of his actions, although written thousands of years earlier, will be completely and accurately fulfilled during the final seven years. Additionally, the words concerning him are more numerous than those of any of the other kings or leaders documented in Daniel 7–12. Through the abundance of scripture written about him, God emphasizes that he will eventually take center stage as the next, and final, man to rule the earth as one man. This vile man will be allowed to punish Israel, as well as the entire world, through the permissive will of God. The world destruction is the result of the astonishing sins and downward fall of mankind in general. In parallel with the destruction of the nations and Israel, God will purge and purify the called of Israel as he fulfills his promises to their fathers.

The prophecies concerning the vile man/Antichrist continue to the end of the chapter.[156] The king will arise from the remnants of the Seleucia, or the modern-day Syrian Empire, in the latter days, fulfilling the prophecy: *"Out of one of them (One of the four kingdoms left from Alexander the Great) shall come a little horn who will wax exceedingly great toward the south; toward the east, and toward the pleasant land."*[157] The scriptures list him as a vile, despised, or contemptible individual—a person afforded little worth. He is not given the honor of the kingdom or the respect of his constituents, but he will come in at a time of careless security and will quickly rise to power. The phrase *"He is not given the honor of the kingdom"* describes the unwillingness of his people, his own constituents, and the world in general to have him as leader or king. Somehow, he seizes the leadership of the nation against the will of the people. The seizure is done either through political manipulation, military action, a trusted powerful ally, or a combination of all three. The way he obtains the

---

[156] See E. W. Bullinger, *Companion Bible*, Daniel 11:21.
[157] Daniel 8:8–9.

kingdom is through a series of slippery promises and flatteries to his constituents and the nations, which will be appealing but in turn deceiving the world. Through this guise of deception, he comes into power and begins his meteoric rise to power and prominence.

Daniel 11.22: "*And with the arms of a flood shall they be overflown from before him, and shall be broken; yea, also the prince of the covenant*". This is a summary statement that characterizes what will shortly come to pass after the rise to power of the vile man and as the final seven years play out. The term *"arms of a flood,"* uses the analogy of a flood to indicate how he will overpower the nations of the world, or their capacity to fight. The description is analogous to a flood quickly destroying everything in its path. It will be the overflowing power from him, through the supernatural force of Satan, that will bring this this horrific destruction to pass. God in one verse summarizes his powerful reign. The ultimate destruction will come in the final three and one-half years but is alluded to in the first section of his rise to power to emphasize the coming impending destruction. This type of supernatural destruction has never occurred on the earth; it is called *"diverse,"* meaning that it is different from anything before it.[158] The same destruction is alluded to in Revelation 12:12: "*Therefore rejoice, ye heavens, and ye that dwell in them. Woe to the inhabiters of the earth and of the sea! for the devil is come down unto you, having great wrath, because he knoweth that he hath but a short time.*" The power that will be given to the Antichrist will be satanic supernatural forces—forces that will quickly overflow the region, the world, and those that dwell therein.

The supernatural destruction of the earth will occur in the second half of the last seven years. The verb *"overflown,"* used in verse 22, is translated from the Hebrew stem *"Nifal,"* indicating a reflexive action. The stem indicates that the subject of the verb both carries out and receives the action. The statement relates to spiritual agencies at work swaying and rearranging the nations into proper alignment for world domination. The vile man will increase in popularity with those who follow him. There will be masses of people who will be

---

[158] Daniel 7:19.

swayed and cast under the spiritual spell of the Antichrist, their loyalty increasing with each passing day. People and fighters will come to help him. He begins with few people; thus, he is referred to in other scriptures as the *little horn;* a leader who grows stronger with time. He grows stronger in time and begins to overflow, conquering neighboring nations, especially to his east, to his south, and in the land of Israel. He will also destroy *the prince of the covenant,* or the leader instrumental in bringing about a compromising agreement with those around him. The vile man will be identified in time as he fulfills these very scriptures written about him. Two interesting words in this section are *"covenant"* (Daniel 11:22) and *"league"* (v. 23). The words describe distinctive characteristics of the same event. The league is associated with an agreement that he makes with a powerful nation and marks the rising of the vile man to powerful heights. God's central focus for this entire section is Israel and the fulfillment of the promises he made to their fathers. The desolation and destruction of the Gentile nations will take place in parallel with God's dealing with Israel, but God's focus in the Old Testament is Israel and Daniel's people; the final days being an extension of God's dealings with Israel. The book of Revelation has a worldlier focus and records the end of Gentile rule on the earth, as well as the time of Jacob's trouble and what the end times means to Israel. Considering this, it is probable that Israel will somehow be closely involved in all this activity, even in the first half of the final seven years. The exact way this unfolds is not completely revealed in scripture; neither is it important for our understanding. As the prophetic events unfold and scriptures march to their fulfillment, the meaning will be clearly understood by the wise alive during those days. Additionally, Israel may not be initially involved but will become more involved as time and events march forward. The one constant through this will be God's Words being fulfilled, with not one jot or tittle falling to the ground.

Daniel 11.23: *"And after the league made with him he shall work deceitfully: for he shall come up, and shall become strong with a small people."* He is a man of small beginnings and begins with a small group of people, resulting in the reference to him as *"the little horn"* or *"a man of small beginnings."*[159] He makes a league and covenant—a strong alliance with a strong, powerful nation—marking the beginning of the final time. The league with a powerful ally marks the beginning of the first of two seven-year periods. It will be this league that will join him, both militarily and politically, to another country or countries. The new alliance will allow him to subsequently increase his power and become strong in his ambitions and conquests. The league marks a sort of turning point in his power, and through the league he becomes more powerful with time. The following verses relate his ascent to world dominion through the league that he makes with a powerful nation. The action of rising (in bold below) is used in each of these verses, indicating the rising to power of the Antichrist, and marking the beginning of the first of two seven-year periods. These verses should be considered together and are associated with the same rising of the Antichrist. Consider the following:

> I considered the horns, and, behold, there **came up among them** another little horn, before whom there were three of the first horns plucked up by the roots: and, behold, in this horn were eyes like the eyes of man, and a mouth speaking great things. (Daniel 7:8 KJV)
>
> And out of one of them **came forth** a little horn, which waxed exceeding great, toward the south, and toward the east, and toward the pleasant land. And it waxed great, even to the host of heaven; and it cast down some of the host and of the stars to the ground, and stamped upon them. Yea, he magnified himself even to the prince of the host, and by him the daily sacrifice was taken away, and the place of his sanctuary was cast down. And an host was given him against the daily sacrifice by reason of

---

[159] Daniel 7:8; 8:9.

transgression, and it cast down the truth to the ground; and it practised, and prospered. Then I heard one saint speaking, and another saint said unto that certain saint which spake, How long shall be the vision concerning the daily sacrifice, and the transgression of desolation, to give both the sanctuary and the host to be trodden under foot? And he said unto me, Unto two thousand and three hundred days; then shall the sanctuary be cleansed. (Daniel 8:9–14 KJV)

And in the latter time of their kingdom, when the transgressors are come to the full, a king of fierce countenance, and understanding dark sentences, **shall stand up.** And his power shall be mighty, **but not by his own power:** and he shall destroy wonderfully, and shall prosper, and practise, and shall destroy the mighty and the holy people. And through his policy also he shall cause craft to prosper in his hand; and he shall magnify himself in his heart, and by peace shall destroy many: he shall also stand up against the Prince of princes; but he shall be broken without hand. And the vision of the evening and the morning which was told is true: wherefore shut thou up the vision; for it shall be for many days. (Daniel 8:23–26 KJV; my emphasis)

And I saw when the Lamb opened one of the seals, and I heard, as it were the noise of thunder, one of the four beasts saying, Come and see. And I saw, and behold a white horse: and he that sat on him had a bow; and a crown was given unto him: and **he went forth conquering, and to conquer.** (Revelation 6:1 KJV; my emphasis)

These verses all relate to the same rising of the little horn at the time of the end, originally initiated by the league that he makes with a strong nation and then his eventual rising to war during the first half of the final seven years. The word "league" is derived from a Hebrew word ("hit-hab-berut") that means "to join through some type of magical charm." Daniel 11:23 is the only place it is used in this form. The allurement of the vile man/Antichrist and his ability to provide fine and slippery promises allows him to make allied relationships. His allure and charm also entice those to deal with him and make agreements with him. God uses the word "league" to emphasize a strong documented relationship with strong Gentile nations that will effectually strengthen his position. The league marks the beginning of the Antichrist coming up and becoming strong with a small group of people eventually initiating the last days and the first of two seven-year periods.

Daniel 11.24: "He shall enter peaceably even upon the fattest places of the province; and he shall do that which his fathers have not done, nor his fathers' fathers; he shall scatter among them the prey, and spoil, and riches: yea, and he shall forecast his devices against the strong holds, even for a time." The word *"peaceably"* here is better translated as *"without warning"* or *"at a time of peace and leisure."* That is, it is not the Antichrist who promises peace, but it is the Antichrist who attacks and disturbs the peace and tranquility of the region without warning. Verse 24 is a general statement regarding his conquering strategy, which he will employ. It is stated that he will share and distribute the spoils of his worldly dominion with allies. Now armed with mutual agreements and with strong, powerful allies through the league, he plans for the right time to begin invasions of nearby countries. He will overflow with his followers and gain footholds of power in strong cities that are assumed to be secure and at rest with him. It will be a time when peace is highly desirable and sought after, but the peace he promises will only be short lived. Stated another way, he will enter unexpectedly into provinces without warning at a time of ease. The provinces he enters into are not mentioned, but there is no doubt, in accordance with this scripture, that they are those to the east and the south of his own country, and, eventually, the pleasant land of Israel.[160] The latter half of this verse identifies his unique characteristic—the basis for loyalty among his followers. The process was not followed by his ancestors—his father's father—but is listed in the latter part of the verse. The process is one of sharing the spoils of conquests with his followers, having the effect of hardening their loyalty toward him. Their undying loyalty will be instrumental to his initial successes; his followers will be willing to risk their lives for his cause. He utilizes and gains strength outside of his inner circle through a series of fine promises and actions: the sharing of the spoils of war, a league made with an ally, and a covenant. He will eventually gain control of the fertile parts of the province, but only for the time appointed by God. Obtaining dominion in these provinces could also be a reference to the failures of his ancestors—his father and his father's father. The sharing of the spoils and gains with his followers is the mechanism that summons huge masses of supporters—a virtual flood of followers. After his remarkable rise to power and conquest, he gains much spoil and divides it among his followers as well as others that rise with him. He will also secretly forecast, or plan attacks, and strategize against strongly held lands and people, but only for the time allotted by God.

Daniel 11.25: "And he shall stir up his power and his courage against the king of the south with a great army; and the king of the south shall be stirred up to battle with a very great and mighty army; but he shall not stand: for they shall forecast devices against him." Sometime after the league which begins the initial seven-year period and after the beginning of the final seven-year period, the Antichrist begins his assault on the nations. It is clear that the time of sorrows of Matthew 24 and the beginning of the twenty-three hundred days of Daniel 8.9 and 8.23 will begin before the arising and attacking which will be carried out by Antichrist. The same rising of Antichrist agrees with the opening of the first seal of Revelation 6.2; the white horse conquering. It is at this time that he rises up with powerful allies that he begins to show his true intentions. The hidden inner desire of this madman had always centered on world dominion. He now

---

[160] Daniel 8:9.

rises up against the king of the South, a leader south of the Seleucid Empire (Syria), his home. The statement "king of the south" could mean any king south of the Syrian empire. Recall that the first half of chapter 11 depicts the Egyptian (involving Ptolemy, king of the South) and Syrian (involving Seleucid, king of the North) wars. It would not be a surprise if this was once again the case in the last days. In any event, these two powers engage in a significant confrontation with great armies on either side. This event will once again reinforce the accuracy of the Word of God and the realization of the days that are upon the inhabitants of the world. Those with the wisdom of God's Word will understand and prepare accordingly. The time frame is still the first 3.5 years of the last seven years and after the beginning of the twenty-three-hundred days. The king of the South does not win and does not make a stand in this battle. His inner circle of friends forecast devices or devise plots against him. The plots are listed in verse 26 and are centered on those closest to him—those who eat with him. Another verse to consider is Daniel 8:9, which states that the little horn rises up and replaces three horns, or leaders of countries, *"to the south, the east, and to the pleasant land"*: the land of Israel.[161] These two verses reveal his initial aspirations of occupying neighboring countries to the South and East, as well as the pleasant land.

Daniel 11.26: "*Yea, they that feed of the portion of his meat shall destroy him, and his army shall overflow: and many shall fall down slain*". The friends and allies of the king of the south forecast or devise plots against him. The ensuing treason causes the king of the south to be defeated but also causes the death of many. "They that feed of the portion of his meat shall destroy him" indicates those who, up until this point, acted as his friends and confidants. Those who eat with him will be the ones who betray and provide for the destruction of him and his country. The observation will be unmistakable in the last days by those wise to these scriptures.

Daniel 11.27: "*And both these kings' hearts shall be to do mischief, and they shall speak lies at one table; but it shall not prosper: for yet the*

---

[161] Daniel 8:9.

end shall be at the time appointed". Both the vile king of the North (Syria) and the king of the South shall have their hearts set to do mischief through deceptive plans of conquest. The king of the South will not be destroyed but will be alive to meet with the Antichrist, speaking lies with him in a meeting between the two of them. The key is the word for "destroy" in verse 26; it is a word indicating how his power to rule will be broken. In any event, their plans will be thwarted by God's timetable. The exact time these two kings speak lies at one table will be clear at the time of the end. The general timing will be sometime in the first half of the final seven years and after the beginning of the final twenty-three-hundred days. The other point of interest in this verse is that the world powers will fail to stop his invasion of a neighboring country. After his successful invasion, he seems to make some sort of a pact with the king of the south—the same king that he just defeated. The agreement seems to have a time sequence attached to it that, if allowed to be kept, would run beyond God's timetable. God states that the agreement will not stand, but God's timetable, the sequence of events of the last seven years, will stand. However, this will not be the case when he invades the South the second time as noted in Daniel 11:29–30. When the second invasion occurs, world powers, as we will see, do begin to take action to stop his advances. The events up to this point occur during the first half of the last seven years—the first forty-two months after the beginning of the final seven years. The two kings will meet, their intentions bent on doing evil, lying to one another in the process. God will be privy to their hearts' intentions. God understands the intentions of mankind—not just the outward intentions but also the inward intentions. The scripture goes on to say that God's end-time timetable will dominate regardless of the best-made plans of political leaders: "The end shall be at the appointed time." This once again links this section of scripture to the time of the end—that is, the last seven years. God assures us that although these fearful events and plans are conspired between these two kings (and there may be others), God's timetable will stand. All events listed by God in these scriptures will be fulfilled in minute detail, as documented by God's prophets. This will be the beacon of hope for the wise alive during these dreadful times. A solace to those alive and who love God during these horrible times is that one can always remember that these horrible times have an end. The seven-year time period allotted by God will be followed by the everlasting kingdom of our Lord and Savior, Jesus Christ. God, through these scriptures, gives his people fair warning for those with "eyes to see and ears to hear."

Daniel 11.28: "Then shall he return into his land with great riches; and his heart shall be against the holy covenant; and he shall do exploits, and return to his own land." After these events and actions with the king of the South, the vile man returns from his southern conquests with great spoil and success. With respect to time, it is the latter half of the first 3.5 years of the last seven years. It is also important to note that although God focuses this section of his scripture on the actions of the king of Seleucia (the vile man), it is likely that other kingdoms and dominions will be at war with one another. This would explain how the Antichrist is allowed to invade unchecked by other world powers. The vile man's success breeds pride and arrogance, which continues to grow in his heart, unabated during this entire period. It is at this time that he begins to multiply his hatred toward God, God's people, and the land of Israel. His innate hatred, no doubt, is exasperated through his growing allegiance and walk with Satan. His destiny is to hate God and all of what God stands for, including God's covenant, God's law, and God's creation. The idea to attack and supplant God and his covenant is embedded in him by Satan, the father of lies. The "holy covenant" in this verse is different from the "covenant" mentioned in 11:22 and 9:27, which does not include the word "holy." The expression "holy covenant" refers to the covenant set apart by God. It includes God, his law, and all he stands for, including the people who adhere to his covenant. It involves the agreement between God and his people and about their relationship with him. In this context, the people are the remnant of believing Israel—those who fear and reverence God in accordance with Old Testament law. Remember that the entire prophecy of all seventy weeks of years concerns Israel and their end. For this reason, the focus of this verse is the remnant of the blessed seed of Jacob. Verse 28 also relates to the time when the vile man begins to believe himself to be divine. He will begin to exhibit his disdain for God and God's covenant people, eventually laying claim to the divine himself. The vile man, in his heart, anticipates world dominion through his continual relationship with and worship of Satan. Through this relationship, the vile man will acquire more of the characteristics of Satan—especially his hatred for anything related to God. Part of this hatred manifests itself in persecution of the people of God as he plans to destroy anything related to God. He returns to his own land with this new strategy—that is, hatred for the true God and world dominion in his heart.[162]

Daniel 11.29,30: "At the time appointed he shall return, and come toward the south; but it shall not be as the former, or as the latter. For the ships of Chittim shall come against him: therefore, he shall be grieved, and return, and have indignation against the holy covenant: so shall he do; he shall even return, and have intelligence with them that forsake the holy covenant." The time appointed indicates that this is still God's timetable; God is the one allowing this to occur, because of man's wickedness on the earth. The vile man, although a wild beast, is still subject to God's permissive will and God's timetable. This verse marks the approach of the time for the events associated with the middle of the last seven years, which are now quickly approaching. Once again, the Antichrist comes against the South toward the end of the first 3.5 years. This second time that he comes against the South will not have the same result as the first; he is met with resistance from the ships of Chittim.[163] In this occurrence, the scripture states that he comes against the South—not the king of the South, but the South itself. This suggests that he comes against some other country, or multiple countries, south of his own country. One of the countries that he begins to take aim at will be the land of Israel—the pleasant land. It is Israel, and especially Jerusalem, as we will see, where several of the final seven-year midweek events and temple atrocities will take place. Chittim, in this verse, stands for the isles of the sea—specifically, in this case, the Mediterranean Sea. The nations and the

---

[162] Daniel 8:12; 7:25.
[163] Isles of the Mediterranean Sea.

THE LAST DAYS AND THE VILE MAN OF DANIEL

rest of the world are now leery of this man and his deception. The nations begin to send strong forces and military ships to attack and destroy him; he is now considered to be a foe to the stability of the world and needs to be removed. The nations are gathering for war with him; the Antichrist is just as defiant and gathers forces of his own. Chittim refers to lands in and around the Mediterranean Sea—ships from foreign lands. The ships will be associated with strong Gentile nations probably associated with the lion, bear, and leopard of Daniel 7. The scripture is silent as to how his allies react to the new threat against him. His own actions become the scripture focus from this point onward. He begins to exhibit his true intentions in plain view of the nations.

After this turn of events, the vile man becomes enraged and focuses his attention and anger toward God and his Old Testament covenant people and their land. At this point, no doubt, he is being directed by Satan to act against God himself and God's people and land. The assault begins with his hatred of God's Word and God's covenants with Israel. He begins his assault by allying himself with those who hate God and the Jewish nation—those looking to breach God's holy covenant as well. There will also be those in Israel who despise God's law. Israel will be divided into two factions: those who love God and those who disdain God and his word.

Daniel 11:30 represents the last verse depicting the events of the first half (first 3.5 years) of the last seven years.[164] Beginning with verse 31, the events of the middle of the last seven years and the final forty-two months begin; this is the worst time in human history. The final forty-two months will then be followed by the everlasting kingdom of our Lord and Savior, Jesus Christ.

Daniel 11.31: "And arms shall stand on his part, and they shall pollute the sanctuary of strength, and shall take away the daily sacrifice, and they shall place the abomination that maketh desolate." This now begins the events of the midst of the seventieth week of Daniel's prophecy of seventy sevens of weeks.[165] *"Arms shall stand on*

---

[164] Daniel 9:24.
[165] Daniel 9:24.

his part" has been translated several different ways and needs to be better understood. The word "arms" in this verse is a Hebrew word, "זְרֹעִים," and is associated with the supernatural arm of the Lord in many other scriptures. *"Arms"* used in the plural is also associated with powerful armies. The first usage of a word in the Word of God is always important and typically contains critical information for interpretation. The first usage of the Hebrew word for "arms" is found in Genesis 49:24; *the arms of Joseph are said to be made powerful by the hands of the mighty God of Jacob.* The word "arms," taken together with the words "to stand," indicates a continual powerful standing, or enduring, of the vile man. There are also translations that associate the word "arms" with "seed" or "offspring."[166] The supernatural offspring translation is offered here because it agrees with other areas of scripture. A sister verse to Daniel is found in Revelation 17:11, which lists the Antichrist as the eighth king, who "proceeds from the seventh, or originates from the seventh."[167] The eight kings of Revelation 17 will be examined with our study of Revelation 17. For now, it is important to understand that this verse agrees that the eighth king which originated from the seventh. Revelation 13 and 17, when compared with Daniel 11:31 and Matthew 24:15, agree that the vile man is now a powerful, conquering supernatural force standing up at the holy place in Jerusalem. This section of Daniel is also cross-referenced by the Lord in Matthew 24:15. Examining the context of Daniel 11 after verse 31 reveals that something has changed in the power of the Antichrist; he has now become stronger and now continually conquering. We shall see that the change is that of new supernatural abilities possessed by the Antichrist after a miraculous resurrection and as listed in Revelation 13 and 17. This will be pointed out when we get to that section in Revelation. Once again it is comparing the same events in different sections of scripture adding additional information to the same man and painting the picture that God wants to paint.

---

[166] Theological Dictionary of the Old Testament; *G. Johannes Botterweck, Helmer Ringgren, Heinz-Josef Fabry; vol 4, p 143.*
[167] Revelation 17:11.

These verses in Daniel, taken together with Revelation 13 and 17, paint a picture of the seventh king, the beast, being assassinated around the time of the midst of the seventieth week. After his assassination, he comes back to life as the eighth king in supernatural form—an unstoppable supernatural force. After his supernatural transformation, in one hour, he gives power to the ten kings, as mentioned in Revelation 17:12. The ten kings receive significant supernatural power, which allows them to pollute the sanctuary of strength, as stated in Daniel 11:31. The sections in Revelation 17:12, Revelation 13.3, Daniel 11:31 and Matthew 24.15 all refer to the same time—the middle of the seventieth seven. The *forces* that grow out from the vile man in Daniel 11:31 are likely supernatural forces. These forces, along with the ten kings (horns), now energized with supernatural power provided by the Antichrist, will now begin their mission of worldly domination. The Antichrist is now supernaturally energized by Satan himself, to the astonishment of the world. It is now Satan himself who is directly involved in the affairs of mankind through his instrument, the Antichrist. Satan is now manifested on the earth through the Antichrist being cast out of the heavens, and *he knows that his time is short*.[168] The ten kings, as mentioned earlier, are stated to receive supernatural power after one hour with the beast.[169] In any event, all will be clear to the wise as these events unfold at the midst of the last seven years. One thing is clear: the beast will be operating in the supernatural realm and will thus be different from all other earthly dominions before him. The verses in Daniel after this verse take a decidedly different turn, a supernatural turn, and they begin describing supernatural power. From this point forward, the beast will be permitted to supernaturally destroy the earth and the cities and the nations thereof. A new thing, a supernatural thing, will now be on the earth; this thing has never been on the earth before.

Significant events transpire during the midst of the seventieth seven. We understand that the midst of the week also marks the beginning of the worst time in human history. The worst time includes

---

[168] Revelation 12:12.
[169] Revelation 17:12.

the final forty-two months, encapsulating the great tribulation and the time of Jacob's trouble.[170] The tribulation, or time of insurmountable trouble, begins first with the Jews and Jerusalem's holy place, and then the entire earth is thrown into chaos. The beast, although it has fulfilled all of the scriptures in Daniel 11:21 to this point, will be hidden or not understood by all the wicked of the earth.[171] The final forty-two months will be followed by the setting up of the rulership of the kingdom of Jesus Christ.[172] The midst of the week is alluded to several times in scripture as the time when *the abomination that causes desolation is set up at the holy place in Jerusalem*.[173] This abomination of desolation is so wicked, from God's perspective, that it brings on, by God's permissive will, a Satanic forty-two-month rule on the earth, along with the undiluted wrath of almighty God. The Lord was alluding to this abomination in Daniel when he spoke in Matthew 24:15. He declared in Matthew that flight is the only option when this abomination occurs. Recall that each verse regarding an event (and there are many regarding this event) cannot contradict; each adds additional details. Daniel 11:31 reveals that arms or forces (*seeds or offspring having supernatural power*) shall stand on his (the vile man's) part. The scripture states that supernatural forces from him, or initiated by him, will be used to pollute the sanctuary of strength: the holy place in Jerusalem.

The time is now the middle of the last seven years, and the final forty-two months are now beginning on the earth. The Antichrist is now gone into supernatural form and is about to declare himself God. After many world powers are turned against him, he suddenly comes into this great supernatural power and immediately anoints ten supernatural allies. These ten kings will allow him to grow in power and stature. This is a curious turn of events in the career of the Antichrist, who is now energized by Satan himself and able to perform great satanic miracles. He no longer needs the help of

---

[170] Jeremiah 30:7.
[171] Daniel 12:10.
[172] Daniel 9:27; Revelation 13; Daniel 12:1; Matthew 24:15–22.
[173] Matthew 24:15–22.

the nations and will turn instead to world domination with his ten kings at his side. He will now deceive the world by promoting the great lie: "The Antichrist is God!" He suddenly, as fast as the floods of Noah's time, ushers in the final forty-two months and becomes skilled at effective utilization of evil supernatural powers. He continues to fulfill the scriptures related to his quest for world domination powered by the dragon—Satan himself.[174] He sets up the abomination that makes or causes desolation at the holy place in Jerusalem. The holy place is actually the holy ground atop the temple mount in Jerusalem—the place where God made his everlasting promise to Abraham (see appendix C). The holy place is holy not because of a building but because of Abraham's willingness to offer his son Isaac at this same location. God, in turn, respected Abraham's commitment and promised the Messiah would return to this same place. It would be God's only begotten son who would be sacrificed for the sins of mankind and also for Israel. God's only begotten son will one day deliver Israel, beginning at this place, as foretold in many scriptures.[175] The attempt here is by Satan to occupy the holy place with the Antichrist, the false God, before the arrival of Jesus Christ. The building of the temple on this place came *after* God called it holy and set it apart. The first usage of the Hebrew word for "holy place" has to do with Abraham and his offerings to God after leaving Egypt.[176] God promised Israel that he would have compassion on Israel when they prayed to this place.[177] God also promised that it would be here that the Messiah would deliver Israel.[178] Thus it is fitting that the final forty-two months, 3.5 years, or 1260 days begin at this point, with the Antichrist proclaiming himself God at this same place. The final forty-two months will feature satanic supernatural powers through the Antichrist, along with desolations and destruction on the earth. At the end of the forty-two months,

---

[174] Revelation 13; Revelation 17; 2 Thessalonians 2:8–11.
[175] Read Psalm 2.
[176] Genesis 13:3.
[177] 1 Kings 8:35.
[178] Romans 11:26–27; 2 Chronicles 7; Psalm 2:1.

the reign of our Lord Jesus Christ on the earth will begin. The reign of the Lord Jesus Christ will happen only after the wrath of our holy God upon a sinful world is fulfilled. The spiritual war on earth will cause the supernatural destruction of the cities of the earth grouped as one under the Antichrist, *"Mystery Babylon"*.

Daniel 11.32: "And such as do wickedly against the covenant shall he corrupt by flatteries: but the people that do know their God shall be strong, and do exploits." The vile man, now in his supernatural form, reveals his true intentions: world dominion and the desire to be worshipped as God by all people.[179] To accomplish his divine ambitions, he must first get rid of any memory of the true God. The time period is the beginning of the final forty months, the middle of the seventieth week, and the Antichrist now begins his attack against God and God's people, Israel (Daniel 11:31). Before this time, Israel and the world intended to overthrow this madman and had no respect for him: "They would not give him the honor of the kingdom."[180] Now, beginning in verse 31, his supernatural powers are exhibited, and he takes great vengeance toward the nations of the world. He is in Jerusalem and the land of Israel, and he proclaims himself divine. Verses 32 through 35 describe and differentiate between those faithful in Israel and those unfaithful. Verse 32 begins with "Such as do wickedly against the covenant," describing those who hate God and his everlasting covenant with Abraham's seed. The Antichrist carries out his hatred for the holy covenant mentioned in verse 28. Israel will be divided between those who love God and those who do not. This division in Israel is also alluded to in Revelation 3:9: "Behold, I will make them of the synagogue of Satan, which say they are Jews, and are not, but do lie; behold, I will make them to come and worship before thy feet, and to know that I have loved thee." At the middle of the week, after his attack on Jerusalem and the holy place, he "corrupts by flatteries" those who hate God and his covenant with Israel. The notion of corrupting by flatteries has to do with making deceptive or deceiving promises through soft,

---

[179] Revelation 13; 2 Thessalonians 2:4.
[180] Daniel 11:21.

unassuming words. His ability to captivate, or put under a trance, is referenced here and refers to his supernatural ability, which will now be exhibited to the world. In contrast, "the people (the faithful Jews) who do know their God shall be strong and do exploits." Those of the Jews—the people dedicated and committed to the living God in Israel—through the knowledge and trust in their God, will be strong and do works of righteousness. This will be done in the midst of the terrible evil that is now upon the earth. The Jews who do know their God will do exploits, defying the godless trend of others. These are those whom the Lord writes to in Revelation 2 and 3 in the epistles to the seven churches. The sanctified in Israel will be set apart and receive a mark by God and will form the new embryonic nation of Israel. The new marked-off chosen group within Israel will then be the focus of God, who will now show his strong arm to save and deliver them through the next forty-two months.

There also will be another group, a different group in Israel, accepting the bribes and the allure of the supernatural Antichrist. These will turn against God and his people. The ability of the Antichrist to gain control of nations is related to his supernatural allure, which allows him to gain the popularity of the people through deception and satanic miracles. The miracles will be magnetizing and mesmerizing, such that all those who are not set apart will believe the great lie. The end result will be great division among the nations, beginning in Israel. The chaos and destruction in Israel, beginning at the Holy Place, will lead to a general upheaval, war, famine, and rebellion throughout the world. In the case of Israel, it will be Jew against Jew, but the same behavior will be seen throughout the nations of the world as well.[181] The verses of Daniel 11:32–35 are in repeated alteration and depict the result to the faithful as opposed to the unfaithful in Israel.

Daniel 11.33–35: "And they that understand among the people shall instruct many: yet they shall fall by the sword, and by flame, by captivity, and by spoil, many days. Now when they shall fall, they shall be holpen with a little help: but many shall cleave to them with flatteries.

---

[181] Daniel 11:25–26.

And some of them of understanding shall fall, to try them, and to purge, and to make them white, even to the time of the end: because it is yet for a time appointed." We are now firmly into the final forty-two months of Jacob's trouble.[182] The description is of the Jews in and around Jerusalem, the focus of the revelation given to Daniel. This section must also be compared to parallel descriptions documented in the book of Revelation. Both sections together complement and reveal the significance of the atrocities that occur in the final forty-two months. The one hundred forty-four thousand mentioned in Revelation 7:4 (twelve thousand from each of the twelve tribes of Israel) are now marked and set aside by God, and they begin their period of trial and deliverance, which lasts many days. Verse 35 states that *"some of them of understanding shall fall, to try them, and to purge, and to make them white, even to the time of the end."* God will once again supernaturally protect and deliver the called of Israel, as he once did with his people in Egypt and afterward, in the wilderness. These solemn verses include others besides the one hundred forty-four thousand chosen of God. They shall resist the Antichrist and face death by sword, by flame, by captivity, and by plundering; some of them will die a martyr's death. The many days mentioned are related to the 3.5 years of Jacob's trouble. God, as mentioned throughout the Old Testament and Revelation, shall save and purge his set-apart people—those of believing Israel. The set-apart ones will endure through the forty-two months of Revelation.[183] God does this not because they deserve it but because of the promises he made to their fathers: Abraham, Isaac, and Jacob. The chosen of Israel, after and through this tribulation or purification, will come to a realization that Jesus Christ is their Lord, King, and Savior. God uses the forty-two months of the book of Revelation as a fiery trial, purifying the new embryonic nation of Israel. The new nation is destined to live forever with Jesus Christ as their Lord and David as their resurrected king. They will finally learn to say, *"Blessed is he that cometh in the name of the Lord."* In contrast to the called-out Jews, the

---

[182] Jeremiah 30; Revelation 12.
[183] Revelation 19.

one body of Jesus Christ, the born-again believers will be lifted from the earth. Israel—those specially selected by God—is now once again the center of the attention of God. The purification of the called-out of Israel will now begin; they will be purified not in the same way as those in the body of Christ, through faith, but through the fiery trials of the final forty-two months of Jacob's trouble. They will understand the scriptures written about them and instruct many out of the scriptures of the impending doom. They will also read of their deliverance through the reading of these very scriptures in Daniel, as well as other Old Testament scriptures, and the information given to them in Revelation chapters 2 and 3. They will realize experientially and take warning from God in his word concerning the coming days. The called-out Jews will be persecuted by the Antichrist and Satan himself; some will fall and die. The messages written to the seven churches in Revelation chapters 2 and 3 should be read in reference to these verses in Daniel, and they need to be applied to believing Israel. The message to the seven churches is written to these called-out Jews, who have escaped and left Jerusalem and are now ready to accept their true Messiah, the Lord Jesus Christ. Additionally, God, after these days, will raise up David to be their king. [184] Consider the following associated verses:

> Let us be glad and rejoice, and give honour to him: for the marriage of the Lamb is come, and his wife hath made herself ready. (Revelation 19:7 KJV—Israel purified through the forty-two months of Revelation)
>
> Then I would know the truth of the fourth beast, which was diverse from all the others, exceeding dreadful, whose teeth were of iron, and his nails of brass; which devoured, brake in pieces, and stamped the residue with his feet; And of the ten horns that were in his head, and of the other which came up, and before whom

---

[184] Jeremiah 30:9.

three fell; even of that horn that had eyes, and a mouth that spake very great things, whose look was more stout than his fellows. I beheld, and the same horn made war with the saints, and prevailed against them. (Daniel 7:19–21)

And in the latter time of their kingdom, when the transgressors are come to the full, a king of fierce countenance, and understanding dark sentences, shall stand up. And his power shall be mighty, but not by his own power: and he shall destroy wonderfully, and shall prosper, and practise, and shall destroy the mighty and the holy people. And through his policy also he shall cause craft to prosper in his hand; and he shall magnify himself in his heart, and by peace shall destroy many: he shall also stand up against the Prince of princes; but he shall be broken without hand. (Daniel 8:23–25)

Son of man, when the house of Israel dwelt in their own land, they defiled it by their own way and by their doings: their way was before me as the uncleanness of a removed woman. Wherefore I poured my fury upon them for the blood that they had shed upon the land, and for their idols wherewith they had polluted it: And I scattered them among the heathen, and they were dispersed through the countries: according to their way and according to their doings I judged them. And when they entered unto the heathen, whither they went, they profaned my holy name, when they said to them, These are the people of the LORD, and are gone forth out of his land. But I had pity for mine holy name, which the house of Israel had profaned among the heathen, whither they went. **Therefore say unto the house of Israel, Thus saith the Lord**

GOD; I do not this for your sakes, O house of Israel, but for mine holy name's sake, which ye have profaned among the heathen, whither ye went. And I will sanctify my great name, which was profaned among the heathen, which ye have profaned in the midst of them; and the heathen shall know that I am the LORD, saith the Lord GOD, when I shall be sanctified in you before their eyes.

For I will take you from among the heathen, and gather you out of all countries, and will bring you into your own land. Then will I sprinkle clean water upon you, and ye shall be clean: from all your filthiness, and from all your idols, will I cleanse you. A new heart also will I give you, and a new spirit will I put within you: and I will take away the stony heart out of your flesh, and I will give you an heart of flesh. And I will put my spirit within you, and cause you to walk in my statutes, and ye shall keep my judgments, and do them. And ye shall dwell in the land that I gave to your fathers; and ye shall be my people, and I will be your God. I will also save you from all your uncleanness's: and I will call for the corn, and will increase it, and lay no famine upon you. And I will multiply the fruit of the tree, and the increase of the field, that ye shall receive no more reproach of famine among the heathen. Then shall ye remember your own evil ways, and your doings that were not good, and shall lothe yourselves in your own sight for your iniquities and for your abominations. **Not for your sakes do I this, saith the Lord GOD, be it known unto you: be ashamed and confounded for your own ways, O house of Israel.** Thus saith the Lord GOD; In the day that I shall have cleansed you from all your iniquities I will also cause you to dwell in the cities, and the wastes shall be builded. And the desolate land shall be tilled, whereas it lay desolate in the sight of all that passed by. And they shall say, This land that was desolate is become like the garden of Eden; and the waste and desolate and ruined cities are become fenced, and are inhabited. Then the heathen that are left round about you shall know that I the LORD build the ruined places, and plant that that was desolate: I the LORD have spoken it, and I will do it. Thus saith the Lord GOD; I will yet for this be enquired of by the house of Israel, to do it for them; I will increase them with men like a flock. As the holy flock, as the flock of Jerusalem in her solemn feasts; so shall the waste cities be filled with flocks of men: and they shall know that I am the LORD. (Ezekiel 36:17–38 KJV; my emphasis)

For I would not, brethren, that ye should be ignorant of this mystery, lest ye should be wise in your own conceits; that blindness in part is happened to Israel, until the fulness of the Gentiles be come in. **And so all Israel shall be saved: as it is written, There shall come out of Sion the Deliverer, and shall turn away ungodliness from Jacob: For this is my covenant unto them, when I shall take away their sins. As concerning the gospel, they are enemies for your sakes: but as touching the election, they are beloved for the fathers' sakes.** For the gifts and calling of God are without repentance. (Romans 11:25–29 KJV; my emphasis)

God purifies and saves his people Israel as a nation—not all of them, but those who fear his name. During the time of Jacob's trouble, some are martyred, and some survive and are purified through the fiery trials of Revelation. God does this not because they deserve it but because of his great name's sake (Ezekiel 36:22, 32) and for the sake of the everlasting promises he made to their fathers. The time appointed by God shall stand: forty-two months, 3.5 years, or 1,260 days. After this time, all of God's will and word will be fulfilled concerning Israel, as documented in the prophecy of the seventy sevens of Daniel 9:24.

Daniel 11.36–39: And the king shall do according to his will; and he shall exalt himself, and magnify himself above every god, and shall speak marvellous things against the God of gods, and shall prosper till the indignation be accomplished: for that that is determined shall be done. Neither shall he regard the God of his fathers, nor the desire of women, nor regard any god (previous or present): for he shall magnify himself above all. But in his estate shall he honour the God of forces: and a god whom his fathers knew not shall he honour with gold, and silver, and with precious stones, and pleasant things. Thus shall he do in the most strong holds with a strange god, whom he shall acknowledge and increase with glory: and he shall cause them to rule over many, and shall divide the land for gain.

The focus is once again on the behavior of the Antichrist and in this role as the willful king. The beast has now risen from the dead and is now in supernatural form. Who can destroy the beast? Who can make war with him?[185] The hour of deception for the world has been thrust upon all men. Is he God, and should we worship him? The beast now begins his assault on the world in earnest. He does according to his will, the pattern of which has never been seen on the earth. This results in a supernatural destruction of those on the earth. He follows some of the traits of Alexander, the last man to rule the earth as one man.[186] But even Alexander did not have the indestructible supernatural body that this man will have. The beast will be different from all other ruling dominions ever on the earth before this time. None shall resist his will or shall be able to

---

[185] Revelation 13:4.
[186] Daniel 8:4; 11:3.

stop him.[187] Powered by the dragon, Satan himself, he reveals his earnest desire to be worshipped as God. He will exalt himself and put himself above every God; he will disregard all other gods and religions that have been ever been on the earth; both men and women will buy into the deception. His claim to be God will be supported by a supernatural presence; this is also documented in several other scriptures.[188] Now, firmly into the final forty-two months of the final seven-year period, the worst time in human history begins. The worst character in human history is operating and rising in power, strength, and dominion. He is called the willful king because all that he wills in his heart will be accomplished during the next forty-two months as he works hand-in-hand with Satan. This is Satan's short time of world dominion on the earth. The sins of mankind have finally reached a boiling point; God now allows man to self-destruct. The Antichrist, through Satan, will be allowed to do all things in his heart, and according to his will, through the worship of a *"God of forces."* The time that he operates, in accordance with God's permissive will, is forty-two months. Verse 39 also states: *"he will cause them to rule over many, dividing the land for gain"*. He characteristically divides the spoil with the ten kings, or the horns of the beast. He utilizes this method to obtain victories; using the undying loyalty to gain rulership and to conquer and be victorious. Consider the following: *"He shall enter peaceably even upon the fattest places of the province; and he shall do that which his fathers have not done, nor his fathers' fathers;* **he shall scatter among them the prey, and spoil, and riches:** *yea, and he shall forecast his devices against the strong holds, even for a time"* (Daniel 11:24; my emphasis).

His dividing of the spoil and the land, as well as his worshipping of a strange or unknown God, sets him apart from his father and father's father. He will come to know this strange God in an intimate manner as he increases with glory and success in his endeavors. He is secretly worshipping Satan, a foreign or disguised God that his fathers never knew. He uses the strength of Satan, the god of

---

[187] Revelation 13:4.
[188] 2 Thessalonians 2:3–4; Daniel 7:25; 8:11, 25; Revelation 13:5–6.

forces, to plan and defeat strong fortified nations and even their great armies. Human armies and war machines will prove no match for this supernaturally charged individual, who will overcome his enemies through the power of Satan. Consider what S. R. Miller wrote in his *New American Commentary on Daniel:*

> **11:39** The future dictator "will attack the mightiest fortresses with the help of a foreign god." This "foreign god" is the "god unknown to his fathers" of the previous verse, and Antichrist's god is "foreign" in the sense that this deity was not worshiped by his ancestors. By means of his overwhelming military power (his god), Antichrist will destroy all of those who dare challenge him. The peoples of the world will be so impressed by his might that they will say: "Who is like the beast? Who can make war against him?" (Rev 13:4). Persons who vow allegiance to Antichrist as their king will be rewarded. He "will greatly honor" them, grant them leadership positions ("make them rulers over many people"), and allot them territories to rule ("distribute the land"). The "price" for such rewards includes unquestioning allegiance to Antichrist and his government but may also involve financial payoffs and political favors. p 309 **11:40** The wars of Antichrist are described in vv. 40–45, and the time of this conflict is declared to be "the time of the end" (v. 40). Leupold remarks: "There is nothing in the context that would restrict the force of the word 'end,' and so the end of all things must be meant." Moreover, this battle concludes with the destruction of Antichrist in Palestine (v. 45) followed by the resurrection of the saints (12:2). These events have not yet transpired, and therefore the "end" in view here must be the final

days of the present age. "Chariots and calvary and a great fleet of ships" would be representative of their modern counterparts in this eschatological battle.[189]

The order of destruction regarding the last days is laid out in Matthew and Revelation, along with Daniel, each describing the end from a separate viewpoint, without contradiction. Daniel is instrumental in listing and documenting the initial rise to power of the vile man. After the Antichrist begins his mission, peace is taken from the earth on a worldly scale. After this, poverty, famines, and disease spread upon the face of the earth. The books of Daniel, Revelation, and Matthew all synchronize to the same sequence of last-time events. Consider the following:

> And I saw when the Lamb opened one of the seals, and I heard, as it were the noise of thunder, one of the four beasts saying, Come and see. And I saw, and behold a white horse: **and he that sat on him had a bow; and a crown was given unto him: and he went forth conquering, and to conquer** (rising of Antichrist). And when he had opened the second seal, I heard the second beast say, Come and see. **And there went out another horse that was red: and power was given to him that sat thereon to take peace from the earth, and that they should kill one another: and there was given unto him a great sword** (Wars initiated). And when he had opened the third seal, I heard the third beast say, Come and see. **And I beheld, and lo a black horse; and he that sat on him had a pair of balances in his hand. And I heard a voice in the midst of the**

---

[189] Miller, S. R., *Daniel*, vol. 18 (Nashville, Tennessee: Broadman & Holman Publishers, 1994), 308–9.

> **four beasts say, A measure of wheat for a penny, and three measures of barley for a penny; and see thou hurt not the oil and the wine** (Poverty, Famines and Pestilences; typically associated with war). (Revelation 6:1–6 KJV; my emphasis)
>
> And Jesus Answered and said unto them, take heed that no man deceive you. For many shall come in my name, saying, I am Christ; and shall deceive many. (Antichrist rises) And ye shall hear of wars and rumours of wars (Wars are initiated): see that ye be not troubled: for all these things must come to pass, but the end is not yet. For nation shall rise against nation, and kingdom against kingdom: and there shall be famines, and pestilences, (Poverty, Famines and Pestilences) and earthquakes, in divers places. All these are the beginning of sorrows. (Matthew 24:4–8 KJV)

The scriptures in Daniel speak from the standpoint of Israel and how Israel is affected. The parallel, or sister, scriptures in Revelation 13, Matthew 24, and others need to be read to understand the final sequence of events and the perfection of the Word of God. Daniel focuses on the end from the standpoint of the Jews alive at that time. Revelation focuses on the final forty-two months from the standpoint of the entire world and how this man affects all on the earth. Once again, scripture buildup needs to be understood here. The realization that several scriptures can document the same event, each adding additional information without contradiction, is key to proper interpretation. This process of scripture buildup allows us to fully understand the events of the last days, such that we cannot get it wrong. The Lord states in Matthew 24:4, "*Let no man deceive you.*" Men can deceive only if scripture regarding these times is not understood; right dividing and interpretation of scripture ensures truth.

The terrible time of Jacob's trouble and earthly destruction is now on the earth, triggered by man's overflowing sin. The destruction is self-appointed through the unquenchable sinful desires of mankind.

God allows man to go down this path of destruction and desolation, appointed by and allowed through God's permissive will, because of the accelerating sin of mankind. The destruction will continue *"till the indignation (wrath of God) be accomplished."* The Antichrist is now speaking and performing astonishing supernatural works while declaring himself to be God.[190] His declaration of deity is blasphemy against the Holy Spirit; he thus commits the unforgiveable sin. The final forty-two months continue and will exhaust the true God's indignation, or wrath.[191] The Antichrist will not regard any God that existed before, including those preferred by women. In the place of the true God, he shall honor the god of military power. Consider Miller's explanation of the *God of forces* mentioned in Daniel 11:38:

> The 'god of fortresses' is the personification of war, and the thought is this: he will regard no other god, but only war; the taking of fortresses he will make his god; and he will worship this god above all as the means of his gaining the world-power." Leupold rightly observes that "if men will not have the true god, there must be something to which they will attach the allegiance of their heart."[96] His ancestors did not worship this god of military power ("a god unknown to his fathers"), but Antichrist will. He "will honor" this god of military power by spending lavishly ("with gold and silver, with precious stones and costly gifts") to increase the size and strength of his army. Young asserts: "For religion he will substitute war, and war he will support with all that he has." That Antichrist will engage in war is seen in vv. 40–45; 7:8, 24; and elsewhere in scripture (e.g., Rev 13:4; 16:13–16).[192]

---

[190] 2 Thessalonians 2:7–10.
[191] 2 Thessalonians 2:11–12.
[192] Miller, *Daniel*, 308.

He will honor the God of forces and worship military conquests. In public, he does not honor any God, but in private he pays homage to a strange God—namely Satan himself, disguised as a God of war or death. The Bible states that Satan is the author of death. In the Antichrist, Satan finds a human agent who will be fully devoted to him, bringing on the greatest death and destruction that the earth has ever seen. With this as his foundation of power, and because of the great sin of mankind, he will continue to exponentially increase with power and glory. He will fulfill all of the desires of Satan on the earth for forty-two months. These verses encompass the core of the final forty-two months—supernatural war and destruction unleashed on the earth. Those he corrupted with flatteries in verse 32, and others who pay him homage, shall rule over many. His fully devoted followers will be granted lands (countries) acquired through his conquests. The ten kings mentioned in many other scriptures associated with him are part of this group.[193] Consider the following:

> And the ten horns which thou sawest are ten kings, which have received no kingdom as yet; **but receive power as kings one hour with the beast.**
>
> These have one mind, and shall give their power and strength unto the beast. (Revelation 17:12–14 KJV; my emphasis)
>
> Thus he said, The fourth beast shall be the fourth kingdom upon earth, which shall be diverse from all kingdoms, and shall devour the whole earth, and shall tread it down, and break it in pieces. **And the ten horns out of this kingdom are ten kings that shall arise:** and another shall rise after them; and he shall be diverse from the first, and he shall subdue three kings. And he shall speak great words against the most High, and shall wear out the saints of the

---

[193] Revelation 17:12–14; Daniel 7:23–25; 12:7.

most High, and think to change times and laws: and they shall be given into his hand until a time (one year) and times(two years) and the dividing of time (one-half year; (3.5 years). (Daniel 7:23–25 KJV; my emphasis)

The beast, in his supernatural form, will "*do according to all his will*," and will seek to be worshipped as God. He will be successful for forty-two months. The earth will go through the worst time in human history. The earth will be filled with wars, destruction, famines, earthquakes, pestilences, and death at the hands of a supernatural beast that cannot be destroyed. These solemn verses sum up, in very few verses, the destruction and mayhem that will be on the earth in those days. Satan and his Antichrist will freely operate on the earth without restraint, through the permissive will of the true God. All this destruction is brought on by man because of mankind's rejection of God and of his Christ. Sometime later in the final forty-two months, God's wrath will also arise as the war of supernatural forces is fought on the earth. God's judgments are accurately laid out in the book of Revelation, and needless to say, God will triumph.

Daniel 11.40–43: And at the time of the end shall the king of the south push at him: and the king of the north shall come against him like a whirlwind, with chariots, and with horsemen, and with many ships; and he shall enter into the countries, and shall overflow and pass over. He shall enter also into the glorious land, and many countries shall be overthrown: but these shall escape out of his hand, even Edom, and Moab, and the chief of the children of Ammon. He shall stretch forth his hand also upon the countries: and the land of Egypt shall not escape. But he shall have power over the treasures of gold and of silver, and over all the precious things of Egypt: and the Libyans and the Ethiopians shall be at his steps.

With his ten kings, he continues his assault on the nations of the world, unabated and supernaturally charged. Nothing will be able to save the inhabitants of the earth, those spiritually bare, who are estranged from the true God. The great lie that this man is a god is now thrust upon the inhabitants of the earth. His alluring power and his easy conquest will be addictive to those on the earth. After these things, the time of the end of the final seven years will approach rapidly. Scripture states that both the king of the south and the king of the north will come against the Antichrist. The reason for this is not clear, but it will be clear at the time of the end. God's Word is simply factual at this point, declaring the things that are now on the earth. These verses describe the sequence of events that occur at the end of the last seven years. It must be remembered that in Daniel, these events are always from the viewpoint of the Jewish people and the land of Israel. The Antichrist is now challenged in his supernatural state with a great military of Gentile nations from the north and the south amassing. He will respond with even more death and destruction directed toward the people and nations of the earth. In the few words of these verses, God sums up a great destruction of nations and people. Satan's pure hate and lack of consideration for any form of life will now take center stage through severe supernatural destruction of the Gentile nations. *"He shall also enter into the glorious land"*—that is, the land of Israel. The term indicating that the vile man will "stretch forth his hand" in verse 42 reveals that the Antichrist will now actively engage the world in war.

The book of Jeremiah documents that God's wrath toward Israel will subside only when the will and power of his people (Israel) are diminished.[194] The end referred to in this verse marks the fulfillment of all of God's promises to Israel as noted in Daniel 9:24.[195] The *end a*lso marks the end of the time of the Gentiles, or the Gentile rule over the earth; it is described as the "time of the end." Once again, this is not the end of the world or the end of the second heaven and earth; rather, it is the end of Gentile rule and dominion over the earth. After Gentile rule is put down and the Antichrist is destroyed by the brightness of the coming of the Lord Jesus Christ, the beginning of the everlasting rule of Jesus Christ begins. The beginning of the "time of the end" is marked by Gentile nations pushing at the Antichrist or turning against him for reasons

---

[194] Jeremiah 30; Daniel 12:7.
[195] Daniel 9:24.

not revealed. The pushing against him also marks the beginning of the gathering of the nations for the final battle of Armageddon, as described in Revelation. The end of the seventieth seven will also be marked by the wrath of Satan and his Antichrist, mingled with the wrath of Almighty God against the seat of Satan on earth. God's wrath will be directed toward both the Antichrist and his forces, as well as the forces of the Gentile nations gathered from across the globe. The result of the battle of Armageddon will be the destruction of the Antichrist and the dethroning of Gentile rule over the earth. The end will be followed by the revelation and establishment of the everlasting kingdom of Jesus Christ. After the end of Gentile rule, God fulfills all his promises to Abraham, Isaac, and Jacob, allowing the restoration of the kingdom to Israel. God will also establish the everlasting kingdom of the Lord Jesus Christ, God's only begotten son. The Gentile nations will once again (as in the Old Testament) be relegated to a secondary position to Israel. Consider the following:

> For I would not, brethren, that ye should be ignorant of this mystery, lest ye should be wise in your own conceits; that blindness in part is happened to Israel, until the **fulness of the Gentiles be come in.** And so all Israel shall be saved: as it is written, There shall come out of Sion the Deliverer, and shall turn away ungodliness from Jacob: For this is my covenant unto them, when I shall take away their sins. As concerning the gospel, they are enemies for your sakes: but as touching the election, they are beloved for the fathers' sakes. (Romans 11:25–29 KJV; my emphasis)
>
> For these be the days of vengeance, that all things which are written may be fulfilled. But woe unto them that are with child, and to them that give suck, in those days! for there shall be great distress in the land, and wrath upon this people. And they shall fall by the edge of the sword, and shall be led away captive into all nations: and

Jerusalem shall be trodden down of the Gentiles, **until the times of the Gentiles be fulfilled**. And there shall be signs in the sun, and in the moon, and in the stars; and upon the earth distress of nations, with perplexity; the sea and the waves roaring; Men's hearts failing them for fear, and for looking after those things which are coming on the earth: for the powers of heaven shall be shaken. And then shall they see the Son of man coming in a cloud with power and great glory. And when these things begin to come to pass, then look up, and lift up your heads; for your redemption draweth nigh. (Luke 21:22–28 KJV; my emphasis)

Daniel 11.44–45: "But tidings out of the east and out of the north shall trouble him: therefore he shall go forth with great fury to destroy, and utterly to make away many. ⁴⁵ And he shall plant the tabernacles of his palace between the seas in the glorious holy mountain; yet he shall come to his end, and none shall help him". The end time for Gentile rule and, for that matter, natural man's rule over the earth is now fast approaching. These end times now line up and are in concert with the final time and the final days of the last seven years. In the previous verse, it was the king of the North and of the South. Now alarming news is also coming from the East, representing the gathering of the nations for the final act at Armageddon. The gathering of the nations for destruction was always to occur near the end of the seventieth seven, and now it is clear how the nations will be gathered together. The Antichrist reacts to this offensive stacked up against him by stepping up his aggression against the world. In verse 44, the term "make away many" probably represents millions of people losing their lives—that is, Satan appointing many to extermination. Verse 45 should be read alongside Revelation 16:13, which records frogs as spirits emanating from the dragon, the beast, and the false prophet. The result will be the summoning of the nations to the great battle. Verse 45 goes on to reveal that the Antichrist takes up residence between the seas—the Mediterranean and the Dead Sea—at the holy mount in Jerusalem. He begins his reign of terror in Jerusalem; therefore, it is fitting that Jerusalem would also be where he comes to his end. How he comes to his end is not explained here, but we are not left ignorant of how he comes to his end. Consider the following:

> And then shall that Wicked be revealed, whom the Lord shall consume with the spirit of his mouth, and shall destroy with the brightness of his coming Even him, whose coming is after the working of Satan with all power and signs and lying wonders And with all deceivableness of unrighteousness in them that perish; because they received not the love of the truth, that they might be saved. And for this cause God shall send them strong delusion, that they should believe a lie: That they all might be damned who believed not the truth, but had pleasure in unrighteousness. (2 Thessalonians 2:8–12 KJV)
>
> But with righteousness shall he judge the poor, and reprove with equity for the meek of the earth: and he shall smite the earth with the rod of his mouth, and with the breath of his lips shall he slay the wicked. (Isaiah 11:4 KJV)
>
> And the beast was taken, and with him the false prophet that wrought miracles before him, with which he deceived them that had received the mark of the beast, and them that worshipped his image. These both were cast alive into a lake of fire burning with brimstone. And the remnant were slain with the sword of him that sat upon the horse, which sword proceeded out of his mouth: and all the fowls were filled with their flesh. (Revelation 19:20–21 KJV)
>
> A fiery stream issued and came forth from before him: thousand thousands ministered unto him, and ten thousand times ten thousand stood

before him: the judgment was set, and the books were opened. **I beheld then because of the great words which the horn spake; I beheld even until the beast was slain and his body destroyed and given to the burning flame.** As concerning the rest of the beasts, they had their dominion taken away: yet their lives were prolonged for a season and a time. I saw in the night visions and behold one like the son of man came with the clouds of heaven, and came to the ancient of days, and they brought him before him. And there was given him dominion, and glory, and a kingdom, that all people, nations, and languages, should serve him: his dominion is an everlasting dominion, which shall not pass away, and his kingdom that which shall not be destroyed. (Daniel 7:10–14 KJV; my emphasis)

The above verses make it clear that it is the Lord Jesus Christ, at his coming for Israel, who destroys the Antichrist between the seas in the glorious holy mountain in Jerusalem. None shall help him; nor can anyone help him, since he is smitten by God. His body is not found, since his end is to be thrown alive bodily into the lake of fire. Eternal damnation and hell is the punishment for the unforgiveable sin—blasphemy against the Holy Spirit.[196] These verses reveal that the end of the seventieth seven will be marked by all nations gathering together against the beast in and around Jerusalem. Psalm 2 indicates that although they come together against the beast, they will ultimately be against God and his Christ. The wicked from all nations will be destroyed together with the beast. Consider the following:

> Why do the heathen rage, and the people imagine a vain thing? The kings of the earth set themselves, and the rulers take counsel together,

---

[196] Matthew 12:31.

against the LORD, and against his anointed, saying, Let us break their bands asunder, and cast away their cords from us. He that sitteth in the heavens shall laugh: the Lord shall have them in derision. Then shall he speak unto them in his wrath, and vex them in his sore displeasure. **Yet have I set my king upon my holy hill of Zion. I will declare the decree: the LORD hath said unto me, Thou art my Son; this day have I begotten thee. Ask of me, and I shall give thee the heathen for thine inheritance, and the uttermost parts of the earth for thy possession. Thou shalt break them with a rod of iron; thou shalt dash them in pieces like a potter's vessel.** Be wise now therefore, O ye kings: be instructed, ye judges of the earth. Serve the LORD with fear, and rejoice with trembling. Kiss the Son, lest he be angry, and ye perish from the way, when his wrath is kindled but a little. Blessed are all they that put their trust in him. (Psalm 2:1–12 KJV; my emphasis)

It is clear from the above scriptures that the nations are now in a delusional state. They are gathered together and believe they can usurp God and his son from heaven Jesus Christ. Psalm 2 reveals the outcome of the battle.

The next section of Daniel (Daniel 12.1–13) is the summing up of God's dealing with Israel and his record of his fulfillment of his promises to Abraham, Isaac, and Jacob. The record should be compared with the promises that he promised through his prophet Daniel in Daniel 9.24. The Antichrist is now destroyed and the redemption of Israel as well as God's final placement of Israel in the land is now to be accomplished. The time is the end of the seventieth seven and the enemies of God are put aside, and the Lord Jesus Christ is now beginning his Millennial rule on the earth. The first resurrection of the just is also described here; the redemption of Israel is the focus of this section. Consider:

> And at that time shall Michael stand up, the great prince which standeth for the children of thy people: and there shall be a time of trouble, such as never was since there was a nation even to that same time: and at that time thy people shall be delivered, every one that shall be found written in the book. And many of them that sleep in the dust of the earth shall awake, some to everlasting life, and some to shame and everlasting contempt. And they that be wise shall shine as the brightness of the firmament; and they that turn many to righteousness as the stars for ever and ever. But thou, o Daniel, shut up the words, and seal the book even until the time of the end: many shall run to and fro, and knowledge shall be increased. (Daniel 12:1–4 KJV)

Daniel 12 is the epilogue of the final scenes of the final seven years—especially how God delivers Israel, summarizing their future with the Lord. Recall that the end of the seventy sevens of years is marked by the completion of all the promises God made to Israel through Abraham, Isaac, and Jacob. These promises are summarized and documented in Daniel 9:24 and will be fulfilled at this time. After the last seven years, the new embryonic nation of Israel will be in the land with David as their king and Jesus Christ as their Lord. The timing of chapter 12 is immediately following the destruction of the Antichrist after the final seven years. This section also references the two resurrections of the dead, which are documented in the scriptures by the Lord Jesus Christ. The first resurrection is mentioned here; the seed of Israel throughout time who were faithful to God are raised and placed in the land. David will also be raised as their king at this same time. The section reveals key time sequences contained within and after the final seven years. God begins (see verse 1) by specially naming and commissioning Michael as the great prince who stands and protects God's interests concerning Israel. Compare this to the other verse, in which Michael is specifically mentioned as the minister of God's protection for Israel. This section also depicts a woman to represent Jerusalem and Israel. Consider the following:

> And there appeared a great wonder in heaven; a woman clothed with the sun, and the moon under her feet, and upon her head a crown of twelve stars: And she being with child cried, travailing in birth, and pained to be delivered. And there appeared another wonder in heaven; and behold a great red dragon, having seven heads and ten horns, and seven crowns upon his heads. And his tail drew the third part of the stars of heaven, and did cast them to the earth: and the dragon stood before the woman which was ready to be delivered, for to devour her child as soon as it was born. And she brought forth a man child, who was to rule all nations with a rod of iron: and her child was caught up unto God, and to his throne. And the woman fled into the wilderness, where she hath a place prepared of God, that they should feed her there a thousand two hundred and threescore days. And there was war in heaven: **Michael and his angels fought against the dragon; and the dragon fought and his angels,** And prevailed not; neither was their place found any more in heaven. And the great dragon was cast out, that old serpent, called the Devil, and Satan, which deceiveth the whole world: he was cast out into the earth, and his angels were cast out with him. And I heard a loud voice saying in heaven, Now is come salvation, and strength, and the kingdom of our God, and the power of his Christ: for the accuser of our brethren is cast

down, which accused them before our God day and night. And they overcame him by the blood of the Lamb, and by the word of their testimony; and they loved not their lives unto the death. Therefore rejoice, ye heavens, and ye that dwell in them. Woe to the inhabiters of the earth and of the sea! for the devil is come down unto you, having great wrath, because he knoweth that he hath but a short time. And when the dragon saw that he was cast unto the earth, he persecuted the woman which brought forth the man child. And to the woman were given two wings of a great eagle, that she might fly into the wilderness, into her place, where she is nourished for a time, and times, and half a time, from the face of the serpent. And the serpent cast out of his mouth water as a flood after the woman, that he might cause her to be carried away of the flood. And the earth helped the woman, and the earth opened her mouth, and swallowed up the flood which the dragon cast out of his mouth. And the dragon was wroth with the woman, and went to make war with the remnant of her seed. (Revelation 12:1–17 KJV; my emphasis)

In Revelation 12, Michael stands up for Israel, as also mentioned in Daniel 12:1. Revelation 12 documents what he does when he stands up; Satan and all evil agents are cast out of heaven and relegated to the earth. Contrary to popular belief, the casting out of Satan and his forces happens at the time of the end and not until then. Daniel 12:1 goes on to state that this action of war in heaven will result in a time of trouble, forty-two months, such as there never was since there was the nation of Israel. Revelation 13 describes this time of trouble for the world in minute detail, while Daniel 12:1 speaks of the same time of trouble from the vantage point of Israel. Both records are harmonious, speaking of this same time without contradiction but from different viewpoints. Each adds information; both build on one another. Additionally, Matthew 24 speaks of this time of trouble. Consider the following:

> But pray ye that your flight be not in the winter, neither on the sabbath day: For then shall be great tribulation, such as was not since the beginning of the world to this time, no, nor ever shall be. And except those days should be shortened, there should no flesh be saved: but for the elect's sake those days shall be shortened. Then if any man shall say unto you, Lo, here is Christ, or there; believe it not. For there shall arise false Christs, and false prophets, and shall shew great signs and wonders; insomuch that, if it were possible, they shall deceive the very elect. (Matthew 24:20–24 KJV)

Michael standing up for Israel is one of the themes, if not the main subject, of Revelation 12. The parallel occurrence in heaven is a war in heaven resulting in Satan being cast out of heaven. The fact that Satan now has a seat in the heavens is critical to understanding the events of the last days and is also acknowledged in Ephesians 6. Consider the following:

> Finally, my brethren, be strong in the Lord, and in the power of his might. Put on the whole armour of God, that ye may be able to stand against the wiles of the devil. **For we wrestle not against flesh and blood, but against principalities, against powers, against the rulers of the darkness of this world, against spiritual wickedness in high (Heavenly) places.** Wherefore take unto you the whole armour of God, that ye may be able to withstand in the evil day, and having done all, to stand. Stand

therefore, having your loins girt about with truth, and having on the breastplate of righteousness; And your feet shod with the preparation of the gospel of peace; Above all, taking the shield of faith, wherewith ye shall be able to quench all the fiery darts of the wicked. And take the helmet of salvation, and the sword of the Spirit, which is the Word of God: Praying always with all prayer and supplication in the Spirit, and watching thereunto with all perseverance and supplication for all saints. (Ephesians 6:10–18 KJV; my emphasis)

The casting out of Satan from the heavens will initiate the final forty-two months of the final seven years—the most troubled time in human history for Israel and the world. Revelation 12 exposes how this one event in heaven, the casting out of Satan and his angels, has a cataclysmic effect upon the inhabitants of the earth. His world dominion will last forty-two months and will begin with his being cast out of the heavens, at or about the midst of the last seven years. The casting out of Satan is a requirement for the beginning of the everlasting kingdom of our Lord and Savior, Jesus Christ; his dominion will encompass the heavens and the earth as delivered to him by the Father.

Commentary (Daniel 12:1–4); The end of the seven years; The chosen of Israel Delivered
Daniel 12:1: "*And at that time shall Michael stand up, the great prince which standeth for the children of thy people: and there shall be a time of trouble, such as never was since there was a nation even to that same time: and at that time thy people shall be delivered, every one that shall be found written in the book.*" Verse 1 of chapter 12 first gives a general statement of the events which precipitate the time of the end; that is Michael standing up for Daniel's people, Israel. Revelation 12 gives further explanation as to what this standing up means. Daniel 12:1 explains that Michael will stand up for Israel and cast

out Satan from the heavens, to be relegated to the earth. Revelation 13 explains the corresponding consequences on the earth for the forty-two months during which Satan is relegated to the earth. Both records indicate a time of trouble like nothing on the earth before; Revelation 13 gives the specific details. The time of this casting out is the middle of the final seven years of the seventieth seven. Both records corroborate and complement each other, and they should also be compared to Matthew 24, which describes the same events from a separate viewpoint. Ephesians 6 supports the fact that the devil is indeed in the heavens causing havoc until he is finally cast out at the time of the end. Additionally, Thessalonians alludes to the fact that the devil is holding fast to his position in the heavens, and Satan will do so until he is finally cast out by Michael at the time of the midst of the final seven years. It will be this departure, documented in 2 Thessalonians 2:3 and 2:7, that will initiate the final forty-two months of hell on earth. Consider the following:

> Now we beseech you, brethren, by the coming of our Lord Jesus Christ, and by our gathering together unto him, That ye be not soon shaken in mind, or be troubled, neither by spirit, nor by word, nor by letter as from us, as that the day of Christ is at hand. **Let no man deceive you by any means: for that day shall not come, except there come a falling away first, and that man of sin be revealed, the son of perdition;** Who opposeth and exalteth himself above all that is called God, or that is worshipped; so that he as God sitteth in the temple of God, shewing himself that he is God. Remember ye not, that, when I was yet with you, I told you these things? **And now ye know what withholdeth** (is holding fast) **that he might be revealed in his time. For the mystery of iniquity doth already work: only he who now letteth** (holds fast) **will let, until he be taken out of the way.** And then shall

that Wicked be revealed, whom the Lord shall consume with the spirit of his mouth, and shall destroy with the brightness of his coming: Even him, whose coming is after the working of Satan with all power and signs and lying wonders, And with all deceivableness of unrighteousness in them that perish; because they received not the love of the truth, that they might be saved. And for this cause God shall send them strong delusion, that they should believe a lie: That they all might be damned who believed not the truth, but had pleasure in unrighteousness. (2 Thessalonians 2:1–12; my emphasis)

Daniel 12:2–3: And many of them that sleep in the dust of the earth shall awake, some to everlasting life, and some to shame and everlasting contempt. And they that be wise shall shine as the brightness of the firmament; and they that turn many to righteousness as the stars for ever and ever. Verse 2 of Daniel 12 documents the time of Israel's deliverance for everyone written in the book. There will be living people and dead people found written in the book; both groups will be delivered at the end of the last seven years. The time will be the time of the first resurrection immediately after the seventieth week, or the final seven years. Many who sleep in the dust shall be resurrected, some to everlasting life and some to everlasting contempt. The verse also alludes to the second resurrection, in which all will get up and be judged according to their works. Revelation 20, which also describes both resurrections, should be read in conjunction with this section; both are mentioned here. These verses also show that the dead are dead until they are raised through one of these two resurrections: either the resurrection to eternal life or the resurrection to judgment. The pertinent verses of Revelation 20 are listed below. The resurrection of dead bodies mentioned here is peculiar and is focused on Israel and their deliverance. There will be righteous Jews written in the book in both resurrections; both are mentioned here, although they are one thousand years apart. Recall Daniel's prayer from chapter 9, where he prayed to understand what would happen to his people (Israel), the land, and the holy place in Jerusalem. God answers Daniel's prayer and summarizes the trials and tribulations of Israel, beginning with their building of the temple by Nehemiah (about 250 BC) and running up until these last days in Daniel 12. The prophecy summarizes the events, ending with the resurrection of believing Israel at the end of the final seven years; it skips over the period of the mystery of the one body of Christ in the process. These verses in Daniel 12 complete and fulfill the prophecy of Daniel 9:24 and give full answer to Daniel's prayer documented in the beginning of chapter 9. The many in Israel who will be resurrected to eternal life are those raised as part of the first resurrection and "written in the book." The second group of Jews, those not raised, will suffer shame and everlasting contempt when they are raised. The second group comprises those who will be part of the second resurrection after the millennial reign of Christ. The second group raised will also include those righteous Jews who lived during the millennial kingdom on earth and were written in the book.

All this goes against the popular teaching that those who die immediately go to heaven. This is not what the Bible teaches; tradition of men will, and has, confused the issue. All that have died await one or the other of the resurrections listed in these verses. The only exception to this will be the rapture of the one body of Jesus Christ at his coming in the air for the saints. This is also why what God did in raising Jesus Christ from the dead is the unique defining moment of human history. Jesus Christ is the only one who was raised from the dead and is alive forever; all other Jews and Gentiles await one of the two resurrections. As for the body of Christ, they await the gathering together with the Lord in the air; both those born-again believers alive at the time of his appearance and those who have died since the day of Pentecost will be raptured by the Lord. The gathering together is a special kind of firstfruits to God and to Christ. Concerning the second resurrection of Jews and Gentiles, those who will be part of the final resurrection, they will be judged according to their works. Both of these resurrections are alluded to in John 5 and Revelation 20. Consider the following:

Verily, verily, I say unto you, The hour is coming, and now is, when the dead shall hear the voice of the Son of God: and **they that hear** (not all will hear; this is the first resurrection) shall live. For as the Father hath life in himself; so hath he given to the Son to have life in himself; And hath given him authority to execute judgment also, because he is the Son of man. Marvel not at this: for the hour is coming, in the which **all that are in the graves** (second resurrection) shall hear his voice, And shall come forth; they that have done good, unto the resurrection of life; and they that have done evil, unto the resurrection of damnation. (John 5:25–29 KJV; my emphasis)

And I saw an angel come down from heaven, having the key of the bottomless pit and a great chain in his hand. And he laid hold on the dragon, that old serpent, which is the Devil, and Satan, and bound him a thousand years, And cast him into the bottomless pit, and shut him up, and set a seal upon him, that he should deceive the nations no more, till the thousand years should be fulfilled: and after that he must be loosed a little season. And I saw thrones, and they sat upon them, and judgment was given unto them: **and I saw the souls of them that were beheaded for the witness of Jesus, and for the Word of God, and which had not worshipped the beast, neither his image, neither had received his mark upon their foreheads, or in their hands; and they lived and reigned with Christ a thousand years**. But the rest of the dead lived not again until the thousand years were finished. This is the first resurrection. Blessed and holy is he that hath part in the first resurrection: on such the second death hath no power, but they shall be priests of God and of Christ, and shall reign with him a thousand years. And when the thousand years are expired, Satan shall be loosed out of his prison, And shall go out to deceive the nations which are in the four quarters of the earth, Gog and Magog, to gather them together to battle: the number of whom is as the sand of the sea. And they went up on the breadth of the earth, and compassed the camp of the saints about, and the beloved city: and fire came down from God out of heaven, and devoured them. And the devil that deceived them was cast into the lake of fire and brimstone, where the beast and the false prophet are, and shall be tormented day and night for ever and ever. **And I saw a great white throne, and him that sat on it, from whose face the earth and the heaven fled away; and there was found no place for them. And I saw the dead, small and great, stand before God; and the books were opened: and another book was opened, which is the book of life: and the dead were judged out of those things which were written in the books, according to their works. And the sea gave up the dead which were in it; and death and hell delivered up the dead which were in them: and they were judged every man according to their works** (second resurrection). And death and hell were cast into the lake of fire. This is the second death. And whosoever was not found written in the book of life was cast into the lake of fire. (Revelation 20:1–15; my emphasis)

From the above, we understand that there will be two resurrections concerning the Jews and Gentiles: the first, or former, is the resurrection of the just, which occurs just after the final seven years of Daniel's seventy sevens; the second resurrection occurs a thousand years after and will be the great white throne judgment for all remaining dead. The second resurrection will include all people who ever lived on the earth, and they will be judged according to their works. The ones counted worthy of the first resurrection will shine like the brightness of the firmament and live and reign with Christ for a thousand years. There will also be those who turn many to righteousness (those worthy of the first resurrection), and they will shine like the stars forever and ever. Daniel 12:3 describes the wise as shining like the brightness of the firmament and they that turn many to righteousness as shining like the stars forever and ever. The scripture is related to Daniel 11:33, 35. Consider the following:

> And arms shall stand on his part, and they shall pollute the sanctuary of strength, and shall take away the daily sacrifice, and they shall place the abomination that maketh desolate. And such as do wickedly against the covenant shall he corrupt by flatteries: **but the people that do know their God shall be strong, and do exploits. And they that understand among the people shall instruct many: yet they shall fall by the sword, and by flame, by captivity, and by spoil, many days. Now when they shall fall, they shall be holpen with a little help: but many shall cleave to them with flatteries. And some of them of understanding shall fall, to try them, and to purge, and to make them white, even to the time of the end: because it is yet for a time appointed.** (Daniel 11:31–35 KJV; my emphasis)

Daniel 12:3 describes the deliverance of God's people, Israel, from the supernatural beast, who was in full operation until finally destroyed by the coming of the Lord Jesus Christ for Israel. There will be those who will have instructed many into righteousness: "… *they that be wise and have instructed many into righteousness.*" The wise and understanding of Israel will also have been martyred for their stand during the great tribulation. The first resurrection, or the resurrection of the just, will occur immediately after the destruction of the Antichrist and his confederacy. The first resurrection will consist of all Israel, past and up to the time of the end of the seventy sevens (490) of years for Israel, who are written in the book of life. The group will include all those throughout time who have lived their life in faith toward God. Both of these groups will shine like the stars of heaven and live and reign with Jesus Christ forever and ever. The first resurrection does not include those of Israel who are blotted out of the book because of their unbelief, as God mentioned frequently in the Old Testament. [197] For example, Joab, who was loyal to David for a good portion of his life, was not loyal until the end. He is not mentioned in the list of great men with David, as documented by God in Samuel. He, although a great warrior and defender of David, was not a man of faith from the heart and was therefore rejected by God.[198] Daniel 12:3 completes the angelic prophecy initiated in Daniel 10:11 and gives a full answer to Daniel's prayer and supplications, which began in Daniel 9.[199]

Daniel 12:4: But thou, O Daniel, shut up the words, and seal the book, even to the time of the end: many shall run to and fro, and knowledge shall be increased. In verse 4, the angel gives further instructions to Daniel regarding the words and the prophecy he just received. His specific instructions are to seal the book and the prophecy until the time of the end. Daniel is instructed to shut up the words. A related instruction to seal and shut up is also given in verses 8–10. "Seal and shut up," in this context, is related to the understanding and the interpretation of this prophecy. God states that the words will be understood and interpreted at the time of the end; until then, it would be fruitless to attempt to understand the fullness of the prophecy. There are several things documented, but full understanding will only be at the time of the end. At the time

---

[197] Exodus 32:31–35.
[198] 2 Samuel 23:8.
[199] See Daniel 9:1–23.

of the prophecy contained in Daniel 12, another whole dispensation time period, the mystery of the one body of Jesus Christ, would have to pass before these words reached their fulfillment and were fully understood. For this reason, Daniel is instructed to seal and to shut up the words until the time of the end. Gabriel was instructing Daniel to preserve *"the words of the scroll"*—not merely this final vision but the whole of the associated future last-days revelation. The full instruction and information is focused on those living at the time of the end, when the message will be needed. The people at the time of the end will undergo the horrors of the tribulation, *"a time of distress,"* like no other group in human history. When these horrors occur, the people at that time will need the precious promises contained in the book of Daniel and those contained in the book of Revelation. They will need to know that God will be victorious over the kingdoms of this world, including Satan and the Antichrist. They will also need to know that the suffering will not last forever but will be limited in time and scope; the time is documented by Daniel and Revelation.[200] At the time of the end, the seal will come off of these words to those who are chosen by God to understand. God states that the words are sealed, not understood, until the time of the end. As for the wicked or unbelieving, they will never understand until it is upon them (verse 10). These words of prophecy in Daniel will be studied but will be fully understood only at the time of the end—the time of their fulfillment. When God says that the words are shut up and sealed, he is referring to their understanding and application. Consider the following: *"For the LORD hath poured out upon you the spirit of deep sleep, and hath closed your eyes: the prophets and your rulers, the seers hath he covered.* ***And the vision of all is become unto you as the words of a book that is sealed, which men deliver to one that is learned, saying, Read this, I pray thee: and he saith, I cannot; for it is sealed"*** (Isaiah 29:10–11 KJV; my emphasis).

The second part of verse 4 states, *"Many will run to and fro and knowledge shall be increased."* Verse 4 gives information as to some of the characteristics of the time of the end. "Many shall run to and

---

[200] Miller, *Daniel*, 321.

fro" is an interesting phrase and has a peculiar meaning. The Hebrew word used for "to and fro" ("יְשֹׁטְטוּ") is used several times in the Bible with the general meaning of "one traveling, searching, or striving, with a particular goal in mind." The word indicates, in the general sense, an increase in travel and striving, with mainly worldly goals in mind. One significant usage is in Job 1:7, where Satan is running *"to and fro"* throughout the earth with obvious evil intentions in mind. The second characteristic of the end times revealed in this verse is an increase in knowledge. The word used for "knowledge" here is the Hebrew word ":הַדָּעַת" and is related to knowledge gained either by the Word of God or from the world through the five senses. Interestingly, the first usage of this word in the Bible is in Genesis and is related to the tree of knowledge, representing the knowledge of good and evil apart from the Word of God. It is believed that there is a double meaning here. First, the knowledge of God's Word increases at the time of the end to those God selects, and second, there will also be a general increase in worldly knowledge and communication among nations. The world will see great new inventions and marvels through the increase in knowledge on the earth. Worldly knowledge will be easily accessible and at one's fingertips. The association is as it was in Genesis; the increase of knowledge ultimately increases the sin and rebellion of mankind against God and against each other.

Commentary (Daniel 12:5–13); Daniel's Final Encounter with the Angelic Messenger and the final timelines

The final section in Daniel begins the final encounter with the angelic beings and the conclusion of the structural breakdown of Daniel 10–12 as laid out in the beginning of this section. This section, part A, is logically connected to part A, or Daniel 10:2–21. These two bookends mark off the entire section and fully describe Daniel's encounter with the angelic messengers before and after the revelation given in Daniel 10–12 is documented. The section concludes the revelation of the entire section listed in Daniel 10–12. The beginning and the end of this section reveal how Daniel communicates with the angelic beings and has dialogue with them. Their purpose in appearing to Daniel was to give him *"skill and understanding"* concerning the events of the last days for his people: "***Now I am come to make thee understand what shall befall thy people in the latter days: for yet the vision is for many days.***"[201] The entire section of chapters 10 to 12 is devoted to give Daniel, and those who read and fear God, skill and understanding regarding the last days, with the focus being Daniel's people, Israel. The final section of Daniel 12 concludes the prophecy and presents key times, dates, and event sequences relating to the prophetic message just given to Daniel. Two additional angelic messengers are also mentioned as appearing, one on either side of the river; the original angel is located upon the waters of the river.

Daniel 12:5–7: "Then I Daniel looked, and, behold, there stood other two, the one on this side of the bank of the river, and the other on that side of the bank of the river. ⁶ And one said to the man clothed in linen, which was upon the waters of the river, How long shall it be to the end of these wonders? ⁷ And I heard the man clothed in linen, which was upon the waters of the river, when he held up his right hand and his left hand unto heaven, and sware by him that liveth for ever that it shall be for a time, times, and an half; and when he shall have accomplished to scatter the power of the holy people, all these things shall be finished. The section begins with one angelic being asking the question "*How long shall it be to the end of these wonders?*" Daniel is permitted to listen in on the angelic conversation. The Hebrew word for "wonders", from previous usage in the Bible, is related to supernatural wonders. The angel states that the beginning of the time period is marked by the miraculous satanic resurrection of the Antichrist. It is also clear from this verse that the supernatural events, and the supernatural judgements of God as described in the book of Revelation directed against the beast and his followers, will not be present until the middle of the final seven years. The beginning of sorrows and the twenty-three hundred days will not be related to supernatural crisis, but rather plagues, wars, and peace being taken from the earth as described in Matthew chapter 24: 8-14 and Revelation 6:1-11. The supernatural resurrection of the beast begins the supernatural war on the earth. His resurrection is a supernatural abomination that results

---

[201] Daniel 10:14.

in the supernatural destruction of the earth. The resurrection event begins the onset of a supernatural war on the earth. The event occurs at the time of the middle of the seventieth seven; therefore, the midst of the week is taken to be the starting point. The starting point also synchronizes with the time at which the Jewish sacrifice is taken away and the abomination of desolation is set up at the holy place in Jerusalem. In the above section the angel responds that the time will be time (one year), times (two years), and half a time (six months), or 3.5 years. The 3.5 years referred to in this verse is related to the second part, or the final three- and one-half years. The 3.5 years lines up with all other scriptures that speak of Jacob's trouble. The verse also indicates that one of God's reasons for the timing is to scatter the power of the holy people in Israel. The forty-two months provides for the purification of the called-out Jews; they are purified and made ready to accept the Lord and Savior, Jesus Christ, as their Messiah. They will be made to completely trust in God; no longer relying on any other nation, weapons of war, or any other thing that puts itself above the true God, but on God only. The called-out purified group becomes the new nation of Israel; David is raised as their king, and Jesus Christ is revealed as their Lord. Consider the following:

> Behold, the days come, saith the LORD, that I will raise unto David a righteous Branch, and a King shall reign and prosper, and shall execute judgment and justice in the earth. In his days Judah shall be saved, and Israel shall dwell safely: and this is his name whereby he shall be called, THE LORD OUR RIGHTEOUSNESS. Therefore, behold, the days come, saith the LORD, that they shall no more say, The LORD liveth, which brought up the children of Israel out of the land of Egypt; But, The LORD liveth, which brought up and which led the seed of the house of Israel out of the north country, and from all countries whither I had driven them; and they shall dwell in their own land. (Jeremiah 23:5–8 KJV)

For, lo, the days come, saith the LORD, that I will bring again the captivity of my people Israel and Judah, saith the LORD: and I will cause them to return to the land that I gave to their fathers, and they shall possess it. And these are the words that the LORD spake concerning Israel and concerning Judah. For thus saith the LORD; We have heard a voice of trembling, of fear, and not of peace. Ask ye now, and see whether a man doth travail with child? wherefore do I see every man with his hands on his loins, as a woman in travail, and all faces are turned into paleness? **Alas! for that day is great, so that none is like it: it is even the time of Jacob's trouble; but he shall be saved out of it.** For it shall come to pass in that day, saith the LORD of hosts, that I will break his yoke from off thy neck, and will burst thy bonds, and strangers shall no more serve themselves of him: But they shall serve the LORD their God, and **David their king, whom I will raise up unto them.** Therefore fear thou not, O my servant Jacob, saith the LORD; neither be dismayed, O Israel: for, lo, I will save thee from afar, and thy seed from the land of their captivity; and Jacob shall return, and shall be in rest, and be quiet, and none shall make him afraid. For I am with thee, saith the LORD, to save thee: though I make a full end of all nations whither I have scattered thee, yet will I not make a full end of thee: but I will correct thee in measure, and will not leave thee altogether unpunished. For thus saith the LORD, Thy bruise is incurable, and thy wound is grievous. There is none to plead thy cause, that thou mayest be bound up: thou hast no healing medicines. All thy lovers have forgotten thee;

they seek thee not; for I have wounded thee with the wound of an enemy, with the chastisement of a cruel one, for the multitude of thine iniquity; because thy sins were increased. Why criest thou for thine affliction? thy sorrow is incurable for the multitude of thine iniquity: because thy sins were increased, I have done these things unto thee. Therefore all they that devour thee shall be devoured; and all thine adversaries, every one of them, shall go into captivity; and they that spoil thee shall be a spoil, and all that prey upon thee will I give for a prey. For I will restore health unto thee, and I will heal thee of thy wounds, saith the LORD; because they called thee an Outcast, saying, This is Zion, whom no man seeketh after. Thus saith the LORD; Behold, I will bring again the captivity of Jacob's tents, and have mercy on his wellingplaces; **and the city shall be builded upon her own heap,** and the palace shall remain after the manner thereof. And out of them shall proceed thanksgiving and the voice of them that make merry: and I will multiply them, and they shall not be few; I will also glorify them, and they shall not be small. Their children also shall be as aforetime, and their congregation shall be established before me, and I will punish all that oppress them. And their nobles shall be of themselves, and their governor shall proceed from the midst of them; and I will cause him to draw near, and he shall approach unto me: for who is this that engaged his heart to approach unto me? saith the LORD. And ye shall be my people, and I will be your God. Behold, the whirlwind of the LORD goeth forth with fury, a continuing whirlwind: it shall fall with pain upon the head of the wicked. The fierce anger of the LORD shall not return, until he have done it, and until he have performed the intents of his heart**: in the latter days ye shall consider it.** (Jeremiah 30:3–24 KJV; my emphasis)

Daniel 12:8–13: And I heard, but I understood not: then said I, O my Lord, what shall be the end of these things? ⁹ And he said, Go thy way, Daniel: for the words are closed up and sealed till the time of the end. ¹⁰ Many shall be purified, and made white, and tried; but the wicked shall do wickedly: and none of the wicked shall understand; but the wise shall understand. ¹¹ And from the time that the daily sacrifice shall be taken away, and the abomination that maketh desolate set up, there shall be a thousand two hundred and ninety days. ¹² Blessed is he that waiteth, and cometh to the thousand three hundred and five and thirty days. ¹³ But go thou thy way till the end be: for thou shalt rest, and stand in thy lot at the end of the days. After the information regarding the final three and one-half years, Daniel, in verse 9, indicates his lack of understanding of the prophecy. His lack of understanding is expected, since understanding is reserved for the people at the time of the end, as previously mentioned in verse 4. Verse 10 goes on to give additional details and characteristics depicting the end times. Many of Israel shall be purified through the forty-two months of tribulation, and they shall be made white and tried. Some of these will also be those who God sets apart to be the embryotic nation of Israel who will be placed back into the land after the final seven years are completed. This is also alluded to in Daniel 11:32–35. In any event, great signs and events in the heavens and on the earth will occur, but these will not change any of the behaviors of the wicked, who will continue to perform wicked acts. All these scriptures will enlighten those called of God and are full of wisdom, but in contrast, they will in no way be understood by the wicked. Verse 11 goes on to define the starting point of the 3.5 years listed in days, not years, so as to prevent confusion and dispel any notion of a day equal to year theory. The 3.5 years is equal to 1,260 days in accordance with the Jewish calendar of 360 days per year. Curiously, the scripture adds 30 and 45 days, respectively, to the 1,260 days, in verses 11 and 12.

The beginning point for all the time periods is taken to be the time when the abomination that causes desolations on the earth is set up at the holy place in Jerusalem. This beginning point is alluded to in the following verses:

> [15] **When ye therefore shall see the abomination of desolation, spoken of by Daniel the prophet, stand in the holy place, (whoso readeth, let him understand:)** [16] Then let them which be in Judaea flee into the mountains: [17] Let him which is on the housetop not come down to take any thing out of his house: [18] Neither let him which is in the field return back to take his clothes. [19] And woe unto them that are with child, and to them that give suck in those days! [20] But pray ye that your flight be not in the winter, neither on the sabbath day: [21] For then shall be great tribulation, such as was not since the beginning of the world to this time, no, nor ever shall be. (Matthew 24:15–21 KJV; my emphasis).

Verse 11 and 12 of Daniel chapter 12 speaks of two end points; one is after 1,290 days and the second is after 1,335 days; both begin at the time when the abomination that causes desolation is set up in Jerusalem. The 1,290 days terminate when the *"many are purified, and made white, and tried."* The 1,335 days terminate some 45 days later when those who are tried, made white, purified and come into the kingdom that God has prepared for them. This is likely also be the time of the cleansing of the sanctuary. The additional 30 and 45 days; 75 days all together are also associated with the time of the judging of the nations, the first resurrection, and the cleansing of the sanctuary. In any event, the time periods are all initiated by the setting up of the abomination that causes desolation and the completion of the scattering of the power of Israel. The end of the seventy sevens marks the fulfillment of the promises to Daniel concerning Israel and is documented in Daniel 9:24. Consider the promises of Daniel 9:24, which God states will be accomplished at the end of this time period:

- The transgressions, or sins, concerning Israel are finished.
- Expiation or atonement for sin (related to Israel) and the setting on a proper course for Israel is complete.
- Everlasting righteousness is begun in Israel with Jesus Christ, as King of kings and Lord of lords for all, ruling from Zion in Israel.
- The prophecy or vision concerning Israel is completed. All that has been the subject of prophecy from all Old Testament scriptures and the Gospels concerning the last days and Israel's judgment and deliverance is now complete.
- The Most Holy, the Holy of Holies, is anointed.[202]

Interestingly, Psalms 30, 45, and 75 each are likely to be related to the additional days mentioned in these scriptures. The first two psalms are associated with the deliverance and resurrection of the called out of Israel and the setting up of Christ's kingdom on the earth, respectively. The third psalm is associated with the cleansing of the sanctuary. Daniel 12 ends with a promise to Daniel that he will be raised and rewarded at the resurrection of the just—the first resurrection.

The second half of this section deals with times and days, giving more detailed information regarding the final forty-two months. The initial period of time is the *time, times, and half a time* (3.5 years) relating to the tribulation period and ending with the power of the holy people being scattered. The period of time mentioned, as per the Hebrew calendar, is 3.5 years, or 3.5×360 days, or 1,260 days. As mentioned above, the period begins with the abomination that causes desolation set up in Jerusalem and ends when the power of the Holy people; those called of Israel, to be powerless in the earthly sense. The 3.5 years include supernatural power that is given to the Antichrist. This will also be co-terminus with the destruction

---
[202] Daniel 9:24.

of the Antichrist by the brightness of the coming of the Lord Jesus Christ.[203] The Antichrist will only be allowed to rule for 1,260 days or forty-two months.[204] The object is to cause to come to nothing of all that the holy people rely on and they finally trust in God alone and his Son from heaven Jesus Christ. The next period of time mentioned is the 1,290 days of Daniel 12:11. The period also begins with the abomination of desolation set up and ends with Israel's deliverance through resurrection; those who will shine as the brightness of the firmament, and those resurrected from the dead. This is the second event mentioned by the angel in Daniel 12:2. The resurrection will include both the living and the dead; those found written in the book of life will at this time be resurrected to eternal life and be with the Lord. The 1,290 days is thirty days more than the 1,260 days mentioned previously. Interestingly, Psalm 30 relates to the first resurrection, the resurrection of the just, with amazing detail. Piecing this information together, it seems evident that 30 days after the completion of the 1,260 days, the resurrection and judgment of the living and the dead of Israel will be accomplished. The resurrection satisfies, and is associated with, the prophecy of Daniel 12:2. The final period of time mentioned in this section is the 1,335 days of verse 12; this is an additional 45 days beyond the 1,290 days. Psalm 45 explicitly relates to the anointing of the king of the earth, the Lord Jesus Christ. Daniel 12:12 states that those who make it through the 1,335 days are a blessed lot. It indicates that not all will make it through this blessed event. A key to this section is the 1,290 days of Daniel 12:11, which will include the judgment of Israel and the anointing of the king in Psalm 45. The 1,335 days is also 75 days after the 1,260 days. The timing will be understood clearly only at the time of the end and the fulfillment of the scriptures regarding these days. Referring to Psalm 75, it refers to the cleansing of the Sanctuary after the glorious new temple is erected by the Lord Jesus Christ. This point in time is referred to several times in Daniel and

---

[203] 2 Thessalonians 2.8.
[204] See Revelation 13.5.

it is entirely possible that this point is seventy-five days after the destruction of the Antichrist.[205]

In summary, chapter 12 of Daniel lists three important time periods: (1) the time of Jacob's trouble, which lasts 1,260 days, or time, times, and half a time (3.5 years); (2) the time of Israel's judgment and deliverance, which lasts 30 days after the 1,260 days, or 1,290 days; and (3) the time of the ushering in of Jesus Christ as King of kings over Israel and the world. This time will be co-terminus with the cleansing of the Sanctuary. The Lord Jesus Christ will now rule with his chosen forever and ever.

Section 2, References 7 and 8: Attributes Associated with the Antichrist (Daniel 11:21–12:13)

Daniel 11:21–22 states that a vile man or ruler arises in the latter days, centuries after the breakup of Alexander's kingdom, from the remnants of one of the four dominions. Verse 21 fixes the realm to the northern territory, another ruler of the north in and around Syria, or the Seleucid Empire from antiquity. The ruler shall not be given the honor or respect of the citizens or those whose territory he rules. Worldly leaders also will not honor him. He gains the rulership of the realm unexpectedly, or through fine, slippery promises. Verse 22 gives a summary statement as to the destiny of the vile man as he grows in stature and power. The forces and dominions of the earth will be swept away and broken from before him with the veracity and quickness of a raging flood, enveloping all and whatever is in its path. The prince of the covenant will also be swept away from before him.

Daniel 11:23–24 explains that the vile man will make a league with a partner, a strong nation, which will allow him to become strong with a small minority of people. This covenant is also mentioned in Daniel 9.27 in which it states that he is made strong with the agreements for seven years (Note: this is not a seven-year agreement, but an agreement that makes him strong for seven years). Because he becomes strong with a small, or few, people (Daniel 11.23), he is referred to as the little horn who becomes stronger and stronger. One

---

[205] See Daniel 8:14.

of his fundamental characteristics will be deceitfulness—that is, his untrustworthy nature or his being filled with lies and vile aspirations. As he grows in strength and stature, he will enter unexpectedly upon the fertile portions of the area. The idea here is that the nations or dominions surrounding him do not even realize their sovereignty is under attack until it is already too late. Verse 24 identifies just how he is able to do this—by dividing the spoil with his allies and association with a strange god (something his father and his father's father did not engage in). During this time, in his heart, he devises schemes and plans against strong fortified fortresses. The fortresses could be strong nations or superpowers.

In Daniel 11:25–27, after he becomes strong and increases in power and might with the league and covenant of Daniel 11.23, the vile man rises up and eventually begins to attack his southern neighbor with a mighty army. The attack occurs in the first half of the last seven years, or the first half of the seventieth seven, sometime after the beginning of the final twenty-three hundred days of Daniel 8:14. The king of the South engages him in war but is betrayed by his own close friends. This method of insider attack is a crucial characteristic of how he attacks and defeats enemies. His loyalty comes from his promises to divide the spoil with allies. The attack results in many dead. Verse 27 goes on to state that the king of the South will still enter into an agreement or truce with him, the details of which are not disclosed. But their plans are thwarted by the end-time sequence of God.

In Daniel 11:28–30, the vile man again comes toward the South after he returns to his own land with great riches and spoil following his initial attack against the south. In reference to time, the end of the first half of the last seven years is now approaching, with the events of the middle, or "midst," of the seven years looming on the horizon of time. The Antichrist now has his heart set against the holy covenant with God and Israel and the "Holy Place." The word "covenant" here is in the Hebrew construct form with "holy," indicating that the two are bound together; this is not the same as the covenant made by the Antichrist with the many, and referenced in 9:27 and 11:22. His hatred against God is provoked by Satan, who hates God and all that God stands for. The "the ships of Chittum" relates to Gentile military ships that come from afar specifically for the purpose of stopping him. The nations are now gathering against him and his deceitful lies and covenant breaking. He now allies with those who hate God, his law, and God's covenant with Israel.

Daniel 11:31–35 is a series of five verses that summarize the events of the middle of the seventieth seven, or the seventieth week. The focus of attention at the midst of the week will be Jerusalem, the Jews, and the holy place set apart by God. As mentioned earlier, the holy place of God is the place where Abraham was willing to offer up Isaac to God. Because of Abraham's obedience, God set apart the place, which became the ground for the Holy of Holies. God promises that one day the Messiah will come there to save Israel.[206] The Antichrist, during the midst of the week, will attempt to deceive the world by coming there in supernatural form as the great lie that tests the whole world, including Israel.[207] His supernatural deceitful resurrection will deceive the whole world as he states that he is God at the Holy place in Jerusalem (See Matthew 24:15, Thessalonians 2: 1–4, Revelation 13:1–3, Revelation 17:6–8).

Daniel 11:36–39 depicts, in short order, the supernatural character of the Antichrist during the final forty-two months. Daniel chapter 11 from this point forward takes a decidedly different turn for the vile man. Before this he is documented to be on the defensive, but after these events he becomes the willful king in which all that he attempts is successful as well as his deceitful declaration to be God. Daniel does not give great detail as to this transition, but God informs us of this supernatural transition in other sections of scripture such as Thessalonians and Revelation chapters 13 and 17. The end of the age of man's rule on earth and of the world has been theorized by many men and philosophers throughout the history of men on the earth, but not one of them even comes close to these amazing events documented in God's Word. The supernatural destruction listed in the book of Revelation is scoffed at and dismissed as not being

---

[206] Psalm 2:6
[207] 2Thessalonians 2:11

possible in the time of man on the earth. It is for this reason, even God considers these evens as his strange work. Consider:

> Therefore thus saith the Lord GOD, Behold, I lay in Zion for a foundation a stone, a tried stone, a precious corner stone, a sure foundation: he that believeth shall not make haste. Judgment also will I lay to the line, and righteousness to the plummet: and the hail shall sweep away the refuge of lies, and the waters shall overflow the hiding place. And your covenant with death shall be disannulled, and your agreement with hell shall not stand; when the overflowing scourge shall pass through, then ye shall be trodden down by it. From the time that it goeth forth it shall take you: for morning by morning shall it pass over, by day and by night: and it shall be a vexation only to understand the report. For the bed is shorter than that a man can stretch himself on it: and the covering narrower than that he can wrap himself in it. For the LORD shall rise up as in mount Perazim, he shall be wroth as in the valley of Gibeon, **that he may do his work, his strange work; and bring to pass his act, his strange act.** Now therefore be ye not mockers, lest your bands be made strong: for I have heard from the Lord GOD of hosts a consumption, even determined upon the whole earth (Isaiah 28:16-22; my emphasis).

The beast will exalt himself and declare himself to be God to the world. He will also be energized by Satan, and therefore able to do all according to his will. Supernatural miracles energized by Satan will enable him to deceive those who do not know God. This will continue until the wrath or indignation and anger of God toward a world that rejects him and his son Jesus Christ is accomplished;

forty-two months. God has determined to accomplish his purpose in this manner. The Antichrist will not worship any other God that was worshipped on the earth before. This includes his father's and ancestors' gods, as well as any gods worshipped by any other people on the earth, including any god that women may respect or worship. He will declare himself greater than them all. He will, however, worship a god of fortresses associated with war—a god not known by his fathers or ever worshipped before. He will worship a new god in a solitary place—a new god associated with war and the conquering of strong fortresses. Through this god, he will be able to overthrow strong nations and any other group that may stand in his way. Those who stand with him and his god will be rewarded with land, dominion, and power. He will worship Satan.

In Daniel 11:40–43, with the forty-two months and God's indignation now coming to an end, the nations begin to push back against the Antichrist. Both the king of the South and the king of the North will push against him. The first attack will come from the king of the North, who will have a great army. In response to this, his wrath toward the earth and the earth dwellers will multiply; he will pass or occupy adjacent countries, destroy many countries and people.

Daniel 11:44–45 tells us that, toward the end of the last seven years, the vile man is alarmed by those that gather against him, and he responds with even more death, destruction, and extermination of people. He comes to his end between the Mediterranean Sea and the Dead sea, at the glorious holy mountain. He will be destroyed by the Lord Jesus Christ at his coming.[208] Once the Antichrist is destroyed, the armies of the world, who are already come together will now attempt to destroy the Lord Jesus Christ which will lead to their final demise. The events of Psalm 2, which should be read in relation to this section in Daniel, will now play out at the end of the seventieth seven.

Daniel 12:1–12:4 states that at the time of the end, or the worst time in human history, the archangel Michael stands up and defends

---

[208] 2Thessalonians 2:8

the chosen, or set apart seed, of Israel. The seven years now being completed, and the Antichrist now destroyed, the first resurrection, or the resurrection of the just, is immediate. Additionally, the Lord Jesus Christ will now begin his everlasting earthly reign. Those of Israel written in the book of life will be resurrected and raised from the dead, as well as those purified through the last seven years. Each group shall be given its reward from God through Jesus Christ. Those not written shall suffer loss. At this point, all of what God promised to Israel through Daniel's prophecies (see Daniel 9:24) shall have been completed and fulfilled. The thousand-year reign of Jesus Christ now begins, and those that are worthy and chosen will shine like the brightness of the firmament and like the stars forever and ever. Daniel is further instructed to seal the words and shut up the book until the time of the end, indicating the fruitlessness of trying to interpret these scriptures until they begin to occur on the earth. Additionally, the last days will be characterized by the unbelieving earth dwellers running to and fro, being busied by all the worldly knowledge that will be available. They will also search the scriptures to try to understand the times but will be left in ignorance.

In Daniel 12:5–12, the end of the angel's revelation and discourse is now complete. Daniel hears two angels discussing the times of the end. Verse 6 reports that one angel asked the other the length of time of the wonders (supernatural events) that were just reported. The second angel reported that it would be "times, time and a half" (3.5 years). The time will end when the Antichrist completely destroys the power of the holy people—those called of Israel. The angel again states that the words of this prophecy are sealed until the time of the end, not to be understood before then. Only those who are called and enlightened by God will understand the times and the sequence of events of the end; none of the wicked or unbelieving will understand. The angel ends the discourse by setting time limits in days: 1,260, 1,290 and 1,335 days. The additional time is likely associated with the setting up of the everlasting kingdom of Jesus Christ and his coming to judge the living and the dead at the end of the seven years as well as the cleansing of the sanctuary. In verse 13, God assures Daniel that he will stand in the lot with the resurrection of the just,

THE LAST DAYS AND THE VILE MAN OF DANIEL

the first resurrection, at the end of the seven years. It will be at this time that God raises of Israel those written in the book of life.

In summary, the following key informational points can be gathered from Section II, References 7 and 8:

1. The Antichrist will be a despicable, vile man—a man given little regard to. He will be looked down upon. He will rise up in the last days as a ruler in, or around, Syria: the remaining ancient Seleucid Empire from antiquity. He will rise in the stead of the last ruler of the north, north of Israel, as stated in Daniel 11:20, but this will occur in the last days. The vile man, or the Antichrist, the future and final ruler of the North, will rise in the latter time, when the sin of man has reached its pinnacle. The vile man will initially act in a similar fashion as Antiochus IV, who foreshadowed his life, but he then will follow and fulfill all of Daniel 11:21–45. The latter-day king of the North, the vile man, will exhaust and fulfill all the scriptures written of him beginning in Daniel 11:21 and continuing until his death in Daniel 11:45. (See Daniel 11:20–21.)
2. The vile king will arise from the remnants of the Seleucid Empire (modern-day Syria and thereabouts) in the latter days. He will rise from one of the four dominions left from Alexander's empire, fulfilling the prophecy: *"Out of one of them* (one of the four kingdoms left from Alexander the Great) *shall come a little horn who will wax exceedingly great toward the south, toward the east, and toward the pleasant land."*[209] The scriptures list him as a vile, despised, or contemptible creature—a person who is afforded little worth. (See Daniel 8:9, 11:21.)
3. He will not be given the honor or dignity of the kingdom or the backing of his citizens. He obtains leadership status through military power, deception, a disguise of slippery

---

[209] Daniel 8:9.

promises, and cunning craftiness. He arises at a time of careless security. (See Daniel 11:21.)

4. He is destined to grow strong; beginning with a small people, he grows strong through an initial alliance or league with an ally, through which he obtains troops and weapons. He will be given a host and an army, which will grow stronger and stronger in time. The mass of people will overflow into the region and break neighboring nations, sweeping into power with the power of a flood of followers, emphasizing his fast ascension to power. (See Daniel 11:22.)

5. The prince or leader of the covenant made with strong nation(s) will also be swept away from before him without any active action by him. (See Daniel 11:22.)

6. He will join himself with a strong ally through a partnership, allowing him to grow stronger and stronger in time. Beginning with a small people, a minority of people, he will increase in strength and force with time. For this reason, he is called the little horn who grows stronger and stronger. Through all of this, he will act deceitfully and dishonestly. The league and the covenant partner him with a particularly strong nation. The league or covenant marks the beginning of the first of two seven-year periods. The second and final seven-year period begins at the midpoint of the first seven-year period (see appendix D: The Final Timelines). The final twenty-three hundred days will begin approximately 220 days after the final seven years begin for Israel. Since the cleansing of the sanctuary is associated with the end of the twenty-three hundred days (see Daniel 8:14), the 220 days may be extended by 75 days in accordance with Daniel 12:12. The league and covenant mark the beginning of the prophecy concerning the Antichrist.

7. He conquers land that his ancestors were not able to conquer—fertile places and countries. These places eventually include the land of Israel. The conquering is done unexpectedly, or at a time of careless security. He

divides the spoil from his conquests among his allies and friends—the ones he initially made the alliance or league with as well as with others. He devises plans to take over strongholds or strong countries, but only for the time appointed by God. (See Daniel 11:24.)

8. He attacks the king of the South—that is, the king south of Syria, who makes no stand. Both kings will have hosts and armies; the host of the vile man will win this altercation. Treason from inside the ranks of the king of the South will be a contributing factor. (See Daniel 11:25–26.)

9. The king of the South and the vile man meet sometime toward the end of the first 3.5 years. They both have their hearts set on doing mischief. Their plans will not be fruitful. (See Daniel 11:27.)

10. He returns to his own land, but in his heart, he begins to reveal his true intentions of his hate for God and God's holy covenant. This ultimately will manifest itself in his declaration of being God in verse 36. Toward the middle of the seven years, he once again comes against the south, but this time the nations are leery of his actions and begin to take steps to stop him through ships sent to intercept and restrain him. In response to this, he is enraged and returns to his land and counsels with those who disregard God's covenant and law. The time is appointed by God, signifying that God is still omnipotent and his timetable will be followed even during Jacob's trouble. (See Daniel 11:27–30.)

11. At the midpoint of the final seven years, or the midst of the week, he sets up the abomination that causes desolation at the holy place in Jerusalem. The abomination that causes desolation is never accurately defined in scripture, but Revelation 13 and 17, 2 Thessalonians 2:3–4, and other scriptures indicate the notion of the vile man, or the Antichrist, declaring himself god after being assassinated and miraculously coming back from the dead through a Satanic miracle. The result will be some type of living

supernatural idol, through which he will go on to declare himself God at the holy place in Jerusalem. This event marks the midst of the week and the beginning of the final forty-two months. He also restricts or stops the Jews from engaging in any prayer or sacrifice in Jerusalem. The vile man now possesses supernatural powers, which he uses to gain world dominion. The scripture alludes to this with the phrase *"forces from him shall appear,"* indicating that seeds or powers arise, or are raised from him, that greatly enhance his powers to rule and to take down many. The world will now be subject to rule by a theocracy governed by a false supernatural god, the Antichrist, backed by satanic powers. (See Daniel 11:31.)

12. He corrupts with flatteries, or deceives with slippery promises, those of the Jews in Israel who disregard God's covenant or law. He basically puts people under a trance as his supernatural powers begin to escalate. The Jews, who know their God, will resist his attempts to deceive and will begin to do godly works; God begins a purification process for the chosen of Israel. Many of those of the Jews who stand faithful to God will be martyred. These faithful will also understand the times and the seasons and will be teachers of many and turn many to God. The tribulation, also known as Jacob's trouble, will continue for 3.5 years. (See Daniel 11:32–33.)

13. In parallel with the increase in power of the vile man, the time of Jacob's trouble fast approaches, and God separates out his chosen few of Israel and begins to deliver them and purify them through the forty-two months of Revelation. Israel's chosen begin to finally understand Jesus Christ as their Lord and King; martyrdom, destruction, and eternal life being the price and reward. God also uses the time of Jacob's trouble to purge and purify the chosen of Israel, the bride of Christ, for the time of judgment. (See Daniel 11:34–35.)

THE LAST DAYS AND THE VILE MAN OF DANIEL

14. The vile man will perform all in his heart, honoring the god of military conquests, who is disguised as Satan himself. He declares himself god and disregards the true God and all other so-called gods of his fathers or any other things worshipped as god—even the gods desired by women. He increases in glory and power and fulfills all his desires—mainly those of world dominion and to be worshipped as God. Through his god, Satan, he will conquer the nations and peoples of the earth as one supernaturally energized man. The destruction will continue until the true God's wrath toward man is completed; this will last forty-two months. He shall cause his chosen few to rule over many and divide the nations of the earth to spoil. (See Daniel 11:36–38.)

15. He divides the lands to those who pay him homage and honor; they are given lands and nations to rule as a reward. He prospers and conquers for forty-two months; increasing in glory and strength and supernatural power during this time. (See Daniel 11:39.)

16. At the time of the end, near the close of the last seven years, both the king of the North and the king of the South come against the Vile man and turn on him. He shall enter adjoining lands and conquer. He shall also enter the chosen land of Israel as well as the land of Egypt. He will have the Libyans and Ethiopians as his allies. A great many will be given to destruction. The masses will continue to build against him, which will cause him to become even more infuriated, and he will destroy and plunder those on the earth. (See Daniel 11:20–43).

17. He overthrows many countries and destroys many people. He has power over riches, weapons, and war machines created by the Gentile nations. Bad tidings cause him to exterminate even more people. He comes to his end between the seas—the Mediterranean and the Dead Sea—in the glorious land of Israel and the holy mountain. None shall help him; this signifies that he will be smitten by God

and destroyed by Jesus Christ himself at his coming for Israel.[210] (See Daniel 11:44–45.)

18. After the destruction of the Antichrist and the time of the end of the last seven years, Jesus Christ comes to judge the living and the dead—the living who persevere and make it through the final forty-two months, and the dead who are raised up of Israel and are written in the book of life. Their rewards are given to them, and they shine like the brightness of the sky above. These are they who turn many to righteousness. Daniel is instructed to seal and shut up the words. The last times will be characterized by a great increase in knowledge and the busyness of people on the earth. (See Daniel 12:1–4.)

19. In the final angelic discourse with Daniel, the angels give the last time in days, as well as years, to dispel any notion that days are anything other than twenty-four-hour days; and years, actual years. Revelation 13:5 also gives the time in months—forty-two months—representing, once again, 3.5 years. The time periods given are "times, time and a half of time" (3.5 years), 1,290 days, and 1,335 days. Each time has significance and represents events that take place at the end of the last seven years. (See Daniel 12:5–13).

Section 3: 2 Thessalonians Chapter 2:1–13: References 9, 10, and 11

"The Man of Sin", "The Son of Perdition", "The Wicked or Lawless One"

We now move to the New Testament references to the vile man. As will be seen in these verses a decidedly different description of the vile man is documented which was only alluded to in the Old Testament. The additional information concerns his supernatural nature and more specific information as to how he obtained this nature. Additionally, the spiritual realities of Satan and his actions and his casting out of the heavens is now openly addressed. In the Old Testament, the spirit of God was not in man and therefore they

---

[210] 2 Thessalonians 2:8–9.

were unable to understand spiritual realities. For this reason God did not expand on this topic. The understanding of this reality also provides a clue as to why God instructed Daniel to not document all that he saw in his visions. In the New Testament, God puts his spirit in man via a new birth and places the believer into the body of Jesus Christ. The new creature in Jesus Christ can now understand spiritual realities. God now reveals spiritual realities to those who can discern spiritual realities. Consider the following verses written to the body of Christ:

> But as it is written, Eye hath not seen, nor ear heard, neither have entered into the heart of man, the things which God hath prepared for them that love him. But God hath revealed them unto us by his Spirit: for the Spirit searcheth all things, yea, the deep things of God. For what man knoweth the things of a man, save the spirit of man which is in him? even so the things of God knoweth no man, but the Spirit of God. Now we have received, not the spirit of the world, but the spirit which is of God; that we might know the things that are freely given to us of God. Which things also we speak, not in the words which man's wisdom teacheth, but which the Holy Ghost teacheth; comparing spiritual things with spiritual. **But the natural man receiveth not the things of the Spirit of God**: for they are foolishness unto him: neither can he know them, because they are spiritually discerned. But he that is spiritual judgeth all things, yet he himself is judged of no man. For who hath known the mind of the Lord, that he may instruct him? But we have the mind of Christ (1Corin 2:9-16).

Those without the spirit (in the above verses the natural man) cannot understand spiritual realities, in fact unless the spirit of

God is within a man these verses will become foolishness and be meaningless. The Jew and Gentile in the Old Testament did not have the spirit born into them via a new birth so they were unable to grasp spiritual realities. God's chosen people in the Old Testament, the Jews, were fighting a physical battle and required to keep the law for their national blessing. In the New Testament the Lord Jesus Christ declares that he is the end of the law to those who have the spirit. Not that the body of Christ does not keep the law, but now they live by the higher calling of walking by the spirit of God which is now in them through a new birth. God directs the body of Jesus Christ that it is no longer a physical battle but a spiritual battle (read Ephesians chapter 6). God instructs the believer in Jesus Christ that greater is he that it is in you (the spirit of God) then he that is in the world.[211] This was not the case in the Old Testament. At the time of the end, those without the spirit of God will continue to mock and poke fun at these New Testament verses as well as the judgements documented in the book of Revelation which are spiritual in nature. God states none of the wicked will understand.

The first New Testament reference to the vile man is in 2 Thessalonians chapter 2 and includes three new titles for the Antichrist. These three titles will be handled together since all three are contained in the same chapter in 2 Thessalonians. Reference 9, 10 and 11 in Thessalonians is the first direct New Testament reference to the vile man, or the Antichrist. The references listed in this section of Thessalonians are those of *"The Man of Sin" or "Son of Perdition," and the Wicked, or Lawless One."* All three of these titles are portrayed in 2 Thessalonians 2:3–8. A new title is introduced here in the New Testament, but the red thread of the unique character of the Antichrist continues to carry through and is in harmony with all Old Testament scriptures. His main attribute, which is common to all of the Bible records, is his claim to be god. He will make this claim while standing at the holy place—that is, the holy mountain of God. The Antichrist standing supernaturally at the holy place, deceiving the world as a false god, will be the greatest abomination ever on

---

[211] 1 John 4:4

earth. This behavior will be the distinguishing behavior marking the vile man and setting him apart from every other vile leader before him. The event will also mark the beginning of the worst tribulation ever to be experienced on earth. Consider the following:

> And this gospel of the kingdom shall be preached in all the world for a witness unto all nations; and then shall the end come. **When ye therefore shall see the abomination of desolation, spoken of by Daniel the prophet, stand in the holy place, (whoso readeth, let him understand:)** Then let them which be in Judaea flee into the mountains: Let him which is on the housetop not come down to take anything out of his house: Neither let him which is in the field return back to take his clothes. And woe unto them that are with child, and to them that give suck in those days! But pray ye that your flight be not in the winter, neither on the sabbath day: For then shall be great tribulation, such as was not since the beginning of the world to this time, no, nor ever shall be. And except those days should be shortened, there should no flesh be saved: but for the elect's sake those days shall be shortened. (Matthew 24:14–22 KJV; my emphasis)

The true God uses scripture buildup in his word to add information to each of the records. It is this scripture buildup, the scriptures taken together, that leads to an accurate depiction of the beast. Although there are indirect references in the Gospels, it is not until this section in Thessalonians that a direct reference to the man of sin is alluded to in the New Testament. In discussing New Testament records, careful division of the Word of God is required to understand what is written to the church of the one body of Jesus Christ (from the book of Acts to Jude), as opposed to what is written to the Jews in the Gospel period. The Old Testament records concerning the Antichrist are typically written to those without the spirit and therefore have a different flavor than the New Testament records. The New Testament records begin to reveal the evil satanic spiritual powers at work; those that are energizing the Antichrist. God reveals these truths to those who have the spirit because it is those with the spirit who can now understand the deeper things of God with regard to the Antichrist. The revelation given in the four Gospels (Matthew, Mark, Luke and John) presented the Lord to Israel as their Messiah and King; he was subsequently rejected by his own people. The Pauline Epistles reveal the period of the mystery of the one body of Jesus Christ sequentially, directly following the Gospel period. It is the Pauline epistles which are now referenced to (i.e. Thessalonians) and it is these epistles which are written to those with the spirit of God.

The mystery period, beginning on the day of Pentecost, began a period of time not revealed or accounted for in the Old Testament or in the Gospels. The section is written to a new people, a peculiar people—the church of the one body of Jesus Christ and those with the spirit of God residing in them. Refer to chapter 3 for the details of the Mystery period of time. The distinction and separation of the body of Christ cannot be overstated and is critical to understanding the last days and right division of the Word of God.

Proper understanding of the biblical records that reveal the behavior of the Vile Man a right division of the Word of God. The scriptures written to the body of Christ (the Pauline Epistles) are written to born-again believers consisting of Jews and Gentiles, with no difference between the two. Understanding this fundamental premise is required to rightly divide the references regarding the man of sin. Consider the following section in Thessalonians:

> Now we beseech you, brethren, by the coming of our Lord Jesus Christ, and by our gathering together unto him, That ye be not soon shaken in mind, or be troubled, neither by spirit, nor by word, nor by letter as from us, as that the day of Christ is at hand. Let no man deceive you

by any means: for that day shall not come, except there come a falling away first, **and that man of sin be revealed, the son of perdition;**

Who opposeth and exalteth himself above all that is called God, or that is worshipped; so that he as God sitteth in the temple of God, shewing himself that he is God. Remember ye not, that, when I was yet with you, I told you these things? And now ye know what withholdeth that he might be revealed in his time. For the mystery of iniquity doth already work: only he who now letteth will let, until he be taken out of the way. And then shall that Wicked be revealed, whom the Lord shall consume with the spirit of his mouth, and shall destroy with the brightness of his coming: Even him, whose coming is after the working of Satan with all power and signs and lying wonders, And with all deceivableness of unrighteousness in them that perish; because they received not the love of the truth, that they might be saved. And for this cause God shall send them strong delusion, that they should believe a lie: That they all might be damned who believed not the truth, but had pleasure in unrighteousness. But we are bound to give thanks always to God for you, brethren beloved of the Lord, because God hath from the beginning chosen you to salvation through sanctification of the Spirit and belief of the truth: (2 Thessalonians 2:1–13 KJV; my emphasis)

Reference 9,10,11: 2 Thessalonians 2: 1–13; Commentary: "The Man of Sin," "The Son of Perdition," and "The Wicked or Lawless One."

Chapter 2 of 2 Thessalonians contains scriptures written to the church of the body of Christ. Verse 1 indicates the scope and subject matter of the chapter—*the coming of the Lord Jesus Christ and our gathering together unto him.* The chapter has to do with future times, including the time of the gathering together, or rapture, of the one body of Jesus Christ. Additionally, the gathering together in the twinkling of an eye is only understood by those with the Spirit of God. The rapture is indeed a reality and is documented by Paul through the revelation of Jesus Christ. [212] Paul first states, through the revelation of Jesus Christ, that we should not be troubled by either spiritual or human means, or by a book or letter supposedly from him or from other believers. Paul reveals that, in the future, premature statements will be made that the day of Christ's return and our gathering together (rapture) is at hand. Paul warns of the deception of men regarding these truths, which will be many and varied through the coming years. The scripture then goes on to give preconditions as to what will usher in the rapture of the body of Christ, the great Day of the Lord, and our gathering together unto him. The day will also include the wrath of almighty God. These significant events all occur at the time of the season of the end of man's rule on the earth—the last seven years. These end times are also associated with the rise of the Antichrist on the earth as alluded to in the scriptures in 2 Thessalonians. The scriptures state in verse 3 that the following two preconditions must be met before the rapture occurs on the earth:

- There will be a falling away, a departure of Satan from the heavens, causing a general apostasy and rejection of God and his word on the earth. Satan will be removed from the heavens and relegated to the earth beginning the fall of mankind from the true God and the general apostasy on the earth. Revelation 12 should be read in association with these events. Satan will be ejected by God's forces. (See Revelation 12.)
- After the departure or ejection of Satan and his spirits from heaven, the man of sin, the Antichrist, will be revealed by the Word of God. Additionally, after the ejection, man

---

[212] 1 Corinthians 15:52.

will become increasingly corrupt as documented in several sections of scripture. It is this apostasy and rejection of God which is alluded to in 2 Thessalonians.

These two conditions are likely intrinsically tied to the same time period at the time of the end; they will occur at the time of the middle of the last seven years. After the ejection of Satan, the final forty and two months will suddenly be thrust upon the earth-dwellers. It is at this time that the Antichrist will be revealed on the earth by the one behavior which is common to all scriptures written about this beast; the Antichrist *"Who opposeth and exalteth himself above all that is called God, or that is worshipped; so that he as God sitteth in the temple of God (Holy Place), shewing himself that he is God."* There will be a man who will rise up during the last days who will oppose and exalt himself against God and declare himself God. An egotistical and proud man, through his own ego and pride, will elevate himself above all God's creation and state that he is God while sitting in the holy place in Jerusalem as a supernatural being! He will commit the unforgiveable sin; declaring he is god. He will also rise from the dead through a great satanic supernatural miracle (more on this when we examine the records in Revelation). Related scriptures place this event, in time, as the marked event that occurs in the middle of the seventieth week of Daniel's prophecy of seventy sevens of years. The abomination mentioned in verse 4 also ushers in the final forty-two months of the second half of the seventieth seven, or Jacobs's time of trouble. The red thread that runs through all scriptures related to the Antichrist is always the unforgiveable sin; a man declaring himself god. The event will be a man—the beast or vile man—declaring himself to be god at the holy place in Jerusalem. Consider the following:

> Thus he said, The fourth beast shall be the fourth kingdom upon earth, which shall be **diverse from all kingdoms**, and shall devour the whole earth, and shall tread it down, and break it in pieces. And the ten horns out of this kingdom

are ten kings that shall arise: and another shall rise after them; and **he shall be diverse from the first**, and he shall subdue three kings. And he shall speak great words against the most High, and shall wear out the saints of the most High, and think to change times and laws: and they shall be given into his hand until a time and times and the dividing of time (3.5 years). But the judgment shall sit, and they shall take away his dominion, to consume and to destroy it unto the end. And the kingdom and dominion, and the greatness of the kingdom under the whole heaven, shall be given to the people of the saints of the most High, whose kingdom is an everlasting kingdom, and all dominions shall serve and obey him. (Daniel 7:23–27 KJV; my emphasis)

And in the latter time of their kingdom, when the transgressors are come to the full, a king of fierce countenance, and understanding dark sentences, shall stand up. **And his power shall be mighty, but not by his own power: and he shall destroy wonderfully, and shall prosper, and practise, and shall destroy the mighty and the holy people. And through his policy also he shall cause craft to prosper in his hand; and he shall magnify himself in his heart, and by peace shall destroy many: he shall also stand up against the Prince of princes; but he shall be broken without hand.** (Daniel 8:23–25 KJV; my emphasis)

I will ascend above the heights of the clouds; I will be like the most High. (Isaiah 14:14 KJV; my emphasis)

Son of man, say unto the prince of Tyrus, Thus saith the Lord GOD; Because thine heart is lifted up, and thou hast said, I am a God, I sit in

> the seat of God, in the midst of the seas; yet thou art a man, and not God, though thou set thine heart as the heart of God. (Ezekiel 28:2 KJV; my emphasis)
>
> For thou hast said in thine heart, I will ascend into heaven, I will exalt my throne above the stars of God: I will sit also upon the mount of the congregation, in the sides of the north. (Isaiah 14:13 KJV; my emphasis)
>
> And the king shall do according to his will; and he shall exalt himself, and magnify himself above every god, and shall speak marvellous things against the God of gods, and shall prosper till the indignation be accomplished: for that that is determined shall be done. (Daniel 11:36 KJV; my emphasis).
>
> And he opened his mouth in blasphemy against God, to blaspheme his name, and his tabernacle, and them that dwell in heaven. (Revelation 13:6 KJV)
>
> And there was given unto him a mouth speaking great things and blasphemies; and power was given unto him to continue forty and two months. And he opened his mouth in blasphemy against God, to blaspheme his name, and his tabernacle, and them that dwell in heaven. (Revelation 13:5–6 KJV)

From these verses, the unmistakable characteristic of the vile man, the Antichrist, is his declaring himself to be God, which is blasphemy against God—the unforgiveable sin. The sin of blasphemy against God will not be forgiven in this age or in the next.[213] Additionally, we are informed that he will have powerful spiritual help (from Satan, his agents, and the false prophet), which will establish and confirm

---

[213] Matthew 12.31

him through strong signs and wonders, to deceive those that dwell on the earth. These works will be done by the false prophet, or the beast from the earth, as documented in Revelation 13:11–18. Only the elect of God will not be deceived. The passage in 2 Thessalonians 2:6 goes on to give additional information regarding the "*mystery of iniquity,*" which will, as stated in scripture, be revealed at the proper time.

The revelation of this awful beast has an appointed time that was appointed by the true God. His actions will not be revealed until his appointed time. God states that the time of the beast will be when the iniquities (sins and transgressions) of the people of the earth have reached their full end and the abomination and stink of sin comes up before God, resulting in God's judgment.[214] Verses 6–8 inform us that the manifestation of Satan on the earth, through the Antichrist, will one day be revealed on the earth. Before being manifested on earth, according to 2 Thessalonians 2:7, he continues to hold fast to his place in the heavens. He will continue to do so until he is cast out of the heavens and relegated to the earth. The words translated as "withholdeth" and "letteth" in the verses 6 and 7 of the KJV are derived from the same Greek word, "*katecho,*" meaning *"to hold something fast."* The translation of 2 Thessalonians 2:6–7 is obscured through wrong English translation in several Bible versions. It should be translated as follows: *"And you know what is holding him fast (Satan) that he might be revealed in his time, for the mystery of iniquity (or lawlessness) is already at work (because of Satan's hold in the heavens). Only he who is holding fast (Satan, to his position in the heavens) will do so until he is cast out of the midst (removed from the heavens via the spiritual war, as documented in revelation 12)."*[215] It is Satan who is now in the heavens creating havoc and deceiving the people of the earth. The deception is toward those who are blind to the Lord Jesus Christ. But one day, in accordance with Revelation 12:7–9, God will remove Satan and his angels from his place in the heavens and cast him onto the earth. The time of this casting out will

---

[214] Daniel 8:23.
[215] See Bullinger, *Commentary on Revelation*, 407–8.

be at or about the middle of the seventieth week of Daniel's seventy sevens. Consider the following:

> Finally, my brethren, be strong in the Lord, and in the power of his might. Put on the whole armour of God that ye may be able to stand against the wiles of the devil. For we wrestle not against flesh and blood, **but against principalities, against powers, against the rulers of the darkness of this world, against spiritual wickedness in high (text: heavenly places).** Wherefore take unto you the whole armour of God, that ye may be able to withstand in the evil day, and having done all, to stand. Stand therefore, having your loins girt about with truth, and having on the breastplate of righteousness; And your feet shod with the preparation of the gospel of peace; Above all, taking the shield of faith, wherewith ye shall be able to quench all the fiery darts of the wicked. And take the helmet of salvation, and the sword of the Spirit, which is the Word of God: Praying always with all prayer and supplication in the Spirit, and watching thereunto with all perseverance and supplication for all saints. (Ephesians 6:10–18 KJV; my emphasis)
>
> **And there was war in heaven: Michael and his angels fought against the dragon; and the dragon fought and his angels, And prevailed not; neither was their place found any more in heaven. And the great dragon was cast out, that old serpent, called the Devil, and Satan, which deceiveth the whole world: he was cast out into the earth, and his angels were cast out with him.**

> *And I heard a loud voice saying in heaven, Now is come salvation, and strength, and the kingdom of our God, and the power of his Christ: for the accuser of our brethren is cast down, which accused them before our God day and night. And they overcame him by the blood of the Lamb, and by the word of their testimony; and they loved not their lives unto the death. Therefore rejoice, ye heavens, and ye that dwell in them.* **Woe to the inhabiters of the earth and of the sea! for the devil is come down unto you, having great wrath, because he knoweth that he hath but a short time** *(42 months)*. (Revelation 12:7–12 KJV; my emphasis)

What these verses state emphatically, and without contradiction, is that the devil and his angels are in the heavens, causing havoc with God and his people on the earth. The current condition is related to the mystery of iniquity which has been at work since the fall of man. This is the same mystery of iniquity that is now working on the earth as referenced in 2 Thessalonians 2:6–7. God states that this condition will continue until Satan and his angels are cast out of the heavens and constrained to the earth at some point during the last seven years. The time of his casting out is predictably the middle of the last seven years. His casting out results in great tribulation on the earth for forty-two months (see Revelation 13), until he is destroyed by the brightness of the coming of the Lord Jesus Christ.[216] The passage in 2 Thessalonians 2 supplies an important link between Revelation 12 and 13. The passage in 2 Thessalonians 2:6 reveals that he is "holding fast" to his place in the heavens and that he will one day be cast out. Revelation 12 reveals when and where he will be cast—that is, to the earth at the time of the middle of the last seven years. Revelation 13 reveals the result of his casting out: great tribulation to the people on the earth (Revelation 13) and, at the same time, cleansing in the heavens. His casting out, as revealed in Revelation 12, will also mark the beginning of the everlasting kingdom of our Lord Jesus Christ and his saints.[217] Combining 2 Thessalonians 2 with Revelation 12

---

[216] 2 Thessalonians 2:8.
[217] Revelation 12:10; also see Bullinger, *Commentary on Revelation*, 406–7.

and 13, it is safe to theorize that Satan will be cast out of the heavens and then, immediately after his casting out, the Lord Jesus Christ will occupy the heavens with his saints; the body of Christ. Chapter 2 of 2 Thessalonians, combined with Revelation 12 and 13, provides God's critical timeline and roadmap with respect to the deliverance of the body of Christ. First the devil and his spirit agents are cast out of the heavens; then the firstfruits of God, the body of Christ, are raptured from the earth and placed in the cleansed heavens. In parallel with this, there will be forty-two months of great tribulation on the earth. This condition will continue on the earth until Satan and his spirit agents are captured and chained at the end of the final forty-two months.

The passage in 2 Thessalonians 2:9–12 goes on to inform us of the link between the vile man, the Antichrist, and Satan. The unique attribute that will distinguish the reign of the vile man/Antichrist from all other previous kingdoms and dominions on the earth will be his supernatural ability. His supernatural ability will be manifested on the earth through great miracles, signs, and wonders. The end result of the deception will be the deceiving of those on the earth into believing the great lie: that a man energized by Satan is god. The scripture is clear in verse 9 that Satan is behind all the evil miracles that will be observed on the earth during the last days. The satanic miracles will have the effect of deceiving the people on the earth. It should be clear from these verses that miracles, in and of themselves, are not all initiated by the true God; this is the case only for those that result in glory to God and to his son, Jesus Christ. The miracles, signs, and wonders of 2 Thessalonians 2 will falsely point to a man impersonating God. They are supernatural lies allowed by God to deceive people on the earth because of sin of the grossest kind. The judgment is toward the people who have turned their hearts from God and will not believe the truth of God's Word. The greatest lie that will be set forth will be the vile man's, or the Antichrist's, miraculous resurrection from the dead; this is the lie that will try all people on the earth. The deceptive resurrection of the Antichrist is documented clearly in several scriptures in the New Testament—especially the book of Revelation. Consider the following:

And I stood upon the sand of the sea, and saw a beast rise up out of the sea, having seven heads and ten horns, and upon his horns ten crowns, and upon his heads the name of blasphemy. And the beast which I saw was like unto a leopard, and his feet were as the feet of a bear, and his mouth as the mouth of a lion: and the dragon gave him his power, and his seat, and great authority. **And I saw one of his heads as it were wounded to death; and his deadly wound was healed: and all the world wondered after the beast.** And they worshipped the dragon which gave power unto the beast: and they worshipped the beast, saying, Who is like unto the beast? who is able to make war with him? And there was given unto him a mouth speaking great things and blasphemies; and power was given unto him to continue forty and two months. And he opened his mouth in blasphemy against God, to blaspheme his name, and his tabernacle, and them that dwell in heaven. And it was given unto him to make war with the saints, and to overcome them: and power was given him over all kindreds, and tongues, and nations. And all that dwell upon the earth shall worship him, whose names are not written in the book of life of the Lamb slain from the foundation of the world. (Revelation 13:1–8; my emphasis)

And the angel said unto me, Wherefore didst thou marvel? I will tell thee the mystery of the woman, and of the beast that carrieth her, which hath the seven heads and ten horns. **The beast that thou sawest was, and is not; and shall ascend out of the bottomless pit, and go into perdition: and they that dwell on the earth shall wonder, whose names**

were not written in the book of life from the foundation of the world, when they behold the beast that was, and is not, and yet is. And here is the mind which hath wisdom. The seven heads are seven mountains, on which the woman sitteth. And there are seven kings: five are fallen, and one is, and the other is not yet come; and when he cometh, he must continue a short space. And the beast that was, and is not, even he is the eighth, and is of the seven, and goeth into perdition. And the ten horns which thou sawest are ten kings, which have received no kingdom as yet; but receive power as kings one hour with the beast. These have one mind, and shall give their power and strength unto the beast. These shall make war with the Lamb, and the Lamb shall overcome them: for he is Lord of lords, and King of kings: and they that are with him are called, and chosen, and faithful. (Revelation 17:7–14 KJV; my emphasis)

For nation shall rise against nation, and kingdom against kingdom: and there shall be famines, and pestilences, and earthquakes, in divers places. All these are the beginning of sorrows. Then shall they deliver you up to be afflicted, and shall kill you: and ye shall be hated of all nations for my name's sake. And then shall many be offended, and shall betray one another, and shall hate one another. And many false prophets shall rise, and shall deceive many. And because iniquity shall abound, the love of many shall wax cold. But he that shall endure unto the end, the same shall be saved. And this gospel of the kingdom shall be preached in all the world for a witness unto all nations; and then shall the end come. **When ye therefore shall see**

the abomination of desolation, spoken of by Daniel the prophet, stand in the Holy Place, (whoso readeth, let him understand:) Then let them which be in Judaea flee into the mountains: Let him which is on the housetop not come down to take any thing out of his house: Neither let him which is in the field return back to take his clothes. And woe unto them that are with child, and to them that give suck in those days! But pray ye that your flight be not in the winter, neither on the sabbath day: For then shall be great tribulation, such as was not since the beginning of the world to this time, no, nor ever shall be. And except those days should be shortened, there should no flesh be saved: but for the elect's sake those days shall be shortened. **Then if any man shall say unto you, Lo, here is Christ, or there; believe it not. For there shall arise false Christs, and false prophets, and shall shew great signs and wonders; insomuch that, if it were possible, they shall deceive the very elect.** (Matthew 24:7–24 KJV; my emphasis)

These verses state emphatically that the vile man/Antichrist (beast) will die his death and then, after a short period of time, come up again through a miraculous satanic resurrection. After his resurrection, he shall go into perdition or destruction; that is, he will be destroyed by God, but not until his forty-two-month rule on earth runs its course. After his resurrection, which will occur about the midst of the seventieth week, he will claim deity, deceiving the unbelieving world. The world will then be faced with believing the lie or dying the death. The great lie is alluded to in 2 Thessalonians 2:11 as strong delusion sent from God. The lie is sent because mankind, in general, will not believe the truth of Jesus Christ, the one and only son of God crucified and raised from the dead for our sins. Only those written in the book of life from the foundation of the world will be able to withstand the great lie. *"And except those days should be shortened, there should no flesh be saved: but for the elect's sake those days shall be shortened.* ***Then if any man shall say unto you, Lo, here is Christ, or there; believe it not. For there shall arise false Christs, and false prophets, and shall shew great signs and wonders; insomuch that, if it were possible, they shall deceive the very elect***" (Matthew 24:22–24 KJV; my emphasis).

2 Thessalonians 2:13 reverts back to addressing the body of Christ and those that are sanctified through faith in Jesus Christ. God reassures them of their salvation through faith in Christ. Additionally, God reiterates that he has chosen them from before the foundation of the world to be sanctified and set apart through faith; therefore, they are not to be included in his wrath toward mankind.[218] The bulk of the book of Revelation, and the first part of 2 Thessalonians 2, is centered on God's fulfilling of promises made to Abraham, Isaac, and Jacob. All of his promises concerning Israel and God's chosen people, the Jews, will be fulfilled at the end of the seven years. The church of the body of Christ will also have been raptured before the wrath of God truly is on the earth. Discerning these foundational truths will allow the Word of God to speak through right cutting, or right division, in accordance with whom it is written to.[219]

Section 3, References 9, 10, and 11: Attributes Associated with the Antichrist (2 Thessalonians 2:1–17)

In 2 Thessalonians 2:1–4, Paul writes through the revelation of Jesus Christ that the Day of the Lord, when the Lord reigns on earth, will not come on the earth until two specific events occur:

    a.   the apostasy or falling away—the casting of Satan and his angels out of the heavens and the subsequent lawlessness of mankind. This lawlessness will begin in earnest at the initiation of the twenty-three hundred and will reach a pinnacle during the final forty and two months of Revelation

---

[218] Ephesians 1:3–10.
[219] 2 Timothy 2:15.

    b.   the man of sin's—the vile man's/Antichrist 's—revelation on the earth through a supernatural resurrection and his claim to be god

Both events are associated with the last seven years. More specifically, they are associated with the final forty-two months of the last seven years. The final seven years will be followed by the thousand-year reign of Jesus Christ on the earth. Paul states, through revelation, that regardless of what you hear or are taught, these two events on the earth will occur before the gathering together of the body of Christ. Verse 4 of 2 Thessalonians Chap 2 documents how the vile man/Antichrist will be revealed; he will be positively identified through his declaration that he is god as he stands at the holy place of God (he holy place of God being the temple mount in Jerusalem). He will be in supernatural form. It is important to note that the temple mount area is holy with or without a Judean temple built on the site. The mount is holy because of what Abraham was willing to do with his son Isaac at this holy place, and it has nothing to do with physical buildings that came later.

In 2 Thessalonians 2:5–7, Paul states through revelation what he already told them previously concerning the *"holding fast"*—that is, what is holding fast and who is holding fast. The first holding fast is documented in verse 6 and is in the neuter gender, while the second *"holding fast"* is in verse 7 and is in the masculine gender. This second one indicates that someone is indeed holding fast to a position. In this case, Satan is holding fast to his position in the heavens. Revelation chapter 12 sheds additional light as to the timing and end of this *"holding fast."* Consider the following regarding this section of scripture:

    a.   At the time of the middle of the last seven years, the one who is holding fast (Satan and his angels) in the heavens will be taken out of the way or cast out of the midst. Then the lawless or vile man/Antichrist will be revealed in totality through his declaration of the divine.[220]

---

[220] Revelation 12: 7–9

b. It is these two events that are keeping the lawless one from being revealed—physically manifested. The mystery of lawlessness occurs even today; the outcropping of this lawlessness manifests itself through Satan's covert or clandestine actions. At the time of the end, when he is cast out of the heavens, during the middle of the last seven years, he will be physically revealed. The main event will be the supernatural revelation of the Antichrist/vile man around the time of the midst of the seventieth week.

c. This section indicates that there is an appointed time for the Antichrist/vile man to operate and have dominion. We understand that the appointed time has to do with the sins of mankind saturating to a point of overflowing; only God knows the timetable of when he will put the last days, or the end times, into motion. We do know that it is at this time when Satan and his followers will be cast out of the heavens.

d. As stated earlier, verse 6 indicates that something is "holding fast the Antichrist" from being revealed. The Greek word for "hold fast" is *"katecho,"* and this is used both in verse 6 and in verse 7. In verse 6, it is used in the neuter gender, indicating a place or thing holding fast and restraining. In verse 7, the verb is masculine, indicating that *"he"* is also holding fast to something. The section states that the Thessalonians were instructed by Paul, but we are not so instructed in this section in accordance with the secret of God. We can only theorize through other scriptures that it is the *"Abyss or the Bottomless Pit"*[221] that is holding him fast and that he (Satan) is also holding fast to his position in the heavens, until he is cast out by Michael, God's agent, as documented in Revelation 12.[222]

---

[221] See Bullinger, *Companion Bible* and *Commentary on Revelation*.
[222] Revelation 12:7; Ephesians 6:12; Revelation 11:7.

2 Thessalonians 2:8–13 begins to describe what transpires on the earth when the *"holding fast or restraining power"* is taken out of the way; the time when Michael stands up and casts out Satan and his angels from the heavens.[223] After this, hell on earth reigns for the next forty-two months and the man of sin is revealed in a superhuman form. He will immediately declare himself to be god, or divine, at the holy place in Jerusalem. This is again proclaimed in verse 4 with the result of the lie having dire consequences on the earth as described in verses 8–12. Verse 8 states that it will be the Lord Jesus Christ who will finally destroy the beast at the end of the forty and two months of intense tribulation on the earth. God puts the more important consequence of his declaration of the divine although, in accordance with time, it occurs last in the sequence documented in 2 Thessalonians. The scripture is clear that it is the Lord Jesus Christ who will destroy the Antichrist, but he will not do so until the reign of the devil on the earth for forty-two months is complete. The deceptive lie on the earth will be enormous and will be supported by satanic miracles of every kind and in every place (verses 9–12). The only way to refute the fantastic deception of the days of God's wrath will be flight and an accurate understanding of the Word of God. God's wrath is now poured out on all people on the earth through his permissive will. God will allow the deception of the lie mentioned in 2 Thessalonians 2 in response to the sin of mankind and their corporate rejection of the truth, his son, The Lord Jesus Christ was crucified, died, and was then raised to save mankind. Mankind states that the earth evolved from nothing and that God had nothing to do with it, but scripture states it is God who made the heavens and the earth. God did create the heavens and the earth for his pleasure, but God takes no pleasure in man's rebellion during this evil time.[224] Finally, 2 Thessalonians 2:13, God, at the time of the end, will differentiate between the ungodly and the godly. God, through his son Jesus Christ, will also save us from the wrath

---

[223] Revelation 12: 7–9
[224] Revelation 4:11.

to come on the earth.[225] The remainder of 2 Thessalonians chapter 2 declares how pleasing and accepted those of the body of Jesus Christ are to God in contrast to those who will suffer the wrath declared earlier in the chapter. They are the called-out ones to God; the ones who God knew before the foundations of the world and specially set aside to be objects of his mercy. God will also comfort the hearts of those living during these times as he has done to all those before this time and who are set apart by God.

In summary, the following key informational points can be gathered from Section III, references 9, 10, and 11:

1. Satan is holding fast to his position in the heavens and will continue to do so until he is cast out by Michael during the last seven years—specifically around the middle of the last seven years. Before being cast out, he is able to deceive the world through his powerful position in the heavens. After his casting out by Michael, he manifests himself on the earth through a great satanic miraculous resurrection carried out by the Antichrist/vile man. (See 2 Thessalonians 2:6–7.)
2. The revelation of the beast on the earth will be unmistakable. After Satan is cast from the heavens, he energizes his instrument the Antichrist who will then declare himself god at the holy place in Jerusalem.
3. The end of mystery period and the rapture of the body of Jesus Christ from the earth (those born-again of the spirit of God) will not occur until two significant events occur on the earth. The events are listed below and will occur at or about the middle of the final seven years of Daniel's seventy-sevens of weeks prophecy:[226]

---

[225] 1 Thessalonians 1:10
[226] Daniel 9:24

    a. The devil and his followers are cast from the heavens to the earth, causing those on the earth to be deceived and fall away from the true God.
    b. The Antichrist will declare himself god at the holy place in Jerusalem.

4. Satan, through the Antichrist, will perform great miraculous lying wonders and feats on the earth, deceiving the people on the earth into believing he is God. He will be destroyed only by the Lord Jesus Christ at his coming for Israel, after the final forty-two months. (See 2 Thessalonians 2:8–9.)
5. All who reject the truth of God will be deceived by the miracles and lying wonders of the Antichrist. The people of the earth will believe the lie put forth by Satan and will be subject to the wrath of the true God.
6. God will set apart those who are sanctified by belief in Jesus Christ; they will be objects of his mercy even during these troublous times.

Section 3: Revelation Chapter 12:13–13:18: Reference 12
"The Beast with Seven Heads and Ten Horns"

The book of Revelation will now be examined with respect to the vile man. The book of Revelation introduces the description of the Antichrist as a wild beast that cannot be tamed. Revelation also contains specific information regarding his miraculous rising from the dead and the deception that it causes throughout the world. The world, under his rule, seems incredulous or impossible to envision. This is all explained by the supernatural nature of the beast. The Old Testament scriptures only allude to the fact that his kingdom will be diverse (changed, altered, transformed) from all other Gentile dominions which existed before his time.[227] His kingdom and dominion will now be better understood as to its inherent supernatural nature through the scriptures contained in the book of Revelation. The book of Revelation supplies the missing

---

[227] Daniel 7.23

ingredients which provide light to all the other scriptures examined to this point concerning the beast. The previous scriptures can now be looked at from a different and separate vantage point; that of the supernatural nature of the Antichrist. As this is done, we are given clearer understanding concerning previous Old Testament scriptures with respect to this beast of a man who will have his brief dominion on the earth. Up to this point, before the book of Revelation, all seemed explainable, yet difficult to understand based on human nature and the Gentile dominions which existed before on the earth. But now, in the book of Revelation, a new characteristic of the vile man/Antichrist is introduced; that of a supernatural beast energized by Satan himself. He cannot be appeased, and his desire is to be worshipped by those on the earth will be fulfilled by those not written in the lamb's book of life. They will fully support the beast and appease their insatiable desires and lusts. It will be this Antichrist who will now direct, and eventually own, those on the earth who will not believe the truth of God's Word.

The scriptures in the book of Revelation provide a culmination, or climax point, concerning God's controversy with the nations, the rebellion of mankind, and his final dealings with Satan. All the heavens and all the earth are involved and judged. The beast, the rebellion of mankind, the spiritual agents, and the resultant judgment of God are all present. The beast and God's final dealings with Israel; the called of Israel, also become central to the story that God tells in Revelation. The body of Christ is said to be saved from God's wrath, so the rapture of the body of Christ is also an event which will take place in and around this time before the wrath of God.

Revelation 12 and 13 contain the most revealing scriptures documenting the actions and behaviors of the Satan and his Antichrist during the final forty-two months. Horrific details regarding the vile man/Antichrist's short time (forty-two months) as ruler over all the nations and people on the earth are recorded. His actions on earth begin in Revelation 12:13 after Satan and his evil agents are cast out of heaven by Michael, as also documented in 2 Thessalonians 2:3 and 2:7. The focus of Revelation chapter 12 and part of chapter 13 is that of the warring between the woman and the wild beast which reaches its climax in the last days. As stated earlier, one of the main themes of the last days of man's dominion is God's final dealings and deliverance of believing Israel. The woman is here represented as the woman clothed with the sun and the moon under her feet, and upon her head a crown with twelve stars. The time has now come for God to cleanse the heavens of the rebellious Satan, who up until now has enjoyed the power associated with his place in the heavens. It is no coincidence that these events are documented in the book of Revelation; the time of the last seven years of Daniels seventy-sevens of weeks prophecy. The time of Gentile judgment, the rapture of the mystical Body of Christ and the time of God's deliverance of believing Israel is all coincident with these last days. Revelation chapter 12 focuses on the last of these: Israel's deliverance and the fulfillment of the prophecy documented in Daniel 9.24. The first step for this fulfillment is God giving the order to Michael the archangel to rise up and war against Satan and his forces, resulting in Satan's expulsion from the heavens. It is necessary for Satan to be expelled from the heavens before the Mystical Body of Christ can be raptured and placed in the heavens under the Lordship of Jesus Christ. Once these great truths are understood, the events of the last days documented in the book of Revelation become clear. It should also be clear that all of these heavenly and earthly biblical events occur in and around the same time. It is the expulsion of Satan and his spiritual forces from the heavens which give rise to the power and dominion of the Antichrist on the earth. It is also the expulsion of Satan and his heavenly forces which also allows the heavens to be occupied with the mystical Body of Christ. It should be clear that after Satan and his forces are cast from the heavens and relegated to the earth, he immediately gives power to his Antichrist and the ten kings or horns who are empowered with him and proceeds to attack the woman—the believing remnant of Jacob and his seed. These scriptures depict the actions in heaven and earth during the time of the middle of the last seven years. Two visions are contained in Revelation chapter 12 and chapter 13. The first vision is the vision that occurs in the heavens and the heavenly pronouncements; Revelation 12.1 to Revelation 12.12. The second vision is the result of the heavenly activities in chapter 12 which document the resulting earthly events. The earthly vision is documented in Revelation 12:13 to 13:18, describing the devil's attack against those on the earth, is best understood when the section is divided into the following three parts:

1. The dragon and his attack against the woman, Israel, and the remnant of her seed (Revelation 12:13–13:1)
2. The Antichrist and his ten kings or horns now energized by Satan and rise to dominance against the nations of the world for the final forty-two months (Revelation 13:2–13:18)
3. At this same time the heavens are cleansed and are now ready to receive the mystical Body of Christ

All three sections support and provide additional detail regarding the vile man/Antichrist, and each does not contradict any previous scripture given in either the Old or New Testament. The expulsion of Satan in chapter 12 is necessary before the deliverance of the Body of Christ as stated in 3 above. The beast is said to speak blasphemous words against God and his people, declaring himself to be God. His declaration of the divine; the core characteristic in each of the scriptures written about him, is once again documented in these scriptures. The details in this section reveal specifics concerning events that occur on the earth during the final forty-two months of the final seven years. Whereas Revelation 13 describes what results on the earth concerning the Gentile nations, as per the wild beast's supernatural transformation, the same time is also documented in Daniel 11:31 to 45, but with the focus on God's deliverance of Israel. The two sections together present a very accurate picture through scripture buildup of the actions and behaviors of the Antichrist.

Revelation 13 also introduces a second beast, the false prophet, who is only alluded to in previous scriptures but is manifestly documented in Revelation 13. The first half of the last seven years is covered in Daniel 11:21–30 and contained in the outline of Daniel 11. In this section, Revelation 12 and 13, God focuses on the second forty-two months. The second forty-two months will give rise to the horrific supernatural career of the vile man/Antichrist and his dominion over the earth. God also specifically identifies his power source as the dragon, or Satan, while introducing the false prophet. The core of our study includes the entire body of work describing the last seven years, which is focused primarily on the Antichrist. Revelation 12 and 13, along with Daniel 11, is fundamental and central to the information God gives regarding the Antichrist/vile man and his destructive career. The essential information provided by God specifically focuses on Israel; however, all earth-dwellers, the heavens and earth, and all of God's creation will be affected. Daniel 11 describes in great detail the first forty-two months of the career of the beast: his rise to power, his deceitfulness, and his attacks against neighboring countries. In contrast, Revelation accurately documents the second forty-two months, or the supernatural career of the beast and the false prophet. Daniel and Revelation, taken together, assemble a composite sketch or blueprint that minutely identifies the character of the vile man/Antichrist. Daniel 11 identifies the initial rise to power of the beast in mortal form, while Revelation 13 identifies his supernatural dominion over the earth during the final forty-two months.

Daniel 11:32–44 documents, from an observer's standpoint, his actions during the final forty-two months. Revelation 13 provides additional information with respect to the supernatural result on the earth and how the earth dwellers will be corporately affected. As far as his initial identification, he is revealed only to those skilled in understanding and rightly dividing the Word of God. Through this means, he will be identified well before the final forty-two months, or the midst of the final seven years. To the world, this man will rise as a typical vile dictator not much different from other deceitful dictators who have previously risen to power on the earth. The vile dictator will virtually go unnoticed as he steps through and satisfies the scriptures written of him. He will create havoc and turmoil, and through his craft or deceitfulness, he shall spiritually spread throughout the world. But his true identity will be unknown until the time of his dominion on earth—the midst of the seventieth week. The time will catch all those on the earth who are not written in the Lamb's book of life off guard similar to the time before the flood. The final Antichrist will behave as other previous vile, despicable, deceitful leaders; he will exhibit no special distinguishing attributes during his rise to power. The only means of identification during the first forty-two months will be his systematic fulfillment of the words God has written about him in Daniel 11. The main and only tool to identify his rise to power and prominence will be through the right division of the Word of God—especially Daniel 11:21 and onward. Those of understanding, and believers of God's Word, will pay close attention to his actions and compare them to the scriptures written about him. It will be his actions, as he fulfills God's prophecy, that will give him away and identify him well before the midst of the seventieth seven of years. During the first part of these final seven years, the world will seem to finally come together as one and arrive at some sort of relative peace, even making great strides through covenants of peace and treaties; but destruction and terror will replace the relative peace in the twinkling of an eye. Consider the following:

> For when they shall say, Peace and safety; then sudden destruction cometh upon them, as travail upon a woman with child; and they shall not escape. **But ye, brethren, are not in darkness, that that day should overtake you as a thief. Ye are all the children of light, and the children of the day: we are not of the night, nor of darkness. Therefore let us not sleep, as do others; but let us watch and be sober.** For they that sleep sleep in the night; and they that be drunken are drunken in the night. But let us, who are of the day, be sober, putting on the breastplate of faith and love; and for an helmet, the hope of salvation. **For God hath not appointed us to wrath, but to obtain salvation by our Lord Jesus Christ,** Who died for us, that, whether we wake or sleep, we should live together with him. Wherefore comfort yourselves together, and edify one another, even as also ye do. (1 Thessalonians 5:3–11 KJV; my emphasis)

The entire thirteenth chapter of Revelation gives us a detailed account of the final forty-two months, or the last half of the seventieth week of Daniel's prophecy. Revelation, in general, is focused on the final twenty-three hundred days of the final seven years—especially the final forty-two months. It reveals the actions and behaviors of the beast after his supernatural resurrection at the time of the middle of the seventieth week. After the supernatural resurrection of the beast from the dead, he will, in short order, take control of the nations of the earth. Additionally, he will pursue Israel, the remnant of the seed of Abraham, Isaac, and Jacob. What follows is earthly destruction and desolation on a grandiose scale. The book of Revelation details the war on the earth. Satanic forces will be operating through the Antichrist and the false prophet. These forces will then be coupled with God's plagues on the earth, directed against Satan and his followers. The whole earth, as well as Israel, will be significantly affected to the point of near extinction. Consider the following: *"For then shall be great tribulation, such as was not since the beginning of the world to this time, no, nor ever shall be. And except those days should be shortened, there should no flesh be saved: but for the elect's sake those days shall be shortened"* (Matthew 24:21–22 KJV).

The final forty-two months reveal the time of Jacob's trouble, which is frequently alluded to in the Old Testament.[228] The final forty-two months also represent God's final dealings with the kingdoms of the world, including the fulfilling of all promises made to the Patriarchs of Israel. The time period represents God's final dealings with Israel, the holy place in Jerusalem, and the rule of the Gentiles. The church will also be raptured from the earth during the time of the end, but this will occur before the full wrath of God. In short, all three groups—Jews, Gentiles, and the church of Jesus Christ—will be affected and changed forever. Consider the following: *"Esaias also crieth concerning Israel, Though the number of the children of Israel be as the sand of the sea, a remnant shall be saved:* **For he will finish the work, and cut it short in righteousness: because a short work will the Lord make upon the earth.** *And as Esaias said before, Except the*

---

[228] Jeremiah 30:7 (read the entire chapter regarding this same time).

Lord of Sabaoth had left us a seed, we had been as Sodoma, and been made like unto Gomorrha" (Romans 9:27–29 KJV; my emphasis).

The terrible beast will be in supernatural form for the last half of the final week of Daniel's prophecy, as set forth in Daniel 9:24 (forty-two months; 1,260 days; time, times, and half a time). The supernatural nature of the beast allows the horrific scenes described in Revelation 13 to occur unfettered. One may ask, how can these things be? The answer lies in the satanic supernatural nature of the beast; Satan gives him power, through the dragon, to subdue the earth. The powers are granted to the beast by the prince of darkness, who has just been cast down to the earth and removed from heavens. These satanic powers and miracles, which will come to the earth during the final forty-two months, have never been encountered on the earth before and will not be allowed again after this time. The prophecy concerning the beast will begin with the first of two seven-year terms. The first begins with the league or covenant with a great nation or people. The beast will then begin to fulfill the scriptures of Daniel 11:23 and onward. As the beast fulfills the scriptures written about him, he will unknowingly provide the infallible evidence that he is indeed the beast. As these scriptures are satisfied, the time of the final seven years will follow the script documented by God beginning in Daniel 11:21 and onward. The final seven-years will move slowly, but methodically, toward the catastrophic events that will surely occur during the middle of the last seven years. In the midst of the last seven years, or after 3.5 years, he will cause the sacrifice and the oblation to cease at Jerusalem and place the abomination of desolations at the holy place in Jerusalem. He will come back from the dead through a satanic resurrection and then will create havoc on the earth for the final forty-two months. At the end of the forty-two months, he will be destroyed by the brightness of the coming of the Lord Jesus Christ.

The subjection of the world to the beast and the flight of the chosen of Israel are the subject of Revelation 12 and 13. These scriptures, together with previous scriptures mentioned in this work, provide the scriptural information, through scripture buildup, to accurately know the sequence of end-time events. God will not leave his people in the dark; nor will that day come upon God's people as a thief. The terrible fourth beast of Daniel 7:23 will rise and begin to take total control over the earth and all of its kingdoms. Revelation 13:1–3 picks up the story just after the beast is miraculously raised from the dead through a great satanic miracle. The time of these events is documented as occurring at the time of the middle of the last seven years. God uses the image of *his deadly wound being healed* to indicate his miraculous resurrection. The great satanic resurrection will be the catalyst that will promote the lie that a man is god, which will deceive all people not written in the book of life. Those on the earth not written in the book of life will be required to worship this resurrected man as God or suffer the consequences. The beast will increase with power and take dominion over the earth from the midpoint of the seventieth week onward to the end of the seven years. Consider the following:

> And then shall that Wicked be revealed, whom the Lord shall consume with the spirit of his mouth, and shall destroy with the brightness of his coming: **Even him, whose coming is after the working of Satan with all power and signs and lying wonders, 10 And with all deceivableness of unrighteousness in them that perish; because they received not the love of the truth, that they might be saved. And for this cause God shall send them strong delusion, that they should believe a lie: That they all might be damned who believed not the truth, but had pleasure in unrighteousness.** (2 Thessalonians 2:8–12 KJV; my emphasis)

The following is the great central section of the book of Revelation depicting God's primary purpose of expelling Satan, delivering the Body of Christ, and final deliverance of believing Israel.

And when the dragon saw that he was cast unto the earth, he persecuted the woman which brought forth the man child. And to the woman were given two wings of a great eagle, that she might fly into the wilderness, into her place, where she is nourished for a time, and times, and half a time, from the face of the serpent. And the serpent cast out of his mouth water as a flood after the woman, that he might cause her to be carried away of the flood. And the earth helped the woman, and the earth opened her mouth, and swallowed up the flood which the dragon cast out of his mouth. And the dragon was wroth with the woman, and went to make war with the remnant of her seed, which keep the commandments of God, and have the testimony of Jesus Christ. **And I stood upon the sand of the sea, and saw a beast rise up out of the sea, having seven heads and ten horns, and upon his horns ten crowns, and upon his heads the name of blasphemy. And the beast which I saw was like unto a leopard, and his feet were as the feet of a bear, and his mouth as the mouth of a lion: and the dragon gave him his power, and his seat, and great authority. And I saw one of his heads as it were wounded to death; and his deadly wound was healed: and all the world wondered after the beast. And they worshipped the dragon which gave power unto the beast: and they worshipped the beast, saying, Who is like unto the beast? who is able to make war with him? And there was given unto him a mouth speaking great things and blasphemies; and power was given unto him to continue forty and two months. And he opened his mouth in blasphemy against God,**

to blaspheme his name, and his tabernacle, and them that dwell in heaven.

And it was given unto him to make war with the saints, and to overcome them: and power was given him over all kindreds, and tongues, and nations. And all that dwell upon the earth shall worship him, whose names are not written in the book of life of the Lamb slain from the foundation of the world. If any man have an ear, let him hear. He that leadeth into captivity shall go into captivity: he that killeth with the sword must be killed with the sword. Here is the patience and the faith of the saints. And I beheld another beast coming up out of the earth; and he had two horns like a lamb, and he spake as a dragon. And he exerciseth all the power of the first beast before him, and causeth the earth and them which dwell therein to worship the first beast, whose deadly wound was healed. And he doeth great wonders, so that he maketh fire come down from heaven on the earth in the sight of men, And deceiveth them that dwell on the earth by the means of those miracles which he had power to do in the sight of the beast; saying to them that dwell on the earth, that they should make an image to the beast, which had the wound by a sword, and did live. And he had power to give life unto the image of the beast, that the image of the beast should both speak, and cause that as many as would not worship the image of the beast should be killed. And he causeth all, both small and great, rich and poor, free and bond, to receive a mark in their right hand, or in their foreheads: And that no man might buy or sell, save he that had the mark, or the name of the beast, or the number of his name. Here is wisdom. Let him that hath understanding count the number of the beast: for it is the number of a man; and his number is Six hundred threescore and six. (Revelation 12:13 to 13:18; my emphasis)

Reference 12: Revelation 12:13–13:18 Commentary: "The Beast with Seven Heads and Ten Horns."

In Revelation 12:13 and 12:14, the time is the midst of the last seven years, and the dragon, Satan, and the fallen angels have been forcibly removed from the heavens as per Revelation 12:9 and cast to the earth. He now understands that his time is short, specifically three and one-half years or 42 months. With the knowledge that his time is short, he now ratchets up his hate and destruction on the earth which is the new home he is relegated to. It is entirely believable that before this time he actually believed that he would have his place in the heavens forever. Revelation 12:13 through Revelation 13 summarizes the result of the casting out of Satan from the heavens to the earth, from the perspective of both Jews and Gentiles. The effect to the called-out Jews, the one hundred forty-four thousand, is flight from Israel and Jerusalem and into the wilderness as depicted in Revelation 12.13. In the wilderness, they are to be protected and fed by God for forty-two months—the final forty-two months.[229] The effect to the Gentiles is war, death, famine, and destruction—the nations of the earth submitting to the world domination of the beast as a supernatural being.[230] Satan's attack against the Jews on the earth is consistent with his attacks against the Jews throughout time. Once again, Satan attempts to disrupt the promises of God that he gave to Abraham, Isaac, and Jacob concerning the remnant of their seed. The Old Testament promise was that they should be in the land forever. God will save a remnant of their seed in these, the last days. After the last seven years, it will be this remnant, the new embryonic nation of Israel, who will live in the land. Satan once again attempts to thwart God's promise by attacking the woman and her seed.

---

[229] Revelation 12:13–17, Matthew 24:15–28, Mark 13:14–23; Bullinger, *Commentary on Revelation*, 413–17.
[230] Revelation 13:1–18.

These last days are referenced several times in the Old Testament, documenting this very time of Jacob's trouble.[231] The flight of Israel and the scriptural references relating to these last-time events are documented clearly in the Old Testament; God sees the end from the beginning. The scripture references are to provide instruction for the chosen of the house of Israel—especially Revelation 2 and 3. These scriptures need to be rightly divided as to whom they are written to in order for them to be fully understood. The dragon persecutes the woman, Israel, who brought forth the man-child, the promised seed, Jesus Christ. The woman goes into the wilderness again during this last time; this exodus will be similar to that of Egypt, but this time it is an exodus from the beast and his kingdom. The scriptures are clear that, once again, called-out Israel will be in the wilderness and will be given supernatural help from God for sustenance. The woman being given the two wings of a great eagle is the same reference that God used in Exodus 19:4 and Deuteronomy 32:11 and 12 to describe Israel's flight. In those Old Testament scriptures, God supernaturally delivered Israel from Egyptian slavery. The "*eagle's wings*" represent the divine swiftness with which divine miraculous help will come to them. The time period in the wilderness, and this help from God, will last the entire 3.5 years of the Antichrist's reign. The time pinpoints both the time of flight of Israel and the time of Satan being cast from the heavens—the middle of the seventieth seven. The three-and one-half years agrees with Daniel 7:25 and 12:7. The beginning of the last three and one-half years also correlates well with 2 Thessalonians 2:4. There are many mainstream Christian religions which erroneously believe that Satan was cast from the heavens centuries ago, but this is not what the scriptures teach. In fact, it will be his casting from the heavens which will initiate the horrific events associated with the time of the end; that is, the final forty-two months.

In Revelation 12:15–17, Satan uses his powers to pursue the woman through the use of a literal "*flood.*" God protects the remnant of the seed of the woman through a supernatural miracle of opening the earth to swallow the "*flood.*" God protects the remnant of Israel,

---

[231] See Hosea 2:14–15; Exodus 14:5; 15; Joshua 24:6; Lamentations 14; Zephaniah 2.

while Satan continues his vain attempt to thwart God's will. Satan's devices are now open and understood to those on the earth with the wisdom of the Word of God; he is now cast from the heavens and can no longer deceive the nations through his once powerful position in the heavens. He continues his assault against the remnant of the woman's seed, as he has done throughout the ages, knowing his time is short. He continues to vainly believe that he has the ability to thwart the will of God. God's will is to protect the remnant of the woman in accordance with his everlasting promises to Abraham, Isaac, and Jacob. The war on the earth, the ultimate war between the forces of God and the forces of Satan, will now continue for the next three- and one-half years unabated. Revelation 12.17 also states the called and faithful seed of the woman, Israel, will now have the testimony of Jesus Christ. This alludes to the fact that beginning of their conversion, and the veil being taken from their eyes, is now in the process of being fulfilled.

Revelation 13:1 begins with the condition of things on the earth at the beginning of the last forty-two months of the seventieth seven—the middle of the last seven years. The beast has now been on the earth for the first forty-two months fulfilling the prophecy of Daniel 11:21–32, but he has been doing so in his mortal form. The time is also coincident with the expulsion of Satan from the heavens and his new knowledge that his time is short. Satan will now energize the Antichrist in supernatural form and exercise all of his evil spiritual power on the earth through the Antichrist. It is now time for the final forty-two months to begin, which is initiated by the beast being assassinated at the holy place in Jerusalem. A short period of time after his assassination, he is miraculously raised from the dead through a satanic miracle and goes on to destruction. The time is also the midpoint of the final seven years. Chapter 13 summarizes the actions of the two beasts—that is, the one from the sea (the beast, or the Antichrist [vv. 1–10]) and the one from the earth (the false prophet [vv. 11–18]). Chapter 13 records the result on the earth of the casting out of Satan (Revelation 12:7–9) and his angels from the heavens. Satan, the dragon, will initially attack the woman, Israel, and her seed, and then will attack the inhabitants of the earth. Dark, ominous, and evil supernatural events will now increase to the point of overflowing, with rapidity, as the final forty-two months ensue. Satan is ousted from the heavens and relegated to the earth with great wrath. Once on the earth, he immediately begins to create havoc on the earth. He does this by first pursuing the woman, or the lost sheep of the house of Israel, and then by raising the terrible beast, who is to have rulership over the inhabitants of the earth for the final forty-two months. The vantage point in time is the middle or midst of the last seven-year period. Satan has just been cast out of the heavens, as documented in Revelation 12, and is relegated to the earth. Consider the following:

> And there was war in heaven: Michael and his angels fought against the dragon; and the dragon fought and his angels, And prevailed not; **neither was their place found any more in heaven. And the great dragon was cast out, that old serpent, called the Devil, and Satan, which deceiveth the whole world: he was cast out into the earth, and his angels were cast out with him. And I heard a loud voice saying in heaven, now is come salvation, and strength, and the kingdom of our God, and the power of his Christ: for the accuser of our brethren is cast down, which accused them before our God day and night.** And they overcame him by the blood of the Lamb, and by the word of their testimony; and they loved not their lives unto the death. **Therefore rejoice, ye heavens, and ye that dwell in them. Woe to the inhabiters of the earth and of the sea! for the devil is come down unto you, having great wrath, because he knoweth that he hath but a short time.** And when the dragon saw that he was cast unto the earth, he persecuted the woman which brought forth the man child. (Revelation 12:7–13 KJV; my emphasis)

Satan, being cast out of heaven with all of his angels, now begins his assault on the people of the earth. In verse 1, the dragon (i.e., Satan) is standing upon sand of the sea and contemplating his next steps after pursuing the woman and being cast out of the heavens. Verse 1 of chapter 13 depicts the wild beast rising to power and taking control over the seven heads and ten horns. The seven heads and ten horns represent the integration of the nations of the earth who will now be forced to support the wild beast. This is Mystery Babylon—that is, Babylon representing the conglomeration of nations similar to their first rising in Babylon in support of the great rebel Nimrod. The study of the seven heads and ten horns will be delayed until our study of Revelation 17. In general, the heads represent strong, powerful Gentile nations, and the horns represent individual Gentile kings or rulers. The three great dominions (lion, bear, and leopard), together with the wild beast, will form the initial core governance for this new world order. The true horror, when the beast takes solitary supernatural control, will begin at the middle, or midst, of the seventieth seven of years. The beast's dominion will then have all power transferred to him as he declares himself God in supernatural form. This is the great lie that the true God allows because of the sins of man, which have now reached into the heavens, as documented in 2 Thessalonians 2:11.

Revelation 13:2 and 3 describes what John saw in the vision: a multifaceted beast resembling a leopard and having the feet of a bear and the mouth of a lion. God, in this verse, points us back to Daniel 7, which gives additional information as to the origin of these final gentile dominions: the bear, the lion, and the leopard. God uses this method to incorporate Daniel 7 with Revelation 13, cementing the subject matter and integration of both chapters with the last times. That is, one cannot be understood without the other, and both describe the conditions at the time of the end. Daniel 7 reveals the origin of these wild animals, which represent latter-day Gentile dominions or countries: how they arise, what characterizes their dominion, and what their end will be. Additionally, Daniel 7 reveals the wild animals as Gentile nations or countries that rise to power in the latter days. Daniel 7 recounts their history, their rising, and their behavior in the latter days. Revelation 13 reveals their conglomeration under the unified power of a corporate beast. It is then stated that one of the heads of the corporate beast has a deadly wound and that his deadly wound is healed. This new individual or, wild beast, the Antichrist, who has just been raised from the dead through a great satanic miracle now becomes the focus of the rest of Revelation 13. Verse 3 states *"**And I saw one of his heads as it were wounded to death; and his deadly wound was healed: and all the world wondered after the beast**"* (Revelation 13:3 KJV; my emphasis). The deadly wound being healed represents the deceitful and Satanic resurrection of the Antichrist, and the lying works of Satan. This evil event also marks the initiation of the final forty-two months. The time is the midst of the seventieth seven; the beast is on the earth, powered by the dragon: Satan. The results of this condition will be the destruction and desolation of all those on the earth not written in the book of life. This time will also result in the setting up of the abomination that God states causes desolation or destruction on the earth. The destruction of the Antichrist is now certain as well. The result will be spiritual war on the earth mingled with the wrath of God. Consider the following verses, which speak of this same event:

> When ye therefore shall see the abomination of desolation, spoken of by Daniel the prophet, stand in the Holy Place, (Note: This refers to the supernatural resurrection of the beast or Antichrist; whosoever readeth, let him understand): Then let them which be in Judaea flee into the mountains: Let him which is on the housetop not come down to take anything out of his house: Neither let him which is in the field return back to take his clothes. And woe unto them that are with child, and to them that give suck in those days! But pray ye that your flight be not in the winter, neither on the Sabbath day: For then shall be great tribulation, such as was not

since the beginning of the world to this time, no, nor ever shall be. And except those days should be shortened, there should no flesh be saved: but for the elect's sake those days shall be shortened. Then if any man shall say unto you, Lo, here is Christ, or there; believe it not. For there shall arise false Christs, and false prophets, and shall shew great signs and wonders; insomuch that, if it were possible, they shall deceive the very elect. (Matthew 24:15–24 KJV)

And arms shall stand on his part, and they shall pollute the sanctuary of strength, and shall take away the daily sacrifice, **and they shall place the abomination that maketh desolate.** (Daniel 11:31 KJV; my emphasis)

And then shall that Wicked be revealed, whom the Lord shall consume with the spirit of his mouth, and shall destroy with the brightness of his coming: **Even him, whose coming is after the working of Satan with all power and signs and lying wonders, And with all deceivableness of unrighteousness in them that perish; because they received not the love of the truth, that they might be saved. And for this cause God shall send them strong delusion, that they should believe a lie: That they all might be damned who believed not the truth, but had pleasure in unrighteousness.** (2 Thessalonians 2:8–12 KJV; my emphasis)

And the angel said unto me, Wherefore didst thou marvel? I will tell thee the mystery of the woman, and of the beast that carrieth her, which hath the seven heads and ten horns.

The beast that thou sawest was, and is not; and shall ascend out of the bottomless pit, and go into perdition: **and they that dwell on the earth**

> **shall wonder, whose names were not written in the book of life from the foundation of the world, when they behold the beast that was, and is not, and yet is.** (Revelation 17:7–8 KJV; my emphasis)
>
> And the beast that was, and is not, even he is the eighth, and is of the seven, and goeth into perdition. (Revelation 17:11 KJV)

These supporting verses make it clear that the wild beast will suffer some type of assassination and then be miraculously raised from the dead and go into perdition or destruction. The time period will be the midst, or middle, of the final seven years. The event will usher in the final forty-two months and the beginning of the end of man's dominion on the earth. From this point forward, the Antichrist/vile man will begin his forty-two-month horrific rulership over the earth. The forty-two months will be immediately followed by the everlasting kingdom of our Lord and Savior, Jesus Christ.

Verse 4 of chapter 13 indicates the captivating nature of the beast in supernatural garb. He will be enticing, fascinating, alluring, interesting, and tempting. Mankind finally receives a sign—the sign it has been looking for throughout the ages. Unfortunately, it will mean destruction to all those who chose to believe the great lie and worship the final wild beast. The beast, now in supernatural form, cannot be destroyed by man's weapons, since he already died the first death. Regarding this, the scripture is clear and asks the question in verse 4, "*Who is like unto the beast? who is able to make war with him?*" The implied answer is that no one on the earth is like the supernatural beast and no one can successfully make war with him. Verse 4 establishes his immutable supernatural power, setting the stage for the rest of the chapter. The chapter goes on to tell of his supernatural dominion, and what this kingdom, this new thing, will mean to the people on the earth who are not written in the book of life. The beast, in his resurrected state, will be wonderful and alluring and enticing to the people of the earth. The fascination with him will be worldwide. He will seemingly possess the answers to life from the dead and promise to give them to those who will worship him. Satan finally finds someone he can work through, supposedly, completing his plans of world domination. The entire population of the world—of those who reject God and his son, Jesus Christ—will be greatly deceived by the lie.

> And there was given unto him a mouth speaking great things and blasphemies; and power was given unto him to continue forty and two months. And he opened his mouth in blasphemy against God, to blaspheme his name, and his tabernacle, and them that dwell in heaven. And it was given unto him to make war with the saints, and to overcome them: and power was given him over all kindreds, and tongues, and nations. And all that dwell upon the earth shall worship him, whose names are not written in the book of life of the Lamb slain from the foundation of the world. If any man have an ear, let him hear. He that leadeth into captivity shall go into captivity: he that killeth with the sword must be killed with the sword. Here is the patience and the faith of the saints. (Revelation 13:5–10)

Verses 5 and 6 state and reinforce all other verses associated with the beast; he will declare himself God through public statements of blasphemy, committing the unforgiveable sin. *His reign will be a definite time of forty-two months.* Consider the following: "*Wherefore I say unto you, All manner of sin and blasphemy shall be forgiven unto men: but the blasphemy against the Holy Ghost shall not be forgiven unto men.* **And whosoever speaketh a word against the Son of man, it shall be forgiven him: but whosoever speaketh against the Holy Ghost, it shall not be forgiven him, neither in this world, neither in the world to come**" (Matthew 12:31–32 KJV; my emphasis)

The beast now begins a campaign of public blasphemy, speaking and lobbying, declaring himself God to the world. His evidence to the world is his supernatural nature, which stuns and amazes. The lie of his resurrection is the event that will try the whole world. The only ones who will not be deceived are those who are written in the book of life. All others will submit and worship him or face certain death. Verse 5 states that his dominion will continue for forty-two months, as stated and documented throughout this work and in several other scriptures. The people of the earth are left with the supernatural spectacle of a powerful supernatural being who cannot be defeated. He demands worship by the nations and peoples of the earth. Satan has finally found someone who will fully worship him and allow all of Satan's evil intentions to be carried out. This being coupled by Satan's casting out from the heavens to the earth becomes the perfect storm for Satan to fulfill his ultimate goal–to be worshipped as God, even if it is for a short time. He now has his way through the embodiment of the Antichrist for a short time—forty-two months. These verses once again line up with several other Old Testament and New Testament verses that speak of these very days and his claim to be God. Consider what is written in Daniel:

> After this I saw in the night visions, and behold a fourth beast, dreadful and terrible, and strong exceedingly; and it had great iron teeth: it devoured and brake in pieces, and stamped the residue with the feet of it: and it was diverse from all the beasts that were before it; and it had ten horns. **I considered the horns, and, behold, there came up among them another little horn, before whom there were three of the first horns plucked up by the roots: and, behold, in this horn were eyes like the eyes of man, and a mouth speaking great things** (blasphemies against God). (Daniel 7:7–8 KJV; my emphasis)
>
> And the ten horns out of this kingdom are ten kings that shall arise: and another shall rise after them; and he shall be diverse from the first, and he shall subdue three kings.

And he shall speak great words (blasphemies) against the most High, and shall wear out the saints of the most High, and think to change times and laws: and they shall be given into his hand until a time and times and the dividing of time (3.5 years; 42 Months). (Daniel 7:24–25 KJV)

Now that being broken, whereas four stood up for it, four kingdoms shall stand up out of the nation, but not in his power. And in the latter time of their kingdom, when the transgressors are come to the full, a king of fierce countenance, and understanding dark sentences, shall stand up. **And his power shall be mighty, but not by his own power: and he shall destroy wonderfully, and shall prosper, and practise, and shall destroy the mighty and the holy people. And through his policy also he shall cause craft to prosper in his hand; and he shall magnify himself in his heart, and by peace shall destroy many: he shall also stand up against the Prince of princes; but he shall be broken without hand.** And the vision of the evening and the morning which was told is true: wherefore shut thou up the vision; for it shall be for many days. (Daniel 8:22–26 KJV; my emphasis)

And arms shall stand on his part, and they shall pollute the sanctuary of strength, and shall take away the daily sacrifice, **and they shall place the abomination that maketh desolate.** And such as do wickedly against the covenant shall he corrupt by flatteries: but the people that do know their God shall be strong, and do exploits. And they that understand among the people shall instruct many: yet they shall fall by the sword, and by flame, by captivity, and by spoil, many days. Now when they shall fall, they shall be holpen with a little help: but many shall cleave to them with flatteries. And some of them of understanding shall fall, to try them, and to purge, and to make them white, even to the time of the end: because it is yet for a time appointed. And the king shall do according to his will; and he shall exalt himself, and magnify himself above every god, and shall speak marvellous things against the God of gods, and shall prosper till the indignation be accomplished: for that that is determined shall be done. Neither shall he regard the God of his fathers, nor the desire of women, nor regard any god: for he shall magnify himself above all. (Daniel 11:31–37 KJV; my emphasis)

The distinguishing characteristics of the first beast are his statements of blasphemy and demand of worship and adoration from the peoples of the earth. His claim to be God in supernatural form identifies his character and is the red thread common to the majority of the scriptures written about him.

Revelation 13, verses 7 through 9, goes on to give additional details of the Antichrist/vile man's rulership. He will be the enemy of all that worship the true God—the saints. He will make war and overcome the saints during his appointed time. His success against the saints is also documented in several other scriptures, including Daniel 11:31–37. All that dwell on the earth, except for the elect of God written in the book, will worship and serve the beast or face death.[232] These scriptures are plain and need no interpretation; they simply need to be believed. They depict the rapidity of these world-changing events that take place after the miraculous satanic resurrection of the beast. The scriptures are silent as to the method by which the Antichrist/vile man accomplishes these feats in such a brief period of time. It is clear, however, that the beast will be supported

---

[232] Exodus 32:32; Daniel 12:1; Isaiah 4:3.

by all of Satan's supernatural power and legions of evil spirits, who will now dwell on earth. Verse 9 makes known that dedicated understanding, applied skill, and the right division of the Word of God will be required to fully understand these times. God gives another appeal to those on the earth not to worship the beast. If any man can hear and understand what is happening on the earth, turn and change now! These final pleas will be heeded by some, but most will turn from them. The Word of God must be allowed to speak without any doctrinal or religious clouds. All words of God must be built upon and proved from previous scriptures; there cannot be one contradiction. The scripture, as originally spoken and written through God's appointed prophets, is inherently perfect and must be interpreted with adherence to its innate perfection. In this work, and regarding this man, the inherent perfection must be adhered to without contradiction. Consider the following: *"Whom shall he teach knowledge? and whom shall he make to understand doctrine? them that are weaned from the milk, and drawn from the breasts. For precept must be upon precept, precept upon precept; line upon line, line upon line; here a little, and there a little"* (Isaiah 28:9–10 KJV). Verse 9 states that without accurate understanding of the Word of God, deception is a certainty. The decision to worship or not to worship the beast will now be highly individual.

Verse 10 reiterates the certainty of the coming judgments and the notion that no one will be able to escape these judgments. During these times, it will be critical that the saints exhibit patience endurance and faith for spiritual survival.

Verses 11–18. In verses 11 to 18 another, second, beast is alluded to who rises from the earth as opposed to the first beast that rises from the sea. This second beast seems to be some type of great religious leader who rises after the first beast. The second beast is only thinly described up to this point in prior scriptures. God's reasoning for this is not revealed. That the second beast appears on the earth during these last times is clearly marked by God. The reason for his rising is also clearly indicated in this section of scripture. The second beast is also a supernatural force and is distinguished from the first best in that he is called a false prophet; some type of great religious leader whose religion is to minister to the first beast and require those on the earth to worship the first beast.

> And I beheld another beast coming up out of the earth; and he had two horns like a lamb, and he spake as a dragon. And he exerciseth all the power of the first beast before him, and causeth the earth and them which dwell therein to worship the first beast, whose deadly wound was healed. And he doeth great wonders, so that he maketh fire come down from heaven on the earth in the sight of men, And deceiveth them that dwell on the earth by the means of those miracles which he had power to do in the sight of the beast; saying to them that dwell on the earth, that they should make an image to the beast, which had the wound by a sword, and did live. And he had power to give life unto the image of the beast, that the image of the beast should both speak, and cause that as many as would not worship the image of the beast should be killed. And he causeth all, both small and great, rich and poor, free and bond, to receive a mark in their right hand, or in their foreheads: And that no man might buy or sell, save he that had the mark, or the name of the beast, or the number of his name. Here is wisdom. Let him that hath understanding count the number of the beast: for it is the number of a man; and his number is Six hundred threescore and six. (Revelation 13:11–18)

Revelation 13:11 introduces the second beast from the earth. The second beast is alluded to in other scriptures, but not as clearly as in Revelation 13. Verses 11–18 reveal the actions and behaviors of this second beast, which arises after the first. The second beast will be religious in nature, the two horns representing his testimony. He speaks as a dragon, with deceit and false intentions. The first beast is political; the second, the false prophet, is religious in nature.[233] The false prophet will arise out of the earth, as opposed to the first beast, who rises out from the sea. Both of these are individuals and are to be taken as individuals; they are not representative of some other contrived interpretation of man. Revelation 13:11–18 is the clearest scripture depicting the work of the false prophet—his intentions, his allegiance, and his new requirements for the earth dwellers. The two beasts together complement each other and are unified in their requirement that men pay worship to a false god. During their time, they will attempt to remove any evidence of the true God from the earth. Laws will be changed, and all reference to the true God will be stamped out. The deception that they will provide will be overwhelming; none will be able to resist other than those written in the book of life. The work of the false prophet will be to make people worship the first beast, who was killed and whose deadly wound was healed. The false prophet will be given miraculous powers and perform supernatural feats in the sight of men. Revelation 13:11–18 openly manifests the second beast, who organizes a new religion dedicated to worshipping the first beast. The second beast is only alluded to in other sections of scripture, but here he is clearly exposed by the Word of God. The second beast is similar to the first; he is superhuman and energized by Satan. He will eventually call on all the peoples of the earth to worship the first beast, supporting his claim that he is God. The second beast is also referred to in other scriptures as the false prophet. [234] The Lord Jesus Christ refers to this false prophet in Matthew 24:24: *"For there shall arise false Christs, and false prophets, and shall show great signs and wonders; insomuch that, if it were possible, they shall deceive the very elect."*

This second beast will be supernatural in nature and will be in unison with the dragon and the first beast in purpose and power. His mission will be to religiously cause the earth to worship the first

---

[233] Revelation 16:13; 19:20.
[234] Revelation 16:13; 19:20; 20:10.

beast—ultimately Satan. As the world sinks further into spiritualism, infatuated with the supernatural, the result will be these two terrible supernatural beasts. The two beasts will be supernatural beings that will bring on ultimate destruction and desolation. The second beast will again be a spirit being operating through the facilities of a man—a man obsessed with the spiritual power of Satan. Eight times in this section is the expression "*he causeth*" used of this false prophet, citing him as an efficient agent of the first beast.[235] His mission is to fulfill the desires of the first beast and of the dragon that energizes both beasts. Verse 12 states that those on the earth are required to worship, and grant divine homage to, the first beast. The basis for this worship is the miraculous resurrection of the first beast, who had his deadly wound healed. The false prophet initiates a new false religion that leaves out the one true God, forcing all on the earth to worship this abomination or be killed. The combination of man's altruistic philanthropy, skill, and wisdom with the new addition of satanic spirit agency will give rise to this new religion. Such an outcome seems implausible at first, but it will not only be possible but also guaranteed by the Word of God. Regarding these times, the Lord states in Matthew, and it is again stated in Revelation 12, "*Woe to those on the earth.*"

The verses of Revelation 13:13 and 14 state that the false prophet works great signs and even causes fire to come down from heaven in the plain view of men. These works are nothing new in scripture; signs and miracles are no assurance of God's doings or proof of the divine. Such works have been performed before in the sight of men and documented in the Word of God.[236] The works of Satan's agents in this section should not be considered godly, but satanic, in nature. In contrast, theology typically teaches the opposite. The miracles will add legitimacy, believability, and deception to those on the earth not written in the lamb's book of life. Man has always been

---

[235] See Bullinger, *Commentary on Revelation*, Print Basis: F.H. Revell, 1909 Rights: Public Domain; CCEL Subjects: All; Kregal Publications, PO Box 2607, Grand Rapids, Mi 49501; 1993; pg 433.

[236] Exodus 7:11; 2 Timothy 3:8.

searching for a sign—some sort of supernatural sign—to convince them of the reality of God. Mankind finally receives supernatural signs from Satan. The signs will encourage those on the earth to worship the beast; they will ultimately worship Satan and completely leave out God. Those who do worship and indulge in the deception of the beast will be dammed forever. The core of the worship will be centered on his miraculous resurrection, in which he was killed by the sword and lived. All other religions and forms of worship will be disassembled. The new religion will leave out God and elevate man and, ultimately, Satan.

Satanic worship will be the evil result of man delving into the supernatural for signs, miracles, and wonders. Although these events occur in the end times, the same lie from Genesis 3:4 will be popularized: "*You shall not surely die.*" The ultimate result of man's infatuation with the supernatural, without God, will be obsession with the beast and the false prophet. Mankind will be forced to worship the beast through the deception provided by the false prophet to sustain his daily life. The false prophet orchestrates the making of an image of the beast—he that had his deadly wound healed.

Verse 15 predictively moves to the physical idolatry of the last times. In all previous world religions man has always formulated or created some type of idol or physical appearance which they ultimately worshipped. The inner heart of Man without the true God requires some type of physical appearance to pay homage to. This new religion will be no different, except with a supernatural flavor. An image is now created depicting the first beast to be worshipped and admired by the peoples on the earth. This new beastly image will then both breathe and speak. Once this image is constructed, the false prophet will have power, satanic power, to give life to the beast. The beast will both breathe and speak. The world, and those of the world seeking after signs, will find the newly created image alluring and magnetizing. The signs finally come, and they result in the most horrible time in human history. Consider the following:

> And when the people were gathered thick together, he began to say, **This is an evil**

generation: they seek a sign; and there shall no sign be given it, but the sign of Jonas the prophet. (Luke 11:29 KJV)

Even him, whose coming is after the working of Satan with all power and signs and lying wonders, And with all deceivableness of unrighteousness in them that perish; because they received not the love of the truth, that they might be saved. **And for this cause God shall send them strong delusion, that they should believe a lie: That they all might be damned who believed not the truth, but had pleasure in unrighteousness.** (2 Thessalonians 2:9–12 KJV; my emphasis)

2 Thessalonians 2:11 and 12 explains why God allows Satan's ultimate evil to occur. They would not believe the truth of God sending his only begotten son to the earth to save the earth. As God waits an extended amount of time for man to repent and accept his son, mankind becomes more corrupt, growing worse and worse with time. Man becomes so bad that God simply allows the evil imagination of the heart of man to bring on the most horrible end—supernatural destruction from Satan. The *"Mystery of Iniquity"* has always been there, but it is allowed to fully manifest itself in the last days.[237] Damnation on the earth follows for those not written in the lamb's book of life. In contrast to the signs of the false prophet, the signs wrought by the Lord are always signs predicted by the Word of God and related to what Messiah was to perform.[238] Jesus Christ fulfilled and identified himself as the Son of God by fulfilling prophecy written about him, not by supernatural powers. Additionally, the supernatural powers that he wrought through God always honored and gave glory to the true God. The lying wonders that will be wrought by the false prophet will pay homage to the beast and Satan. Supernatural

---

[237] 2 Thessalonians 2:7.
[238] Matthew 11:1–6.

works and miracles, one from the other, are distinguished through this fundamental truth. The ones that give glory to God and his son, Jesus Christ, are from the Lord; all others are not from God but from Satan. Revelation 13 identifies the beast and false prophet through infernal Satanic attributes, signs, and wonders performed in the sight of men, ultimately giving glory to Satan.

Revelation 13:15 reveals the new religion; there is an ultimate "living" idol for those on the earth to feast on, fulfilling the desires of their fleshly minds. The false prophet will require an image to be made to the beast that will have life, speech, and breath. The result of this great miraculous wonder will be to cause all on the earth to worship the beast or be killed. These signs and wonders are hard to imagine, but all can be explained by the supernatural makeup of the new world order energized by Satan himself. Consider the following:

> Then I would know the truth of the fourth beast, **which was diverse** (different and of another kind or class) from all the others, exceeding dreadful, whose teeth were of iron, and his nails of brass; which devoured, brake in pieces, and stamped the residue with his feet; And of the ten horns that were in his head, and of the other which came up, and before whom three fell; even of that horn that had eyes, and a mouth that spake very great things, whose look was more stout than his fellows. I beheld, and the same horn made war with the saints, and prevailed against them; Until the Ancient of days came, and judgment was given to the saints of the most High; and the time came that the saints possessed the kingdom. Thus he said, The fourth beast shall be the fourth kingdom upon earth, **which shall be diverse from all kingdoms,** and shall devour the whole earth, and shall tread it down, and break it in pieces. And the ten horns out of this kingdom are ten kings that shall arise:

and another shall rise after them; and he shall be diverse from the first, and he shall subdue three kings. And he shall speak great words against the most High, and shall wear out the saints of the most High, and think to change times and laws: and they shall be given into his hand until a time and times and the dividing of time. (Daniel 7:19–25 KJV; my emphasis)

Revelation 13:16 and 17 makes known that the false prophet will be armed with a new religion and supported by miraculous signs and wonders, and then he will make a lifelike image that all will be forced to worship, the alternative being certain death. The false prophet commands all on the earth to acquire a sign, or mark, imbedded into their flesh—their right hand or their forehead. The mark will be their validation that they are willing to worship the beast. The mark will also bring on certain eternal destruction for all who receive it. The religion now becomes personal, or individual; survival now seems to depend upon the worship of the beast. The trial that tries the whole earth is now reality on the earth. All not written in the book of life will be faced with a personal decision: either live and worship the beast or die the death. Although life seems to be a good decision here, death would be a far better decision to escape future eternal damnation. All people, regardless of class, religion, gender, royalty, or monetary standing, are tasked with the same decision. This is the decision that tries the whole earth. Consider the following: *"Because thou hast kept the word of my patience, I also will keep thee from the hour of temptation, which shall come upon all the world, to try them that dwell upon the earth"* (Revelation 3:10 KJV).

There are now two peoples on the earth: the worshippers of the beast and those who reject the beast. The dwellers on the earth will either worship the beast or not worship and pay the consequences. Refusing to worship results in being ostracized from society and cut off from life's necessities. It will come down to individual decisions and will result in man being against man, individual being against individual. Failure to worship the beast will lead to death. Obedience will lead to eternal damnation.

Revelation 13:18 documents a curious attribute attributed to the beast; he will have a number, and the number will be 666. The number of the beast has been dissected and investigated for over two thousand years as to its meaning. Many agree that the number is associated with a name—that is, the inherited *mortal* name of the beast when he is actively on the earth. The best explanation is captured in the following excerpt from E. W. Bullinger:

> The words imply that the calculation is possible but difficult. The task is generally undertaken on the assumption that the problem is to be solved by Gematria; i.e., by reckoning (after the manner of the Hebrews and Greeks, who had not Arabic numerals) a letter as being put for the corresponding number for which it stood. But this is enumeration, not computation; and the vast number of names which have been thus formed forbid us either to increase the number, or to select from it. We believe the clue is to be found in the statement that it is "man's number." The number Six (with its multiples) is peculiarly man's number. It is first mentioned in connection with man (for man was created on the sixth day). Six, therefore, is to man what the "hall-mark" is to silver. It is man's hall-mark; stamping everything which it is used in connection with as pertaining to man. The great defiers of God have been so stamped. Goliath was six cubits in height, his spear's head weighed six shekels, and he had six pieces of armour. Nebuchadnezzar's Image was sixty cubits in height, and six cubits wide; and six instruments of music summoned its worshippers.

... The great significance of this number is seen when we remember that the secret symbol of the great ancient Pagan mysteries was SSS or 666; and that to-day it is the secret connecting link between them and their revival in Spiritism and Theosophy which aim at the union of all religions in one. The number 666 is expressed in the Greek by the letters χξϛ′. The first symbol stands for 600, the second for 60, and the third for 6. The last is not a real letter, but was a mark invented by the Greeks to represent 6. They called it (stigma*), and it is not without significance that, as associated with man, the word has come to be used in a bad sense. * Stigma is a sign usually made on the body (especially on the forehead and hands) by branding or puncturing, on slaves, soldiers, &c. It was especially used as a symbol of the god whom they served (Lev. xix. 28; xxi. 5. Deut. xiv. 1. 3 Macc. ii. 29) and supposed to be protective. This explains the use of the word in Gal. vi. 17. Paul regarded his wounds and scars received in the service of his Lord and God as not only being marks of his servitude, but marks implying that he was under God's protection. (Compare Isaiah xlix. 16. Ezekiel ix. 4. Exodus xiii. 9, 16).[239]

The method of using gematria, as mentioned in the above excerpt, reveals a considerable number of names of whose letters amount to 666. Most of the names can be set aside and are of no consequence. Additionally, when additional languages are involved—that is, besides Hebrew and Greek—the number of

---

[239] Bullinger, *Commentary on Revelation*; Print Basis: F.H. Revell, 1909 Rights: Public Domain; CCEL Subjects: All; Kregal Publications, PO Box 2607, Grand Rapids, Mi 49501; 1993; pp 439–440.

names increases exponentially. Since languages do not transliterate on a one-to-one basis, the process will not yield the same numbers from one language to another. It is a flawed effort, therefore, to attempt to add the letters from modern European languages and compare them to their ancient roots. The only other explanation is that the verse is pointing to a test of a person being investigated. Gematria is not a means by which a name is to be discovered, but it will be a test and a proof by which the name may be identified based on a man's other fulfillment of scriptures. Once a man is deemed as beginning to fulfill the scriptures of the vile man/Antichrist, his name must then be tested to determine authenticity. This test will serve as a proof as to his identity. The test must conform to scripture; that is, it must be calculated. This is difficult but possible using gematria. In accordance with Revelation 13.18, It will be a mind with wisdom of the Word of God—knowledge of how the man has already fulfilled several of the scriptures written of him—that will be able to identify him. The wisdom of God is placed into a man or woman who seeks first the kingdom of God. This wisdom cannot be found on earth, but it is only wisdom which God places into a man or woman as he chooses.

Section 3, Reference 12: Attributes Associated with the Antichrist (Revelation 12:13–13:18)

1. Revelation 12:12–18 records events on the earth after the war in heaven—after the casting out of Satan from the heavens to the earth. Satan is finally cast out of the heavens, and all of his access to the powers provided by his place in the heavens is removed with his being cast to the earth. Satan will never again have a place in the heavens from this time onward. His place in the heavens, up to this point, allowed him to disguise and manipulate events upon the earth with the heavenly powers provided him. Now, after his casting out during the last days, he will be openly manifested on the earth through the beast and the false prophet. The time of Satan's being cast out occurs on or about the midst of the last seven years of Daniel's prophecy recorded in Daniel 9:24. Consider the following verses, which allude to Satan's hold in the heavens:

   > For we wrestle not against flesh and blood, but against principalities, against powers, against the rulers of the darkness of this world**, against spiritual wickedness in (text: Heavenly) high places**. (Ephesians 6:12 KJV; my emphasis)
   >
   > Remember ye not, that, when I was yet with you, I told you these things? And now ye know what withholdeth that he might be revealed in his time. For the mystery of iniquity doth already work: **only he who now letteth will let, until he be taken out of the way (text: removed from the midst). And then shall that Wicked be revealed, whom the Lord shall consume with the spirit of his mouth, and shall destroy with the brightness of his coming.** (2 Thessalonians 2:5–8 KJV; my emphasis)

Satan is cast out of the heavens and to the earth. Woe to the inhibitors of the earth from this time on. After Satan's casting to the earth, he first attempts to annihilate the source of the man-child—the woman, or the faithful remnant of the house of Israel. God interferes with Satan's plans by protecting the woman for the final forty-two months through supernatural miracles and supernatural protection. God remembers his everlasting promises to Israel and their fathers. God will save Israel through a remnant that will be protected through the final forty-two months. God begins to bring about this great deliverance. It will be this remnant that will form the embryotic nation of Israel in the process. The deliverance will be on par with the deliverance at the time of Moses in Egypt. In fact, the plagues that come upon the entire earth, and those who dwell therein, in the last days are eerily similar to the plagues which came upon Egypt the first time God supernaturally delivered Israel. Revelation 12:17 states that this remnant of Israel are the ones who *"keep the commandments of God and have the testimony of Jesus Christ."* The remnant represents the chosen of the house of Israel and those of Israel who will accept Jesus Christ as their Lord and Savior. These are also the one hundred forty-four thousand numbered in Revelation 7:3–8. The Lord marks them with seals on their foreheads for protection through the final forty-two months.[240] The eyes of these one hundred forty-four thousand are opened; God delivers them, feeds them, and protects them during the final forty-two months. The one hundred forty-four thousand are also the ones addressed "to the seven churches" in Revelation 2 and 3.

2. In Revelation 13:1–4, The dragon, after his attempt to destroy the woman, turns his attention to the Gentile nations and begins his assault on the nations. John first sees a seven-headed, ten-horned beast arising from the sea and

---

[240] Revelation 7:3–8.

standing on the sand of the sea. The seven heads and ten horns are now together and represent the conglomeration of nations and individual rulers under the power and sway of the resurrected beast, who is now energized by Satan. This is Mystery Babylon, which is similar to the first gathering of nations from Genesis 11. The beast of Revelation 13 has the characteristics of a lion, bear, and leopard, pointing us back to Daniel 7, which describes these wild animals and the places they came from in more detail. The wild animals and their heads represent strong Gentile nations, while the horns represent individual rulers appointed by the beast. The time is the middle of the week, and the beast has just been miraculously resurrected; *"his deadly wound was healed."* The world wonders after the supernatural beast; the great deception, the lie, has begun on the earth.

3. In Revelation 13:5–10, the beast now begins his mission, declaring himself God and convincing the unlearned and unknowing on the earth through the great signs and wonders that he works on the earth. Not all will succumb to his declarations, and thus wars will break out. Nevertheless, he will prevail for his little season, having been appointed by God to rule over all the earth. He will also antagonize and persecute the saints. The beast will blaspheme and take law and order from the earth. Through supernatural means, he will supernaturally prove to those on the earth, through deceit and supernatural works, that he is God. The only hope is to be written in the lamb's book of life; all others who live will believe the lie and worship the beast or face death.

4. In Revelation 13:11–18, the false prophet from the earth arises in support of the beast and becomes the religious portion of the new earthly dominion. The false prophet will be energized by Satan, will be superhuman in nature, and will exercise the same power as the first beast. The Lord Jesus Christ warned of false prophets and false Christs and their great power to deceive, in reference to

this very time.[241] The false prophet will have great power to deceive and will religiously convince the world, through his supernatural power, to worship the beast. The object of worship will be the great miraculous resurrection of the first beast. All on the earth will be required to worship the beast. The false prophet then commands an image to be created in honor of the beast, which he subsequently gives life to; along with both speech and breath. Once again, those who will not worship will be condemned to death. The deception will be highly individual: you must receive a mark, or you will not be permitted to eat, work, or live; in effect, you will be ostracized from society and hunted as an infidel. If you receive the mark, you will suffer eternal damnation. The temptation and lie will extend across all socioeconomic boundaries; none on the earth will escape this time of temptation.

In summary, the following key informational points can be gathered from Section II, reference 12:

1. Satan is cast out of the heavens at or about the middle of the last seven years and is cast to the earth. Once on the earth, he attacks the remnant seed of the woman. The remnant seed will be the chosen one hundred forty-four thousand individuals of the seed of Abraham, Isaac, and Jacob—twelve thousand from each tribe of Israel who are chosen by God and protected by God for 3.5 years or 42 months. God helps the remnant and protects them supernaturally. The dragon, frustrated in his attempt to destroy the remnant of Israel, turns his wrath to the Gentile nations in the form of a wild beast. The wild beast rises and takes possession of six heads, which are representative of strong, powerful nations; the beast himself is the seventh head. The beast will also appoint ten horns, representing

---

[241] Matthew 24:5, 11, 24; Mark 13:22.

ten anointed individuals energized by the beast, to have dominion over the earth. The characteristic of this wild beast will be blasphemy against God. (See Revelation 13:1.)

2. The wild beast, now possessing seven heads and ten horns, will be characterized by a lion, bear, and leopard. These gentile nations, or beasts, will be the same lion, bear, and leopard (strong, powerful countries or dominions) described in Daniel 7. The seventh head will be the final head to be added, and this will be the wild beast in supernatural form, newly resurrected from the dead. Recall that the wild beast will be assassinated and then miraculously raised from the dead through a satanic miracle. Initially, the wild beast, or seventh head, will be confederate with the other heads and horns, but it will eventually annihilate the other heads, or dominions, and take complete control with his ten horns.[242] The world will wonder after the wild beast, struggling to understand the supernatural miracle that was witnessed. (See Revelation 13:3.)

3. The wild beast is now worshipped and given divine homage by those not written in the book of life—the unlearned and unknowing on the earth. The earth worships the dragon, or Satan, via the wild beast. The devil, finally, for a short season, receives the worship that he craves. The wild beast, the Antichrist/vile man, is now vocal and opens his mouth in blasphemy against God, the heavens, and God's tabernacle. All not written in the book of life will worship Satan, or the dragon, through the wild beast and through the lifelike image created in his honor. If the worship of the beast is rejected, rejection from society and death will be the result. The beast will declare war and successfully destroy those who will not capitulate or who still pay homage to the true God. (See Revelation 13:4–8.)

---

[242] Daniel 7:7.

Section 3: Revelation Chapter 17: 1–18: Reference 13

"The Beast That Was, and Is Not, and Is Again" God's Description of the Beast and the Great Whore.

The second detailed occurrence documenting the behavior of the beast in the New Testament is contained in Revelation chapter 17. It is this vision of the beast and his doings and his association with the great whore and the nations that has resulted in the abundance of diverse interpretations over the years. The varied and many interpretations of Revelation 17 make it one of the most controversial chapters of the entire Bible. The chapter has to do with a vision that John received from one of the seven angels who held the seven vials. Recall that in chapter 16, John saw the angels pouring out the vials and the results on the earth. This led up to the pouring out of the seventh vile in which God remembers the great Babylon of Genesis chapter 11.[243] Our method for interpretation is the same as we have presented throughout this work. First, we will examine the context and to whom it is written, second, we will examine how the chapter fits into the Canon of the book of Revelation and the bible as a whole, thirdly, we will compare this section to the previous sections of this book concerning the Antichrist to assure that there are no contradictions. Finally, we will gather all the additional information that God provides about the Antichrist/vile man and include it in the final description of the Antichrist. I am confident that these simple keys to interpretation will enlighten the reader to the identity of Antichrist and allow the reader to come to an accurate understanding of the truths presented in Revelation chapter 17.

Setting the structure and the context, we first need to step back to chapter 16, and then chapter 11, to review how the pouring out of the vials complete the Mystery of God and are also the consequence of the sounding of the seventh trumpet from way back in Revelation 11.15. The importance of the sounding of the seventh trumpet has led God to expand on the details of what occurs in both the heavens and the earth giving the bitter-sweet details by way of interlude. The interlude begins with the history of God's methodology of saving the

---

[243] Revelation 16.19

earth and, especially, his called-out ones as he details in chapter 12. Historically, God takes us back to the beginning of the time of man on the earth and brings us to the time of the book of Revelation; that is, the last times when these scriptures in Revelation begin their fulfillment. In parallel with the final days, the beast and the false prophet will rise on the earth and rule the earth with the hatred of Satan as described in chapter 13. After this, God's chosen and set apart ones are described in chapter 14. Then God's great judgments on the earth are described in detail beginning in Revelation chapter 15 and 16. As part of this, God remembers great Babylon from Genesis chapter 11. Once again, God gives additional information by way of interlude as to what he sees in the last days which reminds him of great Babylon (Revelation 17). He then proceeds to destroy the great whore and Babylon who, together, make up the corporate beast and the nations of the world respectively (Revelation chapters 17,18). After the destruction of Babylon, the kingdoms of the earth are become the kingdoms of Our Lord and of his Christ forever and ever; God has now made the earthly kingdoms his footstool (Revelation chapters 19–22). God's description and time sequence here is perfection and only needs to be believed and understood to give fair warning to those called out by the Almighty.

Reverting back to Revelation 11.15, the sounding of the seventh trumpet begins the above series of events which will culminate in the *"The kingdoms of this world are become the kingdoms of our Lord and of his Christ; and he shall reign forever and ever,"* as stated in verse 15. Further, the events of Chapters 17 and 18 provide description, by way of interlude, what is meant by the great whore, and her judgment (chapter 17) and what is meant by the fall of Babylon (the fall of the nations of the world) as described in chapter 18. Recall that in Revelation chapter 16, the seventh vial was poured onto the earth leading to lightnings, thunders, and great commotions on the earth. The lightnings, thunders, and commotions are the same as the result of the seventh trumpet of Revelation 11.19, but God adds the additional information with respect to the first six vials. After Revelation chapter 16, God explains what he means by Babylon, while also introducing a great whore that will be present on the earth at the time of the end. It is the same seventh trumpet, but it is now the seventh vial being poured out describing the culmination of what will occur on the earth after the sounding of the seventh trumpet. *"Great Babylon"* no doubt refers to the gathering of nations, first in Genesis 11, and now during the final time of the beast as he corporately gathers the nations together as one. It is with this backdrop that we now examine the parenthesis of Revelation 17 explaining several of the characters who will rise during the time of the end.

The angel in Revelation chapter 16 verse 19 declares that great Babylon comes into God's remembrance, and describes earthly catastrophes, but the angel does not inform us as to what is meant by great Babylon and its fall. God, in chapters 17 and 18, gives further explanation as to what Babylon is and what its fall means to those on the earth. The vision is given to John in the first century, but the vision is associated with the last days and what will occur in the future (future to John) in *"the Day of the Lord."*

> And there came one of the seven angels which had the seven vials, and talked with me, saying unto me, Come hither; I will show unto thee the judgment of the great whore that sitteth upon many waters: With whom the kings of the earth have committed fornication, and the inhabitants of the earth have been made drunk with the wine of her fornication. **So he carried me away in the spirit into the wilderness: and I saw a woman sit upon a scarlet coloured beast, full of names of blasphemy, having seven heads and ten horns. And the woman was arrayed in purple and scarlet colour, and decked with gold and precious stones and pearls, having a golden cup in her hand full of abominations and filthiness of her fornication:** And upon her forehead was a name written, MYSTERY, BABYLON THE GREAT, THE MOTHER OF HARLOTS AND ABOMINATIONS OF

THE EARTH. And I saw the woman drunken with the blood of the saints, and with the blood of the martyrs of Jesus: and when I saw her, I wondered with great admiration. And the angel said unto me, Wherefore didst thou marvel? **I will tell thee the mystery of the woman, and of the beast that carrieth her, which hath the seven heads and ten horns. The beast that thou sawest was, and is not; and shall ascend out of the bottomless pit, and go into perdition: and they that dwell on the earth shall wonder, whose names were not written in the book of life from the foundation of the world, when they behold the beast that was, and is not, and yet is.** And here is the mind which hath wisdom. The seven heads are seven mountains, on which the woman sitteth. And there are seven kings: five are fallen, and one is, and the other is not yet come; and when he cometh, he must continue a short space. **And the beast that was, and is not, even he is the eighth, and is of the seven, and goeth into perdition. And the ten horns which thou sawest are ten kings, which have received no kingdom as yet; but receive power as kings one hour with the beast. These have one mind, and shall give their power and strength unto the beast.** These shall make war with the Lamb, and the Lamb shall overcome them: for he is Lord of lords, and King of kings: and they that are with him are called, and chosen, and faithful. And he saith unto me, The waters which thou sawest, where the whore sitteth, are peoples, and multitudes, and nations, and tongues. **And the ten horns which thou sawest upon the beast, these shall hate the whore, and shall make her desolate and naked, and shall eat her flesh, and**

burn her with fire. For God hath put in their hearts to fulfil his will, and to agree, and give their kingdom unto the beast, until the words of God shall be fulfilled. And the woman which thou sawest is that great city, which reigneth over the kings of the earth. (Revelation 17:1–18; my emphasis)

Reference 13: Revelation 17:1–18 Commentary: "The Beast that was and is not and is again."

The answer as to why great Babylon comes to the remembrance of God is recorded in Revelation 17. The time is sometime during the middle of the last seven years, and the nations come together once again in unison, for a unified reason. The result is a conglomeration of nations as one. The human eye sees a great stride toward peace in the world; the nations are one and seemingly promoting peace. What God sees is listed in chapter 17 of Revelation—*a whore, that great city*, being supported by a beast with seven heads and ten horns. It is chapter 17 that describes the great whore, *Mystery Babylon*; and chapter 18 which documents the fall of great Babylon. The fall of great Babylon occurs with the pouring out of the seventh vial, but the description of what it is and how it falls is provided by way of interlude. The description of what it is, is listed in chapter 17, and the statement as to how it falls is in chapter 18—it is the result on the earth of the pouring out of the seventh vial of chapter 16. Chapter 16:17–21 generally details the result of the pouring out of the seventh vial, depicting the fall of the nations and the commotions that come on the earth. The angel declares that great Babylon comes into God's remembrance, and describes earthly catastrophes, but the angel does not inform us as to what is meant by great Babylon and its fall. God, in chapters 17 and 18, gives further explanation as to what Babylon is and what its fall means to those on the earth. The vision is given to John in the first century, but the vision is associated with the last days and what will occur in the future (future to John) in *"the Day of the Lord."*

The vision of chapter 17 given to John describes what will occur in the last days, specifically, characteristics of major players on the earth who will be involved in the rebellion against God. The picture is one of a whore supported by a beast with seven heads and ten horns and nations and tongues. The vision is different from John's previous or later revelations since in this vision John is transported into an actual scene on the earth which is occurring and progressing within the vision. As mentioned earlier, this will be the scene in the last days; a conference of world leaders who gather together to support the whore: Jerusalem. The conference will be attended by the leaders of the great nations of the earth, including the seven heads (individual leaders) and the ten horns (kings). The chapter reveals that there are at least two time periods depicted in the vision. The first event, that of Revelation 17:1–6, encompasses the state of affairs at the time of the middle of the last seven years. The seven heads and ten horns (nations and peoples of the earth) are all shown in unison, supporting the whore. The scene is reminiscent of Genesis 11, the first Babylon, in which all the nations of the earth came together as one. This explains why great Babylon comes to the remembrance of God in Revelation 16:19. The whole homogenized picture represents *"the great city; Babylon,"* the nations and peoples on the earth, including the great city of Jerusalem. The vision depicts the people on the earth in unison and in relative peace and safety. Their sense of peace and safety is surely attributed to the nations and peoples of the earth coming together in a false type of harmony and togetherness. This will be an antidote as to gathering storm which is now, at this time of the last days, beginning to envelop the earth. The Gentile nations on the earth have finally come together as one; people of the earth believe that this is just in time to save the crumbling earth. The time is one of peace and safety, because the earth is finally in unison for a common purpose. Revelation 17 suggests that the gathering could take place several times before the middle of the seventieth seven of weeks of years; the middle of the last seven years. This final gathering is described here and is also parallel with Revelation 13.1–2, in which they are all together as one, and, the seventh head, the Antichrist, is about to be raised from the dead and take control of the earth with his ten kings. The scriptures suggest that the final gathering of these nations will be immediately before the beginning of the final forty and two (42) months of the final seven years. Recall, the time mentioned is just after the pouring out of the seventh vile of Revelation 16; that is, before God's judgment via the seventh vial of chapter 16. This is probably also the time in which they say on the earth, "*Peace and safety*," as stated in 1 Thessalonians 5:3, *but sudden destruction is slated to come,* as per the latter part of 1 Thessalonians 5:3. The second-time perspective, Revelation 17:7 to the end of the chapter, is the time when the sixth ruler, or head, "*is*," and five of the seven heads have already fallen. The second-time perspective happens before the first; God puts the more important of the two first. The second-time perspective shows the condition of things on the earth during a representative meeting in the first half of the last seven years. God then goes onto explain what the meeting signifies and what each of the players will do during the remainder of the seven years. At the time of this meeting, the seventh head has not yet come, and the eighth, the beast, will eventually be produced from the seventh. The beast, once he comes into manifestation, will then go into perdition or destruction.

In Revelation 17.1,2: The vision begins with one of the seven angels assigned to pour out the vials in chapter 16 taking John aside to explain to him further details as to why the seventh vile is poured out on the earth. The angel ties the 16th chapter of Revelation to the 17th chapter to give further explanation as to why the vials, especially the seventh vial, is poured out on the earth. We are not told which of the seven angels from chapter 16, but it may be safe to assume that is was the seventh. In any event, the angel begins to explain to John, by way or interlude, the meaning of "*Mystery Babylon*" which God states that he remembers in chapter 16. The angel initially speaks of *"the judgment of a great whore which sitteth upon many waters."* This initial description identifies for us the main focus of the chapter: *"the great whore."* From Old Testament scriptures, other parts of the book of Revelation, and the context of chapter 17 it is understood that this whore is indeed Jerusalem. A major theme of the book of Revelation is God's final dealings with Israel during the last seven-year period.

In chapter 17 God expands for us the meaning of great Babylon and how this relates to his final dealings with Israel and Jerusalem. The angel is about to give John information regarding the condition of things on the earth during the last times, especially with respect to his covenant people Israel.

In Revelation 17:3,4, John is carried away by the spirit to a vision of the future time of the end prepared by God to teach John. The vision is one of a woman who is sitting upon a scarlet-covered beast having seven heads and ten horns. The two main characters in the vision are now introduced in their order of importance to God: the woman and the corporate beast. We understand from previous scriptures in Revelation, that the woman is indeed Jerusalem and the corporate beast to be the Gentile nations under the sway of the Antichrist. The vision is the same as Revelation 13.1–2, but at different times within the last seven years. The vison of Revelation chapter 13 is just after the time of the Antichrist's miraculous resurrection from the dead at the time of the middle of the last seven years. Revelation 17 depicts the woman sitting upon the beast with seven heads and ten horns, but the beast has not yet been resurrected. God clearly states this in verse 8. It will become increasingly clear through the remainder of this chapter, and referencing previous scriptures in the Old Testament and the book of Revelation, that this vision is indeed a great gathering of nations represented by individuals in support of Jerusalem during the time of the end. There will be several gatherings of the same representative nations at various times during the final twenty-three hundred days. The individuals and nations will go through a type of metamorphosis until the time of the middle of the last seven years in which the supernatural Antichrist will take the reins of rulership over the earth for the final forty-two months. In verse 4 the woman is described in more detail in order for God to enlighten us as to the identity of the woman. The attire of the woman is that of a whore as God has already told us in verse 1. We also are told in verse 18 that this woman is the *"great city which reigneth over the kings of the earth."* Revelation chapter 17 documents the woman is a whore, the great city, and it is she who reigneth over the kings or leaders of the earth. As discussed earlier, one of the main themes of Revelation is that of God and his final dealings with Israel. With this in mind we are transferred back to the Old Testament; there we see the prophecy of this woman in all of her glory described as Jerusalem: the great city. One of the many scriptures that should be read regarding this woman is the entire chapter of Ezekiel chapter 16. In Ezekiel chapter 16 God gives the whole history of Jerusalem as a woman with the same garb as that described in Revelation 17. The chapter goes on to describe the nation of Israel from its uneventful beginning until God's final deliverance during the time of the end. The woman in Revelation 17 is also said to have *a golden cup in her hand full of abominations of the earth.* It is this cup, which is attractive and alluring as gold, that the nations drink of in Jeremiah 51.7 (read Jeremiah 51) that makes the nations drunk and to go mad. The cup is also in the hand of the woman, attracting those who partake to the woman. The abomination of idolatry is spoken of in this chapter. The same chapter in Jeremiah is speaking of this same time in which the fall of Babylon, the nations, is shortly to follow. It is this same mystery Babylon which God is now about to judge in Revelation 16:19.

In Revelation 17:5–9, God further identifies the woman and the beast that carries her in one description as *"Mystery, Babylon the Great, the Mother of Harlots and Abominations of the Earth."* The description is written on her forehead but represents the entire woman and the beast that supports her. It is stated that the image of both the woman and the supporting beast is a mystery (*Musterion*: Greek); that is, a secret symbol or a secret sign. The whole picture represents, or is responsible for, the harlots and the abominations of the earth. Of interest is that the woman is pictured together with the beast and the nations, indicating that God draws no distinction, at least initially, between the woman, the great city Jerusalem, and the world powers at the time of his final judgment regarding great Babylon. Jerusalem suffers the same fate as the other nations of the world who will be judged at this juncture in time. The scriptures in Revelation 17 and throughout the Old Testament do not contradict this. The chapter describes the corporate beast, which now includes Jerusalem to be supported by the beast and the nations in the latter days. God states that the conglomeration of nations represented by *"Mystery Babylon"* is the fountain head, or the source, of the abominations and idolatrous harlotries of the earth. In verse 6, John further sees the woman drunk and mad with the same cup that she is holding; drinking her own wine, which is also shared with the nations as stated in Jeremiah 51.7. It is clear that, at this time, God apportions no difference between the woman and the other nations of the world. John is said to be perplexed and filled with wonder at the spectacle the God had just showed him of the woman and the beast. His wonderment leads the angel to give him further information with respect to the vision of the woman and beast in verses 7 through 9. The interpretation goes on for the rest of chapter 17. The angel's interpretation will now render all other interpretations null and void. The angel first informs John that he will explain the meaning of the woman and the beast which shall be upon the earth during the last seven years. An important key is that in verse 3, John fist sees the end result of the corporate beast in all its glory; the heads and horns all together at the time of the middle of the final seven years. The vision is intensely individual and represents a select group of people, kings or leaders, all assembled to support Jerusalem: *the whore*. The assembled group will now go through several changes as the final twenty-three hundred days unfold. The vision of the seven heads and ten horns will be complete at the time of the middle of the last seven years, just before the supernatural rising of the Antichrist at the time of the middle of the last seven years. The interpretation of the angel will now take us through several of these meetings ending up with the group resembling Revelation 17.2 and Revelation 13.1. The angel now goes onto give John more detailed information regarding the supernatural beast or Antichrist along with the woman being supported. The angel explains their history, and their future; all within the final seven years, and especially the final forty-two months. One significant difference between Revelation 17 and Revelation 13, in which the same beast is referred to, is that the woman, Jerusalem is now added to the image collaborating with the beast. The angel now gives additional information, without contradiction, and completing the picture, or vision, given by God in his word.

In verse 8, the beast is first described as the Antichrist, or the same seventh head in Revelation 13.3; the one who dies and lives again. In verse 8 he is the one *who was* (existed before in the flesh) *and is not* (dies the death or is assassinated around the middle of the final seven years) *and then is again* (ascends out of the bottomless pit in supernatural form) to enter into destruction or perdition. God now verifies in two sections of scripture the reality of a supernatural resurrection which deceives the whole world.[244] It is stated that the world will wonder in amazement at this spectacle; and why not? An event never before seen on the earth during the time of man on the earth is now in open view for all of the earth dwellers. The Lord Jesus Christ was raised by God to eternal life at the right hand of God and seen only by those who God chose. The Antichrist will be satanically raised to eternal destruction and will be seen by the world. God, through the angel, gives additional focused details concerning the beast in verse 9, but states that it will only be understood by the wisdom which God imparts. This wisdom must line up with the accuracy of the Word of God concerning this event and mentioned in other areas of God's Word. "*He who has wisdom*" is also a term mentioned in Revelation 13.18 and in the same form as Matthew 24:15; therefore, tying the three chapters together. In Matthew 24:15, it is the words "*to understand*" which associates this section. "*understand*" has the meaning to observe attentively. All three occurrences have the common denominator of the raising of the Antichrist back to life and then his awful rule for the next forty and two months.

In verse 9, the angel states that there are seven heads, or kings, which represent seven mountains. These are not seven kings over and above the seven heads, but, rather, there are the seven kings who represent the seven heads which are mountains. Further information from the angel is now introduced which states that the seven heads are seven mountains. These mountains are not ordinary great piles of rocks but are representative of great powerful Gentile nations. Mountains are many times in the Word of God representative of powerful dominions. Jeremiah 51:25 and Daniel 2.35 are a few

---

[244] Revelation 13:3

examples where mountains are used for great dominions. Jeremiah 51 refers to great Babylon and Daniel 2 refers to the kingdom of the Lord Jesus Christ during the millennial period. The great Gentile dominions of Revelation 17 look to be superpower nations. They may also be what separates the leaders of the other nations (the waters) from the heads in Revelation 17:1. Therefore, if we work this from back to front, we have seven mountains represented by heads, and each head represented by a king or leader. The entire vision is symbolic, or secret sign, of an occurrence on the earth. The occurrence is a great group of world leaders on the earth assembling in Jerusalem to support the Jewish nation. As we shall see from Revelation chapter 17, there will be several meetings of the same leaders during the first half of the final seven years. During these days, the leaders will go through a transition as indicated by the angel's interpretation in Revelation 17. At the time of the middle of the seven years, the assemblage of leaders will resemble that of Revelation 13:1–3 and Revelation 17:3. The vision will be complete with all seven heads and ten horns in unison supporting the woman or whore. It will be at this time when the people will say, *"we have finally achieved peace and security."*[245]

In Revelation 17:10–18, the angel gives the most detailed information in the Word of God about this group of leaders and the great city that they support. The angel's interpretation goes on to give further details concerning the seven kings, who represent seven mountains (great Gentile powers), and who are depicted as the heads of the great beast. Key to our understanding is that these kings are individuals; representative of great nations who rise during the last time. They are now come together during the last days in support of the woman or whore (that great city). Verse 10 is extremely informative with respect to the time that it represents. The time is the first half of the last seven years and covers the time that these kings first get together in Jerusalem until the time when five of the kings are fallen and, one is, and the other (the seventh) has not yet come. The vision is related to the twenty-three-hundred-day vision

---

[245] 1 Thessalonians 5:3.

given in Daniel 8:14 and Daniel 8:22–26. The transition of these kings begins with a gathering, or meeting in Jerusalem, twenty-three hundred days before the cleansing of the sanctuary. The transition, or the falling of the first five Gentile dominions, represented by kings or leaders, will be complete at the time of the middle of the final seven years; a short time before the Antichrist rises to supernatural power. It is this snapshot in time, what looks to be their second gathering, that John observed in Revelation 17.10. This second gathering of these representative great powers and nations of the world will feature many of the same players, but will now take up their positions as documented in Revelation 17:10. The word *fallen in verse 10* is the Greek word **pípto** and is a verb in the aorist tense and the indicative mood. The verb inflected in this way has the meaning of a snapshot in time, in this case, an event on the earth. The verb to fall has the meaning of falling from a higher position to a lower position; not necessarily to die a death. In its first usage in Matthew 17.6, it is in relation to the disciples hearing a voice from heaven concerning Jesus as the son of God, causing them to *fall down* in respect, or worship of the Lord Jesus Christ. The meaning in Revelation 17:10 relates to the same falling down from a higher position to a lower position. From these references, as well as what is documented in Daniel, it seems that these great dominions will suffer some type of fall from their lofty positions and then become lesser powers that at the beginning of the final twenty-three hundred days.[246] In any event, the meaning will be clear at the time of its fulfillment in the last days. We are told that five of the seven kings are fallen from their lofty positions. It is then documented that the one is, the sixth; that is, still in the same position as the beginning of the vision, but more powerful attributing to the fall of the previous five. The seventh has not yet come; or, up to this point, he is not yet assembled with the other six. The focus of this section now is directed on the seventh head or king. We will see that it is the seventh king who becomes the most important in terms of the interpretation in this section. The importance of the seventh also aligns with Revelation chapter 13, in which most of

---

[246] Daniel 7

the chapter describes the doings of the seventh head. We are told the seventh has not yet come and that when he does assemble with the other six kings, who are representing heads or mountains; that is, representative of great Gentile dominions, he must continue a short space. The short space, or short time, is short relative to the time spoken of in this verse; that is, the final twenty-three hundred days. He is said to be a seventh head, however, we will see that the reference is to the awful terrible beast slated to rise and rule the earth as the last, and final, and most destructive Gentile dominion to date. His rule will be for forty and two months.[247] Curiously, from verse 10, it is also clear that the seventh will, at some point, be welcomed into the fold with the other six heads. We are not told why he was not welcomed earlier, but it seems he was not initially recognized. A key to this may be his characteristics as being Vile and rejected with no honor given him, at least initially, by the other heads. [248]In any event, he does eventually assemble with the others as the seventh head.

Verse 11 states that the eighth will be the *beast who was, and is not*. It is this eighth king who now becomes the main character of the chapter. His importance also lines up with Revelation chapter 13, as well as the references to him in Daniel 7, 8, and 11. It is stated that *"he is an eighth and is of the seven."* The key to this interpretation is that the seventh and eighth king are the same individual; the seventh is the beast in his mortal form, and the eighth is the beast in his supernatural form. The word used for *of* in verse 11 is the Greek word ἐκ *ek* and has the meaning:

> If something is in something else, then the separation from it is expressed with ek, out of, while if it is near it, on it, with it, then apó is used. Ek is used either in respect of place, time, source, or origin[249]

---

[247] Revelation 13.5
[248] Daniel 11.21
[249] Zodhiates, S. (2000). *The complete word study dictionary: New Testament* (electronic ed.). Chattanooga, TN: AMG Publishers.

From this definition, and the previous sections relating to the wild beast, we can surmise that the seventh head will be together with the other six heads for a short time before being assassinated. The seventh, after his assassination, will be raised from the dead and become the supernaturally charged eighth—the *"wild beast,"* who will be *out from* the seventh king. The point here is that there are seven heads, but God goes on to describe an eighth which emerges from the seventh, articulating the supernatural nature of the eighth. Afterward, the beast, in his supernatural state, goes on to wreak havoc in the world for the following forty-two months. It is also stated that he will *go into perdition or destruction.* He will commit blasphemy against God, which is the unforgiveable sin, and therefore there will be no cure for him; he is doomed to be cast into the lake of fire and burn forever. After this spectacle, the supernatural beast will then take control of the nations of the world—Mystery Babylon.

In verse 12 and 13, the angel gives further information regarding the ten horns which make up the beast in verse 3. The angel states that, at this point in time in the vision, the ten horns have not received a kingdom as yet. It is further stated that these ten kings will receive power from the beast to be kings and leaders in a very short time—one hour—with the beast. Verse 13 emphatically states the allegiance between the beast and the ten kings: *"They will have one mind and give their power and strength to the beast."* The reference here is to the short-term future. We see in verse 12 the curious relationship between the supernatural beast and his cabinet of leaders appointed by him; the ten kings. In fact, it will be these ten kings who will rise with the beast, after his miraculous resurrection. Other sections of scriptures allude to this, but it is here in verse 12 where God makes it clear through the angel. Consider the following scriptures and how they indirectly suggest this relationship between the beast and the ten kings or leaders, and also provides additional information through scripture buildup. Each section should be read to capture the context of each of the verses below, Consider:

> And whereas thou sawest the feet and toes, part of potters' clay, and part of iron, the kingdom shall be divided; but there shall be in

it of the strength of the iron, forasmuch as thou sawest the iron mixed with miry clay.

⁴² And as the toes of the feet were part of iron, and part of clay, so the kingdom shall be partly strong, and partly broken. ⁴³ And whereas thou sawest iron mixed with miry clay, they shall mingle themselves with the seed of men: but they shall not cleave one to another, even as iron is not mixed with clay. ⁴⁴ And in the days of these kings shall the God of heaven set up a kingdom, which shall never be destroyed: and the kingdom shall not be left to other people, but it shall break in pieces and consume all these kingdoms, and it shall stand for ever.

(Daniel 2:41–44 KJV; my emphasis)

⁷ After this I saw in the night visions, and behold a fourth beast, dreadful and terrible, and strong exceedingly; and it had great iron teeth: it devoured and brake in pieces, and stamped the residue with the feet of it: and it was diverse from all the beasts that were before it; and it had ten horns. (Daniel 7:7 KJV; my emphasis)

³⁷ Neither shall he regard the God of his fathers, nor the desire of women, nor regard any god: for he shall magnify himself above all. ³⁸ But in his estate shall he honour the God of forces: and a god whom his fathers knew not shall he honour with gold, and silver, and with precious stones, and pleasant things. ³⁹ Thus shall he do in the most strong holds with a strange god, whom he shall acknowledge and increase with glory: and he shall cause them to rule over many, and shall divide the land for gain.

(Daniel 11:37–39 KJV; my emphasis)

And I stood upon the sand of the sea, and saw a beast rise up out of the sea, having seven heads and ten horns, and upon his horns ten crowns, and upon his heads the name of blasphemy. (Revelation 13:1 KJV)

These verses allude to the close relationship between the wild beast and his ten horns. It will be these ten horns empowered by the beast who will rule the earth for forty and two months. It also becomes clear that the other six heads, who are not crowned by the beast, and are strong Gentile nations, will fade into obscurity beneath the rulership of the wild beast and his ten horns.

Verse 14 continues the narrative by supplying the information with respect to the end of the ten horns, together with the beast. It is stated that these ten horns, together with the beast, will rise up in war against the Lamb. God fast forwards to show the end of the beast and his ten horns to indicate the more important information first with respect to these ten horns and the wild beast. They are supernatural beings and it will be the Lord Jesus Christ who will finally destroy them without the help of Man, or without hand as stated in Daniel 8.25 which is also a parallel verse to these actions of the beast.

Verse 15 then completes the description or the remaining member of the vision given to John in verse 2: *"the many waters."* The waters are identified as peoples and nations and tongues. From our understanding of the heads and horns; these peoples and nations and tongues are also together at the great peace conference in Jerusalem supporting the whore. These nations and peoples and tongues are marked off from both the superpower nations and the ten kings—the heads and horns, respectively. The additional nations and tongues show us that it is the whole of the peoples of the earth who will be joined in unison in an effort to eradicate God and bring peace to the earth, similar to the first gathering in Babylon, and as described in Genesis 11.

Verse 16 and 17 goes on to identify the actions of the ten horns who are intrinsically tied to the wild beast and that it is God who allows the destruction of Jerusalem due to its whoredoms. God provides the information that it will be these ten kings, or horns, appointed by the beast, who will attack the woman and burn her with fire and destroy her. Ezekiel 16 should also be read in connection with this verse which gives the further description of God's judgement of the great whore: *Jerusalem*. Verse 17 shows how it is God who judges the whore and it is God who puts these actions into the heart of the ten kings to fulfill all of these prophecies recorded before in the Old Testament.

Verse 18 identifies the woman as that *"great city"* as mentioned earlier. The first mention of this term in the book of Revelation is in Revelation 11.8 and refers to Jerusalem. Consider:

> "And their dead bodies shall lie in the street of the great city, which spiritually is called Sodom and Egypt, where also our Lord was crucified. (Revelation 11:8 KJV).

The vision of Revelation 17 was a future prophecy to John, but it will be contemporary to those on the earth when the vision actually occurs on the earth in the last days. The actual vision is an ongoing account of God's judgement of *Mystery Babylon* and the *"Great whore who will sit upon many waters."* The vision will progress through various stages but will encompass the twenty-three hundred days as documented in Daniel 8.9–14 and affect all the peoples of the world.

The book of Revelation, and the book of Daniel, both inspired by God, must be in concert and synchronized without contradiction. That there will be an event on the earth, a symbolic peace conference, and a Babylon-type gathering of nations before the beast comes fully into power is confirmed in Revelation 17:10–15. The series of events is also confirmed in Daniel 8:13, 14, and 26. Revelation 17:9 states that wisdom is required, from the Word of God, to comprehend the vision and the interpretation. The wisdom that God mentions is not the conventional wisdom brought about by the imaginations of man, but rather wisdom that comes from the revealed Word of God. For this reason, all theories not supported or documented by the Word of God may be unceremoniously dismissed. The actual time of the vision during the last seven-year period is also pinpointed to a time when all of these conditions are met. Wisdom, once again, is required to fully understand.[250]

Resolving the issue of the time of the vision requires examination and comparison with other sections of scripture, especially Old Testament scriptures. Recall that one of the main focal points of the book of Revelation is God's final dealing with, and the deliverance of, Israel. The core point is that God will fulfill all of his everlasting promises he made to Abraham, Isaac, and Jacob. The book also closes out, and is a type of bookend for, the promises that God made to Daniel—especially the completion of the promises with respect to the seventy weeks of years. The book of Revelation, together with the Old Testament scriptures, reveals how God fulfils *all* of his promises to Israel. It should be clear that the book of Revelation is intensely related to the Hebrew Old Testament. The Jewish pageantry, the temple, the frequent references to Jewish culture, and Hebrew Old Testament references drive this point home. Consider the following excerpt from E. W. Bullinger's Commentary on Revelation:

> The Hebrew character of the book (the book of Revelation) is shown in its use of idioms, expressions, words and phrases, which cannot be called Greek; and indeed is called by many "bad Greek." Professor Godet in his Studies on the New Testament, says, p. 331: "The only serious objection that can be urged against the authenticity of the Apocalypse, lies in the difference which is observable between its style, and that of the fourth Gospel. The latter is free from Aramaic expressions, the former is saturated with them." And again (p. 351), "the Apocalypse bears, from one end of it to the other, the character of a Hebrew prophecy." The argument based on this fact by the opponents of

---

[250] Revelation 17:9.

the Apocalypse is dealt with by scholars in various ways. But the subject is not one which would be of general interest to grammar. Those who wish to see the subject exhaustively treated are referred to the Commentary on the Apocalypse, by Moses Stuart, who devotes over twenty pages to it (pp. 190–210). There is however another side to the question: and that is, that, while the enemies use the fact against the Book itself, we use it against the popular interpretation of it. Though the language is Greek, the thoughts and idioms are Hebrew; and this links it on, not to the Pauline epistles, but to the Old Testament, and shows that its great subject is God's final dealings with the Jew and the Gentile; and not the Church of God. Connected with this fact there is another that emphasizes it in a remarkable manner. It is not only Hebrew in character as to its linguistic peculiarities, but especially in its use of the Old Testament. Only those who have most intimate acquaintance with the Old Testament can properly understand the Apocalypse. But all who know anything of old Testament history cannot fail to detect the almost constant reference to it. All the imagery - the Temple, the Tabernacle, the Ark of the Covenant, the Altar, the Incense, the heads of the twenty-four courses of Priests.[251]

The importance of God's final dealings with his chosen people—the seed of Abraham, Isaac, and Jacob—cannot be overstated, as it is one of the main themes of the Apocalypse. The Gentile is also dealt with in finality, but the church of God is left out. The church

---

[251] Bullinger, *Commentary on Revelation,* 50–62. Print Basis: F.H. Revell, 1909 Rights: Public Domain; CCEL Subjects: All; Kregal Publications, PO Box 2607, Grand Rapids, Mi 49501; 1993

of God is left out because they will have been previously raptured from the earth before the judgment scenes of Revelation reach their climax. The church of the one body of Jesus Christ, or the church of the born-again believers, is *not* the subject of the book of Revelation. Those who have received the gift of God through faith have eternal life, and according to Romans, nothing can separate them from God's love through Christ Jesus. This book of Revelation is written to those Jews and Gentiles who wish to repent and believe at the time of the end. The book also provides a blessing to all who read and comprehend. To understand further, read Bullinger's *Commentary on Revelation*—especially the introductory section, in which several proofs are presented.

The key to Revelation 17 is identifying the two visions that occur within the last seven-year period and their association with Daniel 8–12. Revelation 17:10–15 alludes to a time before the midst of the week and associates the time to a point after the beginning of the last seven years; the twenty-three hundred days. Examining these verses, it becomes clear that the first vision given to John occurs when the sixth king, or leader, is ruling. The first five Gentile dominions represented by kings, or rulers, have fallen from higher positions to ones of lesser degree. The sixth has not yet "*fallen*" and is still in a powerful position. The other information from the vision is that the ten kings have yet to receive power at the time of the vision, or at this first point in time. It is clear from Revelation 17:10–15 that this portion of the vision occurs on the earth sometime before the midst of the last seven years—a particular point in time on the earth. "*Five kings (or leaders) are already fallen*" and "*one king is*" and "*one is to come*" (Revelation 17:10). The beast, at the time of the middle of the seven years, will have been assassinated and supernaturally raised from the dead; he has gone on to destruction and is beginning his destructive course. The key to understanding is realizing that there are two points in time mentioned in the chapter. The one point in time is the middle of the week, when the beast is in control of the seven heads and ten horns supporting the whore. The second point in time—actually chronologically first, but second in importance—is early in the first half of the last seven years. This second point in time is when the beast has not yet come, the ten kings have not received their power as kings, and only five of the representative heads have fallen.

The vision seen by John in Revelation 17:3–7 is God's future summation, or his perspective, as to what occurs on the earth at the time of the midst of the last seven years. These verses build on, and give additional information to, Revelation 13:1–3. The second part of the vision, Revelation 17:10–15, reveals a second point in time, though it is actually first chronologically. This second vision will be a vision in which God gives early warning to those who understand the scriptural references to the vile man. The vision represents a conglomeration of nations coming together and representing some type of unified statement of peace. Man sees a great step forward for peace—the ultimate solution to bring peace about on the earth. God sees the gathering of nations, and it reminds him of the Babylon of Genesis 11—the last time men attempted to unify together for a common cause. The gathering at Babylon of Genesis was disrupted by God through language diffusion. God states in Genesis that if men come together as one, nothing evil is out of their reach or restrained from them.[252] The ultimate evil, which was avoided in the Babylon of Genesis, will come to pass in the last days as documented in the book of Revelation: *Mystery Babylon is fallen*. God allows destruction and desolations on the earth, owing to the excessive sins of mankind and their rejection of his son, Jesus Christ. *"Mystery Babylon"* is a term described and coined by God in Revelation 17. The mystery of what Babylon would have produced in Genesis will now be openly manifested in the last days. The mystery of what transpires when men come together as one without God will now be unleashed throughout the earth; that is, supernatural destruction. The earth dwellers, those who do not know God at the time of the fulfillment of Revelation 17, and who will not repent of their behavior, will be the victims of the worst time in human history. They will receive firsthand knowledge of the *"mystery of iniquity"*—that is, what happens when ultimate evil is unleashed on the earth. The unfortunate reality of the fall of

---

[252] Genesis 11:6.

Mystery Babylon lies in the words and events God uses to describe the horrible events of the book of Revelation. *Mystery Babylon* will produce Satan unleashed on the earth, along with God's undiluted wrath marshaled against Satan and his followers.

The time of the second part of the vision, given in Revelation 17:10–15, first in terms of time, will occur prior to the midst of the last seven years. Additionally, the twenty-three hundred days mentioned in Daniel 8:14 is also contained within the final seven years. It is likely that the twenty-three-hundred-day vision of Daniel 8:14 will begin with the opening of five of the seven seals, producing the judgment scenes of Revelation. The period of time is a painstakingly long and slow fall into the judgement scenes documented in the book of Revelation. The process of unleashing of the seven seals on the earth also runs parallel to the statements of our Lord in Matthew 24:

> For nation shall rise against nation, and kingdom against kingdom: and there shall be famines, and pestilences, and earthquakes, in divers places.
> [8] All these are the beginning of sorrows.
> (Matthew 24:7–8 KJV)

It is the seventh of these seals that documents the fall of Mystery Babylon as described in Revelation 17 and 18. The peace conference of Revelation 17 occurs on the earth and depicts a time prior to the middle of the seven years. The conference reveals that at the time of the Revelation 17 vision, five of the seven leaders representing the seven heads have fallen, one is, and the other has not yet come.

In conjunction and parallel with Revelation 17, the seals of Revelation 6 are opened and run their course throughout the final twenty-three hundred days. It is the opening of the first seal that begins the rise of the Antichrist to power. The opening of this first seal also begins the final twenty-three hundred days, summarizing the judgment time encompassing the opening of all subsequent seals. There is reason to believe that several of these seals will be opened together and will transition through the twenty-three hundred days ending with the cleansing of the sanctuary, as stated in Daniel chapter 8.

The first vision of Revelation 17 provides the identity of actual individuals who will be empowered during the twenty-three hundred days; it is a sort of pre-curtain call of the characters and their future behaviors throughout the remainder of the final days. The world will see a great gathering of nations bringing "*peace and safety*" to the earth; there will be a feeling of world peace. But God sees "*Mystery Babylon*" and gives fair warning to his people, those who rightly divide his word and are *awake*, of what is about to occur on the earth. In Revelation 17:3–7, God's Word looks forward in time to the role these players will actually play during the time of the midst of the week and onward. There will be a gap in time between both events—the initiation of the twenty-three hundred days and the midst of the week. The time gap represents God's fair warning to those who fear him on the earth. During the time gap, the seventh head, or leader, will come and rule for a short time. As time progresses, toward the midst of the week, he will receive his death wound and subsequently have his death wound healed. After he is miraculously raised from the dead through a great satanic miracle, he will come back as the eighth king—the supernatural beast.

God warns his people, those who rightly divide his word, of the coming apocalypse—the impending doom and destruction about to occur on the earth. After the twenty-three-hundred-day vision begins, the Antichrist will gather strength, but there will still be a gap in time before he rules the earth for the final forty-two months. The rule of the beast on the earth will begin at the time of the middle of the last seven years and will mark the rule of Satan—and Satan's agent: the Antichrist. The midst of the week will represent the supernatural beast coming to power. He will come to power initially with seven heads and ten horns and then will rule the earth with his ten kings. Additionally, Revelation 17 states that at the time of the middle of the week, the beast is supporting the whore, the great city. This condition does not last, for he will appoint his ten supernatural kings, and they will destroy the whore and burn her with fire. The sixth king, or head, will also fall to the beast before the ten kings receive their supernatural power from the beast. The eighth king, or head, will rise as the beast and will be numbered with the seven.

Revelation 17, together with similar verses in Daniel, provides the searchers of scripture critical information as to the origin and history of the beast with the seven heads and ten horns. Both books cover the time period from the opening of the seals at the beginning of the twenty-three hundred days and through the sounding of the trumpets and the pouring out of the vials. The time period is documented in Daniel 8:13–14 as covering the twenty-three hundred days. The end of these things will usher in the Day of the Lord—the day when Jesus Christ comes in glory to rule the earth. The great truth is that both sections, Daniel 8 and Revelation 17, will need to be accurately understood together to fully comprehend the information given by God regarding the last time. The event that initiates the twenty-three hundred days will be the opening of the first seal of Revelation 6.2 and the initial gathering of the nations is support of Jerusalem.

It will be only the Word of God that will allow God's people to understand these events—those who make the right division of the Word of God and who love God, called according to his purpose. The casting call will be visible only to those with skillful understanding of the Word of God: "***here is the mind which hath wisdom***" (Revelation 17:9 KJV)." To the world and those dwelling on the earth, the great conference of nations may look like a stride for peace that offers hope for the nations of the earth. To those with a keen and skillful understanding of God's Word, the conference will confirm the reality of the last days and the trouble on the doorstep. The conference will also be coincident with the beginnings of sorrows on the earth, including wars famines and plagues. The sorrows and evil will continue for the next twenty-three hundred days. They of understanding will be able to understand the general time period, for the sequence of events on the earth is documented in the scriptures. Those endued with scriptural knowledge will be warned as to the coming times: the horror of a wild beast and the wrath of our Holy God, both of which will shortly be on the earth. The time will be marked by several events in time: (1) the beast becoming strong with a strong powerful nation (2) the twenty-three-hundred-days beginning after the beginning of the final seven years and the initial gathering of leaders of the nations. These three events will unmistakably mark both the identity of the beast on the earth and the time period as the middle of the seven years draw near. After these three events on the earth, the next critical event will be the events at the time of the middle of the last seven years marking the initiation of the horrible final forty-two months. Additionally, after the beginning of the twenty-three hundred days, the times of sorrows will continue to intensify on the earth as the opening of the seals in heaven take effect on the earth. At the end of the final forty-two months, God will then set up the kingdom of his dear son, Jesus Christ. A disciplined understanding of God's Word will be required to fully understand the time sequence that God provides in his word. God assures us that none of the wicked (unbelievers) will understand the significance of any of these events.[253]

Daniel 8 and Revelation 17 together provide the information needed to properly interpret the last times. The two books have been critically aligned together by God, and both together unlock the door for proper interpretation. The time frame in Daniel 8, the twenty-three hundred days, instructs us as to the final time frame for the events of Revelation. The twenty-three hundred days begins with the opening of the first three of the seven seals listed in Revelation 6 and ends with the cleansing of the sanctuary in Jerusalem. Additionally, the time frame is the first of several events on the earth; this is further evidence of the last time being present on the earth. It is probable that Daniel saw the same vision seen in Revelation 17—*the beast with seven heads and ten horns supporting the whore*—but Daniel was told not to write it down. Daniel was not to write down his vision but only to give information as to the timing of the vision. Revelation 17 gives the detailed information regarding the vision, but Daniel 8 gives the timing. God uses the information documented in Revelation 17 and Daniel chapters 7–12 to give information about the behavior of those seen in the vision. The individuals depicted in the vision will

---

[253] Daniel 12:10.

fulfill all of what God speaks of them, with not one word falling to the ground.

Daniel 7 and 8 link the Gentile kingdoms to the final Gentile kingdom of the Antichrist and associate both with the last days and the final twenty-three-hundred-day revelation on Earth. Recall, in Daniel 8:15, Daniel overhears a conversation between two of God's angels discussing a vision that is to occur in the last days. The vision represents the events taking place for the final twenty-three hundred days before the cleansing of the sanctuary. Revelation chapter 17 encapsulates the twenty-three hundred days, beginning with the opening of the first seal and ending with the cleansing of the Sanctuary.

The opening of the seals constitutes the beginning of the twenty-three hundred days, the beginning of the judgments of God, who now begins to forcibly take back the earth from Satan and give it to his dear son, Jesus Christ. The *Mystery Babylon* metaphor is symbolic of kings, individual leaders, or dignitaries representing nations and countries all coming together as one at the conference. These are the leaders who gather for this peace event—*Mystery Babylon* of Revelation 17—and when they do, God will reveal their identities. The *Mystery Babylon* representation is hard-hitting and drives home the point of what God wishes to communicate. This gathering and coming together of the nations of the world, and God's remembrance of Babylon, in accordance with Revelation 16:19 will be one of several reasons why God's wrath is kindled against the nations. The event represents God's use of poetic license.

The twenty-three-hundred-day vision revealed to Daniel covers the whole of the opening of the seven seals, and their consequences to the earth dwellers. The connection between the book of Revelation and the book of Daniel should now be clear to the lover of God. It is evident that both books, together, complement and support each other, and both are required for proper interpretation of the Word of God. Both sections together—Revelation 17 and Daniel 8—pinpoints the time of significant events taking place on the earth twenty-three hundred days before the cleansing of the sanctuary. The eyes of God see a great whore, *Mystery Babylon*, supported by a seven-headed, ten-horned beast and the nations of the world—a conglomeration of nations and rulers. The conglomeration is similar to that judged by God in Genesis 11; thus, the name *Mystery Babylon*. It will be this *Mystery Babylon*, described in Revelation 17, that will soon be judged, rejected, and destroyed by God, as documented in Revelation 18. The time period of twenty-three hundred days, listed in Daniel 8, fits the time period carved out in Revelation chapters 6 and 17. Both sections are required to be understood together; each individual section cannot be understood without the other. Once understood, a significant sign, or warning post, is established to "*the mind which has wisdom*" (Revelation 17:9).

Revelation 17 provides the information regarding the reason for the judgement of great Mystery Babylon and those who will take part in the vision: the judgment and fall of "*Mystery Babylon.*" Additionally, the specific details will not be completely understood until the time of the end. God uses the two chapters together, both Daniel 8 and Revelation 17, to demonstrate his omnipotence and all-knowing nature. That is, God gives information about an event at least twenty-four hundred years before it actually occurs on the earth.

John, in Revelation 17, saw the vision of the seven-headed, ten-horned beast supporting the woman, or whore. Daniel was told that there would be a vision, how long it would last, and what would transpire during the final twenty-three hundred days. The angel summarized to Daniel in chapter 8 the actions of the *little horn* and the time period of judgments, trials, and tribulations on the earth. Daniel was instructed to seal, not document, the particular vision that he saw. John saw the beast and whore, *Mystery Babylon*, on the earth; John was given the names and specific information concerning the vision. John also documented the particulars of the actions, tasks, and assignments of the characters and how they would progress through the last seven years. John documented what he saw, all of which will be fulfilled during the final twenty-three hundred days. Additionally, John was given the revelation regarding the seven seals, the trumpets, and the final seven vials. The end point of the revelation in both sections is clear; it is the cleansing and then rebuilding of the sanctuary—the end of the last seven years for Israel.

As mentioned, the integration and understanding of the books of both Daniel and Revelation are paramount to understanding the vision of *Mystery Babylon*, the whore supported by the beast in Revelation 17. The foundation of why Babylon comes to the remembrance of God in Revelation 16:19 should now also be understood. These foundational truths being understood, we can now examine the vision of Revelation 17. Consider the following:

> And there came one of the seven angels which had the seven vials, and talked with me, saying unto me, Come hither; I will shew unto thee the judgment of the great whore that sitteth upon many waters: With whom the kings of the earth have committed fornication, and the inhabitants of the earth have been made drunk with the wine of her fornication. **So he carried me away in the spirit into the wilderness: and I saw a woman sit upon a scarlet coloured beast, full of names of blasphemy, having seven heads and ten horns. And the woman was arrayed in purple and scarlet colour, and decked with gold and precious stones and pearls, having a golden cup in her hand full of abominations and filthiness of her fornication:** And upon her forehead was a name written, MYSTERY, BABYLON THE GREAT, THE MOTHER OF HARLOTS AND ABOMINATIONS OF THE EARTH. And I saw the woman drunken with the blood of the saints, and with the blood of the martyrs of Jesus: and when I saw her, I wondered with great admiration. (Revelation 17:1–6; my emphasis)

"There came one of the seven angels which had the seven vials"; The vision of Revelation 17 is preceded by the pouring out of the seven vials in Revelation 16. The seven vials represent the third

woe on earth, as indicated by the progression of the judgments in the book of Revelation. The final vial, which is poured out in Revelation 16:17, is followed by the fall of *Mystery Babylon*, or the cities of the nations of the earth. The pouring out of the seventh vial in Revelation 16:17 is what brings to remembrance to God great Babylon. The meanings of both Babylon and its fall are explained and expanded in Revelation 17 and 18, respectively. God, through this further explanation, clarifies why the seventh vial is necessary. The fall of *Mystery Babylon* is a great cataclysmic event on the earth. The fall of *Mystery Babylon* after the pouring out of the seventh vial is so catastrophic that God inserts two chapters, Revelation 17 and 18, to explain what it means to the earth dwellers. Its fall literally summarizes the collapse of the cities of the nations throughout the world, as well as the disruption and fall of the peoples of the earth. The seventh seal leads to the seven trumpets and, finally, the pouring out of the seven vials. There is an informational interlude between the sounding of the seventh trumpet in Revelation 11:15 and the actual results of its sounding in Revelation 16—the pouring out of the seven vials. There is another informational interlude between the pouring out of the seventh vial in Revelation 16:17 and the ultimate effect of its pouring out, recorded in Revelation 18 and 19. Revelation 16 ends with the seventh vial being poured out, the cities of the nations falling, and the kings of the earth and the armies of the earth gathered at Armageddon. Jerusalem is also numbered with the falling of the nations in Revelation 16:17–19. Revelation 16:19 reveals great Babylon coming into remembrance before God, with Babylon representing the rebellion of the nations. Revelation 17 supplies the information as to why judgment has come—that is, why Babylon came into remembrance before God. Revelation 17 reveals "*Mystery Babylon*"—where it came from, how it will be judged, and how it is related to Jerusalem. It is the whore who is judged in Revelation 17 and the nations who are judged in Revelation 18. Revelation 18 categorizes the judgment of the world as a whole and what the judgment means on the earth to those still alive.

Babylon's fall is associated with the destruction of the cities of the nations of the earth, including the inhabitants of Jerusalem—

those not protected by God. The subject of the vision seen by John in Revelation 17 is a whore supported by a beast and the nations of the earth. The beast is the same beast of Revelation 13, possessing seven heads and ten horns. The beast, however, is not fully manifested until the middle, or midst, of the seventieth seven. In contrast, the point in time recorded in Revelation 17:10 and onward is a time before the beast comes into power or is fully manifested as the wild beast. The whore is stated to sit upon the beast and upon many waters, the latter of which represent peoples, nations, and tongues. God's initial requirement to the reader is that the understanding of the vision requires wisdom—that is, wisdom beyond what God already has documented in this section. The wisdom required is related to what is written in other sections of scripture, especially the book of Daniel. The vision of Revelation 17 and all of its symbolic imagery is vivid and clear.

The initial observation with respect to Revelation 17 is that the actual vision is representative of Gentile powers, peoples, places, and things on the earth. The chapter represents two separate viewpoints and two separate perspectives for the same event on the earth. The two perspectives are God's perspective and man's perspective. Consider the following: *"For my thoughts are not your thoughts, neither are your ways my ways, saith the LORD. For as the heavens are higher than the earth, so are my ways higher than your ways, and my thoughts than your thoughts"* (Isaiah 55:8–9 KJV).

To God, who sees the end from the beginning, it is *Mystery Babylon*, which is symbolic of man's futile attempt at unified peace without God. God's Word states that this deceptive unity will bring on a frightful end—the same end that was avoided in Genesis 11. God goes on to give details regarding the actions and final events regarding the great city. He also describes the fateful end for all those present at the misguided gathering of nations. The predicted end of what transpires after this conference will be tragic; it will not be the peace and oneness that man anticipates. The end will be what God states in the follow-up chapters in Revelation: utter destruction of the whore, the nations, and the cities, and tragic results to those on the earth. In short, the conference gives way to the end of man's rule on the earth, the beginning of sorrows, and, finally, the ushering in of the everlasting Day of the Lord. The Day of the Lord will shortly be on the earth; this is the day when the Lord is present and ruling on the earth, but not before the worst time in human history.

According to Revelation 16:19, something on the earth brings Babylon to God's remembrance. Revelation 17:5 follows up on Revelation 16:9 and explains why God remembers Babylon and what is meant by *Mystery Babylon*. Revelation 18 describes the fall of *Mystery Babylon*, which represents the fall of the cities of the nations and the fall of Gentile rule on the earth. What is the significance of Babylon to God? To understand, we must journey back to Genesis 11 and consider the first record regarding the first rebellion at Babylon. The story of the tower of Babel is documented in Genesis 11. Consider the following:

> And the whole earth was of one language, and of one speech. And it came to pass, as they journeyed from the east, that they found a plain in the land of Shinar; and they dwelt there.
>
> And they said one to another, Go to, let us make brick, and burn them throughly. And they had brick for stone, and slime had they for morter. And they said, Go to, let us build us a city and a tower, whose top may reach unto heaven; and let us make us a name, lest we be scattered abroad upon the face of the whole earth. And the LORD came down to see the city and the tower, which the children of men builded. And the LORD said, Behold, the people is one, and they have all one language; and this they begin to do: and now nothing will be restrained from them, which they have imagined to do. Go to, let us go down, and there confound their language, that they may not understand one another's speech.
>
> So the LORD scattered them abroad from thence upon the face of all the earth: and they

left off to build the city. Therefore is the name of it called Babel; because the LORD did there confound the language of all the earth: and from thence did the LORD scatter them abroad upon the face of all the earth. (Genesis 11:1–9 KJV)

The similarities between Revelation 17 and Genesis 11 are significant. Both document a conglomeration of nations, and both are viewed from two different perspectives: one of God's and one of Man's. In Genesis, God intervenes to prevent man from destroying himself. God states that nothing, *no evil*, will be restrained from man if he continues on his course of uniting all peoples. If this unification continues, then the ultimate of evils will result. The issue at hand is man's attempt to bring the nations together as one, giving rise to heathenism, idolatry, spiritualism, and every evil thing. The result of all this would be a new universal religion without God—a methodical religious system of idolatrous worship ending with the loss of individual freedoms. The other interesting outcome of the first Babylon documented in Genesis 11 is the building of a city—a secure place of peace and safety. Genesis 11 then describes God's response to all this—to preserve and protect mankind from himself through language diffusion and the scattering of man on the earth.

The similarities are striking between Revelation and Genesis. In Revelation, the city will be built and the nations will come together as one. Revelation 13 and 17 go on to document the result—the ultimate of all evils on the earth, a supernatural being who methodically destroys the nations of the earth and those on the earth and sets up a universal religion. The Antichrist's kingdom will evolve into a systematic idolatrous system of worship in which all individual freedoms are removed; men will be forced to worship or die. This great city, *Mystery Babylon*, represents the cities and nations of the world, which also bring on God's remembrance of the Babylon of Genesis 11. The nations are then judged and destroyed in Revelation 18; this is the result of the pouring out of the seventh vial of Revelation 16:19. The fall of *Mystery Babylon*, as described in Revelation 18, will also bring to an end Gentile rule on the earth. In

Genesis, the city was never finished, due to the intervention of God to preserve mankind on the earth. The word *"city,"* in the Hebrew context of Genesis 11, is symbolic for a safe habitation or a defended fortification—a place of safety where people can find protection. The etymology of the word for "city" in Revelation 17 is the same, but on a much grander scale. *Mystery Babylon* includes all the nations of the earth and the cities thereof. Their protection and safety are now advanced by the coming together of the nations—something attempted but not accomplished in the first Babylon of Genesis 11. The ultimate result of the oneness of the nations will be the stripping of individualism for the good of the whole. Somewhere in the fray, God is forgotten and man is elevated. The end result is a new religious system that excludes God and elevates the pride of man. Thorough all of this, Satan is working his magic to ultimately receive his long-sought-after worship. In Genesis 11, God intervenes to stop man before this madness and destruction come into manifestation; thus, as noted in Genesis 11:8, *"they left off building the city."* In Revelation 17, the building of the city is allowed to reach its frightful and tragic end. The result of building *Mystery Babylon* will be two horrible supernatural beasts: one from the sea, and one from the earth. They both will change the earth forever. In *Lange's Commentary on the Holy Scripture*, J. P. Lange states the following concerning Babylon:

> Genesis Chapter 11: 1. Vers.1 and 2. The settling in the land of Shinar.—The whole earth, that is, the whole human race.—One language and one speech (Lange more literally, one lip and one kind of words). The form and the material of language were the same for all.—From the East (Lange renders, towards the East).—From the land of Ararat, southeast (מדקמ as one word: the land of, or from the East).—A plane.—For them, as they came from the highlands, the plane was the low country, a valley plane (העקב).—Shinar, the same as Babylonia, though extending farther northward.—And they dwelt there.—The

preference for the hill country does not appear to have belonged to the young humanity. Under the most obvious points of view, convenience, fertility, and easier capability of cultivation, seem to have given to these children of nature a preference for the plain. Even at this day do the uncultivated inhabitants of the hills sometimes manifest the same choice. In this respect Babylon had for them the charm of extraordinary fruitfulness. ZAHN ("Kingdom of God," p. 86) gives extracts from Hippocrates and Herodotus in proof of the singular productiveness of this land of the palm, where the grain yields from two hundred to three hundred fold. Thence came luxury, which was followed by the cultivation of the paradisaical gardens (Gardens of Semiramis) and a life of sensuality, together with a sensual religious worship.

2. Vers. 3 and 4. The building of the tower.—They said one to another, Go to.—Expressive of an animated, decided undertaking.—Let us make brick.—The plain was deficient in stones, whereas, on the contrary, it abounded in a clayey soil which would serve for making bricks, and asphaltum, which was good for mortar. They burnt them to stone instead of merely hardening them in the sun, which otherwise was the more obvious practice.—And they said (again) Go to.—Their success in preparing bricks for their dwellings encouraged them to go farther. They resolved upon the building of a city, and a tower whose top may reach, etc. At the ground of this there evidently lies the impression of immensity as derived from the Babylonian plane, which actually, in its great extent, as some travellers have described it, gives the conception of the sublime.

The visible middle point of the same must have been the tower, standing up as a sign of unity for the whole human race. According to the representation, therefore, the words, "even to the heaven," would mean that the heaven was regarded as something that could be reached; although at a later period such language occurs in a hyperbolical sense.—And let us make us a name.—The expression עָשָׂה לוֹ שֵׁם denotes the appointing or establishing for one's self a signal of renown (Isaiah 63:12, 14; Jeremiah. 32:20). The sign of security shall be for them, at the same time, a sign of their fame, and thus, doubtless, would they give themselves a name as a people.—Lest we be scattered abroad.—Not only as a visible signal, but by the glory of its fame shall the tower hold them together. This is the expression of the political and popular feeling of antiquity; in the pride of the national spirit the individual is lost with his strength and his conscience. **Such is the characteristic feature of Babel everywhere, whether upon the Euphrates, the Tiber, or the Seine. The individual with his convictions, his freedom, his personality, must be wholly sacrificed to the name of uniformity, whether it be worldly or ecclesiastical. What is said here relates not merely to an ungodly, arbitrary, ambitious, individually titanic undertaking, but to the first introduction of that atheistical principle which would not merely promote the prosperity and authority of the whole in connection with the well-being and the freedom of the individual person, but also make the individual an involuntary sacrifice to a unity, which becomes, in that way, a false unity, as well as a false idol placed on the**

> throne of the living God,—and this whether it be called Babel, Rome, the Church, or "la grande nation." GÖETHE:
>> "Be it truth, or be it fable,
>> That in thousand books is shown,
>> All is but a tower of Babel,
>> Unless love shall make them one."
>> Or we may adopt as a various reading,
>> When love of glory makes them one.
>
> The question here relates to the destruction, in their very principles, of the Shemitic call to religion, and the Japhethic tendency to civilization, by a Hamitic confounding of religion and culture, to the obstruction of the true progress of the world and of the state, by resolving the constitution of human history into an immovable Hamitic naturalism.[254]

Man believes that the nations coming together and working jointly will result in their long-sought-after peace on earth—the permanent establishment of peace and security on the earth.[255] This is the sacrifice of the individual, and individualism, for the good of the unified whole. The mindset represents man at the pinnacle of his pride, deliberately without the true God and going on to create his own God. This is exactly what occurs in Revelation at the time of *Mystery Babylon*. God intervenes in Genesis 11 to save man from the ultimate destruction—the ultimate evil they would have brought on to themselves through their coming together to build the city. In Revelation 17, at the time of the end, or at the time of the last days of man's rule on the earth, the nations will once again gather under the guise of unified peace on the earth—that is, seeking peace and

---

[254] J. P. Lange, P. Schaff, T. Lewis, and A. Gosman, "Genesis" in *A Commentary on the Holy; 2008 Scripture* (Bellingham, Washington: Logos Bible Software) 363–64.

[255] 1 Thessalonians 5:3.

security through unified cooperation. What follows is the pinnacle of evil and destruction—forty-two months of hell on Earth. God's response to the second Babylon-type gathering, *Mystery Babylon*, is not to intervene but to let the will of man take its frightful course. The result is that the evil that was restrained in Genesis 11 by the Lord is now thrust upon the earth dwellers during the last days of man's rule on earth. At the end, after the forty-two months of hell and destruction on the earth, God finally sends his son, Jesus Christ, to destroy the Antichrist and his confederacy. God's intervention at Babylon, documented in Genesis 11, was to introduce language to confuse the masses. The language diffusion restricted man from the ultimate evil, putting it off for another day. In Revelation 17, God does not intervene but allows the evil of the oneness of mankind, enabled by latter day technology, to come to its predicted end—the end being the supernatural hell on earth described in the final forty-two months of the seventieth seven.

The result of man coming together in a unified fashion is the loss of personal freedoms and individualism. They will be replaced by a heathen religious system in which the true God is excluded. A similar coming together was exemplified in Daniel 2 with the worship of an image made by Nebuchadnezzar, who at that time ruled the nations. All men were forced to worship the image or face certain death. The final coming together of the nations during the horrible times of the last days will result in the unified worship of the beast; the alternative being death or banishment from society. The outcome of what happens in Revelation 13 and 17 is the very thing that God saved man from through language diffusion in Genesis 11.

The interpretation of the vision given by the angel and seen by John in Revelation 17 is listed below. Complete understanding of the vision will require knowledge—the pure knowledge and wisdom provided by the Word of God. God states that we are approved by him when we rightly divide his word.[256]

The summation of Revelation 17 is the general information that God provides concerning the players present for the vision on the

---

[256] 2 Timothy 2:15.

earth during the great unified gathering of nations on the earth at the time of the end. The interpretation of the vision provides information regarding the future actions of the participants mentioned in the vision. The predicted actions will be fulfilled as the final twenty-three hundred days and the final forty-two months unfold. Additional assumptions can be collected from the information in Revelation 17, together with previous references in the Word of God. Consider the following additional information:

1. The beast is the same personage as the one known as the vile man, the Antichrist, and all other similar titles that have been used in this work.
2. The beast has two phases. The first phase is as the seventh of the seven kings, in mortal or human form. The second phase is as the eighth king, the supernatural beast. The seventh and eighth are separated in time as two individuals, since the beast is in two different forms.
3. The seven kings are representative of the seven mountains, or the seven heads of the beast, on which the woman sits. The seven mountains represent powerful Gentile nations.
4. The beast was, is not, and is again; he ascends out of the bottomless pit after his death and rising again in supernatural form. His rising in supernatural form causes those on the earth to wonder at the great satanic miracle. It is important to note that God allows this because of the sins of mankind. The same fact is supported in Revelation 13:1–3.
5. Revelation 17:10 pinpoints a particular point in time—a time before the vision of Revelation 17:3 and a time initiated by the twenty-three hundred days of Daniel 8:14. The reality of the second of these time periods is supported by the following statements:

    a. Five of the seven kings have fallen, the sixth is, and the seventh has not yet come.

b. The ten horns are ten kings that have received no kingdom as yet but (will) receive power as kings after one hour with the beast. The hour with the beast will occur sometime in the future—specifically at the midpoint of the seventieth seven.

6. The vision is a conglomeration of people, nations, and leaders on the earth. The kings, the beast, the horns, and the nations are people and nations present at the time of the gathering together on the earth. The vision is effectively a dress rehearsal of the players and what they will accomplish during the next forty-two months. The actual event depicted by the vision will also serve as a warning to the lover of God who has wisdom to understand. God will give fair warning of what will occur during the final seven years—especially the final twenty-three hundred days which will begin the time of sorrows and lead to the final forty-two months. This warning can be heeded only through rightly dividing the Word of God. He who has eyes to see and ears to hear will understand.

7. The woman, or whore, and the seven heads are the two members representing things other than actual individuals. The seven heads, however, are represented by individual kings. The woman, which represents the great city, is supported by the beast, the nations, and the ten kings. The woman, which is the great city on the earth, will be destroyed or allowed by God to be burned with fire. The destruction of the great city, including the woman, Mystery Babylon, will also be an actual event on the earth; the event is summarized in Revelation 18. Jerusalem is also counted and included in Mystery Babylon and is depicted as a whorish woman.

8. Mystery Babylon represents the entire vision of the whore, nations, ten kings, and seven heads together. Mystery Babylon is collectively the great city—the nations of the earth under the sway of the Antichrist at the time

of the end, including Jerusalem. It is this great Mystery Babylon that is judged and destroyed as part of the pouring out of the seventh vial, as documented in Revelation 18.

Revelation 13 and 17 predict the final days as a day when the beast, the wild beast, is allowed to have dominion over the earth for forty and two months. The beast is the figure commonly referred to as the vile man, or the Antichrist. "The beast" is the name given to him by God after his miraculous resurrection during the final forty-two months. Note: the Antichrist is not referred to as equivalent to the beast at any time in the Bible, his appearance as the beast is first mentioned in Revelation; the book which provides the additional information to the believer, building on the previous usages in scripture, especially the book of Daniel. Consider:

> Little children, it is the last hour, and as **you have heard that Antichrist is coming,** so now many Antichrists have come. Therefore we know that it is the last hour. They went out from us, but they were not of us; for if they had been of us, they would have continued with us. But they went out, that it might become plain that they all are not of us. But you have been anointed by the Holy One, and you all have knowledge. I write to you, not because you do not know the truth, but because you know it, and because no lie is of the truth. **Who is the liar but he who denies that Jesus is the Christ? This is the Antichrist, he who denies the Father and the Son. No one who denies the Son has the Father. Whoever confesses the Son has the Father also.** Let what you heard from the beginning abide in you. If what you heard from the beginning abides in you, then you too will abide in the Son and in

the Father. And this is the promise that he made to us—eternal life (my emphasis).²⁵⁷

Another area of interest, with respect to Revelation chapter 17, are the feet and toes of the great beast of Daniel chapter 2. Recall, these toes are the first indication of the ten kings who will rule with Antichrist during the final Gentile dominion on the earth. God states that this final kingdom will be partly strong and partly weak, indicating that it will not be fully understood until the last days—especially the final forty-two months. The ten kings will most probably be individual kings or leaders who will represent countries in and around Syria—the country that produced the beast. The final powerful Gentile dominion will be powerful nations mixed with weak Gentile nations. We do know from Revelation 17 that the ten kings will receive power, supernatural power, after one hour with the beast.²⁵⁸ The ten kings will have a supernatural power base given to them by the beast. Daniel 2 goes on to state that in the days of these ten kings, or the final days of man's rule on the earth, the true God will set up a kingdom—the kingdom of the Lord Jesus Christ, which will never be destroyed.²⁵⁹

Revelation 13 gives information as to the origin of the beast along with the ten horns. The beast, at the time of the middle of the last seven years—the time of Revelation 13:1–3—is listed as one but is composed of seven heads and ten horns. The beast is also said to be fashioned after a lion, bear, and a leopard. This reference should at once point us back to Daniel 7, which traces the history and identity of the lion, bear, and leopard. The animals represent powerful Gentile nations that rise during the last days. John states that this is what he saw in the vision of Revelation 13. Putting together Revelation 13 with Daniel 7, the beast rises from among the ten horns and humbles

---

[257] 1 John 2:18–25. Scripture taken from *The Holy Bible, English Standard Version*. Copyright © 2000; 2001 by Crossway Bibles, a division of Good News Publishers. Used by permission. All rights reserved.
[258] Revelation 17:12.
[259] Daniel 2:44

three kings, or horns, and then becomes the seventh powerful head, numbered with the other six heads. The heads are representative of six powerful Gentile rulers, representing the lion, bear, and leopard. The beast is also listed as the *little horn,* who rises and becomes strong, and then becomes the seventh head, speaking blasphemous words. He is the seventh head in mortal form, and in accordance with Revelation 17:11, the seventh head receives his deadly wound (his assassination) and is then miraculously resurrected from the dead. He then becomes the eighth head. *The eighth head actually emanates from the seventh head but is now the eighth head in supernatural form.* The seventh and eighth kings are the same individual in two different forms.[260] It is stated that the seventh head is wounded to death by the sword and then brought back to life as the eighth king. The assassination and miraculous resurrection of the seventh, and then eighth, king is the focus of the events of the middle of the last seven years. This singular midweek event will be the incident that will try the whole world.[261] Is this human really some kind of a god?

Revelation 13:1–3 and 17:3 identify the same picture, or metaphor, of the condition of the earth at the time of the middle of the seventieth seven. The beast is shown with all seven heads and ten horns. One of the seven heads, the seventh, has been assassinated and is now the eighth king in resurrected form. He will now go on to rule the earth, having no mercy on the earth dwellers and being full of rage and hate. Before his final destruction at the end of the final forty-two months, he will have dominion over the earth.

Genesis 11 documents man's willingness to build a great city. The assembly of nations and their coming together under the great rebel Nimrod was thwarted by the language diffusion sent by the hand of God. The city was to be a fortified collection of nations, which would give man a great name that would last forever. There was also to be a great tower collectively constructed by the nations, its top reaching to the heavens. Revelation 17 reveals another city that is constructed of nations, and peoples, leaders, and tongues.

---

[260] Revelation 17:11.
[261] 2 Thessalonians 2:11

God depicts the last city as a great whore: "*The Mother of harlots and abominations of the earth.*"

The stamp on the head of the woman (the great city) no doubt refers to the original ancient Babylonian rebellion in Genesis 11 led by Nimrod. The name "Nimrod" itself means "rebellious" or "prone to rebellion." His plan was to unify the nations as one against God, making himself their great warrior or leader. His ultimate goal was to usurp the authority of God. Symbolically, the name on the woman's forehead represents the nations, the beast, and the woman, not just the woman only. The entire picture—that is, the woman, the beast, and the gathering of nations—is depicted as *Mystery Babylon*. This is why Babylon comes to remembrance before God, since it reminds God of the same worldly rebellion documented in Genesis 11. A new rebel, the Antichrist, will, in the last days, lead the nations in another rebellion against God. The conglomeration of nations supporting the woman and the beast brings to God's memory the first rebellion listed in Genesis 11.[262] The nations once again gather together against God with their new warrior, the Antichrist. The similarities are striking, but the results will be quite different. The first rebellion was interrupted by God and diffused by language. The last rebellion shall go further, not interrupted by God. The result will be the ultimate evil that the true God intervened in and prevented in Genesis.

To further understand the significance of the *woman* in Revelation 17, it is critical to understand what is suggested by *Mystery Babylon*. It is worth our while to look into the word used for "Mystery" in Revelation 17:5. The word "*Mystery*" is translated from the Greek word "μυστήριον," which means, "A secret revealed to one who is initiated to understand." The first usage of this word is in Matthew 13:11: "He answered and said unto them, because it is given unto you to know the mysteries of the kingdom of heaven, but to them it is not given."

The mystery of the woman, beast, nations, heads, and horns is not to be taken at face value. The "*Mystery*," or *secret*, will be

---

[262] Revelation 16:19.

revealed to those initiated and knowledgeable of God's Word. As stated earlier, it will be the remembrance of the first Babylon, and what the first Babylon represented, that is critical to understanding what happens on the earth during the last days. The "Mystery" is solved through prayer and diligent effort in assembling together all that God has revealed through his word regarding the first Babylon and now *Mystery Babylon.*

There are two cities mentioned by name in the book of Revelation: Babylon and Jerusalem. These two cities sum up God's dealings with the Jews and the Gentiles. The first city, Babylon, has its parallel references in the Old Testament, as attested to, and was initially representative of the gathering of Gentile nations as a whole, in opposition to God. The references in the Old Testament are similar to those in Revelation.[263] The question is not whether it is great Babylon, but what it represents at the time of the vision in Revelation 17. The second city mentioned in the book of Revelation is Jerusalem. Jerusalem is center stage for a significant portion of God's Word in the Old Testament in connection with God's chosen people, Israel. It should be to no one's surprise that Jerusalem, during the last days, is once again mentioned when God, once and for all, deals with his covenant Old Testament people, Israel. These two cities are the only two mentioned by proper names in the book of Revelation. It is fitting that that these two cities would be the focus of attention in the last days. These two cities, and what God reveals about them in the Old Testament, are key to understanding God's *secret-symbol Babylon* as written down by John in Revelation 17. The treasure of truth that God has revealed in the Old Testament will make known the secret of Revelation 17. God uses the word "secret" or "mystery" to indicate that a keen understanding of the Word of God will be required.

Jerusalem, in the Old Testament and after the time of David, is represented several times as a whorish woman. The children of Israel, and their land and city, were married to God; they are the only nation on earth with this pedigree. Because of their continual

---

[263] Isaiah 13; 51; Revelation 18.

rejection of the true God—the God who gave birth to them and saved them—they adulterated themselves. Their adultery was not taken lightly by God, who saved them and caused them to be a people. Several times in the Old Testament, the city of Jerusalem is declared to be morally unfit: a whore, judged at the time of their transgressions. Revelation 17 records another city, supported by a beast and many nations, that is once again judged in the last days. The city is judged as a whore according to Old Testament law and is given the appropriate Old Testament penalty for adultery. The references in Ezekiel 16 and 23, Jeremiah 4, and Isaiah 1 are most informative with respect to the identity of the whorish woman; they must be read in their entirety for proper understanding regarding the identity of the woman. Additionally, the whole of Hosea should be read in relation to this subject. The records depict a symbolic woman, the apple of God's eye, who in time trusts in her own beauty, quickly moving into adulterous relationships. The woman, as portrayed in Ezekiel 16, was once a beautiful bride but goes on to become a whore, or prostitute, with time. The woman is then judged, and after her debt has been paid in accordance with the law, she is finally and mercifully given an everlasting inheritance. Ezekiel 16 and 23 summarize Jerusalem, its inception, its fall, its judgment, and, finally, its deliverance, rebirth, and redemption. The references are listed below because of their significance to the understanding of this section. The important sections of Ezekiel 16 and 23 are in bold and underlined to indicate the relationship between the Old Testament references and the woman of Revelation 17. Consider the following:

> Again the word of the LORD came unto me, saying, **Son of man, cause Jerusalem to know her abominations,** And say, Thus saith the Lord GOD unto Jerusalem; Thy birth and thy nativity is of the land of Canaan; thy father was an Amorite, and thy mother an Hittite. And as for thy nativity, in the day thou wast born thy navel was not cut, neither wast thou washed in

water to supple thee; thou wast not salted at all, nor swaddled at all. None eye pitied thee, to do any of these unto thee, to have compassion upon thee; but thou wast cast out in the open field, to the lothing of thy person, in the day that thou wast born. And when I passed by thee, and saw thee polluted in thine own blood, I said unto thee when thou wast in thy blood, Live; yea, I said unto thee when thou wast in thy blood, Live. I have caused thee to multiply as the bud of the field, and thou hast increased and waxen great, **and thou art come to excellent ornaments**: thy breasts are fashioned, and thine hair is grown, whereas thou wast naked and bare. Now when I passed by thee, and looked upon thee, behold, thy time was the time of love; and I spread my skirt over thee, and covered thy nakedness: yea, I sware unto thee, and entered into a covenant with thee, saith the Lord GOD, and thou becamest mine. Then washed I thee with water; yea, I throughly washed away thy blood from thee, and I anointed thee with oil. **I clothed thee also with broidered work, and shod thee with badgers' skin, and I girded thee about with fine linen, and I covered thee with silk. I decked thee also with ornaments, and I put bracelets upon thy hands, and a chain on thy neck. And I put a jewel on thy forehead, and earrings in thine ears, and a beautiful crown upon thine head. Thus wast thou decked with gold and silver; and thy raiment was of fine linen, and silk, and broidered work; thou didst eat fine flour, and honey, and oil: and thou wast exceeding beautiful, and thou didst prosper into a kingdom.** And thy renown went forth among the heathen for thy beauty: for it was perfect through my comeliness, which I had put upon thee, saith the Lord GOD.

But thou didst trust in thine own beauty, and playedst the harlot because of thy renown, and pouredst out thy fornications on every one that passed by; his it was. And of thy garments thou didst take, and deckedst thy high places with divers colours, and playedst the harlot thereupon: the like things shall not come, neither shall it be so. Thou hast also taken thy fair jewels of my gold and of my silver, which I had given thee, and madest to thyself images of men, and didst commit whoredom with them, And tookest thy broidered garments, and coveredst them: and thou hast set mine oil and mine incense before them. My meat also which I gave thee, fine flour, and oil, and honey, wherewith I fed thee, thou hast even set it before them for a sweet savour: and thus it was, saith the Lord GOD. Moreover thou hast taken thy sons and thy daughters, whom thou hast borne unto me, and these hast thou sacrificed unto them to be devoured. Is this of thy whoredoms a small matter, That thou hast slain my children, and delivered them to cause them to pass through the fire for them? And in all thine abominations and thy whoredoms thou hast not remembered the days of thy youth, when thou wast naked and bare, and wast polluted in thy blood. And it came to pass after all thy wickedness, (woe, woe unto thee! saith the Lord GOD;) That thou hast also built unto thee an eminent place, and hast made thee an high place in every street. Thou hast built thy high place at every head of the way, and hast made thy beauty to be abhorred, and hast opened thy feet to every one that passed by, and multiplied thy whoredoms.

Thou hast also committed fornication with the Egyptians thy neighbours, great of flesh; and hast increased thy whoredoms, to provoke me to anger. Behold, therefore I have stretched out my hand over thee, and have diminished thine ordinary food, and delivered thee unto the will of them that hate thee, the daughters of the Philistines, which are ashamed of thy lewd way. Thou hast played the whore also with the Assyrians, because thou wast unsatiable; yea, thou hast played the harlot with them, and yet couldest not be satisfied. Thou hast moreover multiplied thy fornication in the land of Canaan unto Chaldea; and yet thou wast not satisfied herewith. How weak is thine heart, saith the Lord GOD, seeing thou doest all these things, the work of an imperious whorish woman; In that thou buildest thine eminent place in the head of every way, and makest thine high place in every street; and hast not been as an harlot, in that thou scornest hire; But as a wife that committeth adultery, which taketh strangers instead of her husband! They give gifts to all whores: but thou givest thy gifts to all thy lovers, and hirest them, that they may come unto thee on every side for thy whoredom. And the contrary is in thee from other women in thy whoredoms, whereas none followeth thee to commit whoredoms: and in that thou givest a reward, and no reward is given unto thee, therefore thou art contrary. Wherefore, O harlot, hear the word of the LORD: Thus saith the Lord GOD; Because thy filthiness was poured out, and thy nakedness discovered through thy whoredoms with thy lovers, and with all the idols of thy abominations, and by the blood of thy children, which thou didst give unto them;

Behold, therefore I will gather all thy lovers, with whom thou hast taken pleasure, and all them that thou hast loved, with all them that thou hast hated; I will even gather them round about against thee, and will discover thy nakedness unto them, that they may see all thy nakedness. And I will judge thee, as women that break wedlock and shed blood are judged; and I will give thee blood in fury and jealousy.

And I will also give thee into their hand, and they shall throw down thine eminent place, and shall break down thy high places: they shall strip thee also of thy clothes, and shall take thy fair jewels, and leave thee naked and bare. They shall also bring up a company against thee, and they shall stone thee with stones, and thrust thee through with their swords. And they shall burn thine houses with fire, and execute judgments upon thee in the sight of many women: and I will cause thee to cease from playing the harlot, and thou also shalt give no hire any more. So will I make my fury toward thee to rest, and my jealousy shall depart from thee, and I will be quiet, and will be no more angry. Because thou hast not remembered the days of thy youth, but hast fretted me in all these things; behold, therefore I also will recompense thy way upon thine head, saith the Lord GOD: and thou shalt not commit this lewdness above all thine abominations. Behold, every one that useth proverbs shall use this proverb against thee, saying, As is the mother, so is her daughter. Thou art thy mother's daughter, that lotheth her husband and her children; and thou art the sister of thy sisters, which lothed their husbands and their children: your mother was an Hittite, and your father an Amorite. And thine elder sister is Samaria, she and her daughters that dwell at thy left hand: and thy younger sister, that dwelleth at thy right hand, is Sodom and her daughters. Yet hast thou not walked after their ways, nor done after their abominations: but, as if that were a very little thing, thou wast corrupted more than they in all thy ways.

As I live, saith the Lord GOD, Sodom thy sister hath not done, she nor her daughters, as thou hast done, thou and thy daughters. Behold, this was the iniquity of thy sister Sodom, pride, fulness of bread, and abundance of idleness was in her and in her daughters, neither did she strengthen the hand of the poor and needy. And they were haughty, and committed abomination before me: therefore I took them away as I saw good. Neither hath Samaria committed half of thy sins; but thou hast multiplied thine abominations more than they, and hast justified thy sisters in all thine abominations which thou hast done. Thou also, which hast judged thy sisters, bear thine own shame for thy sins that thou hast committed more abominable than they: they are more righteous than thou: yea, be thou confounded also, and bear thy shame, in that thou hast justified thy sisters. When I shall bring again their captivity, the captivity of Sodom and her daughters, and the captivity of Samaria and her daughters, then will I bring again the captivity of thy captives in the midst of them: That thou mayest bear thine own shame, and mayest be confounded in all that thou hast done, in that thou art a comfort unto them. When thy sisters, Sodom and her daughters, shall return to their former estate, and Samaria and her daughters shall return to their former estate, then thou and thy daughters shall return to your former estate. For thy sister Sodom was not mentioned by thy mouth in the day of thy pride, Before thy wickedness was discovered, as at the time of thy reproach of the daughters of Syria, and all that are round about her, the daughters of the Philistines, which despise thee round about. Thou hast borne thy lewdness and thine abominations, saith the LORD. For thus saith the Lord GOD; I will even deal with thee as thou hast done, which hast despised the oath in breaking the covenant. **Nevertheless I will remember my covenant with thee in the days of thy youth, and I will establish unto thee an everlasting covenant.**

Then thou shalt remember thy ways, and be ashamed, when thou shalt receive thy sisters, thine elder and thy younger: and I will give them unto thee for daughters, but not by thy covenant. And I will establish my covenant with thee; and thou shalt know that I am the LORD: That thou mayest remember, and be confounded, and never open thy mouth any more because of thy shame, when I am pacified toward thee for all that thou hast done, saith the Lord GOD. (Ezekiel 16:1–63 KJV; my emphasis)

The word of the LORD came again unto me, saying, Son of man, there were two women, the daughters of one mother: And they committed whoredoms in Egypt; they committed whoredoms in their youth: there were their breasts pressed, and there they bruised the teats of their virginity. And the names of them were Aholah the elder, and Aholibah her sister: and they were mine, and they bare sons and daughters. Thus were their names; Samaria is Aholah, and Jerusalem Aholibah. And Aholah played the harlot when she was mine; and she doted on her lovers, on the Assyrians her neighbours, Which were clothed with blue, captains and rulers, all of them desirable young men, horsemen riding upon horses. Thus she committed her whoredoms with them, with all them that were the chosen men of Assyria, and with all on whom she doted: with all their idols she defiled herself. Neither left she her whoredoms brought from Egypt: for in her youth they lay with her, and they bruised the breasts of her virginity, and poured their whoredom upon her. Wherefore I have delivered her into the hand of her lovers, into the hand of the Assyrians, upon whom she doted. These discovered her nakedness: they took her sons and her daughters, and slew her with the sword: and she became famous among women; for they had executed judgment upon her. And when her sister Aholibah saw this, she was more corrupt in her inordinate love than she, and in her whoredoms more than her sister in her whoredoms. She doted upon the Assyrians her neighbours, captains and rulers clothed most gorgeously, horsemen riding upon horses, all of them desirable young men. Then I saw that she was defiled, that they took both one way, And that she increased her whoredoms: for when she saw men pourtrayed upon the wall, the images of the Chaldeans pourtrayed with vermilion, Girded with girdles upon their loins, exceeding in dyed attire upon their heads, all of them princes to look to, after the manner of the Babylonians of Chaldea, the land of their nativity: And as soon as she saw them with her eyes, she doted upon them, and sent messengers unto them into Chaldea. **And the Babylonians came to her into the bed of love, and they defiled her with their whoredom, and she was polluted with them, and her mind was alienated from them. So she discovered her whoredoms, and discovered her nakedness: then my mind was alienated from her, like as my mind was alienated from her sister.** Yet she multiplied her whoredoms, in calling to remembrance the days of her youth, wherein she had played the harlot in the land of Egypt. For she doted upon their paramours, whose flesh is as the flesh of asses, and whose issue is like the issue of horses. Thus thou calledst to remembrance the lewdness of thy youth, in bruising thy teats by the Egyptians for the paps of thy youth. **Therefore, O Aholibah, thus saith the Lord GOD; Behold, I will raise up thy lovers against thee, from whom thy mind is alienated, and I will bring them against thee on every side; The Babylonians, and all the Chaldeans, Pekod, and Shoa, and Koa, and all the Assyrians with them: all of them desirable young men, captains and rulers, great lords and renowned, all of them riding upon horses. And they shall come against thee with chariots, wagons, and wheels, and with an assembly of people, which shall set against thee buckler and shield and helmet round about: and I will set judgment before them, and they shall judge thee according to their judgments. And I will set my jealousy against thee, and they shall deal furiously with thee: they shall take away thy nose and thine ears; and thy remnant shall fall

by the sword: they shall take thy sons and thy daughters; and thy residue shall be devoured by the fire. They shall also strip thee out of thy clothes, and take away thy fair jewels. Thus will I make thy lewdness to cease from thee, and thy whoredom brought from the land of Egypt: so that thou shalt not lift up thine eyes unto them, nor remember Egypt any more. For thus saith the Lord GOD; Behold, I will deliver thee into the hand of them whom thou hatest, into the hand of them from whom thy mind is alienated:

And they shall deal with thee hatefully, and shall take away all thy labour, and shall leave thee naked and bare: and the nakedness of thy whoredoms shall be discovered, both thy lewdness and thy whoredoms. I will do these things unto thee, because thou hast gone a whoring after the heathen, and because thou art polluted with their idols. Thou hast walked in the way of thy sister; therefore will I give her cup into thine hand. Thus saith the Lord GOD; Thou shalt drink of thy sister's cup deep and large: thou shalt be laughed to scorn and had in derision; it containeth much. Thou shalt be filled with drunkenness and sorrow, with the cup of astonishment and desolation, with the cup of thy sister Samaria.

Thou shalt even drink it and suck it out, and thou shalt break the sherds thereof, and pluck off thine own breasts: for I have spoken it, saith the Lord GOD. Therefore thus saith the Lord GOD; Because thou hast forgotten me, and cast me behind thy back, therefore bear thou also thy lewdness and thy whoredoms. The LORD said moreover unto me; Son of man, wilt thou judge Aholah and Aholibah? yea, declare unto them their abominations; That they have committed adultery, and blood is in their hands, and with their idols have they committed adultery, and have also caused their sons, whom they bare unto me, to pass for them through the fire, to devour them. Moreover this they have done unto me: they have defiled my sanctuary in the same day, and have profaned my sabbaths. For when they had slain their children to their idols, then they came the same day into my sanctuary to profane it; and, lo, thus have they done in the midst of mine house. And furthermore, that ye have sent for men to come from far, unto whom a messenger was sent; and, lo, they came: for whom thou didst wash thyself, paintedst thy eyes, and deckedst thyself with ornaments, And satest upon a stately bed, and a table prepared before it, whereupon thou hast set mine incense and mine oil. And a voice of a multitude being at ease was with her: and with the men of the common sort were brought Sabeans from the wilderness, which put bracelets upon their hands, and beautiful crowns upon their heads. Then said I unto her that was old in adulteries, Will they now commit whoredoms with her, and she with them?

Yet they went in unto her, as they go in unto a woman that playeth the harlot: so went they in unto Aholah and unto Aholibah, the lewd women. And the righteous men, they shall judge them after the manner of adulteresses, and after the manner of women that shed blood; because they are adulteresses, and blood is in their hands. For thus saith the Lord GOD; I will bring up a company upon them, and will give them to be removed and spoiled. And the company shall stone them with stones, and dispatch them with their swords; they shall slay their sons and their daughters, and burn up their houses with fire. Thus will I cause lewdness to cease out of the land, that all women may be taught not to do after your lewdness. And they shall recompense your lewdness upon you, and ye shall bear the sins of your idols: and ye shall know that I am the Lord GOD. (Ezekiel 23:1–49; my emphasis)

But if ye refuse and rebel, ye shall be devoured with the sword: for the mouth of the LORD hath spoken it. **How is the faithful city become an harlot! it was full of judgment; righteousness lodged in it;** but now murderers. Thy silver is become dross, thy wine mixed with water. (Isaiah 1:20–22 KJV; my emphasis)

I beheld the earth, and, lo, it was without form, and void; and the heavens, and they had no light. I beheld the mountains, and, lo, they trembled, and all the hills moved lightly. I beheld, and, lo, there was no man, and all the birds of the heavens were fled. I beheld, and, lo, the fruitful place was a wilderness, and all the cities thereof were broken down at the presence of the LORD, and by his fierce anger. For thus hath the LORD said, The whole land shall be desolate; yet will I not make a full end. For this shall the earth mourn, and the heavens above be black: because I have spoken it, I have purposed it, and will not repent, neither will I turn back from it. The whole city shall flee for the noise of the horsemen and bowmen; they shall go into thickets, and climb up upon the rocks: every city shall be forsaken, and not a man dwell therein. **And when thou art spoiled, what wilt thou do? Though thou clothest thyself with crimson, though thou deckest thee with ornaments of gold, though**

> **thou rentest thy face with painting, in vain shalt thou make thyself fair; thy lovers will despise thee, they will seek thy life. For I have heard a voice as of a woman in travail, and the anguish as of her that bringeth forth her first child, the voice of the daughter of Zion, that bewaileth herself, that spreadeth her hands, saying, Woe is me now! for my soul is wearied because of murderers.** (Jeremiah 4:23–31 KJV; my emphasis)

The parallels with the whorish woman of Revelation 17 are significant. The following parallels are listed:

- The whore of Revelation 17 represents a city. The whore of Ezekiel 16 and 23, as well as Isaiah 1:20–22, represents a city—Jerusalem. (See Ezekiel 16:3; Isaiah 1:20–22.)
- The whore of Revelation 17 is arrayed in purple and scarlet color and decked with gold and precious stones and pearls. The whore of Ezekiel 16 is dressed with gold, fine silver, and a costly chain around her neck (pearls), and she is dressed in white. (See Ezekiel 16:10–13.)
- The whore of Revelation 17 is judged by God and given the punishment of a whore in accordance with the law of God. The whore of Ezekiel 16 is judged by God and given the punishment of a whore in accordance with the law of God.[264]
- The whore, the beast, and the nations of Revelation 17, *Mystery Babylon*, are together responsible for the sinning of the nations. The whore of Ezekiel 16 was responsible, symbolically, for the corruption of nations.
- The whore of Revelation 17 is supported by the nations and the beast at the midpoint of the last seven years. It will be the beast and the ten kings who will eventually burn her

---

[264] Leviticus 21:9.

with fire and leave her naked and bare. The whore of Ezekiel 16, as with the whore of Revelation 17, is surrounded by those who love her and those who hate her before being judged. Those that she longed for will destroy her and burn her with fire. (See Ezekiel 16:37.)
- The whore of Revelation 17 is judged, found naked, and burned with fire; her flesh is eaten. The whore of Ezekiel 16 is judged, found naked, burned with fire, and stoned. (See Ezekiel 16:37–41.)

The scriptures reveal that Jerusalem is part of the makeup of *Mystery Babylon* as portrayed in Revelation 17. In relation to this, the book of Hosea should be read in its context. The general story is of a woman who leaves her husband to go whoring after other men. After a long time, her husband searches and finds her naked and bare on the auction block in a faraway Gentile nation. He has pity on her and buys her back and brings her home. The analogy is that of wayward Israel; in the end, God will save a remnant of them because of his promises to their fathers. Consider the verses below in Hosea, in which God describes Israel as a wayward woman who is judged. But through all of this, God saves a remnant of Israel and lures them into the wilderness and pleads with them there. These verses describe how God saves Israel at the time of the end; but he saves only a remnant, whom he draws out of the land and into the wilderness. He then cares for them as he did when he took them out from Egypt and led them himself. These verses will be fulfilled at the time of the end in their entirety. These verses should also be compared to Revelation 12, which describes the same event occurring at the time of the end. Consider the following:

> And I will not have mercy upon her children; for they be the children of whoredoms. For their mother hath played the harlot: she that conceived them hath done shamefully: for she said, I will go after my lovers, that give me my bread and my water, my wool and my flax,

mine oil and my drink. Therefore, behold, I will hedge up thy way with thorns, and make a wall, that she shall not find her paths. And she shall follow after her lovers, but she shall not overtake them; and she shall seek them, but shall not find them: then shall she say, I will go and return to my first husband; for then was it better with me than now. For she did not know that I gave her corn, and wine, and oil, and multiplied her silver and gold, which they prepared for Baal. Therefore will I return, and take away my corn in the time thereof, and my wine in the season thereof, and will recover my wool and my flax given to cover her nakedness. And now will I discover her lewdness in the sight of her lovers, and none shall deliver her out of mine hand. I will also cause all her mirth to cease, her feast days, her new moons, and her sabbaths, and all her solemn feasts. And I will destroy her vines and her fig trees, whereof she hath said, These are my rewards that my lovers have given me: and I will make them a forest, and the beasts of the field shall eat them. And I will visit upon her the days of Baalim, wherein she burned incense to them, and she decked herself with her earrings and her jewels, and she went after her lovers, and forgat me, saith the LORD. **Therefore, behold, I will allure her, and bring her into the wilderness, and speak comfortably unto her. And I will give her vineyards from thence, and the valley of Achor for a door of hope: and she shall sing there, as in the days of her youth, and as in the day when she came up out of the land of Egypt. And it shall be at that day, saith the LORD, that thou shalt call me Ishi; and shalt call me no more Baali. For I will take away the**

names of Baalim out of her mouth, and they shall no more be remembered by their name. And in that day will I make a covenant for them with the beasts of the field, and with the fowls of heaven, and with the creeping things of the ground: and I will break the bow and the sword and the battle out of the earth, and will make them to lie down safely. And I will betroth thee unto me for ever; yea, I will betroth thee unto me in righteousness, and in judgment, and in lovingkindness, and in mercies. I will even betroth thee unto me in faithfulness: and thou shalt know the LORD. And it shall come to pass in that day, I will hear, saith the LORD, I will hear the heavens, and they shall hear the earth; And the earth shall hear the corn, and the wine, and the oil; and they shall hear Jezreel. And I will sow her unto me in the earth; and I will have mercy upon her that had not obtained mercy; and I will say to them which were not my people, Thou art my people; and they shall say, Thou art my God. (Hosea 2:4–23 KJV; my emphasis)

The other point of interest in the book of Revelation with regard to Jerusalem is the information given to us in Revelation 21:9–27 in which an angel, probably the same angel noted in Revelation 17:1, who comes to John in the same way as in Revelation 17 and reveals.. *"a bride who has made herself ready."* When this is put together with the whore of Revelation 17 it drives home the point that Jerusalem will go through a major transition through the time of Jacob's trouble or the final forty-two months of Revelation. The new occupants of this new city will be the remnant of the house of Israel who God calls out and purifies through the forty-two months of the tribulation. The whore who was once identified in Revelation 17 is now a bride who has made herself ready for God and his Christ. The allegory is almost unmistakable and will be understood by those with the wisdom the God provides. Consider the bride of Revelation 21:

> 9 And there came unto me one of the seven angels which had the seven vials full of the seven last plagues, and talked with me, saying, Come hither, I will shew thee the bride, the Lamb's wife. 10 And he carried me away in the spirit to a great and high mountain, and shewed me that great city, the holy Jerusalem, descending out of heaven from God, 11 Having the glory of God: and her light was like unto a stone most precious, even like a jasper stone, clear as crystal; 12 And had a wall great and high, and had twelve gates, and at the gates twelve angels, and names written thereon, which are the names of the twelve tribes of the children of Israel: 13 On the east three gates; on the north three gates; on the south three gates; and on the west three gates. 14 And the wall of the city had twelve foundations, and in them the names of the twelve apostles of the Lamb. 15 And he that talked with me had a golden reed to measure the city, and the gates thereof, and the wall thereof. 16 And the city lieth foursquare, and the length is as large as the breadth: and he measured the city with the reed, twelve thousand furlongs. The length and the breadth and the height of it are equal. 17 And he measured the wall thereof, an hundred and forty and four cubits, according to the measure of a man, that is, of the angel. 18 And the building of the wall of it was of jasper: and the city was pure gold, like unto clear glass. 19 And the foundations of the wall of the city were garnished with all manner of precious stones. The first foundation was jasper; the second, sapphire; the third, a chalcedony; the

fourth, an emerald; 20 The fifth, sardonyx; the sixth, sardius; the seventh, chrysolite; the eighth, beryl; the ninth, a topaz; the tenth, a chrysoprasus; the eleventh, a jacinth; the twelfth, an amethyst. 21 And the twelve gates were twelve pearls; every several gate was of one pearl: and the street of the city was pure gold, as it were transparent glass. 22 And I saw no temple therein: for the Lord God Almighty and the Lamb are the temple of it. 23 And the city had no need of the sun, neither of the moon, to shine in it: for the glory of God did lighten it, and the Lamb is the light thereof. 24 And the nations of them which are saved shall walk in the light of it: and the kings of the earth do bring their glory and honour into it. 25 And the gates of it shall not be shut at all by day: for there shall be no night there. 26 And they shall bring the glory and honour of the nations into it. 27 And there shall in no wise enter into it any thing that defileth, neither whatsoever worketh abomination, or maketh a lie: but they which are written in the Lamb's book of life. (Revelation 21:9–27 KJV)

The two cities, Jerusalem and Babylon, represent *Mystery Babylon*. The second city, Babylon, is not just the geographical city of Babylon but is the mass of nations and tongues, *secret Babylon*, which represents all that assemble as one in the last days. Revelation 17 depicts the woman supported by the nations and tongues and the beast all together as one. The woman herself will be judged as described in Revelation 17; Babylon, or the nations, will be judged in Revelation 18. The book of Revelation is clear that all nations will be judged and will fall during the final forty-two months of the final seven years. Consider the following:

And the seventh angel poured out his vial into the air; and there came a great voice out of the temple of heaven, from the throne, saying, It is done. And there were voices, and thunders, and lightnings; and there was a great earthquake, such as was not since men were upon the earth, so mighty an earthquake, and so great. **And the great city was divided into three parts, and the cities of the nations fell: and great Babylon came in remembrance before God, to give unto her the cup of the wine of the fierceness of his wrath. And every island fled away, and the mountains were not found.** And there fell upon men a great hail out of heaven, every stone about the weight of a talent: and men blasphemed God because of the plague of the hail; for the plague thereof was exceeding great. (Revelation 16:17–21 KJV; my emphasis)

Jerusalem is referred to frequently in the Old Testament as a whore to be judged by God in the last days. But after the final judgment, God will save a remnant of those of the lineage of Abraham, Isaac, and Jacob. God will place the remnant once again in the land with Jesus Christ as their Lord of lords. The end for Jerusalem will be that of a spotless bride—the bride of Christ. At that time, God will make Israel an eternal habitation for his people. But before all this, the final judgments of the final forty-two months occur on the earth—the wrath of God directed against fallen mankind. This time will see the short dominion of *Mystery Babylon*, headed up by the wild beast, his ten kings, and Satan, which will take center stage and rule over the earth. In Revelation 17, the great city, Jerusalem, is numbered with the nations and judged as the same as documented in Hosea. The judgment will fulfill all the Old Testament scriptures. The ten kings, who gave their power to the beast, will hate the whore, burn her with fire, and leave her naked and bare. Consider the following concerning Babylon from Lenski's interpretation of St. John's Revelation:

> The seventh πληγή or blow is the fall of Babylon the Great. This was summarily announced in 14:8: "There fell, there fell, Babylon, the Great!" and now we see her fall. "Babylon" = the entire antichristian empire which was built up by the dragon, Satan, through the beast, the entire antichristian power (13:1–10), and by this power through the second beast, the entire antichristian propaganda (13:11–18), called the pseudo-prophet in 16:13. The kings from the sunrisings (v. 13) and the kings of the whole inhabited earth (v. 14) are viewed as her vassals, as powers that are parts of her empire, likewise the cities that fell (v. 19) plus the islands and the mountains (v. 20). Regarded as a great city, she has many vassals and thus constitutes the antichristian empire; viewed as "Babylon," she is still the antichristian empire. Whether she is only a unit (14:8) or is surrounded by many satellites, Babylon is no less than the whole antichristian empire. Papal Rome, Judaism, all paganism that rejects the gospel, all the secret, oath-bound, deistic organizations, all that deny Jesus Christ and the expiating blood of the Lamb, and all worldly indifferentists who also remain mere dwellers on the earth (3:10; 6:10; 8:13; 11:10; 13:8, 12, 14; 17:8) are parts of Babylon, constitute Babylon.[265]

---

[265] R. C. H. Lenski, *The Interpretation of St. John's Revelation*, (Columbus, Ohio: Lutheran Book Concern, 1935), 481.

The vision of Revelation 17 is multifaceted and reveals the condition of the nations of the earth, including Jerusalem and Israel, at the time of the midpoint of the last seven years. Jerusalem, at the time of the end, is numbered with the nations and included as part of *Mystery Babylon*. It is believed that both cities—Babylon, representing the Gentile nations, and Jerusalem, representing God's holy place—will be numbered together and part of the corporate conglomeration of nations. As such, both are judged and both fall—Jerusalem in the latter part of Revelation 17, and the Gentile nations in Revelation 18.

The Gentile nations, the beast with the seven heads, the ten horns, and the whore coming together for so-called peace and security represents the condition of the nations at the time of the end. The woman, or the whore, represents Jerusalem at the time of the middle of the last seven years. Revelation 18 describes the fall of *Mystery Babylon*—the entire fall of all its members together. The fall of Jerusalem is described separately in the latter part of Revelation 17, but how this happens and what it means for the nations to fall is expanded and explained in Revelation 18. The book of Revelation once again separates Jews and Gentiles as in the Old Testament, the church of Jesus Christ having already been raptured from the earth. It is the gathering of nations in the last days which brings to remembrance before God the Babylon of Genesis 11. The gathering becomes an abomination before God and subsequently brings on God's wrath. The result of God's wrath is the pouring out of the seventh vial, which results in the cataclysmic fall of *Mystery Babylon*; the Gentile nations and Jerusalem fall in desolation and destruction at the hands of the wild beast.

The vision given to John by Jesus Christ and documented in Revelation 17 accurately informs us that there are seven heads, ten horns, and many nations supporting a whorish city. The assembling of nations in the latter first half of the final seven years will be in response to a great common cause that brings the nations together for a unified purpose. The events on the earth will cause the nations and cities of the world to come together as one, reminding God of the first gathering at Babylon.[266] The vision of the beast supporting the whore reveals the condition of the nations of the earth at the time of the middle of the final seven years.

The one hundred forty-four thousand of those of the lineage of Abraham, Isaac, and Jacob, handpicked by God, will then, at the end of the seven years, be made ready for the Lord through God's purification plan. The marriage ceremony is recorded in Revelation 19:7, but this takes place after the completion of the final seven years. The purification will take place during the fiery trials of the events of the book of Revelation; the final forty-two months. During these troubled times, God will supernaturally deliver the remnant of believing Israel called out according to the purpose of God, ultimately setting them in their land with their anointed Messiah. God delivers and protects them through the final forty-two months of hell that will come to the earth.[267] The event is similar to what occurred in Egypt with Moses and his deliverance of Israel through the wilderness at God's direction and God's protection. The one hundred forty-four thousand, the bride of the lamb, will be the new embryotic nation of Israel, with Jesus Christ as their Messiah, David as their king, and Jerusalem as their center. Jerusalem will be central for the next thousand years. Through this time period, the everlasting reign of Jesus Christ as King of kings and Lord of lords will prevail, and it will last forever; the reign of natural man will end.[268] In this way, God will fulfill all unfilled promises to Israel given to the prophets in the Old Testament. God is not a man; he does not lie.

A central focus of Revelation is the transition of Jerusalem from a brutish whore, judged and punished by God, to a chaste virgin made ready for the marriage of the lamb. God marks and protects one hundred forty-four thousand Jews of the physical lineage of Abraham, Isaac, and Jacob; twelve thousand from each of the tribes of Israel.[269] The one hundred forty-four thousand then become

---

[266] Revelation 16:19.
[267] Revelation 19:6–9.
[268] Revelation 7:3–8.
[269] Revelation 7:1–8.

the embryotic nation of Israel, and God goes on to fulfill all of his everlasting promises given to Abraham, Isaac, and Jacob. God also fulfills all of the Old and New Testament prophecies concerning Israel and Jerusalem—both judgments and eternal blessings. In spite of all Israel's disobedience and all the passage of time, God fulfills the covenant he made with Abraham and reaffirmed with Isaac and Jacob. God is not a man; he does not lie. His thoughts are far above our thoughts, and his ways are above our ways. One day to God is like a thousand years, and a thousand years are like one day. His promises do not fade because of time, but he will fulfill all that he has said and all that is written by his prophets. God will not allow one jot or tittle of his entire word to be left unfulfilled. The death of Abraham, Isaac, and Jacob, and the disobedience of the majority of their descendants, does not annul or disavow the everlasting covenants and promises. But before the blessing that God has promised, there will occur the judgment of the wicked, and the purification of those who will inherit the promise will take place on the earth.

The covenant given to Moses was conditional for those of Israel under the law. We know that Israel, as a nation, went after strange gods and suffered the consequences that God laid out in the Mosaic law. In contrast, the everlasting promises made to Abraham, Isaac, and Jacob before the Mosaic law were unconditional and shall reach all of their fulfillment during these last times. A main theme of the book of Revelation is the description of how God fulfills all of the everlasting promises that God promised Abraham, Isaac, and Jacob. God fulfills his promises not because Israel deserves it but because God made unconditional promises to their fathers. To understand why Jerusalem and God's chosen are a central theme in God's final book of Revelation, consider the following everlasting and unconditional promises listed below. The everlasting promises given to the Patriarchs have never been fulfilled. The same promises will be fulfilled at the close of the book of Revelation.

God's everlasting covenant with Abraham, Isaac, and Jacob before the covenant of the law made to their descendants through Moses is the focus of the following verses:

And He took him (Abraham) outside and said, "Now look toward the heavens, and count the stars, if you are able to count them." And He said to him, "So shall your descendants be." **Then he believed in the LORD; and He reckoned it to him as righteousness**. And He said to him, "I am the LORD who brought you out of Ur of the Chaldeans, **to give you this land to possess it**." And he said, "O Lord God, how may I know that I shall possess it?" So He said to him, "Bring Me a three year old heifer, and a three year old female goat, and a three year old ram, and a turtledove, and a young pigeon." Then he brought all these to Him and cut them in two, and laid each half opposite the other; but he did not cut the birds. And the birds of prey came down upon the carcasses, and Abram drove them away. Now when the sun was going down, a deep sleep fell upon Abram; and behold, terror and great darkness fell upon him. And God said to Abram, "Know for certain that your descendants will be strangers in a land that is not theirs, where they will be enslaved and oppressed four hundred years.

"But I will also judge the nation whom they will serve; and afterward they will come out with many possessions. "And as for you, you shall go to your fathers in peace; you shall be buried at a good old age. "Then in the fourth generation they shall return here, for the iniquity of the Amorite is not yet complete." And it came about when the sun had set, that it was very dark, and behold, there appeared a smoking oven and a flaming torch which passed between these pieces. **On that day the LORD made a covenant with Abram, saying, "To your descendants I

have given this land, From the river of Egypt as far as the great river, the river Euphrates". (Note: This covenant is a blood covenant that God made with Abraham and not dependent on anything or anybody; God made it and God will fulfill it. The covenant was made with Abraham before the law was given to Moses; therefore not dependent on the keeping of the Law; a separate agreement between God and Abraham). (Genesis 15:5–18 NASB; my emphasis)

And there was a famine in the land, beside the first famine that was in the days of Abraham. And Isaac went unto Abimelech king of the Philistines unto Gerar. And the LORD appeared unto him, and said, Go not down into Egypt; dwell in the land which I shall tell thee of: Sojourn in this land, and I will be with thee, and will bless thee; for unto thee, and unto thy seed, I will give all these countries, **and I will perform the oath which I sware unto Abraham thy father; And I will make thy seed to multiply as the stars of heaven, and will give unto thy seed all these countries; and in thy seed shall all the nations of the earth be blessed; Because that Abraham obeyed my voice, and kept my charge, my commandments, my statutes, and my laws.** (Genesis 26:1–5; my emphasis)

And Jacob went out from Beersheba, and went toward Haran. And he lighted upon a certain place, and tarried there all night, because the sun was set; and he took of the stones of that place, and put them for his pillows, and lay down in that place to sleep. And he dreamed, and behold a ladder set up on the earth, and the top of it reached to heaven: and behold the angels of God ascending and descending on it. And, behold, the LORD stood above it, and said, **I am the LORD God of Abraham thy father, and the God of Isaac: the land whereon thou liest, to thee will I give it, and to thy seed; And thy seed shall be as the dust of the earth, and thou shalt spread abroad to the west, and to the east, and to the north, and to the south: and in thee and in thy seed shall all the families of the earth be blessed.** And, behold, I am with thee, and will keep thee in all places whither thou goest, and will bring thee again into this land; for I will not leave thee, until I have done that which I have spoken to thee of. (Genesis 28:10–15 KJV; my emphasis)

For I would not, brethren, that ye should be ignorant of this mystery, lest ye should be wise in your own conceits; that blindness in part is happened to Israel, until the fullness of the Gentiles be come in. **And so all Israel shall be saved: as it is written, There shall come out of Sion the Deliverer, and shall turn away ungodliness from Jacob: For this is my covenant unto them, when I shall take away their sins.** As concerning the gospel, they are enemies for your sakes: but as touching the election, they are beloved for the fathers' sakes. **For the gifts and calling of God are without repentance** (change). **For as ye in times past have not believed God, yet have now obtained mercy through their unbelief: Even so have these also now not believed, that through your mercy they also may obtain mercy.** For God hath concluded them all in unbelief, that he might have mercy upon all. O the depth of the riches both of the wisdom and knowledge of God! how unsearchable are his judgments, and his ways past finding out! For who hath known the mind of the Lord? or who hath been his counsellor? Or who hath first given to him, and it shall be recompensed unto him again? For of him, and through him, and to him, are all things: to whom be glory forever. Amen. (Romans 11:25–1 KJV; my emphasis)

And ye shall perish among the heathen, and the land of your enemies shall eat you up. And they that are left of you shall pine away in their iniquity in your enemies' lands; and also in the iniquities of their fathers shall they pine away with them. If they shall confess their iniquity, and the iniquity of their fathers, with their trespass which they trespassed against me, and that also they have walked contrary unto me; And that I also have walked contrary unto them, and have brought them into the land of their enemies; **if then their uncircumcised hearts be humbled, and they then accept of the punishment of their iniquity: Then will I remember my covenant with Jacob, and also my covenant with Isaac, and also my covenant with Abraham will I remember; and I will remember the land.** The land also shall be left of them, and shall enjoy her sabbaths, while she lieth desolate without them: and they shall accept of the punishment of their iniquity: because, even because they despised my judgments, and because their soul abhorred my statutes. **And yet for all that, when they be in the land of their enemies, I will not cast them away, neither will I abhor them, to destroy them utterly, and to break my covenant with them: for I am the LORD their God. But I will for their sakes remember the covenant of their ancestors, whom I brought forth out of the land of Egypt in the sight of the heathen, that I might be their God: I am the LORD.** (Leviticus 26:38–45 KJV; my emphasis)

The timetable for the fulfillment of these promises is listed in Daniel 9:24. All of the promises come to fruition after the destruction of the Assyrian, or the Antichrist, at the end of the seventieth seven. Consider the following: "Seventy weeks are determined upon thy people and upon thy holy city, to finish the transgression, and to make an end of sins, and to make reconciliation for iniquity, and to bring in everlasting righteousness*, and to seal up the vision and prophecy*, and to anoint the most Holy" (Daniel 9:24 KJV).

God made everlasting and unconditional promises to Abraham, Isaac, and Jacob through a blood covenant with Abraham. Understanding the Old Testament in terms of God's promises and the everlasting covenant made to Abraham, Isaac, and Jacob is essential to understanding the Old Testament scriptures and what transpires for Israel during the book of Revelation. The mystery period and the rapture of the of the one body of Jesus Christ must also be rightly divided to understand how God remembers Abraham, Isaac, and Jacob during the last days. The understanding of the everlasting promises is also essential to understanding the book of Revelation. Revelation documents how God, once and for all, fulfills all covenant promises to Abraham, Isaac, and Jacob. God does this in spite of the disobedience of a stiff-necked people. Understanding this explains the many references in the Book of Revelation to

1. the Jews,
2. the Old Testament,
3. the temple,
4. the pageantry,
5. Jerusalem
6. The 144,000; twelve thousand from each of the tribes of Israel
7. the seven scattered Jewish churches, and
8. the salvation of Israel: "The Virgin who has made herself ready for the marriage supper of the Lamb."[270]

---

[270] Revelation 19:8–9.

The church of the one body of Jesus Christ will have been raptured and will be with Jesus Christ before the final seven years come to an end. Once the church of the one body of Christ is raptured, God finishes his final dealings with the Jews, the Gentile nations, and the heavens and the earth.

It should be clear by now that Jerusalem is critical to the events of the book of Revelation and represents God's final dealings with his chosen people, Israel. Jerusalem is numbered with the Gentile nations in the beginning of the last seven years and is represented by a whorish woman and numbered with *Mystery Babylon*. At the end of the seven years, the called of Israel, the chaste bride of Christ, are delivered and are in the land with Jesus Christ as their anointed Messiah in Jerusalem.

If Jerusalem is representative of the Jews and their final end, Babylon is representative of the Gentile nations and their final end. Revelation 17:5 tells us that the name written on the woman's forehead is a "*Mystery*" or "*Secret*" and represents *Mystery Babylon*. The scripture states that *Mystery Babylon* is symbolic and represents a parable that gives understanding to the initiated and wise concerning what God has revealed in his word.[271] Unbelievers and those who do not bring a disciplined understanding of God's Word will be blinded. The vision is symbolic of what God sees from his perspective—a great conglomeration of nations gathering together to unify for peace and, in the process, forget or rebel against God. The nations are effectively stating, "We shall bring peace, and we shall rule the earth and make a great name for ourselves." God says differently. The national rebellion that ensues during the last days will allow Satan to be unleashed on the earth, which eventually brings on God's wrath. The city of Babylon, in Old Testament times, and in the land of Shinar, produced a man who was a great rebel against God—Nimrod. His rebellion against God included the gathering of nations in unison against the almighty. The initial revolt was offset by God through language diffusion in Genesis 10 and 11, the year being approximately 2,200 BC. The term "Babylon," from its origin in

---

[271] Revelation 17:9.

Genesis, has become symbolic of the rebel Nimrod and his unification of the peoples of the earth in revolt. Babylon is mentioned once again, in the book of Revelation, when another national revolt takes place on the earth, producing another man of sin—the Antichrist. In the last days, it is Satan, through his instrument, the Antichrist, who once again orchestrates the nations and the peoples of the earth in a rebellion against the living God.

The book of Revelation documents this second rebellion, in which the nations will gather under one man, who will declare himself God and commit the unforgiveable sin. This second rebellion will not be mitigated through language diffusion as in Genesis; it will be allowed to continue to its horrific end. In Revelation, the rebellion brings on catastrophic disaster until God sends his son at the end of the final forty-two months. The church of the one body of Jesus Christ, made up of born-again believers who were once Jews and Gentiles, will have been raptured from the earth before the wrath of almighty God is on the earth. Those remaining on the earth, both Jews and Gentiles, will face the wrath of God. God will save the called-out Jews, the one hundred forty-four thousand, in fulfillment of his promises to their fathers: Abraham, Isaac, and Jacob. There will also be others who will make it through the final forty-two months of the final seventieth week, but they will do so through fiery trials on the earth.

The use of the term "Babylon" in the book of Revelation is a symbolic representation of Gentile nations of the world and their attempt to unify as one. The symbolic *Mystery Babylon* of the last days will also include Jerusalem initially in its membership. Jerusalem will be numbered with the nations at the beginning of the last seven-year period. The vision of Revelation 17 reveals what God means by *Mystery Babylon*. The concept of *Mystery Babylon* must be understood from both the Old Testament and the book of Revelation. The Old Testament references will be listed below to bring light to why God, during the last days, remembers *Mystery Babylon* in the book of Revelation as he states in Revelation 16:19. The first usage of "Babylon" in the book of Revelation is documented in Revelation 14:8; there God is warning those on the earth, via his angel, about the coming destruction on the earth. The words of these angels form a compendium of what God is going to do in the day of his wrath. The angelic proclamation looks forward to the result of the pouring out of the seventh vial.[272] Consider the following:

> And I saw another angel fly in the midst of heaven, having the everlasting gospel to preach unto them that dwell on the earth, and to every nation, and kindred, and tongue, and people, Saying with a loud voice, Fear God, and give glory to him; for the hour of his judgment is come: and worship him that made heaven, and earth, and the sea, and the fountains of waters. **And there followed another angel, saying, Babylon is fallen, is fallen, that great city, because she made all nations drink of the wine of the wrath of her fornication.** And the third angel followed them, saying with a loud voice, If any man worship the beast and his image, and receive his mark in his forehead, or in his hand, The same shall drink of the wine of the wrath of God, which is poured out without mixture into the cup of his indignation; and he shall be tormented with fire and brimstone in the presence of the holy angels, and in the presence of the Lamb: And the smoke of their torment ascendeth up for ever and ever: and they have no rest day nor night, who worship the beast and his image, and whosoever receiveth the mark of his name. (Revelation 14:6–11 KJV; my emphasis)

The angel proclaims a prophetic warning to the nations that the eminent destruction of Babylon, the nations, is on the doorstep,

---

[272] See Bullinger, *Commentary on Revelation*, 453. Print Basis: F.H. Revell, 1909 Rights: Public Domain; CCEL Subjects: All; Kregal Publications, PO Box 2607, Grand Rapids, Mi 49501; 1993

as described in Revelation 17, 18, and 19. The actual destruction reaches its climax at the pouring out of the seventh vial, resulting in the final destruction of the nations. *Mystery Babylon* is representative of the gathering of nations, including Jerusalem. Initially, Jerusalem is numbered with the nations and is judged and destroyed with the nations. At the time of the Lord's kingdom, at the end of the last seven years, Jerusalem is made chaste and clean. Consider below how Babylon is associated with the nations, especially the Gentile nations, in Revelation 16:

> And the seventh angel poured out his vial (the seventh vial) into the air; and there came a great voice out of the temple of heaven, from the throne, saying, It is done. And there were voices, and thunders, and lightnings; and there was a great earthquake, such as was not since men were upon the earth, so mighty an earthquake, and so great. **And the great city was divided into three parts, and the cities of the nations fell: and great Babylon came in remembrance before God, to give unto her the cup of the wine of the fierceness of his wrath. And every island fled away, and the mountains were not found. And there fell upon men a great hail out of heaven, every stone about the weight of a talent: and men blasphemed God because of the plague of the hail; for the plague thereof was exceeding great.** (Revelation 16:17–21 KJV; my emphasis)

Revelation 16:19 represents the destruction or fall of Babylon, which is also linked to the fall of the nations as the result of the pouring out of the seventh vile. *Mystery Babylon* is represented in Revelation 17 as a gathering of tongues, peoples, nations, and leaders, as well as kings, or horns. The gathering, taken together with the whore, Jerusalem, comprises the whole of *Mystery* or *symbolic Babylon*, as it is referred to throughout Revelation. Revelation 17 explains and interprets what God means by *Mystery Babylon*, which is to be applied whenever Babylon is referenced in the book of Revelation. Revelation 18 reveals the final judgment of *Mystery Babylon* after the pouring out of the seventh vile in Revelation 16.

Revelation 16 takes us to the actual pouring out of the seven vials, which are unleashed after the sounding of the seventh trumpet documented in Revelation 11:15. The vials are poured upon the earth, the seventh vial being the last and deadliest, resulting in the fall of the nations, as documented in Revelation 16:17–21. Examining the results of the pouring out of the previous six vials reveals judgment directed toward the peoples on the earth. The object of all seven final vials is judgment on the earth directed at *Mystery Babylon*. The judgments will be directed to those on the earth—especially those on the earth who worship the beast. The vials represent the height of the wrath of God toward a people who are destroying the earth and who deny the true God, the creator of the heavens and the earth. They insist that God did not create the heavens and the earth, which he did create for his pleasure.[273] The seventh vial, the fall of the nations, is representative of God's wrath toward the nations. The unity of the nations, *Mystery Babylon*, brings to God's memory an eerily similar event—the first rebellion at Babylon, which is documented in Genesis 10 and 11. The scripture states that this remembrance of Babylon brings on "*the cup of the wine of the fierceness of God's wrath.*" The result of this remembrance is the fall of the nations and the peoples of the earth. The fall of the nations and great Babylon, and the judgments associated with the wrath of almighty God, will be the result of the pouring out of the seven vials. The summary of the pouring out—why it happens and what it means to the people of the earth—is listed in Revelation 17, 18, and 19. *Mystery Babylon* has fallen with all its rebellions. The following is a summary list of the last seven vials described in Revelation 16, which collectively represent the third and final woe—God's wrath against man's revolt. Consider the following:

---

[273] Revelation 11;18.

1. The first vial: The grievous sore is inflicted upon the men who worshipped the beast.
2. The second vial: The sea becomes blood, and all souls die in the sea.
3. The third vial: The rivers and fountains of water become blood.
4. The fourth vial: The vial is upon the sun; men are scorched with fire and heat.
5. The fifth vial: Darkness is upon the kingdom of the beast.
6. The sixth vial: The River Euphrates dries up, and all kings and leaders and armies are called to Armageddon.
7. The seventh vial: The great earthquake occurs, and the cities of the nations fall. Hail falls on the people on the earth. Mountains flee, and islands are no more.

Note how each of these vials results in judgment to all on the earth—all labeled as *Mystery Babylon. The city was divided into three, and the nations fell, the islands fled away, the mountains were not found, and great hail fell upon the men of the earth.*[274] The reference to Babylon in Revelation 14 and 16 covers the short description of the judgment and fall of *Mystery Babylon.* The next two references in Revelation 17 and 18 go on to explain the makeup and judgment, or fall, of Babylon. Revelation 17 documents what God means by *Mystery Babylon* and focuses on the judgment of the woman; the whore, who is also part of *Mystery Babylon.* The woman is Jerusalem and describes her judgment; the woman initially is counted together with *Mystery Babylon* and is judged with the rest of the Gentile nations. Revelation 18 details the long description of what is meant by the fall of *Mystery Babylon*, which represents the judgment of the nations of the earth in general.

The next occurrence of Babylon is in Revelation 17, but it has been covered in the previous sections. Revelation 18 describes the consequences of the fall of great Babylon. Revelation 18 gives the meaning and implications of the fall of the nations in Revelation 16.

---

[274] Revelation 16:19–21.

Revelation 18 goes on to describe, in detail, the fall of Babylon. The fall of Babylon, the fall of the nations, is so cataclysmic that God takes an entire chapter to describe exactly what Babylon's fall means. The way of life of all nations and peoples of the earth who are still alive on the earth is now completely changed and will continue to change. The nations are fallen, death is prevalent, famine and war are throughout the earth, and the nations of the earth come to ruin. Psalm 2 and parts of Matthew 24 will reach their fulfillment. Consider the following sections from Matthew 24 and Psalm 2 below:

> When ye therefore shall see the abomination of desolation, spoken of by Daniel the prophet, stand in the Holy Place, (whoso readeth, let him understand:) Then let them which be in Judaea flee into the mountains: Let him which is on the housetop not come down to take anything out of his house: Neither let him which is in the field return back to take his clothes. **And woe unto them that are with child, and to them that give suck in those days! But pray ye that your flight be not in the winter, neither on the sabbath day: For then shall be great tribulation, such as was not since the beginning of the world to this time, no, nor ever shall be. And except those days should be shortened, there should no flesh be saved: but for the elect's sake those days shall be shortened.** (Matthew 24:15–22 KJV; my emphasis)

Additionally, Psalm 2 talks about these very days when kingdoms change and the nations are judged. Consider the following:

> Why do the heathen rage, and the people imagine a vain thing? The kings of the earth set themselves, and the rulers take counsel together, against the LORD, and against his anointed,

> saying, Let us break their bands asunder, and cast away their cords from us. **He that sitteth in the heavens shall laugh: the Lord shall have them in derision. Then shall he speak unto them in his wrath, and vex them in his sore displeasure. Yet have I set my king upon my holy hill of Zion. I will declare the decree: the LORD hath said unto me, Thou art my Son; this day have I begotten thee. Ask of me, and I shall give thee the heathen for thine inheritance, and the uttermost parts of the earth for thy possession. Thou shalt break them with a rod of iron; thou shalt dash them in pieces like a potter's vessel.** Be wise now therefore, O ye kings: be instructed, ye judges of the earth. Serve the LORD with fear, and rejoice with trembling. Kiss the Son, lest he be angry, and ye perish from the way, when his wrath is kindled but a little. Blessed are all they that put their trust in him. (Psalm 2:1–12; my emphasis)

Revelation 18 will now be considered in its entirety. The entire chapter deals with the fall of the nations, who have banded together to usurp God and his Christ. Babylon is now fallen, and its king is about to be judged. The initial reference with respect to the Antichrist is located in Isaiah 14; the reference is to the king of Babylon; Lucifer, Son of the Morning; and the Assyrian (section 1, references 1, 2, and 3).[275] Both Isaiah 14 and Revelation 18 are listed below to show the similarity between the two references, each representing the fall of the nations. Consider these two sections:

> That thou shalt take up this proverb against the **king of Babylon,** and say, How hath the oppressor ceased! the golden city ceased! The LORD hath broken the staff of the wicked,

---

[275] Isaiah 14.

and the sceptre of the rulers. **He who smote the people in wrath with a continual stroke, he that ruled the nations in anger** (i.e. ruled the nations as king of Babylon or king of the nations), **is persecuted, and none hindereth.** The whole earth is at rest, and is quiet: they break forth into singing. Yea, the fir trees rejoice at thee, and the cedars of Lebanon, saying, Since thou art laid down, no feller is come up against us. Hell from beneath is moved for thee to meet thee at thy coming: it stirreth up the dead for thee, even all the chief ones of the earth; it hath raised up from their thrones all the kings of the nations. All they shall speak and say unto thee, Art thou also become weak as we? art thou become like unto us? Thy pomp is brought down to the grave, and the noise of thy viols: the worm is spread under thee, and the worms cover thee. **How art thou fallen from heaven, O Lucifer, son of the morning! how art thou cut down to the ground, which didst weaken the nations!** For thou hast said in thine heart, I will ascend into heaven, I will exalt my throne above the stars of God: I will sit also upon the mount of the congregation, in the sides of the north: I will ascend above the heights of the clouds; I will be like the most High. Yet thou shalt be brought down to hell, to the sides of the pit. **They that see thee shall narrowly look upon thee, and consider thee, saying, Is this the man that made the earth to tremble, that did shake kingdoms; That made the world as a wilderness, and destroyed the cities thereof; that opened not the house of his prisoners?** All the kings of the nations, even all of them, lie in glory, every one in his own house. But thou art cast out of thy grave like an abominable branch, and as the raiment of those that are slain, thrust through with a sword, that go down to the stones of the pit; as a carcase trodden under feet. Thou shalt not be joined with them in burial, because thou hast destroyed thy land, and slain thy people: the seed of evildoers shall never be renowned. **Prepare slaughter for his children for the iniquity of their fathers; that they do not rise, nor possess the land, nor fill the face of the world with cities. For I will rise up against them, saith the LORD of hosts, and cut off from Babylon the name, and remnant, and son, and nephew, saith the LORD.** I will also make it a possession for the bittern, and pools of water: and I will sweep it with the besom of destruction, saith the LORD of hosts.

The LORD of hosts hath sworn, saying, Surely as I have thought, so shall it come to pass; and as I have purposed, so shall it stand: That I will break the Assyrian in my land, and upon my mountains tread him under foot: then shall his yoke depart from off them, and his burden depart from off their shoulders. This is the purpose that is purposed upon the whole earth: and this is the hand that is stretched out upon all the nations. For the LORD of hosts hath purposed, and who shall disannul it? and his hand is stretched out, and who shall turn it back? (Isaiah 14:4–27 KJV; my emphasis)

And after these things I saw another angel come down from heaven, having great power; and the earth was lightened with his glory. And he cried mightily with a strong voice, saying, Babylon the great is fallen, is fallen, and is become the habitation of devils, and the hold of every foul spirit, and a cage of every unclean and hateful bird. **For all nations have drunk of the wine of**

the wrath of her fornication, and the kings of the earth have committed fornication with her, and the merchants of the earth are waxed rich through the abundance of her delicacies. And I heard another voice from heaven, saying, Come out of her, my people, that ye be not partakers of her sins, and that ye receive not of her plagues. For her sins have reached unto heaven, and God hath remembered her iniquities. Reward her even as she rewarded you, and double unto her double according to her works: in the cup which she hath filled fill to her double. How much she hath glorified herself, and lived deliciously, so much torment and sorrow give her: for she said in her heart, I sit a queen, and am no widow, and shall see no sorrow. Therefore shall her plagues come in one day, death, and mourning, and famine; and she shall be utterly burned with fire: for strong is the Lord God who judgeth her. And the kings of the earth, who have committed fornication and lived deliciously with her, shall bewail her, and lament for her, when they shall see the smoke of her burning, Standing afar off for the fear of her torment, saying, Alas, alas, that great city Babylon, that mighty city! for in one hour is thy judgment come. And the merchants of the earth shall weep and mourn over her; for no man buyeth their merchandise any more: The merchandise of gold, and silver, and precious stones, and of pearls, and fine linen, and purple, and silk, and scarlet, and all thyine wood, and all manner vessels of ivory, and all manner vessels of most precious wood, and of brass, and iron, and marble, And cinnamon, and odours, and ointments, and frankincense, and wine, and oil, and fine flour, and wheat, and beasts, and

THE LAST DAYS AND THE VILE MAN OF DANIEL

sheep, and horses, and chariots, and slaves, and souls of men. And the fruits that thy soul lusted after are departed from thee, and all things which were dainty and goodly are departed from thee, and thou shalt find them no more at all. The merchants of these things, which were made rich by her, shall stand afar off for the fear of her torment, weeping and wailing, And saying, Alas, alas, that great city, that was clothed in fine linen, and purple, and scarlet, and decked with gold, and precious stones, and pearls! For in one hour so great riches is come to nought. And every shipmaster, and all the company in ships, and sailors, and as many as trade by sea, stood afar off, And cried when they saw the smoke of her burning, saying, What city is like unto this great city! And they cast dust on their heads, and cried, weeping and wailing, saying, Alas, alas, that great city, wherein were made rich all that had ships in the sea by reason of her costliness! for in one hour is she made desolate. Rejoice over her, thou heaven, and ye holy apostles and prophets; for God hath avenged you on her. And a mighty angel took up a stone like a great millstone, and cast it into the sea, saying, Thus with violence shall that great city Babylon be thrown down, and shall be found no more at all. And the voice of harpers, and musicians, and of pipers, and trumpeters, shall be heard no more at all in thee; and no craftsman, of whatsoever craft he be, shall be found any more in thee; and the sound of a millstone shall be heard no more at all in thee; And the light of a candle shall shine no more at all in thee; and the voice of the bridegroom and of the bride shall be heard no more at all in thee: for thy merchants were the great men of the earth;

for by thy sorceries were all nations deceived. And in her was found the blood of prophets, and of saints, and of all that were slain upon the earth. (Revelation 18:1–24; my emphasis)

The nations are now fallen, and all the inventions of man are judged and destroyed. Men hide themselves from God, and God is about to give the fullness of the kingdoms of the earth to the Lord Jesus Christ. Consider the following excerpt concerning Babylon from E. W. Bullinger's *Commentary on Revelation*:

> In any case we are taken back to the fountain-head, and shown the source and origin of all idolatry. Nimrod is called a mighty hunter. [352] The Targum of Jonathan (an ancient Jewish commentary) interprets this to mean that he was a mighty rebel before the Lord. The Jerusalem Targum reads it as meaning mighty in sin, lying in wait to catch and overthrow men; drawing them away from the worship of the true God, as taught by Shem, to join that taught by Nimrod. Hence, his name became a proverb for any great rebel or Apostate. (Read Gen. x. 9). It is equally impossible to interpret the words of Rome -- and to say that this woman made "the inhabitants of the earth drunk with the wine of her fornication," i.e., made the whole earth partake of her idolatrous system. Neither of Rome, papal or pagan, can this be said. They both drank of her cup; but it is a perversion of all known history, to say that either of them was the tutor of all the nations; and an insult to common sense to apply this to "the inhabitants of the earth for more that 3,000 years before Rome was dreamt of." As Dr. Seiss well puts it, this wine "was already bottled and labelled before the first dispersion. [Gen. xi.]. It

went with that dispersion into every country and nation under heaven. As a matter of fact we find it to this day among all the nations of the earth; affecting, if not controlling their thinking, their politics, their faith, and their worship. Not less than two-thirds of the population of the earth at this hour are Pagan idolaters, driveling under the same old intoxication which came forth from Nimrod and Babylon; whilst the great body of the other third is either Catholic, Jewish, Infidel, or adherents of some tainted and anti-Christian faith and worship. Nor is there a kingdom or government on the face of the whole earth at this hour which does not embody and exhibit more of the spirit of Nimrod than of the spirit, commandments, and inculcations of God. **All the kings of the earth, and all the governments under heaven, have more or less joined in the uncleanness of that same old Babylonian Harlot who had defiled every spot and nook of the whole inhabited world,** notwithstanding that God from the beginning set His seal of wrath upon it. The Jewish whoredoms, and the Papal whoredoms, and the whoredoms of all perverted Christian religionists or other religions, though not entirely letting go the confession of one only God, are still, in essence, the same old harlotry which first found place and embodiment on the banks of the Euphrates. It is the same old Babylon, and her harlot daughters, bearing rule or kingdom upon the dominions of the earth, and intoxicating the inhabitants thereof out of the wine of her fornication." [276]

---

[276] E. W. Bullinger, *Commentary on Revelation*, Kindle edition, Kindle locations 5309–5327; FH Revell, 1909; Rights public domain).

Babylon and the nations have now fallen, and the two great associated cities have now fallen with *Mystery Babylon*. God has now fulfilled the judgment prophecies concerning Jerusalem and the Gentiles, and their cities and nations. Revelation 17 envisions *Mystery Babylon* as the gathering of all nations in support of a whore for a final curtain call on the earth before their final judgment. The great whore and *Mystery Babylon* collectively represent the beast, Jerusalem, and the nations. The vision includes all the peoples of the earth who have been deceived and united in rebellion against God and his Christ. Jerusalem, symbolized by and also part of *Mystery Babylon*, is also numbered with the nations and judged and destroyed together with the nations.

In summary, the vision of Revelation 17 represents two visions of different times on the earth. The visions are gatherings of leaders and kings on the earth and supporting the whore, Jerusalem. The first gathering occurs during the latter first half of the final seven years and is a united conglomeration of nations on the earth gathering for a unified purpose. There will be subsequent gatherings in which the kings and leaders will go through changes over time. Seven kings are identified; they represent seven heads and seven mountains. Five kings will have already fallen, the sixth will be ruling, and the seventh will soon be coming. The final vision represents the conditions on the earth at the time of the middle of the seventieth seven, or 3.5 years after the Antichrist begins his plan to defile Jerusalem. This gathering is depicted in both Revelation 13:1–4 and 17:3. The beast has just been resurrected and is assembled with the other heads and horns. At this final depiction in time, the middle or midst of the final seven years, the six heads and ten horns or kings are all together with the beast and are actively supporting the whore. The conglomeration of nations referenced by the first gathering will be an actual event on the earth—a type of dress rehearsal for the final forty-two months that will follow. God, in Revelation 17, describes the participants and their behavior on the earth in the days that will immediately follow the conference—that is, the final forty-two months. The vision will be understood by those who understand and rightly divide the Word of God. Others, the unbelievers, or those not privy to the accurate division of the Word of God, will be blind to its significance. They will only see a great sign in which they will be deceived into believing that the Antichrist is God. The meetings, and peace conferences as well as the beginnings of sorrows on the earth, will give God's people warning of the days that will immediately follow. The beast, the king of Babylon, will reach the pinnacle of his power during the final forty-two months of the final week. The king of Babylon will declare himself to be God. He will be destroyed by the Lord Jesus Christ at his coming with the saints to the earth in power and great glory, but not before forty-two months of hell on earth. The study and judgment of *Mystery Babylon* fully reveals the implications of Satan's short-lived (forty-two-month) kingdom on the earth. His short forty-two-month rule will be followed by the everlasting kingdom of the Lord Jesus Christ. *Mystery Babylon* can be understood only by a thorough understanding and right division of the Word of God regarding the mystery of the one body—the Jews, Jerusalem, and the nations—represented by *Mystery Babylon*. Once again, the church of the one body of Jesus Christ should not be confused with these judgement scenes concerning the Jews and the Gentiles.

Section 3, Reference 13: Attributes Associated with the Antichrist (Revelation 17)

1. Revelation 17 records a vision given to John by the angel, who had one of the seven last vials. Revelation 17 is an informational interlude that occurs after the pouring out of the seventh vial as documented in Revelation 16:17. The chapter also explains why Babylon comes to God's memory in Revelation 16:19. The pouring out of the seventh vial results in the fall of great Babylon and the fall of the nations. Revelation 17 explains, by way of parenthesis, what and who is meant by Babylon's judgment. The great whore—the woman, and the unification of nations as in original Babylon—is described and judged in Revelation 17. The woman, representing Jerusalem, is also numbered with the nations and documented in Revelation 17. The fall and

judgement of the woman is documented in Revelation 17 and the fall of great Babylon is recorded in Revelation 18.

2. The woman is represented and singled out in Revelation 17, showing that God will initially and separately deal with Jerusalem. Jerusalem will also be numbered with the nations and is judged and destroyed with the other nations of Babylon. The city will be found naked and will be burned with fire.

3. The Antichrist will not be present in his mortal form for the first of these visions in the first half of the final seven years. He will, however, be the seventh king still to come in mortal form, and an eighth in supernatural form. The final peace conference(s) will occur late in the first half of the final seven years. The peace convention will appear to be a unification of nations to rid evil from the earth. The nations will appear to be supporting Jerusalem, and they may very well be in Jerusalem. The first gathering of the nations and six of the seven heads will occur at the beginning of the twenty-three hundred days. From this point forward five will fall and one will remain.

4. The beast is envisioned to be in unison with the nations at the point in time when he has the seven heads and ten horns. The beast is the same beast as that in Revelation 13:1, and the focus will be the seventh head being wounded to death and miraculously resurrected. The key to interpretation is timing. The beast with seven heads and ten horns supporting the whore is the point in time of the middle of the seventieth seven. The point in time of the interpretation, beginning in Revelation 17:7, is during the first half of the final seven years, possibly at the initiation of the final twenty-three hundred days. The angel interprets the condition of the middle of the week from a point in time in the first half of the final seven years. The time will be a period of time before the middle of the week but after the beginning of the last seven years.

5. The middle of the week will be when the deadly wound of the beast, the seventh king, will be healed through a miraculous satanic resurrection also documented in revelation 13:1–3. After the resurrection of the beast, he will become the eighth king and will go on to destruction and be allowed by God to deceive the world. The ones who are not written in the book of life from the foundations of the world will be deceived. (See Revelation 17:8.)
6. The Antichrist will anoint ten kings who, at the time of the first vision, will have no power, but they will receive supernatural power from the Antichrist after one hour with the wild beast. The ten kings, now subservient to the beast, and also referred to as horns, will rule over the earth and destroy the woman and the whore.

In summary, the following key informational points can be gathered from Section 3, reference 13:

1. In the last days, and in the midst of the final seven years, the beast is envisioned together with the nations. He is depicted with the heads and horns as part of a conglomeration of the nations. The beast with his heads and horns initially supports Jerusalem—the woman identified in Revelation 17:6. The first event, or gathering of nations supporting the whore, will occur in the first half of the final seven years; the initiation of the final twenty-three hundred days, but after the beginning of the last seven years. After a timeof transition, five of the seven kings will have fallen, the sixth is still ruling, and the seventh has not yet come. (See Revelation 17:1–18.)
2. God, through his son, Jesus Christ, documents the vision from his perspective. The world sees, at the time of the midst of the final seven years, only a great peace conference on the earth and a significant move toward unity—that is, peace and safety.[277] (See Revelation 17:1–18.)

---

[277] 1 Thessalonians 5:3.

3. The major players for the last days—the heads, the horns, the kings, the people of the earth, and the woman—are identified as part of the vision. God reveals the future for each of the participants—that is, what their roles will be during the final forty-two months. (See Revelation 17:7–18.)
4. The beast is identified as the seventh king, or seventh head, in his mortal form. The beast will then become an eighth king in supernatural form, but he will come out from the seventh. He will then go on to rule for the final forty-two months. (See Revelation 17:10–11).
5. Of the beast, it is stated, "The beast that thou sawest was, and is not; and shall ascend out of the bottomless pit, and go into perdition: and they that dwell on the earth shall wonder, whose names were not written in the book of life from the foundation of the world, when they behold the beast that was, and is not, and yet is." This once again states emphatically that the beast will be part of a great satanic resurrection that will be allowed by God. The deception will be a consequence of man's rejection of God and mankind's insatiable love of sin. (See Revelation 17:8.)

Section 3: Revelation 19:20–21: Reference 14

"[20] And the beast was taken, and with him the false prophet that wrought miracles before him, with which he deceived them that had received the mark of the beast, and them that worshipped his image. These both were cast alive into a lake of fire burning with brimstone. [21] And the remnant were slain with the sword of him that sat upon the horse, which sword proceeded out of his mouth: and all the fowls were filled with their flesh. (Revelation 19:20–21 KJV).

And I saw heaven opened, and behold a white horse; and he that sat upon him was called Faithful and True, and in righteousness he doth judge and make war. His eyes were as a flame of fire, and on his head were many crowns; and he had a name written, that no man knew, but he himself. And he was clothed with a vesture dipped in blood: and his name is called The Word of God.

And the armies which were in heaven followed him upon white horses, clothed in fine linen, white and clean. And out of his mouth goeth a sharp sword, that with it he should smite the nations: and he shall rule them with a rod of iron: and he treadeth the winepress of the fierceness and wrath of Almighty God. And he hath on his vesture and on his thigh a name written, KING OF KINGS, AND LORD OF LORDS. And I saw an angel standing in the sun; and he cried with a loud voice, saying to all the fowls that fly in the midst of heaven, Come and gather yourselves together unto the supper of the great God; That ye may eat the flesh of kings, and the flesh of captains, and the flesh of mighty men, and the flesh of horses, and of them that sit on them, and the flesh of all men, both free and bond, both small and great. And I saw the beast, and the kings of the earth, and their armies, gathered together to make war against him that sat on the horse, and against his army. **And the beast was taken, and with him the false prophet that wrought miracles before him, with which he deceived them that had received the mark of the beast, and them that worshipped his image. These both were cast alive into a lake of fire burning with brimstone.** And the remnant were slain with the sword of him that sat upon the horse, which sword proceeded out of his mouth: and all the fowls were filled with their flesh. (Revelation 19:11–21 KJV; my emphasis)

Reference 14: Revelation 19:20–21 Commentary: "These both were cast alive into the lake of fire burning with brimstone."

The final end and judgment have now come for man's rule on the earth and the short terrifying reign of the wild beast. The beast and the false prophet are judged and are the first to be thrown alive into the lake of fire to endure eternal burning and torment. Note that the beast is joined by the false prophet; both of them committed the unforgiveable sin, blasphemy against God, declaring themselves God or divine. The end of Daniel's seventy sevens of weeks is now complete. All that God promised in Daniel 9:24 is now to be fulfilled, as are many other Old and New Testament scriptures. The twenty-three hundred days are complete, and the sanctuary is cleansed. But before all this, man continues his rebellion against God, continuing in his delusions that he can fight against Almighty God. Man is in a delusional state after the deception on the earth caused by the forty-two-month reign of the Antichrist and the false prophet. This time man's rebellion is directed against the Lord of lords and King of kings. All scripture relating to this time is now approaching final fulfillment, and the rulership of the earth is about to be given to the Lord Jesus Christ and those that are his.

The timeline of Revelation 19 immediately follows the fall of *Mystery Babylon*—the gathering of the nations on the earth and the end of the final forty and two months of Daniel's final seven of years. The remaining scene is one of the kings and armies of the earth, who are now gone mad with Satan's spiritual deception and are gathered together for their great defeat. They are again gathered together as one, and they become delusional in their thoughts against God, believing they can take on and defeat the Almighty.[278] The Lord Jesus Christ has now come and is riding on a white horse, depicted together with the armies of God. His coming to the earth and to Jerusalem is not like his first visit, when he entered the city of Jerusalem humbly on a donkey and was subsequently crucified. This time he comes with the armies of God to destroy those who know not God and to take what has rightfully been given to him by God.

---

[278] Revelation 16:12–14.

All unfulfilled scripture relating to this very time, from both the Old and New Testaments, will now be fulfilled. The related scriptures would be too numerous to list here; however, Psalm 2 and Psalm 110 provide a good summary of these scenes. Consider the following:

> Why do the heathen rage, and the people imagine a vain thing? The kings of the earth set themselves, and the rulers take counsel together, against the LORD, and against his anointed, saying, Let us break their bands asunder, and cast away their cords from us. He that sitteth in the heavens shall laugh: the Lord shall have them in derision. Then shall he speak unto them in his wrath, and vex them in his sore displeasure. Yet have I set my king upon my holy hill of Zion. I will declare the decree: the LORD hath said unto me, **Thou art my Son; this day have I begotten thee. Ask of me, and I shall give thee the heathen for thine inheritance, and the uttermost parts of the earth for thy possession. Thou shalt break them with a rod of iron; thou shalt dash them in pieces like a potter's vessel.** Be wise now therefore, O ye kings: be instructed, ye judges of the earth. Serve the LORD with fear, and rejoice with trembling. Kiss the Son, lest he be angry, and ye perish from the way, when his wrath is kindled but a little. Blessed are all they that put their trust in him. (Psalm 2:1–12 KJV; my emphasis)
>
> A Psalm of David. The LORD said unto my Lord, Sit thou at my right hand, until I make thine enemies thy footstool (the time has now come and God has made the enemies of Christ his footstool). **The LORD shall send the rod of thy strength out of Zion: rule thou in the midst of thine enemies.** Thy people shall be willing in the

day of thy power, in the beauties of holiness from the womb of the morning: thou hast the dew of thy youth. The LORD hath sworn, and will not repent, Thou art a priest for ever after the order of Melchizedek. The Lord at thy right hand shall strike through kings in the day of his wrath. He shall judge among the heathen, he shall fill the places with the dead bodies; he shall wound the heads over many countries. He shall drink of the brook in the way: therefore shall he lift up the head. (Psalm 110:1–7 KJV; my emphasis)

God has now intervened and taken back the earth by force and given the kingdoms of the earth, and all therein, to his son, Jesus Christ. The Lord Jesus Christ destroys the wild beast and the false prophet, who are now thrown bodily into the lake of fire. The following verses below, from other scriptural references within this work, describe the same event from different scriptural vantage points; each is related to the fall of the beast. Observe that the information given in each of the scriptures below builds upon the others without contradiction, adding information and clarifying the same event. Consider the following:

Section 1, References 1, 2, and 3

That thou shalt take up this proverb against the king of Babylon, and say, How hath the oppressor ceased! the golden city ceased! The LORD hath broken the staff of the wicked, and the sceptre of the rulers. He who smote the people in wrath with a continual stroke, he that ruled the nations in anger, is persecuted, and none hindereth. The whole earth is at rest, and is quiet: they break forth into singing ... I will ascend above the heights of the clouds; I will be like the most High. Yet thou shalt be brought

THE LAST DAYS AND THE VILE MAN OF DANIEL

down to hell, to the sides of the pit. They that see thee shall narrowly look upon thee, and consider thee, saying, is this the man that made the earth to tremble, that did shake kingdoms; That made the world as a wilderness, and destroyed the cities thereof; that opened not the house of his prisoners? All the kings of the nations, even all of them, lie in glory, every one in his own house. But thou art cast out of thy grave like an abominable branch, and as the raiment of those that are slain, thrust through with a sword, that go down to the stones of the pit; as a carcase trodden under feet. **Thou shalt not be joined with them in burial, because thou hast destroyed thy land, and slain thy people: the seed of evildoers shall never be renowned** (not buried but thrown into the lake of fire). (Isaiah 14:4–7; 14–20; my emphasis)

Section 2, References 4, 5, 6, 7, and 8

I considered the horns, and, behold, there came up among **them another little horn,** before whom there were three of the first horns plucked up by the roots: and, behold, in this horn were eyes like the eyes of man, and a mouth speaking great things. I beheld till the thrones were cast down, and the Ancient of days did sit, whose garment was white as snow, and the hair of his head like the pure wool: his throne was like the fiery flame, and his wheels as burning fire. A fiery stream issued and came forth from before him: thousand thousands ministered unto him, and ten thousand times ten thousand stood before him: the judgment was set, and the books were opened. **I beheld then because of the voice of the great words which the horn spake: I beheld**

even till the beast was slain, and his body destroyed, and given to the burning flame. (Daniel 7:8–11 KJV; my emphasis).

And in the latter time of their kingdom, when the transgressors are come to the full, a king of fierce countenance, and understanding dark sentences, shall stand up.

And his power shall be mighty, but not by his own power: and he shall destroy wonderfully, and shall prosper, and practise, and shall destroy the mighty and the holy people.

And through his policy also he shall cause craft to prosper in his hand; and he shall magnify himself in his heart, and by peace shall destroy many: **he shall also stand up against the Prince of princes; but he shall be broken without hand** (not destroyed by man but by the Lord Jesus Christ). (Daniel 8:23–25 KJV; my emphasis)

He shall enter also into the glorious land, and many countries shall be overthrown: but these shall escape out of his hand, even Edom, and Moab, and the chief of the children of Ammon. He shall stretch forth his hand also upon the countries: and the land of Egypt shall not escape. But he shall have power over the treasures of gold and of silver, and over all the precious things of Egypt: and the Libyans and the Ethiopians shall be at his steps. But tidings out of the east and out of the north shall trouble him: **therefore he shall go forth with great fury to destroy, and utterly to make away many. And he shall plant the tabernacles of his palace between the seas in the glorious holy mountain; yet he shall come to his end, and none shall help him.** (Daniel 11:41–45 KJV; my emphasis)

Section 3, New Testament References 9 and 10

> For the mystery of iniquity doth already work: only he who now letteth will let, until he be taken out of the way. And then shall that Wicked be revealed, whom the Lord shall consume with the spirit of his mouth, and shall destroy with the brightness of his coming: Even him, whose coming is after the working of Satan with all power and signs and lying wonders, And with all deceivableness of unrighteousness in them that perish; because they received not the love of the truth, that they might be saved. And for this cause God shall send them strong delusion, that they should believe a lie: That they all might be damned who believed not the truth, but had pleasure in unrighteousness. (2 Thessalonians 2:7–12 KJV)

Scripture consistently and accurately portrays the end of the beast/vile man/Antichrist. He is destroyed by the brightness of the coming of the Lord Jesus Christ to the earth at the end of the final seven years, at his coming for Israel. The wild beast and the false prophet are destroyed without hand—that is, without the help of any mortal man, but by the Lord Jesus Christ at his coming for Israel. The beast is a supernatural being and therefore he must be destroyed by the Lord. He is thrown bodily into the lake of fire to burn and be tormented forever and ever. His burial will not be with anyone else who died on the earth. He already died the first death, and his future is to be tormented forever by, figuratively, the second death.

Section 3, Reference 14: Attributes Associated with the Antichrist (Revelation 19:11–21)

1. Revelation 19 documents the end of the beast and his destruction at the end of the final forty-two months. His

end is synchronized and described through many scriptures. He is attacked by the kings of the North and of the South. (See Daniel 11:40.) He comes to his end between the Mediterranean Sea and the Dead Sea, in Jerusalem. (See Daniel 11:45.)
2. The Lord Jesus Christ, King of kings and Lord of lords, will come with the armies of God and destroy the beast and the false prophet. The Lord Jesus Christ will then begin his everlasting rule on the earth. Both the beast and the false prophet will be forever tormented and thrown alive into the lake of fire. (See Revelation 19:20.)

In summary, the following key informational point can be gathered from Section 3, reference 14:

1. The beast is destroyed by the Lord Jesus Christ at his coming. The Lord also destroys the armies gathered at Armageddon. The beast will be thrown alive into the lake of fire. (See Revelation 19:20.)

APPENDIX A

God's Covenant People

THE WORD OF GOD IN the Old Testament is clear concerning blessings to Israel when their Messiah is anointed and accepted by Israel as a nation. His kingdom over Israel, and the world, is one of the central themes of the Old Testament. The promises made to the Patriarchs were everlasting promises that will be fulfilled in totality. God is not a man; he does not lie. Paul's dissertation in Romans 11 and 12 reinforces all Old Testament scriptures concerning Israel and that they still await fulfillment. Romans was written by Paul through revelation he received from Jesus Christ. He wrote concerning the Jews at the time of their dispersion from Israel—the land God promised to their fathers. Their dispersion and removal from the land had no effect on the everlasting promises made to their fathers. The everlasting promises are now held in abeyance but will be fulfilled in the future after the great tribulation, in accordance with God's timetable. The great error in the body of Christ has been to overlook these promises or to claim them for the church. The body of Christ has been the most blessed group of people on the earth, but all of the promises in the scriptures must be rightly divided regarding whom they are written to. The right division of scripture—especially with regard to whom it is written to—is critical for proper interpretation concerning the last days. To understand the last days, the time of the restitution of all things, and the book Of Revelation, right division is a must; without it, significant error will result. Wrong division of scripture has resulted in many flawed and diverse interpretations, causing even the serious searcher of scripture to be frustrated. The church of the one body of Jesus Christ have been given great and precious promises from God, and they are sons and daughters of God through a new birth. The one body of Christ is not the bride of Christ but rather the body of Christ. When God says "body," he means "body," and when he says "bride," he means "bride." A few of the promises given to the body of Christ are recorded in 1 John and Philippians, and these speak of the future of the body of Christ. Consider the following:

> It does not yet appear what we shall be but we know that when he shall appear we shall be like him for we shall see him as he is. (1 John 3:2)
>
> For our conversation is in heaven; from whence also we look for the Saviour, the Lord Jesus Christ: Who shall change our vile body, that it may be fashioned like unto his glorious body, according to the working whereby he is able even to subdue all things unto himself. (Philippians 3:20–21 KJV)

To understand the difference between the bride of Christ (Israel) and the body of Christ (one body composed of former Jews and Gentiles), we must investigate the promises made to the Patriarchs. These promises reveal the significance of the promises made to Israel. The everlasting promises to Israel (the physical seed of Jacob) were made to their fathers by the true God, who cannot lie. God is faithful in everything that he has promised in his word. The Old Testament reveals that God made everlasting promises to Abraham, Isaac, and Jacob, and then suffered through the disobedience of their physical seed. Their disobedience is recorded throughout the Old Testament: the rejection of his law, the killing of his prophets, the worshipping of the Gentile gods, and, finally, the rejection of his son. The disobedience finally resulted in their dispersion in the first century and in the blessings falling upon only a small number of believing Jews (and the rest being blinded). The believing Jews then became part of the body of Christ with the Gentiles. The dispersion did not, and does not, nullify the everlasting promises God made to their fathers concerning the land and the nation. All of God's promises to their fathers will be fulfilled. The dispersion was a result of their following man-made rituals and laws rather than believing God at his word from their hearts. They stumbled at the stumbling block and paid dearly.

The Lord God's continual remembrance of these promises always restrained his hand from completely destroying Jacob's seed; he has always provided and kept a promised physical seed for Abraham.[279] One of the most direct associations linking Israel to the bride of Christ is documented in Revelation 19:7–8 and Revelation 21. But before this, Revelation 17 clearly writes of a great whore who is judged and destroyed by God. Revelation 21 contrasts this with a virgin bride who has made herself ready for her groom after the purification of the tribulation. What is this but the final transition of Israel and Jerusalem from "*not my people*" to the sons of the living God? Consider the following:

> Then said God, call his name Loammi: for ye are not my people, and I will not be your God. Yet the number of the children of Israel shall be as the sand of the sea, which cannot be measured nor numbered; and it shall come to pass, that in the place where it was said unto them, **Ye are not my people**, there it shall be said unto them, Ye are the sons of the living God. Then shall the children of Judah and the children of Israel be gathered together, and appoint themselves one head, and they shall come up out of the land: for great shall be the day of Jezreel. (Hosea 1:9–11 KJV; my emphasis)

---

[279] Romans 11:1–11.

> And there came unto me one of the seven angels which had the seven vials full of the seven last plagues, and talked with me, saying, come hither, I will show thee the bride, the Lamb's wife. And he carried me away in the spirit to a great and high mountain, and showed me that great city, the holy Jerusalem, descending out of heaven from God, Having the glory of God: and her light was like unto a stone most precious, even like a jasper stone, clear as crystal; And had a wall great and high, and had twelve gates, and at the gates twelve angels, and names written thereon, which are the names of the twelve tribes of the children of Israel: On the east three gates; on the north three gates; on the south three gates; and on the west three gates. And the wall of the city had twelve foundations, and in them the names of the twelve apostles of the Lamb. (Revelation 21:9–14)

Contrast this chaste virgin with what the same angel showed John in Revelation 17—the great whore, *Mystery Babylon*. Consider the following:

> And there came one of the seven angels which had the seven vials, and talked with me, saying unto me, Come hither; I will shew unto thee the judgment of the great whore that sitteth upon many waters: With whom the kings of the earth have committed fornication, and the inhabitants of the earth have been made drunk with the wine of her fornication. So he carried me away in the spirit into the wilderness: **and I saw a woman sit upon a scarlet coloured beast, full of names of blasphemy, having seven heads and ten horns. And the woman was arrayed in**

> **purple and scarlet colour, and decked with gold and precious stones and pearls, having a golden cup in her hand full of abominations and filthiness of her fornication: And upon her forehead was a name written, MYSTERY, BABYLON THE GREAT, THE MOTHER OF HARLOTS AND ABOMINATIONS OF THE EARTH. And I saw the woman drunken with the blood of the saints, and with the blood of the martyrs of Jesus: and when I saw her, I wondered with great admiration.** (Revelation 17:1–6 KJV; my emphasis)

The story of Israel is best summarized in Ezekiel 16, where the same transition regarding Israel and Jerusalem is again documented. The chapter portrays Jerusalem as a woman handpicked by God from all the nations of the world to be his bride. In time the bride disavows herself of God and goes off into the uncharted waters of idolatry. The wayward whore, Jerusalem, goes through various stages of abominations before God, symbolizing Israel's Old Testament behavior. The whore is finally judged and destroyed in accordance with Old Testament law. After the judgment, and in the end, God is compassionate and accepts Jerusalem back, remembering his unconditional everlasting promises to their fathers. The great truth here is that God accepts them back because of God's mercy, his loving-kindness, and his forgiveness. The fiery trials of Revelation and Daniel are used as a refiner's fire to purge the called of Israel and make them ready for the marriage feast of the lamb and subsequent return to God.[280] God states that he does this not because they deserve it but because he made promises to their fathers, the Patriarchs. God's plans for and faithfulness to the Patriarchs are remarkable. All his promises to Israel will reach their fulfillment during the last days, at the completion of the final seven years. The final fulfillment documents Jesus Christ coming back to receive his purified bride, who

---

[280] Daniel 11:33–35.

has been cleansed through the fiery trials of the book of Revelation. At his second coming, the remnant of Israel will, from their heart, call on the name of the Lord. The fulfillment of these truths is also documented in Romans 11:26: "*Out of Zion shall come the deliverer to turn ungodliness away from Jacob.*" The veil shrouding Israel's view will be taken away at the end of the last seven years; Jesus Christ will be their Messiah. The verses in the Old Testament must be read with the understanding of these great truths. The book of Revelation, regarding the last days for Israel, will be understood only when the Word of God is rightly divided. An accurate understanding of the period of the mystery of the one body of Christ is also an important key to the right dividing of the Word of Truth. The one body of Jesus Christ will be raptured, or caught away, from the earth by the Lord in the air. The rapture occurs before the coming of the Lord for Israel, and his subsequent earthly reign.

The Old Testament keeps the period of the administration of the mystery of the one body of Christ hidden and secret. Instead the focus is primarily Israel and secondly the Gentiles. The scriptures of Ezekiel 16 include events that have already occurred for Israel, as well as events that will still occur for Israel. The chapter is presented here again to emphasize its critical importance to the right division of the Word of God. This is true of both the Old Testament and the New Testament and, especially, the book of Revelation. This section in God's Word depicts God's remarkable account of the nation of Israel—symbolized by the woman, Jerusalem—from its infancy until its salvation in the last days. Each section is divided in accordance with Israel's history. Consider the following:

> Again the word of the LORD came unto me, saying, Son of man, **cause Jerusalem to know her abominations,** And say, Thus saith the Lord GOD unto Jerusalem; Thy birth and thy nativity is of the land of Canaan; thy father was an Amorite, and thy mother an Hittite. And as for thy nativity, in the day thou wast born thy navel was not cut, neither wast thou washed in

water to supple thee; thou wast not salted at all, nor swaddled at all. None eye pitied thee, to do any of these unto thee, to have compassion upon thee; but thou wast cast out in the open field, to the loathing of thy person, in the day that thou wast born. And when I passed by thee, and saw thee polluted in thine own blood, I said unto thee when thou wast in thy blood, Live; yea, I said unto thee when thou wast in thy blood, Live. I have caused thee to multiply as the bud of the field, and thou hast increased and waxen great, and thou art come to excellent ornaments: thy breasts are fashioned, and thine hair is grown, whereas thou wast naked and bare. Now when I passed by thee, and looked upon thee, behold, thy time was the time of love; and I spread my skirt over thee, and covered thy nakedness: yea, I sware unto thee, and entered into a covenant with thee, saith the Lord GOD, and thou becamest mine. Then washed I thee with water; yea, I thoroughly washed away thy blood from thee, and I anointed thee with oil. I clothed thee also with broidered work, and shod thee with badgers' skin, and I girded thee about with fine linen, and I covered thee with silk. I decked thee also with ornaments, and I put bracelets upon thy hands, and a chain on thy neck. And I put a jewel on thy forehead, and earrings in thine ears, and a beautiful crown upon thine head. Thus wast thou decked with gold and silver; and thy raiment was of fine linen, and silk, and broidered work; thou didst eat fine flour, and honey, and oil: and thou wast exceeding beautiful, and thou didst prosper into a kingdom. And thy renown went forth among the heathen for thy beauty: for it was perfect through my comeliness, which I

> had put upon thee, saith the Lord GOD. (Ezekiel 16:1–14; my emphasis)

The first section of Ezekiel 16 depicts God's analogy of the great city of Jerusalem—a beautiful bride, with God calling her out in her lowliness and bringing her to greatness. We see in this first section all that God made Jerusalem and the children of Israel to be in the day of their original calling out. It was only by the grace of God that they attained this greatness. Notice the analogy of the woman, Jerusalem, being taken from nothing to greatness. The analogy becomes critical to right division of the book of Revelation as we allow God's Word to interpret itself. Further on in Ezekiel, we see this once beautiful woman change dramatically. The woman begins to trust in herself instead of God, and the long, disastrous road down begins. The verses above deal with Israel's rise to power and prominence in the Old Testament; it reaches its high point with Solomon's kingdom. The following verses begin to describe the fall of the same woman from grace. Consider the following:

> But thou didst trust in thine own beauty, and playedst the harlot because of thy renown, and pouredst out thy fornications on every one that passed by; his it was. And of thy garments thou didst take, and deckedst thy high places with divers colours, and playedst the harlot thereupon: the like things shall not come, neither shall it be so. Thou hast also taken thy fair jewels of my gold and of my silver, which I had given thee, and madest to thyself images of men, and didst commit whoredom with them, And tookest thy broidered garments, and coveredst them: and thou hast set mine oil and mine incense before them. My meat also which I gave thee, fine flour, and oil, and honey, wherewith I fed thee, thou hast even set it before them for a sweet savour: and thus it was, saith the Lord

GOD. Moreover thou hast taken thy sons and thy daughters, whom thou hast borne unto me, and these hast thou sacrificed unto them to be devoured. Is this of thy whoredoms a small matter, That thou hast slain my children, and delivered them to cause them to pass through the fire for them? And in all thine abominations and thy whoredoms thou hast not remembered the days of thy youth, when thou wast naked and bare, and wast polluted in thy blood. And it came to pass after all thy wickedness, (woe, woe unto thee! saith the Lord GOD;) That thou hast also built unto thee an eminent place, and hast made thee an high place in every street. Thou hast built thy high place at every head of the way, and hast made thy beauty to be abhorred, and hast opened thy feet to every one that passed by, and multiplied thy whoredoms. Thou hast also committed fornication with the Egyptians thy neighbours, great of flesh; and hast increased thy whoredoms, to provoke me to anger. Behold, therefore I have stretched out my hand over thee, and have diminished thine ordinary food, and delivered thee unto the will of them that hate thee, the daughters of the Philistines, which are ashamed of thy lewd way. Thou hast played the whore also with the Assyrians, because thou wast unsatiable; yea, thou hast played the harlot with them, and yet couldest not be satisfied.29 Thou hast moreover multiplied thy fornication in the land of Canaan unto Chaldea; and yet thou wast not satisfied herewith. How weak is thine heart, saith the Lord GOD, seeing thou doest all these things, the work of an imperious whorish woman; In that thou buildest thine eminent place in the head of every way, and makest thine high place in every street; and hast not been as an harlot, in that thou scornest hire; But as a wife that committeth adultery, which taketh strangers instead of her husband! They give gifts to all whores: but thou givest thy gifts to all thy lovers, and hirest them, that they may come unto thee on every side for thy whoredom. And the contrary is in thee from other women in thy whoredoms, whereas none followeth thee to commit whoredoms: and in that thou givest a reward, and no reward is given unto thee, therefore thou art contrary. Wherefore, O harlot, hear the word of the LORD. (Ezekiel 16: 15–35)

Initially we saw a beautiful woman that God picked from all the nations of the world to be his people and land, but now something has gone terribly wrong. This period represents the fall of Jerusalem, beginning at the end of Solomon's life and continuing to Nebuchadnezzar's invasion and onward. During this time, there were kings in Israel and Judah who did that which was right in the sight of the Lord, but those kings were few and far between. Recall that the mystery of the one body of Jesus Christ is just that—a mystery not revealed in any of the Old Testament scriptures. And it must not be included in any of these scriptures. Attempting to relate these verses to anything except Israel and Jerusalem is wrongly dividing the Word of God and will lead to confusion. The next section describes God's final judgment on the whore, which will not be complete until after the final forty-two months of the end times. In Revelation 17, John is shown the judgment of the great whore. Notice how the woman, or city, in Revelation 17 is strikingly similar (in dress and decor) to the woman depicted in Ezekiel 16. Consider the following from Revelation chapter 17:

And there came one of the seven angels which had the seven vials, and talked with me, saying unto me, Come hither; I will show unto thee the judgment of the great whore that sitteth upon many waters: With whom the kings of the earth have committed fornication, and the inhabitants of the earth have been made drunk with the wine of her fornication. So he carried me away in the spirit into the wilderness: **and I saw a woman sit upon a scarlet coloured beast, full of names of blasphemy, having seven heads and ten horns. And the woman was arrayed in purple and scarlet colour, and decked with gold and precious stones and pearls, having a golden cup in her hand full of abominations and filthiness of her fornication: And upon her forehead was a name written, MYSTERY, BABYLON THE GREAT, THE MOTHER OF HARLOTS AND ABOMINATIONS OF THE EARTH.** And I saw the woman drunken with the blood of the saints, and with the blood of the martyrs of Jesus: and when I saw her, I wondered with great admiration. (Revelation 17:1–6 KJV; my emphasis)

Revelation 17 and Ezekiel 16 both describe the judgment of a city symbolized by a certain whorish woman. In Ezekiel, we know it to be Jerusalem. In Revelation 17, it is a mysterious city, but it is a mystery only to those who fail to put this together from the Old Testament scriptures. Revelation 17 depicts the whore as being numbered with the Gentile nations, *Mystery Babylon*; they are soon both to be destroyed together. It is enticing to look at the abominations throughout the world and try to relate them to this same whore. The disciple of Jesus Christ, or one who follows God's Word with discipline, stays put on what God has revealed in his word and allows God to teach him or her right thinking.

The focus of God, aside from the great period of the mystery of the one body of Christ, is always the lost sheep of the house of Israel. In the last days, God again focuses on his original called-out people, their deliverance, and the promises made to their fathers. God judges his own people first, and then the Gentiles who are without. The judgment arrives on the earth in the last days, when the sins of man are as bad as they were during the time before the flood.[281] Ezekiel 16 goes on to speak of the judgment of the great whore; this is strikingly similar to the judgments listed in Revelation 17. Consider the following:

> Thus saith the Lord GOD; Because thy filthiness was poured out, and thy nakedness discovered through thy whoredoms with thy lovers, and with all the idols of thy abominations, and by the blood of thy children, which thou didst give unto them; Behold, therefore I will gather all thy lovers, with whom thou hast taken pleasure, and all them that thou hast loved, with all them that thou hast hated; I will even gather them round about against thee, and will discover thy nakedness unto them, that they may see all thy nakedness. And I will judge thee, as women that break wedlock and shed blood are judged; and I will give thee blood in fury and jealousy. And I will also give thee into their hand, and they shall throw down thine eminent place, and shall break down thy high places: they shall strip thee also of thy clothes, and shall take thy fair jewels, and leave thee naked and bare. They shall also bring up a company against thee, and they shall stone thee with stones, and thrust thee through with their swords. And they shall burn thine houses with fire, and execute judgments upon thee in the sight of many women: and I will cause thee to cease from playing the harlot, and thou also shalt give no hire any more. So will I make

---

[281] Matthew 24:38.

THE LAST DAYS AND THE VILE MAN OF DANIEL

my fury toward thee to rest, and my jealousy shall depart from thee, and I will be quiet, and will be no more angry.

Because thou hast not remembered the days of thy youth, but hast fretted me in all these things; behold, therefore I also will recompense thy way upon thine head, saith the Lord GOD: and thou shalt not commit this lewdness above all thine abominations. Behold, every one that useth proverbs shall use this proverb against thee, saying, As is the mother, so is her daughter. Thou art thy mother's daughter, that loatheth her husband and her children; and thou art the sister of thy sisters, which loathed their husbands and their children: your mother was an Hittite, and your father an Amorite. And thine elder sister is Samaria, she and her daughters that dwell at thy left hand: and thy younger sister, that dwelleth at thy right hand, is Sodom and her daughters. Yet hast thou not walked after their ways, nor done after their abominations: but, as if that were a very little thing, thou wast corrupted more than they in all thy ways. As I live, saith the Lord GOD, Sodom thy sister hath not done, she nor her daughters, as thou hast done, thou and thy daughters. Behold, this was the iniquity of thy sister Sodom, pride, fullness of bread, and abundance of idleness was in her and in her daughters, neither did she strengthen the hand of the poor and needy.

And they were haughty, and committed abomination before me: therefore I took them away as I saw good. Neither hath Samaria committed half of thy sins; but thou hast multiplied thine abominations more than they, and hast justified thy sisters in all thine abominations which thou hast done. Thou also, which hast judged thy sisters, bear thine own shame for thy sins that thou hast committed more abominable than they: they are more righteous than thou: yea, be thou confounded also, and bear thy shame, in that thou hast justified thy sisters. When I shall bring again their captivity, the captivity of Sodom and her daughters, and the captivity of Samaria and her daughters, then will I bring again the captivity of thy captives in the midst of them: That thou mayest bear thine own shame, and mayest be confounded in all that thou hast done, in that thou art a comfort unto them. When thy sisters, Sodom and her daughters, shall return to their former estate, and Samaria and her daughters shall return to their former estate, then thou and thy daughters shall return to your former estate. For thy sister Sodom was not mentioned by thy mouth in the day of thy pride, Before thy wickedness was discovered, as at the time of thy reproach of the daughters of Syria, and all that are round about her, the daughters of the Philistines, which despise thee round about. Thou hast borne thy lewdness and thine abominations, saith the LORD. For thus saith the Lord GOD; I will even deal with thee as thou hast done, which hast despised the oath in breaking the covenant. (Ezekiel 16: 36–59)

The judgment of the great whore is depicted in the verses above. God gives detailed account of the reason this judgment comes. The comparison to Revelation 17 is strikingly similar and relates to God's final judgment, beginning with his people. The detailed account is not present in Revelation 17 because God already detailed it extensively throughout the whole Old Testament. Revelation 17 deals with the people and players (Gentile nations) that God will use to fulfill this judgment. It is the Old Testament scriptures that give further details and explanation as to the judgment of the great whore. After all this judgment, we then see God once again remembering his promises to the Patriarchs. God finally establishes an everlasting covenant for Israel—not because they deserve it, but because of the everlasting promises he made to their fathers.

> Nevertheless I will remember my covenant with thee in the days of thy youth, and I will establish unto thee an everlasting covenant. Then thou shalt remember thy ways, and be ashamed, when thou shalt receive thy sisters, thine elder and thy younger: and I will give them unto thee for daughters, but not by thy covenant. And I will establish my covenant with thee; and thou shalt know that I am the LORD: That thou mayest remember, and be confounded, and never open thy mouth any more because of thy shame, when I am pacified toward thee for all that thou hast done, saith the Lord GOD. (Ezekiel 16:60–63)

The wayward woman portrayed as Jerusalem, and representative of Israel, is mentioned several other times in the Old Testament, as well as in the book of Revelation. The latter is not as clear, but it will be clear to the believing Jews at the time of the last seven years when these Old Testament verses are assimilated with the book of Revelation. Once again we see the critical link between the book of Revelation and Old Testament Israel; a central focus of the book of Revelation. Revelation 21 speaks of the great city Jerusalem, the virgin bride, coming down from heaven and representing the twelve tribes of Israel. The woman in Revelation 21 is listed as a bride who has made herself ready. The transition from Revelation 17 to Revelation 21 is remarkable; the wayward whore is judged by God and then, after the time of Jacob's trouble, transformed into a chaste virgin, ready for the marriage feast of the lamb. God fulfills all remaining unfulfilled promises to Israel from antiquity. The cleansing and the making ready of the bride is God's doing, and it is wonderful for those with ears to hear and eyes to see.

One other compelling section of the Old Testament scripture will now be examined. The record is in Hosea, in which God tells Hosea to take a bride and have children even though the bride is a harlot. The bride leaves Hosea several times for others, but in time, Hosea is instructed to buy back his bride, or harlot, from slavery. The buying back occurs after she goes whoring in foreign nations with strange men. The story is an actual representation of the nation of Israel and the evolution of their relationship with God; it reflects their going after idols and abandoning the true God. After all of their atrocities, and whoring with other idols, God rescues them, buys them back, and establishes his covenant with them forever. The story is one of the infinite mercy of God toward a people that he called out. The story is true and will be played out at the time of the end. The whole book of Hosea describes this story and is revealing in this context. A portion of chapter 1 is listed below. Consider the following:

> The word of the LORD that came unto Hosea, the son of Beeri, in the days of Uzziah, Jotham, Ahaz, and Hezekiah, kings of Judah, and in the days of Jeroboam the son of Joash, king of Israel. The beginning of the word of the LORD by Hosea. And the LORD said to Hosea, Go, take unto thee a wife of whoredoms and children of whoredoms: for the land hath committed great whoredom, departing from the LORD. So he went and took Gomer the daughter of Diblaim; which conceived, and bare him a son. And the LORD said unto him, Call his name Jezreel; for yet a little while, and I will avenge the blood of Jezreel upon the house of Jehu, and will cause to cease the kingdom of the house of Israel. And it shall come to pass at that day, that I will break the bow of Israel in the valley of Jezreel. And she

> conceived again, and bare a daughter. And God said unto him, Call her name Loruhamah: for I will no more have mercy upon the house of Israel; but I will utterly take them away. But I will have mercy upon the house of Judah, and will save them by the LORD their God, and will not save them by bow, nor by sword, nor by battle, by horses, nor by horsemen. Now when she had weaned Loruhamah, she conceived, and bare a son. Then said God, Call his name Loammi: for ye are not my people, and I will not be your God. Yet the number of the children of Israel shall be as the sand of the sea, which cannot be measured nor numbered; and it shall come to pass, that in the place where it was said unto them, Ye are not my people, there it shall be said unto them, Ye are the sons of the living God. Then shall the children of Judah and the children of Israel be gathered together, and appoint themselves one head, and they shall come up out of the land: for great shall be the day of Jezreel. (Hosea 1: 1–11)

One item God often uses in the analogies in his word is the wedding feast. The culmination of the book of Revelation is the long-awaited marriage of the lamb to his purified bride. The final feast will include the friends of the bride, the friends of the groom, the body of Christ, and, of course, the bride, who has made herself ready. The book of Revelation begins with Israel ("*not my people*"), depicted as the wayward woman, and ends with the great wedding feast of the lamb, in which Israel is purified through the fiery trials of the book of Revelation. Revelation corresponds directly with the story of Hosea ("*not my people*") and then transitions to the children of Israel being "*sons of the living God.*"

Throughout the centuries, wise people who have rightly divided the Word of God have uniformly understood that the final days would focus on Israel, and especially Jerusalem. The called of

Israel and Jerusalem will be blessed with the blessings spoken of by all of the Old Testament prophets. All of the judgments pronounced against her must also be totally fulfilled; the Word of God cannot be broken. Romans 11:26 drives home this point: *"And so all Israel shall be saved: as it is written there shall come out of Zion the deliverer and shall turn away ungodliness from Jacob."*

The veil will be taken away from Israel in the latter days, when the fullness of the Gentiles is come in. The veil was placed upon national Israel by God because of their unbelief. The veil distorts their sight: *"seeing, they may not see, and hearing, they may not understand."* Right division of the Word of God concerning Israel is critical to proper interpretation of the book of Revelation. Once this is understood, the believer is enlightened and can accurately understand the events and the focus of God in the last days concerning the Jews and the Gentiles. Right division will also allow fulfillment of God's will for the one body of Jesus Christ concerning the last days: *"That day shall not overtake us as a thief, for we are all children of the light and of the day."*[282] In addition, the lover of God will know what to look for and what to watch for in the last days: *"Therefore I say to watch and be sober."*[283] The Word of God is flawless and promotes clear understanding when it is rightly divided; if the scripture is rightly divided, we will know what to watch for.

Some additional related scriptures are listed below for reference. The everlasting promises made to Abraham, Isaac, and Jacob, and their descendants, will be fulfilled exactly and precisely as the Lord has set them forth. God's heart toward Israel and the land is clearly conveyed through right division concerning these promises. The Lord Jesus Christ will come back as Lord of lords and King of kings to rule over Israel and the world. God is not slack concerning his promises; all of them, even those made thousands of years ago to the Patriarchs, will be fulfilled.

God's initial promise to Abraham in Genesis reveals the future plan for Israel and all the nations of the earth. God's promises focus

---

[282] 1 Thessalonians 5:4.
[283] 1 Thessalonians 5:6.

on the gifts and deeds bestowed on the few to benefit the many. God's promises may be summed up this way: the declaration and assurance of God made at first to Abraham, Isaac, and Jacob and then to the whole nation of Israel is that (1) he would be their God, (2) they would be his people, and (3) he (God) would dwell in their midst. The blessing of land and of growth of a nation as well as the call to bless the nations was part of the promise to Abraham. Added to these promises were a series of divine actions in history that assured Israel of their authenticity. The words and deeds of God began to constitute the continuously unfolding divine plan by which all the peoples and nations would benefit from God's calling out of the nation.

The promises to Abraham and his promised seed are immediately applicable to this study. Recognition of these promises clearly reveals God's plan for the land and the people of God, in whom he made everlasting promises. The promises are not bound by a time limit; the everlasting theme of the promises transcends time and will have everlasting implications.

The promise to Abraham is as follows:

> And, behold, the word of the LORD came unto him, saying, This shall not be thine heir; but he that shall come forth out of thine own bowels shall be thine heir. And he brought him forth abroad, and said, **Look now toward heaven, and tell the stars, if thou be able to number them: and he said unto him, So shall thy seed be. And he believed in the LORD; and he counted it to him for righteousness. And he said unto him, I am the LORD that brought thee out of Ur of the Chaldees, to give thee this land to inherit it.** And he said, Lord GOD, whereby shall I know that I shall inherit it? And he said unto him, Take me an heifer of three years old, and a she goat of three years old, and a ram of three years old, and a turtledove, and a young pigeon. And he took unto him all these, and divided them

in the midst, and laid each piece one against another: but the birds divided he not. And when the fowls came down upon the carcases, Abram drove them away. And when the sun was going down, a deep sleep fell upon Abram; and, lo, an horror of great darkness fell upon him. And he said unto Abram, Know of a surety that thy seed shall be a stranger in a land that is not theirs, and shall serve them; and they shall afflict them four hundred years; And also that nation, whom they shall serve, will I judge: and afterward shall they come out with great substance. And thou shalt go to thy fathers in peace; thou shalt be buried in a good old age. But in the fourth generation they shall come hither again: for the iniquity of the Amorites is not yet full. And it came to pass, that, when the sun went down, and it was dark, behold a smoking furnace, and a burning lamp that passed between those pieces. **In the same day the LORD made a covenant with Abram, saying, Unto thy seed have I given this land, from the river of Egypt unto the great river, the river Euphrates: The Kenites, and the Kenizzites, and the Kadmonites, And the Hittites, and the Perizzites, and the Rephaims, And the Amorites, and the Canaanites, and the Girgashites, and the Jebusites.** (Genesis 15:4–21 KJV; my emphasis)

Additional Promises to Abraham, Isaac, and Jacob can be found in the following verses:

> Neither shall thy name any more be called Abram, but thy name shall be Abraham; for a father of many nations have I made thee. And I will make thee exceeding fruitful, and I will

make nations of thee, and kings shall come out of thee. **And I will establish my covenant between me and thee and thy seed after thee in their generations for an everlasting covenant, to be a God unto thee, and to thy seed after thee. And I will give unto thee, and to thy seed after thee, the land wherein thou art a stranger, all the land of Canaan, for an everlasting possession; and I will be their God.** And God said unto Abraham, Thou shalt keep my covenant therefore, thou, and thy seed after thee in their generations. This is my covenant, which ye shall keep, between me and you and thy seed after thee; Every man child among you shall be circumcised. And ye shall circumcise the flesh of your foreskin; and it shall be a token of the covenant betwixt me and you. (Genesis 17:5–11 KJV; my emphasis)

God establishes Abraham's promise to Isaac: Sojourn in this land, and I will be with thee, and will bless thee; for unto thee, and unto thy seed, I will give all these countries, and I will perform the oath which I sware unto Abraham thy father; And I will make thy seed to multiply as the stars of heaven, and will give unto thy seed all these countries; and in thy seed shall all the nations of the earth be blessed; Because that Abraham obeyed my voice, and kept my charge, my commandments, my statutes, and my laws. (Genesis 26:3–5 KJV)

And, behold, the LORD stood above it, and said, I am the LORD God of Abraham thy father, and the God of Isaac: the land whereon thou liest, to thee will I give it, and to thy seed; And thy seed shall be as the dust of the earth, and thou shalt spread abroad to the west, and to the east, and to the north, and to the south:

and in thee and in thy seed shall all the families of the earth be blessed. And, behold, I am with thee, and will keep thee in all places whither thou goest, and will bring thee again into this land; for I will not leave thee, until I have done that which I have spoken to thee of. (Genesis 28:13–15)

And (God) said unto me, Behold, I will make thee fruitful, and multiply thee, and I will make of thee a multitude of people; and will give this land to thy seed after thee for an everlasting possession. (Genesis 48:4)

Seeing that Abraham shall surely become a great and mighty nation, and all the nations of the earth shall be blessed in him? For I know him, that he will command his children and his household after him, and they shall keep the way of the LORD, to do justice and judgment; that the LORD may bring upon Abraham that which he hath spoken of him. (Genesis 18:18–19)

These promises were made to the Patriarchs, the fathers of Israel. The promises that God made to them are still real and are still truth today. All of them will be fulfilled exactly as God spoke them into being through holy men of God, who were moved by the Holy Spirit. God is not a man; he does not lie. All will be fulfilled accurately and completely. These are everlasting promises made concerning the land and the people. Every word will come to pass exactly the way it is set forth in the above promises. *"The lord is not slack concerning his promise, as some men count slackness; but is long-suffering to us ward, not willing that any should perish, but that all should come to repentance."*[284]

---

[284] 2 Peter 3:9.

APPENDIX B

The Holy Place and the Abomination of Desolation of Matthew 24

THE LORD JESUS CHRIST IN Matthew 24:15, warns those in Jerusalem that when they see the abomination of desolation set up, or standing, in the holy place, flight will be the only option for survival. The Lord quotes Daniel as the origin of the prophecy and associates the event with the last days for Israel. The event is so cataclysmic that the Lord instructs all of believing Israel to vacate Jerusalem and Judea for the mountains when this event occurs. Matthew 24 contains several prophetic passages associated with the last days, especially as related to Israel. In Matthew 24:4–22, the Lord answers the apostles' question stated in Matthew 24:3 regarding the end of the age. Recall their question: "*And as he sat on the mount of Olives, the disciples came unto him privately, saying, Tell us, **when shall these things be? and what shall be the sign of thy coming, and of the end of the world?***" The Lord's response was as follows:

> And Jesus answered and said unto them, Take heed that no man deceive you. ⁵ For many shall come in my name, saying, I am Christ; and shall deceive many. ⁶ And ye shall hear of wars and rumours of wars: see that ye be not troubled:

for all these things must come to pass, but the end is not yet. ⁷ For nation shall rise against nation, and kingdom against kingdom: and there shall be famines, and pestilences, and earthquakes, in divers places. ⁸ All these are the beginning of sorrows. ⁹ Then shall they deliver you up to be afflicted, and shall kill you: and ye shall be hated of all nations for my name's sake. ¹⁰ And then shall many be offended, and shall betray one another, and shall hate one another. ¹¹ And many false prophets shall rise, and shall deceive many. ¹² And because iniquity shall abound, the love of many shall wax cold. ¹³ But he that shall endure unto the end, the same shall be saved. ¹⁴ And this gospel of the kingdom shall be preached in all the world for a witness unto all nations; and then shall the end come. ¹⁵ **When ye therefore shall see the abomination of desolation, spoken of by Daniel the prophet, stand in the holy place, (whoso readeth, let him understand:)** ¹⁶ Then let them which be in Judaea flee into the mountains: ¹⁷ Let him which is on the housetop not come down to take any thing out of his house: ¹⁸ Neither let him which is in the field return back to take his clothes.

¹⁹ And woe unto them that are with child, and to them that give suck in those days! ²⁰ But pray ye that your flight be not in the winter, neither on the sabbath day: ²¹ For then shall be great tribulation, such as was not since the beginning of the world to this time, no, nor ever shall be. ²² And except those days should be shortened, there should no flesh be saved: but for the elect's sake those days shall be shortened. (Matthew 24:4–22 KJV)

God counsels Israel to flee as the only course of action when the *abomination that causes desolation* is set up *at the holy place in Jerusalem*. The abomination that causes desolation, the most significant world changing event of the end times, the satanic resurrection of the Antichrist, will occur at the time of the middle of the last seven years. Before this occurs on the earth, there will be a time of sorrows which will begin well before the middle of the last seven years. The time of the beginning of sorrows referenced by our Lord in Matthew 24:8 will be initiated at the beginning of the final twenty-three hundred days as stated in Daniel 8:14. The time of sorrows is also the time when the first four of the seals of Revelation 6 are opened and the sorrows associated with wars, famines, pestilence, and the initial rise of antichrist to power; causing death to a quarter of all those on the earth will occur to those on the earth. After the seals are first opened on the earth, those who know the lord will preach the gospel to all those on the earth for the next 1,040 days, or until the rise of the Antichrist and his final rule at the time of the middle of the final seven years.

The rising from the dead of this false messiah is identified as the abomination that causes desolation on the earth. Where is the holy place where this event happens? What will be the warning signs? The answers must be revealed in the Word of God, or else there is no answer until God reveals the meaning. There are references in the Bible to a holy place throughout scripture. References to this holy place must be properly examined to accurately understand God's Word. The scripture also states in Matthew 24:15, "*Whosoever readeth, let him understand.*" The Greek word translated as "understand" means "To pay focused attention to; to consider accurately." God instructs in Matthew that the meaning is not obvious and must be examined in his word to get to the accurate interpretation. The Greek words for "holy" and "place" have their roots from the Greek words "*hagios*" and "*topos*," respectively. Together the words form a unique meaning: *"A holy sanctified set-apart place in the eyes of God."* The word "place" and the instruction for Israel to flee to the mountains puts the location of the holy place on the earth, but at a place that is considered holy, or set apart to God. The scripture states that it is a *place*; a building or temple is not mentioned. There are three key verses that document the same event at the holy place; they are Matthew 24:15, Daniel 11:31, and 2 Thessalonians 2:4. Each one expresses the idea of a place, not a physical temple. To get an understanding of the holy place, we must explore the similar scriptural references—especially those associated with the last seven years for Israel. First, we will explore Matthew 24 itself to understand the time and context. Matthew 24 contains significant information concerning the last seven years for Israel. The focus of the seals and the results of their opening is further restricted to the final twenty-three hundred days. In fact, the entire last seven years encompassing the final twenty-three hundred days—the successive openings of the seals as documented in Revelation 6—is summarized in Matthew 24. The following parallels can be gathered from a comparison of both chapters:

Matthew 24	The order of seals in Revelation	Revelation 6
Matthew 24:4–5	First: the false Christ	Revelation 6:1–2
Matthew 24:6–7	Second: wars	Revelation 6:3–4
Matthew 24:7	Third: famines	Revelation 6:5–6
Matthew 24:7	Fourth: pestilences	Revelation 6:7–8
Matthew 24:8–14	Fifth: martyrdoms	Revelation 6:9–11
Matthew 24:29–30	Sixth: signs in heaven of advent	Revelation 6:12–17

Matthew 24:4-30 summarizes the first six seals summarized in Revelation 6. The events take us up to the signs immediately preceding the second advent of the Lord in his glory at the end of the seventieth seven. The first five of these seals are associated with the time between the initiation of the twenty-three hundred days and the middle of the final seven years. The similarities of Revelation 6 and Matthew 24 are deliberate, and both associate and describe the final seven years—especially for Israel. To understand the holy place and the *Abomination of (that causes) Desolation*, relevant scriptures must be examined in the Word of God. The book of Revelation and the

book of Daniel represent the core of what God would have us know about the last days. They also provide relevant information regarding the holy place, as both record critical information with respect to the holy place. In Matthew 24:15, the Lord instructs us to look to the book of Daniel to understand the events of the last days. The Lord himself, through this instruction, acknowledges that the book of Daniel contains significant information regarding the last days.

The holy place referenced in Matthew 24:15 does not reference any building; rather, it references a place on the earth that God considered holy or set apart. If God meant to refer to a building, he would have referred to a building in Matthew 24:15. The place mentioned in Matthew 24:15 is holy to God with or without a building or temple on its premises. God uses separate Greek words to distinguish the temple building from a place that is holy to God. The Greek word used for "place" in Matthew 24:15 is the Greek word "*topo*," which is the root of the English word "topographical," meaning *"A place on the earth."* The crucial point here is that this is a place that is holy to God, regardless of what is on it. The question then becomes, what place on Earth is holy to God?

The Old Testament scriptures describe how God calls out Israel as his special people. Through this special calling of a nation, all the nations on the earth would be blessed. The called Israelites were to be a "*holy people*" unto the Lord with a land and city that God would bless forever. The original promise was given to Abraham, who was willing to offer his son at the place determined by God. The place of Abraham's attempted sacrifice of his son Isaac became a special place to God. The same place eventually became the place where God instructed David to build the temple. The place was also where God stated to Solomon that he would always remember what Abraham was willing to do in sacrifice and obedience. The scripture states that when God remembered what Abraham was willing to do for God, at the place determined by God, he would turn from his wrath toward Israel—if they repented from their sin.

The holy place is then traced back in the Old Testament to an area atop Mount Sion in modern-day Jerusalem. God calls the place holy throughout his word, as you will see in the scriptures that follow.

The holiness of the place was associated with Abraham's willingness to offer his only son, Isaac, at the very same place. God's response to Abraham's sacrifice and willingness to offer his son Isaac was to offer his only begotten son—the Lord Jesus Christ—for the sins of the many, sparing Isaac, and Abraham's grief, in the process. The key point is that the place was holy long before any building was built upon it. The holy place is defined as the place where Abraham was willing to offer his son, his only son of promise, to God. The sacrifice was made in obedience to the request from God. God relented in his request to offer Isaac, but he understood that a man on the earth, Abraham, was willing to offer his son to God. In the end, God did offer his only begotten son for the sins of mankind because of what Abraham was willing to do. The same holy place became the place where David was instructed to build the temple in Jerusalem. Subsequently, the first and second Jewish temples were built at this holy place. The Holy of Holies within the temple marked the exact rock where Abraham was willing to offer Isaac. So, the place was holy to God before a building or temple was erected because of what Abraham was willing to do. Consider the following:

> And Abraham said, My son, God will provide himself a lamb for a burnt offering: so they went both of them together. **And they came to the place which God had told him of;** and Abraham built an altar there, and laid the wood in order, and bound Isaac his son, and laid him on the altar upon the wood.
> And Abraham stretched forth his hand, and took the knife to slay his son And the angel of the LORD called unto him out of heaven, and said, Abraham, Abraham: and he said, Here am I. And he said, Lay not thine hand upon the lad, neither do thou any thing unto him: for now I know that thou fearest God, seeing thou hast not withheld thy son, thine only son from me. And Abraham lifted up his eyes, and looked, and behold behind

him a ram caught in a thicket by his horns: and Abraham went and took the ram, and offered him up for a burnt offering in the stead of his son. And Abraham called the name of that place **Jehovahjireh: as it is said to this day, In the mount of the LORD it shall be seen.** And the angel of the LORD called unto Abraham out of heaven the second time, And said, By myself have I sworn, saith the LORD, for because thou hast done this thing, and hast not withheld thy son, thine only son: That in blessing I will bless thee, and in multiplying I will multiply thy seed as the stars of the heaven, and as the sand which is upon the sea shore; and thy seed shall possess the gate of his enemies. (Genesis 22:8–17 KJV)

The place where Abraham was willing to offer Isaac to God caused God to set apart the place as holy. The word proclaimed by God as *"Jehovahjireh,"* when translated, means, *"The place where God is seen."* This is Mount Moriah, which is the place where God instructed David to build the temple. The significance of this place cannot be overstated; it is also the place where the Lord will come and be seen and revealed on earth after the final forty-two months. It became a *holy place* because of what Abraham was willing to do in obedience to God. It is also the place where God promised to give his only begotten son, and then send his only begotten son in the last days, for the sins of mankind. Since it was God who instructed Abraham to go to this certain place, the place may have a special significance to God. Whatever the significance to God, it is clear that God went out of his way to instruct Abraham to go to this certain place. There are many theories as to why God picked this place, but of more importance is that Abraham was willing to offer his son—his only son of promise—to God. God requested the ultimate of Abraham, and Abraham was willing to obey; Abraham believed and obeyed God. From that day forward, God observed the place as holy.

The *holy place* is located atop Mount Moriah. Consider this excerpt from the *Baker Encyclopedia of the Bible*:

> Moriah.
>
> Name used twice in the OT. Abraham was sent to sacrifice his son Isaac in "the land of Moriah" (Gn 22:2). Because in the narrative it is said that the ram was "provided" in the place of Isaac (vv 8, 14) when God "appeared" to Abraham, it has been suggested that the form of the name "Moriah" may be connected with this. (The Hebrew verb ra'a can have meanings "see," "provide," "appear," and the ending -iah is the shortened form of the name of the Lord which is found in many Hebrew names.)
>
> In 2 Chronicles 3:1 Mt Moriah is the place of Solomon's temple, specifically identified with the threshing floor of Ornan the Jebusite (cf. 2 Sm 24; 1 Chr 21), but not explicitly with the place of Abraham's sacrifice. Some, however, see in the description of the Lord's appearing to David a reminder of his appearing to Abraham there. The Jewish historian Josephus (Antiq. 1.13.2, 7.13.4) clearly connects the place of the temple with the place where Isaac was offered up, as does the 2nd-century B.C. Book of Jubilees (18:13). Samaritan tradition linked Moriah with Mt Gerizim. Muslim tradition connects the Dome of the Rock which stands today on the site of the Jerusalem temple with Abraham's sacrifice of Isaac on the great rock under the dome of the mosque.[285]

---

[285] W. A. Elwell and B. J. Beitzel, *Baker Encyclopedia of the Bible* (Grand Rapids, Michigan: Baker Book House, 1988), 1488–89.

The rock on Moriah where God instructed Abraham to offer Isaac became a "*Holy,*" or sanctified, place to God. The place was holy to God before the foundation of a temple was built. The place is still holy although the temple was destroyed. At the dedication of the first temple in Jerusalem, Solomon asked God to keep the place holy and to listen to the prayer of his people when they prayed to this place. God also stated that he would dwell there forever. Consider the following: *"And it came to pass, when Solomon had finished the building of the house of the LORD, and the king's house, and all Solomon's desire which he was pleased to do, That the LORD appeared to Solomon the second time, as he had appeared unto him at Gibeon. And the LORD said unto him, I have heard thy prayer and thy supplication that thou hast made before me: I have hallowed this house, which thou hast built, to put my name there forever; and mine eyes and mine heart shall be there perpetually"* (1 Kings 9:1–3 KJV)[286]

The holy place is also the place God showed mercy to David; that is, he had mercy on Israel and Jerusalem after David prayed for relief from the curse, as recorded in the Old Testament.[287] It is evident that the holy place is where God grants grace and mercy to Israel because of God's remembrance of Abraham's willing sacrifice. The place also marks the location where Messiah is to come to save Israel after the tribulation.[288] Relating to this, and referring back to Matthew 24:15, and 2 Thessalonians 2:4, it is also the place where the devil tries to inhabit and declare himself to be God, attempting to occupy the holy place before the return of the Lord Jesus Christ. He does this by setting the *abomination of (that causes) desolation at the same holy place through his possessed instrument, the Antichrist.*[289] This is why the abomination that causes desolation, or the supernatural vision of the supernatural Antichrist, at the holy place is so desolating. The devil tries to occupy the *holy place* in the last days with his supernatural instrument, the Antichrist, who declares

---

[286] Read 1 Kings 8–9.
[287] 2 Samuel 24:15–21.
[288] Romans 11:26.
[289] 2 Thessalonians 2:4; Daniel 11:31.

himself God. The devil, understanding the scriptures, does this at the same place God promises to send his son, Jesus Christ. The devil, in effect, attempts to occupy the holy place with his supernatural being, who declares himself God at the same place where God states his son will be revealed and seen by all the earth. The appearing of the resurrected Antichrist at this place begins the final forty-two months of the worst time in human history.

Matthew 24:15 states, "*Whoso readeth let him understand.*" The scripture does not leave us wondering where the holy place is; this must be understood through careful examination of the Word of God. The evidence is overwhelming that the holy place is Mount Moriah in Jerusalem—Abraham's place of sacrifice to God. As stated earlier, the place is holy without a temple constructed on Mount Moriah. The scriptures state that, at the time of the end, an *abomination that causes desolation* will be set up at this very place. It is further stated that after the setting up of this *abomination that causes desolation*, desolations and destruction will follow for forty-two months. The Lord instructs the believing Jews in Matthew 24:16–18 to take flight from Jerusalem and Judea; this is presented as the only option that will be available when this event occurs on the earth at the time of the middle of the last seven years. The holy place is now understood to be the original Mount Moriah, where Abraham was willing to offer his only son of promise to God. The setting up of the *abomination that causes desolation*, as recorded in Matthew 24:15, is the catalyst that causes the destruction of the earth. What is this *abomination that causes desolation*? When does it occur? How long does it last? What characteristics are we to look for?

Matthew 24 lists many details associated with last seven years for Israel, and ultimately the end of Gentile rulership of the world. The section is divided into two, as with many of the references to the final seven years of Daniels seventy-sevens of years prophecy. The first section begins with the *beginning of the time of sorrows and ends at the time of the setting up of the abomination that causes desolations on the earth*. The section is initiated at the beginning of the twenty-three hundred days after the start of the final seven years. This section is captured in Matthew 24:4–14. The second section references the final forty-two months, the worst time in human history on the earth. The second section is captured in Matthew 24:15–28. Matthew 24:16 and onward also documents the dispersion of the Jews, those called of God, to leave Jerusalem and the land of Israel. It will be this group which will be protected by God, and who God will plead with once again in the wilderness. Additionally, Revelation 2 and 3 are addressed to these dispersed Jews and will ultimately make up the seven churches of the Jews scattered after their dispersion from Jerusalem and Israel. The dispersion of the Jews in the last days is the result of their obedience to the Lord concerning his instruction in Matthew 24:16–18. These believing Jews, at the time of the end, will understand these very words spoken by the Lord in Matthew 24, and they will obey his instruction to vacate Jerusalem and the land of Israel. They will understand that this is the time of the vengeance of the living God. They will see these judgments recorded in the book of Revelation coming on the earth: the seals, the trumpets, and the vials. They will understand the parallels of the book of Daniel (their prophet), the Gospels and the book of the Revelation of Jesus Christ referencing the same last-time events. References regarding the seals and the judgments parallel with Matthew 24 are also found through careful comparison of Revelation 6 and Daniel 9–12.

The book of Daniel contains two important references to the *abomination that causes desolation*, as referenced by the Lord in Matthew 24:15. The first reference gives information as to when this event occurs and what takes place at the time of this event. Consider the following: "And he shall confirm the covenant with many for one week: and in the midst of the week he shall cause the sacrifice and the oblation to cease, **and for the overspreading of abominations he shall make it desolate, even until the consummation, and the determined shall be poured out upon the desolate**" (Daniel 9:27 KJV; my emphasis).

Daniel 9:27 lists certain actions of the Antichrist before, during, and after the setting up of the *abomination that causes desolation.* The actual initiation of the action against the holy place that eventually causes desolations to occur on the earth will begin at the middle, or midst, of the last seven years. It is important to understand that there are two seven-year periods referenced in the Old Testament Scriptures. The first seven-year period begins with the Antichrist making a league or covenant with a great super-power nation in which he strengthens himself for seven years.[290] The second seven year period begins at the midst, or the middle, of the first seven-year period, and is the seven-years identified as the final seven years in Daniels 9.24 prophecy. The final seven years is the beginning of the planning of the Antichrist to end the Jewish daily sacrifice, through abominations and desolations on the earth. It is this supernaturally raised Antichrist, *the abomination that causes complete destruction on the earth*, which initiates the beginning of the final forty-two months. This time is alluded to in the latter half of Daniel 9:27, and is described as the *consummation;* the time in which God is determined to pour out his undiluted wrath on the earth. This is also known as the wrath of God toward an evil and rebelling generation. The destruction and wrath of God will continue for the following forty-two months. The timing is consistent with other scriptures, while additional events occur at the middle, or midst, of the last seven years. It is this abomination set up at the holy place in Jerusalem that is the catalyst for the wrath of God on the earth. The events consist of the Jewish sacrifice coming to an end and Jerusalem and Judea falling into the hands of enemies of God. Following this is the overspreading of abominations causing desolations on the earth. Matthew 24 correlates well with Daniel 9:27 as well as Daniel chapter 11 and 12 as to the sequence of events of the last days. Daniel 12.11 gives additional information as to the timing of the setting up of the abomination that causes desolation. Daniel 9:27, in effect, states that desolations will continue and spread on the earth until the complete destruction decreed by God is complete; the final forty-two months—the second part of the last seven years. Once again, this is corroborated with the other scriptures regarding days, months, and years, all adding up to 3.5 years, forty-two months, or 1,260 days.

---

[290] Daniel 11.23, Daniel 9.27.

THE LAST DAYS AND THE VILE MAN OF DANIEL

The second important reference concerning the abomination that causes desolation in Daniel is listed in Daniel 11. Consider the following:

> For the ships of Chittim shall come against him: therefore he shall be grieved, and return, and have indignation against the holy covenant: so shall he do; he shall even return, and have intelligence with them that forsake the holy covenant. **And arms shall stand on his part, and they shall pollute the sanctuary of strength, and shall take away the daily sacrifice, and they shall place the abomination that maketh desolate.** And such as do wickedly against the covenant shall he corrupt by flatteries: but the people that do know their God shall be strong, and do exploits. And they that understand among the people shall instruct many: yet they shall fall by the sword, and by flame, by captivity, and by spoil, many days. Now when they shall fall, they shall be holpen with a little help: but many shall cleave to them with flatteries. And some of them of understanding shall fall, to try them, and to purge, and to make them white, even to the time of the end: because it is yet for a time appointed. And the king shall do according to his will; and he shall exalt himself, and magnify himself above every god, and shall speak marvellous things against the God of gods, and shall prosper till the indignation be accomplished: for that that is determined shall be done. Neither shall he regard the God of his fathers, nor the desire of women, nor regard any god: for he shall magnify himself above all. (Daniel 11:30–37 KJV; my emphasis)

Daniel 11:21–45 describes in detail the behavior of the Antichrist, or vile man, for the entire last seven years of the prophecy of seventy sevens. The man who fulfills these actions, the vile man, will be unmistakable to those who rightly divide the Word of God. The events of Daniel 11:31, Daniel 9:27, Matthew 24:15, 2 Thessalonians 2:3–4, Revelation 13, and Isaiah 10.23 all reference the same time—the last time—and the same events on the earth. It is this same event that occurs at the time of the middle of the seventieth seven, or the midst of the last seven years that initiates the final forty and two months. Each scriptural reference adds additional information, but none of the references are in contradiction. All three speak of an *abomination that causes desolation on the earth*, each placing the event at the holy place in Jerusalem. Daniel 9:27 and 11:31 state that the Jewish daily sacrifice will be terminated at the same time the abomination of desolation is set up. Daniel 11:31 gives additional details as to the events that occur at the middle of the last seven years. Daniel 11:31 also adds events occurring just prior to and events occurring just after the setting up of the abomination in Jerusalem. Through these actions, the vile man is positively identified. The key to the identification of the man of sin is listed in Daniel 11:21–31. His behavior will be unmistakable, and as he fulfills all of what God foretells in Daniel 11, he will be revealed to those who rightly divide the Word of God.

Daniel 11:21–45 can now be split into two-time sections in accordance with the splitting of the last seven years. The last seven years include two 3.5-year sections divided by the midweek setting up of the abomination that causes desolation. The middle of the week can now be pinpointed and forecast accurately, through events that occur in the first forty-two months as documented in Daniel 11:21–31. The initialization of the prophecy concerning the Antichrist begins with the covenant, or resolution, that strengthens the vile man with the many (strong).[291] Daniel 11:32–45 then goes on to describe the events of the final forty-two months. Daniel 11:31–37, Matthew 24:15, and 2 Thessalonians 2:3–9 provide information as

---

[291] Daniel 9:27.

to what the abomination that causes desolation actually is. Consider the following:

> When ye therefore shall see the abomination of desolation, spoken of by Daniel the prophet, stand in the holy place, (whoso readeth, let him understand:) Then let them which be in Judaea flee into the mountains: Let him which is on the housetop not come down to take anything out of his house: Neither let him which is in the field return back to take his clothes. And woe unto them that are with child, and to them that give suck in those days! But pray ye that your flight be not in the winter, neither on the sabbath day: For then shall be great tribulation, such as was not since the beginning of the world to this time, no, nor ever shall be. And except those days should be shortened, there should no flesh be saved: but for the elect's sake those days shall be shortened. (Matthew 24:15–22 KJV)
>
> And the king shall do according to his will; and he shall exalt himself, and magnify himself above every god, and shall speak marvellous things against the God of gods, and shall prosper till the indignation be accomplished: for that that is determined shall be done. Neither shall he regard the God of his fathers, nor the desire of women, nor regard any god: for he shall magnify himself above all. (Daniel 11:36–37 KJV)

Compare these verses to 2 Thessalonians:

> Let no man deceive you by any means: for that day shall not come, except there come a falling away first, and that man of sin be revealed, the son of perdition; **Who opposeth and exalteth**

himself above all that is called God, or that is worshipped; so that he as God sitteth in the temple (Greek: naos; dwelling place) of God, shewing himself that he is God. Remember ye not, that, when I was yet with you, I told you these things? And now ye know what withholdeth that he might be revealed in his time. For the mystery of iniquity doth already work: only he who now letteth will let, until he be taken out of the way And then shall that Wicked be revealed, whom the Lord shall consume with the spirit of his mouth, and shall destroy with the brightness of his coming: Even him, whose coming is after the working of Satan with all power and signs and lying wonders. (2 Thessalonians 2:3–9 KJV; my emphasis)

The middle of the final seven-year period is marked by an event that occurs at the holy place in Jerusalem. The Antichrist/vile man occupies the holy place in Jerusalem and declares himself to be God, removing all sacrifices to the true God by the faithful Jews in Jerusalem. He then goes on, for the next forty-two months, to cause desolations on the earth and the destruction of the nations. He does this through supernatural miracles, energized by Satan. Revelation 13 and 17 give further information as to the abomination that causes desolation. As stated earlier, the holy place is Mount Moriah in Jerusalem, which was made holy by the declaration of God to Abraham at the time Abraham was willing to offer his only son of promise, Isaac. The middle of the week is now upon the earth, and the beast is about to come into supernatural form at the holy place in Jerusalem, declaring himself a god. Consider the following:

> And I stood upon the sand of the sea, and saw a beast rise up out of the sea, having seven heads and ten horns, and upon his horns ten crowns, and upon his heads the name of

blasphemy. And the beast which I saw was like unto a leopard, and his feet were as the feet of a bear, and his mouth as the mouth of a lion: and the dragon gave him his power, and his seat, and great authority. **And I saw one of his heads as it were wounded to death; and his deadly wound was healed**: and all the world wondered after the beast. And they worshipped the dragon which gave power unto the beast: and they worshipped the beast, saying, Who is like unto the beast? who is able to make war with him? And there was given unto him a mouth speaking great things and blasphemies; and power was given unto him to continue forty and two months. And he opened his mouth in blasphemy against God, to blaspheme his name, and his tabernacle, and them that dwell in heaven. And it was given unto him to make war with the saints, and to overcome them: and power was given him over all kindreds, and tongues, and nations. And all that dwell upon the earth shall worship him, whose names are not written in the book of life of the Lamb slain from the foundation of the world. If any man have an ear, let him hear. (Revelation 13:1–9; my emphasis)

The beast that thou sawest was, and is not; and shall ascend out of the bottomless pit, and go into perdition: and they that dwell on the earth shall wonder, whose names were not written in the book of life from the foundation of the world, **when they behold the beast that was, and is not, and yet is.** And here is the mind which hath wisdom. (Revelation 17:8–9 KJV; my emphasis)

Revelation 13 and 17 state that the beast had a deadly wound, or was dead, and then came back to life, ascending out of the bottomless pit. He then goes onto destruction and creates havoc on the earth for the next forty-two months. The destruction refers to both him and the destroying of the nations of the world, who are forced to worship him or face death. The event occurs at the middle of the last seven-year period since he is listed as continuing with the abomination for forty-two months. The forty-two months pinpoints his satanic resurrection, or abomination before God, to the time of the middle of the last seven years. The beast, in this supernatural state, declares himself God and is subsequently worshipped as God by those who are not written in the book of life. The abomination that causes desolation is the satanic resurrection of the beast at the holy place in Jerusalem. Stated differently, the abomination that causes desolation will be the beast in supernatural form standing at God's holy place. He will declare himself God at the same place Jesus Christ is prophesied to come and deliver Israel. [292] The supernatural nature of the beast will deceive all the unbelieving Jews and the nations of the world. "*Who is able to make war with him*"? No one, since he will not be flesh and blood but a great spiritual power.[293] His supernatural destruction of the world is why his kingdom, and that of his followers, is called diverse, or different, from all the previous Gentile kingdoms of the earth. He will be allowed to operate for the next forty-two months, during which supernatural destruction of the earth will be a common thing.

The previous verses summarize the events of the middle of the last seven years. At the time of the middle of the last seven years, the following events will take place:

1. The beast will end the sacrifice of the Jewish people—the remnant of faithful Jews at Jerusalem—to the one true God.
2. The beast will cause the abomination that causes desolation to stand at the holy place. He will be raised from the dead and declare himself to be god at the holy place.

---

[292] Romans 11:26–27; Psalm 2.
[293] Revelation 13:4.

3. The holy place in Jerusalem will be the location for a supernatural being standing and declaring himself to be God, deceiving the whole world in the process. The holy place is the same place where Abraham was willing to offer Isaac to God. The event is marked as the abomination that causes desolation.
4. Desolations, or destruction, will then begin in Jerusalem after the beast declares himself God at the holy place in Jerusalem, and it will spread to all the nations of the world for the next forty-two months.
5. The forty-two-month rule of the beast will be diverse, or different, from all other dominions that have previously been on the earth. The dominion of the beast will be supernaturally energized. The final forty-two months will be the worst time in human history.
6. The forty-two-month rule will be worse than the flood of Noah's time, since at that time death was allowed. For the last forty-two months, men will seek death but not be allowed to die; they will be required to suffer.[294]

---

[294] Revelation 9:6.

APPENDIX C

The Twenty-Three Hundred Days of Daniel 8:14

WHEN GOD GIVES TIME PERIODS in prophecy, he gives them as information to be used by those skilled in the right division of the Word of God. Time periods represent important guideposts that reveal key aspects of prophecy; they are critical for proper understanding and interpretation. Every Word of God has been purified and is perfect, providing doctrine, reproof, and correction to those who love and seek God. In Daniel 8:14, God mentions a peculiar period of time that lasts twenty-three hundred days in length. The twenty-three hundred days represents the time period of a vision seen by Daniel and discussed by two angelic beings in verse 13. The vision itself is partially listed in Daniel 8:9–12 and is associated with the last seven years of Daniel's seventy sevens of years prophecy. The end of the twenty-three hundred days, as indicated in the Word of God, is clear and is marked by the cleansing or rededication of the holy place in Jerusalem or the sanctuary, as stated clearly in the vision.[295] The beginning of the twenty-three hundred days is marked by the opening of the seals of Revelation chapter 6. The beginning

---

[295] Daniel 8:14.

of the twenty-three hundred days is also the beginning of sorrows as documented by the Lord in Matthew 24:4–14.

As the time progresses through the twenty-three hundred days, the vile man/Antichrist will rise up to war and begin making military gains against the south, the east and the pleasant land (Israel). He will rise to a powerful position on the earth only to be destroyed by the Lord at the end of his short, forty-two-month rule. The twenty-three hundred days begin long after he enters into a league with a powerful ally.[296] The entire twenty-three hundred days will begin a few hundred days after the beginning of the final seven years and may extend slightly after the final seven years to the dedication and cleansing of the new Jerusalem Temple Sanctuary. The final seven years encompass two thousand five hundred and twenty days (2,520), which include the final forty-two months; the rule of the Antichrist. The twenty-three-hundred-day time period is important to God and has significance, as all of the words of God. God also does not give information concerning times and seasons unless there is profitable doctrine, reproof, or correction; used by those skilled in understanding of the Word of God. The parallel verses that also are associated with this time can be listed as follows. Additionally, the initiation of the time of sorrows, as stated below, is the time of the beginning of the twenty-three hundred days. The words in bold italics below represent the time of the beginning of the twenty-three hundred days, also known as the beginning of sorrows, up until the time of the middle of the last seven years:

> And as he sat upon the mount of Olives, the disciples came unto him privately, saying, Tell us, when shall these things be? and what shall be the sign of thy coming, and of the end of the world? ⁴ And Jesus answered and said unto them, Take heed that no man deceive you. ⁵ For many shall come in my name, saying, I am Christ; and shall deceive many. ⁶ **And ye shall hear of wars and**

---

[296] Daniel 8:9, Daniel 11.23.

rumours of wars: see that ye be not troubled: for all these things must come to pass, but the end is not yet. ⁷ For nation shall rise against nation, and kingdom against kingdom: and there shall be famines, and pestilences, and earthquakes, in divers places. ⁸ <u>All these are the beginning of sorrows.</u> ⁹ Then shall they deliver you up to be afflicted, and shall kill you: and ye shall be hated of all nations for my name's sake. ¹⁰ And then shall many be offended, and shall betray one another, and shall hate one another. ¹¹ And many false prophets shall rise, and shall deceive many. ¹² And because iniquity shall abound, the love of many shall wax cold. ¹³ But he that shall endure unto the end, the same shall be saved. ¹⁴ And this gospel of the kingdom shall be preached in all the world for a witness unto all nations; and then shall the end come. ¹⁵ When ye therefore shall see the abomination of desolation, spoken of by Daniel the prophet, stand in the holy place, (whoso readeth, let him understand:) ¹⁶ Then let them which be in Judaea flee into the mountains: ¹⁷ Let him which is on the housetop not come down to take anything out of his house: ¹⁸ Neither let him which is in the field return back to take his clothes. ¹⁹ And woe unto them that are with child, and to them that give suck in those days! ²⁰ But pray ye that your flight be not in the winter, neither on the sabbath day: ²¹ For then shall be great tribulation, such as was not since the beginning of the world to this time, no, nor ever shall be. ²² And except those days should be shortened, there should no flesh be saved: but for the elect's sake those days shall be shortened. ²³ Then if any man shall say unto you, Lo, here is

Christ, or there; believe it not. ²⁴ For there shall arise false Christs, and false prophets, and shall shew great signs and wonders; insomuch that, if it were possible, they shall deceive the very elect. (Matthew 24:3–24 KJV)

⁴ Tell us, when shall these things be? and what shall be the sign when all these things shall be fulfilled?

⁵ And Jesus answering them began to say, Take heed lest any man deceive you: ⁶ **For many shall come in my name, saying, I am Christ; and shall deceive many. ⁷ And when ye shall hear of wars and rumours of wars, be ye not troubled: for such things must needs be; but the end shall not be yet. ⁸ For nation shall rise against nation, and kingdom against kingdom: and there shall be earthquakes in divers places, and there shall be famines and troubles: these are the beginnings of sorrows. ⁹ But take heed to yourselves: for they shall deliver you up to councils; and in the synagogues ye shall be beaten: and ye shall be brought before rulers and kings for my sake, for a testimony against them. ¹⁰ And the gospel must first be published among all nations. ¹¹ But when they shall lead you, and deliver you up, take no thought beforehand what ye shall speak, neither do ye premeditate: but whatsoever shall be given you in that hour, that speak ye: for it is not ye that speak, but the Holy Ghost. ¹² Now the brother shall betray the brother to death, and the father the son; and children shall rise up against their parents, and shall cause them to be put to death. ¹³ And ye shall be hated of all men for my name's sake: but he that shall endure unto the end, the same shall be saved.**

¹⁴ But when ye shall see the abomination of desolation, spoken of by Daniel the prophet, standing where it ought not, (let him that readeth understand,) then let them that be in Judaea flee to the mountains: ¹⁵ And let him that is on the housetop not go down into the house, neither enter therein, to take any thing out of his house: ¹⁶ And let him that is in the field not turn back again for to take up his garment. ¹⁷ But woe to them that are with child, and to them that give suck in those days! ¹⁸ And pray ye that your flight be not in the winter. ¹⁹ For in those days shall be affliction, such as was not from the beginning of the creation which God created unto this time, neither shall be. ²⁰ And except that the Lord had shortened those days, no flesh should be saved: but for the elect's sake, whom he hath chosen, he hath shortened the days. ²¹ And then if any man shall say to you, Lo, here is Christ; or, lo, he is there; believe him not: ²² For false Christs and false prophets shall rise, and shall shew signs and wonders, to seduce, if it were possible, even the elect. ²³ But take ye heed: behold, I have foretold you all things. ²⁴ But in those days, after that tribulation, the sun shall be darkened, and the moon shall not give her light, 25 And the stars of heaven shall fall, and the powers that are in heaven shall be shaken. ²⁶ And then shall they see the Son of man coming in the clouds with great power and glory. ²⁷ And then shall he send his angels, and shall gather together his elect from the four winds, from the uttermost part of the earth to the uttermost part of heaven. (Mark 13:4–27 KJV)

The beginning of sorrows marks the beginning of the final twenty-three hundred days and is documented in Matthew 24:8, Mark 13.8, and Luke 21:9. In addition to the scripture sections above, the beginning of sorrows, or the twenty-three hundred days, is also marked by the opening in heaven of the first five of the seven seals documented in Revelation chapter 6. These first five seals are parallel in time to the wars, famines, and pestilences which the Lord Jesus documented in the gospels listed above. The first seal is listed in Revelation 6:2—the white horse commissioned to conquer on the earth is reflective of the Antichrist/Vile man increasing in power on the earth and rising up to begin his conquests. The second seal to be opened in heaven is listed in Revelation 6:3—the red horse indicating the proliferation of wars and peace taken from the earth. The third seal is listed in Revelation 6:5—the black horse initiating the famines developing throughout the earth; the collateral damage associated with the first two seals. Revelation 6:8 then represents the fourth seal—the pale horse indicating death to a quarter of those on the earth through plagues, wars, and famines. Death is predictable and the result of the opening first three seals. The fourth seal also indicates that the first three seals, together with the fourth, may well be opened simultaneously on the earth, or closely together, as the beginning of sorrows as the Lord prophesied in the gospels begin to take hold on the earth. It will also be during the initial part of these twenty-three-hundred days that five of the great Gentile nations of Revelation 17:10 will fall from once prominent positions to that of lower degree. How this occurs will only be known at the time of the end, but it may be related to the overspreading of abominations as mentioned in Daniel 9.27. Additionally, there may well be an initial meeting of these heads at the time of the beginning of the twenty-three hundred days bringing great Babylon to God's remembrance. The twenty-three hundred days are now underway, and sorrows begin to multiply on the earth. In parallel with this will be the declaration of the Gospel to all on the earth as a final warning before the final forty and two months, the worst time in human history. Once again, all of the records regarding this time speak of this persecution of the saints and those who declare the gospels. The final declaration during this time will be the final chance for those on the earth to receive salvation through a new birth in Jesus Christ, the free gift of God. It is clear that the beginning of the twenty-three hundred days up until the middle of the final seven years will be filled with unrest via the beginning of sorrows listed in Matthew chapter 24 and the first five of the seven seals of Revelation chapter 6. We also understand that this will be a time of acute tribulation before the total destruction of the final forty and two months. It is stated that God gives over power to Antichrist for the final forty and two months.[297] Before the final forty and two months and after the beginning of the twenty-three hundred days, God uses this time period to warn those on the earth to once again seek the truth regarding God and his creation. It is also during this time period that the Gospel will be preached to all on the earth one last time. We also understand that the supernatural events will only be unleashed after the middle of the final seven years.

The initiation of the twenty-three hundred days begins some 200–275 days after the beginning of the final seven years of Daniel 9.24 (see Appendix D: *The Final Timelines*). The first four seals are initiated at the time of the beginning of the final twenty-three hundred days. The fourth seal summarizes the result on the earth of the opening of the first three seals on the earth, death to a quarter of those on the earth. It is also interesting that God *instructs not to hurt the oil or the wine during the famines, plagues and wars which come upon the earth.*[298] In effect, there will be famines, wars and plagues, or diseases, on the earth, but the oil and the wine will not be affected. Oil, wine, and corn are always mentioned in the Old Testament as being abundant during times of plenty,[299] however, during this time, it is famine, together with wars and plagues which will be on the earth, God states the oil and wine will not be disrupted. The fifth seal of Revelation 6:9–11 represents the persecution of the saints during the time when the gospel is preached to the whole world. The idea is that the initiation of sorrows will not be completely debilitating

---

[297] Revelation 13.7
[298] Revelation 6:6
[299] Deuteronomy 11.14, Deuteronomy 28.51

or cause a complete disruption of daily life. This effectively will allow for the Gospel to be preached to the whole world. The time of this final preaching of the Word of God will begin at the beginning of the twenty-three hundred days and last until the time of the supernatural resurrection of the Antichrist, the middle of the last seven years. Those who will obey and preach the Word of God will be workers together with God as the world begins to search for answers concerning the things which will now be manifested on the earth. After the supernatural raising of the Antichrist, the nations, and the people of the earth, will be given to the rule of the Antichrist for the next 42 months.[300] The reality of the preaching of the Gospel to the world at this time period is also alluded to in several salient sections of scripture. The following are some of these sections; the sections highlighted represent these times:

> [5] For many shall come in my name, saying, I am Christ; and shall deceive many. 6 And ye shall hear of wars and rumours of wars: see that ye be not troubled: for all these things must come to pass, but the end is not yet. 7 For nation shall rise against nation, and kingdom against kingdom: and there shall be famines, and pestilences, and earthquakes, in divers places. **8 All these are the beginning of sorrows. 9 Then shall they deliver you up to be afflicted, and shall kill you: and ye shall be hated of all nations for my name's sake. 10 And then shall many be offended, and shall betray one another, and shall hate one another. 11 And many false prophets shall rise, and shall deceive many. 12 And because iniquity shall abound, the love of many shall wax cold. 13 But he that shall endure unto the end, the same shall be saved. 14 And this gospel of the kingdom shall be preached in all**

---
[300] Revelation 13:5.

the world for a witness unto all nations; and then shall the end come. 15 When ye therefore shall see the abomination of desolation, spoken of by Daniel the prophet, stand in the holy place, (whoso readeth, let him understand:). (Matthew 24:5–15 KJV; my emphasis)

For many shall come in my name, saying, I am Christ; and shall deceive many. 7 And when ye shall hear of wars and rumours of wars, be ye not troubled: for such things must needs be; but the end shall not be yet. 8 For nation shall rise against nation, and kingdom against kingdom: and there shall be earthquakes in divers places, and there shall be famines and troubles: **these are the beginnings of sorrows. 9 But take heed to yourselves: for they shall deliver you up to councils; and in the synagogues ye shall be beaten: and ye shall be brought before rulers and kings for my sake, for a testimony against them. 10 And the gospel must first be published among all nations.**

11 But when they shall lead you, and deliver you up, take no thought beforehand what ye shall speak, neither do ye premeditate: but whatsoever shall be given you in that hour, that speak ye: for it is not ye that speak, but the Holy Ghost. 12 Now the brother shall betray the brother to death, and the father the son; and children shall rise up against their parents, and shall cause them to be put to death. 13 And ye shall be hated of all men for my name's sake: but he that shall endure unto the end, the same shall be saved. 14 But when ye shall see the abomination of desolation, spoken of by Daniel the prophet, standing where it ought not, (let him that readeth understand,) then let

> **them that be in Judaea flee to the mountains.** (Mark 13:6–14 KJV; my emphasis)
> ⁹ But when ye shall hear of wars and commotions, be not terrified: for these things must first come to pass; but the end is not by and by. ¹⁰ Then said he unto them, Nation shall rise against nation, and kingdom against kingdom:
> ¹¹ And great earthquakes shall be in divers places, and famines, and pestilences; and fearful sights and great signs shall there be from heaven. ¹² **But before all these, they shall lay their hands on you, and persecute you, delivering you up to the synagogues, and into prisons, being brought before kings and rulers for my name's sake. ¹³ And it shall turn to you for a testimony. ¹⁴ Settle it therefore in your hearts, not to meditate before what ye shall answer: ¹⁵ For I will give you a mouth and wisdom, which all your adversaries shall not be able to gainsay nor resist. ¹⁶ And ye shall be betrayed both by parents, and brethren, and kinsfolks, and friends; and some of you shall they cause to be put to death. ¹⁷ And ye shall be hated of all men for my name's sake. ¹⁸ But there shall not an hair of your head perish. ¹⁹ In your patience possess ye your souls**. ²⁰ And when ye shall see Jerusalem compassed with armies, then know that the desolation thereof is nigh. (Luke 21:9–20 KJV; my emphasis)

These sections noted above are all in agreement as to the great commission in which God will cause disruptions on the earth and work with those who will preach the resurrection of Jesus Christ to all nations. After this, the middle of the seven years and the undiluted wrath of God will be on the earth for the following forty and two months. In the Old Testament, the content and scope as to what happens during the twenty-three hundred days is contained between the two verses marking the beginning and the end of the period as recorded in Daniel 8:9–12. The vision that Daniel sees is also related to the opening of the seals of Revelation 6 and also the beginning of sorrows as documented in the gospels as documented above. As time progresses, the sorrows and birth pangs will grow stronger on the earth. The sequence of sorrows will continue until the middle of the last seven years, in which time the abomination causing desolation will be set up at the holy place in Jerusalem. It will be sometime after the middle of the seven years that the church of the one body of Jesus Christ will be raptured from the earth. The world will be left to the Jews and the Gentiles; of which salvation will only be through the grace of God and the works the Lord mentions in Revelation chapters 2 and 3.

The vision and events of the twenty-three hundred days and the final seven years will have far-reaching implications while also providing proper understanding of times, seasons, people, and the consequences in the days that follow. The actuality of the twenty-three hundred days unfolding on the earth will accurately proclaim the nearness of the Day of the Lord and the vengeance of our God soon to be on the earth. To the church of the One Body of Jesus Christ it will also indicate the nearness of the gathering together of the saints. Once the importance of the final twenty-three hundred days is understood, the desire to understand the events associated with the time period promotes a desire for proper understanding and proper interpretation. Through the years, the twenty-three-hundred-day vision has morphed into several different unrelated interpretations by a multitude of interpreters. A number of them regard the days as something other than twenty-four-hour days in spite of the explicit reference to evenings and mornings documented by God in Daniel 8:26. This verse was purposely inserted by God to ward off misinterpretation and make it clear that God is speaking of twenty-four-hour days. The days must be taken literally, since the angel himself is explicit in stating that they represent mornings and evenings.[301]

---

[301] Daniel 8:26.

We will now look closely at the origin of the twenty-three-hundred-day vision in Daniel chapter 8. The first part of Daniel 8 describes earthly Gentile dominions represented by the ram and the he-goat, which represent Medo-Persia and the rule of Alexander the Great (Greece), respectively. After Alexander's breakup, as recorded in Daniel 8, four dominions are left and are divided from Alexander's dominion. Out of one of these dominions—in the latter, or last, days—a "*little horn*" rises; this is the Antichrist, or vile man. The chapter goes on to describe the actions of the "*little horn*" in detail, which include the twenty-three-hundred-day vision documenting his actions on the earth. The focus of the entire chapter is dedicated to giving information regarding the dominion of the Antichrist, the final, and by far the fiercest, Gentile dominion on the earth. The ram, the he-goat, and the four dominions simply give information as to the origin of the "*little horn*," which is the focus of the chapter. The information provided in Daniel 8, including the twenty-three-hundred-day vision, is critical to the understanding of the last days and the book of Revelation—especially Revelation 17.

Daniel 8:9–27 will now be listed, beginning with the little horn rising in the last days, and eventually taking us up to the Lord's coming and the cleansing of the sanctuary. The section should be divided into two segments: the initial vision concerning the *little horn* (verses 9–15), and the interpretation of the *little horn* and his actions (verses 17–27). The twenty-three hundred days is critically interwoven into the prophecy and is therefore associated with the last days and the *little horn*. Curiously, the twenty-three-hundred-day vision is listed in both the vision and the interpretation of Daniel 8, binding it to the events of the last days. The twenty-three-hundred-day vision is unique and is not listed anywhere else in the Word of God except in Daniel chapter 8. Whereas the final seven years, the forty-two months, and the 1,260 days are all mentioned several times in scripture, the twenty-three hundred days is mentioned only once in Daniel 8. Consider the following:

> And out of one of them came forth a little horn, which waxed exceeding great, toward

the south, and toward the east, and toward the pleasant land. And it waxed great, even to the host of heaven; and it cast down some of the host and of the stars to the ground, and stamped upon them. Yea, he magnified himself even to the prince of the host, and by him the daily sacrifice was taken away, and the place of his sanctuary was cast down. And an host was given him against the daily sacrifice by reason of transgression, and it cast down the truth to the ground; and it practised, and prospered. Then I heard one saint speaking, and another saint said unto that certain saint which spake, **How long shall be the vision** (hazon; prophecy or entire prophetic vision) **concerning the daily sacrifice, and the transgression of desolation, to give both the sanctuary and the host to be trodden under foot? And he said unto me, Unto two thousand and three hundred days; then shall the sanctuary be cleansed.** And it came to pass, when I, even I Daniel, had seen the vision, (hazon; prophecy or entire prophetic vision that was seen) and sought for the meaning, then, behold, there stood before me as the appearance (mareh(h); physical sighting; in this case of the mighty warrior) of a man (arrogant mighty warrior; not the angel). And I heard a man's voice between the banks of Ulai, which called, and said, Gabriel, make this man to understand the vision (mareh(h); physical sighting; in this case of the mighty warrior). So he came near where I stood: and when he came, I was afraid, and fell upon my face: but he said unto me, **Understand, O son of man: for at the time of the end shall be the vision (hazon; prophecy or entire prophetic vision that was**

seen). Now as he was speaking with me, I was in a deep sleep on my face toward the ground: but he touched me, and set me upright. And he said, Behold, I will make thee know what shall be in the last end of the indignation: for at the time appointed the end shall be. The ram which thou sawest having two horns are the kings of Media and Persia. And the rough goat is the king of Grecia: and the great horn that is between his eyes is the first king. Now that being broken, whereas four stood up for it, four kingdoms shall stand up out of the nation, but not in his power. **And in the latter time of their kingdom, when the transgressors are come to the full, a king of fierce countenance, and understanding dark sentences, shall stand up. And his power shall be mighty, but not by his own power: and he shall destroy wonderfully, and shall prosper, and practise, and shall destroy the mighty and the holy people. And through his policy also he shall cause craft to prosper in his hand; and he shall magnify himself in his heart, and by peace shall destroy many: he shall also stand up against the Prince of princes; but he shall be broken without hand. And the vision of the evening and the morning which was told is true: wherefore shut thou up the vision; (hazon; prophecy or entire prophetic vision that was seen) for it shall be for many days.** And I Daniel fainted, and was sick certain days; afterward I rose up, and did the king's business; and I was astonished at the vision, (mareh(h); physical sighting; in this case of the mighty warrior) but none understood it. (Daniel 8:9–27 KJV; my emphasis)

Daniel 8:14 is the only biblical reference to the twenty-three-hundred-day time period. The context of the chapter includes a vision future to Daniel, seen by Daniel, of the dominions of Medo-Persia (the ram with two horns) and Alexander the Great (the he-goat). The fall of Alexander's dominion results in four lesser dominions that rule in the stead of Alexander. In the latter time of their kingdom, and when the sins of mankind have reached their full, out of one of these four dominions a little horn, or king, will arise: the Antichrist. The little horn represents the arrival of the Antichrist/vile man, who rises in the latter days—that is, the last days of man's rule on earth. The vile man, the *little horn*, is stated to rise and become powerful with a small people; thus, he grows stronger with time.[302] Daniel 11:20 states that the *little horn* rises from the northern Seleucid (Syrian) kingdom, but he does so at the time of the end. The time of the *little horn's* rise will be a time when *transgressions are come to a full*. These transgressions represent the rebellious sins of mankind being filled to overflowing—that is, a time when sin will dominate man's thinking and actions: the time of the end.[303] Other scriptures state that the *little horn* rises during the final seven years of Daniel's prophecy of seventy sevens. The prophecy of the *little horn* and of the final seven years begins in Daniel 8:9 and continues through verse 17. Further interpretation of Daniel 8:9–17 is provided by the angel and listed in Daniel 8:23–26.

The twenty-three hundred days of Daniel 8:14 is associated with the last seven years and the rising of the *little horn as well as the beginning of sorrows on the earth*. The last seven years include 2520 days (360×7) and terminates with the destruction of the vile man by the Lord Jesus Christ. The vile man will be destroyed by the brightness of the coming of the Lord Jesus Christ. The twenty-three hundred days represent evenings and mornings, indicating that they are actual twenty-four-hour days and not symbols of some other unit of time. The twenty-three hundred days are contained in the last seven years and begin some 220-275 days after the beginning of the

---

[302] Daniel 11:21.
[303] Daniel 8:23.

final seven years; the cleansing or rededication of the sanctuary will mark the end of the twenty-three hundred days. The beginning and subsequent events of the twenty-three hundred days; the beginning of sorrows, will be marked by the opening of five of the seven seals of Revelation chapter 6. There will be a time of about 1,340 days in which these seals will change the way of life on the earth. The birth pangs of a woman in labor will grow stronger and stronger with time. This will also be the time when the Word of God and salvation through Jesus Christ will be preached to all on the earth. At the time of the middle of the seven years, there will forty-two months, 1,260 days of hell on earth as Satan and his followers will be cast to the earth.

Referring back to Daniel chapter 8, it is stated that the "vision" given to Daniel in Daniel chapter 8 will last twenty-three-hundred mornings and evenings (days). The vision here may very well represent the vision or the prophecy given to John from our Lord; that is, the book of the Revelation of Jesus Christ. The judgments will begin with the opening of the seals and last up to and including the destruction of the Antichrist, and the subsequent cleansing of the Sanctuary. The time period for this will be twenty-three hundred days.

The first Hebrew word translated as "vision" in this chapter is from the Greek "hazon," which means *"To speak under the influence of divine inspiration, with or without reference to future events—to prophesy, to make inspired utterances."*[304]

The second word translated as "vision" in this section is the Hebrew word "mare(h)," which has the following definition: *"The act of seeing with the eye (Ge 2:9);* **2.** *LN 24.1–24.51* **a sight***, i.e., what is seen with the eye (Ecclesiastes 6:9);* **3.** *LN 58.14–58.18* **appearance**, *form, i.e., the visual form which is seen."*[305]

---

[304] J. P. Louw and E. A. Nida, *Greek-English Lexicon of the New Testament: Based on Semantic Domains*, vol. 1, 2nd ed., electronic ed. (New York: United Bible Societies, 1996), 439 (Hereafter "*Semantic Domains.*")

[305] J. Swanson, *Dictionary of Biblical Languages with Semantic Domains: Hebrew (Old Testament)*, electronic ed. (Oak Harbor: Logos Research Systems, Inc., 1997).

Both of the Hebrew words need to be understood in the context of their usage to attain proper interpretation of the Word of God, especially regarding Daniel 8. The list below identifies and explains each of the usages of the word "*vision*" in the context of its corresponding Hebrew word in Daniel 8. Each usage is derived from one or the other of the Hebrew words "hazon" and "mareh," and each, in its context, has important contextual significance, providing critical meaning to the verse. Understanding the meaning of the word "vision" in each unique contextual usage is essential for proper understanding of Daniel 8. This is especially true regarding the twenty-three-hundred-day vision, which was revealed to Daniel in chapter 8. Let's look at each instance of the word "vision" beginning in Daniel 8:13; that is, let us determine which Hebrew word is used, how it is used, and the context surrounding each verse. It will be helpful if you have a Bible open to Daniel 8 while going through each usage. Consider the following:

1. In Daniel 8:13–14, one angel asks the other angel the length of time of the prophetic vision ("hazon") concerning the rise of the vile man and his conquests. It is stated that he conquers to the south, the east, and the pleasant land and accomplishes the removal of the daily sacrifice and the transgression causing desolation. Because of this, both the sanctuary and the host will be trodden underfoot. The context here is a question of a prophetic vision and the time period that it describes—that is, twenty-three hundred days. The time period includes the rising of the vile man, which is marked by his conquering toward the South, the East, and the pleasant land. After he rises and begins to conquer territory, he will eventually stop the daily sacrifice and set up the transgression of desolation at the holy place in Jerusalem. We know from related scriptures that he will set up the transgression of desolation, but this event will not occur until the time of the middle of the final

seven years.[306] After the middle of the final seven years, the destruction, or desolations, of Jerusalem will then last the remainder of the final seven years. Sometime after this, and after the completion of the twenty-three hundred days, the sanctuary, or holy place in Jerusalem, will be cleansed. The cleansing and rededication of the sanctuary will mark the end of the twenty-three-hundred days and occur at the same time as the end of the final seven years. The angel states that at the end of the twenty-three hundred days, the sanctuary will be cleansed (also meaning rededication), completing the vision or prophecy of the twenty-three hundred days. From this it is clear that the twenty-three hundred days begin shortly after the beginning of the final seven years. The timelines are also shown in appendix D of this work.

By the time the Antichrist makes a league with a strong ally,[307] beginning the last time, he will have already fulfilled many of the scriptures written of him. At the time of the beginning of the final twenty-three hundred days, the Antichrist will initiate the process of rising up against the South, the East, and the pleasant land. The words of God in Daniel 8, and all those relating to the vile man, must be fulfilled accurately and acutely. We know from Daniel 12:10–13 that there are events that extend beyond the last seven years. In Daniel chapter 12 the angel speaks of the extension of the seven years represented by thirty and forty-five days.[308] Interestingly, Psalms 30, 45, and 75 (30+45) represent the raising of the dead, the anointing of the Lord, and the cleansing of the sanctuary, respectively. In any event, it will be understood by those who seek God's Word and are alive during those frightful times. The word "vision" here (verse 13) is derived from the Greek word

---

[306] Daniel 11:31; Matthew 24:15.
[307] Daniel 11.23
[308] Daniel 12:11–12.

"hazon," which means, "To speak under the influence of divine inspiration, with or without reference to future events—to prophesy, to make inspired utterances."[309]

2. *"And it came to pass, when I, even I Daniel, had seen the vision, (**hazon; prophecy or entire prophetic vision that was seen**) and sought for the meaning, then, behold, there stood before me as the **appearance (mareh(h)); physical sighting**. And I heard a man's voice between the banks of Ulai, which called, and said, Gabriel, make this man to understand the **vision (mareh(h); physical sighting)**"* (Daniel 8:15–16; my emphasis). In the first part of the verse, Daniel searches for the interpretation of the prophecy (vision) he has just seen. After this, suddenly and unexpectedly, he sees a vision ("mareh") that startles him and stands before him. Verse 16 instructs Gabriel to work with Daniel so he might understand the meaning of the vision ("mareh") he had just seen. Note: The first word usage of "vision" in verse 15 is derived from "hazon," which means, "To speak under the influence of divine inspiration, with or without reference to future events—to prophesy, to make inspired utterances."[310] The second and third usages of "vision" in verse 16 are derived from "mare(h)," which has the meaning, "The act of seeing with the eye (Ge 2:9); **2.** LN 24.1–24.51 **a sight**, i.e., what is seen with the eye (Ecclesiastes 6:9); **3.** LN 58.14–58.18 **appearance**, form, i.e., the visual form which is seen; (my emphasis)."[311]

Daniel sees an actual real-time figure or image that startles him. The appearance that Daniels sees somehow represents twenty-three hundred days of which Daniel is not to reveal in his writings. Daniel questions the

---

[309] Louw and Nida, *Semantic Domains*, 439.
[310] Ibid.
[311] Swanson, Dictionary of Biblical Languages with Semantic Domains: Hebrew (Old Testament), electronic ed. (Oak Harbor: Logos Research Systems, Inc., 1997).

appearance, and in the verses and chapters that follow, Daniel seeks to understand the meaning.

3. *"So he came near where I stood: and when he came, I was afraid, and fell upon my face: but he said unto me, Understand, O son of man: for at the time of the end shall be **the vision (hazon; prophecy or prophetic vision give to Daniel concerning the last days.)**"* (Daniel 8:17). Gabriel begins to detail and interpret the prophecy ("hazon") concerning the appearance Daniel saw and how it relates to the end times. The vision or appearance that he saw represents biblical prophecy and will be fulfilled at the time of the end.

4. *"And he said, Behold, I will make thee know what shall be in the last end of the indignation: for at the time appointed the end shall be"* (Daniel 8:19). Gabriel states that he will make Daniel understand what will occur in the last seven years, including the twenty-three hundred days. He reiterates that the last days are appointed by God and will occur exactly how and when God prescribes. The majority of Daniel 8 relates to the last days; the exception to this in chapter 8 of Daniel is the ram and the he-goat, which in effect recount the history of the little horn. Consequently, even the ram and the he-goat are associated with the last days, since they give historical account as to the origins, although thousands of years earlier, of the final little horn.

5. *"The ram which thou sawest having two horns are the kings of Media and Persia. And the rough goat is the king of Grecia: and the great horn that is between his eyes is the first king. Now that being broken, whereas four stood up for it, four kingdoms shall stand up out of the nation, but not in his power"* (Daniel 8:20–22). Gabriel recounts the prophetic vision beginning with the ram (Medo-Persia) and the he-goat (Alexander and Greece). The ram and the he-goat are mentioned only to set the stage for the vile man, who will arise thousands of years later at the time of the end. It is his rising and behavior that becomes the focus of the chapter 8. Historically, the Medo-Persian Empire was conquered by Alexander, and after his

death, his kingdom was divided into four dominions. The four dominions were far inferior to his original kingdom. The angel states that the little horn will rise from the original foundation of Alexander, but that it will do so thousands of years later and that it will come out of one of the four dominions formed after Alexander's death. We know from other scriptures that the Antichrist will arise from the residual northern, or Seleucid (Syrian) kingdom in the last days.

6. *And in the latter time of their kingdom, when the transgressors are come to the full, a king of fierce countenance, and understanding dark sentences, shall stand up. And his power shall be mighty, but not by his own power: and he shall destroy wonderfully, and shall prosper, and practise, and shall destroy the mighty and the holy people"* (Daniel 8:23–24). Gabriel begins to give specific details regarding the rise, the power, and the defiance of the little horn. The description unmistakably identifies the little horn as the vile man, or the Antichrist, who will rise in the last days. His foundation is the dominion of Alexander, who, as one man, ruled the nations. He, the Antichrist, will be the next "one man" to rule the nations. He is described as a king of fierce countenance and understanding of difficult political situations. He is filled with intrigue and despised by many, but he is a man of increasing power and craftiness. He rises when the sins, or the transgressions, of man have reached their full—the time of the end. This is a time when God determines in his heart that the sins of mankind are as horrific as the time before the flood recorded in Genesis.[312] The vile man is stated to have mighty power that is not his own. The destruction he will be responsible for will be beyond human comprehension, as indicated by the Hebrew word translated as *"wonderfully"* in the verse. The word has to do with causing amazement or showing oneself

---

[312] Matthew 24:37.

to be marvelous. The special power given to him comes both through others who ally with him as well as through power provided by Satan himself. The power will also manifest itself through many alliances with outsiders—that is, outlaw groups and rogue nations. His power is allowed to increase through God's divine permission, owing to the manifest and extensive sins of mankind. The power he will use is both the power provided by allied powerful nations and the power of Satan, the dragon himself. It will be this supernatural power from Satan that will supernaturally affect situations and sway the minds of millions of people on the earth. God, because of the great sin of mankind at the time of the end, does not intervene to stop the vile man's rise to power but allows men to gather together in a way similar to the first gathering at Babylon. The vile man will destroy wonderfully, through powerful alliances with other nations, all orchestrated by the supernatural power provided by Satan. The vile man will be successful in all that he does and will prevail throughout his end-times career—especially the final forty-two months. He shall destroy nations considered mighty and powerful, as well as some of the holy, or set-apart, ones. The nations will simply be in amazement and caught off guard by his power and ability; probably not even aware that it is the Vile man who will be supernaturally swaying the earth to be re-organized to be used by him after his satanic resurrection. This will become especially evident at the time of the beginning of the twenty-three hundred days when his supernatural powers become evident; but not understood by the world.

7. *"And through his policy also he shall cause craft to prosper in his hand; and he shall magnify himself in his heart, and by peace shall destroy many: he shall also stand up against the Prince of princes; but he shall be broken without hand"* (Daniel 8:25). He shall cause craft or deceit to prosper, or to succeed, in place of truth (i.e., man's truth). He will cleverly use his new power through shrewd decisions to successfully deceive the

world and its rulers, while also causing commotions to the unsuspecting inhabitants on the earth. He will consider himself to be great, superior to others, even God. He will make deceitful or treacherous speech to prosper. Through utilization of his proud arrogance, he will, while there is a sense of careless security, unexpectedly cause the destruction of many as he comes upon rulership of the world. Finally, he will raise up his hand against God and his son, but he will be destroyed by the Lord Jesus Christ at his coming.

8. *"And the vision (**mareh(h);** physical sighting;) of the evening and the morning which was told* (by the angel manifested to him) *is true: wherefore shut thou up the vision;* (hazon; prophecy or entire prophetic vision that was seen) *for it shall be for many days"* (Daniel 8:26). Verse 26 assures Daniel that the vision ("mareh") and the biblical prophecies represented by it are true. Daniel is further instructed to seal, conceal, or shut up the vision (hazon), for it will not come to pass for many days. The instruction from the angel is not to reveal the actual vision and the prophecy it represents. Later, Daniel does come to an understanding of the prophecy that it represents in the subsequent chapters. Daniel, curiously, does document the time frame that it represents suggesting early on that it must be other parts of scripture that will need to be understood to complete the puzzle. The genius of this is that God intrinsically ties this section together with the book of Revelation as in other sections of Daniel. Understanding of both books will be required for proper interpretation. This also will require the reader and searcher of scripture to understand that the book of Daniel and the book of Revelation are critically tied together in God's purpose. The first and third usages of "vision" in verse 26 are derived from "mare(h)": "the act of seeing with the eye (Ge 2:9); **1** "sight, appearance, vision. 1A sight, phenomenon, spectacle, appearance, vision. 1B what is seen. 1C a vision (supernatural). 1D sight, vision

(power of seeing)."[313] The second usage of "vision" in verse 26 is derived from "hazon": 1C vision, oracle, prophecy (divine communication). 1D vision (as title of book of prophecy).[314]

9. *"And I Daniel fainted, and was sick certain days; afterward I rose up, and did the king's business; and I was astonished at the vision,* (mareh); (issues relating to the last times and the wars on the earth, and the description of the Antichrist) *but none understood it"* (Daniel 8:27). Daniel reveals his astonishment at the vision ("mareh") of the last times events, but none understood the vision. In Daniel 10:1, Daniel states that he finally understands the vision of the mighty, warlike, imposing figure and the wars and commotions he represents on the earth from the additional information given him by the angel in chapters 9 and 10. Although Daniel has understanding, he does not reveal the vision in accordance with the angelic instruction. Daniel states only that he had understanding and that it concerned a long warfare.[315] As stated earlier, The usage of "vision" in this verse is from "mare(h)": "the act of seeing with the eye" (Genesis 2:9)

The above scriptures reveal what the Bible has to say about the twenty-three hundred days documented in Daniel 8:14. It is clear that the twenty-three hundred days are concerned with a vision of a time of a great war and tribulation on the earth at the time of the rising of the Antichrist during the last days. The Antichrist is depicted in the book of Revelation and many other sections of scripture. Some of his significant behaviors and actions and how he garnishes support are described in Revelation 13 and 17. The rising

---

[313] Strong, J. (1995). *Enhanced Strong's Lexicon*. Woodside Bible Fellowship; *Hebrew word number 4758*

[314] Strong, J. (1995). *Enhanced Strong's Lexicon*. Woodside Bible Fellowship; *Hebrew word number 2377.*

[315] See Daniel 10:1.

and the strengthening of the beast is consequent with the same event recorded in Revelation 6:2; the beast is commissioned, through a heavenly command, to rise up and conquer on the earth; initially to the South, the East and the pleasant land (Israel). The rising to power of the beast, the initial opening of the seals of Revelation chapter 6, marks the beginning of the twenty-three hundred days. The sequence of events that terminate the last days begins with the destruction of the beast by the Lord Jesus Christ. The events that follow, after the final seven years and the cleansing of the sanctuary, will be the raising of the dead associated with the first resurrection as indicated in the book of Revelation and the book of Daniel, as well as Psalm 30. Shortly after this will come the anointing of the Lord Jesus Christ as Lord of lords and King of kings (Psalm 45).

The initiation of the last twenty-three hundred days begins with the opening in heaven of the seals of Revelation chapter 6. The events associated with the opening of the seals on the earth will begin to empower the beast and prepare him for world domination. The 2,300 days are now beginning and life on the earth will now change and continue to change dramatically. This is also the beginning of sorrows on the earth. The meetings of the nations depicted in Revelation chapter 17 begins to occur at the time of the initiation of the twenty-three hundred days; the members and their dominions transitioning and changing until five of these dominions fall from once lofty positions to lower positions on the earth.

Associating Revelation chapter 17 with Daniel chapter 8, the following information can be arrived at when taken together:

1. The beast, the seven heads, and the ten horns are all present in both sections.
2. The timing is the last seven years—specifically sometime in the beginning of the last seven years; approximately 220-275 days after the beginning of the last seven years (Note: The additional 30 and 45 or 75 days recorded in Daniel chapter 12[316] could add to this 220 days which would push

---

[316] Daniel 12:12.

out the cleansing of the sanctuary. Considering this, the 220 days could be pushed out to approximately 295days after the beginning of the final seven years. This will become clear at the time of the fulfillment).

3. The vision in Revelation 17, as interpreted by the angel, will require several hundred days to be fulfilled. The days and the vision of Revelation are directly related to the 2,300 days of Daniel 8:14.
4. God states in Revelation 17:9 that wisdom is required to understand the vision or to put it together with other sections of scripture. The wisdom required is that of right division of the Word of God and realizing God understands the end from the beginning. It is the book of Daniel which provides the missing details of the book of Revelation.
5. Understanding of both Revelation 17 and Daniel 8 together is required to fully understand the meaning of both sections of scripture. True understanding will require both Jews and Gentiles to realize Jesus Christ, the author of the book of Revelation which he received from God, as the true Messiah.
6. It must be made clear that the seven heads of Revelation chapters 13 and 17 are Gentile nations who will be involved in rulership of Gods' land and people. It is for this reason that God does not mention other Gentile nations in his Word since God is always focused on his land and people. This reality is also why God only mentions a handful of Gentile nations in the Old Testament.

The vision documented by Daniel beginning in Daniel 8:9 is a vision of future last-time cataclysmic events that will actually occur on the earth. The vision was understood by Daniel, but Daniel was not to write it down in his prophecy; he was to write only that it would take twenty-three hundred days to complete. The twenty-three hundred days begin with the beginning of sorrows on the earth and then the Antichrist rising up to war with the kings of the South, the East, and the pleasant land. The beginning also marks the initial opening of the first five seals of Revelation 6.2. The seals and how they envelop the earth is at the discretion of God, but it will be God who will ultimately give the commands to go forth. Additionally, after the beginning of the final twenty-three hundred days, and sometime during the first half of the final seven years, there will be a worldly gathering including many representatives of nations, six of the seven heads, and kings who have yet to receive power. The gathering will depict the corporate beast made up of the seven heads, ten horns, the whore, and many nations. After some time and toward the middle of the final seven years, five of these kings, and their powerful nations, will fall from a once prominent status. One of these kings will still be ruling and still will maintain prominent status as a superpower nation. This superpower nation is thought to be the bear of Revelation 13 and Daniel chapter 7. It will be the bear, the feet of the wild beast of Revelation 13.2, who the wild beast will utilize to crush the remaining five strong nations after their fall.[317]

The peace conference with the many will fulfill the vision of Revelation 17. The initial meeting will initiate the final twenty-three hundred days. At the beginning of the twenty-three hundred days all six superpower nations will be ruling. As the days mount toward middle of the final seven years, the opening of the seals and the weakening of the nations will occur until five of the nations will fall from powerful nation status. At that time, thought to be toward the middle of the seven years, one, the bear, will continue superpower status. The meetings of the nations will appear to be a great move forward for the nations of the world, as they will finally acquire some degree of peace on earth through unity. The meeting will serve, at least on the surface, to unify Jerusalem, the Jews, the Gentiles, and the nations of the world. The event, in the eyes of God, will bring to remembrance *Mystery Babylon* and begin to stir God's ire.[318] The visions that John and Daniel saw are congruent; they are synchronized in time, yet they are thousands of years apart. The common theme is one of a great warfare on the earth led by the Antichrist for the final forty and two months of the final

---

[317] Daniel 7.7
[318] Revelation 16:19.

seven years. The rebellion represents Satan's rebellion on earth after his being cast out of the heavens as documented in Revelation 12:9. The scripture states that he will manifest himself as pure hatred to those on the earth because he knows his time is short. Evil men will carry out this wickedness through the use of spirit mediums and supernatural power. The meeting of the nations and superpowers will be a warning sign to all those who love God and understand his word. *"None of the wicked will understand, but the wise shall understand."*[319] The wise will understand the signs of the times from the Word of God as God's Word methodically, but unmistakably, moves toward final fulfillment.

---

[319] Daniel 12:10.

APPENDIX D

The Final Timelines

To get a better visual understanding as to the synchronization of the timelines associated with the last times set forth by God in the book of Daniel and Revelation, consider the following diagrams depicting division of the seventy sevens of years prophecy given to Daniel in Daniel 9:24. Figure 1 depicts the overall timeline of the entire seventy sevens of years from the time of its initial prophecy, to the cutting off of the Messiah at or about 29AD (69 sevens of years, or 434 years, completed), and then the final seven years associated with the last days. From our study, we know that the *Mystery of the One Body of Jesus Christ* began after the resurrection of Jesus Christ in the first century and continues to this day (2020). This Mystery period is depicted in the diagram (Figure 1) as occurring between the 69th and 70th week of years. The last seven years is associated with the time of the end of Man's rule on earth and held in abeyance by God until the time of the end. We know that at the end of the seventy sevens, several realities for Israel will come to pass as stated in Daniel's prophecy. Consider (Daniel 9:24–27 KJV):

> **Seventy weeks are determined upon thy people and upon thy holy city, to finish the transgression, and to make an end of sins, and to make reconciliation for iniquity, and to**

> bring in everlasting righteousness, and to seal up the vision and prophecy, and to anoint the most Holy. **25** Know therefore and understand, that from the going forth of the commandment to restore and to build Jerusalem unto the Messiah the Prince shall be seven weeks, and threescore and two weeks: the street shall be built again, and the wall, even in troublous times. **26** And after threescore and two weeks shall Messiah be cut off, but not for himself: and the people of the prince that shall come shall destroy the city and the sanctuary; and the end thereof shall be with a flood, and unto the end of the war desolations are determined. **27** And he shall confirm the covenant with many for one week: and in the midst of the week he shall cause the sacrifice and the oblation to cease, and for the overspreading of abominations he shall make it desolate, even until the consummation, and that determined shall be poured upon the desolate.

In relation to the prophecy of Daniel 9:24, after Figure 1, the attention focuses on the final seven years: the last days of man's rule on the earth. Figure 2 is an exert from Appendix 90 in EW Bullinger's work *"The Companion Bible"*, which shows the synchronization of all the time periods in the book of Daniel, and how each of them are in concert with all other prophecies. Although there are a few changes in figure 2 based on further study and the time of the end approaching, the fact that Mr. Bullinger saw these time periods and their synchronization in the early 20th Century is extraordinary in itself.

Figure 3 is a graphical representation of Daniel chapter 11:21–45 depicting how the text of this section lines up with final seven years and the last days. Figure 4 is a diagram showing the breakdown of the last days and the final seven years, beginning with the initial covenant or league between the Antichrist and a great Gentile nation (the beginning of the Last Days record) and takes us up to the end of the final seven years as well as the events shortly after the final seven years. The final seven years still awaits complete fulfillment (2020). As shown in figure 4, the 2,300 days lie within the final seven years. Additionally, the figure shows clearly the two seven-year periods and how the second, and final, seven-year period of Daniel 9:27, begins at the time of the middle of the first seven-year period.

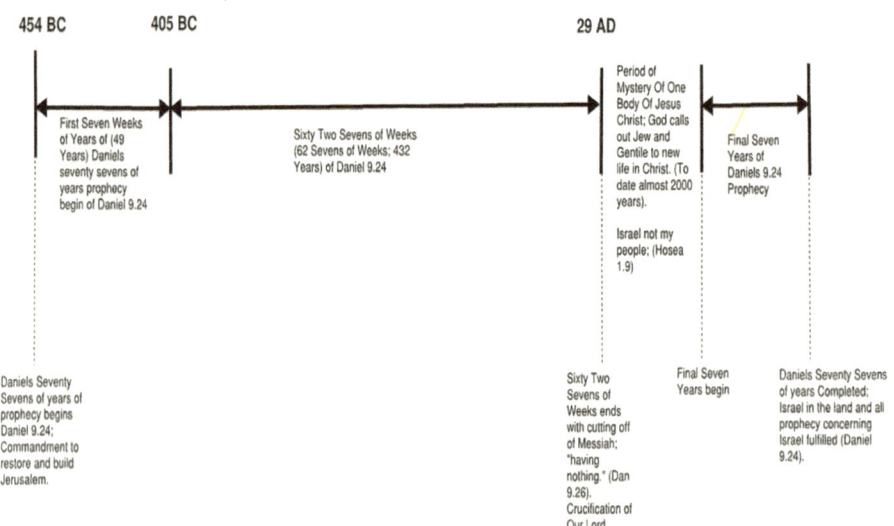

Figure 1: The Seventy Weeks of Daniel

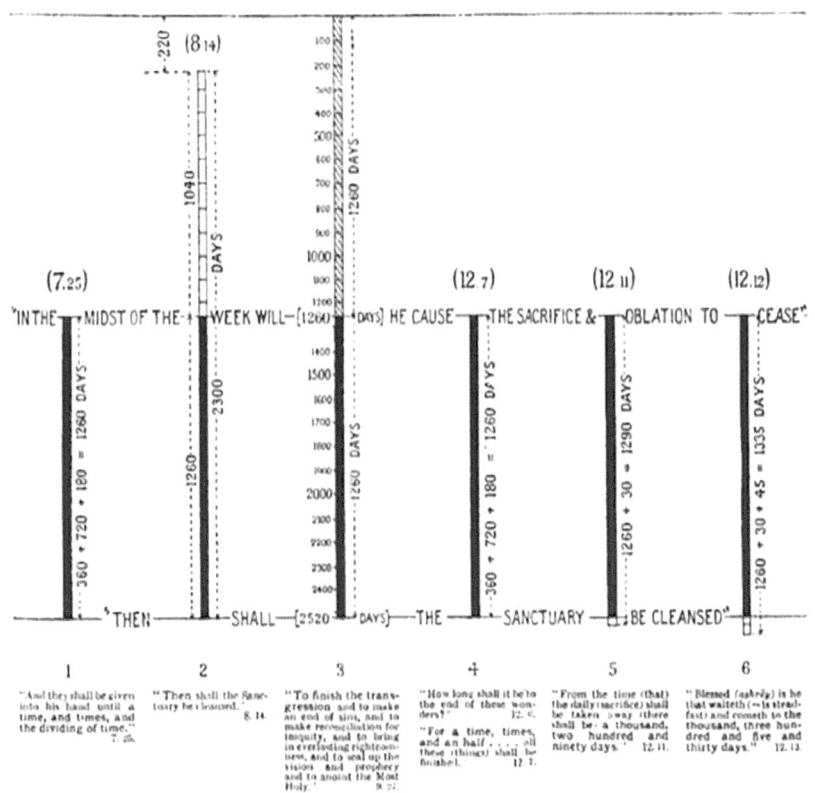

Figure 2: The Times Listed in Daniel[320]

---

[320] Bullinger, *Companion Bible Appendix 90*. King James Version, published in 1990 by Kregel Publications; PO Box 2607, Grand Rapids, Michigan 49501.

Vile Man Rises to Power as King of the North

²¹ And in his estate shall stand up a vile person, to whom they shall not give the honour of the kingdom: but he shall come in peaceably, and obtain the kingdom by flatteries. ²² And with the arms of a flood shall they be overflown from before him, and shall be broken; yea, also the prince of the covenant. ²³ And after the league *made* with him he shall work deceitfully: for he shall come up, and shall become strong with a small people. ²⁴ He shall enter peaceably even upon the fattest places of the province; and he shall do *that* which his fathers have not done, nor his fathers' fathers; he shall scatter among them the prey, and spoil, and riches: *yea*, and he shall forecast his devices against the strong holds, even for a time.

Final Seven Years Begins: First 3.5 years

²⁵ And he shall stir up his power and his courage against the king of the south with a great army; and the king of the south shall be stirred up to battle with a very great and mighty army; but he shall not stand: for they shall forecast devices against him. ²⁶ Yea, they that feed of the portion of his meat shall destroy him, and his army shall overflow: and many shall fall down slain. ²⁷ And both these kings' hearts *shall be* to do mischief, and they shall speak lies at one table; but it shall not prosper: for yet the end *shall be* at the time appointed. ²⁸ Then shall he return into his land with great riches; and his heart *shall be* against the holy covenant; and he shall do *exploits*, and return to his own land. ²⁹ At the time appointed he shall return, and come toward the south; but it shall not be as the former, or as the latter. ³⁰ For the ships of Chittim shall come against him: therefore he shall be grieved, and return, and have indignation against the holy covenant: so shall he do; he shall even return, and have intelligence with them that forsake the holy covenant.

Middle or Midst of Final Seven Years

³¹ And arms shall stand on his part, and they shall pollute the sanctuary of strength, and shall take away the daily *sacrifice*, and they shall place the abomination that maketh desolate. ³² And such as do wickedly against the covenant shall he corrupt by flatteries: but the people that do know their God shall be strong, and do exploits.

THE LAST DAYS AND THE VILE MAN OF DANIEL

> [Final 3.5 years or 42 Months]
>
> ³³ And they that understand among the people shall instruct many: yet they shall fall by the sword, and by flame, by captivity, and by spoil, *many* days. ³⁴ Now when they shall fall, they shall be holpen with a little help: but many shall cleave to them with flatteries. ³⁵ And *some* of them of understanding shall fall, to try them, and to purge, and to make *them* white, *even* to the time of the end: because *it is* yet for a time appointed. ³⁶ And the king shall do according to his will; and he shall exalt himself, and magnify himself above every god, and shall speak marvellous things against the God of gods, and shall prosper till the indignation be accomplished: for that that is determined shall be done. ³⁷ Neither shall he regard the God of his fathers, nor the desire of women, nor regard any god: for he shall magnify himself above all. ³⁸ But in his estate shall he honour the God of forces: and a god whom his fathers knew not shall he honour with gold, and silver, and with precious stones, and pleasant things. ³⁹ Thus shall he do in the most strong holds with a strange god, whom he shall acknowledge *and* increase with glory: and he shall cause them to rule over many, and shall divide the land for gain. ⁴⁰ And at the time of the end shall the king of the south push at him: and the king of the north shall come against him like a whirlwind, with chariots, and with horsemen, and with many ships; and he shall enter into the countries, and shall overflow and pass over. ⁴¹ He shall enter also into the glorious land, and many *countries* shall be overthrown: but these shall escape out of his hand, *even* Edom, and Moab, and the chief of the children of Ammon. ⁴² He shall stretch forth his hand also upon the countries: and the land of Egypt shall not escape. ⁴³ But he shall have power over the treasures of gold and of silver, and over all the precious things of Egypt: and the Libyans and the Ethiopians *shall be* at his steps. ⁴⁴ But tidings out of the east and out of the north shall trouble him: therefore he shall go forth with great fury to destroy, and utterly to make away many. ⁴⁵ And he shall plant the tabernacles of his palace between the seas in the glorious holy mountain; yet he shall come to his end, and none shall help him.[321]

Figure 3: Daniel 11: 21–45 Timeline

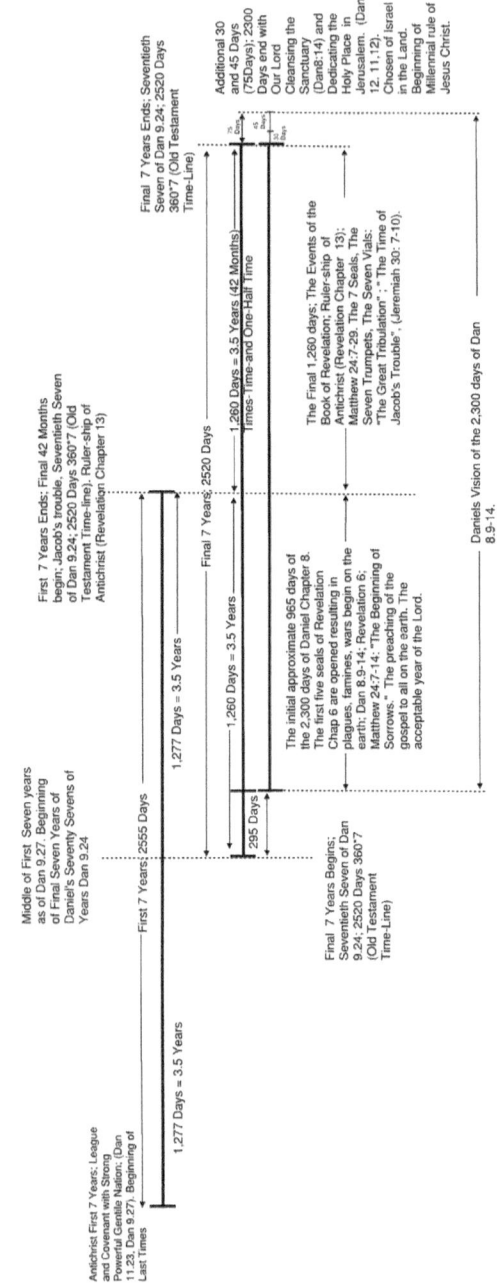

Figure 4: The Last Days and Final Seven Years Timeline

The first timeline above, figure 1, diagrams the prophecy of seventy sevens of weeks of years (70×7, or 490, years) given to Daniel in Daniel 9:24. In figure 1, we know that it is not the Lord who makes an agreement, or breaks a covenant with the many. The Lord had no part in either event. The time of the last seven years is therefore marked off from the other sixty-nine sevens of years and still awaits final fulfillment. It is unfortunate that this interpretation is, rather, the exception to a good deal of the commentaries regarding these interpretations. To properly interpret these scriptures, one must believe that God, who sees the end from the beginning, documented these events in the book of Daniel thousands of years before their fulfillment on the earth. If we err, we will err on the side of believing God at his word, understanding that all scripture must fit together perfectly for it to be the revealed Word of God. The issue is one of believing the scriptures and the power of God; this is typically the stumbling block for many authors of commentaries. Not believing God at his word, or believing his words are the words of men, is the first step in the path down. The starting point for the prophecy concerning the last days or final time (See Figure 4) is the prophecy concerning the covenant or league that the Antichrist makes with a great nation.[322] After the covenant, two additional significant events will follow, the first will be the beginning of the final seven- years at the time of the middle of the first seven-year period. Secondly, after the beginning of the second seven-year period, after approximately 295 days, the beginning of the twenty-three hundred days of Daniel 8:14 will begin. It will be this time period in which God begins to unleash judgements on the earth in accordance with the first five seals of Revelation 6 and the consequences described in Matthew 24:7–14. God's judgements will be on the earth and the body of Christ will be workers to together with God and the Lord Jesus Christ to assure that all on the earth confronted and given the opportunity to believe the truth of the Word of God. Specifically:

---

[322] Daniel 9.27.

> **⁹ That if thou shalt confess with thy mouth the Lord Jesus, and shalt believe in thine heart that God hath raised him from the dead, thou shalt be saved. ¹⁰ For with the heart man believeth unto righteousness; and with the mouth confession is made unto salvation. ¹¹ For the scripture saith, Whosoever believeth on him shall not be ashamed. ¹² For there is no difference between the Jew and the Greek: for the same Lord over all is rich unto all that call upon him.**

After approximately 965 days from the beginning of the final twenty-three hundred days, and after the those on the earth are confronted with the truth of the Gospel of Jesus Christ the final forty-two months of the Antichrist rule on the earth will begin. The time will be the worst time in human history as spiritual warfare between Satan and the judgements of God; his wrath, are poured out on the earth. This is summarized in Matthew 24:15–24 and the judgements of the seals, trumpets and the vials described in the book of Revelation of our Lord Jesus Christ. This time will be diverse or different from any other time in human history in that it will be supernaturally charged. Once the time lines are understood which were crafted from both the Old and New Testament records, the timeline will be a beacon to those on the earth during this time to understand the times and the seasons; that there will be an end in accordance with the will of God.

Once again, the scriptures concerning this time were analyzed with respect to the last seven years with each record adding additional information. Through this process the scriptures can then be pieced together harmoniously. The time between the cutting off of the Messiah and the league that the Antichrist makes with a strong nation is separated in time by thousands of years, as figure 1 above indicates. The time between these two events is known as the hidden time of the mystery of the one body of Christ. The time was hidden in the Old Testament.

Figure 2 illustrates all the specified periods of time in the book of Daniel in relation to the seventieth seven—the last seven years of Daniel's prophecy. The figure reveals the remarkable synchronization of all passages in Daniel dealing with the last days—especially the last seven years for Israel. The perfection of the Word of God is unmistakable. The time is listed in days, times, and years such that the time cannot be misinterpreted. The time is also listed in months in Revelation 13, also documenting the same time period. The perfection of the Word of God is clear when these verses are rightly divided with respect to the mystery of the one body of Jesus Christ; our only responsibility is to ingest them and believe them and then let God bless us through faith.

Once the foundation of the time periods is understood, the scriptures are clear as to their meaning; God then gives ample warning to the believer. If men choose to be ignorant, they will choose ignorance no matter what is recorded in the Word of God. God states that there will be believers who will be awake (understand these times) and there will those who will be asleep (oblivious to the times and the seasons).[323] Figure 4 also represents another interesting time period; that of the twenty-three hundred days of Daniel 8:14. The events of this time period are further explained in Appendix C. The events occurring on the earth during these times will be warning signs for those on the earth who are awake and understand the warnings given by God.

The story of the revelation, or manifestation on the earth, of the Lord Jesus Christ in the last days will require understanding of both the Old and New Testaments with a good deal of the information contained in the book of Daniel and the book of Revelation. The majority of the foundational work for this book was built upon these relevant sections of scripture. God deliberately structured his word in this fashion for his own reasons. The instruction that Jesus Christ provides to the Jews is documented in Revelation 2 and 3. God saves twelve thousand Jews from each of the tribes of Israel, for a total of one hundred forty-four thousand who are marked by God

---

[323] 1 Thessalonians 5:10

for protection during the last time and the final forty-two months. These marked out individuals, of the physical seed of Abraham, Isaac and Jacob will become the first fruits of the new nation of Israel after the time of the tribulation. It is only God who knows their identities; they will be the called out of God after the church of the one body of Jesus Christ is raptured from the earth. The first fruits of the nation of Israel will not be all that make it through the final seven years, but they are a remnant that become the nucleus of the new nation of future blessed Israel—the bride of Christ. Through this remnant, God begins the fulfillment of the everlasting promises made to Abraham, Isaac, and Jacob. Daniel gives the time period of twenty-three hundred days, and the Lord Jesus Christ, in Revelation 2 and 3, provides instruction to the Jews to preserve the called Israelites of God in those tragic days.

Understanding Revelation 17 and Daniel 8 is required to accurately and rightly divide the overall meaning of the last days. Right interpretation is paramount to the one hundred forty-four thousand Jews and the additional souls that God calls out in the last days. The called-out Jews will be required to study the book of Revelation to get instruction during the terrible events of the last days. This instruction to the Jews, in those tragic days, will be given by the Lord Jesus Christ in the book of Revelation; they will finally follow, obey, and understand him to be their Messiah. The entire book of Revelation will give instruction and direction concerning the days of Jacob's trouble. The instruction is given to Israel after they, as instructed by the Lord in Matthew 24:16–18, leave Jerusalem in the last days. Once scattered, they will gravitate to seven locations, as depicted in Revelation 2 and 3, and begin to follow their Messiah. These words in Daniel and Revelation have been staring men in the face for thousands of years, but they will come to full realization only when the time of the end approaches. The Word of God will be the guide—the only guide—for those called by God in the last days. To God be the glory.

The timelines of all the figures above are accurate and very informative as to the progression of the sequence of events during the last days. However, the twenty-three hundred days and the other events of the last seven years give rise to the need of another timeline—namely, the textual timeline of the last seven years broken down into its three significant parts. Figures 3 and 4 above represent a textual and graphical guideline, respectively, of the same final seven years of Daniels seventy-sevens of years. Daniel 11:21–45 gives the most detailed information regarding the behavior of the Antichrist, and the sequence of events on the earth from the vantage point of Israel and the Jews and during the last days. The reader is walked through the final behaviors of the vile man as he unknowingly progresses through, and fulfills, the scriptures written about him in the Word of God. The prophecy includes the important events—important to God—of both the initial and final forty-two months, as well as the midst of the week. Daniel 11:21–45 is listed and outlined in its entirety above in figure 3. The section (figure 3) is partitioned into four significant periods of time: the beginning of the last days, the first 3.5 years, the middle of the last seven years, and the final 3.5 years. The information contained in figures 3 and 4 above works to further our understanding from the Word of God concerning the specific behaviors of the Antichrist. God has given his people several signposts and, amazingly, has listed for us significant behaviors of this vile man as he fulfills his ill-fated mission on the earth. God has also given accurate times, days, and years for us to accurately understand. The purpose is for us to glean from, and then seek, the Lord's will with respect to his will for our lives, if alive during these times. The direction and guidance from the Word of God will be critical for those alive during the tragic last days described by God.

APPENDIX E

The Seven Heads and Ten Horns of Revelation and Daniel

THE SEVEN HEADS AND TEN horns of Revelation and Daniel are associated with the last days and the beast when he rises to power during the final seven years—especially the final forty-two months. They will be inspired by Satan, and their mission will be as instruments utilized by the beast during the final forty-two months. They are mentioned and described in both the Old Testament and the Book of Revelation. As noted earlier, the book of Revelation complements the book of Daniel; both books touch on the seven heads and ten horns, as well as their association with the beast and the Antichrist. The books work hand in hand to reveal key information regarding the seven heads and ten horns. To develop a keen understanding of the seven heads and ten horns, the seventy weeks of years listed in Daniel 9:24 must first be understood. Daniel's revelation from God focused on the final seventy weeks of years, which are concerned with the Jews' affairs: the land, Jerusalem, and the holy place. The climax or God's final dealings with the Jews occurs during the final seven years which are associated with the last days of mankind's rule over the earth. It is these final seven years which will include enormous and amazing supernatural judgements of God. The final seven years are divided into two 3.5-year sections, as depicted in figure 4 of appendix

D. The first sixty-nine of these weeks of years begins on or about 454 BC and ends with the cutting off of the Messiah, his crucifixion, which occurred approximately AD 29. The first part of the prophecy of the seventy weeks of years is historical to us in this day and time (2020). After the first sixty-nine weeks of years, Daniel's prophecy skips over the time of the mystery of the one body of Jesus Christ (which has lasted about two thousand years to date) and moves to the last seven years as it relates to the Jews and Jerusalem; this is the final week, or final seven years.

It is Daniel's seventieth week of years (the final seven years), which details specific events focused on Israel and the deliverance of the Jews, their land, the city, and the holy place of God in Jerusalem. The deliverance of the Jews is the focus of Daniel's prophecy regarding the seventy sevens of years. The prophecy in Revelation concerns the Jew, the Gentile, and the entire heavens and the earth. Both the books of Daniel and Revelation mention the seven heads and ten horns in one way or another. Revelation expands on the last week—especially the final forty-two months of Daniel's Prophecy for Israel, while also giving specific details concerning the end of the rule of the Gentiles. The book of Revelation is written to believing Israel and to the Gentiles who choose to fear God. The church of the one body of Jesus Christ is raptured from the earth before the wrath of almighty God is unleashed during the final forty-two months. After the last seven years, God appoints his son, Jesus Christ, as King of kings and Lord of lords and ruler over the heavens and the earth. The book of Revelation, at the end of the final seven years, fulfills all of the prophecy written to Israel by all the Old Testament prophets. Although the final seven years focus on Israel both in Daniel and Revelation, the effects of the unleashed evil and God's final judgments on the earth will affect the entire world. God specially fulfills all promises made to Israel. God will ensure that all prophecies and promises to the Patriarchs are fulfilled in his Word.

In Revelation, after the rapture of the one body of Christ, the middle wall of partition is once again restored, and Jew and Gentile are once again separated. Whereas there was no difference between Jew and Gentile in the time of the body of Christ; that is, whosoever believed on the Lord Jesus Christ and confessed him as Lord and Savior was rewarded with eternal life and make up the same body of Christ; no difference between Jew and Gentile.[324] In contrast, the book of Revelation, after the rapture of the one body of Jesus Christ, once again separates Jew and Gentile. The church of the body of Christ is removed and raptured from the earth before the great day of the wrath of Almighty God. The rapture of the church of the one body of Christ will complete the mystery period as revealed to the apostle Paul. These foundational truths from the Word of God must be understood before we move forward regarding the seven heads and the ten horns.

The Satan-inspired seven heads and ten horns of the beast are first mentioned together in Revelation 12:3. The vision of Revelation 12 is associated with the fourth vision in heaven and on earth, as seen by John. The fourth vision that John saw concerned the woman, the child, and the dragon as it first played out in the heavens. Revelation 12 records the old dragon, Satan, being cast out of the heavens and relegated to the earth. It must be understood that this casting out occurs at or about the middle point of the final seven years. Revelation 13 then expounds upon the corresponding consequences on the earth of the vision in heaven. The scene is played out first in the heavens and then on the earth; these events are documented in Revelation 12 and 13, respectively.

The seven heads and the ten horns encompass the governance of the dragon, or Satan, as stated in Revelation 12:9. Fundamentally, it must be understood that there are heavenly realities and earthly realities, the heavenly realities being far above the earth. Several times in scripture, the events in heaven precede, or give birth to, events on the earth. Revelation 12 and 13 form a pair of visions: one in heaven, in chapter 12, and the subsequent result on the earth, in chapter 13. The book of Revelation, and its heavenly visions and subsequent earthly visions, records judgments or declarations in heaven, and the resulting consequences on the earth. It is clear in these vision pairs that all judgments are initiated in the heavens, under the rulership of

---

[324] Galatians 3.28.

God, and have consequences on the earth. There are many examples of this in the Word of God—figures of heavenly realities that have representative or corresponding consequences on the earth. In fact, the entire book of Revelation encompasses seven pairs of visions of heavenly realities and their resulting consequences on the earth. The realities in heaven are first, and their result is what occurs on the earth. A good example of this, outside of the book of Revelation, is documented in the book of Hebrews, in which Moses is directed to pattern an earthly tabernacle and the Holy of Holies after the original in the heavens. Consider the following:

> Now of the things which we have spoken this is the sum: We have such an high priest, who is set on the right hand of the throne of the Majesty in the heavens; A minister of the sanctuary, and of the true tabernacle, which the Lord pitched, and not man. For every high priest is ordained to offer gifts and sacrifices: wherefore it is of necessity that this man have somewhat also to offer. For if he were on earth, he should not be a priest, seeing that there are priests that offer gifts according to the law: **Who serve unto the example and shadow of heavenly things, as Moses was admonished of God when he was about to make the tabernacle: for, See, saith he, that thou make all things according to the pattern shewed to thee in the mount.** But now hath he obtained a more excellent ministry, by how much also he is the mediator of a better covenant, which was established upon better promises. (Hebrews 8:1–6 KJV; my emphasis)

Heavenly realities are mentioned in the Bible several times throughout God's Word. In some of these instances, God reveals how heavenly realities are related to earthly realities. It is no secret, to those who humbly handle the Word of God, that Satan is the god of this world.[325] It is also true that Satan has infiltrated the heavens and will hold on to his place in the heavens until he is cast out by Michael, the archangel, as documented in Revelation 12:7.[326] The time of Satan's being cast out of the heavens is pinpointed by God in Revelation 12:7 as the middle of the last seven years. This timeline agrees with all other scriptures written on the subject—especially the books of Daniel and Revelation. In fact, it is this casting out that is the main catalyst for the cataclysmic events that occur on the earth during the final forty-two months. It is clear from God's Word concerning the middle of the last seven years that cataclysmic events occur. It is also clear that Michael, the archangel, casts Satan from the heavens during the middle of the last seven years.[327] The scripture is also clear that something supernatural occurs and changes things for the next forty-two months on the earth: "*Woe to the earth and the inhabitants of the earth and the sea! For the devil is come down unto you, having great wrath, because he knoweth that he hath but a short time.*"[328]

After the casting of the devil and his spirit agents from the heavens to the earth at the time of the middle of the last seven years, momentous changes will occur on the earth. One of the first things is the devil setting up an earthly government—the seven heads and the ten horns. The heads and horns, a group of Gentile countries and rulers, will become the instruments of the beast as allotted by Satan for worldly dominion and rulership. The only question is, who will make up this governance group? It has been Satan up until this point, who was able to avail both the heavens (to some extent) and the earth for his use. Through his power in the heavens, he destructively manipulated the events on the earth and had the ability to indirectly hide the source of that evil. Once cast out of the heavens (in Revelation 12:7), he will be relegated to the earth for the next forty-two months. He will then manifest himself through the seven heads and ten horns, headed up by the supernatural beast

---

[325] 2 Corinthians 4:4.
[326] Ephesians 6:12.
[327] Revelation 12:7–8.
[328] Revelation 12:12.

on the earth. The supernatural beast will then be destroyed by the brightness of the coming of the Lord Jesus Christ at the end of the final forty-two months.

The scriptures in Revelation 12 and 13 describe two separate groups, Jews and Gentiles, who are persecuted by the dragon when he is cast onto the earth. The two groups are purposely listed independently in Revelation 12 and 13. Since they are now independent of each other, God now deals with each separately. The first group mentioned is the seed of the woman, or the remnant of the house of Israel. Once cast from the heavens, the devil attempts to persecute the woman and her seed. God helps the woman and protects her for the final forty-two months of the devil's reign on earth. God protects her in much the same way he protected Israel at the time of their exodus from Egypt. They escape to the wilderness, and God pleads with them there to return to him, fulfilling the scriptures in Revelation and many Old Testament scriptures. After the casting of Satan and his angels to the earth, Satan immediately pursues the woman, Israel. There will be a called-out people, or remnant of Israel, who will be of the physical lineage and seed of Abraham, Isaac, and Jacob. God will protect these one hundred forty-four thousand Jews—twelve thousand from each of the tribes—and will set his seal of protection on them in the wilderness. The scene is historically similar to how God saved his chosen people from Egyptian tyranny at the time of Moses. Satan, frustrated with his fruitless attack against the woman, then sets up his governance to rule the earth for the next forty-two months.

The second group mentioned in Revelation 12 and 13 are the Gentiles on earth at the time of the middle of the seventieth week. The resulting tragedies, consequent with Satan's being cast to the earth, are documented in Revelation 13. The satanic governance on earth will be represented by the seven-headed, ten-horned beast, as described in Revelation 13:1. Satan's first order of business with respect to the Gentiles is to establish his governance on the earth: the beast, the seven heads, and the ten horns. God does not reveal many details regarding the beast in the heavens, how this entity came to be, or the heavenly disruption it represented to God. God does acknowledge, however, that it does exist and that the devil and his ability to manipulate will come to an end with his being cast out of the heavens. The timing will be the middle point of the last seven years. The casting out will be accomplished and led in the heavens by Michael, as stated in Revelation 12:7–9. The reality of the heavens is beyond our understanding, and therefore God did not burden us with the details. God does reveal and provide details as to the makeup and the result of this evil governance on the earth. God also reveals that it is the devil, being cast out of the heavens, that initiates the final forty-two months of hell on earth. God provides this crucial information for us to assimilate and digest.

The dragon, the seven heads, and the ten horns represent the prince of the power of the air, which will openly manifest itself on the earth at the time of the middle of the last seven years. The corporate beast represented by their leader, the Antichrist, is now destined to rule the people of the earth for the next forty-two months. The allure of Satan will be irresistible to the earth dwellers who know not God or his Christ. As the earth dwellers become more interested in the supernatural, God allows them to become infatuated with a seemingly supernatural man declaring himself to be God. Although these events seem to be impossible or part of some science fiction movie; nevertheless, the scriptures clearly document this. Our responsibility is to believe what is stated in the Word of God. All who are not written in the book of life will willingly become followers of the beast or face death and destruction. The seven-headed, ten horned beast represents Satan's previous governance in heaven, which is now established on the earth. The initial verses in Revelation 13 give the details of the corporate governance of Satan on the earth. God initially tells of the origin of the beast on the earth—his seven heads and ten horns. Historically, the beast will be composed of the same seven heads and ten horns mentioned and prophesized in Daniel 7, 8, 9, 10, and 11. It is Daniel 7 that first introduces us to powerful Gentile nations who rise in the last days and are represented by wild beasts; the bear, lion with eagles wings, and leopard in the chapter. It will be these same wild animal-likened Gentile nations, introduced in Daniel 7, who arise and rule in the last days before the Antichrist takes control with his ten kings (horns). The fourth terrible beast in Daniel 7 is composed of the previous three Gentile dominions with ten additional leaders, or horns. It is also important to understand that God only mentions Gentile nations in relation to their association or their ruling of the Holy Place in Jerusalem. This explains why the multitude of other Gentile nations are never mentioned in the Bible. Understanding this also reveals to us that it will be this governance of the seven heads and ten horns who will be associated with the governance of the Holy Place in Jerusalem at the time of the end.

The corporate governance of the nations and leaders introduced to us in Daniel 7 are the same as those described by God in the first few verses of Revelation 13. The model used in both sections, Revelation 13 and Daniel 7–11, will consist of human agents, nations, and peoples with a supernatural flavor. The book of Revelation—especially Revelation 13 and 17—provides the additional information required to interpret Daniel 7, 8, 9, 10, and 11. The corporate beast model of Revelation 13 takes a dramatic and ominous turn in Revelation 13:3. One of the heads of the corporate beast is wounded to death, *and his death wound is healed.* The wild beast, or the Antichrist, is now the center of attention and is wounded to death; but then, in defiance of all worldly explanation, *he has his deadly wound healed.* The reality of this is that he, the vile man/Antichrist, is assassinated in his mortal form at or about the time of the middle of the last seven years. He then supernaturally rises from the dead as the wild beast. He is now alive in supernatural form and declares himself God, thus committing the unforgiveable sin—blasphemy against the Holy Spirit. Revelation 13 then goes on to document the forty-two-month earthly dominion of Satan on the earth as he utilizes his new instrument of destruction—a supernatural beast with seven heads and ten horns. Of note in Revelation 13 is that the other six heads are no longer mentioned beyond Revelation 13.3, but it is now the wild beast with the false prophet as well as the ten horns or kings who receive supernatural power[329] and who will now rule the earth for the

---

[329] Revelation 17.12

next forty and two months. The chapter suggests that the transition will occur fairly quickly after the middle of the final seven years. The other six heads representing the six strong Gentile nations will fade into obscurity; subservient to the beast and probably warring with each other. Daniel chapter seven also states that it will be the bear, the feet of the corporate beast, that will be used to stamp or destroy the other five heads.[330] God's Word also suggests this in Revelation 17 in which it is stated that one is ruling and the other five have fallen in stature.[331]

The earthly model is now the focus of our attention. The seven heads and ten horns will reveal in plain sight the deep-seated evil that lies behind the hate of Satan. Satan's hate and disdain extend to God and all his creation, including man. Whereas while in the heavens Satan disguised his hateful horrific actions and abominations on the earth, now, after his being cast out, they will be openly manifested and amplified, since he knows his time is short. Satan will be stripped of his heavenly power but not his supernatural power and ability to hide his evil root core. The dominion of Satan will be revealed in plain sight on the earth in all its destructiveness. The wise will understand from the scriptures that this indeed will be Satan's final stand on earth. Those not written in the book of life will fall prey to the allure of the wild supernatural beast.

To understand the earthly model, we will examine the references to the seven heads and ten horns in scripture. The following verses are the documented references in the scripture of the seven heads and ten horns. Of note is the reality that the seven heads appear together only in the book of Revelation. Although the heads and the nations that they represent are alluded to in Daniel 7, the actual mention of them as a unified governance structure is found only in Revelation 13 and 17. The ten horns, in contrast, trace their origin to the Old Testament—especially the book of Daniel. The references to the unified seven heads and ten horns are listed in the order in which they appear in scripture. The first occurrence is related to the

---

[330] Daniel 7.19
[331] Revelation 17.10

origin of the seven heads and ten horns in the heavens as they are first explained in Revelation 12:

> And there appeared a great wonder in heaven; a woman clothed with the sun, and the moon under her feet, and upon her head a crown of twelve stars: And she being with child cried, travailing in birth, and pained to be delivered. **And there appeared another wonder in heaven; and behold a great red dragon, having seven heads and ten horns, and seven crowns upon his heads.** And his tail drew the third part of the stars of heaven, and did cast them to the earth: and the dragon stood before the woman which was ready to be delivered, for to devour her child as soon as it was born. (Revelation 12:1–4 KJV; my emphasis)

The first mention of the seven heads and ten horns is associated with the heavenly vision that depicts a sign in the heavens of the dragon, the woman, and the twelve stars. God makes clear in Revelation 12:9 the identity of the dragon—that is, Satan, the devil, the old serpent: he that deceived the entire world. The woman, the twelve stars, the sun, and the moon are understood as Israel, the twelve tribes, and the man-child—that is, the Lord Jesus Christ. This should also be clear from the references in the Old Testament. The one special verse in the Old Testament that should be considered concerning the woman, the sun, the moon, and the twelve stars is the vision seen by Joseph in Genesis 37:9–11. Joseph sees the sun and the moon and the eleven stars (Joseph himself being the twelfth) paying obeisance to him. Jacob correctly interprets the vision as one that describes Jacob, his twelve sons, and their mother paying obeisance to him. Once more, God drives the point home that the interpretation is true because they did indeed pay tribute to him when he was second in command to Pharaoh. The sun, the moon, and the twelve stars represent Israel. The twelve stars represent the zodiacal signs symbolizing the tribes of Israel. And now, at the time of the middle of the last seven years, God, at long last, is going to bring to pass what the stars and zodiacal signs have been describing all along. The stars, which God created to tell a story, are now going to fulfill their story that God intended them to tell. God created the heavens, and God takes this time in Revelation 12 to drive home the point that they did tell a story and that it will come to pass exactly how God designed for it to come to pass. This will occur despite all the evil devised by mankind via worshiping the sun, moon, and stars. Through the years, the stars have been corrupted by Satan through astrology and other methods to hide their story. But God now reiterates that the true story told in the heavens is his story, and that his plans for them, and the story that he designed for them to tell, will come to pass exactly and precisely as he planned. The scripture states that the stars and the sun and the signs in the heavens were created by God for signs and the giving of knowledge.[332]

The dragon is said to have seven heads and ten horns in the heavens, as explained in Revelation 12:9. The section goes on to explain that the great red dragon is the old serpent called the devil (meaning "slanderer") and Satan (meaning "adversary"). He has seven heads and ten horns, and his color is red—the color of blood and death. The heads and horns represent the universality of the earthly dominion that is about to be on the earth. Once this heavenly governance is cast to earth, it takes the form of seven earthly heads and ten earthly leaders combined as a corporate beast upon the earth. The corporate beast will eventually be energized by the supernatural beast.

Revelation 12 depicts the spiritual nature of the dragon in heaven. Satan has a position in the heavens, and through his powerful position in the heavens up until this point, he has been able to manipulate events on the earth. God states emphatically in this section, and in others, that Satan has rulership over the earth until he is cast out of the heavens and finally destroyed. Only those born again and set apart to Jesus Christ can stand against Satan, and this

---

[332] See Genesis 1:14; Psalm 19.

can occur only when they rely on their gift from God—the gift of the Holy Spirit. Satan is depicted as the *prince of the power of the air*, the *Prince of this world*, and *the god of this world*.[333] This point is further driven home through the words of our Lord in the book of Luke. The Lord does not dispute Satan's claim in Luke 4:5–8 that Satan had rulership over the earth; he only states, *"Thou shalt worship the Lord thy God and him only shalt thou serve."*[334]

The dragon in Revelation 12 is said to be red in color—the color of fire and of blood, symbolizing the dragon's cruelty and bloodthirstiness. [335] The heads, horns, and crowns are the "signs" of Satan's earthly power and governance body. Satan's corporate governance body is united in Satan and is delivered to whomsoever he wills.[336] Thus, briefly, the woman's enemy is set before us in Revelation 12. The first occurrence speaks to us as to the origin of the seven heads and ten horns as belonging to Satan's earthly dominion and originally present with him in the heavens. Revelation 12 documents his being cast out of the heavens by God through Michael, the archangel.

To fully understand Satan's being cast out of the heavens, we need to understand how Satan obtained his place in the heavens in the first place. Satan, a heavenly being, was granted dominion over the earth after Adam, the proprietor over the earth, fell into sin and delivered it to him. Genesis 3 documents the fall of Adam and the transfer of the power over the earth to God's archenemy, Satan. In Revelation 12, that dominion is once again the center of reference and is about to be disannulled by God. War in heaven is initiated by Michael, the archangel, and Satan is finally cast out of the heavens and, subsequently, into the earth. The notion that Satan is not in a powerful position in the heavens is not true and will lead only to confusion and misinterpretation of scripture. Revelation 12 clearly paints the picture of Satan in the heavens until he is cast

---

[333] Ephesians 2:2; John 12:31; 14:30; 16:11; 2 Corinthians 4:4.
[334] Luke 4:8.
[335] John 8:44; 1 John 3:12.
[336] Luke 4:6–7; Revelation 13:2.

out by Michael, the archangel, during the last days. Satan's access to heavenly power is the one of the major reasons for the sorrow and hardship in the earth. How Satan manipulates the events on the earth is unclear, but that he does so is clear from the scriptures. His presence in the heavens also assists him in disguising his actions and the reality of his existence. That Satan is in the heavens is clear from scripture; Ephesians 6:12 states, "*We wrestle not against flesh and blood, but against principalities, against powers, against the rulers of the darkness of this world, against **spiritual wickedness in high (text: heavenly) places.***" Satan is in the heavens and first needs to be cast out of the heavens for God to move on with his plan of salvation. All this is done in accordance with God's timetable. The casting out of Satan from the heavens occurs at the midpoint of the last seven years of Daniel's prophecy of seventy sevens of weeks.

The dragon, after his ejection from heaven, pursues the woman—that is, the believing promised seed of Israel. Satan's plan throughout the ages has been to stop the seed of the woman. The seed of the woman is the Lord Jesus Christ—the promised seed, as declared by God in Genesis 3:15. Satan's plan, throughout time, has always been to prevent the birth of the Lord Jesus Christ. Once God declared in Genesis that a seed would be born to the woman that would crush the head of Satan, symbolizing all of his plans and power, Satan sought to destroy the seed of the woman. The scriptures state in Genesis 3:15 that it will be the devil that bruises the heel of the Lord, but the Lord will crush the head of Satan. Satan knew from the scriptures that it was this seed, the seed of Jesus Christ, that would one day conquer and destroy him. Satan, throughout the Old Testament, partially because he knew of his fate as documented in Genesis, always attempted to destroy all the seed of Israel through various means. If he could destroy Israel, he could stop the promised seed as promised to Abraham, Isaac, Jacob, and, finally, David. After he failed and the Messiah was born into the world, he attempted to destroy the seed of Christ at Calvary through the crucifixion. The attempt seemed successful; however, God raised Christ from the dead to sit at his right hand and initiated the church of the one body of Christ. Part of Genesis 3:15 was now fulfilled—the bruising of the heel of the seed of the woman. The second part looms and will be fulfilled at the end of the final seven years. In the last days, when the devil is cast out of the heavens, Satan once again attempts to destroy the woman; Why? The reason is simple, and the scriptures are clear; God, in the last days, will save the remnant of the seed of the woman, the called-out Jews, and place them in the land in fulfillment of the promises made to their fathers. Consider the following:

> For if thou wert cut out of the olive tree which is wild by nature, and wert graffed contrary to nature into a good olive tree: how much more shall these, which be the natural branches, be graffed into their own olive tree? **For I would not, brethren, that ye should be ignorant of this mystery, lest ye should be wise in your own conceits; that blindness in part is happened to Israel, until the fulness of the Gentiles be come in. And so all Israel shall be saved: as it is written, There shall come out of Sion the Deliverer, and shall turn away ungodliness from Jacob: For this is my covenant unto them, when I shall take away their sins.** As concerning the gospel, they are enemies for your sakes: but as touching the election, they are beloved for the fathers' sakes. For the gifts and calling of God are without repentance. For as ye in times past have not believed God, yet have now obtained mercy through their unbelief: Even so have these also now not believed, that through your mercy they also may obtain mercy. For God hath concluded them all in unbelief, that he might have mercy upon all. (Romans 11:24–32 KJV; my emphasis)

Jesus Christ saves Israel at the time prepared by God when they finally accept him as their Messiah in the last days. Satan understands this reality and will once again attempt to thwart the promises of

God through his attack on the woman in the last days. The Lord Jesus Christ has always represented the demise of Satan, as stated very early on in Genesis 3:15. Thus the heads and the horns in Revelation 12 are a "sign" of Satan's power in the heavens and eventually on the earth and over mankind, especially during the last days. Satan's first order of business was always to destroy the seed of the woman, the Lord Jesus Christ. When this fails, after his ouster from the heavens, Satan sets his sights on the woman herself, the remnant seed of the woman, who will be in the land forever as promised by God. Revelation 12 and 13 maintains the order important to God. God lists the Jews first and how God protects them through the forty-two months of Revelation and as documented in Revelation 12. Revelation 13 then moves on to describe how the beast affects the Gentiles through the world dominion of the beast. The second order of business, the Gentiles, will be ruled by the seven-headed, ten-horned beast and then ultimately face the wrath of almighty God. The beast will rule the earth with cruelty and massive destruction, changing and rearranging the relative order of society on the earth. Everyday life will radically change for all on the earth. All that man has trusted in will fail, and survival will come down to worship of the beast. If they worship, they will be doomed to destruction; if they do not worship, they will be ostracized from society.

The beast will rule the earth through death, fear, and destruction. The nations and relative order of society will begin to change at the time of the beginning of the final twenty-three hundred days—the beginning of sorrows on the earth. This will continue until the middle of the final forty-two months, at which time the beast in supernatural form will begin his deadly rule on the earth. Those who attempt to resist his rule and the worship of the beast will face death and persecution. Those who willingly worship the beast will face eternal damnation. Business as usual on the earth is about to change in a cataclysmic way.

The second occurrence of the seven heads and ten horns together is related to earthly power after the casting out of the dragon from the heavens and his relegation to the earth. The second occurrence describes how the Gentile nations will be affected by the new Satanic order on the earth. The second occurrence is the earthly manifestation of the beast with seven heads and ten horns. Unlike the first heavenly representation, the earthly manifestation is explained in much more detail in several scriptures, beginning in Revelation 13. Revelation 13:1–3 begins to summarize the newly ordained forty-two-month governance set up on earth immediately after the casting out of Satan from the heavens. Revelation 13 gives the horrible details of what it means to have Satan's evil governance on the earth—woe to the people on the earth!

> And I stood upon the sand of the sea, and saw a beast rise up out of the sea, **having seven heads and ten horns, and upon his horns ten crowns,** and upon his heads the name of blasphemy. And the beast which I saw was like unto a leopard, and his feet were as the feet of a bear, and his mouth as the mouth of a lion: and the dragon gave him his power, and his seat, and great authority. And I saw one of his heads as it were wounded to death; and his deadly wound was healed: and all the world wondered after the beast. And they worshipped the dragon which gave power unto the beast: and they worshipped the beast, saying, Who is like unto the beast? who is able to make war with him? And there was given unto him a mouth speaking great things and blasphemies; and power was given unto him to continue forty and two months. And he opened his mouth in blasphemy against God, to blaspheme his name, and his tabernacle, and them that dwell in heaven. And it was given unto him to make war with the saints, and to overcome them: and power was given him over all kindreds, and tongues, and nations. And all that dwell upon the earth shall worship him, whose names are not written in the book of life of

the Lamb slain from the foundation of the world. (Revelation 13:1–8 KJV; my emphasis)

Revelation 13:1–4 represents, in a few verses, the new conditions on earth that will have their beginning at the midpoint of the final seven years. The seven-headed, ten-horned beast is about to take control of the whole earth. One man—the supernatural beast, the vile man, the Antichrist—has just been raised from the dead through a great satanic miracle. The Satan-inspired resurrection occurred at the holy place in Jerusalem—the place that God foretold of the return of the Lord but is now confederate with the presence of the beast, declaring himself a false god. This event is also ominously known as the ***abomination which will cause desolation or destruction on the earth.***[337] The beast will now assume full control and, with his ten horns, will go on to conquer the earth and make her desolate. The beast is said to rise from the sea—the same sea that the four winds of heaven strove upon to bring up the four powerful Gentile dominions in Daniel 7. Revelation 13:1–4 is an expansion of the fourth terrible beast documented in Daniel 7. In Daniel 7, the fourth beast rises consecutively after the lion, bear, and leopard listed in the first part of the chapter. Daniel 7 identifies the origin of the three previous beasts or Gentile dominions that rise before the beast in the last days. The lion with eagle's wings, the bear who raised himself on one side, and the leopard with the four heads are documented and described with more detail in Daniel 7. In Revelation 13:1–2, the Gentile beasts, or dominions, are depicted as being in unison with the beast, but their history is left out. Consequently, Revelation 13:1–2 needs to be examined together with Daniel 7 to gain full understanding of what God would have us know concerning these beasts.

Revelation 13:1–4 identifies the conditions on the earth at the time of the middle of the seventieth seven. The beast has just come into power and is shown in unison with the three powerful Gentile dominions, or superpowers, of Daniel 7. Both Daniel 7 and Revelation 13 explain that the beast, in the last days, is made up

---

[337] Matt 24:15

of the previous three powerful Gentile dominions, ten horns, and a resurrected seventh head. The wild beast is the supernaturally charged seventh head, and as such, it stuns those on the earth with wonderment. The wild beast and the great superpowers and kings of the earth—the lion (one head), the bear (one head), the leopard (four heads), the ten horns—and the peoples of the earth have now come together as one; this is *Mystery Babylon*. To God it is reminiscent of the first Babylon of Genesis 11.[338] The six heads—made up of the lion, bear, and leopard—have associated themselves with, and are depicted in unison with, the seventh head, who has just been miraculously raised from the dead. The seven heads, along with the ten horns, now represent the governance foundation for the dragon as he sets up his forty-two-month terrible dominion on the earth—the worst time in human history.

The seven heads and ten horns were not specifically defined while Satan wielded his power from his place in the heavens. God, now, in Daniel chapters 7–12, along with Revelation 13 and 17, gives further information about and explanation to the meaning of the earthly seven heads and the ten horns and their terrible nature. The beast, taken together with its seven heads and ten horns, represents the governance body of Satan on the earth, which will last forty-two months.[339] The governance body that was once in the heavens is now reestablished on the earth; it is symbolic of the former heavenly rule. This reality is stated by God in Revelation 12:9–12:

> And the great dragon was cast out, that old serpent, called the Devil, and Satan, which deceiveth the whole world: he was cast out into the earth, and his angels were cast out with him.
> And I heard a loud voice saying in heaven, Now is come salvation, and strength, and the kingdom of our God, and the power of his Christ: for the accuser of our brethren is cast

---

[338] Revelation 16:19.
[339] Revelation 13:5.

down, which accused them before our God day and night. And they overcame him by the blood of the Lamb, and by the word of their testimony; and they loved not their lives unto the death. Therefore rejoice, ye heavens, and ye that dwell in them. **Woe to the inhabiters of the earth and of the sea! for the devil is come down unto you, having great wrath, because he knoweth that he hath but a short time;** (Rev 12:9–12; my emphasis).

Daniel's prophecy reveals that of the seven heads, six of them originated from the Gentile superpowers that rise before the final seven-year period. The seventh head, or the head that was wounded to death and whose deadly wound was healed, is the wild beast himself, a man raised from the dead, empowered by Satan and in supernatural form. Recall that the heads represent mountains or strong superpower dominions that come together under the beast to rule the earth in the last days.[340] The beast, now on the earth, turns his attention to the earth and the Gentile kingdoms of the earth. In Revelation 13:1, the dragon contemplates his next move and his final earthly strategy. The result is the rising of the beast with seven heads and ten horns from the sea. It is also important to understand that at the time of the middle of the seven years, five of the seven heads will have fallen from once prominent positions on the earth. This reality occurring between the beginning of the twenty-three hundred days and the middle of the seven years. In effect, the five fallen nations will be easily dismissed by the wild beast.

Revelation 13:1–2 declares that the beast is like a leopard with feet like those of a bear, and his mouth is that of a lion. The searcher of scripture will immediately associate these beasts with the same beasts documented in Daniel 7. The same beasts were documented and explained, through a vision, in Daniel 7. Once again, we see the extraordinary relationship between the book of Revelation and the

---

[340] Revelation 17:9.

book of Daniel; both describe the last days of man's rule on earth. Chapter 4, section 2, reference 4 of our study documents the vision of the four beasts that Daniel saw in Daniel 7. In Daniel 7, the wild animals, or Gentile dominions, rise in consecutive order and are identified as Gentile kingdoms, or dominions, that arise prior to the appearance of the last terrible wild beast. The last terrible wild beast will then unify the previous three beasts—the lion, the bear, and the leopard with the four heads—into a power base for his world dominion, as summarized in Revelation 13:2. Six of the seven heads mentioned represent the six corporate heads of the lion, the bear, and the four-headed leopard (see Daniel 7) all acting together as one. The seventh head is that of the recently resurrected wild beast, who was assassinated and miraculously came back to life: "*his deadly wound was healed.*"[341] The seven heads represent the conglomeration of Gentile dominions or rulership on the earth during the last days. The three wild animals, or earthly Gentile dominions, will arise on the earth prior to the last days, but at the last time, and will be immediately followed by the wild beast, who will unify these governments under the vile man/Antichrist. The rulership of the wild beast under the supernatural power of the Antichrist will last for the final forty-two months. The final terrible beast represents the final Gentile dominion over the earth and, after their dominion is revoked, will bring the time of the Gentiles to an end.

The scripture depicts the wild beast, the seventh head, as having ten horns protruding out of his head. This indicates that the ten horns will be subservient or part of the wild beast and also share in his supernatural power. This cannot be said for the other six heads which will eventually fade into warring with each other and relative obscurity. The horns, as used in the scriptures, represent strong, powerful individuals, kings, or leaders. The ten horns are ten individually picked kings, or leaders, who will receive supernatural power from the beast after "*one hour with the beast.*"[342] To understand the horns, we must look at the scriptures and their usages in other

---

[341] Revelation 13:3.
[342] Revelation 17.

section of scripture. Horns are interpreted by God through their previous usage in his word. In Daniel 8:20–21, God interprets horns to be representative of powerful kings or leaders of countries. Historically, the initial horns listed in the beginning of Daniel 8 represent the two kings of Medo-Persia and the first king of Greece, Alexander the Great. It is clear from previous scripture usage that horns represent strong, powerful leaders, such as powerful kings or rulers.[343] The critical question regarding these final ten horns is, who are they? They are listed as rising together in the last days and, as documented in Revelation 17:12, they receive supernatural power from the beast after one hour with the supernatural beast.

Historically, we look again to the book of Daniel to gain a fuller understanding of the ten horns of Revelation. The ten horns, or ten kings, are first mentioned as the feet and toes of the last Gentile dominion associated with the great image described in Daniel 2. The latter chapters of Daniel also mention the horns and the beast several times, along with part of the last Gentile dominion. The horns are again mentioned in Revelation 13 and 17, where they are associated with the last days and the final Gentile dominion of the beast. Each time the ten horns are mentioned, in both Old and New Testaments, they need to be interpreted as part of the last days scenario. Once again, we can accumulate all the verses containing the ten horns and understand what God reveals through scripture buildup. The following are the documented verses associated with the ten horns in sequential order in the Word of God. Each verse relates to the ten horns, or kings. The verses are listed here, but it is suggested that the reader spend some time reading the verses in their contexts.

> And whereas thou sawest the **feet and toes** (ten kings), part of potters' clay, and part of iron, the kingdom shall be divided; but there shall be in it of the strength of the iron, forasmuch as thou sawest the iron mixed with miry clay. And as the **toes of the feet** were part of iron, and part of clay,

---

[343] Daniel 8:20–21.

THE LAST DAYS AND THE VILE MAN OF DANIEL

so the kingdom shall be partly strong, and partly broken. And whereas thou sawest iron mixed with miry clay, they shall mingle themselves with the seed of men: but they shall not cleave one to another, even as iron is not mixed with clay. And in the **days of these kings** shall the God of heaven set up a kingdom, which shall never be destroyed: and the kingdom shall not be left to other people, but it shall break in pieces and consume all these kingdoms, and it shall stand for ever. (Daniel 2:41–44 KJV; my emphasis).

After this I saw in the night visions, and behold a fourth beast, dreadful and terrible, and strong exceedingly; and it had great iron teeth: it devoured and brake in pieces, and stamped the residue with the feet of it: and it was diverse from all the beasts that were before it; **and it had ten horns.** (Daniel 7:7KJV)

And of the **ten horns** that were in his head, and of the other which came up, and before whom three fell; even of that horn that had eyes, and a mouth that spake very great things, whose look was more stout than his fellows. (Daniel 7:20 KJV; my emphasis)

And **the ten horns** out of this kingdom are ten kings that shall arise: and another shall rise after them; and he shall be diverse from the first, and he shall subdue three kings. (Daniel 7:24 KJV; my emphasis)

And there appeared another wonder in heaven; and behold a great red dragon, having seven heads **and ten horns,** and seven crowns upon his heads. (Revelation 12:3 KJV; my emphasis)

And I stood upon the sand of the sea, and saw a beast rise up out of the sea, having seven heads and **ten horns**, and upon his horns ten crowns, and upon his heads the name of blasphemy. (Revelation 13:1 KJV; my emphasis)

So he carried me away in the spirit into the wilderness: and I saw a woman sit upon a scarlet coloured beast, full of names of blasphemy, having seven heads and **ten horns**. (Revelation 17:3 KJV; my emphasis)

And the angel said unto me, wherefore didst thou marvel? I will tell thee the mystery of the woman, and of the beast that carrieth her, which hath the seven heads and **ten horns.** (Revelation 17:7 KJV; my emphasis)

And the **ten horns** which thou sawest are ten kings, which have received no kingdom as yet; but receive power as kings one hour with the beast. (Revelation 17:12 KJV; my emphasis)

And the **ten horns** which thou sawest upon the beast, these shall hate the whore, and shall make her desolate and naked, and shall eat her flesh, and burn her with fire. (Revelation 17:16 KJV; my emphasis)

The beast in his mortal form and as a man is first represented as a little horn—a man of small beginnings who is not given the honor of the kingdom.[344] The ten horns, rulers, or kings, that arise in the last days are always associated with the head of the wild beast and not with the other six heads of the seven-headed beast.[345] As noted earlier, the first six heads represent Gentile dominions (the lion, the bear, and the leopard with four heads) that will rise in the last days before the rising of the wild beast. The six heads of these Gentile dominions will join forces with the seventh head, the beast, after his miraculous resurrection at the time of the middle of the last seven

---

[344] Daniel 8:9; 11:21.
[345] Daniel 7:7.

years. The seventh head, or wild beast, is made diverse through the supernatural powers afforded him by Satan. The seventh supernatural head wrestles control from the other six heads, and then goes on to rule the earth with the ten horns with whom supernatural power is also given in one hour with the beast. The deception and mayhem of the wild beast and ten horns will go on for forty-two months. The destruction will continue until the wild beast is destroyed by the Lord Jesus Christ at the end of the final forty-two months.[346] The beast, with his ten horns, will destroy the earth, tread it down, and break it into pieces. Only those called by God, written in the book of life, will be able to withstand the final deception. The wild beast, together with the ten horns, will make up the seventh head. Regarding the ten horns, they are stated to give their power unto the beast until all the words of God are fulfilled. It will be the ten horns, or kings, after being given supernatural power from the wild beast, that will be responsible for the destruction of Jerusalem, the sanctuary, and the people of the land. [347]

From the verses that describe the ten horns above, the following can be gleaned:

1. The ten horns are ten individual powerful kings or leaders who rise along with the beast in the last days. (See Revelation 13:1.)
2. The ten horns are associated with the beast of the last days and are given power as kings at one and the same hour with the beast. These events will transpire when the beast receives his supernatural power—in the middle of the last week, or at the midpoint of the last seven years. (See Revelation 17:12.)
3. The ten horns will agree with the beast and give their power unto the beast until God's Words are completely fulfilled. (See Revelation 17:12, 17.)

---

[346] 2 Thessalonians 2:8.
[347] Daniel 9:26, Revelation 17:16.

4. At the end of the forty-two-month rule of the beast and the ten kings, God will set up his everlasting kingdom with Jesus Christ as the anointed King of kings and Lord of lords on the earth. (See Daniel 2:43–44.)
5. The identities of these ten kings will be known only at the time of the end—the time of their actual rising on the earth. These kings will, however, be identified by these very verses when they do arise.
6. The ten kings will arise before the beast. The beast will rise initially as a little horn, or ruler, and he will subdue three of the original ten kings as he rises to become the seventh head. (See Daniel 7:24.)
7. The scriptures suggest that these ten kings will probably all be from the same area in and around Syria, and all from the Middle East. Daniel 7:7–8 states that the little horn, the beast, comes up *among* the other horns. This indicates that beast will be associating with the other ten horns in some capacity before he rises up and becomes the wild beast. We know from Daniel 11 that the beast will be another king of the North—a Syrian king or leader rising to power in the last time. The man of sin will rise as a Syrian leader and then appoint ten kings who will receive supernatural power to rule the earth with the wild beast. We conclude that the ten horns, which eventually become joint rulers with the beast, will be from the same area of the world as the beast as he rises to power. Consider the following:

> After this I saw in the night visions, and behold a fourth beast, dreadful and terrible, and strong exceedingly; and it had great iron teeth: it devoured and brake in pieces, and stamped the residue with the feet of it: **and it was diverse from all the beasts that were before it; and it had ten horns. I considered the horns, and, behold, there came up among them another little horn, before whom there were three of**

the first horns plucked up by the roots: and, behold, in this horn were eyes like the eyes of man, and a mouth speaking great things. (Daniel 7:7–8 KJV; my emphasis)

The final occurrence in the Bible of the seven-headed, ten-horned beast is recorded in Revelation 17:3. The record details the most information regarding the corporate unified seven heads and ten horns—their origin, their actions, and their end. Revelation 17 reveals a vision to John of a woman supported by a beast with seven heads and ten horns; the entire image is labeled *Mystery Babylon*. The revelation is given to John by one of the seven angels who have the seven vials. The placement in scripture of this vision is significant. Recall that in Revelation 16, the final wrath of almighty God is played out on the earth through the pouring out of the seven vials. During the pouring out of the seventh vial in Revelation 16:19—the final vial, which results in the fall of all the nations—great Babylon comes into remembrance before God.[348] Revelation 17 and 18 explain, by way of parenthesis, why great Babylon came to God's remembrance (Revelation 17), and what the fall of great Babylon really means (Revelation 18).

Revelation 17 reveals the history and the future of the beast, the woman, the ten horns, and the seven heads. The chapter also describes what actually happened on the earth to bring *Mystery Babylon* into the remembrance of God, as stated in Revelation 16:19. The vision given to John in Revelation 17 is divided into two real-time events that occur on the earth during the final seven years. The theme is consistent—*Mystery Babylon and the judgment of the great whore*. Both events relate to different points in time with respect to the evolution of *Mystery Babylon*. Both events provide interpretation regarding the heads, the horns, the woman, and the waters. The second event, in time, is listed first in the chapter because it is more significant. The second event records the condition of things at the time of the middle of the seventieth week. The seven-headed beast, with the seven heads

---

[348] Revelation 16:19.

and the ten horns, is portrayed as supporting the whore together with the nations and peoples of the world. The picture adds significant information to all previous scriptures regarding the beast and gives additional information as to what will occur during the middle of the final seven years, once again without contradiction. The central point of all of these events is played out during the middle of the last seven years and builds upon all previous information contained in God's Word. The first event in time describes what will lead up to the events of the middle of the seventieth week. Revelation 17:8–18 provides additional information with respect to this event. The main players will be the wild beast, the woman, the ten horns, and the seven heads. Following are the salient points that God would have us understand:

1. The woman, or the whore, is identified as the great city and is supported by the beast. From previous scriptures and the Old Testament, we understand this woman to be Jerusalem.[349]
2. The whore will be burned with fire and left naked and bare during the final forty-two months.
3. The ten horns are discussed in detail as to what they will accomplish and their transition from obscurity to powerful agents of the beast during the final forty and two months.
4. The Gentile nations and tongues are pictured together with the wild beast, or under the sway of the wild beast.
5. The heads are identified as mountains representing powerful Gentile dominions as distinct from the other Gentile nations.
6. Seven representative kings representing these powerful Gentile nations are identified as being present.
7. The ten horns, or ten kings, will make war with the lamb, and the lamb will overcome them.

---

[349] Ezekiel 16

8. The beast was, is not, and yet is. The reference here is to his miraculous resurrection and subsequent deception of the nations and peoples.

Revelation 17:3–6 relates to the same event at the same approximate time as the vision given to John in Revelation 13:1–3; this takes place during the middle of the seven years. Revelation 17:3–6 builds upon Revelation 13:1–3 and the references in Daniel giving the additional information listed above. God states clearly that the next verses in the book of Revelation, Revelation 17:9–18, will require wisdom to be understood. The wisdom is the perception to rightly divide the Word of God through an accurate understanding of God's documented timeline events, both the Old and New Testaments. To understand, observe that the seven-headed, ten-horned beast and the nations are acting together as one corporate body in Revelation 17:1–3. The cooperative support represents the conditions on the earth at the midpoint of the seven years. Beginning in Revelation 17:9, the angel gives information concerning a different time—a time that is well before the middle of the seven years. The players from verses 1–3—the beast, the heads, the horns, the woman, and the waters or nations—are all included, but the time is different. In Revelation 17:9–18, additional information is provided regarding the evolution of the seven heads, the ten horns, the beast, the woman, and their interaction. God goes back in time to reveal to us how the midweek crisis came to be and what will be the end for the whore, the ten horns, and the beast.

It is Revelation 17:9–18 that represents an earthly meeting before the beast comes into power. In fact, at this time, probably sometime before the the middle of the final seven years, the beast is documented as not yet being incorporated into the seven heads and ten horns.[350] The first meeting may also be in and around the beginning of the twenty-three hundred days. It is clear that the meeting of the nations and leaders of the earth occurs sometime before the middle of the seven years, and that the beast has not yet come into power on

---

[350] Revelation 17:10.

the earth. There will be at least two or maybe more meetings between the beginning of the final twenty-three hundred days and the final 1,260 days. This is evidenced by the transition of the members as time moves forward to the middle of the final seven years. It is also clear that the meetings will involve the woman (Jerusalem) and the nations of the world somehow all coming together for an apparent peace conference, or some other type of event which unites them together. It should also be clear that not long after these meetings, the beast will come into power, and at the time of his resurrection, the middle of the last seven years will be thrust upon the world. This would seem to indicate the final meeting taking place sometime late in the first half of the seven years but after the beast becomes strong with an ally during the initiation of the final twenty-three hundred days. (See figure 4)

In brief, the vision is one of giving detail regarding all of the players as they go through their transition from mere obscurity to supernatural rule and then defeat at the hands of the son of God. The whore is also judged and dealt with in accordance with God's Old Testament law. The whore, Jerusalem, is burned with fire and left naked and bare (Ezekiel 16 should be read in connection with this event). The transition of the city from a whore to the bride of Christ, the new Jerusalem, is completed in Revelation 21:2, in which the new Jerusalem, the bride of Christ, has made herself ready for her husband.

In summary, Revelation 17:9–18 represents another vision on earth, which the Lord reveals to John through his angel. This will be a peace conference, but there is nowhere in scripture that pinpoints the actual time of this meeting. It is clear that it will be sometime in the first half of the final seven years but before the middle of the seven years. This meeting will reveal six of the seven heads, the ten kings, the whore, and the nations, all of whom will be supporting each other and a common cause. The event will be a type of casting call documented by God to secretly alert those with wisdom and understanding of God's impending wrath. The alert will be a warning of the impending doom and destruction that will soon (in days) be coming to the earth—woe to the inhabitants of the earth! The casting call, or peace convention, will identify the significant members who will shortly come into power on the earth. The characters described by God in Revelation 17:3–6 will be formally introduced at this first vision, and they will effectively fulfill the vision represented by Revelation 17:9–18. Their future actions are summarized and will peak at the middle of the seven years with the rising of first the corporate beast and then the wild beast of Revelation 17:1–3.

God refers to the great corporate whore and all of its members as *Mystery Babylon*, the mother of all abominations of the earth. The judgment of great Babylon is not restricted to one city but to all the inhabitants and all the nations of the earth—all those listed in Revelation 17:1–3. Mystery Babylon is God's way of characterizing the gathering of the nations as one. God uses the same city, Babylon, from Genesis 11.

The whole of Revelation 17 answers, by parenthesis, the question of why Babylon came to God's remembrance in Revelation 16:19. The section also reveals the judgment of Jerusalem. The result of their gathering and God's judgment against the nations is recorded in Revelation 18. As the first Babylon was led by the mighty rebel Nimrod, the second Babylon will be led by a mighty warrior, the Antichrist. The chapter also provides prophecy as to the eventual outcome of their rebellion on Earth. The vision and prophecy represented by Revelation 17:9–18 will be a gathering of the nations, which will appear like a great stride forward toward peace for the nations of the earth. But God's view is very different. Consider God's summary in contrast to that of man as you read Revelation 17 below. Consider the detailed information given by God (listed below) regarding the ten horns, the seven heads, and the whore (also known as the great city).

> And there came one of the seven angels which had the seven vials, and talked with me, saying unto me, Come hither; I will shew unto thee the judgment of the great whore that sitteth upon many waters: With whom the kings of the earth have committed fornication, and the

inhabitants of the earth have been made drunk with the wine of her fornication. **So he carried me away in the spirit into the wilderness: and I saw a woman sit upon a scarlet coloured beast, full of names of blasphemy, having seven heads and ten horns.** And the woman was arrayed in purple and scarlet colour, and decked with gold and precious stones and pearls, having a golden cup in her hand full of abominations and filthiness of her fornication: And upon her forehead was a name written, MYSTERY, BABYLON THE GREAT, THE MOTHER OF HARLOTS AND ABOMINATIONS OF THE EARTH. And I saw the woman drunken with the blood of the saints, and with the blood of the martyrs of Jesus: and when I saw her, I wondered with great admiration. And the angel said unto me, **Wherefore didst thou marvel? I will tell thee the mystery of the woman, and of the beast that carrieth her, which hath the seven heads and ten horns. The beast that thou sawest was, and is not; and shall ascend out of the bottomless pit, and go into perdition: and they that dwell on the earth shall wonder, whose names were not written in the book of life from the foundation of the world, when they behold the beast that was, and is not, and yet is. And here is the mind which hath wisdom. The seven heads are seven mountains, on which the woman sitteth. And there are seven kings: five are fallen, and one is, and the other is not yet come; and when he cometh, he must continue a short space. And the beast that was, and is not, even he is the eighth, and is of the seven, and goeth into perdition. And the ten horns which thou sawest are ten kings,**

> **which have received no kingdom as yet; but receive power as kings one hour with the beast. These have one mind, and shall give their power and strength unto the beast. These shall make war with the Lamb, and the Lamb shall overcome them: for he is Lord of lords, and King of kings: and they that are with him are called, and chosen, and faithful.** And he saith unto me, The waters which thou sawest, where the whore sitteth, are peoples, and multitudes, and nations, and tongues. **And the ten horns which thou sawest upon the beast, these shall hate the whore, and shall make her desolate and naked, and shall eat her flesh, and burn her with fire. For God hath put in their hearts to fulfil his will, and to agree, and give their kingdom unto the beast, until the words of God shall be fulfilled.** And the woman which thou sawest is that great city, which reigneth over the kings of the earth. (Revelation 17:1–18 KJV; my emphasis)

John, through the Holy Spirit, is shown a vision on the earth describing the events on the earth that will shortly come to pass as part of the last seven years. As stated earlier, the vision is a type of casting call for the characters who will soon come to power on the earth. Those of an accurate understanding of the Word of God will receive the warning that God gives—understanding the events from the Word of God.

The middle-of-the-week event, the abomination that will lead to desolations on the earth, will test all men on the earth. The event will be the supernatural appearance of the Antichrist at the holy place in Jerusalem; *he will have just been raised from the dead and will be declaring himself to be God*. The initial event, the gathering of the nations before the midweek event, is described in Revelation 17:10 and is characterized by the gathering of nations for peace. The leaders of the nations will consist of six of the seven heads listed in Revelation 13 and 17, all ten kings (horns), and many of the nations of the world. The focus of the vision of Revelation 17 features a woman atop a seven-headed, ten-horned beast, together with many nations and peoples of the earth. God describes the gathering as *"Mystery Babylon the Great, the Mother of Harlots and Abominations of the Earth."* The woman is pictured as being unified with the nations, and she is also considered a harlot at the time of the initial vision. The wise will understand the interpretation of the vision—that it reveals information regarding what will shortly occur on the earth. The climax will be the rise of the corporate beast at midweek. The angel's interpretation, beginning in verse 7, reveals God's version, the true version, which describes how God sees the events on the earth. The world sees a great stride forward that, in the world's view, will contribute to world peace. God sees the event as the ultimate evil, bringing to fruition God's wrath toward the earth, the wicked men who rule it, and Satan. The vision itself will identify satisfactorily, through the interpretation of Revelation 17 and other previous records, the actual earthly players taking part in the vision. In Revelation 17:8, the angel reveals that the beast *was, is not, and is again*, signifying how the wild beast/vile man/Antichrist will rise from the dead and deceive the whole earth. Verse 9 states, *"The seven heads are seven mountains on which the woman sitteth."* God uses mountains in the Bible as a figure (symbol or metaphor) for a kingdom or dominion of power. Consider the following verses, which exemplify this symbolism. The first verse in Jeremiah speaks directly of the seven mountains of *Mystery Babylon*.

> And I will render unto Babylon and to all the inhabitants of Chaldea all their evil that they have done in Zion in your sight, saith the LORD. **Behold, I am against thee, O destroying mountain, saith the LORD, which destroyest all the earth:** and I will stretch out mine hand upon thee, and roll thee down from the rocks,

and will make thee a burnt mountain. (Jeremiah 51:24–25 KJV; my emphasis)

And the mountain symbolic of the dominion of Jesus Christ is referred to in Daniel 2:35 KJV:

> Then was the iron, the clay, the brass, the silver, and the gold, broken to pieces together, and became like the chaff of the summer threshingfloors; and the wind carried them away, that no place was found for them: **and the stone that smote the image became a great mountain, and filled the whole earth (my emphasis).**

Assembling this information together with the interpretation of the angel, the seven heads represent seven mountains or world superpowers, on which the woman sits. The seventh head will be the beast; first in mortal form and then the eighth in supernatural form. They are seven powerful Gentile dominions that come together in the last days comprising the corporate beast. The seven heads and the nations of the world come together as one in the last days, and God compares them to the coming together at Babylon in Genesis 11.

It is clear, at the point in time of the first vision, that Jerusalem is numbered with the other nations of *Mystery Babylon* and is depicted as a whore disowned by God. Six of the seven heads will be present for the confederate conference of nations. Additionally, Revelation 13:3 illustrates the conditions on the earth at the midpoint, or midst, of the seven years, when the beast has just come into power, in supernatural form, after being raised from the dead. At the midpoint of the seven years, all seven of the heads will be present, and the seventh will have just been resurrected from the dead. Notice how Revelation 17:10 states that only six of the seven heads are present and that the seventh has not yet come. This indicates the two independent time periods as referenced by God in his word. The fact that there are two independent time periods listed in Revelation 17 is of critical importance for proper interpretation regarding the interpretation of Revelation 17.

Revelation 17:12 states that the ten horns are ten kings, or leaders, who have received no kingdom as of yet but will receive power as kings after one hour with the beast. The power that will be given to the ten kings will occur when the beast rises from the dead at the midst of the week, or 1,260 days before the destruction of the beast. Revelation 17:13 goes on to state that it will be these ten kings, or individual leaders, who will, together with the beast, make war with the lamb and be destroyed by the lamb.[351] The ten horns, or leaders, will be responsible for destroying the whore, making her desolate and naked, eating her flesh, and burning her with fire. The same judgment is prophesied in Ezekiel 16:38–45; both sections speak of the same time of judgment for Jerusalem. Consider the following:

> And I will judge thee, as women that break wedlock and shed blood are judged; and I will give thee blood in fury and jealousy. And I will also give thee into their hand, and they shall throw down thine eminent place, and shall break down thy high places: they shall strip thee also of thy clothes, and shall take thy fair jewels, and leave thee naked and bare. They shall also bring up a company against thee, and they shall stone thee with stones, and thrust thee through with their swords. **And they shall burn thine houses with fire, and execute judgments upon thee in the sight of many women: and I will cause thee to cease from playing the harlot,** and thou also shalt give no hire any more. So will I make my fury toward thee to rest, and my jealousy shall depart from thee, and I will be quiet, and will be no more angry. Because thou hast not remembered the days of thy youth, but hast fretted me in all these

---

[351] Revelation 17:14.

> things; behold, therefore I also will recompense thy way upon thine head, saith the Lord GOD: and thou shalt not commit this lewdness above all thine abominations. Behold, every one that useth proverbs shall use this proverb against thee, saying, As is the mother, so is her daughter. Thou art thy mother's daughter, that lotheth her husband and her children; and thou art the sister of thy sisters, which lothed their husbands and their children: your mother was an Hittite, and your father an Amorite. (Ezekiel 16:38–45 KJV)

God, in Ezekiel 16, pronounces judgment against Jerusalem because of departing from true God and worshipping strange gods. This was, and is, the sin of adultery, in which God declares them adulterers, resulting in God's final judgments. Additionally, the final judgement regarding *Mystery Babylon* will also be carried out during the last days and as described in Revelation 18. Revelation 17 depicts seven heads which are coexistent with each other and are listed in the vision as seven mountains who together support the woman at the time of the vision. Of the seven kings, it is stated that the first five are fallen, the sixth is ruling, and the seventh has not yet come. This indicates that the seventh, the beast in mortal form, will not be present at the conference but will become the seventh in due time. The scripture also states that five of the powerful Gentile dominions are fallen; that is, they have fallen from a higher state to a lower state. They have not been destroyed or killed, as many interpret this to mean. The key word in the verse is the Greek word used for "fallen" in verse 10. "Fallen," from the *Complete Word Study Dictionary*, has the following meaning: "***4098. πίπτω píptō; fut. pesoúmai, 2d aor. épeson, aor. épesa (Revelation 1:17; 5:14). To fall. (I) Particularly, to fall from a higher to a lower place, spoken of persons and things.***"[352] Based on this definition it is clear that the

---

[352] Zodhiates, S. (2000) *Complete Word Study Dictionary*; New Testament (electronic ed.). Chattanooga, TN: AMG Publishers; 1992; word #4098

sixth head at the time of the vision will be ruling or still at the peak of its power. The other five heads will still be empowered, but not as powerful as they once were. How this occurs on the earth is probably related to the opening of the seals of Revelation chapter 2. God is clear that these nations will fall from once prominent positions on the earth. It is likely that the sixth head that is ruling is the bear, the feet of the corporate beast,[353] since it states in Daniel that the beast will destroy the residue (the other five heads) ***with the feet of it***.[354]

The complete true meaning of this event will be evident only at the time of its fulfillment. Those with wisdom of the Word of God regarding these verses will understand perfectly well at that time; until then, it is fruitless to speculate. Six of the seven kings are present for the conference, and one, the seventh, is still to come. Five of the leaders representing powerful Gentile nations will be present, but their nations will have fallen from a higher position to a lower position. The sixth is ruling at the time of the conference; more powerful than the other five, and the seventh has not yet come. From these verses, God has provided ample information to piece together this conference on the earth, and how it relates to Revelation 17. When the seventh comes, he will have a short rule before giving way to the eighth—the wild supernatural beast. The wild beast is stated to emanate from (Greek "*ek*") the seven or the seventh. The beast will be in his mortal form as the seventh king, and then he will be killed. After this, the seventh king will be raised from the dead as the supernatural eighth king, the wild beast. Although seven mountains, represented by seven kings, are mentioned, there is also an eighth king stated to exist in the same section. The key to this puzzle is understanding that the seventh and the eighth kings are the same person in two different forms. The seventh king is the mortal form of the beast, and the eighth king is the supernatural form of the beast, now called the wild beast.

To summarize, the seven heads represent six powerful Gentile nations or powerful dominions on the earth and the seventh being

---

[353] Revelation 13.2.
[354] Daniel 7.7.

the beast; all gathered together at the time of the end and present for a conference showing unity for Jerusalem. The heads from Daniel 7 and Revelation 13 resemble a lion with eagles' wings (nation 1), a bear (nation 2), and a leopard with four heads (nations 3, 4, 5, and 6).[355] The seventh head is the beast, first in mortal form and then, as the eighth king, in supernatural form. It is the supernatural form of the beast, the eighth king, who will give supernatural power to the ten kings, or horns, and rule the earth with cruelty for forty-two months. The beast will come back to life at the midst, or middle, of the last seven years, and he will go on to create hell on earth for the next forty-two months. At the end of the forty-two months, Jesus Christ will destroy the beast with the brightness of his coming. [356]

The peace conference, which occurs on the earth during the last time, is marked by a gathering of nations and powers on the earth, and it will symbolize the conference laid out by God in Revelation 17. The first meeting or conference will be held sometime after the beginning of the last seven years and at, or shortly after, the beginning of the final twenty-three hundred days. The time will also be some time after the beast begins to rise through a league with a powerful ally. The league with the powerful ally marks the beginning of the first of two seven-year periods and marks the beginning of the entire period known as the last days. The beginning of this time period will only be known by God and it will be God who will set it into motion at his own discretion. Once it is put into motion, or initiated, the sequence of events will follow exactly as laid out in the Word of God. The nations, kings, and peoples of the earth are represented by seven heads, ten kings, and a number of dignitaries from the other nations of the earth. The meeting will also concern the woman, Jerusalem. All of these characters will be present at the conference, unified, and symbolizing to God *Mystery Babylon*. The entire vision recorded in Revelation 17 is God's perspective of what is about to occur on the earth. The mind with wisdom realizes God's thoughts to be much higher than those of man. To man, the conference represents a great

---

[355] Daniel 7:4–6; Revelation 13:1–2.
[356] 2 Thessalonians 2:8.

stride forward toward peace and unity on Earth. To God, the meeting represents destruction and wrath about to envelop the earth. God thinks and sees differently than man, his thoughts being so much higher than man's. The conference and prophecy concerning the members, and their action henceforth, continues through the middle of the seventieth week and throughout the final forty-two months. The central characters present for the meetings in Revelation 17—the horns, the heads, the nations, and the whore—are taken through their past, present, and future behaviors. Revelation 17 also documents the beast himself, although he is not present for the conference, he will, in short time become the center of attraction. The reference also takes the reader through the beast's evolution through time. Following is a summary of the transition of each of the members of the vision, in accordance with Revelation 17:7–18.

1. *The beast:* At the beginning of the conference, the beast is in mortal form, but he is not present for the initial peace summit. He initially is a king or leader of his country on the earth. He will, for whatever reason, not be invited to the conference, but in time he will be the seventh head and transition to the eighth—the supernatural wild beast. The transition from the mortal seventh king to the supernatural eighth king will take place at the time of the middle of the seven years. The beast will support the great city and, in collaboration with the other members, will support the whore at the middle of the seven years. The beast is the seventh king in mortal form but the eighth in supernatural form. The beast is assassinated and raised from the dead, and he then becomes the eighth king in supernatural form. His death will probably last only a few days before his seemingly miraculous satanic rise from the dead. He will then go on to declare himself as divine and subsequently deceive the world for the final forty-two months. The beast will also be responsible for energizing the ten kings

with supernatural power as he goes on to orchestrate the destruction of Jerusalem; the city and the sanctuary.[357]

2. *The ten horns or kings:* The ten horns are individual men who begin with no power at the beginning of the vision but transition to ten powerful supernatural kings after spending one hour with the supernatural beast. Their power to rule supernaturally is received almost simultaneously with the supernatural power of the beast at the middle of the seven-year period. The power they receive from the beast is then used to destroy the whore—to burn her with fire and eat her flesh. The ten horns will also be responsible for the destruction of the nations; they will be at one with the beast and will rule the earth. These ten horns are given supernatural power from the beast to destroy. These ten kings, or horns, may be considered the beast's cabinet appointees when he comes into power. Revelation 17:14 gives the details concerning the final end of the ten horns; they will be crushed by the Lord Jesus Christ himself.

3. *The whore:* The whore (that great city, Jerusalem) is the focus of the initial meetings of the corporate beast and is depicted, initially, as being supported by the corporate beast. The final meeting in which the whore is supported by the corporate beast occurs late in the first half of the final seven years. At the time of the initial meeting pictured in the vision, she is considered by God as a whore engaged in worship and paying homage to other gods; this is a direct violation of God's greatest commandment to her: "*Thou shalt love the lord thy God and him only shalt thou worship.*" At the time of the middle of the seven years, or thereafter, the whore is destroyed through fire, and she will be left desolate and naked at the hands of the ten supernatural horns. The judgment will be allowed by God's permissive will.[358] The burning and destruction of the whore is in

---

[357] Daniel 9.26
[358] Revelation 17:16–18.

accordance with the judicial judgment of a whore in the Old Testament.[359]

4. *The seven heads:* The seven heads are seven mountains—powerful Gentile nations. The seven heads are represented by seven kings, and six of the kings are in power at the time of the peace conference at or near the middle of the final seven years. Five of the nations will fall from a higher state to a lower state, and one will still be ruling at the time of the middle of the final seven years. The transition from the five nations being prominent and powerful to a fallen state will occur between the initiation of the final twenty-three hundred days and the middle of the final seven years. The beast, initially not at the peace conference, will complete the seven heads and will shortly come to power. The beast will then be the eighth in supernatural form, having come out from the seventh head. The Word of God is silent concerning the future of the other six heads after the middle of the week. God's silence concerning these nations indicates that their power will pale in comparison with that of the wild beast and his ten kings. The seventh head, the wild beast, will assume total earthly rule with his ten handpicked kings, or horns, continuing through the final forty-two months. The wild beast will be destroyed by The Lord at his coming for Israel after the forty-two months are completed. The countries represented by the bear, lion, and leopard, the other six heads, will exist for a short time after the Lord Jesus Christ comes into power in accordance with Daniel 7:12.

In summary, Revelation 17:9–18 relates the progression of the seven heads, the ten horns, the beast, the nations, and the woman through the various transitions that will take place in the final days, beginning with the initiation of the twenty-three hundred days. All scriptures associated with the final unifying event, *Mystery Babylon*—

---

[359] Leviticus 21:9; Ezekiel 16.

especially the related scriptures in Daniel and Revelation—must be combined to fully rightly divide the Word of God. Understanding the special focus given to Israel, and God's everlasting promises he made to their fathers, easily resolves a good deal of apparent confusion. The last days will end the controversy that God has with the Gentile nations and Israel. The church of God, the born-again believers, will be raptured from the earth. Their rapture will occur sometime after the middle of the final seven years and after the wild beast declares himself to be a God.[360] The true God, in the short time of forty-two months, will change the status of all three groups: Jews, Gentiles, and the church of God. Additionally, after the Lord Jesus Christ destroys the wild beast, all rulership of the earth will be transitioned to the Lord Jesus Christ as King of kings and Lord of lords. And so, God's statement and promise that he will make a short work on the earth will come to pass. Consider the following:

> As he saith also in Osee, I will call them my people, which were not my people; and her beloved, which was not beloved. And it shall come to pass, that in the place where it was said unto them, Ye are not my people; there shall they be called the children of the living God. Esaias also crieth concerning Israel, Though the number of the children of Israel be as the sand of the sea, a remnant shall be saved: **For he will finish the work, and cut it short in righteousness: because a short work will the Lord make upon the earth.** And as Esaias said before, Except the Lord of Sabaoth had left us a seed, we had been as Sodoma, and been made like unto Gomorrha. (Romans 9:25–29 KJV; my emphasis)

A powerful telescope is a good analogy for the way God focuses in on the events of the last days. The first thing you do to properly

---

[360] 2 Thessalonians 2:3,4.

utilize a telescope is get an idea as to what you would like to look at. You next point the finderscope in the general direction of the object that you would like to view. The crosshairs are then used to adjust the object in the finderscope as you zero in on the object. You then focus in with the main scope of the instrument to get the object in full view and close up. Finally, you continue to increase the lens strength so as to get the most powerful and closest view. The closest view would not mean anything if each step were not properly followed. And so, it is with the Word of God; God continues to give more and more detailed information on the same subject as the biblical student continues to study and rightly divide his word. Each scripture relating to the same event gives additional details—here a little, there a little. The searcher of the word continues to read, believe, study, and work the Word of God relating to the same event, to the point of clear understanding and proper interpretation of God's revealed prophecy. The references, taken as a whole, provide a clear view of what God's Word is portraying. With respect to the same subject or event, no two scriptures can contradict one another, but each provides its own unique information regarding the subject or event.

APPENDIX F

The Four Latter-Day Beasts

THE WORD OF GOD IN Daniel 7 mentions four latter-day beasts that will arise from the sea in the last days. The four beasts are first mentioned in Daniel 7, and they are mentioned again in Revelation 13:1–3. The beasts are represented by a bear, a lion with eagle's wings, and a leopard with four heads.[361] The fourth and final beast is the final kingdom of the Antichrist—the same one that appears in the last days. The beasts have caused a great deal of confusion through many and varied interpretations handed down through the years. The interpretations relate to who they are, what they represent, and when they will arise. God makes it clear that these same beasts, which are first revealed in Daniel 7 and are present once again in Revelation 13, arise at the time of the end. Since they are mentioned in Revelation 13 as being contemporary with the final wild beast, it is clear that they are associated with the last days and the time of the final Gentile dominion of the Antichrist. Recall that God uses wild beasts in his word to describe Gentile nations, which God represents as wild, untamed animals, since their governments will not be ruled by God's ways and Word. There are scores of believers in each of the nations of the world, but the rulers and governments of the nations, as a whole, are confederate against God, his ways, and his law.

---

[361] Daniel 7:4–7.

The beasts first mentioned in chapter 7 of Daniel—the lion with eagle's wings, the bear, and the leopard with the four heads—represent Gentile superpower nations. This reality of wild beasts symbolizing Gentile nations is first evidenced in Daniel 8, when God first introduces the ram and the he-goat as being powerful Gentile nations. The ram and the he-goat, as interpreted by God in Daniel 8, represent the Medo-Persian Empire and the dominion of Alexander the Great, respectively. The four beasts associated with the last days—the lion, the bear, and the leopard with the four heads—are first mentioned by God in Daniel 7. They are powerful Gentile nations that rise from the sea in the last days and, at least initially, support the beast, as documented in Revelation 13 and 17. The sea is interpreted for us in Daniel 7:17 and Revelation 17:15; the nations of the earth The beasts are end-times Gentile dominions, and God, knowing the end from the beginning, documents them thousands of years earlier in the book of Daniel. And why not? God, who knows the end from the beginning, has always given those who love him fair warning of impending destruction via his prophets and servants. The truth is that God does give his servants, sons, and daughters critical knowledge of what will occur just prior to the day when he sends his son, Jesus Christ, to rule the heavens and the earth.

The interpretation of both sections of scripture, Daniel and Revelation, each documenting the four latter-day beasts, must start with the understanding that God binds these two sections (Daniel 7–12 and Revelation 13 and 17) together in his word. These scriptures reveal how God knows the end from the beginning. Time, to God, is simply a dimension—a dimension that God is outside of. God associates the four beasts with the last days, binding together Daniel with Revelation; one is dependent on the other for proper interpretation. The fact that these beasts are part of the last-times final Gentile dominion necessarily rules out that these beasts existed before—that is, in the Old Testament. They existed only in Old Testament future prophecy—not in actuality. The beasts will rise in the last days and fulfill all scriptures that describe them in both the Old and New Testaments. This fundamentally fuses Daniel 7 with Revelation 13 and 17 for proper interpretation. The four beasts are part of the events of the last days, and they are revealed in the Old Testament as proof that God sees all time from the outside in.

In Daniel 7, Daniel receives a vision from God regarding the last days of man's rule on the earth and also the events that will take place on the earth during the last days. The remaining chapters in Daniel are all related to Daniel's initial vision of the four latter-day beasts. The vision portrays what transpires during the last days and final seven years of man's rule on earth. Daniel 7 is especially concerned with Daniel's people, Israel. Daniel is instructed that four beasts will arise from the sea, representing four superpower Gentile nations that arise in the last days. The four will arise on the earth at the time of the end but before the everlasting kingdom of our Lord Jesus Christ is finally established on the earth. The interpretation requires the records of Daniel 7, Revelation 13, and Revelation 17 to be understood together to achieve proper understanding. In the latter part of Daniel 7, the angel gives a brief interpretation concerning the beasts and their significance.[362] The first key is to understand what God means by beasts rising from the sea as stated in Daniel 7:2 and interpreted in Daniel 7:17. Consider the following: "These great beasts, which are four, are four kings (Dominions and the governmental rulers of such), which shall arise out of the earth" (Daniel 7:17 KJV)

The Word of God symbolizes the sea to represent Gentile nations of the world in several scriptures in the Old Testament as well as Revelation.[363] Revelation 17:15 states, "*The waters that thou saw were peoples, and multitudes, and nations, and tongues.*" God also represents individual Gentile nations, kingdoms, and dominions through the use of beasts or animals, as stated earlier. Considering how God uses animals to represent Gentile nations, the wild animals mentioned in Daniel 7 also represent Gentile dominions. The first three Gentile dominions listed in Daniel 7 will rise out of the nations of the earth during, and immediately preceding, the last days, and before the rising of the final wild beast. Since they rise during the

---

[362] Daniel 7:17.
[363] Isaiah 8:7; 17:12; 27:1; 57:20; Psalm 46:4; Revelation 8:8; 17:15.

last days, they are not interpreted by the angel in Daniel 7, as was done with Medo-Persia and Alexander's dominions. The lion, bear, and leopard of the end times will be understood only at the time of their rising by those looking for them in the last days. They will be understood by God's characterization of them, as well as by the insight that God gives to those who love and respect him.

The final Gentile dominions of Daniel 7, represented by the lion, bear, and leopard, will be present on the earth when the fourth beast—the wild beast, or the Antichrist—comes to supernaturally rule the earth with his ten kings. The fourth beast is the dragon-energized Antichrist (the fourth kingdom mentioned in Daniel 7), who comes into power at the time of the end. There are many and varied interpretations as to whom these dominions of Daniel 7 represent. The fourth beast, the supernatural beast, who is different from all beasts before him, is indeed the dominion of the Antichrist, who is energized by Satan himself. The fourth beast will be easily interpreted, but what about the previous three? Several interpretations attempt to associate the bear, lion, and leopard with previous visions of Daniel and as part of Old Testament Gentile dominions. This is a fallacy and will lead only to confusion and misinterpretation. Some have even gone so far as to relate them to the ram and he-goat mentioned in Daniel 8. The fact that they are different animals, with different characteristics, implies that God intends for them to represent different dominions—in this case, dominions representing a different time. God also states in Daniel 7: that they *"shall arise out of the earth."* The Hebrew stem of the verb *shall arise*, in this context, describes a future rising out from the earth. God's Word is silent as to the identity of these wild animals, except for what is stated of them in Daniel 7:17 and the characteristics given to them in Daniel 7:4–6. The final Gentile dominions of Daniel 7 will be recognized at the time of the end by those trained and skillful in the right division of his Word. Additionally, they will be understood through the characteristics God gives them in Daniel 7. God lists these animals and their associated characteristics because they had not yet come into being at the time the prophecy was given to Daniel. Daniel 7:7

states that these three beasts, or Gentile dominions, whoever they are, will become subservient to the fourth terrible kingdom of the Antichrist. As stated, the first three Gentile nations are not identified but will be understood through God's description of them when they arise in the last days.

By gathering information from the context of Daniel 7 and Revelation 13, it becomes clear that the bear, lion, and leopard are contemporary with one another and will coexist together at the time of the end. Daniel 7 does not mention any of these animals attacking each other; this is in contrast with the he-goat and ram of Daniel 8, who do war with each other. These last-time Gentile dominions will coexist with each other peaceably, at least at first, and then will be assimilated into the kingdom of the beast. They will be present on the earth before, and at the rising of, the final fourth beast. In fact, they will assist in the rising of the Antichrist until the Antichrist becomes a supernatural being and delivers their nations to ruin. Consider the distinct resemblance between the following two sections of scripture (Daniel 7 and Revelation 13):

> And four great beasts came up from the sea, diverse one from another. The first was like a lion, and had eagle's wings: I beheld till the wings thereof were plucked, and it was lifted up from the earth, and made stand upon the feet as a man, and a man's heart was given to it. And behold another beast, a second, like to a bear, and it raised up itself on one side, and it had three ribs in the mouth of it between the teeth of it: and they said thus unto it, Arise, devour much flesh. After this I beheld, and lo another, like a leopard, which had upon the back of it four wings of a fowl; the beast had also four heads; and dominion was given to it. **After this I saw in the night visions, and behold a fourth beast, dreadful and terrible, and strong exceedingly; and it had great iron teeth: it devoured and**

> **brake in pieces, and stamped the residue with the feet of it: and it was diverse from all the beasts that were before it; and it had ten horns.** (Daniel 7:3–7 KJV; my emphasis)
>
> And I stood upon the sand of the sea, and saw a beast rise up out of the sea, having seven heads and ten horns, and upon his horns ten crowns, and upon his heads the name of blasphemy. **And the beast which I saw was like unto a leopard, and his feet were as the feet of a bear, and his mouth as the mouth of a lion: and the dragon gave him his power, and his seat, and great authority.**
>
> And I saw one of his heads as it were wounded to death; and his deadly wound was healed: and all the world wondered after the beast. And they worshipped the dragon which gave power unto the beast: and they worshipped the beast, saying, Who is like unto the beast? who is able to make war with him? (Revelation 13:1–3KJV; my emphasis)

The fourth terrible beast arises during the last days and is initially composed of the previous three—the lion, the bear, and the leopard—as documented in Revelation 13:2. Six of the seven heads of Revelation 13 are derived from these first three beasts: the lion, the bear, and the leopard with four heads. God's Word in Revelation 13:2 describes the condition of the nations and the rulership of the earth at the time of the rising of the fourth beast, and at the time of the middle of the seventieth seven. The fourth beast, led by the great rebel Antichrist, will come into power at the middle, or midst, of the seventieth seven. The fourth beast will arise and take dominion over the earth immediately after the miraculous satanic resurrection of the Antichrist.[364] Revelation 13:2 clearly associates the bear, lion, and

---

[364] Revelation 13:3; Revelation 17:8.

leopard with the last days and with the fourth terrible dominion of the Antichrist. Daniel 7:7 states that the beast will stamp the residue (lion, bear, and leopard) with its feet (the bear). The final beast will be the Antichrist with his ten horns, who are personally appointed by the wild beast, as documented in Revelation 17:12. The first six heads, or six powerful Gentile dominions—the lion, the bear, and the leopard—will fade away into obscurity. It will be the supernaturally charged Antichrist with his supernaturally charged ten kings, or horns, who will have dominion over the earth for the final forty-two months. This is confirmed in both Daniel 7 and Revelation 13 and 17. The other heads and beasts will be destroyed by the final beast and by its feet (the bear). The destruction of the nations will, once again, occur at the time of his coming into power over the earth—the middle of the final seven years.

Daniel 7 provides historical information about the bear, the lion, and the leopard, as well as about the peculiar characteristics of each of the wild animals as per their origins and future. Daniel 7 documents the bear, lion, and leopard as rising consecutively but being in power on the earth together during the end times, before the rise of the final wild beast. Unlike the previous beasts in Daniel, these nations that rise in the last days or dominions do not attack each other, at least initially, but rise consecutively and coexist on the earth together. The scriptures are silent concerning what happens to the lion, bear, and leopard after the middle of the week. War and desolation at the hands of the fourth beast would seem to be what is in store for all on the earth after the wild beast comes into power. It is also stated in Daniel 7:7 that it will be the feet of the beast, the bear, who will trample the other five heads and allow the wild beast to come into total control. This fact in Daniel 7:7, put together with Revelation 17:10, which states that five of the heads will fall, indicates that it will be the bear, in collaboration with the wild beast, which will destroy and war with the other five heads at the time of the end. The turmoil caused by the supernatural rising of the Antichrist, with his ten kings, or horns, will cause the earth and all the nations thereof to descend into total lawlessness and chaos.

After the rising of the fourth beast at the middle of the seventieth seven, the focus of scripture concerns his actions as he goes forth to conquer. The previous three beasts become completely insignificant. It is the fourth terrible beast, led by the Antichrist with his appointed ten horns (now powerful kings), that will rise and assume control of the earth for the final forty-two months.[365] Daniel 7:7 together with Revelation 13:2 states that the fourth terrible beast will stamp the residue (of the remaining beasts) with its feet, indicting how the final wild beast assumes control. It will be the bear, allied with the wild beast, which will initially be utilized to destroy the nations and make them subservient to him. From this it is clear that the wild beast utilizes the bear, the second gentile superpower nation, to destroy the nations and assume control of the earth. After the initial onslaught initialized by the bear, and in coordination with the wild beast, the Antichrist will then rule the earth with his ten kings. The stamping mentioned in Daniel 7:7 by the wild beast is an indication of the transfer of power and dominion from the three previous beasts to the fourth terrible beast, or the Antichrist. The seventh head will reduce the previous six heads and all other nations of the earth to rubble and desolation for the next forty-two months. How this transition takes place we are not told, but the scriptures are clear; the seventh head with the ten horns will supernaturally take control over the entire earth. The previous three Gentile dominions—the lion, the bear, and the leopard—will be incorporated into the fourth beast during the time of the end. The prophecy of the beasts of Daniel 7 is not continuous history but is related to the prophecy of the end-time crisis associated with the last seven years.

The fourth beast of Daniel 7 is stated to be dreadful, terrible, and exceedingly strong, with great iron teeth, and it is the focus of Daniel 7. The previous scriptures in Daniel 7 concerning the three previous beasts are included only to shed light on the fourth terrible beast, providing information as to how the fourth kingdom came into fruition at the time of the end. The focus of Daniel 7 is the fourth terrible beast. The other beasts of Daniel 7 provide historical

---

[365] Revelation 13:5.

information to reveal the initial makeup of the fourth beast. It will be the Antichrist and the ten horns who will compose the fourth terrible beast on the earth. The time frame for these end-time events, including both the rising of the first three beasts and the final forty-two-month rule of the Antichrist, could last for decades. In contrast, the scripture is clear that the fourth beast of the Antichrist and the ten horns will last forty-two months.

The beasts of Daniel 7 arise during the last days and are not interpreted by God, but it is clear that they are powerful Gentile countries. Attempting to interpret these before their presence on the earth is only guesswork and will lead to confusion. The rising of these beasts, or nations, will be recognized by those of understanding and those who rightly divide the word of truth at the time of the end. These nations could be on the earth for several decades before the crisis of the end times is initiated. The verses of Daniel 7 will come to life at the time of the end and will serve as a guidepost to those of understanding regarding the Word of God. The future of these Gentile nations, after the final forty-two months are completed, is also curious. The scripture reveals that these nations continue on the earth, at least for a while, even after the return of Jesus Christ and at the beginning of his millennial rule on the earth. Consider the following:

> After this I saw in the night visions, and behold a fourth beast, dreadful and terrible, and strong exceedingly; and it had great iron teeth: it devoured and brake in pieces, and stamped the residue (lion, bear and leopard) with the feet of it: and it was diverse from all the beasts that were before it; and it had ten horns. I considered the horns, and, behold, there came up among them another little horn, before whom there were three of the first horns plucked up by the roots: and, behold, in this horn were eyes like the eyes of man, and a mouth speaking great things. I beheld till the thrones were cast down, and the

Ancient of days did sit, whose garment was white as snow, and the hair of his head like the pure wool: his throne was like the fiery flame, and his wheels as burning fire. A fiery stream issued and came forth from before him: thousand thousands ministered unto him, and ten thousand times ten thousand stood before him: the judgment was set, and the books were opened. I beheld then because of the voice of the great words which the horn spake: I beheld even till the beast was slain, and his body destroyed, and given to the burning flame. **As concerning the rest of the beasts, they had their dominion taken away: yet their lives were prolonged for a season and time.** I saw in the night visions, and, behold, one like the Son of man came with the clouds of heaven, and came to the Ancient of days, and they brought him near before him. And there was given him dominion, and glory, and a kingdom, that all people, nations, and languages, should serve him: his dominion is an everlasting dominion, which shall not pass away, and his kingdom that which shall not be destroyed. (Daniel 7:7–14 KJV; my emphasis)

The fourth beast stamps the previous three and reduces them to rubble. After the final seven years and, especially, the final forty-two months, the fourth beast is slain. His body is destroyed and given to the burning fire as part of the judgment of God. The parallel verse in Revelation 19:20 tells us that the beast/Antichrist and the false prophet are thrown alive into the burning fire. After these events, the Lord Jesus Christ is given dominion of the kingdoms of the world forever and ever. It is at this time, after the destruction of the beast, that Lord Jesus Christ will have all the nations before him, and they will bow to him. He will also judge the nations, as documented in the scripture, and he will be revealed to all nations. Daniel 7:12 states that the rest of the beasts or nations (*the lion, bear, and leopard*) will have their dominion (governmental rule and authority) taken away, yet their lives were prolonged for a season and a time. This scripture will be fulfilled at the return of the Lord Jesus Christ and at the beginning of his earthly rule. The Word of God is in harmony with these scriptures in Daniel. It is documented several times in scripture that both Jews and Gentiles will be on the earth during the millennial rule of Our Lord Jesus Christ. It is only the one body of Jesus Christ that will be raptured from the earth during the last days.

Consider the following: *"When the Son of man shall come in his glory, and all the holy angels with him, then shall he sit upon the throne of his glory: And before him shall be gathered all nations: and he shall separate them one from another, as a shepherd divideth his sheep from the goats: And he shall set the sheep on his right hand, but the goats on the left. Then shall the King say unto them on his right hand, Come, ye blessed of my Father, inherit the kingdom prepared for you from the foundation of the world"* (Matthew 25:31–34 KJV). The future of these beasts, or superpower Gentile nations, will be to have all of their power and dominion removed and then judged. How this is done is not revealed by God in his word. It is revealed that the church of the body of Jesus Christ will have already been raptured from the earth before the wrath of Almighty God comes upon the earth. The rapture will be initiated by the Lord Jesus Christ, through the power of God. The judgment documented in Matthew is of Gentile nations and the unbelieving Jews. They will be judged in accordance with God's judgment, which he will have transferred to his dear son, Jesus Christ.

The principle of scripture buildup must be employed to rightly divide the Word of God. Scripture buildup is the process in which God, through many separate sections of his word, builds up information regarding an important topic. The book of Revelation builds upon the foundational scriptures laid out in the gospels and Old Testament writings. Each section adds information and builds upon the others. Reading these books together and understanding their unique relationships gives good understanding concerning the time of the end. An accurate knowledge of all related scriptures, especially those in Daniel and Revelation, will develop right interpretation. Accurate interpretation will fend off *"being tossed about with every wind of doctrine, whereby men lie in wait to deceive."*[366] In the book of Revelation, God simply increases the magnification of the twenty-three hundred days and the last half of the seventieth week, as initially documented in the book of Daniel and elsewhere. In Daniel, the first half of the last seven years is emphasized. Both books together clearly depict the whole of the last seven years. In Revelation, the Word of God focuses clearly on specific details that will come to pass in the last days—especially the final forty-two months. The time of the end, as opposed to the church of the one body of Jesus Christ, was not hidden in the Old Testament or the Gospels. The information will not contradict, but will add important events and details to, what was originally foretold in Daniel and elsewhere. The benefit will be that God's people who are alive during those terrible days will have understanding and comfort from the Word of God. The scriptures emphatically state as much in Thessalonians to the church of God: *"That day shall not overtake you as a thief."*[367] When all that God has revealed in his word is interpreted and rightly divided correctly, the believer cannot get the time of the end wrong. Scripture buildup incorporates all records, giving additional information with each new documented record. The end result is an accurate interpretation of the last days. The accurate picture can then be used to obey the Lord's instruction in Luke 21 to "**watch**." Consider the Lord's words in Luke:

> And there shall be signs in the sun, and in the moon, and in the stars; and upon the earth distress of nations, with perplexity; the sea and the waves roaring; Men's hearts failing them for fear, and for looking after those things which are coming on the earth: for the powers of heaven shall be shaken. And then shall they see the Son

---

[366] Ephesians 4:14.
[367] 1 Thessalonians 5:4.

of man coming in a cloud with power and great glory. And when these things begin to come to pass, then look up, and lift up your heads; for your redemption draweth nigh. And he spake to them a parable; Behold the fig tree, and all the trees; When they now shoot forth, ye see and know of your own selves that summer is now nigh at hand. So likewise ye, when ye see these things come to pass, know ye that the kingdom of God is nigh at hand. Verily I say unto you, This generation shall not pass away, till all be fulfilled. Heaven and earth shall pass away: but my words shall not pass away. **And take heed to yourselves, lest at any time your hearts be overcharged with surfeiting, and drunkenness, and cares of this life, and so that day come upon you unawares. For as a snare shall it come on all them that dwell on the face of the whole earth. Watch ye therefore, and pray always, that ye may be accounted worthy to escape all these things that shall come to pass, and to stand before the Son of man.** (Luke 21:25–36 KJV; my emphasis)

God reveals in Revelation the origin and the identity of the beast—where he came from, who he is, and the length of his dominion (forty-two months, or 3.5 years). The information is incorporated together with Daniel to give the believer an accurate representation as to what to watch for in the last days. Revelation 13:2 reveals the final Gentile beast to appear to be made up of a lion, bear, and leopard, along with seven heads and ten horns. Daniel 7 reveals the origin of the four latter-day beasts—where they came from and their peculiar characteristics. Next, we shall consider the second chapter of Daniel, which gives additional information regarding the same fourth terrible beast who rises in the last days to destroy the nations of the world.

In Daniel 2, a vision is given to Nebuchadnezzar and eventually interpreted by Daniel. The vision was that of a great image seen by Nebuchadnezzar in a dream, and it had to do with the rising and falling of great Gentile nations. The nations identified by Daniel revealed Gentile dominions that arise one after the other in a timed sequence, beginning with Nebuchadnezzar. The sequence continues until the rise of the final dominion of the Antichrist, which is represented by the feet and the toes of the great image. The vision goes on to state that this final dominion will be destroyed by *"a stone that becomes a great mountain"*; that is, the Lord Jesus Christ at his coming. Comparing Daniel 2 with Daniel 7 reveals that the fourth beast of Daniel 7 is also the feet and toes of final beast of Daniel 2. Although these two are the same, the similarities between Daniel 2 and Daniel 7 end there. Daniel 7 focuses on the last days and final Gentile dominions that arise in the final time. In contrast, Daniel 2 begins at the reign of Nebuchadnezzar and ends with the final Gentile dominion of the Antichrist—the feet and toes. Daniel 7 provides an additional layer of focus and can be thought of as an expansion of the feet and toes of the great image of Daniel 2. The result is the same in Daniel 2 and Daniel 7; that is, God, through his son, Jesus Christ, will establish his everlasting kingdom on earth at the time of the rise of the final beast and his ten kings. Additionally, it must be understood when reading Daniel 2 that the period of the mystery of the one body of Jesus Christ, including at least two thousand years of time, is again skipped over and hidden by God. The critical difference between the image of Daniel 2 and the Gentile beasts of Daniel 7 is related to time. Daniel 2 encompasses all time from the time of Nebuchadnezzar up until the time of the end, but it skips the time of the mystery of the one body of Jesus Christ. The other commonality of Gentile dominions of Daniel 2 is that they will all have, at one time or another, dominion over Jerusalem and God's holy place. Recall that in the book of Daniel the focus is always directed toward God's people, the land, and the holy place. Daniel 7 is focused only on the unique beasts that rise at the time of the end and become confederate with the wild beast, or the Antichrist, as well as on how they affect the people of God, their land. The

THE LAST DAYS AND THE VILE MAN OF DANIEL

interpretation given to Nebuchadnezzar with respect to the great image he saw in Daniel 2 is now listed below for consideration:

> Thou, O king, sawest, and behold a great image. This great image, whose brightness was excellent, stood before thee; and the form thereof was terrible. This image's head was of fine gold, his breast and his arms of silver, his belly and his thighs of brass, His legs of iron, his feet part of iron and part of clay. **Thou sawest till that a stone was cut out without hands, which smote the image upon his feet that were of iron and clay, and brake them to pieces. Then was the iron, the clay, the brass, the silver, and the gold, broken to pieces together, and became like the chaff of the summer threshingfloors; and the wind carried them away, that no place was found for them: and the stone that smote the image became a great mountain, and filled the whole earth.** This is the dream; and we will tell the interpretation thereof before the king. Thou, O king, art a king of kings: for the God of heaven hath given thee a kingdom, power, and strength, and glory. And wheresoever the children of men dwell, the beasts of the field and the fowls of the heaven hath he given into thine hand, and hath made thee ruler over them all. Thou art this head of gold. And after thee shall arise another kingdom inferior to thee, and another third kingdom of brass, which shall bear rule over all the earth. And the fourth kingdom shall be strong as iron: forasmuch as iron breaketh in pieces and subdueth all things: and as iron that breaketh all these, shall it break in pieces and bruise. **And whereas thou sawest the feet and toes, part of potters' clay, and part of iron, the kingdom**

shall be divided; but there shall be in it of the strength of the iron, forasmuch as thou sawest the iron mixed with miry clay. And as the toes of the feet were part of iron, and part of clay, so the kingdom shall be partly strong, and partly broken. And whereas thou sawest iron mixed with miry clay, they shall mingle themselves with the seed of men: but they shall not cleave one to another, even as iron is not mixed with clay. And in the days of these kings shall the God of heaven set up a kingdom, which shall never be destroyed: and the kingdom shall not be left to other people, but it shall break in pieces and consume all these kingdoms, and it shall stand for ever. Forasmuch as thou sawest that the stone was cut out of the mountain without hands, and that it brake in pieces the iron, the brass, the clay, the silver, and the gold; the great God hath made known to the king what shall come to pass hereafter: and the dream is certain, and the interpretation thereof sure. (Daniel 2:31–45 KJV; my emphasis)

The image of Daniel 2 includes the initial prophecy encompassing Gentile rulership, or the time of the Gentiles, over Jerusalem and the holy place. The time begins with the initial removal of the Jews from their Land, Jerusalem and the Holy Place—the time of Nebuchadnezzar up until the time when the land is given to the Lord Jesus Christ and the remnant twelve tribes called by God to inherit the land: the time of the end. The section lists the time of the Gentiles from the rising of Nebuchadnezzar until the final rising of the ten kings associated with the kingdom of the Antichrist. The prophecy can be compared to an overall initial view of the time of the Gentiles up until the coming of the Lord Jesus Christ and his kingdom on earth. The time of Gentile rule over Jerusalem's Holy Place is also mentioned in Romans 11, which states that at the end of the time of the Gentile rule, the land and Holy Place will once again be given to the remnant Jews and they will once again be in the land. Additionally, Daniel 2 is also focused on the rulership of Jerusalem and the holy place. Consider the following: *"For I would not, brethren, that ye should be ignorant of this mystery, lest ye should be wise in your own conceits; that blindness in part is happened to Israel,* ***until the fulness of the Gentiles be come in.*** *And so all Israel shall be saved: as it is written, There shall come out of Sion the Deliverer, and shall turn away ungodliness from Jacob: For this is my covenant unto them, when I shall take away their sins"* (Romans 11:25–27 KJV; my emphasis).

The Gentile dominions of Daniel 2 represent past kingdoms or dominions and the future dominion of the Antichrist—namely, the feet and the toes of the great image. Once again, the mystery period is skipped over by God in the vision of Daniel 2. The body parts in Daniel 2 represent Gentile dominions, which God allows to have power, strength, glory, and rulership over the holy place in Jerusalem. The time that they represent is the time of the Gentiles—the time when the Gentiles rule over the holy place in Jerusalem. The common theme here is dominion over God's holy place. The Gentile dominions represented in Daniel 2 are Nebuchadnezzar, Medo-Persia, Alexander the Great, and the Roman Empire, depicted by a two-legged split dominion. The final dominion, the dominion of the Antichrist, arises during the last days and is represented by the feet and the toes partly of iron and partly of clay. It is these ten toes, or ten kings, with the Antichrist, that go on to rule over God's holy place for the final forty-two months. Finally, the kingdom of the Antichrist, along with his ten kings, will be destroyed by the Lord Jesus Christ at his coming. This will mark the end of the time of the Gentiles. The mystery of the one body of Christ is represented by the span of time between the Roman dominion and the kingdom of the Antichrist, or the rising of the final ten kings. The first three beasts of Daniel 7, which rise in the last days, are not the same as the four kingdoms written of in Daniel 2. This error has been promoted by many commentaries and leads only to confusion and additional error. The four beasts of Daniel 7 are specifically related to the last days and provide further details regarding the last Gentile dominion of Daniel 2—namely the feet and the toes.

It is the feet and the toes of Daniel 2 that are the only part of the image of Daniel 2 associated with the last days. The feet and toes of Daniel 2 are equivalent to the final terrible beast of Daniel 7. Therefore, the feet and the toes represent the only portion of Daniel 2 that still awaits fulfillment. Daniel 7 expands, or gives additional information concerning, the last and final kingdom of Daniel 2. Observe also that the seven heads are not mentioned in either Daniel 2 or Daniel 7, since God's focus in Daniel is the time of Gentile rule over Jerusalem. The little horn, who grows into the seventh head with the ten horns, is mentioned and will rule over Jerusalem and the holy place in the final time of Gentile rule.[368] The corporate seven heads are associated with the rule over the Gentiles during the last days; therefore, they are not specifically associated with Jerusalem and the holy place. As for the seven heads, six are initially part of the kingdom of the beast but will be overthrown by the beast. Recall that six of the seven heads are the nations associated with the three beasts—the lion, bear, and leopard—which arise during the last days and are described in Daniel 7. Understanding these relationships is critical for right division of the Word of God.

The initial three beasts, or superpower nations/dominions, listed in Daniel 7 will rise as nations on the earth and be coexistent with each other at the time when fourth terrible beast arises during the last days. The three initial beasts of Daniel 7 will be separate powerful governmental dominions on the earth prior to the rise of the fourth beast. The scripture is silent as to their identity, but they will be identified by the people of God alive during the time of the end, through the information God gives in Daniel 7. The fourth beast of Daniel 7 rises and assumes control of the previous three beasts: the lion, bear, and leopard. The fourth beast is different from all previous beasts, in that the final beast is energized through Satan himself and is supernatural in nature. The fourth beast gathers the other Gentile dominions together as one before stripping them of

---

[368] Daniel 7:8.

their governmental rule and taking full control of the earth. The fourth beast, or kingdom of the Antichrist, goes on to rule over the earth for the final forty-two months. After the forty-two months, the fourth beast is destroyed by the Lord Jesus Christ, who afterward sets up his everlasting dominion.

Recall that God represents the final four Gentile dominions of Daniel 7 using symbolic wild animals. The wild animals—the lion, the bear, and the leopard—and the terrible ten-horned wild beast are unclean animals that represent Gentile dominions. Note how the final wild beast, also known as the dragon, is not described by an animal on the earth, since the wild beast will be something different from anything ever on the earth before.

Let's now examine the beasts of Daniel 7 and the distinctive characteristics of each of the beasts. The first beast in Daniel 7 is *like* a lion and has eagles' wings. Consider the following: *"And four great beasts came up from the sea, diverse one from another.* ***The first was like a lion, and had eagle's wings: I beheld till the wings thereof were plucked, and it was lifted up from the earth, and made stand upon the feet as a man, and a man's heart was given to it"*** (Daniel 7:3–4 KJV; my emphasis).

This beast, representing one of the final Gentile dominions, is likened to a lion with eagle's wings; it has the characteristics of both a lion and an eagle. The lion with eagle's wings is not interpreted, but we know that it will be present and will eventually become part of the fourth beast.[369] It will be recognized by the people of the last time who understand and rightly divide the Word of God. The lion with eagle's wings is also represented in Revelation 17 by a mountain that God uses to represent strength and power.[370] This lion-eagle type of nation will be a strong, powerful nation, and it will continue that way for some time until it is made to stand on its feet like a man. The representation speaks of a strong, powerful nation that, over time, falls from its once high and lofty position and is made to stand on its feet like a man. Being made to *"stand on its feet like a man"*

---

[369] Revelation 13:2.
[370] Revelation 17:9.

represents this nation again being numbered with the other nations in ordinary fashion and represents a fall from its once high, lofty, and powerful status.[371] It is thought that this falling from a lofty position will be after the beginning of the final twenty-three hundred days, but before the middle of the final seven years. The falling of this lion-eagle type nation is related to the falling of the five heads of Revelation 17:10; it represents one of the five heads. Eventually this nation will become part of the fourth beast; the fourth beast itself will take away its lofty status. From our previous study, it will be the bear which will finally destroy this nation as depicted in Daniel 7:19. It is worth our while to understand the characteristics of an eagle and lion from the perspective of God's Word.

The term "eagle" refers to several large birds of prey active in the daytime rather than at night. The Hebrew term translated as "eagle" ("*nesher*") also sometimes is translated as "vulture." The eagle, the largest flying bird of Palestine, has a wingspan that may reach eight feet or more. The Palestinian eagle builds great nests of sticks on rocky crags in the mountains (see Job 39:27–28; Jeremiah 49:16). As one of the most majestic birds, it occupies a prominent role in the Bible. The eagle appears in the lists of unclean birds (see Leviticus 11:13; Deuteronomy 14:12). Old Testament writers noted the eagle's swift movement (see Deuteronomy 28:49; 2 Samuel 1:23; Jeremiah 4:13), the sweep and power of its flight (see Proverbs 23:5; Isaiah 40:31), and the eagle's concern for its young (see Exodus 19:4; Deuteronomy 32:11). In the ancient world, the eagle or vulture often was associated with deity. The prophets and apocalyptists chose this bird to play a figurative or symbolic role in their writings (see Ezekiel 1:10; 10:14; Daniel 7:4; Revelation 4:7; 8:13). In Exodus 19:4 and Deuteronomy 32:11, the eagle is used figuratively of God's protection and care. In these passages, God is pictured as a loving parent who redeems and protects His people even as the parent eagle cares for its young. The dove and the eagle are two of the most frequently mentioned birds of the scriptures. They symbolize two basic aspects of the Bible's

---

[371] Daniel 7:4.

THE LAST DAYS AND THE VILE MAN OF DANIEL

message. The dove symbolizes God's activity in the world through His Spirit, while the eagle represents God's care for His people.[372]

The lion is a large, swift-moving cat. The male has a heavy mane. Mentioned approximately 135 times in the Old Testament, the lion is the proverbial symbol for strength (see Judges 14:18). The Bible describes the lion as powerful and daring (see Proverbs 30:30) and distinguished by a terrifying roar (see Isaiah 5:29). It was a sign of the tribe of Judah (see Genesis 49:9; Revelation 5:5). David defended his father's flock against lions and bears (see 1 Samuel 17:34–35). One of the most well-known stories in the Bible is about a young man being cast into a den of lions (see Daniel 6:16–23). Since untamed lions were put in pits, it is possible that Daniel was cast into such a pit. Lions were kept as pets by pharaohs. Hebrew seems to make closer distinctions than does English in the lion family, since five unrelated Hebrew words are translated as "lion." Lions have disappeared from Palestine, with the last one having been killed near Megiddo in the thirteenth century.[373]

The two references documented above of the eagle and the lion reveal from the Word of God characteristics of the lion/eagle type of superpower nation that rises in the last days but before the final terrible wild beast. This Gentile superpower will be present and will be an active contributing factor to the rise of the fourth terrible beast. The lion-eagle type of nation will be a symbol of strength and power in the world. It will also exhibit characteristics of an eagle—namely God's care and protection for his people. The description reveals a strong nation combined with a loving nature for God's people and land. Revelation 13:2 states that at the time of the rise of the last terrible beast, this nation will initially be the mouthpiece, the head, of the terrible beast until the terrible beast assumes full control with his ten horns.[374] After the fourth beast rises, the lion/eagle's strength and power are diminished. The lion-eagle type of beast contributes one head to the seven-headed beast listed in Revelation 13 and 17.

---

[372] *Holman Bible Dictionary*, s.vv. "birds," "eagle."
[373] *Holman Bible Dictionary*, s.vv. "eagle," "lion."
[374] Revelation 13:2.

The second beast, or gentile superpower dominion, mentioned in Daniel 7 is likened to a bear: ***"And behold another beast, a second, like to a bear, and it raised up itself on one side, and it had three ribs in the mouth of it between the teeth of it: and they said thus unto it, Arise, devour much flesh"*** (Daniel 7:5).

The second beast, or superpower Gentile nation, that rises before the last days will have bear-like characteristics. This beast is *like* a bear *(not a bear but like a bear)*. This bearlike Gentile nation will devour much flesh on one side. The flesh that it devours, and in which direction it devours much flesh, is not mentioned; it is only stated that it will devour mainly in one direction. The verse indicates that this nation, through some type of war or through several confrontations, is responsible for the destruction of many people in one direction (i.e., north, south, east, or west). This beast already has three ribs in its mouth indicating that it already has devoured much flesh. It is then ordered, during the last days crisis, to devour more flesh. This aligns with the scriptures regarding the final beast, or kingdom of the Antichrist, in which it is the bear assigned to "*stamp the residue*" of the remaining great nations with the feet *(bear)* of it after they have fallen from prominence.[375]

The bear is a large, heavy mammal with long, thick shaggy hair. It eats insects, fruit, and flesh.

Bears may grow as high as six feet or more and weigh several hundred pounds. In biblical times the bear was a threat to vineyards and to herds of sheep and goats (see 1 Samuel 17:34–35). The two largest and strongest beasts of prey—the bear and the lion—are often listed together in the Bible (see 1 Samuel 17:37). A narrative about Elisha recorded in the Bible depicts the ferocity of the bear (see 2 Kings 2:23–24). Within the last century, the Syrian bear has disappeared from the Holy Land, with the last bear having been killed in Galilee just before World War II. It still survives in Syria, Persia, and Turkey.[376]

---

[375] Daniel 7:19.
[376] *Holman Bible Dictionary*, s.v. "bear."

The second Gentile dominion is likened to a bear—a mighty Gentile superpower nation—that will once again rise at the time of the end. The nation will have bearlike characteristics; it will be very large, fierce, and a flesh eater. The flesh is devoured on one side, or in one direction. The bear has three ribs in its mouth, indicating that the bear, at the time of the end, will have already devoured much flesh before it is commanded to devour a great deal more. Typically, the usage of "rib" in the Bible represents man, in this case, a bear who has already devoured men. In any event, the identity of this great nation will be obvious to those with ears to hear and eyes to see at the time of the end. In summary, the prophecy states that this bearlike Gentile nation will arise from apparent sleep or hibernation and devour much flesh in one direction during the last time. The final details and specifics, and how this unravels, will be fully understood at the time of the end. The bear will contribute a second head to the seven-headed beast in Revelation 13:2. Both the bear and the lion's dominion could span decades before the actual onset of the last seven years. The bear, in Revelation 13.2, is also stated to make up the feet of the fourth terrible beast; allowing it to move or walk. The bear also is the nation that is depicted as stamping the remaining beasts suggesting a type of special relationship with the final wild beast.[377]

The third beast is likened to a leopard with four heads: ***"After this I beheld, and lo another, like a leopard, which had upon the back of it four wings of a fowl; the beast had also four heads; and dominion was given to it"*** (Daniel 7:6).

The last beast, or Gentile superpower entity, to appear during the last days is the leopard with four heads and four wings of a fowl. This third beast appears after, but contemporary with, the first two— the lion with eagles' wings and the bear. This final powerful Gentile nation, which rises in the last days, or the time leading up to the last days, will have the characteristics of a leopard. The leopard will have four separate heads and four wings of a fowl, yet it will be one beast, or dominion. The beast will comprise four significant nations and another four that will be less significant.

---

[377] Daniel 7.7.

The leopard is a large cat with yellow fur with black spots that form patterns. This animal is one of the most dangerous both to animals and human beings. Known for its gracefulness and speed, it was common in Palestine in Old Testament times, especially in the forests of Lebanon, but it is seldom found there now. Five were killed around Jerusalem just before World War II, and one was killed in Southern Palestine near Beersheba soon after the war. The leopard still survives in Israel and is protected by the government. Two locations suggest habitats of leopards: Beth-nimrah ("leopards' house"; see Numbers 32:36) and "waters of Nimrim" ("waters of leopards"; see Isaiah 15:6 and Jeremiah 48:34). In Hosea 13:7, the lurking, noiseless movement of the leopard symbolizes God's wrath. Isaiah illustrated the serene peace of God's kingdom as creating the seemingly impossible occurrence of a leopard lying down with the goat (Isaiah 11:6). Some translate the word normally translated as "leopard" in Habakkuk 1:8 as "cheetah."[378]

The Leopard described in Daniel 7 has four heads that give direction to a swift-moving graceful beast. The beast also is said to have the four wings of a fowl on its back. The dominion will include several nations, including four significant nations, or power bases, represented by the four heads. Notice that this last beast is given dominion; neither of the prior two are given dominion, or at least it is not mentioned. The dominion represents authority over all its constituents to exercise power. The third beast is graceful, powerful, fast, and dangerous. The leopard symbolizes the imminent approach of God's wrath through secretive events. The leopard-like Gentile dominion is built upon a four-mountain type of power base—the four heads. The leopard-like dominion also has other nations besides the four main heads, which are indicated by the wings of a fowl on its back. The speed of this beast suggests that this final four-headed beast will arise shortly, relatively speaking, before the final seven years and grow very quickly. The final leopard-like Gentile nation will also contribute four heads to the seven-headed beast.

---

[378] *Holman Bible Dictionary*, s.v. "Leopard."

THE LAST DAYS AND THE VILE MAN OF DANIEL

The first three beasts, or powerful Gentile nations, of Daniel 7 have now been evaluated. These final three are not the only Gentile countries or dominions that will be present on the earth during the last days, but they represent the core of the superpower nations associated with the final wild, terrible beast. Additionally, they are mentioned since they will be associated with governance over Jerusalem and the Holy Place. It would also not be a stretch to believe that these superpower nations will facilitate the rising of the final, terrible wild beast. The lion, bear, and leopard, when their heads are added together, bring the number of heads to six. The final, or seventh, head of the seven-headed beast in Revelation 13:2 will be the Antichrist, who will start out small and then rise to prominence and power. The final head will only arrive on the scene with the other six heads at the time of the middle of the final seven years. The vile man, or the Antichrist, is said to rise among the first ten kings and subdue three of the first ten. He will subdue three kings or horns and grow into *"a mouth speaking great things and have the eyes of a man."*[379] The final head will also possess the ten horns, or kings. Additional information from Revelation 13 and 17 indicates that the seventh head is wounded to death and his death blow is healed.[380] The seventh head of the fourth terrible beast is documented in Revelation 13 and 17 to supernaturally return from the dead. It is this seventh head, together with the ten horns, or kings, that will crush the previous six heads and rule the earth for the final forty-two months. Consider the following:

> After this I saw in the night visions, and behold a fourth beast, dreadful and terrible, and strong exceedingly; and it had great iron teeth: **it devoured and brake in pieces, and stamped the residue (the remaining three: lion, bear and leopard) with the feet of it:** and it was diverse from all the beasts that were before it; and it had

---

[379] Daniel 7:8.
[380] See Revelation 13:3.

ten horns. I considered the horns, and, behold, there came up among them another little horn, before whom there were three of the first horns plucked up by the roots: and, behold, in this horn were eyes like the eyes of man, and a mouth speaking great things. I beheld till the thrones were cast down, and the Ancient of days did sit, whose garment was white as snow, and the hair of his head like the pure wool: his throne was like the fiery flame, and his wheels as burning fire. A fiery stream issued and came forth from before him: thousand thousands ministered unto him, and ten thousand times ten thousand stood before him: the judgment was set, and the books were opened. I beheld then because of the voice of the great words which the horn spake: I beheld even till the beast was slain, and his body destroyed, and given to the burning flame. As concerning the rest of the beasts, they had their dominion taken away: yet their lives were prolonged for a season and time. (Daniel 7:7–12)

The fourth beast at the time of the end that rises will initially be a combination of the prior three (lion, bear, and leopard). The fourth beast will be, *by far*, the fiercest of all the beasts that have ever been on the earth. The fourth beast is the subject of this study and is the final and fiercest beast to manifest itself on the earth. The beast will be different from all previous beasts or dominions on the earth; it will have supernatural characteristics. The fourth and final terrible beast will be exceedingly strong, dreadful, and terrible. It will have great iron teeth and will be diverse from all the others before it. The fourth and final beast is described as a dragon—that is, an animal having no correlation to any earthly animal. The dragon associates the final beast with a dominion that has never been on the earth before, exemplifying its supernatural characteristics. The lack of understanding of a dragon is consistent with the diverse nature of this terrible final ten-horned beast. The fourth and final beast will rule over the prior three and, initially at least, use the prior three for its power base. The fourth beast is stated to stamp the residue of the prior three beasts with its feet.

In summary, there will be four beasts that will arise from the Gentile nations of the earth in the latter days. The first three beasts will be equivalent to Gentile superpower nations having characteristics of a lion/eagle, a bear, and a four-headed leopard. They will be strong coexistent nations on the earth and will be present on the earth at the time of the rising of the fourth terrible beast. The fourth beast that arises will be the kingdom of the Antichrist and will, initially at least, employ the services, power, and rulership of the prior three. The fourth beast will eventually stamp, or conquer, the previous three beasts, taking their power and dominion from them. The fourth beast will then rule the earth as one dominion. The dominion will continue for forty-two months. The dominion of the Antichrist will be three and one-half years, or forty-two months. The fourth beast of the Antichrist will destroy the earth and break it into pieces. In parallel with this, God's supernatural wrath on earth against the kingdom of the Antichrist and his followers will also be present on the earth. The result will leave the earth in ruins. Woe to the people on the earth during this time. After the three and one-half years, the Antichrist will be destroyed by the Lord Jesus Christ, who will then immediately set up his earthly rule. God's kingdom will remove Gentile dominion and power from the nations. All power will be given to the saints of the highest and his son from heaven, the Lord Jesus Christ. Blessed be our great God and his son from heaven, Jesus Christ.

APPENDIX G

The Millennial Kingdom of Our Lord Jesus Christ

AFTER THE DESTRUCTION OF THE beast and the rapture of the church of God, the millennial kingdom will be present on the earth. "Millennial kingdom" is a biblical term used to describe the time when the Lord Jesus Christ reigns as King of kings and Lord of lords on the earth for the first one thousand years after the destruction of the beast. His reign begins after the destruction of the beast and at the end of the final forty-two months. After the destruction of the wild beast, God initiates the first resurrection, the resurrection of the just, in which he resurrects the just to live and reign with his son, Jesus Christ, during his millennial reign. His millennial reign is followed by the great white throne judgment of God, as described in Revelation 20:11, in which all who ever lived will get up and be judged by God. The white throne judgment is the second resurrection—that is, the judgment of all who have lived on the earth. It is not part of the first resurrection. Both of these resurrections should not be confused with the rapture of the one body of Jesus Christ. The rapture will occur sometime after the middle of the final seven years and is a special resurrection of the one body of Jesus Christ; that is, those who have made Jesus Christ their Lord and Savior through belief in his name and a new birth as sons and daughters of God. The rapture is also part of the hidden Mystery period and therefore not mentioned in the Old Testament, the Gospels or the book of Revelation. It is only mentioned in the writings of apostle Paul and written only to the one body of Jesus Christ. In contrast, the first of the final two resurrections is the resurrection of the just and occurs immediately after the destruction of the beast. The second resurrection, or the great white throne judgment, is the resurrection of the unjust, but it is delayed until after the one-thousand-year reign of the Lord Jesus Christ. Both resurrections are mentioned in the gospel of John. Consider the following:

> For the Father loveth the Son, and sheweth him all things that himself doeth: and he will shew him greater works than these, that ye may marvel. For as the Father raiseth up the dead, and quickeneth them; even so the Son quickeneth whom he will. For the Father judgeth no man, but hath committed all judgment unto the Son: That all men should honour the Son, even as they honour the Father. He that honoureth not the Son honoureth not the Father which hath sent him. Verily, verily, I say unto you, He that heareth my word, and believeth on him that sent me, hath everlasting life, and shall not come into condemnation; but is passed from death unto life. **Verily, verily, I say unto you, The hour is coming, and now is, when the dead shall hear the voice of the Son of God: and they that hear shall live** (first resurrection). For as the Father hath life in himself; so hath he given to the Son to have life in himself; And hath given him authority to execute judgment also, because he is the Son of man. Marvel not at this: **for the hour is coming, in the which all that are in the graves shall hear his voice, And shall come forth; they that have done good, unto the resurrection of life; and**

they that have done evil, unto the resurrection of damnation (second resurrection). (John 5:20–29 KJV; my emphasis)

The two resurrections are also described and alluded to in the book of Acts and also in the book of Hebrews. Consider the following:

> And have hope toward God, which they themselves also allow, that there shall be a resurrection of the dead, **both of the just and unjust**. And herein do I exercise myself, to have always a conscience void of offence toward God, and toward men. (Acts 24:15–16 KJV; my emphasis)
>
> Women received their dead raised to life again: and others were tortured, not accepting deliverance; **that they might obtain a better resurrection.** (Hebrews 11:35 KJV; my emphasis)

In John 5:20–29, the Lord documents two separate and distinct resurrections. The first resurrection is a select group of those who hear the voice of the Son of God and shall live; that is, they will live eternally with the Lord (see v. 25). The second group is *all* who are in the graves, who will be resurrected and judged according to their works, some to the resurrection of life and some to the resurrection of damnation (see vv. 28–29). The two resurrections are separated by one thousand years; the first occurs after the destruction of the beast, and the second, the great white throne judgment, occurs after the millennial rule of the Lord Jesus Christ.

During the Lord's millennial reign, Satan will be chained and unable to deceive the nations. After the thousand years, Satan will be set loose for a short season and allowed to deceive the nations on the earth.[381] He will then be destroyed by the Lord Jesus Christ. Following

---

[381] See Revelation 20:7–8.

his destruction, the great white throne judgment of God will take place. God will judge all people from all time that were not raised at the time of the resurrection of the just.[382] After the final judgment, the Lord will rule forever and ever on a new heaven and new earth created by God. The thousand-year reign of our Lord Jesus Christ is considered the Day of the Lord, or the day that the Lord rules on the earth. All earthly dominion will be taken away from the nations and given to the son of God. The Lord will rule with the resurrected saints: those who persevered through the tribulation period and those written in the book of life. The millennial kingdom begins with the destruction of the Antichrist by the Lord at his coming for Israel. The destruction of the Antichrist will be coincident with the setting up of the glorious kingdom of Jesus Christ on the earth. Revelation 20:1–6 documents this thousand-year reign. Consider the following:

> And I saw an angel come down from heaven, having the key of the bottomless pit and a great chain in his hand. And he laid hold on the dragon, that old serpent, which is the Devil, and Satan, and bound him a thousand years, And cast him into the bottomless pit, and shut him up, and set a seal upon him, that he should deceive the nations no more, till the thousand years should be fulfilled: and after that he must be loosed a little season. And I saw thrones, and they sat upon them, and judgment was given unto them: and I saw the souls of them that were beheaded for the witness of Jesus, and for the Word of God, and which had not worshipped the beast, neither his image, neither had received his mark upon their foreheads, or in their hands; and they lived and reigned with Christ a thousand years. But the rest of the dead lived not again until the thousand years were finished. This is the first resurrection.

---

[382] See Revelation 20:11–15.

> Blessed and holy is he that hath part in the first resurrection: on such the second death hath no power, but they shall be priests of God and of Christ, and shall reign with him a thousand years. And when the thousand years are expired, Satan shall be loosed out of his prison, And shall go out to deceive the nations which are in the four quarters of the earth, Gog and Magog, to gather them together to battle: the number of whom is as the sand of the sea. (Revelation 20:1–8 KJV)

The destruction of the beast will mark the end and fulfillment of Daniel's prophecy of seventy sevens as documented in Daniel 9:24. It will also mark the beginning of the thousand-year reign of our Lord. At the end of the final forty-two months, God fulfills all promises to Abraham, Isaac, and Jacob. Consider the following:

> Seventy weeks (weeks of years or 490 years) are determined upon thy people and upon thy holy city, to finish the transgression, and to make an end of sins, and to make reconciliation for iniquity, and to bring in everlasting righteousness, and to seal up the vision and prophecy, and to anoint the most Holy. (Daniel 9:24 KJV)

The promises made to Israel in Daniel 9:24 will be fulfilled only at the end of the seventy weeks of Daniel's prophecy. Once again, the time of the mystery of the one body of Christ is skipped over. The promises made to Israel's fathers are reserved for the Day of the Lord and will come into concretion only at the start of the millennial kingdom of Jesus Christ. It is interesting to note that the disciples also knew of the blessings that would come to Israel. It is for this reason that the disciples went to our Lord before his ascension in the first century AD with the question that was burning in their hearts. Their question was regarding the future of Israel and had to do with the promises God made to their fathers in the Old Testament. Their question to the Lord is documented below in the book of Acts.

> For John truly baptized with water; but ye shall be baptized with the Holy Ghost not many days hence. When they therefore were come together, **they asked of him, saying, Lord, wilt thou at this time restore again the kingdom to Israel?** And he said unto them, it is not for you to know the times or the seasons, which the Father hath put in his own power. But ye shall receive power, after that the Holy Ghost is come upon you: and ye shall be witnesses unto me both in Jerusalem, and in all Judaea, and in Samaria, and unto the uttermost part of the earth. (Acts 1:5–8 KJV; my emphasis)

The disciples knew from the Old Testament that there would be a glorious end for Israel. They could not piece together when the millennial kingdom would come, but they knew that it would absolutely come through their knowledge of Old Testament prophecy. The future of Israel is made clear through the scriptures—especially the Old Testament scriptures. Not understanding the new time that was coming on the earth; the time of the one body of Jesus Christ, which was kept hidden in God, they asked the Lord the question concerning Israel. In contrast, the future of the church of the body of Christ is eternal life and sons of God through Jesus Christ. But what function the one body of Christ takes on in the future is not as clear. The church of the body of Jesus Christ, the most blessed group on the earth, will be raptured from the earth and will live with the lord eternally in the heavenlies.[383] The future of the born-again believers is not yet revealed, as stated in 1 John 2. Consider the following:

> Behold, what manner of love the Father hath bestowed upon us, **that we should be called**

---
[383] Ephesians 1:3

the sons of God: therefore the world knoweth us not, because it knew him not. **Beloved, now are we the sons of God, and it doth not yet appear what we shall be, but we know that, when he shall appear, we shall be like him; for we shall see him as he is.** And every man that hath this hope in him purifieth himself, even as he is pure. (1 John 3:1–3; my emphasis)

Before the Day of the Lord and the wrath of God, the one body of Jesus Christ, made up of called-out former Jews and Gentiles, will be raptured from the earth. When these called out of Jesus Christ are raptured from the earth, the remaining Jews will once again be the focus of God's attention. The Jews and Gentiles will once again be separated and will be treated differently. In Acts 1 the Lord did not deny the glory that would come to Israel. He answered their question in Acts 1:6, knowing that another time was coming, and the final glory of Israel was to be held in abeyance. He knew that the period of the mystery of the one body of Christ would now be upon the earth until the fullness of the time of the Gentiles was come in. The removal of the church, or the rapture of the one body of Christ, will occur in the same time frame as the last days but before the wrath of Almighty God on the earth. After the rapture, or removal of the church, the blindness will be taken away from national Israel and they will understand Jesus Christ as their Messiah. Romans 11 discusses the interaction between the body of Christ and the Jews. Consider the following:

For I would not, brethren, that ye should be ignorant of this mystery, lest ye should be wise in your own conceits; that blindness in part is happened to Israel, until the fullness of the Gentiles be come in. And so all Israel shall be saved: as it is written, There shall come out of Sion the Deliverer, and shall turn away ungodliness from Jacob: **For this is my covenant unto them, when I shall take**

> **away their sins.** As concerning the gospel, they are enemies for your sakes: but as touching the election, they are beloved for the fathers' sakes. **For the gifts and calling of God are without repentance.** (Romans 11:25–29 KJV; my emphasis)

The Bible documents clearly that our Lord and Savior, Jesus Christ, will establish his millennial kingdom on earth. The kingdom will begin with blindness being taken away from the bride of Christ—Israel. The blindness will be taken away after the destruction of the Antichrist and the end of the times of the Gentiles—the end of the final forty-two months. The Lord will come to the holy place in Jerusalem at the end of the final forty-two months. Consider the following sections, which speak of these very days:

> O sing unto the LORD a new song; for he hath done marvellous things: his right hand, and his holy arm, hath gotten him the victory. The LORD hath made known his salvation: his righteousness hath he openly showed in the sight of the heathen. **He hath remembered his mercy and his truth toward the house of Israel: all the ends of the earth have seen the salvation of our God.** Make a joyful noise unto the LORD, all the earth: make a loud noise, and rejoice, and sing praise. Sing unto the LORD with the harp; with the harp, and the voice of a psalm. With trumpets and sound of cornet make a joyful noise before the LORD, the King. Let the sea roar, and the fulness thereof; the world, and they that dwell therein. Let the floods clap their hands: let the hills be joyful together Before the LORD; for he cometh to judge the earth: with righteousness shall he judge the world, and the people with equity. (Psalm 98 KJV; my emphasis)

Why do the heathen rage, and the people imagine a vain thing? The kings of the earth set themselves, and the rulers take counsel together, against the LORD, and against his anointed, saying, Let us break their bands asunder, and cast away their cords from us. He that sitteth in the heavens shall laugh: the Lord shall have them in derision. Then shall he speak unto them in his wrath, and vex them in his sore displeasure. **Yet have I set my king upon my holy hill of Zion. I will declare the decree: the LORD hath said unto me, Thou art my Son; this day have I begotten thee. Ask of me, and I shall give thee the heathen for thine inheritance, and the uttermost parts of the earth for thy possession. Thou shalt break them with a rod of iron; thou shalt dash them in pieces like a potter's vessel.** Be wise now therefore, O ye kings: be instructed, ye judges of the earth. Serve the LORD with fear, and rejoice with trembling. Kiss the Son, lest he be angry, and ye perish from the way, when his wrath is kindled but a little. Blessed are all they that put their trust in him. (Psalm 2 KJV; my emphasis)

When the Son of man shall come in his glory, and all the holy angels with him, then shall he sit upon the throne of his glory: And before him shall be gathered all nations: and he shall separate them one from another, as a shepherd divideth his sheep from the goats: And he shall set the sheep on his right hand, but the goats on the left. Then shall the King say unto them on his right hand, Come, ye blessed of my Father, inherit the kingdom prepared for you from the foundation of the world. (Matthew 25:31–34 KJV)

THE LAST DAYS AND THE VILE MAN OF DANIEL

At the completion of the seventy sevens of years of Daniel's prophecy, all that God promised to the patriarchs—Abraham, Isaac, and Jacob—will have been fulfilled. As of today, most of these promises documented in the Old Testament have yet to be fulfilled. The promises made to Israel are separate and distinct from the promises made to the church of God or the body of Jesus Christ. Trying to insert the church of the body of Christ into the Old Testament promises for Israel, or even the book of Revelation, creates confusion and wrong division of the Word of God. The error leads to additional error, subsequently distorting the Word of God. The result of this wrong division of the Word of God is putting the body of Christ once again on the seat of judgment and justification by works instead of the safety of righteousness through faith. The church of the body is saved by the grace of God—that is, God's unmerited divine favor. We have been saved by faith in his son, Jesus Christ, through the grace of God. Conversely, salvation by faith is not the standard in the book of Revelation; works is once again the order of the day. The book of Revelation is written to certain Jews and those Gentiles who will be redeemed out of the time of crisis on the earth. The church of the body of Christ will be raptured from the earth before the great final judgments of God come upon the earth as described in Revelation.

The book of Revelation is the culmination of judgment for Jew and Gentile, not the church of the one body of Jesus Christ. At the time of the book of Revelation, the separation of the Jew and Gentile is once again enforced, and God goes on to fulfill all promises made to the Patriarchs. The Jews' rejection of the Messiah is reversed; he is accepted by the called out of Israel who have made themselves ready for his second coming. The remnant will now become, after the destruction of the Antichrist, the embryotic nation of Israel, which will be present with him during his millennial kingdom. Consider the following: *"Verily I say unto you, All these things shall come upon this generation. O Jerusalem, Jerusalem, thou that killest the prophets, and stonest them which are sent unto thee, how often would I have gathered thy children together, even as a hen gathereth her chickens under her wings, and ye would not!* **Behold, your house is left unto** *you desolate. For I say unto you, Ye shall not see me henceforth, till ye (national Israel) shall say, Blessed is he that cometh in the name of the Lord"* (Matthew 23:36–39 KJV; my emphasis).

National Israel, at the completion of the seventy weeks, will finally learn the reality of their Messiah and learn to say **"Blessed is he who comes in the name of the Lord."** Their house—that is, the temple at the holy place in Jerusalem—is left desolate until that time. Their house is not left desolate forever, but for a specific period (to date it has been about two thousand years). The right division of the Word of God dispels confusion and wrong teaching. In the millennial period, the Gentile nations will receive their blessings through Israel. The church of the one body will already have been raptured from the earth and will only be a memory as to its earthly existence. All these events—except, of course, the hidden church of Christ—are clearly stated in many Old Testament scriptures. All of God's Word must, and will, absolutely be fulfilled with astounding accuracy and precision. Consider the following: *"And there was given me a reed like unto a rod: and the angel stood, saying, Rise, and measure the temple of God, and the altar, and them that worship therein.* ***But the court which is without the temple leave out, and measure it not; for it is given unto the Gentiles: and the holy city shall they tread under foot forty-two months"*** (Revelation 11:1–2 KJV; my emphasis).

During the last seven years, the Holy of Holies in Jerusalem is once again established, and the Jewish remnant are set apart. Taking a rod and measuring is a figure of speech used by God to indicate the construction process. The final building of the temple fulfills the Old Testament prophecy in Ezekiel. Consider the following:

> In the five and twentieth year of our captivity, in the beginning of the year, in the tenth day of the month, in the fourteenth year after that the city was smitten, in the selfsame day the hand of the LORD was upon me, and brought me thither. In the visions of God brought he me into the land of Israel, and set me

upon a very high mountain, by which was as the frame of a city on the south. And he brought me thither, **and, behold, there was a man, whose appearance was like the appearance of brass, with a line of flax in his hand, and a measuring reed; and he stood in the gate**. And the man said unto me, Son of man, behold with thine eyes, and hear with thine ears, and set thine heart upon all that I shall show thee; for to the intent that I might show them unto thee art thou brought hither: declare all that thou seest to the house of Israel. And behold a wall on the outside of the house round about, and in the man's hand a measuring reed of six cubits long by the cubit and an hand breadth: so he measured the breadth of the building, one reed; and the height, one reed. Then came he unto the gate which looketh toward the east, and went up the stairs thereof, and measured the threshold of the gate, which was one reed broad; and the other threshold of the gate, which was one reed broad. And every little chamber was one reed long, and one reed broad; and between the little chambers were five cubits; and the threshold of the gate by the porch of the gate within was one reed. He measured also the porch of the gate within, one reed. (Ezekiel 40:1–8 KJV; my emphasis)

The period of the mystery of the one body of Christ will have already been received up into glory before the millennium reign of our Lord Jesus Christ. The rapture of the body of Christ marks the end of salvation through the gift of God as he established in Romans 10.9 and the new birth of Jews and Gentiles whose new identity becomes the one body of Jesus Christ; each an individual member of his body. The end times, the final seven years, and the final forty-two months of those seven years is the time of the wrath of our Holy God upon all the wicked of the earth. The called-out remnant of Israel will be saved by God in similar fashion to the way he saved them out from Egypt, as documented in Genesis. God states that he does this for his name's sake and because of the promises that he made to the Patriarchs centuries before. God does not do this because of their obedience or righteousness, but because he promised it to their fathers. Consider the following:

> Son of man, when the house of Israel dwelt in their own land, they defiled it by their own way and by their doings: their way was before me as the uncleanness of a removed woman. Wherefore I poured my fury upon them for the blood that they had shed upon the land, and for their idols wherewith they had polluted it: And I scattered them among the heathen, and they were dispersed through the countries: according to their way and according to their doings I judged them. And when they entered unto the heathen, whither they went, they profaned my holy name, when they said to them, These are the people of the LORD, and are gone forth out of his land. **But I had pity for mine holy name, which the house of Israel had profaned among the heathen, whither they went. Therefore say unto the house of Israel, Thus saith the Lord GOD; I do not this for your sakes, O house of Israel, but for mine holy name's sake, which ye have profaned among the heathen, whither ye went. And I will sanctify my great name, which was profaned among the heathen, which ye have profaned in the midst of them; and the heathen shall know that I am the LORD, saith the Lord GOD, when I shall be sanctified in you before their eyes.** For I will take you from among the heathen, and gather you out of all

countries, and will bring you into your own land. Then will I sprinkle clean water upon you, and ye shall be clean: from all your filthiness, and from all your idols, will I cleanse you. A new heart also will I give you, and a new spirit will I put within you: and I will take away the stony heart out of your flesh, and I will give you an heart of flesh. And I will put my spirit within you, and cause you to walk in my statutes, and ye shall keep my judgments, and do them. And ye shall dwell in the land that I gave to your fathers; and ye shall be my people, and I will be your God. I will also save you from all your uncleannesses: and I will call for the corn, and will increase it, and lay no famine upon you. And I will multiply the fruit of the tree, and the increase of the field, that ye shall receive no more reproach of famine among the heathen. Then shall ye remember your own evil ways, and your doings that were not good, and shall lothe yourselves in your own sight for your iniquities and for your abominations. **Not for your sakes do I this, saith the Lord GOD, be it known unto you: be ashamed and confounded for your own ways, O house of Israel.** Thus saith the Lord GOD; In the day that I shall have cleansed you from all your iniquities I will also cause you to dwell in the cities, and the wastes shall be builded. And the desolate land shall be tilled, whereas it lay desolate in the sight of all that passed by. And they shall say, This land that was desolate is become like the garden of Eden; and the waste and desolate and ruined cities are become fenced, and are inhabited. Then the heathen that are left round about you shall know that I the LORD build the ruined places, and plant that that was desolate: I the LORD have spoken it, and I will do it. Thus saith the Lord GOD; I will yet for this be enquired of by the house of Israel, to do it for them; I will increase them with men like a flock. As the holy flock, as the flock of Jerusalem in her solemn feasts; so shall the waste cities be filled with flocks of men: and they shall know that I am the LORD. (Ezekiel 36:17–38 KJV; my emphasis)

The Lord God fulfills all promises to the Patriarchs at the time of the millennial rule of the Lord Jesus Christ. David is raised as their king, and Jesus Christ is their Lord. They will be in the land of Israel forever and will be blessed by God. *God does this not because they deserve it but for his holy name's sake.* In Old Testament Egypt, it was the Lord God dealing with a defiant pharaoh who would not let the people of God go. In Revelation it will be a defiant world under the delusion of the Antichrist who will not let the people of God go. In the end, the remnant Jews called of God are in the land, and all the promises to their fathers are fulfilled. God reverts to a similar time when he delivered his people, Israel, supernaturally from the tyranny of Egypt. In the last days, God once again supernaturally delivers the remnant of Israel; the firstfruits, 12,000 from each of the tribes or 144,000, and then those that are his at his coming. They will be delivered from the tyranny of the vile man/Antichrist. God will feed and protect them and lead them with a pillar of fire, hiding them for forty-two months. They will be purified and made ready for their savior, Jesus Christ. They will then be counted as the earthly firstfruits of Israel in the millennial age.

The millennial kingdom will feature both Jew and Gentile on the earth. The church of the one body of Jesus Christ will have been raptured from the earth and be with the Lord. The Jews will once again be favored over the Gentile. God will fulfill all the promises to Abraham, Isaac, and Jacob. The prophets—Isaiah, Ezekiel, and many others—speak of this same glorious time for Israel. Consider the following:

The Spirit of the Lord GOD is upon me; because the LORD hath anointed me to preach good tidings unto the meek; he hath sent me to bind up the brokenhearted, to proclaim liberty to the captives, and the opening of the prison to them that are bound; To proclaim the acceptable year of the LORD, and the day of vengeance of our God; to comfort all that mourn; To appoint unto them that mourn in Zion, to give unto them beauty for ashes, the oil of joy for mourning, the garment of praise for the spirit of heaviness; that they might be called trees of righteousness, the planting of the LORD, that he might be glorified. **And they shall build the old wastes, they shall raise up the former desolations, and they shall repair the waste cities, the desolations of many generations. And strangers shall stand and feed your flocks, and the sons of the alien shall be your plowmen and your vinedressers. But ye shall be named the Priests of the LORD: men shall call you the Ministers of our God: ye shall eat the riches of the Gentiles, and in their glory shall ye boast yourselves.** For your shame ye shall have double; and for confusion they shall rejoice in their portion: therefore in their land they shall possess the double: everlasting joy shall be unto them. For I the LORD love judgment, I hate robbery for burnt offering; and I will direct their work in truth, and I will make an everlasting covenant with them. And their seed shall be known among the Gentiles, and their offspring among the people: all that see them shall acknowledge them, that they are the seed which the LORD hath blessed. I will greatly rejoice in the LORD, my soul shall be joyful in my God; for he hath clothed me with the garments of salvation, he hath covered me with the robe of righteousness, as a bridegroom decketh himself with ornaments, and as a bride adorneth herself with her jewels. For as the earth bringeth forth her bud, and as the garden causeth the things that are sown in it to spring forth; so the Lord GOD will cause righteousness and praise to spring forth before all the nations. (Isaiah 61:1–11 KJV; my emphasis)

The word that Isaiah the son of Amoz saw concerning Judah and Jerusalem. And it shall come to pass in the last days, that the mountain of the LORD'S house shall be established in the top of the mountains, and shall be exalted above the hills; and all nations shall flow unto it. And many people shall go and say, Come ye, and let us go up to the mountain of the LORD, to the house of the God of Jacob; and he will teach us of his ways, and we will walk in his paths: for out of Zion shall go forth the law, and the word of the LORD from Jerusalem. **And he shall judge among the nations, and shall rebuke many people: and they shall beat their swords into plowshares, and their spears into pruninghooks: nation shall not lift up sword against nation, neither shall they learn war any more.** (Isaiah 2:1–4 KJV; my emphasis)

Following the destruction of the Antichrist, the following events will take place on the earth at the start of the millennium kingdom of our Lord Jesus Christ:

1. The first resurrection, or the resurrection of the just, and the judgment of the Gentile nations will take place on the earth. The judging will be accomplished by God through his son Jesus Christ, his holy angels, and his disciples. The first

resurrection includes those saved out of the tribulation as well as the saints written in the Lord's book of life; including the Old Testament believers. Consider the following:

> Let the heathen be wakened, and come up to the valley of Jehoshaphat: **for there will I sit to judge all the heathen round about.** (Joel 3:12 KJV; my emphasis)
>
> When the Son of man shall come in his glory, and all the holy angels with him, then shall he sit upon the throne of his glory: **And before him shall be gathered all nations: and he shall separate them one from another, as a shepherd divideth his sheep from the goats: And he shall set the sheep on his right hand, but the goats on the left.** (Matthew 25:31–33 KJV; my emphasis)
>
> And I saw thrones, and they sat upon them, and judgment was given unto them: and I saw the souls of them that were beheaded for the witness of Jesus, and for the Word of God, and which had not worshipped the beast, neither his image, neither had received his mark upon their foreheads, or in their hands; **and they lived and reigned with Christ a thousand years. But the rest of the dead lived not again until the thousand years were finished. This is the first resurrection. Blessed and holy is he that hath part in the first resurrection:** on such the second death hath no power, but they shall be priests of God and of Christ, and shall reign with him a thousand years. (Revelation 20:4–6 KJV; my emphasis)
>
> Verily, verily, I say unto you, The hour is coming, and now is, **when the dead shall hear the voice of the Son of God: and they that hear shall live. For as the Father hath life in himself; so hath he given to the Son to have life**

> **in himself; And hath given him authority to execute judgment also, because he is the Son of man. Marvel not at this: for the hour is coming, in the which all that are in the graves shall hear his voice, And shall come forth; they that have done good, unto the resurrection of life; and they that have done evil, unto the resurrection of damnation.** (John 5:25–29 KJV)

The resurrection of the just is also called the first resurrection and will occur immediately before the millennial kingdom of Jesus Christ is established. The resurrection of the just will include the redeemed of the tribulation period who died during that time. The group will also include the redeemed and lovers of God during the Old Testament times.

2. The lion will lie down with the lamb.

> The wolf also shall dwell with the lamb, and the leopard shall lie down with the kid; and the calf and the young lion and the fatling together; and a little child shall lead them. And the cow and the bear shall feed; their young ones shall lie down together: and the lion shall eat straw like the ox. And the sucking child shall play on the hole of the asp, and the weaned child shall put his hand on the cockatrice' den. (Isaiah 11:6–8 KJV)

3. The earth will be fruitful, as it was before the fall in Genesis 3. Evil will exist but will be restricted. Mankind will live long fruitful lives, but death will still be present.

> But be ye glad and rejoice forever in that which I create: for, behold, I create Jerusalem a rejoicing, and her people a joy. And I will rejoice in Jerusalem, and joy in my people: and the voice

of weeping shall be no more heard in her, nor the voice of crying. There shall be no more thence an infant of days, nor an old man that hath not filled his days: for the child shall die an hundred years old; but the sinner being an hundred years old shall be accursed. And they shall build houses, and inhabit them; and they shall plant vineyards, and eat the fruit of them. They shall not build, and another inhabit; they shall not plant, and another eat: for as the days of a tree are the days of my people, and mine elect shall long enjoy the work of their hands. They shall not labour in vain, nor bring forth for trouble; for they are the seed of the blessed of the LORD, and their offspring with them. And it shall come to pass, that before they call, I will answer; and while they are yet speaking, I will hear. The wolf and the lamb shall feed together, and the lion shall eat straw like the bullock: and dust shall be the serpent's meat. They shall not hurt nor destroy in all my holy mountain, saith the LORD. (Isaiah 65:18–25 KJV)

Behold, the eyes of the Lord GOD are upon the sinful kingdom, and I will destroy it from off the face of the earth; saving that I will not utterly destroy the house of Jacob, saith the LORD. For, lo, I will command, and I will sift the house of Israel among all nations, like as corn is sifted in a sieve, yet shall not the least grain fall upon the earth. All the sinners of my people shall die by the sword, which say, the evil shall not overtake nor prevent us. In that day will I raise up the tabernacle of David that is fallen, and close up the breaches thereof; and I will raise up his ruins, and I will build it as in the days of old: That they may possess the remnant of Edom, and of all the heathen, which are called by my name, saith the LORD that doeth this. Behold, the days come, saith the LORD, that the plowman shall overtake the reaper, and the treader of grapes him that soweth seed; and the mountains shall drop sweet wine, and all the hills shall melt. And I will bring again the captivity of my people of Israel, and they shall build the waste cities, and inhabit them; and they shall plant vineyards, and drink the wine thereof; they shall also make gardens, and eat the fruit of them. And I will plant them upon their land, and they shall no more be pulled up out of their land which I have given them, saith the LORD thy God. (Amos 9:8–15 KJV)

And when the thousand years are expired, Satan shall be loosed out of his prison, And shall go out to deceive the nations which are in the four quarters of the earth, Gog and Magog, to gather them together to battle: the number of whom is as the sand of the sea. And they went up on the breadth of the earth, and compassed the camp of the saints about, and the beloved city: and fire came down from God out of heaven, and devoured them. (Revelation 20:7–9 KJV)

The millennium demonstrates God's victory over sin and his complete faithfulness to his people. Following this time, a rebellion will occur, but God will have victory. He will then judge all those who ever lived upon the earth and were not part of the first resurrection. Thus, the first thousand-year period, when the Lord Jesus Christ triumphs over evil, is present on the earth. The time will be a time of peace and fulfillment of God's promises to his people. At the end of the thousand years, evil and death are finally eradicated, and a new heaven and earth are created by God. The last heaven and earth will be for those whom God judges worthy to live and who are written in God's book. Blessed be the Lord God and his son from heaven, Jesus Christ, forever.

APPENDIX H

The Composite Description and Identification of the Beast

THE PREVIOUS SECTIONS COMPLETE THE scriptures that identify the actions and behaviors of the beast and the events of the last days. The scriptures identify the events surrounding the rising of the beast in the last days until his destruction by the Lord Jesus Christ. The beast and the false prophet are then, after the final seven years, unceremoniously disposed of in the lake of fire. The scriptures examined in this work do not exhaust what God states about the last days but provide critical keys enabling the searcher of scripture to recognize the final beast when he appears on the world stage. The critical keys will enable the searcher of scripture and lover of God to also identify the events of the last days and then the last seven years as they progress through their sequence. Attentiveness to these critical keys will identify the last times and the seasons—especially the rising of the beast and the times of sorrows as described by our Lord Jesus Christ. God's Word effectively provides keys to our understanding regarding the last time and season of the end times. The referenced scriptural information, both from the Word of God and summarized below, provides an accurate profile revealing a vivid focused picture of the last days and the rising of the beast. The references are critically tied to the Word of God, as they must be for an accurate account of the truth. From the time frame perspective, the backdrop is Daniel's prophecy of seventy sevens of weeks (years) given in Daniel 9:24.[384] The time frame encompasses the whole of the rule of the Gentiles, from the removal of Israel from the land—the time of Nebuchadnezzar—up until the anointing of the Messiah by embryotic national Israel after the final seven years. The crowning of the Messiah by Israel, or the wedding feast of Revelation 19:7–9, occurs at the conclusion of the last seven years.

The initiation of the last seven years is in God's hands, but when God does initiate the final seven years, the time will follow the sequence of events laid out by the Word of God. The sequence of events will be in accordance with what is documented by God in both the Old and New Testament scriptures—especially the book of Daniel and Revelation. For convenience, all attributes and behaviors of the beast from the previous reference sections will be listed below. From these attributes, a composite narrative is assembled and documented after the list of attributes below. The narrative will accurately describe the beast and his rising in the last seven years from the Word of God. The time frame when the beast rises, the last days, will also be unmistakable as the judgments of God progress forward in time. The attributes will be listed and accounted for in the narrative. The methodology will allow the reader to cross-reference the narrative from the scriptural reference sections it was derived from, for clarification purposes. The attributes from each of the reference sections are listed as follows:

Cumulative List of Attributes

<u>Section 1, Reference 1, 2, and 3 (Isaiah 14)</u>

1. The Antichrist, or king of Babylon, will eventually direct his anger against Israel. He will direct his anger against Israel, but a remnant of Israel will be saved from destruction; this

---

[384] Daniel 9:24.

THE LAST DAYS AND THE VILE MAN OF DANIEL

is the purpose that God has purposed upon the whole earth (see vv. 1–4, 25–27).
2. He will represent Satan on Earth, arrogance, pride, destruction, and a claim to be God (see vv. 9–14).
3. He will be brought down to hell and will be the first to be cast into hell and not buried in the earth (see vv. 15–20).
4. He will narrowly be considered, and the power he once had will be scoffed at (see v. 16).
5. He is described as the man that made the world (Mystery Babylon) a wilderness, indicating how he will destroy the nations and cities therein (see v. 17).
6. After his rulership of the nations of the world and their subsequent destruction, the nations will be no more; the rule over the earth will be given to the true God and his Christ (see vv. 21–23).
7. He will rise from the Assyrian territory (the Seleucid Empire, now Syria) and grow in strength and power, finally ruling over all the earth.
8. He will be destroyed in the land of Israel (see v. 25).

<u>Section 2, Reference 4 (Daniel 7:1–27)</u>

9. The fourth latter-day beast, or kingdom, headed by the Antichrist will be dreadful, terrible, and extremely strong Gentile dominion. It will have great iron teeth and nails of brass, and it will devour, stamp, and break into pieces the residue of the three prior contemporary beasts, or nations: the lion, bear, and leopard (see v. 7).
10. The fourth latter-day beast will be different from all the rest of the beasts (dominions or kingdoms) that preceded it on the earth. The fourth beast, headed by the Antichrist, will have, after his miraculous resurrection, supernatural characteristics not ever seen on the earth before; hence it shall be different (see v. 7).
11. The beast will have ten horns, or rulers—representative kings or rulers appointed by the beast. The Antichrist will

arise as a little horn and will replace or subdue three of the first ten horns. The horns he replaces are identified as those of the South, the East, and the pleasant land—that is, Israel, the center of compass in the eyes of the true God (see vv. 7–8).

12. The little horn will declare himself God and speak blasphemies against God and his people, and he will be allowed to rule, deceive, and destroy for forty-two months.[385] (see vv. 8, 25)

13. The beast, Antichrist, or vile man will be destroyed by the Lord Jesus Christ at the end of the final forty-two months of the seventieth seven-year period. The beast will be destroyed by the brightness of the coming of the Lord Jesus Christ, who will set up his millennial kingdom immediately after the destruction of the beast. The beast will then be judged by God and thrown into the lake of fire forever and ever.[386] (see vv. 11–14, 27)

14. The Antichrist, or little horn, will make war with the saints of the most-high and will prevail against them. The destruction of the nations by the Antichrist, and the enmity against God and his people, will begin at the time of the middle of the seventieth week and continue for the final forty-two months[387] (see vv. 19, 21, 23, 25).

15. The Antichrist will wear out the saints of the most-high and will change times and laws, including the covenant law of God given through Moses and the prophets. Lawlessness will increase and abound on the earth. He will do according to his will for time, times, and half of time—three and one-half years (see v. 25).[388]

---

[385] Daniel 7:7, 19, 20, 24; 8:9.
[386] Daniel 7:11; 2 Thessalonians 2:8; Revelation 19:20.
[387] Daniel 7:21; 11:31–35; 12.11.
[388] Daniel 7:25; 11:31–36.

Section 2, Reference 5 (Daniel 8:1–27)

16. The Antichrist will arise from one of the four dominions remaining after the death of Alexander the Great—the northern kingdom of the Seleucids. But this will occur thousands of years later, in the latter days.[389] The four dominions referenced in the Word of God and remaining after the fall of Alexander include (1) the Seleucid Empire, or modern-day Syria (North), (2) the Ptolemies, or modern-day Egypt (South), (3) Asia Minor (East), and (4) Greece (West) (see v. 9).
17. The Antichrist will be the next man to rule the earth as one man and declare himself to be a god. He will follow in the steps of Alexander the Great, the last man to rule as one man. This is what is foreshadowed in Daniel 8:9 (see v. 9).
18. The Antichrist is depicted as a little horn or a man of small beginnings who rises in the last days from one of the four residual dominions of Alexander's reign—the northern kingdom.[390] His rise is marked by the league he makes with a Gentile superpower, which also marks the beginning of the events of the last days. Within these last days will be the twenty-three hundred days and the final seven years (see v. 9). The covenant or league will begin before both the final seven years and the final twenty-three hundred days.
19. The Antichrist will grow and become exceedingly great toward the South, the East, and the glorious land, or the land of Israel itself. (Note: God's center of the compass on the earth is always the Holy of Holies in Jerusalem) (see v. 9).[391]
20. The Antichrist will become great and will affect even the stars, or the angels of heaven. The Antichrist will cast down a third of the stars, or angels, from heaven, revealing how

---

[389] Daniel 8:9.
[390] Daniel 11:23.
[391] Daniel 8:9.

he is cast out of heaven with his evil angels and cast to the earth (see v. 10).[392]

21. The Antichrist will magnify himself even to God himself—the God of the starry host.[393] He will believe in his heart that he is a god through powerful miracles. He will magnify himself in his heart (see vv. 11, 25).
22. He will make covenants, or promises, of peace, acting deceitfully, which will have the opposite effect; that is, doing so will cause the destruction of many people and nations (see v. 25).
23. The Antichrist will take away the daily sacrifice in Jerusalem. This could be a prayer sacrifice in Jerusalem. The sanctuary—the Holy of Holies in Jerusalem—is also cast down. These events are associated with the midst of the seventieth week (see v. 11).[394]
24. The Antichrist will be given a military host from those he allies with, and he will initially use this host to stop the daily sacrifice in Jerusalem. He will then use the military host and his supernatural powers to accomplish his will (see v. 12).
25. The Antichrist will cast down to the ground God's truth—the laws and practices given through Moses and the prophets. These events begin to occur at or about the middle of the seventieth week, or the final seven years of Daniel's prophecy of seventy weeks of years (see v. 12).[395]
26. He shall rise to power in the last days when the sins of the people, and of the world, have reached their limit—that is, when the world overflows with sin as in the time of Noah before the flood (see v. 23).[396]

---

[392] Revelation 12:4; Daniel 8:10.
[393] Daniel 8:10; 11:36; Revelation 13; 2 Thessalonians 2:4.
[394] Daniel 8:11; 11:31.
[395] Daniel 8:12; 11:31–32.
[396] Matthew 24:38.

27. He shall be the final Gentile ruler of the earth. He will be a ruler or leader of fierce countenance, or of hard countenance (i.e., impudent, unashamed in trampling down, without fear of God or man, and having no compassion for any human being) (see v. 23).
28. His power shall be great, but he will not attain it by his own power; he will be assisted by a strong superpower, other allies, and by Satanic evil spirits. All of this will be orchestrated by Satan and evil spirits to destroy the nations and people of the earth "wonderfully"—that is, through supernatural means.[397] Satan's power will be unbridled through him (see v. 24).[398]
29. He shall understand dark sentences or conceal his purpose behind ambiguous words, using dissimulation, forming an artifice (see Daniel 8:25). The unfolding of these qualities is also presented in Daniel 8:24–25 (see v. 23).
30. The power he uses is power from Satan and Satan's ability to affect situations supernaturally, or beyond human effort. The result of this special power will result in fearful destruction, and he shall succeed in what he does. He shall cause mighty men, mighty nations, and the saints to be conquered (see v. 24).
31. By his shrewd understanding, discerning, and feeling of superiority, he shall make deceitful or treacherous speech to prosper under his hand, completely in his control. He will consider himself to be superior and divine. Through utilization of this proud arrogance, he will, without warning, and while there is an air or careless security, unexpectedly cause the destruction of many peoples and nations. Finally, he will raise himself up against God and his son, Jesus Christ, bringing on his own destruction without

---

[397] Revelation 13:2; 2 Thessalonians 2:9–10.
[398] 2 Thessalonians 2:9.

the help of man but by the brightness of the coming of the Lord Jesus Christ (see vv. 23–25).[399]

Section 2, Reference 6 (Daniel 9:20–10:1)

32. Seventy sevens of years (490 years) are determined, or cut off, for Israel to fulfill all promises made to their fathers. 483 of those years have been fulfilled and are in the past; the last seven-year period remains to be fulfilled (2020) and will be initiated in accordance with God's timetable. The mystery period of the one body of Jesus Christ lies between the sixty-ninth and the seventieth weeks (see v. 24).
33. The prince, or the Antichrist, will come and destroy the city (Jerusalem) and the sanctuary (the holy place) at the time of the end. This event will begin to take place sometime near the middle of the first of two seven-year periods. At the time of the middle of the final seven year period the event will actually occur in Jerusalem. (see v. 26, 27).
34. The Antichrist will make a strong covenant or league with a strong nation which will initiate the end times events as documented by God in his word. This covenant will initiate the first of two seven-year periods; the second seven-year period beginning at the time of the middle of the first (see timelines). The covenant will strengthen the Antichrist both politically and militarily for the duration of the first seven-year period. The covenant or league begins the prophecy concerning the Antichrist and the last days.
35. The Antichrist will begin to cause the sacrifice and oblation by the Jews in Jerusalem to cease during the initial part of the final twenty-three-hundred days. The emptiness at the site of the sacrifice will be related to the *"overspreading of abominations"* as documented in Daniel 9:27. This overspreading will also begin the time of sorrows as indicated in Matthew 24:8. The middle of the first of

---

[399] 2 Thessalonians 2:8.

two seven year periods will also mark the beginning of the second and final seven-year period. It will be this final seven-year period which will complete the seventy-sevens of years (490 years) prophecy of Daniel 9.24 for Jerusalem and the Jews. As stated earlier, the middle of the first seven-year period will also mark the beginning of the final seven-year period. The abominations and rebellions against the holy place will also begin to intensify at this time. What exactly this is will be clear to those alive at the time of the end. Whatever it is, it will be begin its downward turn as part of the events that take place during the final twenty-three hundred days. The middle of the seven-year covenant mentioned in this verse can be considered the middle of the first of two seven-year periods (see v. 27 and timelines).

36. The events beginning in the middle or midst of the first seven-year period which will occur simultaneously with the beginning of the second seven-year period (see timeline) will continue to intensify until the middle of the last seven years. The middle of the second seven-year period will be followed by 3.5 years, 1,260 days, and 42 months of desolation and destruction on the earth—the same destruction documented in the Gospels and Revelation (see v. 27b).

Section 2, References 7 and 8 (Daniel 11:21–12:13)

37. The Antichrist will be a despicable, vile man—a man given little regard to. He will be looked down upon. He will rise up in the last days as a ruler in, or around, Syria, the remaining ancient Seleucid Empire from antiquity. He will rise in the stead of the last ruler of the North, north of Israel, as stated in Daniel 11:20, but this will occur in the last days. The vile man, or the Antichrist, the future and final ruler of the North, will rise in the latter time when the sin of man has reached its pinnacle. The vile man will initially act in a similar fashion to Antiochus IV, who

foreshadowed his life, but he then will follow and fulfill all of Daniel 11:21–45. The latter-day king of the North, the vile man, will exhaust and fulfill all the scriptures written of him beginning in Daniel 11:21 and continuing until his death in Daniel 11:45 (see Daniel 11:20–21).

38. The vile king will arise from the remnants of the Seleucid Empire (modern-day Syria) in the latter days. He will rise from one of the four dominions left from Alexander's empire, fulfilling the prophecy: *"Out of one of them* (one of the four kingdoms left from Alexander the Great) *shall come a little horn who will wax exceedingly great toward the south, toward the east, and toward the pleasant land."*[400] The scriptures list him as a vile, despised, contemptible creature—a person who is afforded little worth (see Daniel 11:21; 8:9).

39. He will not be given the honor, or dignity, of the kingdom or the backing of his citizens. He obtains leadership status through military power, deception, a disguise of slippery promises, cunning craftiness, and a covenant with a superpower nation. He arises at a time of careless security (see Daniel 11:21).

40. He is destined to grow strong, beginning with a small people—the little horn. He then grows strong through an initial alliance, or league, with an ally, through which he obtains troops and weapons. It is this league that begins his rise to power and the first of two seven-year periods. At the time of the middle of the first seven-year period, the second seven-year period will begin. At this time the Antichrist will begin his plotting against Jerusalem and the Jewish sacrifice, fulfilling the scriptures of Daniel 9.27. After the beginning of the final seven-year period the prophecy regarding the twenty-three hundred days of Daniel 8.14 will begin shortly thereafter. The time of the beginning of the twenty-three-hundred days will mark the initiation of

---
[400] Daniel 8:9.

the opening of the first four seals of Revelation 6.2 in no particular order. These seals will run the gamut of the final twenty-three hundred days and also mark the beginning of the time of sorrows as stated by the Lord in Matthew 24.8; that is, beasts, plagues, famines, and wars causing death to one-quarter of those on the earth.[401] He will be given a host and an army that will grow stronger and stronger in time. The mass of people will overflow into the region and break neighboring nations, sweeping into power like a flood of followers. The flood analogy emphasizes his fast ascension into power. However, the time period and warfare will have a long duration, only gradually evolving as the twenty-three hundred days march forward (see Daniel 11:22, Daniel 8.9–14).

41. The prince, or leader of the covenant that he makes with the many nations, will also be swept away from before him without any active determination by him (see Daniel 11:22).

42. He will adjoin himself to a strong ally through a partnership, allowing him to grow stronger and stronger in time. Beginning with a small people, a minority people, he will increase in strength and force with time. For this reason, he is called the "*little horn*" who grows stronger and stronger. Through all of this, he will act deceitfully and dishonestly. The league is a partnership made with him that allows him to grow in strength and power (see Dan 11:21-23).

43. He conquers land that his ancestors were not able to conquer—fertile places and countries—eventually including the land of Israel. The conquering is done unexpectedly, or at a time of careless security. He divides the spoil from his conquests among his allies and friends— the ones he initially made the alliance or league with, as well as others. He devises plans to take over strongholds or

---

[401] Revelation 6:8

strong countries, but only for the time appointed by God (see Daniel 11:24).

44. After the beginning of the final seven years, he girds up his power and attacks the king of the South—that is, the king south of Syria—who makes no stand. Both kings will have hosts and armies; the host of the vile man will win this altercation. Treason from inside the ranks of the king of the south will be a contributing factor (see Daniel 11:25–26).

45. The king of the South and the vile man meet sometime toward the end of the first 3.5 years. They both have their hearts set on doing mischief. Their plans will not be fruitful (see Daniel 11:27).

46. He returns to his own land, but in his heart, he begins to reveal his true intentions of his hate for God and God's holy covenant. This ultimately will manifest itself in his declaration of being god in verse 36. Toward the middle of the seven years, he once again comes against the South, but this time the nations are leery of his actions and begin to take steps to stop him through ships sent to intercept and restrain him. In response to this, he is enraged and returns to his land and counsels with those who disregard God's covenant and law. The time is appointed by God, signifying that God is still omnipotent and his timetable will be followed even during Jacob's trouble (see Daniel 11:27–30).

47. At the midpoint of the final seven years, or the midst of the week, he sets up the abomination which causes desolation at the holy place in Jerusalem. The abomination that causes desolation is never accurately defined in scripture, but Revelation 13 and 17 and 2 Thessalonians 2:3–4, as well as other scriptures, indicate the notion of the vile man, or the Antichrist, declaring himself God after being assassinated and miraculously coming back from the dead through a Satanic miracle. The result will be some type of supernatural idol, through which he will go on to declare himself God at the holy place in Jerusalem. This event

THE LAST DAYS AND THE VILE MAN OF DANIEL

marks the *midst of the week* and the beginning of the final forty-two months. He also restricts or stops the Jews from any prayer or sacrifice in Jerusalem. The vile man now possesses supernatural powers that he uses to gain world dominion. The scripture also alludes to this with the phrase **"forces from him shall appear,"** indicating that seeds or powers arise, or are raised from him, that greatly enhance his powers to rule and to take down many. The world will now be subject to rule by a theocracy; it will be governed by a false supernatural god, the Antichrist, backed by satanic powers (see Daniel 11:31).

48. He corrupts with flatteries, or deceives with slippery promises, those of the Jews in Israel who disregard God's covenant, or law. He basically puts people under a trance as his supernatural powers begin to escalate. The Jews, who know their God, will resist his attempts to deceive and begin to do godly works; God begins a purification process for the chosen of Israel. Many of those of the Jews who stand faithful to God will be martyred. These faithful will also understand the times and the seasons; they will be teachers of many and will turn many to God. The tribulation, also known as Jacob's trouble, will continue for 3.5 years (see Daniel 11:32–33).

49. In parallel with the increase in power of the vile man, the time of Jacob's trouble fast approaches and God separates out his chosen few of Israel. Through this process, God begins to deliver them and purify them through the final forty-two months of Revelation. Israel's chosen begin to finally understand Jesus Christ as their Lord and King—martyrdom, destruction, and eternal life being the price and reward. God also uses the time of Jacob's trouble to purge and purify the chosen of Israel, the bride of Christ, for the time of judgment (see Daniel 11:34–35).

50. The vile man will perform all in his heart, honoring the god of military conquests disguised as Satan himself. He declares himself God and disregards the true God and

all other so-called gods of his fathers or any other thing worshipped as god—even the gods desired by women. He increases in glory and power and fulfills all his desires—mainly those of world dominion and to be worshipped as God. Through his god, he will conquer the nations and peoples of the earth as one supernaturally energized man. The destruction will continue until the true God's wrath toward man is completed—forty-two months. He shall cause his chosen few to rule over many and divide the nations of the earth to spoil (see Daniel 11:36–38).

51. He divides the lands to those who pay him homage and honor; they are given lands and nations to rule as a reward. He prospers and conquers for forty-two months, increasing in glory and strength and supernatural power during this time (see Daniel 11:39).

52. At the time of the end, and near the close of the last seven years, both the king of the North and the king of the South come against the vile man and turn on him. He shall enter adjoining lands and conquer. He shall enter the chosen land of Israel as well as the land of Egypt. He will have the Libyans and Ethiopians as his allies. A great many will be given to destruction. The masses will continue to build against him, which will cause him to become even more infuriated, destroying and plundering those on the earth (see Daniel 11:20–43).

53. He overthrows many countries and destroys many people. He has power over riches, weapons, and war machines created by the Gentile nations. Bad tidings cause him to exterminate even more people. He comes to his end between the seas—the Mediterranean and the Dead Sea—in the glorious land of Israel and the holy mountain. None shall help him, signifying how he will be smitten by God and destroyed by Jesus Christ himself at his coming for Israel (see Daniel 11:44–45).[402]

---

[402] 2 Thessalonians 2:8–9.

54. After the destruction of the Antichrist and the time of the end of the last seven years, Jesus Christ comes to judge the living and the dead, the living being those who persevere and make it through the final forty-two months, and the dead being those who are raised up of Israel and are written in the book of life. Their rewards are given them, and they shine like the brightness of the sky above. These are they who turn many to righteousness. Daniel is instructed to seal and shut up the words. The last times will be characterized by a great increase in knowledge and the busyness of people on the earth (see Daniel 12:1–4).

55. In the final angelic discourse with Daniel, the angels give the last time in days, as well as years, to dispel any notion that days are anything other than twenty-four-hour days and that years are anything other than actual years. Revelation 13 also gives the time in months—forty-two months—representing, once again, 3.5 years. The time periods given are "times, time and a half of time" (3.5 years), 1,290 days, and 1,335 days. Each time has significance and represents events that take place at the end of the last seven years (see Daniel 12:5–13).

Section 3; References 9, 10, and 11 (2 Thessalonians 2:1–17)

56. Satan is holding fast to his position in the heavens and will continue to do so until he is cast out by Michael during the last seven years—specifically around the middle of the final seven years. Before he is cast out, he is able to deceive the world through his powerful position in the heavens. After his being cast out by Michael, he manifests himself on the earth through a great, miraculous satanic resurrection carried out by the Antichrist/vile man (see 2 Thessalonians 2:6–7).

57. Satan, through the Antichrist, will perform great, miraculous lying wonders and feats on the earth, deceiving the people on the earth into believing he is a god. He will

be destroyed only by the Lord Jesus Christ at his coming for Israel, after the final forty-two months (see 2 Thessalonians 2:8–9).

58. All who reject the truth of God will be deceived by the miracles and lying wonders of the Antichrist. The people of the earth will believe the lie put forth by Satan and will be subject to the wrath of the true God. The rapture of the one body of Jesus Christ will not occur until apostasy or lawlessness begins to increase and abound on the earth and the man of sin is revealed as he declared himself God in Jerusalem.

Section 3, Reference 12 (Revelation 12:13–13:18)

59. Satan is cast out of the heavens at or about the middle of the last seven years and is cast to the earth. Once on the earth, he attacks the remnant seed of the woman. The remnant seed will be the physical seed of Jacob, especially the chosen one hundred forty-four thousand individuals of the seed of Abraham, Isaac, and Jacob—twelve thousand from each tribe of Israel chosen by God and protected by God for 3.5 years. God helps the remnant and protects them supernaturally. The dragon, frustrated in his attempt to destroy the remnant of Israel, turns his wrath to the Gentile nations in the form of a wild beast. The wild beast rises and takes possession of six heads, which are representative of strong, powerful Gentile nations, the beast himself being the seventh head. The beast will also appoint ten horns, representing ten anointed individuals energized by the beast to have dominion over the earth. The characteristic of this wild beast will be blasphemy against God (see Revelation 13:1).

60. The wild beast, now possessing seven heads and ten horns, will be characterized by a lion, bear, and leopard. These Gentile nations, or beasts, will be the same lion, bear, and leopard (strong, powerful countries or dominions)

described in Daniel 7. The seventh head will be the final head to be added and will be the wild beast in supernatural form, newly resurrected from the dead. Recall that the wild beast will be assassinated and then miraculously raised from the dead through a satanic miracle. Initially the wild beast, or seventh head, will be confederate with the other heads and horns, but it will eventually annihilate the other heads, or dominions, and take complete control.[403] The world will wonder after the wild beast, struggling to understand the supernatural miracle that was witnessed (see Revelation 13:3; Revelation 17.8).

61. The wild beast is now worshipped and given divine homage by those not written in the book of life—the unlearned and unknowing on the earth. The earth worships the dragon, or Satan, via the wild beast. The devil, finally, for a short season; that is, forty and two months, 1,260 days and 3.5 years, receives the worship that he craves. The wild beast/Antichrist/vile man is now vocal and opens his mouth in blasphemy against God, the heavens, and God's tabernacle. All not written in the book of life will be forced to worship Satan, the dragon, through the wild beast and through the lifelike image created in his honor. The beast will declare war and successfully destroy, or ostracize, those who will not capitulate, or who still pay homage to the true God (see Revelation 13:4–8).

Section 3, Reference 13 (Revelation 17:1–18)

62. In the last days, and at the midst of the final seven years, the beast is envisioned together with the nations. He is pictured with the heads and horns as part of a conglomeration of the nations. The beast supports Jerusalem, the woman, also characterized as the whore in Revelation 17:1. There will be an initial gathering of the heads at the time of the

---

[403] Daniel 7:7.

beginning of the final twenty-three hundred days. The next gathering of the heads will take place late in the first half of the final seven years but after the beginning of the last seven years. At the time of this next event, five of the seven nations represented by kings will have fallen from a once prominent position to that of lower degree. The fall of these nations will be directly attributed to *"beginning of sorrows"* [404] associated with God's first judgements; the opening of the seals of Revelation chapter 6. The transition of these nations from once powerful positions to a fallen status will begin to take place at the beginning of the final twenty-three hundred days. Their fall will continue until the middle of the final seven years, at which time they will have fallen to a less prominent state of being as described in Revelation 17.10. These kings who represent one-time great dominions have now fallen to a lesser degree in power. The sixth dominion is ruling, indicating it is more powerful than the others. This sixth head is probably associated with the strong Gentile nation represented by the bear, the feet of the corporate beast, in Daniel 7 and Revelation 13. It will be the feet of the wild beast that will be used by the Antichrist to destroy the other five Gentile nations (See Daniel 7.7). The seventh, at the time of the conference of nations, has not yet come; that is, not yet present with the other heads of state, but will shortly come into this inner circle of leaders and, initially at least, be accepted as a world leader (see Revelation 17:1–18).

63. God, through his son, Jesus Christ, documents the vision from his perspective. The world sees only a great conference of nations coming together for a common purpose on the earth and a significant move toward unity—that is, peace and safety (see Revelation 17:1–18).[405]

---

[404] Matthew 24:7,8.
[405] 1 Thessalonians 5:3.

64. The major players for the last days—the heads, the horns, the kings, the people of the earth, and the woman—are identified as part of the vision. God reveals the future for each of the participants—that is, what each of their roles will be during the final forty-two months (see Revelation 17:7–18).

65. The beast is identified as the seventh king, or seventh head, in his mortal form. The beast will then become an eighth head in supernatural form, but he will come out from the seven or the seventh. He will then go on to rule for the final forty-two months (see Revelation 17:10–11).

66. Of the beast, it is stated, *"The beast that thou sawest was, and is not; and shall ascend out of the bottomless pit, and go into perdition: and they that dwell on the earth shall wonder, whose names were not written in the book of life from the foundation of the world, when they behold the beast that was, and is not, and yet is"* (Revelation 17:8). This once again states emphatically that the beast will be part of a great satanic resurrection that will be allowed by God. The deception will be a consequence of man's rejection of God and mankind's insatiable love of sin.

Section 3, Reference 14 (Revelation 19:11–21)

67. The beast is destroyed by the Lord Jesus Christ at his coming. The Lord also destroys the armies gathered at Armageddon. The beast will be thrown alive into the lake of fire (see Revelation 19:20).

Composite Narrative and Description of the "Wild Beast" from the Sections of This Work

As we provided earlier, with respect to the last days of Man's rule on earth, God has utilized, through his prophets, the literary tool of scripture buildup in his word to describe, through several sections of scripture from Genesis to Revelation, the same events or events which transpire during the time we know as the last days of Man's rule on earth. We understand that the scriptures are perfect truth and given to us through the prophets that God handpicked; holy men of God who spoke as they were moved by the Holy Spirit. Further, no scripture concerning the same event can contradict, but each of the scriptures can build on previous scriptures providing missing information and details in that when the whole of the references are assembled together a unique and accurate picture of the revelation that God has provided shines forth out of the darkness of man's many and varied interpretations. Based on the preceding sections of this work regarding the last days and the Vile man who rises to power before the return of the Lord Jesus Christ, the following synopsis integrates all of the references from both Old and New Testaments to build a composite picture of the events of the last times.

The Events Identifying the Approach of The Last Times.

The last days will be a time when the sins of man reach up into heaven and subsequently bring on God's righteous judgment. Contrary to man's opinion that times are progressing and man is improving, God states that the times will grow worse and worse and that evil men will grow worse and worse.[406] Although technology and knowledge will improve and increase, the heart of man will continue to deteriorate and grow worse and worse. It will be the increased knowledge and advanced technology associated with the latter days that will assist the beast in controlling the nations of the earth, but before this, the advances in technology will accelerate the unifying of the nations similar to the unifying at Babylon as described in Genesis 11. The last times will be characterized by self-centered man denying God and seeking to be his own god. The following scriptures reveal the evil behavior of man on the earth just prior to the initiation of the last days—the last seven years. The events of the last days and actions of the beast are cross-referenced to the above Cumulative List of Attributes (CLA) for convenience. Consider the following:

---

[406] 2 Timothy 3:13.

This know also, that in the last days perilous times shall come. For men shall be lovers of their own selves, covetous, boasters, proud, blasphemers, disobedient to parents, unthankful, unholy, Without natural affection, trucebreakers, false accusers, incontinent, fierce, despisers of those that are good, Traitors, heady, highminded, lovers of pleasures more than lovers of God; Having a form of godliness, but denying the power thereof: from such turn away. For of this sort are they which creep into houses, and lead captive silly women laden with sins, led away with divers lusts, Ever learning, and never able to come to the knowledge of the truth. (2 Timothy 3:1–7 KJV)

Yea, and all that will live godly in Christ Jesus shall suffer persecution. But evil men and seducers shall wax worse and worse, deceiving, and being deceived. But continue thou in the things which thou hast learned and hast been assured of, knowing of whom thou hast learned them. (2 Timothy 3:12–14 KJV)

Verily I say unto you, This generation shall not pass, till all these things begin to be fulfilled. Heaven and earth shall pass away, but my words shall not pass away. But of that day and hour knoweth no man, no, not the angels of heaven, but my Father only. But as the days of Noe were, so shall also the coming of the Son of man be. For as in the days that were before the flood they were eating and drinking, marrying and giving in marriage, until the day that Noe entered into the ark, And knew not until the flood came, and took them all away; so shall also the coming of the Son of man be. Then shall two be in the field;

the one shall be taken, and the other left. Two women shall be grinding at the mill; the one shall be taken, and the other left. Watch therefore: for ye know not what hour your Lord doth come. (Matthew 24:34–42 KJV)

But thou, O Daniel, shut up the words, and seal the book, even to the time of the end: **many shall run to and fro, and knowledge shall be increased.** Then I Daniel looked, and, behold, there stood other two, the one on this side of the bank of the river, and the other on that side of the bank of the river. And one said to the man clothed in linen, which was upon the waters of the river, how long shall it be to the end of these wonders? And I heard the man clothed in linen, which was upon the waters of the river, when he held up his right hand and his left hand unto heaven, and sware by him that liveth for ever that it shall be for a time, times, and an half; and when he shall have accomplished to scatter the power of the holy people, all these things shall be finished. And I heard, but I understood not: then said I, O my Lord, what shall be the end of these things? **And he said, Go thy way, Daniel: for the words are closed up and sealed till the time of the end. Many shall be purified, and made white, and tried; but the wicked shall do wickedly: and none of the wicked shall understand; but the wise shall understand.** And from the time that the daily sacrifice shall be taken away, and the abomination that maketh desolate set up, there shall be a thousand two hundred and ninety days. Blessed is he that waiteth, and cometh to the thousand three hundred and five and thirty days. But go thou thy way till the end be: for

> thou shalt rest, and stand in thy lot at the end of the days. (Daniel 12:4–13 KJV; my emphasis)

The last days will be characterized by sin and sinfulness increasing on the earth. This condition continues until God finally steps in and his wrath ensues. His judgements will begin with the opening of the first five seals of Revelation chapter 6; the beginning of sorrows as spoken by the Lord in Matthew chapter 24 and also the beginning of the twenty-three hundred days of Daniel 8:14. This timeframe suggests a slow sorrowful decline of the peoples on the earth as plagues, famines and wars and general lawlessness as "iniquity abounds (increases). These conditions will now become the new normal on the earth. As noted in Daniel 12:4, people will be preoccupied with daily activities associated with great strides in human knowledge and their pursuit of pleasure. To the believer and lover of God, these times will be hard, difficult, and even grievous to live through. The last days feature mankind becoming progressively more self-centered and God-rejecting. In the midst of these hard times, God, at his own discretion, initiates the events of the last times and then the last seven years, which have been held in abeyance since the first century. None of the wicked shall understand this initiation, but the wise will understand as God's Word marches on to fulfillment.

In addition to man's evil behavior and rejection of God, the last times will feature the consecutive rising of three great Gentile dominions, as depicted and documented in Daniel 7. The dominions are described as a lion with eagle's wings, a bear who rises on one side and devours much flesh, and a leopard with its four main heads (see appendix F for further explanation). Before the initiation of the last seven years, these three dominions will be on the earth and ruling. These three dominions do not attack each other but coexist up until their absorption into the kingdom of the beast. The dominions will be revealed by the Word of God at the time that they rise on the earth, and especially during the last time. It would seem that the rise of these three great Gentile dominions would span 50–100 years before the initiation of the last days. Once they rise, they will have the characteristics given to them by God in Daniel chapter 7.

ROBERT PELLETIER

The Initial Rising of the Antichrist

Now with the sins of man increasing on the earth and the three great Gentile dominions in place, the stage is set for God to put the last times and the last seven years in motion; but he will do so at his own discretion. The time when God initiates the last days is completely at his own discretion, as the Lord notes in Acts 1:6–7. When God does initiate the last seven years, the events that transpire will follow God's order as documented in his word, with the wise understanding the times and the specific events from the Word of God. The book of Daniel provides the foundational scriptures for examining the rise of the beast. The vile man of Daniel 11, beginning in Daniel 11:21 and continuing to the end of the chapter, is foundational for proper interpretation regarding the wild beast, his rise, and his subsequent rule. These verses include the time up until the destruction of the beast—that is, the giving of his body to the burning flame as documented at the end of Daniel 11. Daniel 11:21 and onward recounts the actions of the beast—both his initial rising and then the first 3.5-year mortal career and his final forty-two-month career as described in the book of Revelation. The time period from his initial rising until his destruction after the final forty and two months will span greater than twelve years. The last days will officially begin with the beast strengthening himself through a league, or covenant, with a powerful Gentile nation. The end times will continue up to the time when he is destroyed at the appearance of Jesus Christ. It is important to realize that the beginning of this time is not related to one particular event, but several events in time in which the words and events of the words of God continue to be satisfied. This method of a sort of triangulation of the events of the last times will give those with wisdom of the Word of God fair warning concerning the time of the end. The initial event beginning this sequence of event will be the rising of a vile despicable king of leader in and around the country north of the land of Israel; the Seleucid empire, but thousands of years after the time of the dominions left after the time of Alexander the Great. This will satisfy the requirement of the origin of the Vile man and his characteristic behavior (ref 37 CLA). This rising will satisfy the first requirement from the Word of God. The period of time between his initial rising and the covenant or league he makes with a strong Gentile nation; that is, the beginning the first of two interrelated seven-year periods, could span months or years. He will rise and be a despicable, devalued leader; a man associated with atrocities of war and the hatred of his people and many other leaders of the earth. This condition will continue for a while and then will come the first of two seven-year periods in which the second seven-year period will begin at the middle, or midst, of the first seven-year period (see timelines and ref 31 CLA). The beginning of the first seven-year period will be marked by a league or covenant that the vile man will make with a great Gentile superpower nation. This covenant or league with a strong ally will allow him to become a stronger conquering force for the whole of the first seven years (ref 34 CLA). Daniel 12 gives additional information as to the times and the seasons, as well as God's judgment and God's deliverance of the called of Israel. The profile provided here will follow Daniel 11:21 onward and will include the other sections of this work to support the sequence of events. The Word of God can have no contradictions. The Word of God is inherently perfect and accurate in its original written form.

In summary, the prophecy concerning the last days begins with a league or covenant between the beast and great nations as noted in Daniel 9.27 and Daniel 11.23. It is this league of Daniel 11.23 that will have the effect of strengthening the beast and will also initiate the first of two seven-year periods. During the midst of this first seven-year period (Daniel 9.27), the final seven years of Daniel 9.24 will be initiated. Both of these seven-year periods must be clearly understood (see Appendix D: The Final Timelines). The initial covenant or league will allow the beast to strengthen himself throughout the first seven-year period (ref. 31 CLA). The Hebrew word for "*covenant and league*" used in these verses is described as a binding resolution with a great nation(s) which allows the beast to strengthen himself for seven years (ref. 31 CLA). Piecing this together we now understand that the beast himself, in his mortal form, initially begins his ascent to power from a particular remnant of Alexander the Great's dominion, but this occurs thousands of years after that dominion has ended. Daniel 8 documents that the beast will proceed from one of the four dominions remaining after the fall of Alexander the Great (ref. 17 CLA). The four dominions are verified through antiquity and also the Word of God (ref. 17 CLA). The king of the North, or the Seleucid Empire (now Syria), is stated to bring forth the little horn, or the man of small beginnings, but this will occur thousands of years after the Seleucid Empire has ceased to exist (ref. 36 CLA). The Seleucid Empire (the northern empire) is now (today) known substantially as Syria (ref. 36 CLA). Daniel 11:21 begins to shed light on the rise of the beast—his actions and behaviors.

As discussed, the vile man is described as a vile (despicable, contemptible, and given little worth) man—a man of small beginnings who rises out of the ashes of the Seleucid Empire, which is now in and around (2020) Syria. The reference to him is as one who starts with small beginnings; thus, he is known as the *little horn*. He is associated with a minority people that grow in numbers and strength with time. That he is a man of small beginnings and a *little horn* is referenced in Daniel 8:9 and 7:8, respectively (ref. 39 CLA). He will come not from a superpower but from a lesser country and a minority people, thus he is a little horn who grows with time. It is also stated that he does not receive the honor of the kingdom, indicating his being at odds with his own people and the majority of the other nations of the world (ref. 38 CLA). He comes into power unexpectedly and without warning, but with cunning and craftiness. He will eventually begin to utilize special spiritual resources and display keen insight characterized by trickery (refs. 37, 38 CLA). The initial rise of the beast does not fit well with an anticipated great earthly ruler, or the picture that many have attached to his rising, but God will bring about the fulfilling of his word exactly as he has documented it. The idea that a covenant and league is made concerning him, combined with no honor from his own people, gives rise to the realization that he, initially at least, will be at odds with the world at large. There will be, however, his supporters and allies, who will encourage him and stand by him. The divisions will set the stage for future wars associated with the last times, as documented in the Word of God. In contrast to the many secular writings depicting him as an acceptable and desirous leader, the scriptures reveal, initially at least, that he is not at all welcome on the world stage, except by his allies and friends.

The vile man will act deceitfully and craftily as he rises and becomes more powerful. He will scheme and deceitfully take advantage of the world leaders as they bicker with one another as to his intentions. He will continue to make slippery promises that cannot be completely enforced or verified by those dealing with him (ref. 38 CLA). The first of two seven-year periods are initiated at the time of a league or covenant which allows him to become stronger with time, he grows in strength and power. At the time of the midst of the initial seven-year period, the final seven years will begin. Additionally, approximately 220 to 295 days after the beginning of the final seven-year period, the twenty-three-hundred-day time period of Daniel 8.14 will begin. The initiation of this time period will also mark the opening in Heaven of the first five seals as documented in of Revelation 6:2—he on the white horse given power to conquer, the plagues, famines, and peace taken from the earth as lawlessness abound and men will hate one another and men will kill one another. The opening of the seals begins to fulfill the scriptures of Matthew 24:8–15. The beast now rises up in courage and begins his aggression toward the nations. The beginning of the twenty-three hundred days also begins the *overspreading of abominations* on the earth which will lead to the Jerusalem oblation and sacrifice to become desolate or empty (refs. 35, 41 CLA). Additionally, the beginning of the twenty-three hundred days will also mark the beginning of sorrows on the earth as documented by the Lord in Matthew 24:8. There will also be an initial meeting of six of the seven heads mentioned in Revelation 17:10. From this point forward, five of the seven heads, or great Gentile nations, will begin to fall from prominence on the earth as stated in this verse. The twenty-three-hundred days will also be a time of acute hardships on the earth to allow the Gospel to be preached to all the earth to give a final opportunity, before the end, for those on the earth to receive salvation through Jesus Christ. The salvation which will be preached will be as per Romans 10:10:

> **Rom 10:9, 10** That if thou shalt confess with thy mouth the Lord Jesus, and shalt believe in thine heart that God hath raised him from the dead, thou shalt be saved.
>
> Rom 10:10 For with the heart man believeth unto righteousness; and with the mouth confession is made unto salvation.

This will be served as an end-times warning to receive salvation through faith in Jesus Christ before the horrible events of the final 1,260 days and the wrath of our Holy God (see Appendix D: The Final Timelines).

The league with the ally will change the course of events in his favor in the initial stages of his rise to power (refs. 39, 41 CLA). The vile man, now armed with a covenant and a league with an ally, begins his outward conquests and secretly plans world dominion with his superpower ally. He will do what his fathers or father's fathers have not done—successfully expand his dominion while rewarding allies with the spoils of war and political conquests (ref. 42 CLA). Through his policy of sharing spoils, he receives both undying loyalty and the ability to increase in power and strength. The policy will result in successful conquests as the time continues within the entirety of the initial seven-year period. It is this first seven years and his covenant with a superpower that affords him a powerful military position. At the time of the of the middle of the first seven-year period, the second seven-year period will begin (ref. 35 CLF); that is the final seven-years. The first seven years -and for that matter during the entirety of the last days, the vile man's actions will appear as if everything that he does miraculously falls into place, but Satan and his spiritual agents will be in the background, pulling the strings.

The Beginning of First 3.5 Years of the Final Seven Years

The vile man, now firmly established with the covenant, the league, and the policy of sharing the spoils, ponders his position. He now plans for his broader ambitions of extending his borders through annexing neighboring countries. The neighboring countries will be to the South, to the East, and the pleasant land. The time frame is now the first half of the last seven years. As noted in Daniel 9:27, the vile man strengthens himself with a covenant with the great for a seven-year period (the first seven-year period). In the middle of this time period, Daniel 9:27 states that he begins his ambitions of attacking and stopping the Jewish daily sacrifice in Jerusalem (see Appendix D: the timelines). He will eventually do this in time, but his new ambitions in his heart will initiate the beginning of the first half of the final seven-year period. This final seven-year period is identified as the final seven-years of Daniel 9:24 and its completion will fulfill all that God promised the chosen seed of Israel in Daniel 9:24. The final seven years will unceremoniously begin with abominations and a more intense hatred for the Jewish land and people for the first 220–295 days. Not much will change leading up to and after the beginning of the final seven years, with the exception of the time growing more and more unstable in the world. There will be wars and rumors of wars as well as more instability within the land of Israel. This will continue until the beginning of the final twenty-three hundred days documented in of Daniel 8:14.

The Beginning of the Final 2,300 Days

The twenty-three hundred days of Daniel 8:14 is a peculiar period of time documented by Daniel. The time period is extensively studied in Appendix C. A brief description will be listed here to allow for the proper flow of the time process in this last time analysis. The time period has been wrestled with by numerous commentaries; so many that it is fruitless to enumerate all of the diverse interpretations regarding this time. As concerning the meaning of days in the verse, it is clear that the days mentioned by the Lord are indeed twenty-four-hour days since this is clearly indicated by the angel in Daniel 8:26 that they *"days and nights."* Referring to Daniel 8:14, It is also clear that the end of the 2,300 days is marked by the cleansing of the sanctuary in Jerusalem. The context of this section of scripture, along with the fact that this cleansing can only be performed by the

Lord Jesus Christ at his coming for Israel, undoubtably identifies this time period with the last times and within the final seven years. The final seven years will encompass 2,520 (7*360) days. The Jewish year included 360 days and an additional jubilee year in which the additional days were added.

Additional instructions from the angel to Daniel in chapter 8 were that this was a vision that concerned the last or latter time. The section is also referencing the actions of the vile man during the final seven years. The angel also states that the vision shall be *"shut-up"* or not documented by Daniel. Consider the following section from Daniel chapter 8:

> [23] And in the latter time of their kingdom, when the transgressors are come to the full, a king of fierce countenance, and understanding dark sentences, shall stand up. [24] And his power shall be mighty, but not by his own power: and he shall destroy wonderfully, and shall prosper, and practise, and shall destroy the mighty and the holy people. [25] And through his policy also he shall cause craft to prosper in his hand; and he shall magnify himself in his heart, and by peace shall destroy many: he shall also stand up against the Prince of princes; but he shall be broken without hand. [26] **And the vision of the evening and the morning which was told is true: wherefore shut thou up the vision; for it shall be for many days.** [27] And I Daniel fainted, and was sick certain days; afterward I rose up, and did the king's business; and I was astonished at the vision, but none understood it. (Daniel 8:23–27 KJV)

It is clear that the vision concerns the last days and that the vision is also descriptive of the Antichrist. The time period is 2,300 days and ends with the cleansing of the sanctuary; that is, the holy place in Jerusalem. Applying wisdom to these words, and understanding the Word of God, it should be clear that the vision spoken of by the angel is related to the book of Revelation. Daniel was given the days with respect to the book of Revelation, but John, in the first century was given the events of the book of Revelation. Daniel was to shut up the words, but John, in the first century, was to write down what the Lord Jesus revealed to him concerning the last times also known as the book of the Revelation of the Lord Jesus Christ. This effectively requires both sections of scripture, that of Daniel and of Revelation, to both be understood to ingest and understand what God has revealed concerning this time.

With this as our backdrop, we can now piece together the events which open the book of Revelation which is related directly to the 2,300 days of Daniel 8:14. The first five chapters of the book of Revelation open with directions and warnings to those on the earth, and those of the house of Israel. Chapter 5 also describes the heavenly vision of the Lord Jesus Christ, the lion of the tribe of Judah, being the only one able to break the curse of sin and death on the earth. Once the lord God accepts him, he begins to open the seven seals of judgement on the earth. Chapter 6 of Revelation begins the opening of the seals and the consequences on the earth and the earth dwellers. Recall that the book of Revelation is the record of God forcibly taking back the earth from Satan and wicked men and giving it to his Son Jesus Christ, and those who believe on and follow him. For this reason, the judgements of God will appear to be unsettling to casual reader, but they will accomplish the purpose that God planned for them. With this in mind, it is the seals of Revelation chapter 6 which will open the judgements of God against those on the earth and will also initiate the 2,300 days- some 295 days after the beginning of the final seven years. The beginning of these judgements is also parallel with the time of trouble mentioned by our Lord in Matthew 24. The Lord also identifies this initiation in Matthew 24:8 as the *"beginning of sorrows."* Both of these sections together, Revelation chapter 6 and Matthew chapter 24, describe the same judgements on the earth: plagues, famines, war, earthquakes, and peace taken from the earth and lawlessness increasing as the 2,300 days move forward. How this plays out on the earth is not entirely revealed, but that it begins and when it begins is now understood by those who fear God and rightly divide his word. In any event, when these judgements do begin their mission on the earth, it will be unmistakable to those who fear God.

The 2,300 days progress in time evolving into increasing difficulty to those on the earth. Everyday life on the earth will change and continue to change as time progresses toward the middle of the seven years. Recall that power will be given unto the Dragon (Satan) and Antichrist for the final forty-two months, 1,260 days, 3.5 years of the final seven years. Within this time frame they will do according to their will (ref. 61 CLF). The time between the beginning of the 2,300 days and the beginning of the final forty and two months (1,260 days) will be a time in which total control will not be given to Satan. However, this time will be the beginning of sorrows and initial judgements of God via the opening of the seals of Revelation chapter 6. Based on the seals of Revelation 6 in comparison with the beginning of the times of sorrows recorded in Matthew 24:8–14, it is evident that the first five seals will be opened with their consequences on the earth. Gathering together all that we know about this intermediate time of trouble, or increasing sorrow on the earth, the following events will take place during this time period:

1. The five heads (five great Gentile nations) of the seven headed beast of Revelation 13 and 17 will begin to fall from a once prominent positions to a lower position. How this evolves is not clear, but the opening of the seals will certainly be a factor. This will continue until the next meeting of the seven heads, in which five of the heads will have fallen. This can also be cross referenced with the *Lion with Eagles Wings* of Daniel 7:4 being made to stand on its feet like a man and a man's heart was given to it.
2. The sixth head, or great Gentile nation, will not fall, but still retain its power at the time of the next meeting of the seven heads.
3. The time between the initiation of the twenty-three hundred days and the middle of the final seven years (approximately

1000 days; 2,300 -1,260) will be a time of acute tribulation initiated in heaven by God. This time will not have the effect of total devastation but increasing sorrows on the earth. The time will also be a time in which people will be searching for answers to the disruption of normal life on the earth and a time of increasing lawlessness. This period of time will be the time when the one body of Jesus Christ, the born-again believers, will be workers together with God to proclaim the salvation through faith in Jesus Christ to the entire world. After this, and at the time of the middle of the final seven years, will come the worst time in human history, beginning with the resurrection of the beast and the subsequent wrath that follows on the earth for the next 42 months. The following supports this:

a. The third seal of Revelation 6:5–6 indicates that the *oil and wine* will not be affected. This suggests that there will not be complete immobility on the earth.
b. The Lord in Matthew 24:9–14 documents the persecution and hatred of those who witness for Jesus Christ. The Lord goes on in verse 14 to state:

And this gospel of the kingdom shall be preached in all the world for a witness unto all nations; and then shall the end come.

c. The fifth seal of Revelation 6 summarizes the persecution of the saints as well. The sixth seal moves forward to the time of the end in which the stars and the sun are affected by the judgements. These seals are in parallel with what the Lord spoke in Matthew 24. Five will be opened before the *Abomination of Desolation* is set up in Jerusalem indicating the middle of the final seven years.

With respect to the beast on the earth at this time, he will begin to assert his strength on the earth until the cleansing of the sanctuary. For the first seven years it is stated that he strengthens himself with a strong covenant with a powerful ally (ref 34 CLF). During this time, he will continue to be strong with this covenant. As the world begins to be thrown into turmoil after the initiation of the twenty-three-hundred days, and in the first half of the final seven-years, there will be a great gathering of nations for oneness and peace—*Mystery Babylon*. It is this great gathering which will partially fulfill the vision of Revelation 17. The gathering will be a type of curtain call that God will provide for those of understanding to foreshadow what each of the members will do during the final 42 months. With respect to the twenty-three-hundred days consider the translations of Daniel 8:13 using the New Living Version (NLT) and the NIV84 translation are as follows:

> Then I heard two holy ones talking to each other. One of them asked, "How long will the events of this vision last? How long will the rebellion that causes desecration stop the daily sacrifices? How long will the Temple and heaven's army be trampled on? (Daniel 8:13 NLT)
>
> Then I heard a holy one speaking, and another holy one said to him, "How long will it take for the vision to be fulfilled—the vision concerning the daily sacrifice, the rebellion that causes desolation, and the surrender of the sanctuary and of the host that will be trampled underfoot?" (Daniel 8:13 NIV84)

Specifically, the vision that the angel is questioning is generically documented in Daniel 8:9–12 and specifically identified in the book of Revelation. It begins with the strengthening of the Antichrist toward the South, East, and the pleasant land and ends with the cleansing of the sanctuary. The verses in Daniel concerning the twenty-three hundred days are also synchronized with Revelation

6:2, which tells of the opening of the first of the seven seals. It is thought that the first five seals will be opened and perform their desired results between the initiation of the final 2,300 days and the middle of the last seven years. Additionally, Revelation 17:10 describes an additional event after the beginning of the twenty-three hundred days and the final seven years from a different vantage point—that of a gathering of leaders on the earth together to show their unity, especially for Jerusalem. This group is *Mystery Babylon* of Revelation 17. The initial meeting will feature the seven heads intact, but as the final 2,300 days progress, five of the great nations will fall from once prominent status to that of a much lesser degree. The scriptures also suggest that there will be a second meeting of these Gentile nations in which five of these seven leaders of great Gentile powers have fallen to a lesser degree from the height of their power on the earth, the sixth, however, is ruling and more powerful than the others. The seventh, the beast, has not yet fully come into power (ref 62 CLF). God intricately ties the Old and New Testament scriptures to convince the believing Jews, and those with wisdom among his church, to look to the Lord Jesus Christ for further instruction. The beast will arise in the order prescribed by God and laid out by God in his word, specifically as documented in Revelation 17:10.

The vile man, at one time a fairly insignificant figure, is now a cause for concern. Although he is a man of small beginnings, he is showing forward-looking thinking and intelligent scheming. He has already entered into a binding resolution, or covenant, with a great nation, he will make a league with this superpower Gentile nation. He will then cooperate with world powers to comply, and he will finally join their coalition. He will also align himself with carefully picked allies through a league or military alliance (ref. 41 CLA). The covenant will give him legitimacy, strengthening his position. The vile man will use this time for military advantage and to plan his next moves in a political chess game for world dominion (ref. 42 CLA). Additionally, a great many nations will come together in cooperation with each other in an unusual time of collaboration; this group will be *Mystery Babylon*. The uniting of the nations will set the stage for the next significant event within the seven years; the time of the middle of the final seven years.

The seven-year covenant with the many, the league with a superpower ally, the peace conference, and his growing in strength will serve as an unmistakable warning that the final seven years have indeed begun and will fulfill both Old and New Testament scriptures. The hate of the Antichrist, the wrath of God, and the destruction of the earth will begin in earnest after the beast comes into supernatural form at the time of the middle of the last seven years. The final forty-two months will fulfill all of God's prophecies regarding his wrath toward an earth overflowing with evil man. The conference of leaders and nations will fulfill the prophecies of Revelation 17 and will occur sometime later in the first half of the final seven years. In Revelation 17:10, God pinpoints the time of the conference to when six heads represented by kings are present. The first five kings, who are said to be fallen, are alive but the countries they represent have fallen from previously higher positions. The six heads, or leaders; the ten kings; and the many nations will be present for the conference, as noted in Revelation 17. The timing of the conference, as well as the characters involved in the conference, will unknowingly provide the required proof that the last seven years have begun. Man's rule on the earth will shortly come to an end, and none of the wicked will understand.[407] While the world believes that peace and security have finally arrived on the earth, the unity of nations at the peace conference giving them proof, God's Word marches on to fulfillment.[408] Time will now continue toward the mid-seven-year crisis. Man's rule, or man's day, will shortly come to an end and be replaced by the kingdom of the Son of God, the Lord Jesus Christ, but not before the worst time in human history plays out for forty-two months.

Once the initial seals of Revelation chapter 6 are opened, beginning some twenty-three hundred days before the cleansing of the Sanctuary, the vile man begins to implement his plan of dominance. He continues to grow in strength and stature through deceitful ways

---

[407] Daniel 12:10.
[408] 1 Thessalonians 5:3.

and fine, slippery promises (ref. 38 CLA) as the world and earth dwellers begin to struggle with the initial judgements of God from the throne. As time marches forward, the seals increasingly affect those on the earth and the times become difficult. As for the vile man, with the world powers now neutralized, he gathers his strength and courage and initiates an assault against the king of the South (ref. 43 CLA). Why he attacks the king of the South and where he gains this confidence is not documented, but it seems there will be a standoff and division within the six heads, or Gentile powers. It is now that the nations will be re-configured by spiritual powers to come into alignment for domination by the last Gentile beast soon to be ruling the earth. The vile man will now exploit this weakness, believing there will be no repercussions by world powers in response to his attacks. The weakness may be related to the lion with eagles' wings made to stand on its feet as a man (a depraved or weak man), and to its power being in decline.[409] The bear and the four headed leopard are not mentioned to be in decline in Daniel chapter 7, but from the scriptures in Daniel and Revelation 17 it is clear that five of the heads or great Gentile nations will fall and one, the bear will still be left intact. Those alive who fear God at the time of the end will understand the truth of this verse. The king of the South will be a country south of Syria. Which country it is we are not told; we know only that it one to the south. The likely candidates seem to be Lebanon, Jordan, or even Egypt. Although Israel is somewhat south of Syria, Israel seems to be last in the initial series of three lands to be invaded by the beast. God always addresses Israel separately as the pleasant land. The beast will attack and occupy Jerusalem at the time of the midst of the week.[410] The king, or leader, of the South gathers a great army together to repel the advances of the vile man. His warlike maneuvers, however, will come to nothing, due to treason within his ranks—especially by his closest friends (refs. 43–44 CLA). There will be many killed, but the vile man will sit down with the king of the South and discuss the futures of both countries. It is stated that

---

[409] Daniel 7:4.
[410] Daniel 11:30–31.

both kings and leaders *"will have hearts to do mischief and speak lies at one table; but it shall not prosper: for yet the end shall be at the time appointed"*[411] (ref. 44 CLA). Daniel 11:27 indicates that the king of the South is conciliatory in defeat and appears to make some type of an agreement with the vile man. The agreement will have a time frame, but God states in the latter part of verse 27 that their plans will not come to fruition; God's Word and timetable will be carried out as documented in his word.

The vile man has now successfully won a battle with an adjacent nation—the king of the South. The time frame is still the first half of the last seven years, but it is later in the first half of the week and toward the middle of the final seven years. The vile man is becoming stronger and stronger with his allies and is now developing a personal relationship with Satan. Satan ultimately promises him dominion over the earth and those who dwell therein if he will pay him homage. The beast, or vile man, now returns to his own country with the spoils of war. His hate will now be directed against God, his holy place, and God's people. He begins to show his ultimate hatred for God and the people of God. At the same time, he will continue with his secret worship of Satan, which will increase with time (ref. 45 CLA).

The events are now moving swiftly toward the middle of the last seven years. The vile man is becoming stronger and stronger and is now developing a strategy to occupy Jerusalem and the holy place (ref. 45 CLA). Toward the middle of the final seven years, or at the appointed time in God's timetable, the vile man, for a second time, will come against the South. The scripture does not say "the king of the South" but simply "the South." The second incursion will not be like his first triumph against the South (king of the South) or the latter attack. During this second coming against the South, he will be confronted by a superior arsenal of naval ships and weaponry in the Mediterranean Sea (ref. 45 CLA). Unlike the first attack, in which he was not confronted, this second time, for whatever reason, he is confronted with ships and arsenals sent by world powers. The confrontation leads to an enraged vile man, who now begins to show

---

[411] Daniel 11:27.

his hatred for the world and the world powers (ref. 45 CLA). Now, after his confrontation with world powers, he "*has indignation against God's holy covenant.*"[412] His indignation is related to his relationship with Satan, who ultimately plants in the beast a hatred of God and all that God stands for. The Hebrew word translated as *"indignation"* in Daniel 11:30 (KJV) is defined as "Defiant or abhorrent; loathsome or detestable." The vile man now begins to exhibit his true colors and is manifestly overflowing with hatred for mankind and God alike, like his new father, Satan. The initial focus of his hatred is against Israel, God's law, and the holy place, the holy place being the place where God promised that the Messiah would come one day.[413] The vile man, directed by Satan, will return to his own nation and have intelligence, or focus his attention, on those who hate God, God's law, and God's people (believing Israel). The vile man will now cooperate with those who all along wanted to destroy Israel and who also wanted to stop the daily sacrifice of the Jews at the holy place in Jerusalem. The vile man will now initiate an invasion against Israel, Jerusalem, and the holy place. The first 3.5 years, or forty-two months are now coming to an end, and the events of the middle of the week are next to take place in accordance with Daniel 11 (refs. 45–46 CLA).

The Midst, or Middle, of the Last Seven Years

The events of the middle of the last seven years usher in the worst time (forty-two months) of human history. The Lord Jesus Christ states this emphatically several times in the Gospels, and it is corroborated by both Old and New Testament scriptures. The same truth is documented in several Old and New Testament scriptures. Consider the following verses:

> And he shall confirm the covenant with many for one week: **and in the midst of the week** he shall cause (begin to cause) the sacrifice and

---

[412] Daniel 11:30.
[413] Psalm 2:6.

the oblation to cease, and for the overspreading of abominations he shall make it desolate, even until the consummation, and that determined shall be poured upon the desolate. (Daniel 9:27 KJV; my emphasis)

And at that time shall Michael stand up, the great prince which standeth for the children of thy people: **and there shall be a time of trouble, such as never was since there was a nation even to that same time:** and at that time thy people shall be delivered, every one that shall be found written in the book.

And many of them that sleep in the dust of the earth shall awake, some to everlasting life, and some to shame and everlasting contempt. (Daniel 12:1–2 KJV; my emphasis)

When ye therefore **shall see the abomination of desolation, spoken of by Daniel the prophet, stand in the Holy Place, (whoso readeth, let him understand:)** Then let them which be in Judaea flee into the mountains: Let him which is on the housetop not come down to take any thing out of his house: Neither let him which is in the field return back to take his clothes. And woe unto them that are with child, and to them that give suck in those days! But pray ye that your flight be not in the winter, neither on the sabbath day: **For then shall be great tribulation, such as was not since the beginning of the world to this time, no, nor ever shall be. And except those days should be shortened, there should no flesh be saved: but for the elect's sake those days shall be shortened.** (Matthew 24:15–22 KJV; my emphasis)

The Middle of the Last Seven Years in Heaven

The cataclysmic events of the middle of the last seven years in heaven are marked by the casting out of Satan from his heavenly position by Michael, the archangel (refs. 55–56, 58 CLA). Satan, up until this time, has had a presence in the heavens, and now he is finally cast out at the time of the middle of the seven years. His position in the heavens provided deception and disguising of his actions through heavenly power; he secretly manipulated the events of the world. Now, finally, he will engage in manipulation through *Mystery Babylon.* God does not specifically reveal what his casting out of the heavens really means in the heavenly sphere, since it is beyond our human understanding. What we do know is that he will be cast out and relegated to the earth: **"Woe to the inhabitants of the earth and of the sea! for the devil is come down to you, having great wrath, for that he knows that his time is short."**[414] The casting out of Satan will happen near or about the middle of the last seven years. His casting out to the earth causes death, war, destruction, famine, and pestilence to the earth dwellers and eternal damnation to those who worship the beast. Satan knows that the time of his dominion on the earth through the beast is short, forty-two months; therefore, his wrath is intensified.[415] After his being casting to the earth at or about the middle of the last seven years, his first order of business is to pursue the woman and her seed, who still worship the true God.[416] Satan, understanding of the Word of God, knows of the salvation that will finally come to Israel.[417] Subsequently, he attempts to thwart God's plan (refs. 1, 58 CLA). Satan, after his being cast out, first attacks the faithful promised seed of Abraham, Isaac, and Jacob; and then, after this failure, he turns his fury against the Gentile nations and the earth dwellers in general. His accomplice for this destruction

---

[414] Revelation 12:12.
[415] Revelation 12:12.
[416] Revelation 12:13–17.
[417] Romans 11:26.

will be the supernatural beast, the Antichrist, a man committed to him through homage and worship.

The Middle of the Last Seven Years on the Earth

The beast, now strengthened with an army and many followers, is now quickly becoming the personification of Satan on earth. He enters and attacks the pleasant land and Jerusalem with his army, hating God and his covenant people. His desire will be to occupy the holy mount (holy place) in Jerusalem and declare himself God, as directed by Satan. Psalm 79, which speaks of this very time, will come to remembrance with God's people. Consider the following:

> O God, the heathen are come into thine inheritance; thy holy temple have they defiled; they have laid Jerusalem on heaps. The dead bodies of thy servants have they given to be meat unto the fowls of the heaven, the flesh of thy saints unto the beasts of the earth. Their blood have they shed like water round about Jerusalem; and there was none to bury them. We are become a reproach to our neighbours, a scorn and derision to them that are round about us. How long, LORD? wilt thou be angry for ever? shall thy jealousy burn like fire? (Psalm 79:1–5 KJV)

In the process of his aggression toward Israel and Jerusalem, the beast, still in mortal form, receives a death wound by which he is apparently killed. After his assassination, probably two or three days, he is miraculously raised from the dead and stands in the holy place in Jerusalem. He is now a supernatural being just raised from the dead through a satanic miracle, having great wrath toward those on the earth. This singular event will be the great lie that will try the whole earth. The decision to those on the earth is now intensely individual: will you worship the beast, or will you resist and be ostracized and also face probable death? The lie will be perpetrated first in Jerusalem and then throughout the nations of the earth. The event is referred to in Matthew 24:15 as the "*abomination that causes desolations on the earth.*"[418] The Satanic resurrection of the beast brings on God's plagues and wrath (refs. 46, 55, 59, 64–65 CLA). The beast will now be in supernatural form at the holy place in Jerusalem and will declare himself to be God. He will go on to reject all other gods and religions on the earth; all will be forced to worship him as God (refs. 2, 11, 20, 24, 34, 46, 56, 60 CLA) or face a death sentence. He will now be in control of the earth for the next forty-two months. The time will be a time of trial for the entire world. Those on the earth will be in amazement at the events transpiring on the earth.[419] Additionally, many scriptures will be fulfilled—both Old and New Testament scriptures. Consider the following scripture from 2 Thessalonians 2:

> Let no man deceive you by any means: for that day shall not come, except there come a falling away first, and that man of sin be revealed, the son of perdition; **Who opposeth and exalteth himself above all that is called God, or that is worshipped; so that he as God sitteth in the temple of God, shewing himself that he is God.** Remember ye not, that, when I was yet with you, I told you these things? And now ye know what withholdeth that he might be revealed in his time. For the mystery of iniquity doth already work: only he who now letteth will let, until he be taken out of the way. And then shall that Wicked be revealed, whom the Lord shall consume with the spirit of his mouth, and shall destroy with the brightness of his coming: **Even him, whose coming is after the working of Satan with all power and signs and lying wonders, And with all deceivableness of unrighteousness in**

---

[418] Matthew 24:15.
[419] Revelation 13:3–4; 17:8.

them that perish; because they received not the love of the truth, that they might be saved. And for this cause God shall send them strong delusion, that they should believe a lie: That they all might be damned who believed not the truth, but had pleasure in unrighteousness. (2 Thessalonians 2:3–12 KJV; my emphasis)

The Final 3.5 Years or Forty-Two Months on the Earth

The final forty-two months have now begun. The beast is in supernatural form and has declared himself to be God and now proceeds to establish his dominion over the earth with great hatred. The earth dwellers have never witnessed a supernatural dominion such as this before. For this reason, the final dominion is called *"diverse (different) from all others on the earth before."*[420] The beast is a supernatural force and cannot be destroyed by any man. It is believed that, about this time, the church of the one body of Jesus Christ will be raptured to God and removed from the earth. The earth dwellers will now consist of Jews and Gentiles, who will remain on the earth. God once again separates Jews from Gentiles as he fulfills all his everlasting promises made to Abraham, Isaac, and Jacob concerning their seed. Referring to the beast, he now appoints ten kings to rule over the earth, who receive their supernatural power to rule the earth at the same hour the beast is resurrected.[421] The ten kings, to this point not identified as to who they are and where they come from, will be known by the beast and will be given satanic power from the beast to rule over the nations of the earth. The ten kings will also destroy Jerusalem and persecute the people of God. It is also now that all daily prayers by the Jews to the true God will be stopped by the beast in Jerusalem. The wild beast will also deploy the bear, the strong Gentile nation of Daniel 7, to attack and dominate the other Gentile nations. (refs. 13, 22, 32, 34, 45–47 CLA).

---

[420] Daniel 7:19–25.
[421] Daniel 2:44; 7:7, 24; Revelation 17:12.

The middle of the week will also feature a remnant of Abraham's physical promised seed, who will begin to understand their true Messiah, the Lord Jesus Christ. This new group will be marked by the true God for deliverance. These Jews will take heed to the warnings of Jesus Christ listed in Matthew 24:15–25, abandoning Jerusalem and leaving for the wilderness. These will form the seven churches, who will receive instruction from Jesus Christ as per Revelation 2 and 3. They also will form the new embryotic nation of Israel, which will be protected by God for forty-two months. The protection will be like the wilderness protection God provided for them after delivering them from Egyptian tyranny. Consider the words of the Lord Jesus Christ as he writes to these future remnant Jews in Matthew 24:

> And many false prophets shall rise, and shall deceive many. And because iniquity shall abound, the love of many shall wax cold. But he that shall endure unto the end, the same shall be saved. And this gospel of the kingdom shall be preached in all the world for a witness unto all nations; and then shall the end come. **When ye therefore shall see the abomination of desolation, spoken of by Daniel the prophet, stand in the Holy Place, (whoso readeth, let him understand:) 16 Then let them which be in Judaea flee into the mountains: Let him which is on the housetop not come down to take anything out of his house: Neither let him which is in the field return back to take his clothes. And woe unto them that are with child, and to them that give suck in those days! But pray ye that your flight be not in the winter, neither on the sabbath day: For then shall be great tribulation, such as was not since the beginning of the world to this time, no, nor ever shall be.** And except those days should be shortened, there should no flesh be saved: but

for the elect's sake those days shall be shortened. Then if any man shall say unto you, Lo, here is Christ, or there; believe it not. For there shall arise false Christs, and false prophets, and shall shew great signs and wonders; insomuch that, if it were possible, they shall deceive the very elect. Behold, I have told you before. Wherefore if they shall say unto you, Behold, he is in the desert; go not forth: behold, he is in the secret chambers; believe it not. For as the lightning cometh out of the east, and shineth even unto the west; so shall also the coming of the Son of man be. For wheresoever the carcase is, there will the eagles be gathered together. (Matthew 24:11–28 KJV; my emphasis)

The beast will now begin his rule of terror and destruction through supernatural power from Satan. He first destroys Jerusalem and attacks those loyal to God in Jerusalem, stopping any worship of the true God (refs. 47, 35 CLA). The ten kings also receive their power at the same hour with the supernatural beast. The beast and the ten kings will now work in concert to rule and destroy and devastate the earth for the next forty-two months.[422] The six other heads, who up until this point have been the foundation of the beast, are now enemies and will be routinely set aside. *"Who is like the beast? Who is able to make war with him?"*[423] The answer is that no one is like the beast; the beast will have total supernatural control. The beast will also inherit all the weaponry and technology of the six other heads and use it toward their own destruction.

The events of the next forty-two months are filled with war, false messiahs, false prophets, desolation of the cities of the earth, death, destruction, famines, pestilences, and the wrath of Almighty God. Man will be astonished at the things that will come to the

---

[422] Revelation 17;12.
[423] Revelation 13:4.

earth during the final forty-two months. God's wrath will now be actively poured upon the earth through heavenly judgments: the seven seals, the seven trumpets, and the seven deadly vials. The book of the revelation of Jesus Christ will now come to life; all the scriptures previously scoffed at with disbelief, will now methodically be completely fulfilled. The seven seals cover the whole period in brief and in outline. The specific details of the seven seals are supplied by the consequences of the trumpets and the vials. Through this process, God will actively and forcibly take back the earth from evil men inspired by Satan and give his creation to his son, Jesus Christ, and his called-out ones, who are found written in his book. At the end of the forty-two months, the Lord Jesus Christ will receive glory on the earth, which he purchased through his own blood. He obeyed God through his agonizing death on the cross, and now God has given him the earth and those in it for an inheritance. God will fulfill his promise to his son as listed in the Psalms:

> **The LORD said unto my Lord, Sit thou at my right hand, until I make thine enemies thy footstool.** The LORD shall send the rod of thy strength out of Zion: rule thou in the midst of thine enemies. Thy people shall be willing in the day of thy power, in the beauties of holiness from the womb of the morning: thou hast the dew of thy youth.
>
> The LORD hath sworn, and will not repent, Thou art a priest for ever after the order of Melchizedek. The Lord at thy right hand shall strike through kings in the day of his wrath.
>
> He shall judge among the heathen, he shall fill the places with the dead bodies; he shall wound the heads over many countries He shall drink of the brook in the way: therefore shall he lift up the head. (Psalm 110:1–7 KJV; my emphasis)

The times of trouble and supernatural plagues on the earth are all well documented in the Old Testament and the book of Revelation will be fulfilled exactly as written. The initial focus will be Israel and Jerusalem and then the rest of the world. The many references in this work regarding the last forty-two months are listed as follows from the CLA above: *refs 2, 5, 8, 9–14, 19–20, 23–24, 26–27, 29–31, 47–53, 56–60*. Additionally, consider the following:

> Woe unto them that decree unrighteous decrees, and that write grievousness which they have prescribed; To turn aside the needy from judgment, and to take away the right from the poor of my people, that widows may be their prey, and that they may rob the fatherless!
>
> And what will ye do in the day of visitation, and in the desolation which shall come from far? to whom will ye flee for help? and where will ye leave your glory? Without me they shall bow down under the prisoners, and they shall fall under the slain. For all this his anger is not turned away, but his hand is stretched out still. O Assyrian, the rod of mine anger, and the staff in their hand is mine indignation. I will send him against an hypocritical nation, and against the people of my wrath will I give him a charge, to take the spoil, and to take the prey, and to tread them down like the mire of the streets. Howbeit he meaneth not so, neither doth his heart think so; but it is in his heart to destroy and cut off nations not a few. For he saith, Are not my princes altogether kings? Is not Calno as Carchemish? is not Hamath as Arpad? is not Samaria as Damascus? As my hand hath found the kingdoms of the idols, and whose graven images did excel them of Jerusalem and of Samaria; Shall I not, as I have done unto Samaria and her idols, so do to Jerusalem and her

idols? Wherefore it shall come to pass, that when the Lord hath performed his whole work upon mount Zion and on Jerusalem, I will punish the fruit of the stout heart of the king of Assyria, and the glory of his high looks. For he saith, By the strength of my hand I have done it, and by my wisdom; for I am prudent: and I have removed the bounds of the people, and have robbed their treasures, and I have put down the inhabitants like a valiant man: And my hand hath found as a nest the riches of the people: and as one gathereth eggs that are left, have I gathered all the earth; and there was none that moved the wing, or opened the mouth, or peeped. Shall the axe boast itself against him that heweth therewith? or shall the saw magnify itself against him that shaketh it? as if the rod should shake itself against them that lift it up, or as if the staff should lift up itself, as if it were no wood. Therefore shall the Lord, the Lord of hosts, send among his fat ones leanness; and under his glory he shall kindle a burning like the burning of a fire. And the light of Israel shall be for a fire, and his Holy One for a flame: and it shall burn and devour his thorns and his briers in one day; And shall consume the glory of his forest, and of his fruitful field, both soul and body: and they shall be as when a standardbearer fainteth. And the rest of the trees of his forest shall be few, that a child may write them. **And it shall come to pass in that day, that the remnant of Israel, and such as are escaped of the house of Jacob, shall no more again stay upon him that smote them; but shall stay upon the LORD, the Holy One of Israel, in truth. The remnant shall return, even the remnant of Jacob, unto the mighty God.**

For though thy people Israel be as the sand of the sea, yet a remnant of them shall return: the consumption decreed shall overflow with righteousness. For the Lord GOD of hosts shall make a consumption, even determined, in the midst of all the land. Therefore thus saith the Lord GOD of hosts, O my people that dwellest in Zion, be not afraid of the Assyrian: he shall smite thee with a rod, and shall lift up his staff against thee, after the manner of Egypt. For yet a very little while, and the indignation shall cease, and mine anger in their destruction. And the LORD of hosts shall stir up a scourge for him according to the slaughter of Midian at the rock of Oreb: and as his rod was upon the sea, so shall he lift it up after the manner of Egypt. And it shall come to pass in that day, that his burden shall be taken away from off thy shoulder, and his yoke from off thy neck, and the yoke shall be destroyed because of the anointing. He is come to Aiath, he is passed to Migron; at Michmash he hath laid up his carriages: They are gone over the passage: they have taken up their lodging at Geba; Ramah is afraid; Gibeah of Saul is fled. Lift up thy voice, O daughter of Gallim: cause it to be heard unto Laish, O poor Anathoth. Madmenah is removed; the inhabitants of Gebim gather themselves to flee. As yet shall he remain at Nob that day: he shall shake his hand against the mount of the daughter of Zion, the hill of Jerusalem. Behold, the Lord, the LORD of hosts, shall lop the bough with terror: and the high ones of stature shall be hewn down, and the haughty shall be humbled. And he shall cut down the thickets of the forest with iron, and Lebanon shall fall by a mighty one. (Isaiah 10:1–34 KJV)

> Then the LORD will make thy plagues wonderful, and the plagues of thy seed, even great plagues, and of long continuance, and sore sicknesses, and of long continuance. (Deuteronomy 28:59 KJV)
>
> And he said, Behold, I make a covenant: before all thy people I will do marvels, such as have not been done in all the earth, nor in any nation: and all the people among which thou art shall see the work of the LORD: for it is a terrible thing that I will do with thee. (Exodus 34:10 KJV)
>
> I will surely consume them, saith the LORD: there shall be no grapes on the vine, nor figs on the fig tree, and the leaf shall fade; and the things that I have given them shall pass away from them. Why do we sit still? assemble yourselves, and let us enter into the defenced cities, and let us be silent there: for the LORD our God hath put us to silence, and given us water of gall to drink, because we have sinned against the LORD. We looked for peace, but no good came; and for a time of health, and behold trouble! The snorting of his horses was heard from Dan: the whole land trembled at the sound of the neighing of his strong ones; for they are come, and have devoured the land, and all that is in it; the city, and those that dwell therein. For, behold, I will send serpents, cockatrices, among you, which will not be charmed, and they shall bite you, saith the LORD. (Jeremiah 8:13–17 KJV)

The Word of God will be fulfilled exactly as God documented it in his Word, in both the Old Testament and the New Testament. The final forty-two months of man's day will be different from any time in human history. The Word of God provides the important and salient details regarding this terrible time on the earth. Our responsibility is to believe what God has written and realize it will be a time different from all others; a supernatural beast energized by Satan will be king. Satan and his spirit agents will be operating in the supernatural realm on earth and in the sight of men. Deception and false messiahs will be abundant. The final forty-two months will bring God's wrath and indignation and great judgments on the earth: the seals, the trumpets, and the deadly vials.

Two sections of scripture, Daniel 11 and Revelation 13, provide significant information regarding the last forty-two months. Daniel 11 records the last forty-two months regarding the Jews and Jerusalem. Revelation records the consequences for the Gentiles, the earth, and the sea at large. Consider the following:

> And this gospel of the kingdom shall be preached in all the world for a witness unto all nations; and then shall the end come. **When ye therefore shall see the abomination of desolation, spoken of by Daniel the prophet, stand in the holy place, (whoso readeth, let him understand:)** Then let them which be in Judaea flee into the mountains: Let him which is on the housetop not come down to take any thing out of his house: Neither let him which is in the field return back to take his clothes. And woe unto them that are with child, and to them that give suck in those days! But pray ye that your flight be not in the winter, neither on the sabbath day: For then shall be great tribulation, such as was not since the beginning of the world to this time, no, nor ever shall be. And except those days should be shortened, there should no flesh be saved: but for the elect's sake those days shall be shortened. (Matthew 24:14–22 KJV; my emphasis)

THE LAST DAYS AND THE VILE MAN OF DANIEL

The scriptures that Jesus Christ refers in Matthew 24 concerning the abomination that causes desolation above are documented in Daniel and are associated with the middle and completion of the final seven years. Consider the following section of scripture:

> And arms shall stand on his (the beasts) part, and they shall pollute the sanctuary of strength, and shall take away the daily sacrifice, and they **shall place the abomination that maketh desolate.** And such as do wickedly against the covenant shall he corrupt by flatteries: but the people that do know their God shall be strong, and do exploits. And they that understand among the people shall instruct many: yet they shall fall by the sword, and by flame, by captivity, and by spoil, many days. Now when they shall fall, they shall be holpen with a little help: but many shall cleave to them with flatteries. And some of them of understanding shall fall, to try them, and to purge, and to make them white, even to the time of the end: because it is yet for a time appointed. And the king shall do according to his will; and he shall exalt himself, and magnify himself above every god, and shall speak marvellous things against the God of gods, and shall prosper till the indignation be accomplished: for that that is determined shall be done. Neither shall he regard the God of his fathers, nor the desire of women, nor regard any god: for he shall magnify himself above all. But in his estate shall he honour the God of forces: and a god whom his fathers knew not shall he honour with gold, and silver, and with precious stones, and pleasant thing. Thus shall he do in the most strong holds with a strange god, whom he shall acknowledge and increase with glory: and he shall cause them to

rule over many, and shall divide the land for gain. And at the time of the end shall the king of the south push at him: and the king of the north shall come against him like a whirlwind, with chariots, and with horsemen, and with many ships; and he shall enter into the countries, and shall overflow and pass over. He shall enter also into the glorious land, and many countries shall be overthrown: but these shall escape out of his hand, even Edom, and Moab, and the chief of the children of Ammon. He shall stretch forth his hand also upon the countries: and the land of Egypt shall not escape. But he shall have power over the treasures of gold and of silver, and over all the precious things of Egypt: and the Libyans and the Ethiopians shall be at his steps. But tidings out of the east and out of the north shall trouble him: therefore he shall go forth with great fury to destroy, and utterly to make away many. And he shall plant the tabernacles of his palace between the seas in the glorious holy mountain; yet he shall come to his end, and none shall help him. (Daniel 11:31–45 KJV; my emphasis)

And I stood upon the sand of the sea, and saw a beast rise up out of the sea, having seven heads and ten horns, and upon his horns ten crowns, and upon his heads the name of blasphemy. And the beast which I saw was like unto a leopard, and his feet were as the feet of a bear, and his mouth as the mouth of a lion: and the dragon gave him his power, and his seat, and great authority. And I saw one of his heads as it were wounded to death; and his deadly wound was healed: and all the world wondered after the beast. And they worshipped the dragon which gave power unto the beast: and they worshipped the beast, saying, Who is like unto the beast? who is able to make war with him? And there was given unto him a mouth speaking great things and blasphemies; **and power was given unto him to continue forty and two months.** And he opened his mouth in blasphemy against God, to blaspheme his name, and his tabernacle, and them that dwell in heaven. And it was given unto him to make war with the saints, and to overcome them: and power was given him over all kindreds, and tongues, and nations. And all that dwell upon the earth shall worship him, whose names are not written in the book of life of the Lamb slain from the foundation of the world. If any man have an ear, let him hear. He that leadeth into captivity shall go into captivity: he that killeth with the sword must be killed with the sword. Here is the patience and the faith of the saints. And I beheld another beast coming up out of the earth; and he had two horns like a lamb, and he spake as a dragon. And he exerciseth all the power of the first beast before him, and causeth the earth and them which dwell therein to worship the first beast, whose deadly wound was healed. And he doeth great wonders, so that he maketh fire come down from heaven on the earth in the sight of men, And deceiveth them that dwell on the earth by the means of those miracles which he had power to do in the sight of the beast; saying to them that dwell on the earth, that they should make an image to the beast, which had the wound by a sword, and did live. And he had power to give life unto the image of the beast, that the image of the beast should both speak, and cause that as many as would not worship the image of the beast should be killed.

> And he causeth all, both small and great, rich and poor, free and bond, to receive a mark in their right hand, or in their foreheads. And that no man might buy or sell, save he that had the mark, or the name of the beast, or the number of his name. Here is wisdom. Let him that hath understanding count the number of the beast: for it is the number of a man; and his number is Six hundred threescore and six. (Revelation 13:1–18 KJV; my emphasis)

God's wrath, which comes to the earth in response to the beast ruling and the general rejection of God by the earth dwellers, is contained in the seals, trumpets, and vials documented in the book of Revelation. The judgments of God documented in the book of Revelation are listed below as they appear in the book of Revelation. God's judgments start with the opening of the first of the seven seals (Revelation 6:1), which open and initiate God's forceful takeover, or the taking back, of the kingdoms of the world. The seals are a summary in brief of the whole period of the Tribulation; they correspond exactly with the last great prophecy of Christ, which is listed in Matthew 24:4–30.

The seven seals are as follows:
- **first seal:** The white horse is the Antichrist given power to conquer his foes (see Revelation 6:1, 2).
- **second seal:** With the red horse, peace is taken from the earth so its inhabitants will kill one another (see Revelation 6:4).
- **third seal:** The black horse is famine and dearth on the earth (see Revelation 6:5–6).
- **fourth seal:** The pale horse is death given to the fourth part of the earth via sword, famine, pestilence, and the beasts of the earth (see Revelation 6:7).

- **fifth seal:** Those faithful to Jesus Christ and God are killed; they will wait in death for their redemption (see Revelation 6:9–11).
- **sixth seal:** The great convulsion of the heavens and the earth occurs immediately after the tribulation of those days and just before the personal advent of Christ.[424] The sixth seal takes us up to the end but does not include the actual Apocalypse, or unveiling of the Lord (see Revelation 6:12–16). The sixth seal is also coterminous with the seventh trumpet, as listed in Revelation 11:17 and part of the proceedings after the seventh seal is opened. The seventh seal begins a new set of judgments listed as trumpets and vials.
- **seventh seal:** The seventh seal begins a new set of judgments listed as trumpets and vials. The seventh seal expands on the first six and gives additional information. It will culminate with the revelation of Jesus Christ as King of kings and Lord of lords on the earth. The seventh seal is opened (see Revelation 8:1) and gives way to the seven trumpets.

The seven trumpets are as follows:
- **the first trumpet:** Hail and fire fall to the earth, mixed with blood. A third of the trees and all green grass on the earth is burned up (see Revelation 8:7).
- **the second trumpet:** A burning mountain is cast into the sea. A third of the sea becomes blood. A third of sea life dies, and a third of ships in the sea are destroyed (see Revelation 8:8–9).
- **the third trumpet:** A burning star falls on a third of the rivers, turning them to wormwood (poisonous water) (see Revelation 8:10–11).
- **the fourth trumpet:** A third of the sun is smitten, along with a third of the moon and stars (see Revelation 8:12).

---

[424] Matthew 24:29.

- **the fifth trumpet (first woe trumpet):** A star falls from heaven, a pit is opened, man is tormented by special locusts released on the earth for five months, and men seek death but will not find it (see Revelation 9:1–11).
- **the sixth trumpet (second woe trumpet):** The four Euphratean supernatural angels are released to destroy a third of men with fire, brimstone, and smoke. The two witnesses are interposed as to their mission, their time, and their death and resurrection (see Revelation 9:13–11:14).
- **the seventh trumpet (third and final woe trumpet, sounded in heaven):** (See Revelation 11:15.) The seven vials, which make up the last seven plagues, are poured on the earth. The reason for the vials and judgments are interposed in chapters 12, 13, and 14. The results of the vials being poured out are listed in Revelation 16:1.

The seven vials are listed as follows:
- **The first vial:** A noisome and grievous sore falls upon the men who have the mark of the beast (see Revelation 16:2).
- **The second vial:** The sea becomes blood, and every living soul dies that was in the sea (see Revelation 16:3).
- **The third vial:** The rivers and fountains (man's drinking water supply) become blood.
- **The fourth vial:** Men (mankind) are scorched with vehement heat, and they blaspheme the name of God.
- **The fifth vial:** The kingdom of the beast becomes darkened.
- **The sixth vial:** The Euphrates dries up, making way for the gathering of the kings and armies on the great day of Almighty God. The beast and his spirit agents, as frog, are the gatherers of the armies to the slaughter at Armageddon.
- **The seventh vial:** The great earthquake occurs, and God shakes the entire earth, Babylon comes to remembrance, mankind hides from God, the nations fall, certain mountains are removed, islands flee, and great hailstones fall upon men. The end of this is the revelation of the son

of God regarding the battle on earth, as documented in Revelation 19:11 (see Revelation 16:17–20).

The war now on earth will be played out between God and Satan. God, through plagues and marvelous supernatural wonders, will bring the nations, *Mystery Babylon*, and the kingdom of the beast to nothing. God foretells of these days throughout the Old and New Testaments, and the day for their fulfillment has finally come. The following are some of the references to the Day of the Lord—the day when everything done will exalt the Lord and debase man: Isaiah 2:12; 13:6–18; Ezekiel 13:5; Joel 1:15; 2:1, 11; 3:14; Amos 5:18, 20; Obadiah 15, Zephaniah 1:7, 14; Malachi 4:5; Ezekiel 30:3, Zechariah 14:1, 17; 1 Thessalonians 5:2; 2 Thessalonians 2:2. These prophetic references, as well as others in both the Old and New Testaments, refer to these same forty-two months. The time period and judgments will be fulfilled exactly as written down; not a Word of God will fall to the ground unfulfilled.[425]

The End of Man's Day

In 1 Corinthians 4:3, Paul, through revelation given to him by Jesus Christ, mentions how it was a very small thing for him to be judged by man in the day when man was ruling. He was alluding to the fact that before the Day of the Lord, or the day when the Lord will be exalted, it is man who judges. The day of man, or when man rules on the earth, has an end and is linked to the judgments in Revelation when God forcibly takes back the earth and gives it to his son, Jesus Christ. Paul documents this in 1 Corinthians 4:

> Let a man so reckon us as officers of Christ, and stewards of the secrets of God, and as to the rest, it is required in the stewards that one may be found faithful, **and to me it is for a very little thing that by you I may be judged, or by man's**

---
[425] 2 Peter 1:21–22.

> **day, but not even myself do I judge**, for of nothing to myself have I been conscious, but not in this have I been declared right -- and he who is discerning me is the Lord: so, then, nothing before the time judge ye, till the Lord may come, who will both bring to light the hidden things of the darkness, and will manifest the counsels of the hearts, and then the praise shall come to each from God. (1 Corinthians 4:1–5 YLT; my emphasis)

The end of the beast—that is, his kingdom on earth and man's day of ruling—will all end together at the completion of the final forty-two months. The end also marks the completion of Daniel's prophecy of seventy sevens of years documented in Daniel 9:24. The supernatural beast is destroyed by the coming of the Lord Jesus Christ. Consider the following:

> …The son of perdition; Who opposeth and exalteth himself above all that is called God, or that is worshipped; so that he as God sitteth in the temple of God, shewing himself that he is God. Remember ye not, that, when I was yet with you, I told you these things? And now ye know what withholdeth that he might be revealed in his time. For the mystery of iniquity doth already work: only he who now letteth will let, until he be taken out of the way. **And then shall that Wicked be revealed, whom the Lord shall consume with the spirit of his mouth, and shall destroy with the brightness of his coming.** (2 Thessalonians 2:3–8 KJV; my emphasis)

The seventy weeks of years is complete with the destruction of the wild beast—the Antichrist. All of what is prophesied in Daniel 9:24 concerning those called out of Israel will have been accomplished.

Consider the following: *"Seventy weeks are determined upon thy people (Israel) and upon thy holy city, to finish the transgression, and to make an end of sins, and to make reconciliation for iniquity, and to bring in everlasting righteousness, and to seal up the vision and prophecy, and to anoint the most Holy"* (Daniel 9:24 KJV).

At the end of the seventy weeks—specifically the last seven years, which are marked by the destruction of the beast—the prophecies of Daniel 9:24, along with many of the prophecies concerning the last days, will be completed. The deliverance of Jacobs's seed will be complete, and all that God promised for Israel in Daniel 9:24 will have been fulfilled. The promises will now be enjoyed by those called out by the Lord who are written in the Lord's book of life. The promises of Daniel 9:24 concerning Israel are listed below and will reach their fulfillment after the final seven years of Daniel's seventy sevens of years:

- The transgression will be finished.
- The dominance of sin will be ended.
- Reconciliation will be made for iniquity.
- Everlasting righteousness will be brought in.
- Vision and prophecy will be fulfilled.
- The Most Holy will be anointed.

God will now place those who are called out from the house of Jacob in the land with Jesus Christ as their anointed Messiah. God will also raise David from the dead to be their king. The called out of Israel will consist of those raised from the dead at the resurrection of the just and also those sealed and protected by God through the final forty-two months of the tribulation period. The group will make up the new Israel, who will live with Jesus Christ as King of kings and Lord of lords. In contrast, the church of the body of Christ will have already been raptured and given new bodies, and they will be forever with the Lord, as their inheritance is in heaven and not on earth. What exactly the church of the body of Christ will be doing is still not entirely clear, but this will become clear after their rapture from the earth. Consider the flowing verses that refer to the church of the body of Christ:

> For our conversation is in heaven; from whence also we look for the Saviour, the Lord Jesus Christ: Who shall change our vile body, that it may be fashioned like unto his glorious body, according to the working whereby he is able even to subdue all things unto himself. (Philippians 3:20–21 KJV)
>
> Behold, what manner of love the Father hath bestowed upon us, that we should be called the sons of God: therefore the world knoweth us not, because it knew him not. **Beloved, now are we the sons of God, and it doth not yet appear what we shall be: but we know that, when he shall appear, we shall be like him; for we shall see him as he is.** And every man that hath this hope in him purifieth himself, even as he is pure. (1 John 3:1 KJV; my emphasis)

As for the new embryotic nation of Israel, consider the following:

> And at that time shall Michael stand up, the great prince which standeth for the children of thy people (Israel): and there shall be a time of trouble, such as never was since there was a nation even to that same time: **and at that time thy people shall be delivered, every one that shall be found written in the book. And many of them that sleep in the dust of the earth shall awake, some to everlasting life, and some to shame and everlasting contempt. And they that be wise shall shine as the brightness of the firmament; and they that turn many to righteousness as the stars for ever and ever.** (Daniel 12:1–3 KJV; my emphasis)

THE LAST DAYS AND THE VILE MAN OF DANIEL

The end of the last seven years is marked by three unique time periods, all of which are documented in Daniel 12. Consider the following:

> And I heard the man clothed in linen, which was upon the waters of the river, when he held up his right hand and his left hand unto heaven, and sware by him that liveth for ever that it shall be for a **time, times, and an half; (3.5 years)** and when he shall have accomplished to scatter the power of the holy people, all these things shall be finished. And I heard, but I understood not: then said I, O my Lord, what shall be the end of these things? And he said, Go thy way, Daniel: for the words are closed up and sealed till the time of the end. Many shall be purified, and made white, and tried; but the wicked shall do wickedly: and none of the wicked shall understand; but the wise shall understand. **And from the time that the daily sacrifice shall be taken away, and the abomination that maketh desolate set up, there shall be a thousand two hundred and ninety days. Blessed is he that waiteth, and cometh to the thousand three hundred and five and thirty days.** But go thou thy way till the end be: for thou shalt rest, and stand in thy lot at the end of the days. (Daniel 12:7–13 KJV; my emphasis)

All three times are mentioned in Daniel 12:7–13: the 3.5 years (1,260 days), the 1,290 days, and the 1,335 days. The first period is marked by the destruction of the beast by the Lord. The second and third time periods will probably be associated with the first resurrection of the dead—the resurrection of the just—and the setting up of the kingdom of the Lord Jesus Christ, respectively. The cleansing of the Sanctuary is also associated with this extended time. The setting up of the Lord's kingdom includes the judging of the nations and the cleansing of the holy place and the nuptials associated with the wedding feast of the lamb. Consider the following: *"When the Son of man shall come in his glory, and all the holy angels with him, then shall he sit upon the throne of his glory: And before him shall be gathered all nations: and he shall separate them one from another, as a shepherd divideth his sheep from the goats: And he shall set the sheep on his right hand, but the goats on the left. Then shall the King say unto them on his right hand, Come, ye blessed of my Father, inherit the kingdom prepared for you from the foundation of the world"* (Matthew 25:31–34 KJV).

The time of man's day is ended. God has vacated Satan from the heavens and placed him and his followers in chains. The church of God has been raptured and gathered together into the heavens. The Lord Jesus Christ has destroyed the beast and his followers and has set up his everlasting kingdom on the earth. The once powerful nations are no more and have been judged and weeded out. The new nation of Israel is in the land, and God has fulfilled all his promises made to Abraham, Isaac, and Jacob. The earth will now enjoy one thousand years of relative peace and healing, with the Lord Jesus Christ ruling in justice and righteousness forever. Amen.

www.ingramcontent.com/pod-product-compliance
Lightning Source LLC
Chambersburg PA
CBHW060347080526
44583CB00012B/203